Hypnosis, Will, and Memory
A Psycho-Legal History

The Guilford Clinical and Experimental Hypnosis Series
Michael J. Diamond and Helen M. Pettinati, Editors

Hypnosis, Will, and Memory: A Psycho-Legal History
Jean-Roch Laurence and Campbell Perry

Hypnosis and Memory
Helen M. Pettinati, Editor

Clinical Practice of Hypnotherapy
M. Erik Wright with Beatrice A. Wright

Hypnosis, Will, and Memory
A Psycho-Legal History

JEAN-ROCH LAURENCE
CAMPBELL PERRY
Concordia University

THE GUILFORD PRESS
New York   London

© 1988 The Guilford Press
A Division of Guilford Publications, Inc.
72 Spring Street, New York, NY 10012

All rights reserved

No part of this book may be reproduced, stored in a retrieval system, or transmitted, in any form or by any means, electronic, mechanical, photocopying, microfilming, recording, or otherwise, without written permission from the Publisher

Printed in the United States of America

Last digit is print number: 9 8 7 6 5 4 3 2 1

Library of Congress Cataloging-in-Publication Data

Laurence, Jean-Roch.
   Hypnosis, will, and memory.

   (The Guilford clinical and experimental hypnosis series)
   Includes bibliographies and index.
   1. Hypnosis—History. I. Perry, Campbell W.
II. Title. III. Series. [DNLM: 1. Coercion.
2. Hypnosis—history. BF 1125 L379h]
BF1125.L38   1988   154.7'09   87-19672
ISBN 0-89862-339-1 (cloth)
ISBN 0-89862-504-1 (paper)

Acknowledgments

It would take more than just a few words to convey appropriate thanks to all of the individuals who have helped us in writing this book.

First and foremost, we would like to thank the Natural Sciences and Engineering Research Council of Canada (NSERC) which has for many years provided financial support for the research projects of both authors independently. Without the help of NSERC and its commitment to developing research in Canada, this book would never have seen the light of day.

We would like also to acknowledge the libraries that have so generously opened their inner rooms to the satisfaction of our insatiable curiosity: The Library of Congress in Washington, D.C.; the different libraries of McGill University in Montréal; and probably the one that will remain in our memory as the cradle of our interest, La Bibliothèque Nationale in Paris. More than 2,000 hours were spent by the first author exploring the shelves of this amazing building, and both of us spent almost four years organizing and digesting the information found there. The personnel of these libraries were always courteous, helpful, and most of all very patient.

During the period that the first author was researching the primary French sources, the second one participated vicariously by telephone. We had fantasied for many years about what treasures La Bibliothèque Nationale held, in much the way that the discoverer of a sunken Spanish galleon must fantasize about what will be found when divers are sent down to inspect its contents. In such cases, fantasy usually falls well short of reality, and certainly this was true in our case. The second author became addicted to the telephone and was close to being named a patron saint of the phone company. It was an exhilarating period for both of us as we discussed the potential significance of each new unexpected find, as well as those that had been anticipated.

To the people in France who took interest in our work, our deepest appreciation: Dr. Léon Chertok, Dr. Didier Michaux, and Mrs. Sylviane Gauthier Garnier. To Sylviane, who is now finishing a doctorate in the field of hypnosis, we are particularly indebted. She opened the doors to the many treasures that lay within La Bibliothèque Nationale and introduced the first author to the intricacies of the French mind. Hours of discussion, laughter, and disagreement allowed her and the first author to build a friendship that has survived time and distance. To Sylviane and her family, our very best wishes.

Our interest in the legal investigative use of hypnosis was first whetted when we completed Martin Orne's Forensic Hypnosis Workshop in Chicago at the Society for Clinical and Experimental Hypnosis Meeting of 1980. Over the years, Martin and Emily Carota Orne have always been generous and at times extremely patient in sharing their expertise with us and in helping us to conceptualize the issues more clearly.

Josée Bélanger, a Montréal lawyer who is completing a Master's degree on hypnosis and the law, was invaluable in explaining many of the legal issues surrounding the investigative utilization of hypnosis. She pointed to many complexities that we, who are untrained in law, would otherwise have missed.

We came to know Michael Barnes of the British Broadcasting Corporation while he was making his outstanding four-part documentary series on hypnosis. He quickly developed an expertise on investigative hypnosis, and in the many conversations we had with him in London, Montréal, and on the telephone, we greatly appreciated being able to float our ideas past him as they evolved. We particularly admire his remarkable demonstrations of British tolerance on some of these occasions.

We are indebted to all of these individuals for their assistance in formulating the legal-investigative aspects of this book, and we appreciate their encouragement. The final responsibility, however, for the conclusions reached herein are entirely our own.

We wish to thank also Dr. Ken Bowers and Dr. Patricia Bowers at the University of Waterloo, who sat through many hours of discussion and seminars with the first author listening and commenting thoughtfully on the details of what was to become this book; in addition, we owe many interesting insights to their students who questioned and commented so cogently on the material presented, particularly Debra Hughes, Mary Miller, and Claude Balthazard.

Special thanks to Ms. Andrea Kenney who read and reread the manuscript, suggesting many improvements, pointing to many contradictions: Her help has improved this volume immensely.

In addition, we wish to express our grateful admiration to Danielle Laurence (the first author's sister), and Lavinia Holmes who typed, retyped, corrected, and recorrected the manuscript neatly and without any complaint. In this respect, also, we wish to thank Trenny Cook, of the University of Waterloo, who typed the initial drafts of the first several chapters, and Keith Sicard who helped input corrections during the final frenetic month of this project. Both Trenny and Keith provided major assistance.

Further thanks to all of our friends who have stood steadfastly beside us, tolerating our obsessions, and understanding our ecstasies and agonies. We can only hope that they will enjoy reading this book as much as we have enjoyed the ecstasy of writing it.

We wish, also, to thank the personnel at The Guilford Press, notably Judith Grauman, Marian Robinson, and Carolyn Graham, for the highly professional manner in which they went about processing the book manuscript from the time that we submitted it. We owe a very special debt to Rennie Childress, who copyedited the book with great care, sensitivity, and, most of all, with class.

Finally, our appreciation to Seymour Weingarten, Editor-in-Chief of The Guilford Press, for his patience, and for his trust in our ability to write this book. In addition our thanks to Michael J. Diamond and Helen M. Pettinati, the Editors of The Guilford Clinical and Experimental Hypnosis Series, who, on the basis of reading very rough drafts of the first three chapters, somehow persuaded Seymour that it was publishable.

Neither Seymour, Michael, nor Helen were hypnotized. . . .

Jean-Roch Laurence
Campbell Perry
August 1986

Contents

Introduction   xiii

I. Origins and Development of Animal Magnetism

1. Animal Magnetism, Magnetic Medicine, and Exorcism   3
2. Witchcraft, Religious Fanaticism, and Animal Magnetism: Some Behavioral Aspects of Social Change   24
3. The Mesmerist Movement in France: 1778 to 1784   49
4. The Fall of Mesmerism   73

II. From Mesmerism to Hypnosis

5. Artificial Somnambulism   103
6. Between Science and Religion   126
7. From Europe to America: Times of Change   153

III. The Golden Years of Hypnosis: 1878 to 1905

8. The Entry of Hypnosis into the Judicial System   179
9. The Public Debate: 1884 to 1890   215
10. Europe Meets America: Hypnosis in the Last Years of the Nineteenth Century   263

IV. The Contemporary Use of Forensic Hypnosis

11. The Twentieth Century: Bust Followed by Boom   293

12. Hypnosis in Criminal Law: History Repeated   335

Conclusion   391

Bibliography   397

Index   423

Introduction

During the late eighteenth century in France, Franz Anton Mesmer introduced an innovative method for treating physical illness that was to capture the interest and curiosity of both the scientific community and the general public. He believed that there was an invisible force permeating the universe which he could harness, accumulate in his body, and transmit to sick people with curative effects. This ability of the human body to interact with such an unknown force he called *animal magnetism*. The most important fact about Mesmer is that, despite an erroneous theory, he was able to effect both cures and ameliorations of illness that had defied the best attempts of orthodox medical practitioners of his period.

Mesmer's work constituted the beginnings of what is now called *hypnosis*. The term itself was coined by a Scottish physician, James Braid, in 1843.[1] It is a metaphor derived from the Greek word *hypnos* (sleep) and was devised to draw attention to the apparent parallels between the behavior of the hypnotized person and some aspects of nocturnal sleep. Hypnosis, we now know, has nothing to do with nocturnal sleep. Studies employing the electroencephalogram (EEG), initiated during the 1950s (Aserinsky & Kleitman, 1953), indicate that there are four distinct sleep stages as defined empirically by EEG criteria. These stages alternate cyclically throughout the night. By contrast, no distinct brain psychophysiology has yet been demonstrated for hypnosis. Indeed, the EEG of a hypnotized person is formally indistinguishable from that of a person who is relaxed, alert, with eyes closed. Nevertheless, the term hypnosis is still widely used, even though it is recognized by clinicians and researchers in the field as being based on a misleading metaphor.

More than two centuries have passed since Mesmer's observations first reached the public domain. By contrast, the scientific study of hypnosis under standardized laboratory conditions is of far more recent origin. It can be attributed to the work of the noted American psychologist, Clark L. Hull, who, in collaboration with a small and dedicated group of students, established a hypnosis laboratory at the University of Wisconsin at Madison during the 1920s. The patient and meticulous work of these researchers culminated in a classic text authored by Hull, *Hypnosis and Suggestibility* (1933). Hull subsequently moved to Yale University during the late 1920s, and continued to carry out hypnosis research. During the winter of 1930, he was informed by the employment department of Yale that it would no longer obtain more subjects for him on the grounds that there had been complaints from parents. On subsequent inquiry Hull learned that the real source of opposition to his research was in the School of Medicine; some of its professors had taken a strong stand against hypnosis, maintaining that it was extremely dangerous. In the end, Hull was obliged to abandon the field for other lines of inquiry (J. F. Kihlstrom, personal communication to Campbell Perry, December 18, 1986).

The general public tends to equate hypnosis with the notion of suggestibility, which is a polite way of characterizing a person as gullible and weak willed (and possibly feebleminded). As will be seen in the following chapters, this popular conception of hypnosis can be traced back to the works of Charcot and his colleagues in the late nineteenth century when hypnosis and hysteria were seen as closely related illnesses. Both were thought to be more prevalent in women whose alleged labile nervous systems rendered them more vulnerable to external influence. More recently, laboratory research, spurred on by a new generation of researchers, has revealed a far more complex and fascinating picture of what hypnosis may be in actuality (see, for example, Hilgard, 1977; Orne, 1959; Sheehan & McConkey, 1982). As in all areas of scientific research, there are considerable theoretical disagreements regarding hypnosis, yet there is also a remarkable degree of consensus. Indeed, this consensus is a cornerstone of the present book.

Hypnosis is a situation in which an individual is asked to set aside critical judgment, without abandoning it completely, and is asked also to indulge in make-believe and fantasy (Gill & Brenman, 1959; E. Hilgard, 1977). There are stable individual differences in the ability to do this. Studies, dating from clinical observations in the nineteenth century (Faria, 1819; Bernheim, 1884, 1886) have indicated that approximately 10 to 15 percent of the population is highly responsive to hypnosis (that is, capable of experiencing suggested posthypnotic amnesia), a further 10 to 15 percent is unresponsive, and the remaining majority of 70 to 80 percent is moderately responsive to varying degrees (E. Hilgard, 1965). It follows from this basic observation that the degree to which a person can set aside critical judgment in favor of fantasy and imagination will determine the extent to which he or she experiences alterations, even distortions, of perception, mood, and memory (Orne, 1980).

A number of investigators of different theoretical orientations have converging ideas regarding the nature of the fantasy and make-believe that a hypnotic procedure evokes. Sarbin and Coe (1972) have referred to it as "believed-in imaginings," J. Hilgard (1979) has described it as "imaginative involvement," Spanos and Barber (1974) have described it as "involvement in suggestion-related imaginings," while Sutcliffe (1961) characterized the hypnotized person as "deluded" in a descriptive, nonpejorative sense.

Apart from the different abilities that allow an individual to experience these alterations of perception, memory, mood, and behavior, the contexts in which such modifications are elicited play an important role. Hypnosis is an interactive process: The appropriateness of the context in permitting the establishment of a relationship of trust between hypnotist and subject will favor the elicitation of these abilities. As will be seen throughout this book, hypnosis can best be understood in terms of the factors underlying this interaction. Expectations, beliefs, and motivations are thus aspects of the hypnotic relationship that influence the hypnotized subject's ability to experience suggested phenomena whether it be amnesia, visual and auditory hallucinations, or hypermnesia.

At this point, it would be inappropriate to review the research data that support this view of the nature of hypnosis. Rather, it is sufficient to say that viewing hypnosis in these terms leads to an interesting conundrum. Increasingly, hypnosis is being used clinically as an adjunctive treatment in medicine. Considerable success has been encountered in alleviating such conditions as clinical pain, dermatological conditions, and asthma (Wadden & Anderton, 1982) to mention but a few. Here, it would appear that training patients to deploy their imaginative abilities can be highly beneficial and rewarding—at least sometimes. In the light of this well-documented observation, however, identifying the role played by the different factors in these clinical successes (and failures) is no easy undertaking; contemporary research in hypnosis is only beginning to bring together the different pieces of this intriguing jigsaw puzzle.

Paralleling these clinical data is the claim for comparable success when hypnosis is utilized in the investigation of crimes to enhance the fragmented memories of witnesses and victims and to provide information that may assist police forces in apprehending instigators of crime. To equate the experimental, clinical, and investigative uses of hypnosis can lead to severe misinterpretations of the nature of the hypnotic situation; to ignore the commonalities between each respective use is to open oneself to accusations of severe misunderstanding.

Indeed, many police departments in countries such as the United States, Canada, and Australia have established hypno-investigative units comprised of police officers who have, for the most part, received a brief 32-hour training course in hypnosis. These are offered by private institutes which have tended to ignore recent developments in the areas of both experimental and clinical hypnosis. This enthusiasm for the investigative use of hypnosis which originated in the mid-1970s has created a major controversy within the scientific community: There is mounting concern that a profligate utilization of hypnosis with victims, witnesses, and even self-professed amnesic crime suspects will lead to major miscarriages of justice. Indeed, as our final chapter indicates, a number of close calls have been documented in recent years. What is not known, however, is how many unnoticed injustices have already occurred. If the past and contemporary examples of abuses described in this book are any indication of what may be happening, many surprises are yet to come.

The current interest in the forensic use of hypnosis is far from being new. In the nineteenth century, hypnosis was introduced to the law courts of most European countries with France leading the way. At that time, individuals were prosecuted or exonerated on the sole basis of the hypnotically elicited testimony of a crime victim or witness. Furthermore, a vigorous debate focused on the possibility that a person could be induced to commit a crime or could become the victim of a crime as the result of being hypnotized. This debate was a natural progression of one that had its origins in animal magnetism. From a very early period, there have been allegations that hypnosis (or its antecedents) could be used to sexually seduce women, or more generally, to abolish the willpower of those who submitted to it. The observation that memory could be manipulated during magnetism, and imagination easily enhanced, led to the expression of skepticism about the ability of the highly magnetizable individual to report accurately on external events (Bertrand, 1823). This skepticism was to be echoed by the European medico-legal experts of the late nineteenth century.

Regardless of whether it is claimed that hypnosis can be used to seduce women, to coerce individuals into committing crimes, or to enhance memory, the underlying assumption is basically the same. In all cases, the unspoken premise is that hypnosis can subjugate one's will and/or memory, so that the person becomes an automaton lacking any means of resisting this apparent external "power" when it is deployed by a skillful operator.

These views are still quite prevalent in twentieth-century Western society. Most people have seen stage hypnotists exercise their "powers" over the people who volunteer to appear on stage. Occasionally, newspapers publicize the exploits of men alleged to have seduced women with hypnosis. Quite frequently also, one obtains media accounts of a police investigation that has faltered, only to be brought to a successful culmination by the hypnotically elicited memories of a crime victim or witness. Common assumptions underlying these reports are that the subject of stage hypnosis had no choice but to behave inanely, the seduced woman lost her willpower to decline an unwanted sexual advance, and the passive memory system of the crime victim/witness was released from its amnesia as if by an all-illuminating searchlight which probed one's innermost recesses.

Contemporary research has yet to demonstrate in a satisfactory sense just how, when, and why certain individuals can be harmed by an unscrupulous hypnotist. On the other hand, research and clinical work in the areas of memory and hypnosis in the last 15 years are beginning to bear fruit. Leafing through the history of hypnosis and related phenomena may bring us a few steps closer to understanding these important issues.

In writing this book we were obliged to focus on three basic issues: Why did hypnosis become associated with ideas of power and dominance? What happened in the past that permitted such a pervading belief to become established? And finally, how can the hypnotic situation lead to reports of total submission, compulsion, or lack of control over one's own physical and psychological processes?

For one interested in the history of hypnosis, an initial and obvious landmark can be identified easily. In August 1784, a secret report on the social and moral danger of animal magnetism was submitted, as a warning, to the King of France (Neufchâteau, 1800). When the content of the report is examined, however, the vagueness and the generality of the arguments presented are perplexing. Why was the secret report written? On what observations was it based? Could it be an example of some archaic beliefs superseding the newly adopted scientific orientation of the late eighteenth century?

In seeking to answer these questions, it became apparent that the alleged coercive power of hypnosis, or of eighteenth-century animal magnetism, stemmed from its identification with long-standing beliefs surrounding phenomena such as witchcraft and sorcery, religious fanaticism, and the unabated popular enthusiasm stimulated by the scientific discoveries of each particular era. A complete history of all of these movements will not be presented here, but the similarities in the behaviors of individuals who were labeled through the centuries as either possessed by the Devil or inspired by God, or as recipients of miraculous cures and treatments, magnetized or hypnotized, provide the basis for our analysis of the coercive aura surrounding the phenomenon of hypnosis.

Mesmer's theory can thus be seen as a center point around which an intricate system of beliefs, mostly of religious origin, came to clash with the rising tide of the Enlightenment, which was a symbol of the human desire to question and understand the world in naturalistic terms. Animal magnetism was to represent for the learned man the delicate balance he had to maintain between theistic beliefs and scientific innovations.

The emphasis of the book is upon the psycho-legal aspects of hypnosis but we focus also on when, and how, the phenomenon developed a coercive image. The conceptualization of hypnosis as a coercing agent is rooted in the history of the interaction between its nontraditional aspects as a treatment and the negative reactions to its use from the established medical, religious, and political milieus of the last two centuries. The behaviors and the experiences of the magnetized patient strongly resembled those of the possessed individual (whether it be by God or the Devil). In a similar way, the magnetized patient's behaviors and experiences matched the ones of the hypnotized subject of the late nineteenth century. Needless to say, contemporary subjects of hypnotic experiments perform and report experiences that are closely linked to those of their predecessors. After a long history of insinuations and unsubstantiated accusations, scientific observations and popular beliefs were to be thrust against each other in the legal arena at the end of the nineteenth century . . . and again in the twentieth century. Would Justice be as blind as Destiny?

Hopefully, it is in this continuity of behavior and experience beyond the different proposed explanations where lie some of the answers to the questions posed in this book.

Ariadne's Clew

The book has been divided into four parts in an attempt to guide the reader through the many events that have surrounded the development of animal magnetism and hypnosis. As far as possible, we have attempted to follow the words of those who lived during each period of this history; we let them explain what they were thinking, minimizing our interpretation of the facts (although we realize how difficult it is not to be influenced by our own conceptions). When it was feasible (and almost all of the time, it was) we referred to the original manuscripts and sought to keep translated quotations as close as possible to the original words. When we chose to go along with a secondary source, it was either because the original was not available, an already translated source proved adequate, or the original manuscript was in a language neither of us could understand![2]

Part I (the first four chapters) covers the origins of animal magnetism, as well as some of its antecedents. In Chapter 1, the beginnings of Mesmerism in Vienna are summarized and contrasted with what was known as "magnetic medicine" in earlier centuries. Mesmer's treatment is presented as an attempt to integrate both medical (magnetic medicine) and religious (exorcism) practices of the early eighteenth century. The issues of morality and the alleged danger of Mesmer's doctrine are introduced and linked to previous conceptions surrounding nontraditional therapeutic systems.

The behaviors elicited during mesmeric treatment were not in any way specific to Mesmer's new system. Similar behaviors and experiences could be found in a number of different settings, namely witchcraft and the religious extremist movements that flourished in seventeenth- and eighteenth-century France. Some examples of these movements are reviewed in Chapter 2. What is to be remembered of such movements is the similarity in both behaviors and subjective experiences reported by people who lived through these episodes.

Mesmer's effort to differentiate his theory from spiritualism allowed his movement to grow solid roots within the intelligentsia of his time. By the same token, however, it provoked the ire of the clergy, confusion in the scientific community, and the enthusiasm of the population.

The story of Mesmer in Paris and his struggle to implement his new system is summarized in Chapters 3 and 4. The conceptions of Mesmerism as an immoral and revolutionary political system are emphasized. In 1784, two Royal Commissions of Inquiry were formed to examine the claims of the magnetists. The commissioners debunked the magnetists' claims on both scientific and moral grounds.

Mesmer never recovered from this public debate. His proponents took over and developed his theory along new dimensions. Among them, the Marquis de Puységur was to alter the whole development of the mesmeric system through his discovery of *artificial somnambulism*.

In *Part II*, the transformation of Mesmer's original system into artificial somnambulism and hypnosis is documented. In Chapter 5, it will be seen how this new way of looking at "magnetic phenomena" led in the early nineteenth century to a revival of the conflict between science, religion, and the new therapeutic system. From the beginning, artificial somnambulism was accused of being immoral, and nothing more than quackery. The effect of the unstable political climate during the French Revolution tempered, however, the conflict between the scientific establishment and the adherents to this revised version of magnetism.

The first half of the nineteenth century saw the beginnings of the scientific investigation of what was to become hypnosis. In Europe as well as in the United States, a number of important theoretical and practical innovations accompanied the establishment of hypnosis as a gradually accepted (or, at least, tolerated) medical treatment.

At the same time, however, hypnosis was making its first appearance in the legal system. Lay magnetists were to be accused of illegally practicing medicine as well as of using the new therapeutic as a method of coercing individuals. Meanwhile, in Europe, a number of important writers came to endorse magnetism and hypnosis. Both phenomena were perceived favorably by many medical, legal, and religious authorities. In Chapter 6, the work of investigators such as Faria and Bertrand, who anticipated some of the modern conceptualizations of hypnosis, is reviewed. The astute observations of these practitioners, however, did not solve the conflict between ancient beliefs and newly proposed alternatives.

The same problems that arose in France during the first hundred years of the mesmeric system found their way to England in the mid-nineteenth century. Chapter 7 examines the efforts of investigators such as Esdaile, Elliotson, and Braid to gain the recognition of the British scientific establishment (which was in fact even more distrustful of the new treatment than its French counterpart). Although the battle was not easily won in England, the relabeling of magnetism as hypnosis by Braid and the scientific investigations that he carried out helped to gain public acceptance.

In the United States, animal magnetism became entangled in the Protestant revivalist movement in particular and, more generally, with spiritualism. Two major consequences of these alliances were, on the one hand, to leave the medical profession quite free to use hypnosis therapeutically without theorizing about it, while permitting, on the other hand, the crystallization of spiritualistic approaches into such movements as the Christian Science of Mary Baker Eddy. The United States, however, would not avoid the forensic debate that flourished in Europe, although it showed less panache than did its European counterpart.

Part III examines what has been called the "Golden Years of Hypnosis" in France, from 1878 to 1905. As will be seen in Chapters 8, 9, and 10, hypnosis was to regain scientific acceptability in France by the end of the 1870s. Two main schools of thought evolved, one led by Bernheim in Nancy, the other by Charcot in Paris. Part of the ensuing theoretical debate addressed the use of hypnosis as a coercive agent. For more than 20 years, the medical and psychological literature resonated with the claims of the two schools concerning the dangers of hypnotism. Chapter 8 presents the different theories that prevailed at the time. The old beliefs became incorporated into a new scientific orientation, as if the proverb "If you cannot beat them, join them!" was the only possible solution to the schism between faith and science. Numerous trials took place; innumerable controversies arose. Once again supporters of hypnosis had to wage a public battle that led to its ultimate decline. One famous trial, the Eyraud-Bompard affair, was to be at the core of the final debate between the different schools of thought. This fascinating period of the history of hypnosis is documented in Chapter 9.

In the midst of the European debate, the Americans embarked on a similar journey. A number of trials took place leading to the first major court decision (the Ebanks case) at the end of the nineteenth century. The American experts did not show the same enthusiasm as their European colleagues for hypnosis and the beliefs surrounding it. The courts, in particular, espoused a stern position that led ultimately to the current forensic debate in the United States. Chapter 10 describes the American involvement in this early forensic debate and summarizes the position of both American and European medico-legal experts at the turn of the century.

Finally, in *Part IV*, the contemporary history of forensic hypnosis is reviewed. Most of the questions that surround the current use of hypnosis in the legal system were already asked by our predecessors. They thought and wrote extensively about it; they proposed their own model of the human mind and how it should be dealt with therapeutically and legally. It is fruitful to examine their thinking on these matters for their writings reveal that forensic hypnosis is more than merely a legal or a psychological issue. Implicitly, it is our whole conceptualization of the human mind that is the subject of this debate. It is a challenge for contemporary psychology; once already in the not so recent past irrational claims by both lay and professionally trained hypnotists not only precipitated a decline in the interest given to this most intriguing aspect of human behavior, but cut off a most useful method for studying human consciousness. Contemporary hypnosis research by its interaction with the legal world offers a unique opportunity for looking at human behaviors and experiences in a naturalistic environment. Chapters 11 and 12 present, in a condensed fashion, contemporary research on hypnosis and hypnotizability that has been triggered by its psycho-legal use and abuse. These chapters summarize contemporary events so that the reader can appreciate how the more blatant misunderstandings of the past have taken new forms and shapes, but still pervade its lay and sometimes even its scientific conceptualization.

Whatever theoretical position one is willing to espouse vis-à-vis the different phenomena seen in the investigation of hypnosis, one fact remains certain: If history is any guide, the phenomena will outlive their current explanations.

A Last Word

As Darnton (1984) pointed out recently, it is a nearly impossible task to capture the history of "mentalities," to understand past events through the eyes of those who actually lived them. It would be comforting to demonstrate that attitudes toward hypnosis evolved along with the social changes that took place in Europe and America during the last two hundred years. Unfortunately, attitude formation and popular beliefs are not necessarily determined by social change (Darnton, 1984, p. 259). Clinicians and researchers of each generation have considered their work innovative and creative. We may think and believe that they were deceiving themselves; correspondingly, this may be our own self-deception. Indeed, this represents the inherent difficulty (perhaps impossibility) of understanding the mentalities of centuries past.

NOTES

1. As will be seen in the book, however, terms derived from the Greek word *hypnos* had already been proposed by a French magnetist, Hénin de Cuvillers, in the early 1820s.

2. Most of the original manuscripts were written either in French, English, or Latin, three languages that the present authors are quite familiar with. A handful of eighteenth-century texts, however, were written in German. When possible, we looked for their translation in French or English. If it could not be found, we decided to not use them, rather than risk misinterpretation. The early development of German and Austrian magnetism and related phenomena can, however, be found in the writings of investigators such as Moll and Schrenk-Notzing, whose works have been translated into either French or English.

Hypnosis, Will, and Memory
A Psycho-Legal History

I

Origins and Development of Animal Magnetism

1

Animal Magnetism, Magnetic Medicine, and Exorcism

Mesmer in Vienna

Most of Franz Anton Mesmer's biographers disagree as to his place of birth. Much of the evidence, however, points to Iznang, a small village on the shore of Lake Constance in Austria. He was born on May 23, 1734, the third of nine children. His father, Antonius Mesmer, was a forester in the service of the Archbishop of Constance. In 1752, the 18-year-old Mesmer decided to become a priest. Having obtained a scholarship from the Archbishop, he attended the Jesuit University of Dillingen in Bavaria where he studied for four years. He found himself more interested in science and astronomy, however, and decided to move to Ingolstadt to study these topics. It is not at all clear if he received a degree from Ingolstadt, nor how long he actually studied there. (According to Amadou, 1971, Mesmer received a doctorate of philosophy in 1759.) Following this, he moved to Vienna where he enrolled in law school for a year, before finally opting for medicine in 1760 (Walmsley, 1967).

Very little is known about his life before he established himself as a physician in Vienna in 1766. He had studied medicine under the supervision of Gerard van Swieten, director of the Medical Faculty of Vienna, and Anton de Haën, who was court physician to Empress Maria Theresa at the time, as well as deputy director at the Faculty. Mesmer received his medical degree in 1766 for his thesis on the influence of the planets on human diseases. He was then 32 years old.

Mesmer married Maria Anna von Bosch, a woman from the aristocracy and the young widow of the late imperial advisor Ferdinand von Bosch. She was the daughter of an army apothecary at Court, George Friedrich von Eulenschenk. Maria Anna was Mesmer's elder by ten years. Many saw in their wedding the attraction that Mesmer held for the prestige and glamour of high society (see, for example, Walmsley, 1967). It was with one of Maria Anna's distant relatives, Francisca Oesterlin that he would first employ his magnetic treatment.

Mesmer led the life of a wealthy patrician. His clientele was mainly from the aristocracy and his house was visited by famous musicians among whom were his friends Wolfgang Amadeus Mozart and Christoph Willibald Gluck. He himself played the glass harmonica with some talent, a skill that would come to be a part of his magnetic treatment.

The medical practice of that period was quite rudimentary. The most common medical treatments included leeches, blood letting, cupping glasses, the administration of violent medications such as arsenic and emetics, herbal drugs, and the use of magnets and electricity. Surgery was not as yet recognized by the medical profession. In his early practice, Mesmer was particularly interested in using magnets, electric shocks, and cream of tartar. As will be seen later, he abandoned the use of the first two after his discovery of animal magnetism, but retained the latter. Mesmer, like most physicians of his time, believed that most human diseases were caused by internal obstructions; relieving the bowels with the aid of tartar became a hallmark of his magnetic practice.

Around 1773, Mesmer met with a Jesuit priest, Father Maximilian Hell, who was teaching astronomy in Vienna. Father Hell also had studied magnetic medicine for more than 15 years. He used it to treat various diseases, mainly of nervous origin. He fashioned his own magnets to fit specific human organs believing that their therapeutic value depended upon their shape. Mesmer consulted often with Father Hell and together they experimented with different magnets. Quite soon, however, Mesmer realized that magnets were not a crucial part of the treatment. He wrote in 1773 in the *Mercure Savant d'Altona*:

> I have observed that the Magnetic matter is quite similar to the electric fluid, and like the latter tends to propagate itself through intermediary bodies. Steel is not the only matter that can be used; I have magnetized paper, bread, silk, leather, rocks, glass, water, different metals, wood, men, dogs, in short, everything that I touched to such an extent that it produced on patients the same effects as the magnets. I have filled up bottles with magnetic matter in the same way that it is practiced with the electric fluid. (cited in Amadou, 1971, p. 51)

Early in 1775, Mesmer published his first attempt to systematize what he had observed into a comprehensive theory of animal magnetism. In his "Letter to a Foreign Physician" published in the *Nouveau Mercure Savant d'Altona* Mesmer stated his belief that the therapeutic effects of the magnets were due to a universal fluid that he could accumulate in his body. The physical magnet, or any other means, was but an instrument in allowing this fluid to propagate through the human body. This conclusion, however, produced a clash between Father Hell and Mesmer that proved to be detrimental to the acceptance of Mesmer's discovery by the scientific community. Father Hell claimed that the magnetic effects were due to the magnets and had nothing to do with a "universal fluid." To prove his point, Mesmer abandoned the use of both electricity and magnets in his medical practice in 1776 (Mesmer, 1781).

Mesmer linked his discovery of this universal fluid, and of the human body's ability to accumulate it, to an observation he had made during his adolescence. One day as he was witnessing the bleeding of a patient by a surgeon, he noticed that the rate of blood flow was influenced by the distance that separated himself from the patient. He came to believe that he possessed some qualities similar to those exhibited by healers.

His discovery was rejected by the Academy of Sciences of Berlin which stated bluntly that he was in error, and refused to study the memorandum he had sent to the Academy. It may be coincidental that the president of the Medical Faculty and First Physician of the Empress, Baron Anton von Stoërck, was a very close friend of Father Hell.

Undisputed, however, was the fact that Mesmer produced major effects in his patients. Although disapproving of Mesmer's theory, Steiglehmer, a professor of physics at Ingolstadt, reported that Mesmer produced surprising physical alterations in his presence. He recognized that Mesmer could elicit nervous crises in patients but attributed these phenomena to the patients' imagination. He related the story of one of his friends afflicted for more than seven years by a nervous disease that could be aggravated by mesmeric passes. He had tried it himself on his friend and to his own surprise had been able to reproduce Mesmer's magnetic phenomena.

> I could renew his paroxysm at will, with my hand, with my finger, with a mirror, with my foot, etc., until one of my friends, witnessing the event, distracted the patient, directing his attention to different ideas. At this point the operation and the power I had ceased. I was therefore convinced of what I should think of all this thing. (van Swinden, 1785, Vol. II, p. 198)

Although rejected by the official science of the time, Mesmer's popularity and fame increased quickly.

During the year 1775, he traveled to Switzerland and Swabia where he met with another important healer of the period, Father Johann Joseph Gassner. Gassner represents a transition between the Renaissance and the Enlightenment, a period in which beliefs in supranatural powers influencing man's destiny began to succumb to the glorification of Reason. As will be seen later, Mesmer's treatment was quite close in practice to Gassner's exorcisms, though based upon different theoretical premises.

Gassner: Exorcism Tamed

Johann Joseph Gassner was a Catholic priest of humble origins. Born in 1727, he was ordained into the priesthood in 1750. A few years later he began to suffer from headaches, dizziness, and a variety of other symptoms. He consulted numerous physicians and tried most of the commonly available medicines without any effect. He began to notice that his symptoms worsened each time he was preparing for Mass. This alerted him to the possibility that he might be possessed by the Devil. He resorted to Church exorcism and prayers; to his surprise, the cure was so complete that, for more than 16 years, he did not need any other treatment. He then began exorcising sick people in his parish. His great success rapidly brought him great popularity. He moved from Klösterle in Switzerland to Ellwangen where he stayed for several months before establishing himself in Ratisbonne.

Gassner described himself simply as an exorcist. He distinguished two kinds of illness: natural ones for which a normal physician should be consulted; and preternatural ones caused by the Devil. These latter diseases could be treated only by the Catholic exorcism ritual. Following these principles, Gassner always began his intervention with a trial exorcism (*exorcismus probatorius*) aimed at recognizing the presence or absence of demoniacal influence. If it was recognized that the Devil was not implicated with the illness, the patient was sent to a physician. If the Devil demonstrated his presence, Gassner would proceed with the real exorcism, a ritual that could last from some hours to a number of days. One of Gassner's most celebrated cases (the cure of a young woman, Emilie, the daughter of an officer employed by a well-known German aristocrat) illustrates his procedures and how, to a large extent, his techniques were similar both to those of Mesmer and to those of modern-day stage hypnotists. Indeed, there is a continuity both in patients' behaviors and in their treatments across the different movements of each era (see Anonymous, 1775; Bertrand, 1823; Figuier, 1860, Vol. III, pp. 131–137; Paulet, 1784b, p. 204).

Emilie was a 19-year-old woman suffering from daily convulsive crises that lasted for many hours. The convulsions had first appeared more than two and a half years previously and had been treated successfully by a local physician. She was, however, still suffering from headaches, stomachaches, and certain feelings of melancholia. She sought treatment of these from Father Gassner, then residing in Ellwangen.

To do so, she was obliged to walk for more than 50 leagues (240 kilometers, or 150 miles). After witnessing Gassner's operations for more than two days, she decided to talk to him and proceeded to describe her sufferings. Gassner protested against a medical diagnosis arguing that she was in fact suffering from an illness which was the result of an evil influence (*circumsessio*, an imitation of a natural illness caused by the Devil). To demonstrate his point, Gassner commanded the Devil to show himself in Emilie's right arm, left arm, right foot, and left foot; the Devil obeyed. He asked the Devil to make Emilie scream, turn her eyes upward, and suffer severe convulsions. For more than one minute, Emilie convulsed. Gassner terminated the convulsion with the word *cesset*, and everything immediately returned to normal.

Although Gassner had spoken in German throughout, this word *cesset* (stop or rest) was the first time he had used Latin with Emilie. As will be seen in the next chapter, one of the signs of demoniacal possession was the Devil's ability to understand foreign languages. In this particular case, however, although it was not mentioned in Gassner's report, Emilie understood and spoke Latin due to her good education (see Figuier, 1860, Vol. III).

The trial exorcism had been quite painless and Emilie reported feeling much better.[1] From this, Gassner concluded that she was an appropriate candidate for exorcism and decided to publicize this impending event. He invited more than 20 individuals from the gentry (*gens du monde*) to the ceremony in order to have as many credible witnesses as possible. Rather than proceeding with the curing exorcism, however, he first proceeded to demonstrate how he could control the Devil through Emilie's body. There followed a dramatic demonstration of many phenomena still seen today in stage presentations of hypnosis. Gassner started by eliciting general physical signs of the Devil's presence in Emilie.

These localized and generalized convulsions were provoked by Gassner indicating the location where they ought to appear. Each time he uttered the word *cesset*, the convulsions disappeared. The external manifestations, however, were not enough. Gassner showed that the Devil in Emilie could also control her internal organs. Suggestions were given (in an authoritarian fashion) that her heartbeat should increase, decrease, and become irregular in rapid alternation.

In the same way that physical manifestations could be elicited, emotions and subjective experiences could also be modified. Upon command, Emilie displayed joy and laughter, sadness and tears. With a simple verbal command, Gassner induced pain in different parts of the young woman's body.

Following these emotional displays, Gassner completed his demonstration by showing how the Devil could turn different sense organs on and off. He was anticipating the phenomenon of negative hallucination as well as the hysterical blindness and deafness of later centuries. Emilie lost her sight and hearing as soon as Gassner ordered it.

Finally he asked Emilie to resist the crisis that he would suggest as much as she possibly could, by concentrating on it going away. It is difficult to understand why Gassner gave such a command to Emilie. Was he not demonstrating that she could control the Devil's behavior, albeit through his authority? Keeping in mind, however, that Gassner was a Catholic priest, and that he was performing in front of a highly selective audience, he may have decided to inform them subtly that he had the power to place God on their side.

Gassner then proceeded with the curing exorcism, showing to Emilie what she had to do to conduct it again by herself. The report of her exorcism concluded with 12 signatures of upper-class men, all testifying to the truthfulness of the data reported.

A number of controversies soon began to surround Gassner. He had acquired popularity and had strong support from some of the ruling class; nevertheless, he was looked upon with caution. Inquiries were made into his practice, one of which involved Mesmer. The Prince Elector Max-Joseph of

Bavaria appointed a Commission of Inquiry which invited Mesmer to appear as an expert witness due to his reputation as the discoverer of a new therapeutic modality.

Mesmer arrived in Munich on November 23, 1775. In the following days, he demonstrated that all of Gassner's effects could be reproduced without recourse to the rituals of exorcism. Initially, he explained that the priest was in reality only acting on the patients' imagination. Later, in his 1781 book, he proposed that Gassner possessed a great deal of personal magnetism, but was not aware of it. He wrote: "I said that he was obtaining genuine effects, but he did not know the real cause. I repeat it here" (p. 125). Unfortunately for Gassner, at this period of history where reason was becoming the dominant force among intellectuals and scientists, religious practices were no longer accepted automatically. Following a series of political decisions by the religious authorities who were alarmed by the publicity surrounding their colleague, and the secularization and vulgarization of the exorcism's rituals, Gassner was asked to retire to the small community of Pondorf where he died on April 4, 1779. As Ellenberger has pointed out: "Curing the sick is not enough; one must cure them with methods accepted by the community" (1970, p. 57). By the mid-eighteenth century, France was changing, both intellectually and socially. Darnton (1984) has addressed this issue by documenting the major shift underlying the conceptualization of the "tree of knowledge" that occurred with the publication of Diderot's *Encyclopédie* (1751–1772). The ultimate goal of the new philosophers was "to remove it [knowledge] from the clergy and to put it in the hands of intellectuals committed to the Enlightenment" (p. 209).

At the same time, the work of Jean-Jacques Rousseau was effecting a dramatic change in the life styles of cultivated people. Where the Enlightenment promoted Reason, Rousseauism inspired readers to involve themselves in the pursuit of virtue. The clash of Emotion and Reason became dominant in the thinking of eighteenth-century French high society.

It should be noted that Gassner's technique of exorcism was very similar to those reported during the sixteenth- and seventeenth-century witch-hunts in Western Europe. One of these episodes is illustrated in the next chapter, the possession of the nuns of Loudun. It describes many of the beliefs that were held at the time, as well as the parallel behaviors of both the possessed individual and the mesmerized patient. Gassner's popular image was also a major indication that times were changing. The terror that had accompanied the mere mention of the word "exorcism" had, by this time, vanished almost completely. In the same way that Rousseau conveyed a subjectivistic approach to human conduct, other movements such as German Romanticism, followers of Swedenborg, and the religious wars of the previous century in France all paved the way for the dedramatization of the exorcism ritual. Mesmer was to benefit from the confrontation between Emotion and Reason, becoming the reflection of their interaction on the mind and heart of the population of France at the end of the eighteenth century.

It is also important to recognize that in the exorcism of Emilie, one can find many of the major behaviors and subjective experiences that were later to be associated with hypnosis in the nineteenth century as well as most of the hypnotic behaviors investigated by contemporary researchers. These include rigidity of the body or specific body parts, the manipulation of pain perception, and suggested hallucinations of deafness and blindness.

One other major point is worth noticing in Gassner's procedures. During the exorcism Gassner did not command Emilie directly, but rather addressed himself to the evil force inside her. This semantic sophistication helped to create the experience of an involuntary possession state. This theme was to be repeated throughout the history of hypnosis. While Gassner attributed most of these symptoms to the power of the Devil, Mesmer linked this power to the magnetic fluid and to its agent, the magnetist. That is probably what Gassner intended to demonstrate by his suggestion to Emilie to resist any further crisis. This phenomenon of depersonalization would become a central aspect in the magnetized and hypnotized subject. It was the first time that he addressed Emilie directly. She was to resist the Devil inside herself; and she was to do it through his command. Later on, he showed her what she should do to avoid any further crisis.

Mesmer Leaves Vienna

Although Mesmer eventually triumphed over Gassner, he was still badly treated by the medical profession and the scientific community in general. His conflict with Father Hell, and his rejection by the Faculty of Medicine (presided over by the Baron von Stoërck), contributed to his isolation from the scientific intelligentsia. As if this were not sufficient, Mesmer soon provided his adversaries with an opportunity to attack his integrity as well.

Mesmer at that period was taking several patients into his own home. Three young women were living at his house, among whom was Maria-Theresa Paradis, the 18-year-old daughter of a wealthy and influential civil servant. It may not have helped that she had also been in treatment with von Stoërck for the previous ten years. As can be seen from his 1781 book, Mesmer's accounts of this particular incident added fuel to the claims of his opponents:

> This young lady was eighteen years old. Her parents were well-known; she was herself known by her Majesty the Queen-Empress; she was receiving a pension from her because she had been totally blind since the age of four. The cause of her illness was a complete *gutta serena*.[2] Her eyes projected almost out of the sockets, and were convulsive. She was also melancholic, suffering from liver and spleen obstructions that triggered such delirium and anger that one could not but think of madness. . . . She had taken all sorts of medicines; she had suffered uselessly through more than 3,000 electric shocks; she was treated for more than ten years by M. von Stoërck without success. She had

been declared incurable by the Baron de Venzel, a physician-oculist living in Paris who had examined her in Vienna upon the request of Her Majesty.

If one had to look for an obvious case of blindness, Mlle Paradis was the best example. I gave her back her eyesight. One thousand witnesses, among whom many physicians and M. von Stoërck himself, accompanied by the second president of the Faculty and some of his colleagues came to appreciate this new demonstration and testify to its truth.

Mlle Paradis's father himself thought his obligation was to render these facts public in all Europe and published the details of this interesting cure. His letter can be found in my *Mémoire sur la découverte du magnétisme animal*, translated from German.

It looked impossible to deny such well proven fact. Nevertheless, M. Barth, a professor of anatomy for the eyes, and a cataract surgeon, succeeded in proving it had never happened. After having witnessed twice at my home that she was in fact able to see, he denied it publicly. He dared to say that he had checked her himself, and that Mlle Paradis was ignoring or confounding the names of the different objects presented to her; a simple and unavoidable fact for a person whose blindness goes back to infancy.

That one more person would join the association between M. Ingenhouz and Father Hell, did not trouble me much. Truth was pointing to the extravagance of his contentions. How ignorant I was of the resources of an envious person!

They attempted to withdraw Mlle Paradis from my care while her vision was still imperfect, to stop her from appearing in front of Her Majesty, and prove in such a way that it was a hoax.

To succeed, they had to worry M. Paradis; they made him believe that he would lose the royal pension if his daughter recovered her vision. They persuaded him to take her back from me. At first he acted alone; then, with her mother. The resistance of the daughter, however, made her suffer bad treatments. The father tried to use force; he entered my home with his sword. By the time we had disarmed him, both mother and daughter had lost consciousness. The former out of anger; the latter, because her savage mother had thrown her head first into a wall. Although I was freed from the mother in a couple of hours, the fate of Mlle Paradis really worried me. Continuous convulsions, vomiting, and tantrums returned; she was as blind as before. I was afraid for her life, or at least for her brain. I did not think of revenge which I could have in terms of the law. I thought only of saving this young unfortunate woman who was still under my responsibility.

With the help of the people who had encouraged him, M. Paradis alarmed the whole of Vienna with his protests. I was the subject of the most outrageous slanders. The too easily convinced M. von Stoërck commanded me to send Mlle Paradis back to her parents.

As she could not be moved, I kept her for another month. In the first two weeks, I had the pleasure of restoring her eyesight as it was before this incident. In the last two weeks, I showed her what to do to restore her health and keep improving her vision.

The excuses that M. Paradis presented me, the thanks expressed by the mother to my wife, and their promise to send their daughter back each time I would judge it necessary were all but a lie. Granting them the benefit of the doubt, I allowed their daughter to go to the countryside with them. I never saw her thereafter: It was obviously necessary for her eager parents that this unfortunate person stayed blind or at least look like she was blind. That is what these cruel people were working on.

In this way, M. Ingenhouz and his associates had their own triumph.... (cited in Amadou, 1971, pp. 98-100)

Although it is likely that Mesmer embroidered the story of Mlle Paradis, this episode had dramatic consequences for him. Through the Empress's first physician, Mesmer received a note "ordering him to stop this trickery" (Figuier, 1860, Vol. III, p. 145). This certainly activated his desire to leave Vienna and take residence in Paris. Even granting exaggeration, however, some facts remain certain. It is surprising that following the order by the Empress's physician and President of the Faculty of Medicine, Mesmer kept Mlle Paradis for more than a month. Also surprising is the fact that her father, sword in hand, came to rescue his daughter, but left without her. Whether or not he later apologized to Mesmer cannot be ascertained, but his previous public testimony leaves little doubt; his daughter's vision was restored, at least partially, and M. Paradis had been more dramatic in his recognition of this point than had Mesmer.

M. Paradis's letter to Mesmer can be found in Amadou (1971, pp. 81-84). He appeared to recognize that his daughter had regained her eyesight, and he did not question Mesmer's treatment. Indeed, he judged his daughter's progress to be so dramatic that he asked Mesmer to announce her recovery publicly.

Confirmation of Mesmer's claims in the Paradis case comes from an interesting but unknown book published in Paris in 1839 by a Father Scobardi entitled *Confidential Report on Animal Magnetism and on the Recent Behavior of the Royal Academy of Medicine.* This report was addressed to the Supreme Counsel of the Holy Congregation of The Index.[3] Although a later chapter examines the reaction of the Catholic Church to Mesmerism and hypnosis during the eighteenth and nineteenth centuries, it is relevant to note at this point that this particular book mentions all of the intrigues and plots formulated against Mesmer and the mesmerist movement from the time of his early encounter with Father Hell. For example, in discussing the allegation that Mesmer stole Father Hell's discovery of the therapeutic effects of the magnets, Scobardi stated:

> The situation was critical; the honor of the corps (the Jesuits) was compromised. The Counsel met and decided that Father Hell should *nevertheless* be supported. It was unanimously decided that Mesmer would be continuously harassed and that Magnetism would be proscribed . . . since we had failed to retain it for ourselves. (p. 12, italics in original)

Scobardi also recognized that the congregation played a major role in the episode concerning Miss Paradis. He even stated that it was crucial to do whatever was necessary to ensure that Mesmer would not, even inadvertently, cure the young lady's blindness.

> But what was really at stake here? Was not the idea to prove that Mesmer was an impostor, Magnetism a chimera, and most of all, that one should not quarrel with us with impunity? . . . Could one put up with the presence of one more blind person and the miserable handful of pennies that it costs to achieve such results? (pp. 15-16)

Although it is difficult to evaluate the veracity of Father Scobardi's revelations, it will be seen later that some of the events he cites are troubling.[4]

Following his failures with the scientific community in Germany and Austria, Mesmer spent three months in the country trying to elaborate his magnetic theory. He had not yet formulated the basis of his doctrine and was quite at a loss to explain the success of his treatment. It was during these three months of solitude, according to his own account, that he realized how he should introduce his discovery to the rest of the world.

> The object of my discourse can not be expressed in a objective manner. . . . If I want to be understood, I have to use images, comparisons, approximations. . . . Animal magnetism as I use it is akin to a sixth, *artificial sense*. Senses can not be defined or described; they have to be felt. (1781, p. 23, italics in original)

He left for Paris and arrived there in February 1778.

Magnetic Medicine before Mesmer

It may be asked whether animal magnetism as presented by Mesmer was a discovery. Many of the criticisms that he encountered subsequently in France were centered around the idea that he was merely presenting a new version of an old song. Up to a certain point this criticism is valid. Magnetic medicine was an ancient art; Mesmer's definition of animal magnetism as "the ability of an animal body to be influenced by both celestial bodies and the reciprocal action of surrounding bodies, an ability analogous *to the magnet*. . ." (cited in Amadou, 1971, p. 77, italics in original), can be traced back to the origins of magnetic medicine in the early sixteenth century.[5]

After his encounter with Father Hell, Mesmer clearly separated himself from the physicians using magnets in their therapeutic work. He also called the active agent of his method animal magnetism to better differentiate it from what was then known as mineral magnetism. His theory, however, was essentially rooted in magnetic medicine as it had been known since the fifteenth century.

In 1782, Noël Retz published a small manuscript entitled *A Letter on the Secret of Mr. Mesmer* where he pointed to the similarities between Mesmer's theory and a fifteenth-century medical book written by Thomas Fienus, a physician, which explored the realms of human imagination. Briefly, Fienus proposed that there existed two types of influence on man's imaginative capacity. The first came from inside the person; the second, from the influence of one person on another. In the first case, the success of the influence depended on the natural disposition of the subject. In the second case, the belief that another person had the power to influence the subject was grafted onto his or her natural disposition.

Fienus described a number of illnesses that could be cured using the second type of influence on the imagination of the patient. He argued that both imagination and the beliefs one had in the curing power of the physician were responsible for the successful treatment of these illnesses. This conclusion was presented by Retz as the main explanation of Mesmer's successes. He also pointed out that it was the patient's imagination that allowed him or her to imitate the healthy state depicted by the physician. Imagination and imitation were thus viewed to be the two major elements of mesmeric cures; a conclusion quite similar to that of the report on animal magnetism by the Benjamin Franklin Commission in 1784.

This influence of the imagination on human beings was generally accepted, but could not be explained scientifically in the seventeenth century. Science needed a subtle and mysterious agent that could account for these otherwise inexplicable phenomena.

In 1600, William Gilbert, an English physician appointed to the service of Queen Elizabeth, wrote the first scientific treatise on the magnet entitled *De Magnete*. His treatise was largely acclaimed by physicists, and the magnet became an archetype for the presence of a universal principle in the realm of nature. The principle underlying the magnet was described as a fluid emanating from celestial bodies and penetrating all of the universe. This invisible fluid became the *modus operandi* behind all natural phenomena.

One of the first, if not *the* first physician to hypothesize the presence of a similar fluid in the human body was Paracelsus. He called this force *Magnale*.[6] Born in 1493 in Gaiss, Switzerland (near Swabia), Paracelsus was the first physician to recognize the presence of a preservative and regenerative principle emanating from celestial bodies. According to him, man possessed two types of magnetism. One type attracted the celestial bodies, taking nourishment from them. This part gave rise to man's feelings, wisdom, and thought. A second part attracted the different terrestrial elements and used them in a regenerative way. From that second part came blood and flesh. This state of magnetization in the human body was such that a sick person was attracted to a healthy one in order to restore his or her health. This quality was known as "sympatheism" or "antisympatheism" according to its attractive or repelling quality. Paracelsus could then expand on this principle and talk about the medicinal properties of magnetized objects. Soon, the magnet became endowed with curative properties (cited in Tentzel, 1653). Father A. Kircher's book *Magnes, sive de arte magneticá* (1643) described how magnets were tailored into bracelets or different portable amulets to prevent and/or cure convulsions, pain, and nervous illnesses. From then on, sympathetic or magnetic medicine began to flourish.

Toward the beginning of the seventeenth century a fierce controversy arose between the proponents of magnetic medicine and the clergy. At this time, the clergy still represented a major political force, and it dominated both philosophy and science. Attempts to separate the natural from the supernatural could be an extremely perilous task, as a professor of medicine in Marbourg (Germany), Goclenius, was soon to discover (see Figuier, 1860, Vol. III). He published a treatise in 1608 on the magnetic cure of sores, using a "weapon salve." In this he was following Paracelsus who had been the first to discuss the possibility of manufacturing a salve that possessed magnetic properties. According to Paracelsus, a wound could be cured by rubbing the instrument that had caused it with such a salve. This unusual property would find its equivalent in the doctrine of animal magnetism. It would be through the magnetist that the magnetized individual would be in "rapport" with the world. Everything felt by the magnetist would resonate in his patients. The clergy did not react favorably to such publicized belief. Through the voice of one of its members, Father Roberti, Goclenius's contentions were challenged. In 1615, Roberti wrote his first refutation in a book entitled *Short Anatomy of the Treatise on the Magnetic Cures of Sores by Goclenius.* His main argument was that the efficiency of the weapon salve came from the work of the Devil.

Goclenius replied in his book *The Articulation of the Magnetic Philosophy, Contrasted with the Miserable Anatomy of John Roberti* (1617), arguing that the cures were natural and followed the universal principle of sympatheism. The conflict at that point lost its scientific base and both authors entered the realm of sarcasm, satire, and threats. Roberti replied in 1618 with a book entitled *Goclenius, The Man Who Is Punishing Himself.* Goclenius retorted with *The Stupid Science of Roberti* in 1618. Roberti then proceeded to espouse a clearly defamatory stance, accusing Goclenius of being a Calvinist, which at the time placed the physician in an uncomfortable proximity to the stake.

Roberti followed this with a second libelous pamphlet called *Goclenius the Magician, Seriously Delirious* at which point Goclenius realized that silence was not merely appropriate, but necessary for his survival (see Figuier, 1860, Vol. III, pp. 101–103). Roberti's victory, however, was short-lived. One of Goclenius's followers, J. B. van Helmont decided to attack Roberti. Many authors began to defend magnetic medicine, among whom was Helimontius (one of the first to talk about the possibility of transferring diseases from a patient to an animal, or any other substance). The next major contender, however, came from Scotland.

Robert Fludd believed in the existence of a universal principle from which all was created. The soul was but a small part of this universal principle. Sympatheism and antisympatheism depended on the direction taken by this principle. According to Fludd, man possessed different poles and different magnetisms: positive, negative, moral, and physical. In the case of a positive magnetism between two individuals there was a danger of communicating certain diseases either moral or physical. In this theory can be seen the roots of what Mesmer presented as negative magnetism and the necessity for the magnetist to be in a good physical and mental health. In fact, Mesmer would describe the divisions of the human body as the flux and reflux of the universal fluid running along different poles.

In his book *Philosophia moysaïca* (1638), Fludd provided numerous examples of how illnesses could be transfered from a human body to a tree. Not all trees were thought to be as equally receptive; the oak or willow tree represented the best choice. In order to treat an illness successfully, it was necessary to cut out a piece of the bark, make a hole in the tree, and place either some urine or hair of the diseased person in it. By replacing the bark, the disease would transfer to the tree. (This use of trees later provided an interesting episode in the development of animal magnetism.)

In *Philosophia moysaïca*, there was also a chapter on the role played by the Devil in the human body. Fludd believed in the reality of the Devil, and its ability to interfere with the magnetic quality. This belief, however, did not prevent Father Kircher five years later in 1643 from violently attacking the doctrine presented by Fludd. Kircher and Fludd were by then two well-known scientists who had studied the properties of magnets. It is thus very likely that there was some professional rivalry between the two men that transcended mere religious beliefs. In the early pages of his book, Kircher clearly indicated his distaste for Fludd's views:

> We see men who, because of their inability to produce new and certain experiments on the magnetic qualities, will speculate false and illusory ideas, overrunning schools with all kinds of dreams, fantastic things, untenable lies, that should render them shameful. Take, for example, the use of the infamous Weapon Salve recommended by Goclenius, and a number of other similar practices introduced recently into medical practice. (p. 30)

Kircher rejected the analogy between the magnet and the human body, especially in light of some bizarre and superstitious practices to which it had given rise. One of these practices constituted a major judicial proof of a wife's fidelity. The test consisted in placing a magnetic stone on a woman's body while she was asleep. When she awoke, as she would once the stone had been placed, she would either tenderly embrace her husband, signifying that she was a faithful spouse, or would flee the scene, thereby signifying her infidelity.

Kircher's book contained all the observations that he had performed on sympatheism and antisympatheism as found in nature. For Kircher, there existed a plurality of magnetisms among which he detected what he called *zoomagnetism* or animal magnetism. He referred also to magnetism in remedies, music, imagination, and love. In his description of magnetism in music, Kircher explained how certain instruments can influence diverse passions. He even described the glass harmonica (p. 721) which in a sense deprived Mesmer in advance of any claims of originality in his theory of magnetism.[7]

The acceptance of the notion of sympatheism led to many reports of an incredible nature. One of the most picturesque has been described by a number of authors. A famous sixteenth-century surgeon, Taliacot (professor of medicine in Marbourg), had perfected an intervention that allowed the replacement and correction of defective noses. In one case, a man from Brussels who had undergone the Taliacot intervention returned home, living a normal life. The operation had been a complete success. After a few years, however, his nose became cold and rotten before finally falling off. Nobody could explain the phenomenon until it was learned that the donor, a man from Bologna who had sold a part of the skin of his arm to fashion the new nose, had died at the same time the nose had fallen off. This unmistakably demonstrated the force of sympatheism at play in nature. Even Voltaire wrote a sarcastic poem on Taliacot:

> And so Taliacotus,
> as great as Aesklipios of Etruria
> repaired all the lost noses
> with an admirable technique.
> He could easily take
> A piece of a poor man's ass
> and properly place it upon a stranger's nose.
>
> Often, though, it would happen
> that when the donor died
> the borrower's nose would fall off.
>
> And so in the same coffin
> by justice or just agreement
> the nose of the borrower
> was reunited with the ass of the donor.
> (cited in Figuier, 1860, Vol. III, p. 114)

Of all the philosophers, physicians, and physicists who wrote on magnetism in the fifteenth, sixteenth, and seventeenth centuries, there is one in which Mesmer could have found all of his theory already laid down. Guillaume Maxwell, a Scottish gentleman, is the one person whose theoretical writings most closely resemble those of Mesmer. In fact, most of Mesmer's ideas about magnetism can be found in Maxwell's writings. Maxwell believed in a universal spirit, a unique vital principle, that came from the celestial bodies and could be transmitted to any body having the correct dispositions. It could be used therapeutically and, like Mesmer's system, it was primarily physical. It represented the transposition of a physical force from one living body to another. He wrote of its medical application:

> It is in this domain that one finds all the excellence of magnetic medicine, whose help can be accumulated without any fear of bad consequences or of irritating natural processes. . . . In ordinary medicine, internal medication is used that often has negative consequences. In magnetic medicine, quite to the contrary, the help is always external and comes only from the fortifying side. (1679, p. 199)

Maxwell regarded magnetism as a panacea. All diseases were the result of a decrease in the vital spirit which could be reinstated by magnetic practices. It was also an approach to preventive medicine, which was another of Mesmer's conclusions on the value of magnetic fluid. Maxwell, however, never described all the procedures by which such benefit could be attained. At this time, talismans, mummies, magical boxes, and amulets were used to preserve and use this vital spirit.

One final point should be emphasized. Although many authors had touched on the moral implications of magnetic treatment, and many religious individuals had underscored its similarities with the Devil's action, Maxwell was the first person to point to the specific moral danger of using magnetic medicine. He warned his contemporaries that the use of this vital force could allow absolute dominion over the hearts and minds of women. In his book *De Medicina Magnetica* (1679), he wrote:

> It is not wise to talk about these matters because of the problems it can create. It can especially provide the occasion to satisfy a dissolute passion. Even if we were to talk overtly about this (and of that God disapproves) fathers could not trust their daughters, husbands could not trust their wives and even women could not trust themselves. (cited in Thouret, 1784, p. 60)

Well before Mesmer began practicing in Paris, magnetic medicine was believed to be morally dangerous. No doubt the relation between unorthodox medical practices and some of the beliefs in witchcraft and religious possession that were contemporaneous with the onset of magnetic doctrines helped to shape this apparently unjustified reputation. It must be stated, however, that no single concrete case of abuse was documented in this early period of the history of magnetic medicine.

Mesmer never admitted to having been influenced by these authors. In a letter dated August 16, 1784, Mesmer specifically denied having read Maxwell although he recognized that there could be some coincidental similarities between them. After all, Mesmer was following the scientific and religious trends of his time. The only authors that he seemed to have read were Newton and Mead, both of whom influenced the ideas expressed in his medical dissertation. In fact, most of the clinical cases cited by Mesmer in his thesis were taken directly and without acknowledgement from Richard Mead's 1746 book *De imperio solis ac lunae in corpora humana et morbis in de oriundis* (see Amadou, 1971).

One final precursor of animal magnetism should be mentioned, especially since he is probably the one who most approached Mesmer in terms of his therapeutic practice. Valentin Greatrakes, born in Ireland, was the most well-known and successful faith healer of the seventeenth century.

In 1662, he had the revelation that he could cure *scrofula* (swelling of the lymph nodes especially in the neck region). It must at first have been a surprise since only the kings of France and England were thought to possess this divine gift (Browne, 1684). In the following three years, his gift increased rendering him able to cure a large selection of illnesses including ulcers, wounds, and convulsions. His greatest success, however, was with pain. In April 1665, the clergy, irritated by his successes, promulgated an interdiction to cure. Greatrakes left for England where he met with even greater success. He had no particular theory to account for his curing power; he believed it was a gift from God. He cured by touching, recognizing that he was not effecting miracles but that there was some mysterious salutary influence emanating from his body.

Greatrakes performed his successful treatments in front of the most prestigious people in the British Kingdom: the King of England, the Duke of Buckingham, and the French Ambassador to England, M. de Comminges. In his book, *Observationum medicarum libri tres* (1691), Pechlin presented the testimonies of illustrious medical doctors who had witnessed Greatrakes's cures. As was subsequently the case with Mesmer, Greatrakes could not cure everyone and he had more partial successes than complete ones. One of his techniques was to displace the pain from its actual location to the feet in order to evacuate it from the body. If he was distracted and had to stop, the pain stayed where it was, rather than returning to its original location. When the treatment was resumed, the pain was drained to the toes and dispelled from the body.

As can be seen from this brief summary of magnetic medicine, all the necessary conditions for the establishment of a theory and practice of animal magnetism were present at the time Mesmer started publicizing his therapeutic approach. If Mesmer did not actually invent anything, he had the privileged roles of extending these previous practices into all of the strata of society, and perhaps, more importantly, of attracting the attention of the scientists and physicians of the time to what had been up to then, an obscure therapeutic agent.

Many have said that Mesmerism would not have had such popular recognition if Mesmer had not decided to reside in Paris. The French were enthusiastic for the esoteric and the bizarre as well as for the exciting discoveries of eighteenth-century science. The climate that reigned in France at the time of Mesmer's arrival in Paris will be explored in Chapter 3. It should be noted, however, that none of Mesmer's precursors were French. Most of them came either from Germany or what is now the United Kingdom. The reverse would happen during the following century, as France became the center of the study of animal magnetism. Before tracing the subsequent development of animal magnetism, however, it is necessary to explore briefly two major phenomena of European and mostly French history, as they also had a direct influence on the perception of animal magnetism. In the same way that the witch hunts and religious fanaticism that struck France in the sixteenth, seventeenth, and eighteenth centuries were to provide a panoply of behaviors and experiences that would be role models for the magnetized individuals, magnetic medicine had paved the way, both conceptually and clinically, to the development of animal magnetism.

Appendix: Gassner's Exorcism of Emilie

The following text is a transcript of the exorcism that Gassner performed on Emilie. We followed Figuier's ordering of the text. According to Figuier (1860, Vol. III, pp. 130–138), the text represents a word-for-word transcription of the actual procedures followed by Gassner.

"Praecipio tibi, in nomine Jesu, ut minister Christi et Ecclesiae, veniat agitatio brachiorum quam anteceder habuisti" (I admonish you, in the name of Jesus, as minister of Christ and of the Church, to make the arms move as you did before). Emilie's hands began shaking.

"Agitentur brachia tali paroxismo qualem antecedenter habuisti" (Move the arms to great paroxysm as you did before). She fell back on the chair, and extended her arms, looking very weak.

"Cesset paroxismus" (The paroxysm stops). She stood up suddenly and appeared to be in a good mood.

"Paroxismus veniat iterum vehementius, ut ante fuit et quidem per totum corpus" (May the paroxysm come with violence, as it was before and through the whole body). The crisis recommenced. A surgeon witnessing the scene, Jacques Bollinger, examined Emilie's pulse and found it rapid and intermittent. Her feet raised themselves to table level, and her fingers and arms became rigid; all the muscles and the tendons were so rigid that two strong men were unable to bend her arms. The eyes were completely turned upward. The exorcism continued:

"Cesset paroxismus in momento" (The paroxysm stops immediately). Emilie regained her composure and stated that she was feeling well. She recognized that she had suffered some pain at the beginning but that it had vanished as Gassner continued his demonstration.

"Veniat morbus sine dolore, cum summa agitatione per totum corpus" (May the sickness come without pain, with extreme agitation through the whole body). At the word "corpus" the crisis returned. She became completely rigid again.

"Cesset" (It stops). Everything reverted to normal. Emilie stated that she had not felt any pain.

"Veniat paroxismus cum doloribus, in nomine Jesu moveatur totum corpus" (May the paroxysm come with pain, in the name of Jesus, and move the whole body). Emilie fell back on the chair and became rigid once more.

"Tollantur pedes" (May the feet rise). Emilie pushed on the table so violently that a small statue on it fell to the floor. During this crisis, her pulse was even more intermittent and rapid.

"Redeat ad se" (She returns to herself). She regained consciousness, admitting to having felt terrible pain in her stomach, and in her left arm and foot.

"Veniat maximus tremor in totum corpus, sine doloribus" (A great paroxysm comes in the whole body, without any pain). A great tremor shook her whole body without pain to the previously affected areas of the body. Her eyes closed and her head shook.

"*Veniat ad brachia*" (It comes through the arms). Her arms began shaking.

"*Ad pedes veniat*" (It comes through the feet). Her feet shook also.

"*Tremat ista creatura in toto corpore*" (This creature shakes through her whole body). Her whole body shook.

"*Habeat angustias circa cor*" (She has constrictions around the heart). Emilie lifted her shoulders, her arms extended, her eyes turned upward; her mouth became distorted and her neck swollen.

"*Redeat ad statum priorem*" (She comes back to her prior state). She becomes normal again.

"*Paroxismus sit in ore, in oculis, in fronte*" (Paroxysm comes to the mouth, the eyes, and the forehead). She fell back onto the chair, and her face convulsed. At the word "*cesset*" she reverted to normal.

"*Adsit paroxismus morientis*" (She is near a paroxysm of death). She fell back onto the chair and closed her eyes.

"*Aperti sint oculi et fixi*" (The eyes are opened and stare). Emilie followed the instruction.

"*Paroxismus afficiat nares*" (The paroxysm affects the nose). Her nose turned up and the nostrils widened on each side; her mouth opened.

"*Sit quasi mortua*" (May she be like dead). Her face became very pale, her mouth opened widely, her nose seemed to elongate, the eyes turned upward and appeared lifeless. She gave an apparent death rattle. Her neck and head were so rigid that even strong men could not separate her from the chair on which she was seated. The surgeon had trouble locating her pulse.

"*Pulsus adsit ordinarius, sit modo lenis, sit intermittens*" (The pulse is near normal, and is slow, and is intermittent). One of the witnesses, a professor of mathematics, asked that the pulse be intermittent every second pulse beat, then on every third one, and finally that it became irregular: "*Sit capricans.*" The surgeon verified each demand. The same witness then asked Gassner to make the masseter muscle (lower jaw muscle used in mastication) change.

"*Infletur musculus masseter*" commanded Gassner (Make the masseter muscle change). The surgeon felt a swelling on the left side, but the professor did not feel anything on the right one. But it was not the fault of the Devil. In fact he was out to give them a lesson in both anatomy and grammar. Gassner had said "*Masseter.*" That was the singular form and since there are two of these muscles, the Devil inflated only one. When Gassner repeated the order in the plural form, the Devil complied and both masseter muscles showed swelling. Upon Gassner's command, Emilie went into an apoplectic crisis. After terminating this crisis, he then ordered the young woman to demonstrate anger:

"*Irascatur mihi, etiam verberando me*" (She becomes angry at me, so that she strikes me). Emilie pushed Gassner away.

"*Sit irata omnibus praesentibus*" (She is angry at all present). She demonstrated anger toward the audience.

"*Surgat de sella et aufugiat*" (She gets up from the chair and flees away). She started walking toward the door, but then turned away from it.

"*Fugiat per januam*" (She flees through the door). She walked toward the door and began to open it.

"*Redeat*" (She returns). She came back but used a different chair to sit on.

"*Redeat ad sellam priorem ubi ante fuit, et sedeat*" (She returns to the chair as it was before and she sits). Emilie complied.

"*Redeat ad se, et habeat usum rationis*" (She returns to one self and has the experience of reason). Emilie began talking to the audience saying that she had no awareness of having left her chair.

"*Habeat paroxismum cum clamore, praecipio in nomine Jesu, sec since dolore*" (I admonish in the name of Jesus that she has a paroxysm with cries but without pain). Emilie started moaning.

"*Clamor sit fortis*" (She shouts loudly). Emilie moaned progressively louder. Her body began to shake again.

"*Habeat paroxismum gemens*" (She has a paroxysm of laments). She moaned and appeared to be sad.

"*Habeat dolores in ventre et stomacho*" (She has pains in the abdomen and the stomach). Looking weak, she placed her right hand on her stomach and began moaning.

"*Dolores veniant in caput*" (The pain goes to the head). She touched her head.

"*Habeat dolores in illo pede in quo antea*" (She has pain in the same foot as before). She turned around and moved her left foot as if in pain.

"*Sit melancholica, tristissima, fleat*" (She is melancholic, sad, she weeps). Emilie started crying.

"*Mox rideat*" (She will soon laugh). She began laughing so loudly that she could be heard by the most distant spectator.

"*Cessent dolores omnes, et sit in optimo statu sanitatis*" (All pain stops and she is in a maximum state of health). She smiled.

"*Omnis lassitudo discedat ex toto corpore, sit omnis omnino sana*" (All fatigue leaves the whole body; all is entirely healthy). She stood up in an apparently good mood.

"*Nihil modo audiat*" (Nothing can be heard). When Gassner proceeded to ask her name, she did not answer.

"*Audiat iterum*" (She hears like before). This time she answered Gassner's question.

"*Apertis oculis nihil videat*" (Nothing is seen through the opened eyes). Upon asked what she was seeing, she answered that she could not see anything.

"*Praecipio in nomine Jesu, ut non possis loqui*" (I admonish in the name of Jesus that you will not be able to talk). Asked for her name, she answered twice before becoming mute.

"*Loquatur in nomine Jesu, et habeat usum rationis*" (She talks in the name of Jesus and she has the experience of reason). She regained her speech. Gassner then gave her an interesting new command. She was asked to resist the oncoming crisis as much as she possibly could, by concentrating on its going away. He then said:

"*Perdat usum rationis in nomine Jesu*" (In the name of Jesus, she loses the experience of reason). This order, however, did not produce any effect. Gassner asked her if she was particularly happy. She answered affirmatively with a large smile.

Gassner then proceeded with the curing exorcism, showing to Emilie what she had to do to conduct it again by herself. The report of Emilie's exorcism concluded with 12 signatures of upper-class men, all testifying to the truthfulness of the data reported.

NOTES

1. The complete version of Gassner's exorcism can be found in the Appendix at the end of this chapter. The reading of the complete text conveys more readily the sensational effect that Gassner sought to produce in his witnesses.

2. Under this term the physicians of the day included all cases of blindness in which no signs of disease could be discovered in the eye itself. In Maria-Theresa's case, the blindness was thought to have followed a traumatic event in her childhood.

3. In the Roman Catholic religion, the Index was the body in charge of approving the publication of any book written by a member of the clergy or by any Catholic person seeking Church approval.

4. It is difficult to evaluate the historical validity of Scobardi's book. Part of the problem may reside in the fact that the only apparent version is a French translation, and the name of the translator is not given in full. We have attempted to identify who Scobardi actually was by writing to the *Archivum Romanum* of the Society of Jesus (the Jesuits' congregation) in Rome. We received the following answer:

> In answer to your letter dated October 10th [1985], I have to tell you that I cannot find in the Archival registers *any* jesuit by the name of *Scobardi.* I checked it not only for the XIXth century, but also for the end of the XVIIIth century period during which the consultation on Animal Magnetism demanded by the King of France to the Academy of Sciences had taken place.
>
> This name of SCOBARDI is also unknown to the author of our great classical bibliography: Carlos SOMMERVOGEL, S.I., Library of the Company of Jesus. Brussels–Paris 1890–1909 and of its supplements.
>
> The question must thus be answered, in its entirety, by the negative. (italics and capitals in original)

The letter is signed by Father Edm. Lamalle, S.I., director of the Archives. The letter also bears the number 137/85 and is dated October 22, 1985. This should be the answer to the question. It may not, however, be so.

If the author was not a Jesuit, why did he or she attempt to present him- or herself as one? Is Scobardi a fictional name? Then again who is the alleged translator? In our original request, we had given the information that we had on the translator. The answer did not address this point. It was probably not investigated.

As was mentioned in the chapter, many of the facts reported by "Scobardi" are troubling, and many appear to be corroborated by other authors. His book however, should not, at this point, be considered a reliable source of evidence.

5. The magnet in Greece was called $μάγνηζ$ $λιθοζ$ or for short $μάγνηζ$. Literally this expression means the "stone of the fluid," or "stone of magical spirit." $Μάγνηζ$ is the union of two Phoenician words *mag* and *naz*. The first word *mag* signified in the Orient a pontiff, a high priest possessing power and knowledge. The following Greek and Latin words derive from *mag*: $μάγνοζ$, $μεγαζ$, *magus*, and *magnus*. The second word, *naz* has its roots in Arabic and Hebrew and signifies everything that moves, a thing whose influence can be felt from the outside. The Greek word $νόοζ$ (soul or spirit) derives from it. Although Mesmer probably ignored these etymological roots, it is

fascinating to note how expressive the words "animal magnetism" are. The same derivation can be found in the Sanskrit term *maya*, that signifies "illusion"; the term "animal magnetism" can be defined etymologically as the "illusive or magical influence of the spirit" as Moreau (1891, p. 10) proposed, following Lombard (1819). Even if this etymological analysis is a bit farfetched, and not necessarily exact (or at least not necessarily the only one), it does illustrate the romantic ideas (*à la* Rousseau) that underlined animal magnetism at the time.

6. *Magnale descendit ab astris et ex nullo alio* (*Magnale* descends from the stars and nowhere else).

7. It consisted of five glasses containing different liquids in diverse quantities; water, red and white wine, oil, and brandy, for example. Sound was produced by revolving one's finger around the rim of the glass. When Mesmer played the glass harmonica, he had up to 32 glasses all of which had a thin gold layer on the rim. Subsequently, Benjamin Franklin added some modifications to this basic design.

2

Witchcraft, Religious Fanaticism, and Animal Magnetism: Some Behavioral Aspects of Social Change

If Mesmer's theory had already been proposed by the magnetic healers of previous centuries, and his rituals laid down by the faith healers and the Catholic exorcists, the behaviors and experiences of the magnetized subjects had their antecedents also.

This chapter will not be concerned with the origins of witchcraft or even its possible explanations. Rather, we will attempt here to document the *similarities* between the possessed individual (whether it be by God or the Devil) and the mesmerized or hypnotized subject of subsequent centuries. There is something to be said about the continuity of such behaviors over and above the reflection of shared cultural beliefs. The fact that certain behaviors have been regularly elicited over the last four hundred years in a variety of contexts may give some indication of how the mind functions.

A more pragmatic purpose may be served also. One of the major conflicts in the early nineteenth century concerning the acceptance of magnetism arose between the scientific community and the Catholic clergy. Part of the problem resided in the determination of scientists to use animal magnetism as an explanation for the uncanny similarity between the behaviors of both witches and religious fanatics of earlier centuries. This direct attack upon religious practices gave rise to a bitter struggle between the intelligentsia and religious officialdom.

One of the major arguments raised by the clergy for the rejection of magnetism and later of hypnosis, was its potential for abuse and misuse, particularly in regard to morality. This belief in both the dangers of the technique and the vulnerability of hypnotized individuals (the loss of willpower and the alleged heightened sensual arousal of women) may have arisen from the prejudices and beliefs surrounding witches and witchcraft in general.

Rather than provide an exhaustive review of early witchcraft phenomena, specific examples have been chosen from the literature at large. These best illustrate the relations between the different manifestations of these uncommon behaviors. They are also the most frequently cited by the early magnetists in their attempt to demythologize these phenomena.

In the previous chapter, Father Gassner was introduced as a typical exorcist of the last decades of the eighteenth century. The exorcism procedures that he used were quite typical as well. It is the same type of procedure that had been used during the previous two centuries to evoke manifestations of the Devil. There was no need to change the procedures, since it was successful: A remarkably large number of individuals confessed to being either possessed or under a sorcerer's spell.

By the end of the seventeenth century, torture was not frequently applied in witchcraft trials. This may reflect an important modification in the way the Catholic Church looked at demonic possession at the time. Around this period, the allegedly bewitched individual began to be considered as a victim rather than a culprit. It was supposed that someone was responsible for the victim's possession. This person was the one to be chastized.

The Signs of Witchcraft

During most of the sixteenth and seventeenth centuries in Europe, there was a general belief in witchcraft. No one really disputed the fact that the Devil could manifest itself through a human organism. Although a hallmark of Catholicism, this belief was also found in other Christian religions. No social class was spared altogether. As was seen in the previous chapter, few individuals protested the all encompassing notion of possession.

Accordingly few cases of possession were disputed. Once a possession had been suspected, its origins were sought. The chief determination was whether it originated directly from the Devil or through the intermediary of a sorcerer. The consequences of such a differentiation could be dramatic; the possessed individual was usually spared if the sorcerer could be identified.

Usually, the possessed individual was made to explain his or her own possession. This could be for many people a threatening situation; anyone accused by the possessed of being responsible for his or her condition had no other choice than to undergo the exorcism ritual.

The earliest most complete encyclopedia written on the procedures for recognizing as well as eradicating a possession was the *Malleus Maleficarum* (The Hammer of Sorcerers) written in the fifteenth century by two Dominican priests, Father Heinrich Krämer (Institor) and Father Jakob Sprenger. From that point onward, it became possible to identify potential witches (Trevor-Roper, 1967). Seven different signs or phenomena were thought to be indicative of possession: (1) the ability to know the private thoughts of the exorcist; (2) knowledge and ability to speak unknown languages; (3) knowledge of future events; (4) knowledge of distant events; (5) increased intellectual abilities; (6) increased physical strength; and (7) the possibility of body levitation for a considerable amount of time.

The first six points were, in the next two centuries, to become held widely, though erroneously, as the hallmarks of magnetism, somnambulism, and later on of hypnotism. Even the last point, the ability to levitate would be tentatively explained away as a consequence of the increased physical strength of the magnetized subject (see Bertrand, 1823). If an illness could not be explained or cured by the medical science of the time (given the questionable assumption that it could cure any disease) possession was automatically suspected. People suffering from diseases of nervous origin, pain, and convulsive disorders were prime candidates for the accusation of possession. Needless to say, this belief saved both physicians and moralists from many embarrassing situations. Most of what happened in Europe as well as in the United States during these centuries can and has been tentatively explained in terms of social context and shared cultural beliefs (Spanos, 1983, 1985; Trevor-Roper, 1967). There is strong evidence also, although it was not always the case in Europe, that marginal individuals—older women living alone, for example—were prime targets for accusations of witchcraft. As Darnton (1984) so cogently demonstrated, unproductive members of families from the peasantry in eighteenth-century France (mostly young children and older women) were an economic burden for the community. To relieve the social stress created quite unvoluntarily by these individuals, it was common to have them eliminated through the telling of dark tales at the fireside. In the original version of *Little Red Riding Hood*, for example, the grandmother is killed by the wolf and fed to the little girl before she, herself, suffers an identical fate (Darnton, 1984, pp. 9–15). What is important about the ethnological, anthropological, and sociological views of the witchcraft phenomenon (and of hypnosis later) is the understanding that behaviors can be shaped and modeled by the environment. Shared beliefs, however, do not translate identically for every individual; what remains to be explained is why, for some individuals, the alteration in their subjective perception of reality was such as to lead them to identify themselves as witches or as possessed—a more than dangerous social and psychological position.

Although the *Malleus Maleficarum* described the different behaviors that led to the accusation of witchcraft, these signs were rarely the highlights of the trials. Most often, once an accusation was launched, it was accepted as being true, and accused persons had no other choice than to go through with the trial. They usually had to respond to such accusations as eating newborn infants, having sexual relations with the Devil, spreading diseases to men and animals, being able to fly, and being able to change into animal form. They were also submitted to a physical examination in order to demonstrate the presence of an evil force within them. The physical examination, not to be confused with the tortures that were used to obtain confessions, was usually conducted by physicians. They were, most of the time, looking for specific signs of possession; including brutal muscular spasms that could be the result of possession, the ease with which a violent muscular spasm led to a convulsive crisis, areas of skin analgesia believed to be indicative of the Devil's mark on the body, and signs of nymphomania demonstrable through the insensitivity of the vaginal mucosae (again, signs that would become pathognomonic of hysteria in the late nineteenth century [see Chapter 8]).

The physical signs of possession, however, were not believed to be necessary to establish the fact of possession. Medical doctors who were recognized as expert in determining the naturalness of different symptoms did not always accept that specific physical symptoms were pathognomonic of diabolical possession. Neither did they reject the idea of possession (see Diethelm, 1970). In one of the last reported cases of collective possession in the seventeenth century (in the diocese of Nîmes, France), the Medical Faculty of the University of Montpellier, the most renowned French medical school of the period, was consulted on the relevance of the different physical signs of possession. The prosecutors wanted to know the probability that specific unusual behaviors could be relied upon to determine the genuineness of diabolic possession. Questions were asked concerning the issues of muscular control and pain perception, two areas that had been associated traditionally with the Devil's presence.

The answers provided by the learned society were indicative that the times were changing. A naturalistic explanation was offered to each question. The members of the Montpellier Medical Faculty showed some reservations in their answers, however. They did not deny the possibility of possession altogether; they merely indicated that more appropriate signs and symptoms should be sought.[1]

As indicated in the previous chapter, some individuals attempted to explain these nonnormal phenomena in naturalistic terms, but were often confronted with the general belief in sorcery and witchcraft. Needless to say most of these beliefs were nurtured by the powerful Catholic Church which wanted to preserve its political hold on society. From the Middle Ages to the end of the eighteenth century, however, major shifts in perspective occurred toward individuals exhibiting the traditional behaviors of the possessed person. From the first trials for witchcraft in the Medieval period to the discovery of artificial somnambulism by the Marquis de Puységur in the late eighteenth century five different shifts of perspective can be identified. Very broadly they can be summarized as follows.

1. In the fifteenth and sixteenth centuries, the possessed individual was persecuted. The sorcerers and witches were seen as being under the Devil's influence by their own choice.

2. In the seventeenth and part of the eighteenth century, the possessed

individual became the victim of the spell and, as such, was held mostly not responsible for his or her behavior. It became important in these cases to determine if the spell had been cast by the Devil himself or through the intermediary of a magician or sorcerer. Accordingly, the person most commonly persecuted at this time was not the actual possessed individual, but rather the presumed perpetrator of the possession. The person accused of casting the spell could do nothing but stand trial, hoping to demonstrate that he or she was not responsible for the possession.

This shift in perspective is extremely important since it demonstrates for the first time the possibility that a human being could influence another human being from a distance, thus slowly preparing the entrance of animal magnetism and its recognition by learned societies a hundred years later. The reader will remember that it is also during this period that magnetic medicine flourished. One of its principles was the assumption of a common force influencing individuals.

3. In the last decades of the seventeenth century and the first decades of the eighteenth, following the onset of a religious conflict in France within the Catholic religion, and a second conflict between Catholicism and Protestantism, most of the behaviors that had been hitherto identified with evil influence suddenly were seen as the result of God's intervention. Witches and sorcerers became prophets. This major shift in the religious perspective accompanied by the sudden development of the natural sciences brought forward the fourth period.

4. This period is exemplified by the struggle between Mesmer and Father Gassner, or the onset of Rationalism and the decline of magic and superstition. If the scientific community was not ready to accept animal magnetism as a science, it was more than ready to abandon witchcraft and sorcery as major social forces. The evil force proceeded to become a therapeutic one that could be harnessed by persons who possessed the appropriate state of mind. It is interesting to note that the clergy in general was extremely discreet in the early period of animal magnetism. The perception of it as diabolic was to resurface only in the early nineteenth century. The period of animal magnetism can be seen as the triumph of the rational mind over the religious one, though it proved to be short-lived.

5. The discovery of artificial somnambulism reinjected magical thinking into the politically and socially troubled late eighteenth-century France. It could be described as a God-given sickness. The somnambulist more than anybody else came to represent the confusion between the rational and the magical aspirations of men; embedded in this dramatic illness were the sources of all knowledge.

The remainder of this chapter will briefly describe the periods preceding the beginnings of animal magnetism. Emphasis will be placed upon describing the behaviors of the protagonists rather than their *post facto interpretations.* The first two periods will be illustrated by what was to become the most famous case of "demon mania" in France, the Loudun possession, in which an entire convent became demoniacally possessed.

The Loudun Possession

Before summarizing the facts (as far as can be ascertained) of this particularly dramatic episode of the witchcraft mania in France, it is of interest to look at the description of the nuns' behaviors during their possession as written by a physician, François Pidoux. This physician had visited the convent and witnessed the behaviors of the possessed nuns:

> They are delirious, they shout, they laugh, they cry, they show a very long tongue, they profess obscenities, they utter curses, they provoke many fights, they whirl violently, or observe, standing still; they roll on the ground, they rotate on themselves in complete convulsions without suffering much, they are seized in ecstasy; to questions presented and repeated in Latin, they answer appropriately in their own language. They execute the commands of the priest with the utmost precision. They remain motionless, very stiff, stabbings are not felt, and . . . they are barely breathing, lying as if dead. . . . (cited in Figuier, 1860, Vol. I, pp. 238-239)

It is of course of particular interest to note that this description of the nuns' behaviors is similar to the behaviors exhibited by Gassner's young patient as well as to those that 150 years later, the Benjamin Franklin Commission was to report as demonstrating the power of imagination. Pidoux's report was written in 1634, two years after the onset of the first signs of possession at the convent.

The story of the Loudun possession is typical of the second period described earlier. Although the nuns were the possessed individuals, they identified one man, Urbain Grandier, as being responsible for their possession. Grandier, the parish priest, was thus accused of witchcraft and was obliged to stand trial. By being identified with the Devil's work, he was most likely to be burned. The nuns, although subjected to the usual torments of the Inquisition, were more likely to be punished than killed.

No other trial created as much controversy as this one. It has been presented variously as a political plot to remove Grandier from his parishship, as a truly religious trial, and as a massive hysteria where both political and religious powers became so confused that the execution of the parish priest became necessary. Whatever the real story behind the trial, its facts and fictions remained a matter of speculation for more than two hundred years. In the nineteenth century, most writers on animal magnetism and hypnotism devoted many pages to this famous trial. This, in turn, led to a polemical debate between scientists and religious representatives who attempted to revive the idea that only the Devil or some evil influence could be at work in animal magnetism.

The First Signs of Possession

The Ursuline convent in Loudun had been in existence for a few years when in the spring of 1632, rumors spread to surrounding towns and villages that bizarre events were occurring. Some of the nuns appeared to be noctambulists, walking along the corridors, the roofs, and even entering other nun's rooms. Others were complaining of being harassed by ghosts, some of which used obscene language. The nuns thought they were being troubled by their ex-confessor who had died recently. After talking to their new confessor, the crises increased up to the point where it was decided that some of the nuns were possessed and should be exorcised. The confessor and one of his colleagues well versed in the subtleties of Catholic exorcism began the rituals: For more than ten days, the nuns were questioned and exorcised, but without result. Civil authorities became suspicious of what was happening at the convent. On October 11, 1632, two of the town magistrates decided to inquire.

At the convent, for what would be the first of a long series of crises, they witnessed the Mother Superior exhibiting massive convulsions and replying in Latin to the questions asked by the priests. It was also the first time that Urbain Grandier was named as the person responsible for the possession. The two civil servants, however, were far from convinced of the reality of the possession; on subsequent days they revisited the convent. Each time the story of Grandier's involvement was more detailed than before. Although they suspected trickery from the priest in charge of the exorcism, especially since he was a personal enemy of Grandier, they were confronted continually with the fact that the Mother Superior, Jeanne de Belfiel, seemed to be amnesic for what transpired during her crises. However, though she was interrogated many times, she never contradicted herself.

Why was Urbain Grandier accused? Who was he that he suddenly became the incarnation of the Devil? Grandier was a parish priest in Loudun. For more than ten years he had built himself a less than enviable reputation as a priest. He was known as a good preacher and writer as well as a society man. He was also good-looking and particularly liked seducing women. It was also well-known that he was far from rejecting those who succumbed to his charms. As the author of *Les Diables de Loudun* puts it:

> It was not only rivals that he [Grandier] had to fear, but fathers and husbands, furious and outraged at the bad reputation that his frequent visits to their houses gave them. (cited in Figuier, 1860, Vol. I, p. 96)

His reputation as a seducer caused him many problems, both professionally and politically. He had succeeded during the ten years before the events of Loudun in alienating a number of political and religious figures with his less than moral conduct (at least for a priest). Many officials who testified at his trial were suspected beforehand of wanting to prove him guilty.

It is noteworthy that Grandier had never had any contact with the Ursulines. Since the foundation of the convent, Grandier had never visited the nuns nor been interested in any of their business. The contrary, however, was not necessarily true. The nuns, and particularly the Mother Superior, had heard about the parish priest's feats, both political and romantic. He could very well have inflamed their secluded imaginations; during the Inquisition trial, two young women were to declare that they had felt a forbidden passion for the priest when they received communion from his hands.

As with most of the celebrated trials of that period, three major positions surfaced. For the people in charge of the inquisition, there was no doubt that the nuns were possessed. They exhibited a number of signs, physical and psychological, which will be discussed later, that left little doubt in the inquisitors' minds. The trial, however, had gained such public notoriety that trickery was introduced in order to render the possession more spectacular. Unfortunately, some of the trickery was so fatally flawed that it cast doubts in the minds of a number of people on the genuineness of the events. One night, for example, one of the priests in charge of the exorcism predicted that the demons inhabiting the body of the Mother Superior would lift her off the ground and keep her floating in space for a while. When the people of the town heard of this dramatic event, they came in great numbers to witness it. Soon after the beginning of the ritual on that particular night, the Mother Superior started rising in the air. Unfortunately for the nun and the inquisitors, a curious spectator decided to lift the nun's robe and see for himself that she did not touch the ground. He found that she was standing on the tips of her toes!

Far from being discouraged the priests asked for another sign of the demon's powers. One of the demons, named Béhérit, promised that he would lift the skullcap of Jean Martin de Laubardemont, the inquisitor in charge. On the night in question nothing happened. The audience sat waiting for the feat to occur, but Laubardemont's cap did not move at all. Two witnesses had noticed that Laubardemont had taken a seat in the darkness rather than near the light. They suspected that there could be trickery involved. Accordingly, they climbed up to the church vault where they found a man with a long thread and a hook preparing to send it down to Laubardemont. When he saw the two skeptical witnesses, the accomplice fled.

For the second group of people, who recognized the possibility of possession but did not believe that the events of Loudun were genuine, the sequence of trickeries indicated that they were correct. They began writing letters and pamphlets which described the trial in political terms, especially emphasizing the rivalries between the victim, Grandier, and a number of prosecutors. It took great amounts of energy as well as a royal statement prohibiting any public comment on the irregularities of the inquisition's procedures to silence them.

The third group, by far the least representative of all, was composed of a few physicians who considered the possession to be due to some nervous disease. It may be recalled that the controversy surrounding the use of the physical magnet was ongoing at this time. A few medical and nonmedical professionals had proclaimed the magnet's natural powers, in opposition to the Church position, thus risking the accusation of hereticism. The same phenomenon happened in Loudun. The physicians who were part of the Inquisition trial attempted to oppose some of its conclusions. They were severely reprehended for their disbelief. Only one of them, however, actually resigned.

In 1634, Marc Duncan, a physician from Saumur, a nearby town still known today for its medieval castle, published a book on the events at Loudun. Although not a member of the Inquisition team, he had witnessed the procedures for more than two years. Convinced that possession could occur, he took particular care to document its phenomena in his book. This care can best be understood in terms of the consequences of being a heretic! Nevertheless, he continued to deny the genuineness of the Loudun possession. His entire thesis can be summarized by a sentence he wrote at the beginning of his exposé: "Would it not be possible that, due to lunacy and errors of imagination, they [the nuns] would believe they are possessed when in fact they are not?" (Duncan, 1634, p. 13). Having posited this, he attempted to explain how the nuns' behaviors could be explained as symptoms of a well-known nervous disorder called *melancholia*. His thesis was supported by a British physician, Thomas Brown, who, in his book *Religio Medica* (cited in Figuier, 1860, Vol. I, p. 232) wrote that although he believed that some men could be possessed, many of them were suffering from melancholia. In light of this, it is interesting to examine the symptoms exhibited by the nuns.

Leaving aside the clear trickeries involved, the allegedly possessed nuns exhibited five major symptoms that for Duncan were unmistakable signs of melancholia: analgesia, convulsions, catalepsy, the speaking of unknown languages, and spontaneous amnesia for what had happened during the exorcisms. A sixth sign that was also linked to melancholia, particularly in women, was the display of what was then called *erotomania*, as exemplified by the two women who had felt a forbidden passion at the sight of Grandier.

More to the point: The behavior of the nuns during the exorcism rituals was often related to the presence of a sleep-like state that could account for the amnesia following the crises. Not only were they amnesic, but they showed also, on awakening, few signs of fatigue. Even after their worst convulsions their heart rate was not more elevated than if they had been actually sleeping (reported by a number of contemporary authors cited in Figuier, 1860). The next two excerpts illustrate how the behaviors were described by two different authors present at the time of the exorcisms. Both excerpts emphasize the sleep-like quality of the nun's state:

> In their *drowsiness* they [the nuns] become as flexible, as malleable as a strip of lead; their bodies can be bent in many ways, forward, backward, to the side, even up to the point where their heads touch the ground. They would stay in the position they were placed in until we changed that position. (De Lamenardière, 1634, p. 479, italics added)

This text is certainly reminiscent of what Charcot would later call hysterical and hypnotic catalepsy.

An additional observation provides a more global idea of what the nuns could endure during the procedures. The text was written in 1635 by the King's brother Gaston, the Duke of Orléans, after he had witnessed the performances of the nuns during exorcism for a two-day period. The mere fact that the King's brother traveled to Loudun to witness the exorcism indicated the extent to which these events had become public. It is also a good example of the social pressures that may have helped to reinforce some of the nuns' behaviors. The person exorcised in this case was Madame Claire de Sazilli, a woman from the nobility who had joined the sisterhood a few years earlier. She was also related to Cardinal de Richelieu, probably the most influential political figure in France. In fact, when the political debate surrounding the Loudon possession grew, the Cardinal sent one of his own secretaries, J. M. de Laubardemont, in an attempt to hasten the procedures. The King's brother described one of the exorcisms that he witnessed in the following terms:

> The first demon that came up at the command of Father Elisée *having put her* [Madame de Sazilli] *asleep*, rendered her as flexible as a strip of lead. Following that, the exorcist bent her body in many different ways, frontward, backward, and on both sides in such a way that her head nearly touched the ground. The demon left her in that posture until the position was changed and during that time, which was quite long, she did not breathe by the mouth, but had a short nasal breath. She was also *nearly insensible* since the father pierced the skin of her arm from one side to the other with a needle without her bleeding or showing any feelings. (cited in Figuier, 1860, Vol. I, p. 201, italics added)

We see here that it was not the exorcist who induced a sleep state, but the different demons. Only after the demons had put the nuns to sleep could the usual feats of possession be witnessed. As indicated earlier, the nuns seemed to be amnesic for what had transpired during the crises and learned what they had said only after they had returned to the normal state. One of the most troubling aspects of the whole trial was that, upon hearing their own confessions, a number of them tended to contradict themselves, denying what they had said during the exorcism. They felt such extreme guilt that one of them, Jeanne de Belfiel the Mother Superior, who had initiated the whole process, was stopped one day, *in extremis*, attempting to hang herself. In many of the nun's declarations during and after the trial, they denied being possessed. Sister Agnès, for example, who was affectionately nicknamed the "cute little Devil" because of her beauty and youth, said often "that she was not possessed, that people wanted her to believe that she was, and that she was forced to undergo the exorcisms" (Duncan, 1634, p. 15).

When one considers that the Ursulines who were thought to be possessed were exorcised twice a day for seven years, it is not difficult to imagine how some of them came to believe that they were in fact possessed. A number of other women who were also prosecuted came from the town of Loudun after having found themselves passionately attracted to Urbain Grandier. This erotomania was mainly present in the hallucinations and dreams that the nuns reported and revolved around them being sexually seduced.

One phenomenon is still worth mentioning especially since it returned during the nineteenth century as one of the major aspects of somnambulism: the possibility of thought transference. As indicated earlier, one of the signs of possession was the ability on the part of the possessed individual to read the mind of the exorcist. As with somnambulism, two hundred years later, the exorcists did not notice at the time how they inadvertently cued the possessed people into doing what they were thinking. Although no direct suggestions were given, transcripts of the sessions demonstrate how subtle cuing can lead to the appearances of thought transmission without any of the actors ever suspecting that the whole process was the result of indirect suggestion.

Ironically, nineteenth-century authors in their explanations of the Loudun possession were the first to point out that there was no need to invoke the intervention of the Devil when it was well known that a good somnambulist is able to read the mind of the magnetist. It was not until the end of the nineteenth century that authors such as Janet and Bernheim would begin to point to the ability of certain individuals to be sensitive to subtle cuing. Some earlier writers like Bertrand (1823) proposed an explanation of these events based on an interaction between an exalted imagination and a well-defined context; their words would find no echo.

Although for more than two centuries many different explanations were offered for demonic possession, such behaviors always outlasted the explanations. The following example illustrates that what was thought to be a mental suggestion was nothing but the careful approximative shaping of an appropriate response by the exorcist. It was, however, regarded during the Loudun trial as a dramatic example of the Devil's ability to read the mind of the exorcist. It must be remembered that more than two hundred of these examples were reported, though not all of them are as easily explicable as the following one.

On June 20, 1633, a priest from a neighboring village came to look at the exorcism of Madame de Sazilli. The priest asked the exorcist to demonstrate what was called thought transference by mentally suggesting to her to bring five leaves from one of the garden's rosebushes into the church. The exorcist asked (mentally) and commanded the nun to obey the order (usually through gestures):

> The nun went into the garden and brought back different herbs. She presented them to exorcist, de Morans, with laughter in her voice—"Father, is it what you asked for? I am not a Devil to know your intentions."—The priest answered simply: "*Obedias* [Obey]." She went back to the garden; after a number of trials, she came back with a branch from a rosebush that had six leaves. The exorcist said:—"*Obedias punctualiter sub poena maledictionis*" [Obey right away or fear the malediction]; she tore one of the leaves off and

said:—"I can see that you only want five of them, there was one too many." The priest was so astonished by what he had seen that tears came to his eyes. (De Lamenardière, 1634, p. 22)

With the wisdom of hindsight, it becomes evident that the nun understood the priest's hidden thought through trial and error, and not by thought transference.

Finally, it is of value to provide a brief account of the outcome at Loudun. On August 18, 1634, Urbain Grandier was formally charged with crimes of witchcraft and other malefic deeds and condemned to be burned alive in the public square. He was condemned also to submit to the "ordinary and extraordinary question" to determine if he had any accomplices and what their names were. In Loudun, the extraordinary question consisted of placing two wooden boards around the legs of the individual which were then tightly secured by ropes. Once these were installed, and the ropes tightened, wooden wedges were hammered in between the legs and the boards; the larger the wedges, the greater the pressure on the legs. More often than not, the wedges would cut through the skin and muscles and shatter the bones. In the case of Grandier it is reported that they used the largest wedges they could find. Needless to say, when the boards were removed, both of his legs were broken. He was then taken to the stake where he was burned alive.

The signs of possession did not stop with the death of Urbain Grandier. They continued for nearly five years up to a point where most of the possessed nuns were isolated in different convents, and more importantly, the financial support to the convent at Loudun from the Royal Court of France was stopped. The Mother Superior became so well known that she was presented to the King; she maintained a good reputation until her death.

This sad story was merely the beginning of a number of events that would slowly terminate the epidemics of possession and prepare for the next episode of religious fanaticism. In the second half of the seventeenth century, cases of group possession diminished, and by the end of the century they had disappeared almost completely.

What should be remembered is that, already in the sixteenth and seventeenth centuries, most of the behaviors and beliefs about magnetism on the one hand and witchcraft on the other were already documented. Their explanations varied, however, in line with the major social changes of each era. Most of the behaviors that came to form the basis of Mesmerism and somnambulism can be seen in the witchcraft trials. During the seventeenth and eighteenth centuries, they gradually became the consequences of God's intervention rather than the Devil's work, slowly preparing the evolution toward a rationalistic perspective on these extreme examples of human behaviors. It should be emphasized that these behaviors continued to carry most of the beliefs and superstitions that they engendered during the previous centuries, giving rise even today to some enduring misconceptions about them.

The Jansenist Revolution: God-Given Convulsions

Two major religious revolutions took place in France during the sixteenth, seventeenth, and eighteenth centuries. On one side there was a battle between Roman Catholicism and Protestantism; it occupied most of the seventeenth and part of the eighteenth century in one of the most bloody episodes of religious fanaticism in France. This movement gave rise to the famous Protestant prophets who came to be known as the "Shakers of Cévennes" because of their particular convulsions when possessed by the spirit of God. Most of the behaviors described in the previous section were also exhibited by the Protestant prophets.

The second movement, the Jansenist Revolution, is of greater importance because it happened mainly in Paris and the surrounding area and helped pave the way for Mesmer's acceptance there. It demonstrates the continuity within the same religious context of explaining extraordinary behaviors and events by the intervention of supernatural forces, whether they be perceived as good or evil.

Before discussing the Jansenist convulsionaries, however, it is necessary to summarize briefly the main details of the Jansenist movement, with particular emphasis on the situational background of that period.

Brief Survey of the Jansenist War

The Jansenist war occupied the Catholic Church and the French state for more than a century. Throughout the seventeenth century, political and religious rivalries between the Jesuits on one side and the Jansenists on the other so undermined the social order that a political solution had to be found in order to restore a climate of peace and faith within the French kingdom.[2]

The basic question at issue was the much debated topic of man's free will on earth. In the Catholic Church of the sixteenth and seventeenth centuries, two basic positions could be distinguished: On one side, there were those, like Jansenius, who favored "efficacious grace," that is, the necessity of God's intervention in order for man to obtain salvation. On the other side, there were those who favored "sufficient grace," where God's intervention is so discreet as to leave man with the impression of having a free will with which he could work toward his own salvation. A variant of sufficient grace had been proposed by a Jesuit, Molina, and adopted by the then politically as well as religiously powerful Jesuits: They became known as the *Molinists*.

Jansenism was a reformation movement, opposed to the Jesuits, that recognized the necessity of grace to bring about one's own salvation, while denying free will. Following this basic premise, the Jansenists developed a system of morality that was particularly strict and rigid. In doing so, they directly opposed and combated the morality of the Jesuits whom they perceived as betraying the foundations of Roman Catholicism. The fight between the two factions involved not only the Church but also the State since, in France, the King was Rome's representative. During the century of conflict, most battles were won by the Molinists, until ultimately, at the beginning of the 1800s, the Jansenist movement was finally eradicated and all but silenced.

The conflict was more than academic. A large number of people were imprisoned, exiled, and even excommunicated as the result of their beliefs in Jansenism. Even the ordinary people had to suffer the consequences of this religious conflict. An anecdote illustrates both the universality of the conflict as well as the level of pettiness it had reached by the turn of the seventeenth century. In 1713, Pope Clement XI, in a document called the *Unigenitus Bull*, had condemned the Jansenist position. Every Catholic was obliged to pledge allegiance to the Bull even at the moment of death. Of course, most people were not even aware of the Bull's existence. One day a priest was called to assist a man on his deathbed. The confessor asked him:

—Are you, my son, accepting the Unigenitus Bull?
—Father, I am submitted to the Church.
—This is not the point. Are you condemning the one hundred and one propositions found in the book of Father Quesnel [a well-known Jansenist preacher and writer].
—Alas, Father, I never heard about it. I am a good Christian, and I condemn anything that the Church condemns.
—Come on now, said the confessor, let's talk openheartedly. Are you a Jansenist or a Molinist?
—Neither one nor the other, Father.
—Neither one nor the other! What are you then? Come on, be more specific.
—Father, said the poor man after a few hesitations, I am . . . .
—Yes, my son. . . .
—I am a cabinet maker.
(cited in Figuier, 1860, Vol. I, pp. 297-298)

The conflict lasted until 1720 when finally a document was signed by both parties reaching a compromise between the two positions. The Jansenists, however, were defeated. There was only one solution left: miracles. It was the only way to demonstrate that God did not reject the Jansenist position: only the Church did. The Jansenists' prayers were soon to be answered. The episodes of miracles with convulsions and convulsions without miracles began to occur only a few years after the Jansenist war.

The Deacon François de Pâris

Although the life of François de Pâris is particularly instructive in regard to the Jansenist morality, it was not until after his death on May 1, 1727, that miracles began to happen on his tomb. François de Pâris was born June 30, 1690 in Paris. His childhood was particularly uneventful except for the fact that from a young age he showed his preference for a secluded religious life. Many of his teachers were Jansenist priests. The young François adopted their way of life to such an extent that it became clear to his contemporaries that he would not survive the austere way he had chosen to live his life. He denied himself everything that life had to offer. He would only dress with old clothes, fast as often as possible, and live in conditions of complete destitution. He was noted neither as a thinker nor as a preacher, and contented himself by living a life of self-mortification. He had a talent for finding new ways of increasing the pain of living. Very often friends succeeded in preventing him from self-imposed torture that could easily have killed him. He had pushed the Jansenist morality and way of life to an extreme. Not too surprisingly, he died at the age of 37, of complete exhaustion. His life and death may be the clearest example of a religious suicide. He was looked upon as a saint, especially in the Parisian Jansenist community where his behaviors had aroused admiration. Apparent miracles began to occur soon after his funeral.

François was buried in a small cemetery adjacent to Saint Médard Church. Four months after his death, a tombstone made of a slab of black marble supported by four small one-foot-high columns was placed over the grave. The miracles, however, did not wait for the elegant tombstone to be erected. A number of them occurred immediately following his death. The convulsions did not start immediately. As the number of reported miraculous cures increased, the anxiety of the Jesuits, who believed they had succeeded in eliminating the Jansenists, also increased. A few examples will give an idea of their nature.

A young woman, Mlle Mossaron, had been paralyzed for some time. Her confessor, a Jansenist priest, advised her that impossible cures were to be sought at the Saint Médard cemetery only. Accordingly, she decided to visit it. With the help of a friend, she went to the cemetery to pray on the tomb of the deacon, with no effect on the paralysis. The next day, she returned and succeeded in sitting on a chair to pray; again no miracle occurred. On the third day, she kneeled on the tombstone, and although she felt better, she remained paralyzed. At this point, she thought that she should lie under the stone if a miracle were to occur. After a number of effortful trials, she succeeded in slipping beneath the stone. The miracle happened almost instantaneously; Mlle Mossaron stood up rapidly and began dancing around the tomb and all the way home. There were many eyewitnesses to this miracle, including her physician, her confessor, a neighbor, and an apothecary (see, for example, Figuier, 1860, Vol. I).

Most of the miracles were of a similar nature. They were not particularly different from contemporary religious miracles. Their occurrence did not please the Jesuits who decided to downplay them by equating Jansenism with the work of the Devil. But their political power worked better than their logic. Persecutions were resumed and a number of Jansenist leaders were once again exiled. More than two hundred doctors left the Sorbonne following Jesuit political pressures. The Jansenists, however, could rely on a saint, and François de Pâris was not to disappoint them. As the persecutions began, so did the convulsions at the cemetery. They were quickly interpreted as more divine than the cures themselves.

The first person who demonstrated convulsions was a poor woman, Aimée Pivert. A servant at a nearby print shop, the 42-year-old woman could walk only on crutches and with the greatest difficulty. Having heard about the miracles happening at the Saint Médard cemetery, she decided to visit it. As soon as she began praying on the tombstone, she felt increasing pain throughout her body; her bones were cracking and her whole body convulsed so violently that by-standers thought she was possessed. She returned daily for nine days. Each time she exhibited severe convulsions. On the ninth day, she stood up and walked away from the cemetery leaving her crutches beside the tomb.

A succession of similar scenes followed. The testimony of one of the cured persons, Madeleine Bridan, is a typical example:

> I could not stand up; people lifted me by the arms and placed me on a chair where I lost consciousness. When I awoke, I had just enough strength to tell them who I was, where I was living and explain to them that I had come to the cemetery to make a novena; while praying fervently I had gone into convulsions. Some charitable souls picked me up and laid me down on the tombstone. I stayed there for more than an hour and a half in such terrible convulsions that it took more than three or four persons to restrain me and avoid my falling from the tombstone. For twenty-two days, I felt the same convulsions on the tombstone of the holy deacon. At the high-point of each crisis I would lose consciousness; but it would come back later. I would experience the same thing when I was at home if I drank water that had been mixed with some earth from the deacon's tomb. The convulsions, however, were less violent and I did not lose consciousness. (cited in Figuier, 1860, Vol. I, p. 353)

In her description of the crises, Madeleine Bridan stated also that convulsions increased as she approached the tombstone, becoming progressively more painful each time. The cure occurred finally on the day that she was able to go to the cemetery, sit on the tomb, and not experience any convulsions. As will be seen in the next chapter, these behaviors would be repeated exactly by individuals under Mesmer's magnetic influence; the termination of magnetic convulsions was also the unmistakable sign of a cure.

Before long, everyone in Paris knew about the events at the Saint Médard cemetery. It became a popular site where curious as well as sick people would go to witness the convulsions, even to participate in them. Soon the cemetery and the surrounding streets were filled with people experiencing convulsions. Louis Figuier, the famous French historian, described the scene at the cemetery in the following way:

> The ground of the Saint Médard cemetery and of the neighboring streets is fought over by a large number of girls, women, crippled individuals of all ages

trying to outdo everybody else's convulsions. Here you will see some men moving like real epileptics, whereas further away others swallow little rocks, glass and even burning coals. Over there, women are walking on their heads with all the decency or indecency that such a posture entails. Other women lay down on the ground inviting by-standers to hit them in the stomach and will only be relieved if ten to twelve men fall upon them. It is the beginning of the "assistances"; soon, there will be other types more extraordinary, more deadly. Women and girls just ask men for them. They want pain and pleasure, and some will take the pleasure without the pain. We can see some who place their heads between the legs of young men, lifting and carrying them on their shoulders. . . . (1860, Vol. I, pp. 358–359)

The government did not take long to react. After one month of universal convulsions, on January 27, 1732, the cemetery was closed on the King's order. The following day someone wrote on the door of the cemetery: *"By the King's order, It is forbidden for God to make miracles in this place."* And, replied Voltaire: "What is more surprising is that God obeyed!" (cited in Hammond, 1876, p. 221).

Evicted from the cemetery, the Jansenists attempted to continue the convulsions on a private basis. The police, however, were watching them carefully. During the next month more than three hundred Jansenists were arrested and jailed. The persecution did not stop them: A large number of small underground groups were organized, giving rise to one of the most curious European religious movements, based on a ritual called the "deadly assistances."

The Assistances

Confronted by the power of the law, the Jansenists now needed some justification to continue these scenes of convulsion. No longer was it sufficient to convulse because of the influence of some holy person. The convulsions now became part of a greater plan to demonstrate both the decadence of the Catholic Church and what was to be expected and attained if one conformed to a stricter sense of values. To further the enlightenment of the people, the assistances were developed. The assistances were ritualized acts of violence toward the convulsionaries.

They were of two types: the "small assistances" consisted of fist blows, hitting the convulsionaries with small batons, kicking them, shaking them, or any other imaginative way of hurting them in a relatively unharmful, nonlethal way. The second type, the "deadly assistances," were far more serious. The convulsionaries were hit with heavy batons, iron rods, hammers on the legs, the arms, the chest, the hips. It was a way of saying how corrupt and decadent the Church had become. Some went so far as to be crucified in order to demonstrate how God cared for them. By submitting themselves to treatments that could be lethal, and surviving, they believed that God favored them, preparing their passage into heaven.

The convulsionaries exhibited apparent analgesia, remarkable physical endurance, as well as amnesia for their convulsive crises and the assistances they received. Consider, for instance, the following excerpt from Montgeron, one of the scientific men who witnessed these scenes of theomania and participated in many of them as a helper, that is, as one who administered the assistances. As Figuier (1860) pointed out, Montgeron's writings seem to have minimized the atrocities of these violent displays of behavior. Montgeron was to become interested also in animal magnetism in his later years.

> The fire-log of which I will talk here is a very big iron rod. . . . This fire-log weighs around 29 to 30 pounds. It is with such an instrument that this convulsionary received the most brutal blows, not on the abdomen, but in the pit of the stomach. Since I am not ashamed to have been one of those who have most faithfully followed the convulsionaries, I recognize that I was the helper that an author described as testing the violence of the blows that he had just administered to the convulsionary on a brick wall. I had started as usual by hitting the convulsionary with only moderate strikes; soon however, I was convinced by her moanings that the oppression that she felt in her stomach could only be attenuated by very strong blows, I doubled my efforts. It was in vain that I used all my strength; the convulsionary continued to complain that my strikes were not strong enough, that she did not feel any relief; she then asked me to give the iron rod to a more vigorous man. This man did not spare her anything. Knowing from what I had just done that no blows could be hard enough, he administered her the most terrible strikes in the pit of the stomach, so terrible indeed that the wall behind her was shaken. The convulsionary asked him to give her the 100 strikes that she had originally asked for, not counting in these the sixty I had already administered her. I took back the iron rod, wanting to estimate if my strikes that she found so weak would do anything to a brick wall. After the 25th strike, the brick onto which I was striking broke weakened by the previous strikes. . . . When violent strikes are administered, the iron rod presses so much on the stomach that it looks like it penetrates down to the back, crushing all the internal organs. It is at this point that the convulsionary was shouting in a very contented voice: "Oh! This is good! Oh! This is such a relief! Courage my brother, double your strength if you can!" (cited in Figuier, 1860, Vol. I, pp. 382-383)

Although this account is seemingly exaggerated, many other manuscripts describing even more atrocious scenes can be found. Certain convulsionaries received up to 30,000 blows in the months that they submitted to these treatments.

After the closing of the cemetery, only a few of the religious fanatics continued with their secret meetings. Montgeron related that these groups totaled about four thousand, only five hundred of whom submitted to the assistances. Most of the latter were from the lower social classes whereas the helpers were mainly from the upper classes and the aristocracy. This division of labor was to find its parallel in the animal magnetism movement. The magnetist usually came from the upper classes, whereas the magnetized individual tended to be a member of the lower classes.

Surprisingly enough, these sects continued to conduct their sessions well into the 1760s. Miracles attributed to the deacon François de Pâris were still reported as late as 1787. It is thus not surprising to see that, when Mesmer arrived in France in 1778, the Parisians still had memories of these troubled moments. One of the last sessions of deadly assistances was reported by a well-known eighteenth-century writer, M. de La Condamine, a friend of Benjamin Franklin. After having learned of the continued existence of the convulsionary movement, he asked to witness one of their sessions. M. de La Condamine became a witness of not only deadly assistances, but also of a crucifixion. On April 13, 1759, he went to Le Marais, a borough of Paris, to the home of Sister Françoise. Sister Françoise was 55 years old and had been a convulsionary for the last 27 years. She already had been crucified twice, and had received the assistances on numerous occasions. On this particular night, 24 persons representing all social classes witnessed the session.

In the first part of the session, Sister Françoise received deadly assistances from her spiritual advisor. After one half hour of these physical torments, it was decided that she would undergo a crucifixion. She lay down upon the cross where she was first tied with ropes, an d then nails were driven through her hands and feet. For one hour and a half, she lay there, with the cross elevated approximately four feet above the floor. Then the cross was reversed so that her head was down and her feet up, although not in a completely vertical position. She stayed in that position for another 15 minutes, whereupon the cross was reverted to its original position. Sister Françoise remained on it for another two hours. During this period, she underwent most of the other tortures that are described in the New Testament. For example, at one point, a crown of thorns (made from iron thread) was placed on her head. At the end of the evening, more than three hours and a half after the beginning of the assistances, Sister Françoise descended from the cross.

Few physicians and scientists attempted to understand what was happening to these convulsionaries. One physician, however, Dr. Hecquet, published a book in 1733 where he explained the convulsions in terms of imagination and imitation tendencies, especially in women. He was predating by more than 50 years the Benjamin Franklin Commission report on animal magnetism which would reach similar conclusions. Hecquet explained further that for most of the women who submitted to the assistances, the experience was a sexual one. In their convulsions, according to Hecquet, there was such an exaltation of the genital organs that most of the strikes they received on the abdomen and stomach generated pleasure. Again, in the secret report of the Benjamin Franklin Commission, the magnetic session would be described as a sexual experience. Later on, La Salpêtrière's model of hypnosis incorporated Hecquet's hypotheses in their description of erotogenous zones present in hysterical and hypnotized patients.

The Trials of Animals

Within a century, the signs and behaviors that had been so readily identified with witchcraft and sorcery, became signs of divine intervention. Analgesia, amnesia, and physical feats were the hallmarks of these religious fanatics. Once again, certain physicians, seeking to understand the origins of such behaviors, recognized the role played by the imagination and the tendency of human beings to imitate one another. They also provided different descriptions and labeling of these rituals: Theomania, demonomania, melancholia, hysteria, were all terms implying that individuals exhibiting such behaviors were in some way or another suffering from a disease, or at least had some peculiar characteristics.

In light of the history of animal magnetism, it is important to note that few phenomena arise in a vacuum; the seeds were already planted for Mesmer's arrival in France. The sorcery and witchcraft trials, and the various episodes of religious fanaticism (of which the Saint Médard convulsionaries can be seen as the epitome) prepared Parisians for a subsequent episode.

Before returning to Mesmer, a small digression into the legal world of this period is necessary. In the unfolding history of animal magnetism and hypnosis, experiments using animals were to play an important role in substantiating the belief that there was an unknown fluid that could be communicated during magnetization. This effect demonstrated the power of the human will over the will of an animal. Later on, the results of these experiments would even be used as a demonstration that hypnosis could not be a psychological phenomenon only, but had to effect its influence through some physiological channels. A number of trials were conducted from Medieval times onward against animals. These trials illustrate how moral and penal responsibility was conceived of during these centuries and how it evolved. In a number of witchcraft trials animals were thought to be the Devil in disguise. These trials can be seen as the antecedents of the animal experiments that would gain popularity within the scientific and magnetism communities, whether it be in a context of a scientific endeavor or a stage demonstration of the "power" of hypnosis and magnetism. As Darnton (1968) demonstrated, the beginnings of animal magnetism were plagued by concurrent beliefs in magical and extraordinary phenomena. These were often reinforced by the marvels that surrounded the new scientific discoveries of the period, whether it be electricity, the montgolfiers, or helium gas. The animal trials were to resurface at the end of the nineteenth century when the legal and medical experts would confront each other in courts. The issue at stake would be the difference between the legal and psychological conceptions of the human being (Lemesle, 1900). This issue illustrated the problems linked to the evaluation of moral versus penal responsibility, an issue that is still debated today. The animal trials represent one episode of this enduring debate, and underline the consequences of falling victim to our own sytem of beliefs in evaluating these complex issues. In the animal trials as in the animal experiments of the following century, animals would be endowed with will, reason, and memory, although to a lesser extent than their presumed superior in evolution, man.

Animal trials can be found as early as the twelfth century and as late as the French Revolution. Although the subject may appear frivolous at first glance, it nevertheless reflected the attitudes of the legal system, as well as society in general, when confronted with issues of moral and legal responsibility. (It was not until the mid-nineteenth century that the British courts of law would accept the defense of "not guilty by reason of insanity," the first such case being the trial of Daniel McNaughtan.[3])

In defense of the justice system in France, it must be said that when animals were tried and condemned they benefited from all of the privileges accorded to their human counterparts. They were kept in a common jail and all of their living expenses were paid by the government. All prisoners were treated as equals, with no distinction as to species.

One of the earliest reported animal trials occurred in 1120, in the village of Laon in France. In that year, the Bishop of Laon excommunicated a horde of caterpillars that had invaded the area. It is interesting to note that the Bishop used the same excommunication ritual against the caterpillars as had been used the previous year against married priests by the Reims synod.

In 1454, the Bishop of Lausanne in Switzerland decided to sue leeches that were living in the water of the city of Bern. The Bishop sent the following letter to the Court's judges:

> It would be preferable to capture one of these aquatic worms and to bring it in front of a magistrate. The magistrate could then warn them, all of them, those present as well as those absent, to leave the sites that they have foolhardily occupied and to retire where they will not cause any harm. The magistrate should allow them three days to do so. . . . (cited in Lemesle, 1900, p. 365)

The leeches were officially asked to appear in court, but none were present at the trial. A lawyer was commissioned to defend them, and they were judged *in absentia.* They were asked to leave within three days. When they did not comply with the sentence, they were excommunicated.

In 1522, the inhabitants of the village of Autun prosecuted a plague of rats. This may very well be the most famous of all animal trials for it lasted more than eight years! The rats were summoned to appear in court. Not unexpectedly, they did not comply. Their Court appointed attorney attempted to use every legal means to delay the procedures against the rats. One of his major arguments was that most of his clients lived in the country where there was little opportunity for them to have heard of the Court's summons. The court accepted this argument and decided to publish a second summons which would be read in all the churches of the surrounding localities. When the rats did not obey this second court ultimatum, the judge threatened to prosecute them *in absentia*. The defense lawyer, however, argued that the trip to court required of his clients was long and dangerous. He pointed out that most cats, their mortal enemies, had heard of the summons also and were waiting for the rats. In addition, he argued that it was unjust to accuse all of the rats for the troubles caused by a minority. Finally, however, the rats were condemned. It had taken eight years. . . .

Not all animals, however, were found guilty of the accusations laid against them. In 1720, a female donkey was accused of being an accomplice to a murder that occurred in the village of Vanvres. Her master was the murderer. The donkey had powerful friends in the village, particularly the parish priest and many of the town's officials. Having heard of the court proceedings against the animal, the parish priest and a number of citizens wrote a letter to the Court on her behalf. The letter specified that

> We, the undersigned, parish priest and the inhabitants of the parish of Vanvres, certify that for the last four years that we have known Jacques Ferron's donkey, she has always been wise and had good conduct whether it be at her place or outside. She has never bothered anyone either by her actions or her language. Of such we testify and sign. Done at Vanvres, on September 19th, 1720. Pintuel, parish priest. (cited in Lemesle, 1900, p. 367)

Following the receipt of the letter, the master was found guilty, but the donkey was acquitted.

The long tradition of animal trials represented a small surface element of a much broader set of culturally shared views about religion, witchcraft, and human responsibility. These were progressively being eroded by scientific values which sought to explain unusual events in naturalistic terms. The question of free will, of moral and legal responsibility, and more generally of man's place in nature would be omnipresent in the long and difficult development of science, and in its realization of the unavoidable circularity of previously held beliefs.

One telling example of this dramatic change was documented by Marc Bloch, the contemporary French historian, who investigated the belief that the Kings of France and England had the power to heal certain illnesses. The fact is reported by E. J. Hobsbawm (1985):

> at the coronation of Louis the XVI in 1774 2,400 sufferers from scrofula came forward to be cured of the "king's evil" by the royal touch. But when Charles X revived the ancient ceremonial of coronation at Reims in 1825, and was reluctantly persuaded to revive the ceremony of royal healing also, a mere 120 people showed up. Between the last pre-revolutionary king and 1825 the Shakespearean belief that "there's some divinity doth hedge a king" had virtually disappeared in France. (p. 68)

Paris was to become a major center for much of the intellectual ferment on these basic issues. It was into this cauldron of changing beliefs that Mesmer, in 1778, proceeded to plunge. He was to leave an indelible mark, regardless of whether one sees him as a blatant fraud, a misunderstood genius, or as an admixture of these and other characteristics.

Appendix

The following appendix reports the answers that the University of Montpellier Medical School provided the prosecutors in a case of collective possession in the Diocese of Nîmes (France). Although most of the behaviors questioned were explained in naturalistic terms, there is still, underlying the responses of this learned society, the belief that one did not need physical symptoms to infer possession; it remained an accepted fact, in and of itself.

Questions Submitted to the University of Montpellier

Question: Are body curvatures and movements, as in when the head touches the feet, and similar contortions a valid sign of possession?

Answer: Mimes and jumpers are capable of the most strange movements. They can bend in such a way that we must believe that there is not any posture men and women cannot take with practice. . . . So, such operations only reflect natural strength.

Question: Can the speed with which the head can move frontward and backward be a sure indication of possession?

Answer: This movement is so natural that nothing needs to be said than what was said before of the body movements.

Question: Are the swelling of the tongue, throat, and face as well as the sudden change in color good indicators of possession?

Answer: The inflation and agitation of the chest by interruption are the effects of the aspiration phase of respiration, normal actions of breathing from which no possession can be inferred. The swelling of the throat can come from voluntarily stopping breathing; as for the other parts, melancholic vapors that we find everywhere in the body may be responsible. This can not be seen as a sign of possession.

Question: Can the feelings of stupidity or dizziness or the absence of feelings, like not complaining when one is pinched or pricked, or not moving and even not changing the skin's color, be seen as a sure sign of possession?

Answer: The young Lacedemonian who had his liver eaten by a fox that he had stolen, but pretended not to feel anything, or individuals who were birched to death on Diana's altar without any sign of pain demonstrate that one can willfully sustain needle pricks without shouting. In certain individuals, there are small parts of the skin which are insensitive surrounded by sensitive ones usually due to some previous illnesses. Consequently this effect is useless to demonstrate possession.

Question: Can the complete immobility of the body seen in some allegedly possessed individuals at the beginning of the exorcism and sometimes happening during the strongest convulsions be seen as a sure sign of diabolical possession?

Answer: Body movements are voluntary and whether or not one moves is under voluntary control; this is not a very strong point in favor of possession especially if it is not accompanied by an absence of sensitivity at the same time.

Question: Can yapping, or noises similar to a dog, that come from the breast rather than the throat, be a sign of possession?

Answer: The human condition is so flexible that one can see everyday individuals that can mimic the reasoning, voice, and song of all kinds of animals without even moving their lips. Some can even be found that can form speech and voices in their stomach as if they came from somewhere else: These people are called *eugastronimes* or *eugastriloquists*. This effect is a natural one as shown by *Pasquier* in Chapter 38 of his *Recherches*, where he gives the example of the clown Constantin.

Question: Is it a good sign of possession if the gaze is fixed on a particular object and does not move on either side?

Answer: Eye movements like body movements are natural and voluntary. There is nothing exceptional here.

Question: Can the responses that some possessed individuals voice in French when questioned in Latin be an indication of possession?

Answer: It is certain that hearing and speaking languages that one has not learned is a supernatural fact and may lead one to believe that it could be done through the influence of the Devil, or any other superior cause. It is, however, suspect if only a few questions are answered. Practice, or deception by teaming up with other individuals can be responsible for these answers. The Devil is seen as always responding in French or in the natural language of the one we want to see as a possessed one. This fact cannot by itself be conclusive of the Devil's presence, especially if the questions do not contain many sentences.

Question: Is vomiting objects exactly as they were when swallowed, a sign of possession?

Answer: Del Rio, Bodin, and other authors have said that by using spells, sorcerers can make people vomit nails, needles, and a number of strange things. So in real possessed individuals, the Devil can do the same thing. Vomiting objects as they were when swallowed can be natural in people who have a weak stomach. . . .

Question: If there is no blood following pricking by a lancet, can this be seen as a sign of possession?

Answer: It could be linked to a melancholic disposition in the individual; the blood is so coarse that it cannot leak out from such small wound. That is why many who are pricked by the surgeon's lancet in their veins or natural vessels do not bleed. There is nothing extraordinary here (cited in Aubin, 1716, pp. 247–252).

NOTES

1. A complete transcript of the questions submitted to the Medical School as well as the answers that were provided can be found in the Appendix at the end of this chapter.

2. It was only after the resolution of the conflict in favor of the Jesuit theological position that God decided to give the Jansenists a sweet revenge; one of them proved to be the instrument of miracles (or at least the involuntary instigator of an epidemic of convulsions) in Paris.

3. R. Moran (1981), in his article entitled *Knowing Wrong from Right: The Insanity Defense of Daniel McNaughtan,* reports 12 different ways of spelling McNaughtan's name. We have adopted *McNaughtan* as did Moran since it appears to be the way he signed his name (from bank records). His father used the same spelling.

3

The Mesmerist Movement in France: 1778 to 1784

Mesmer in Paris

Following the events surrounding the treatment of Mlle Paradis and the debacle with Baron von Stoërck, Mesmer decided to leave Vienna for what he considered to be a more than deserved rest. (Contrary to what most historians have written, he was not forced to leave this city [see McConkey & Perry, 1985].) Paris was to be his destination. He prepared himself carefully. First, he obtained from Prince Kaunitz, then State Chancellor of Austria, a letter of introduction addressed to the Austrian Ambassador in Paris, Count de la Merci-Argenteau. Second, he left two of his patients in the care of his wife. These two patients, Ossine and Zwelferine, stayed on at Mesmer's house for the next 16 months and left only after receiving orders from the authorities.

Ironically, in the same month, nearly on the same day, another man was returning to Paris after 22 years of exile and more than 60 years of glory. Voltaire, the patriarch of philosophical skepticism, was returning to die; Mesmer was coming to begin a new life. Voltaire's brother was to become a partisan of animal magnetism, after having been a supporter of Jansenism. The clash between Rationalism and Illuminism was soon to occur.

Mesmer's rest was to be shortlived. Although his arrival in Paris had not been particularly publicized, the medical establishment showed an immediate interest in his work. According to F. M. Grimm (1830), Mesmer arrived in Paris with a second letter of introduction addressed to the Baron d'Holbach. The Baron invited him to a dinner at which many prominent literary figures of the time were to be present. Unfortunately, Mesmer's magnetism did not live up to its reputation: "Perhaps it was him [Mesmer], or perhaps his audience who was insensitive to the marvelous effects of Magnetism; but on that day, he could not influence anybody. Since this unfortunate set-back, he has never returned to M. d'Holbach" (Grimm, 1830, Vol. 10, p. 327).

Quite rapidly disputes arose as to the significance of the cures obtained by Mesmer's procedures. Although in themselves these disputes were not serious, they were nonetheless premonitory of how the relationship between Mesmer and the French scientific community would develop.

These early disputes particularly attracted the attention of French physicians when a letter[1] from Vienna, addressed to Father Hell, was published in the June issue of the *Journal Encyclopédique*. Mesmer expressed shock upon reading it. In his 1779 book, he referred to it in the following terms: "The untruthfulness, the thoughtlessness and the malice of this letter call only for contempt; it is sufficient to read it in order to be convinced of this" (cited in Amadou, 1971, p. 84).

These controversies were noticed by the scientific community, and they soon became the source of a series of attacks on Mesmer's honesty and disinterestedness. In his 1781 book, Mesmer recounted an incident that occurred soon after these events.

> One day as I was busy with patients, someone announced to me the arrival of a president of a sovereign legal court. I saw this tall man dressed as a lawyer who, ignoring the people around me, began questioning me about his diseases in quite an outrageous way. In fact, it was M. [Antoine] Portal, a Paris physician, who happy to have deceived me started telling his story publicly. According to him, he had proven without a doubt that I did not have any of the skills that I claimed to have. I had believed, based on the different sensations he had described feeling, that he was sick, and he was not. Furthermore, I had been taken in by his disguise not noticing that he was not wearing the proper presidential pants. (cited in Amadou, 1971, p. 197)

This incident, though actually trivial at the time, was taken seriously by Mesmer. The fact that well-known personalities behaved in such ways was indicative of the reputation surrounding Mesmer, and of the unwillingness of the French medical establishment to entertain his ideas. As such, Mesmer's reaction may have been congruent with what he felt was going on in the medical societies. His attitude here is revealing, and before going further, a few of his characteristics require comment.

The public and the private images of individuals do not necessarily correspond. In Mesmer's case, the difference is striking. Very little is known of the private Mesmer; he has remained a mystery for more than two hundred years. One can obtain an inkling of his character through his writings where he sometimes expressed his inner feelings. A most revealing passage can be found in his 1781 book.[2] In the following excerpt, he describes his inner state of mind prior to his arrival in Paris, following his bitter encounters with the Viennese scientific establishment:

> A feverish passion overwhelmed my senses. Love did not guide my search for truth anymore. I was anxious. The countryside, the forests, only the most

secluded places attracted me. There, I felt closer to Nature. Extremely agitated, tired of Nature's useless invitations, I sometimes rejected her with violent anger. O Nature, would I say in my crises, what do you want of me? Other times, to the contrary, I imagined embracing her tenderly, asking her, impatiently, enthusiastically, to surrender to my wishes. Fortunately only the trees could witness the vehemence of my accents. I certainly looked like a maniac. (cited in Amadou, 1971, p. 101)

This passage illustrates how isolated and tormented Mesmer felt. He was obsessed by his discovery as someone who understood intuitively its significance, but could not document or explain it. This emotional and intellectual passion isolated him from his wife, his friends, and his colleagues. His impetuous character interfered early on in his marital relationship. In his correspondence, he complained often of his wife's indifference to his work, of her lack of intellectuality, describing her as dull and lacking in imagination. Her extravagance with money irritated him; Mesmer, as will be seen in his public life, was attracted to the acquisition of material possessions. He left his wife after a few years of marriage, but nonetheless kept a sporadic relationship with her. He inherited what was left of her fortune after her death.

Mesmer did not have any intimate friends. His only comfort was in music, where he excelled to a surprising degree. His obsession with his therapeutic system as well as a certain paranoia (partly justified) toward the dishonest intentions of both his adversaries and his supporters, made life around him unpredictable. As Madam Brillon wrote to her good friend Benjamin Franklin in a letter dated November 1, 1779, "in heaven, Mr. Mesmer will content himself with playing the armonica [*sic*] and will not bother us with his electrical fluid" (cited in McConkey & Perry, 1985, p. 124).

Publicly, either through his books or his correspondence, two characteristics of his personality predominated. The first was his sense of honor. To honor one's word was the single most important quality that Mesmer professed to recognize in his fellow men. Whatever the consequences, one must respect his word. Throughout his writings, and especially under the attacks of the scientific intelligentsia, Mesmer would never understand that the politics of "all is fair in love and war" could prevail over the respect for an honorable man. Often perceived as delusions of grandeur, his reactions were articulated in terms of what he construed to be attacks on his honor. It is important to keep this dimension of Mesmer's character in mind when one reads his writings and particularly his comments on the different commissions of inquiry into animal magnetism.

Mesmer's attitude is not surprising. A sense of honor was the trademark of the aristocracy, certainly one of the social classes that he attempted to seduce. What he did not seem to understand, or perhaps had not integrated, were the subtle changes that were taking place in the last decades of eighteenth-century France. People began realizing that political and social power were more a matter of finances than of honor. In some cities (for example, Montpellier), the aristocratic sense of honor was not admired anymore; money and work dominated the new hierarchy of values (Darnton, 1984).

From a different perspective, Rousseauism had invaded all of the social classes and was particularly prominent in Germany and Austria. Germany had not waited for Rousseau to initiate its own reaction to the Enlightenment: Romanticism. It pervaded all fields of human interest from the arts to medicine. Mesmer's description of his state of mind and his desire to live according to Nature's laws summarized well the Romantic ideal. The continuous struggle between money and honor in Mesmer's writings illustrated dramatically the social, cultural, and philosophical changes of the time.

The second characteristic of Mesmer's personality was his complete devotion to his work both as a therapist and as a humanitarian. Beyond the therapeutic use of animal magnetism can be found the bases for some profound social reforms. Not only was Mesmer devoted to the alleviation of individual sufferings, but also to the establishment of a socially egalitarian system that would promote man's well-being. His ideas would find a fertile soil in America; indeed, nowhere else would magnetism become so entangled in the development of new spiritualistic movements (see Chapter 7). He was, however, unaware of the fact that his latent philosophical ideas were thrown into the public arena by some of his more politically oriented followers such as Nicolas Bergasse and Duval D'Espréménil. These two were to be among the most prominent political figures of these prerevolutionary years. This latter quality would nonetheless turn against him. As Grimm (1830) noted in his *Correspondance*, "What really decreased the popularity of the new thaumaturgist within high society was his lack of wit and imagination" (p. 40).

Nonetheless, in the months following his arrival in Paris, Mesmer's popularity with the public increased enormously. People from all social classes could be found at his home, observing or experiencing the new treatment.

One of the individuals who visited Mesmer's house at that time was Jean-Baptiste Leroy, president of the Paris Academy of Sciences. He was the first scientist to contact Mesmer publicly and to voice his interest in the new therapeutic system. From 1778 to 1784, Mesmer's life was oriented toward the recognition of his system by the scientific community, and Leroy's visit was only the first step. Three major scientific institutions existed in Paris, and Mesmer felt compelled to deal with each of them separately, though in this he may have misjudged the situation.

To better understand Mesmer's relationship with the scientific representatives of these institutions, a brief examination of each of them, as well as the relationships that existed between them, is necessary.

The Parisian Medical Establishment

Three major institutions were interested in questions related to medicine: the Paris Academy of Sciences, the Royal Society of Medicine, and the Paris Medical Faculty. The Academy of Sciences did not have much to do with the healing arts. Preoccupied by all of the sciences, but most particularly by the natural sciences, it usually referred any new therapeutic approach to the Medical Faculty. The Paris Medical Faculty was the corporation supervising the teaching and practice of medicine in France, as well as the evaluation of new medication. On the latter point, however, its reputation was less than enviable. It was highly conservative, rejecting most if not all therapeutic innovations. It was vehemently opposed to the introduction of any chemical medications, even when their usefulness had been well established. Not long before Mesmer's arrival in Paris, the Faculty had refused to recognize the benefits of inoculation, especially against smallpox.

When Louis XV died of smallpox, it was realized that he should have been vaccinated against the advice of the Faculty. Following his arrival on the throne, Louis XVI and two of his brothers asked to be vaccinated immediately.[3] Following the tacit rule of the Royal Court that *regis ad exemplar totus componitur orbis*, everyone copied the royal example. This was a major blow to the Faculty's reputation. Irritated by the Faculty's conservatism, the King created the Royal Society of Medicine on April 9, 1776. It was to be a new corporation in charge of regulating the medical profession. The reaction of the Medical Faculty was one of disbelief and profound discontent. The Faculty had not even been consulted.

During the next two years, most physicians who sought progress and evolution in the science of medicine joined the newly formed society. In 1778, the King even asked the Medical Faculty for advice on the proper accreditation procedure with which the new society should be endowed. On June 22, 1778, during one of its regular meetings, the Medical Faculty issued a statement indicating that all Faculty members who would not in the following month resign from the new society would be banned from the Faculty. It ordered the Society to stop its public meetings. Before the end of June, however, it received a royal order to retract its decision, and to cease interfering in the Royal Society's business. At the same time the Faculty was notified that it would no longer be consulted on the accreditation process. This was to prove a fatal blow. The Royal Society obtained its accreditation in August 1778; the Medical Faculty had lost its medical monopoly (see Sabatier, 1835).

Although it may appear at first glance that this political battle had little to do with Mesmer, it proved to be an important event in his search for acceptance by the scientific establishment. It is noteworthy that Mesmer did not take sides publicly in the political struggle. He did not at any time voice his preference for any of the three scientific societies. Quite to the contrary, he treated all of them with the same respect and distance (and sometimes with the same disrespect). As will be seen in the next section, it was not an adept political stance. Mesmer may have thought himself to be above political struggle, but the three societies interpreted his position as an attack on their respective integrities.

His first contact, as mentioned previously, was with the Academy of Sciences through its president, M. Leroy. He asked Mesmer to present his system to the Academy, through his mediation. Mesmer accepted and gave Leroy a copy of his 1779 book, *Mémoire sur la découverte du magnétisme animal.* They agreed that Leroy would present it at one of the regular meetings of the Academy in Mesmer's presence.

Upon arriving at the meeting, however, Mesmer expressed his dismay at the attitudes of the academicians. When his turn arrived to speak, he declined the invitation. He described the scene thus:

> As the academicians were entering the room, they joined different small committees which, I thought, were discussing scientific questions. I thought that when the assembly would be large enough to attain quorum, they would concentrate their attention on only one topic. I was in error. Everyone continued his private conversation. When M. Leroy attempted to talk, he could not obtain either their silence or their attention. When he showed some insistence in his demand, he was rebutted by an impatient colleague who told him to leave the text he was reading on the main desk where interested people could consult it if they so desired. M. Leroy received the same reply on the second topic he proposed. Another of his colleagues asked him to talk about something else because he was bored. Finally a third topic was dismissed as being mere quackery by a third member who had interrupted his own conversation to render such an illuminating decision.
>
> Fortunately, up to that point, nothing had concerned me. I started daydreaming, thinking about the veneration I had always held for the Academy of Sciences. I concluded that when it comes to certain objects, it is essential that they should only be seen from a distance. Admired from afar, but so petty from closer. (cited in Amadou, 1971, pp. 105–106)

The next topic on the agenda was Mesmer's memoire. Mesmer asked Leroy to delay the presentation. If the members could not show respect for their president, how would they receive a complete stranger? Leroy succeeded nonetheless in interesting 12 members of the assembly who stayed after it was dismissed to ask Mesmer some questions. They stated that they wanted, more than anything else, to see some actual experiments. Although Mesmer was not particularly in favor of experimenting in front of people who ignored the theoretical basis of his system, he agreed to demonstrate some of the phenomena of animal magnetism. It was agreed that they would meet at M. Leroy's house for the occasion.

On their arrival, one of the guests, M. A., agreed to serve as a subject; he was suffering from severe asthma attacks. The meeting did not go as well as Mesmer had hoped. The observers would not pay attention, and ridiculed M. A.'s answers. Quite soon, only 5 of the original group of 12 were still present. At that point, M. A. seemed to relax and respond more comfortably to Mesmer's attempts. Among the different phenomena that Mesmer demonstrated that night was the possibility of altering the senses of smell and taste. After having covered M. A.'s eyes, Mesmer moved his fingers under his subject's nose from different directions. According to the directions, M. A.

reported smelling either nothing or sulfur. The same happened to the taste of water; it was identified as wine.[4]

Other experiments, this time with patients, were carried on a few days later in front of two members of the Academy of Sciences. One of the witnesses, M. de Maillebois, although impressed by the demonstration, argued that the patients' imaginations could explain the observed events. Mesmer expressed amazement and irritation. To prove the usefulness of his methods, he agreed to a suggestion by M. de Maillebois to undertake the treatment of a number of patients. He would regret it later, arguing that it was a mistake to believe that obtained cures reinforced the validity of the treatment employed. As he put it in his 1781 book: "Nothing can prove demonstrably that a physician or the medical art cures diseases" (p. 109).

Mesmer did not want merely to prove that animal magnetism could cure diseases. He sought acceptance of his theoretical viewpoint as well as its therapeutic applications. One could say that he failed to take heed of his own beliefs on this matter.

In May 1778, three months after his arrival in Paris, Mesmer left for the village of Créteil with some patients. He had only been in Créteil for 12 days when he heard that the Royal Society of Medicine was preparing to send a commission of inquiry to his clinic. Expressing surprise at this news, Mesmer returned to Paris to clarify the situation.

At this point in time the Royal Society had not yet received its accreditation letters and wanted to ratify its existence by making a public statement. Among the different observers who usually came to Mesmer's clinic in Paris were a few physicians from the newly formed Society. Having heard of the interaction between Mesmer and the Academy, some pressures were exerted by the Society to take charge of the examination of this new doctrine. It was proposed to Mesmer that a commission should be formed to evaluate the usefulness of animal magnetism. Mesmer rejected the commission, but accepted the commissioners. This ambiguous position can be explained by the fact that a medical commission's role was usually to judge the usefulness of a new treatment, whether it be drugs, pills, or diets.

For Mesmer, magnetism was not a technique to be applied in the same way that a drug is prescribed. To him, it was only one beneficial application of a larger system of preserving health and well-being. He thus rejected the commission, but wished for the commissioners to visit his clinic to observe the usefulness of the therapeutic application of magnetism. He also agreed that patients should be examined before their treatment by physicians of the Medical Faculty as had already been requested by the Academy. This was an unfortunate and politically naive arrangement. The Royal Society did not want to interact with the Medical Faculty. Patients were to be sent to the Society where they could be re-examined. Having made these arrangements, Mesmer left for Créteil to resume his patients' treatments.

Only one patient was ever sent to the Society. Realizing that the struggle between the two medical agencies was detrimental to his recognition, Mesmer changed his strategy and sent the Royal Society documents related to each case he was treating; reports of physical examinations, as well as written testimonies of physicians and patients, were included in the package.

On a second visit to the Society, Mesmer was flatly informed that the answer of the Society had been sent to Créteil where it was awaiting his return. When Mesmer returned to Créteil a letter from the perpetual secretary of the Royal Society, M. Félix Vicq d'Azyr, informed him that the Society refused to observe his treatment without first carefully examining all of the patients. Included in the letter were the documents Mesmer had sent to the Society in their original package. It had not even been opened. Although Mesmer replied that he had sent the documents to avoid the competition between the two medical associations, and that the commission had been formed without his consent, he soon discovered that doors were closing on him.

Mesmer continued treating the patients he had brought to Créteil. By the end of that summer, realizing that their treatment was coming to an end, he wrote once again to both the Academy and the Royal Society to invite their representatives to Créteil. He wanted them to observe the results of four months of magnetic treatment. The Academy did not answer. The Royal Society, through its secretary Vicq d'Azyr, sent him a four-line note rejecting his invitation. This episode was the last one between Mesmer and the learned societies until 1784. The timing was wrong as Mesmer himself recognized. Mesmer left Créteil and returned to Paris. It was obvious that the Royal Society was attacking the Medical Faculty and not Mesmer by refusing to even consider the diagnostic reports of patients who had been examined by Medical Faculty members. As for the Academy, it preferred to retreat behind the newly formed Society, arguing that it was solely a question of therapeutics and, as such, belonged to that group's domain of expertise.

At this point Mesmer stated that he would have stopped his attempts to gain recognition by the medical establishment if not for his encounter with Charles D'Eslon who was to become, in the following five years, Mesmer's companion, student, friend, and finally rival (Mesmer, 1781; reported in Amadou, 1971, pp. 125–126).

Mesmer's Relationship with D'Eslon

After this less than encouraging interaction with the medical establishment, Mesmer decided to approach the French government directly rather than trying to reason with the three learned societies. He certainly did not need money. His magnetic treatment, as well as his own financial background, was more than enough to keep him miles away from the poor house. As he himself stated on a number of occasions in his various books, in attempts to reply to the often voiced criticism that he was only trying to make money, he was looking for protection, and for recognition, not financial security.

I need to be protected, and I want to be, but only by the king-father of his people, by the minister who possesses his confidence, by the laws which protect the honest and useful man. I will never be ashamed to be under the protection of such a man; neither will he of me. I will never be, and I don't want to be protected by those with small vision who can only appreciate the value of protection through the money it cost them to acquire it. (Mesmer, 1781; cited in Amadou, 1971, p. 123)

This may have been true; there is no way of knowing. Nevertheless, following his rebuffs from the medical and scientific establishments, Mesmer's desire for what amounted to royal patronage was bound to be perceived as having a profit-making motive.

In September 1778, Mesmer met Charles D'Eslon who was a member of the Paris Medical Faculty as well as first physician appointed to the King's brother, Msgr. Le Comte d'Artois. D'Eslon, in his early 30s, had an excellent reputation as well as many friends in high society. He was more than welcomed by Mesmer who could foresee the advantages of converting such a man to his system. D'Eslon quickly became an ardent advocate of animal magnetism. His devotion to and admiration for Mesmer had no limit. In the only book that he published, *Observations sur le magnétisme animal* (1780), he wrote that his first meeting with Mesmer was entirely the product of chance.[5] "Without me noticing it, the conversation between us became animated; I was soon to realise that apart from a very particular form of knowledge, M. Mesmer possessed a medical knowledge that I could only but envy" (D'Eslon, 1780, pp. 19-20).[6]

D'Eslon proved to be an excellent student as well as a good promoter of animal magnetism. He brought so many patients to the clinic at Place Vendôme that they soon ran out of space. They decided to move to a larger house, the Hôtel Bullion, where they could establish a more suitable clinic. It was large enough to allow people to stay when they needed a more sustained treatment. Fountains, an orchestra, well-designed gardens, four wooden tubs, or "baquets," and later on, a magnetized tree for the benefit of the poor completed the arrangement. It soon became an object of intense curiosity. Not only did Mesmer and D'Eslon publicize their new clinic; they publicized also the private treatment that they offered at their respective homes. Although still an amateur magnetist, D'Eslon seemed to have had complete freedom to practice what he had witnessed in Mesmer's clinic.

The four baquets were among the innovations of the new clinic. The baquet, which was to become the hallmark of mesmeric practice, was an economical method of treating several patients simultaneously. Figuier (1860) summarizes the importance of Mesmer's innovative technique in the following cynical terms:

In fact, mesmerism is nothing without the baquet. Mesmerism without the baquet would be like aristocracy without blazon, poetry without images, geometry without axioms, rhetorics without figures of speech, diplomacy without protocols, medicine without clinical practice and religion without symbols. (Vol. III, p. 46)

Although this literary allusion is exaggerated, it partially reflects the truth. The baquet became central to animal magnetic practice, because it both symbolized the early magnetic movement and represented the availability and equality of treatment for all people. The only segregation occurred between those who had enough money to pay for treatment and those who did not. There was, however, a special baquet that the very poor could attend. They came in such large numbers that it proved necessary to magnetize a tree outside of the clinic to accommodate everyone. In this way rich and poor could profit from magnetism. Mesmer, however, confined his own personal participation to the high society baquets.

To better understand the atmosphere surrounding the new treatment, it is of interest to describe the baquet and what occurred around it. Because of the numerous books that were written at the time, it is possible to obtain a reliable description of the apparatus. Upon arrival at Mesmer's clinic, patients were taken to a dimly lit room which was adorned with heavy drapes and zodiacal and masonic signs painted on the walls. The patients were asked to sit around a table that was the cover of a circular oak box, 18 inches high and 6 feet in diameter. This box, or tub, was the baquet. It contained water, broken glass, and iron filings. Over these objects were placed symmetrical rows of bottles filled with water. In each row, the necks of the bottles alternately converged and diverged from the center of the box. It was believed that the more rows, the greater the curative power from the baquet. The water level was adjusted depending on the type of effects desired. The whole box was covered by a wooden panel which had a number of holes, through which either glass or iron rods protruded. Each rod was bent at an angle that allowed one extremity to be in water while the other could be applied to the patient's body. Since there were often many rows of patients around each baquet, the rods came in varying lengths.

When everyone was in position, a rope was tied loosely around each person sitting at the baquet until it was returned to the tub. This rope provided two functions: First, it permitted the magnetic fluid to circulate through everybody before being redirected into the baquet (a kind of recycling process which is thus certainly not a twentieth-century idea). Second, it was through this rope that the magnetist induced the movement of the magnetic fluid. In order to be effective, the magnetist had to be a part of the chain. Once the magnetist had roped the people together, it was thought that nothing could prevent the dissemination of the magnetic fluid.

Not all of those present, however, could be magnetized to the same degree. In his 1775 article in the *Nouveau Mercure Savant d'Altona*, Mesmer had pointed to the existence of individual differences in the susceptibility to being magnetized. He wrote:

I have noticed also that not all men can be equally magnetized: of ten persons that were present, there was one who could not be magnetized, who stopped the communication of magnetism. On the other hand there was one of these ten persons who was so susceptible to magnetisation that he could not approach a patient within ten feet without causing him tremendous pain. (cited in Amadou, 1971, p. 52)

The responses varied also among people as a function of their previous experiences. The neophytes usually did not feel anything unless Mesmer himself came to magnetize them. For the more experienced patients, there were different types of reaction. Some would laugh, sweat, yawn, shiver; most of them had bowel movements, a sure sign of the effect of the magnetism, though this appears to have been the result of ingesting cream of tartar, a light laxative.

In a small proportion of patients, the effects were more intense. They shouted, cried, fell asleep, or lost consciousness. They sweated profusely; laughter and shivers became convulsive. In all this, Mesmer appeared like the conductor of an orchestra. With his glass or iron rod, he directed the ensemble. In one group, he might stimulate a lazy fluid, in another he might calm a convulsion. At one point, he would retire to the shadows to play his glass harmonica.

According to Mesmer's writings as well as those of a number of observers who have written on the phenomenon, complete crises occurred in approximately one quarter of the patients. For the rest of them, magnetism appeared to produce neither remarkable nor observable effects. The convulsive crisis was one step toward being cured. As Mesmer had noticed, however, a crisis did not have to be convulsive; a number of people would simply fall asleep or lose consciousness. It may also be noted here that Mesmer, and most of those who were to follow him, believed that the effects of magnetism vanished when the diseased organs were cured. Indeed, in healthy individuals, the effects were minimal.

The signs of the onset of a convulsive crisis were unmistakable. Convulsions became violent and mixed with moanings of pain, intense hiccups, and uncontrollable crying. Quite suddenly people would begin searching for each other, either embracing passionately or rejecting each other violently. The most extreme cases were taken to the crisis chamber where Mesmer would attend to them personally (Burdin & Dubois, 1841; Figuier, 1860).

This room was specially prepared to receive convulsive patients. It was carefully padded to allow the most violent convulsions. The only other person present was Mesmer. He forbade entrance to any other worker. Once in the chamber he would personally magnetize or demagnetize patients. The use of the chamber, however, was quickly abandoned by Mesmer's followers, following alleged accusations of immorality, as D'Eslon himself would discover later (D'Eslon, 1784).

Mesmer's magnetic technique was simple. The first step was to establish rapport with the patient. To do this, the magnetist sat in front of the patient with his back facing north, feet and knees touching. He would then place his thumbs over or on the epigastric region, and his fingers on the hypochondriac regions, massaging slowly down the spleen. This first operation usually lasted approximately 15 minutes. Then, depending upon the disease, specific movements or *passes* would be made. For well circumscribed diseases like an ophthalmia, or a headache, the hands would be placed on each side of the body around the diseased part. For more vaguely defined illnesses, it was necessary to apply long current magnetization, in which the hands were pointed, from a distance, toward the body and movements made from the head to the toes. It was not necessary in this latter case to touch the patient directly.

Not surprisingly, people soon began making insinuations as to what was really occurring in Mesmer's clinic. This point will be discussed later, after the relationship between D'Eslon and Mesmer has been discussed in more detail. As will be seen, the Royal Commission of Inquiry's decision to study the practices of D'Eslon rather than those of Mesmer was based partially on opinions regarding the two men's respective moralities.[7] As has often been reported, this decision could also have been influenced by Mesmer's aggressive attitude toward the medical establishment (see Podmore, 1909/1964). There may have been also a political ingredient: Word reached the monarchy that many of Mesmer's followers were injecting revolutionary political doctrines into their discourses on magnetism. This intelligence report appears to have been important in the King's decision to initiate an investigation (Darnton, 1968).

Although D'Eslon worked with Mesmer, they did not share the profits. According to their agreement, Mesmer would teach D'Eslon his magnetic techniques and, in return, D'Eslon would attempt to introduce Mesmer's ideas to the Medical Faculty. D'Eslon himself thought at the time that it was a good political move considering the animosity between the two medical associations. In order to effect this, D'Eslon persuaded Mesmer to make a list of new observations and to write a manuscript which presented his theoretical views. Mesmer was less than enthusiastic, but finally agreed after many months of negotiation. At the end of March 1779, Mesmer wrote to D'Eslon that he was willing to initiate a relationship with the Medical Faculty. While Mesmer was writing his manuscript, D'Eslon was busy writing a clinical counterpart. Mesmer's book was published in 1779, followed by D'Eslon's in 1780.

The negotiations with the Faculty did not run smoothly. The books were not well received. D'Eslon decided to change his strategy. Rather than approaching the Faculty, he decided to contact individual members. He convinced 12 of his colleagues to attend a lecture on magnetism followed by a dinner at his house. At the end of the dinner, after some lively discussion, it was agreed that Mesmer would work with patients in a hospital in order to evaluate better his treatment procedures. When the guests left, however, no hospital appointment had been made. D'Eslon convinced Mesmer to take three of his colleagues to work with him at his clinic. Mesmer accepted. For more than seven months the three physicians observed Mesmer's practice. They proved to be so difficult to convince that Mesmer terminated his relationship with them when he concluded that they would never testify in his favor before the Faculty. He did not know that, privately at least, two of them had indicated a favorable attitude to his procedures.

The publication of D'Eslon's book, however, acted as a necessary warning signal to the Faculty. The Faculty was increasingly concerned that the mesmeric movement was becoming popular, especially since one of their most respected members, D'Eslon, had become a mesmeric adept. Unbeknownst to D'Eslon himself, certain members wished to settle the question once and for all. Since D'Eslon had already demanded a special session on animal magnetism, it was decided that he should get one.

As he would soon come to realize, the Faculty's plan was not to listen to either him or Mesmer. The session was to be held so as better to reprimand him. The session was scheduled for September 18, 1780. It can be seen retrospectively that both Mesmer and D'Eslon suffered from severe naivety. A few days before the publication of D'Eslon's book, a pamphlet written by Jacques de Horne[8] attacked Mesmer's morality. He accused Mesmer of using seductive techniques with his patients, techniques that had nothing to do with the good practice of medicine. A second well-known physician, Jean-Jacques Paulet, editor of the *Gazette de Santé* (*Medical Gazette*), even accused Mesmer of sleeping with his patients (although he wrote in a satirical way). The actual fact, however, was slightly different from the way Paulet reported it. Mesmer, as was his habit with patients who needed a sustained treatment, would sleep *in* the room of a patient, not *with* her. Paulet (1784b) was subsequently to write one of the best critical and humorous books on the history of the mesmeric movement.

The physician who had asked the Faculty to grant D'Eslon an audience was Augustin Roussel de Vauzesmes who, in 1780, was 26 years old. He was a new member of the Faculty and saw the situation as an opportunity to expose what he believed was mere quackery. It was also a wise political move to gain popularity with his older colleagues (Figuier, 1860). When the session began, he was the first person to address the audience in which D'Eslon was present. His memorandum was transcribed in its entirety in Mesmer's 1781 book followed by Mesmer's critique of it. It would be too long and tedious to report all of the material presented by Roussel de Vauzesmes here; some excerpts illustrate the flavor of his intervention.

The main thrust of his argument was to demonstrate that animal magnetism was a sham and that D'Eslon in his affiliation with Mesmer had betrayed both the Faculty and medical ethics. It is important to remember that D'Eslon was present at Roussel de Vauzesmes's lecture, together with an audience of approximately 160 physicians. Among these were the three physicians who had witnessed Mesmer's practice in the previous six months. After summarizing what had happened to Mesmer in Vienna (although most of the facts were slightly distorted), he turned his attention to D'Eslon. He characterized the physician in the following terms:

> I will describe M. D'Eslon as a man whose attitude promotes charlatanism, as someone who insults the learned societies and especially this Faculty, as someone who has betrayed the basic doctrine of the medical school by advocating principles contrary to good medicine, and claimed to support his false principles by presenting cures that are both impossible and ridiculous. (cited in Amadou, 1971, p. 146)

He then proceeded to give examples designed to support his main argument. He directly attacked D'Eslon's book by citing a number of its reports of cures as examples of quackery. Among the patients treated by Mesmer was M. Busson, a well-known Parisian physician, who had recently been cured of a nasal polyp by Mesmer. Roussel de Vauzesmes used this case to illustrate how Mesmer and D'Eslon were distorting the facts of their cures. According to Mesmer, Busson had been abandoned by his physicians as being incurable. He had begun treating him with some success. The polyp was receding, but Busson's health was not improving. He died a few weeks later. The mere fact that he had sought relief from Mesmer, however, had attracted much attention. Two years later, it was still discussed. In a letter, M. Busson is described as

> an excellent citizen. His death is the best example of this statement. Because he knew his end was approaching, he wanted it to be useful to humanity. By deciding to be a victim, he went to M. Mesmer; he did not want to save his life; he wanted to die from his treatment to convince the universe that Animal Magnetism was nothing more than quackery. (Anonymous, 1782, p. 24)

Roussel de Vauzesmes was loudly applauded by the audience. When D'Eslon commenced his presentation, many boos could be heard from the assembly. Nonetheless, he proceeded with his own memorandum. His address was sober, and he sought to base his case on fact. Although he made some attacks on the Faculty's behavior, his case was focused entirely upon Mesmer's work. After his presentation, he left the room, to await the decision of the assembly. When he returned to the room, the president of the assembly read the decision of the Faculty. The decision consisted of four short and pointed statements:

> 1. Injunction to be more careful in the future. 2. A one-year suspension of his voting rights in the Faculty's assemblies. 3. Expulsion at the end of the year from the Faculty if he has not denied his *Observations sur le magnétisme animal.* 4. All of Mesmer's propositions are rejected. (Mesmer, 1781; cited in Amadou, 1971, p. 171)

D'Eslon left the assembly without saying a word; possibly he was in shock.

In his 1781 book, Mesmer summarized his relationship with the Medical Faculty in one short sentence: "The only pleasant aspect of my relationship with the Paris Medical Faculty is the fact that it lasted only one day, and that all of our exchanges were made by letters" (cited in Amadou, 1971, p. 137).

Following this episode, Mesmer ignored the medical establishment and concentrated his efforts upon the French Government. His first attempt, however, proved disastrous. After many negotiations with one of the King's physicians on the possibility of instituting a commission that would examine his practice, the dialogue ceased since, consistent with previously held positions, Mesmer saw no value in it. Apparently discouraged, Mesmer told his patients that he would leave Paris on the following April 15, 1781. This announcement alarmed the Court from which many of his patients were drawn. The Queen herself, through an emissary, informed Mesmer that he should not leave France in such a way as it was not a humane method of treating patients.

This led to one of the most controversial and bizarre aspects of Mesmer's attempts to obtain official recognition. He replied to the Queen that he had more than proven his dedication to France since his arrival. However, because he had not succeeded in his quest for recognition, he had decided to travel for a while. He indicated also that there was still ample time to reach an agreement before the announced date of his departure. A few days after his reply, a representative of the Court reopened negotiations. After a four-hour meeting, both parties agreed on the following: (1) A commission of five members would inquire into the usefulness of Mesmer's practice. If the inquiry found his practices beneficial, the government would recognize them in a ministerial decree. (2) The decree would specify that Mesmer's discovery was useful. (3) The government would then provide a property where a clinic could be placed. (4) Mesmer would receive a 20 thousand *livres*[9] life income on condition that he would not leave France without the King's permission. The agreement also specified that Mesmer would benefit from the decree as soon as the usefulness of his doctrine had been demonstrated.

Mesmer signed the agreement, but insisted on modifying two of its points. For his clinic, he asked for a specific castle and domain. Second, the agreement would be void if the decision of the commission was not known before his announced date of departure. This last point left only one month to conduct the commission and reach a decision. The request for a domain was quite consistent with Mesmer's ideas of permanently establishing the grandeur of his discovery. Two weeks later, he was asked to meet with M. de Maurepas, then State Minister, to discuss the agreement. To Mesmer's surprise, the King had decided to modify some of its terms. Among the changes, the King had agreed to forego the inquiry. In its place Mesmer would teach his methods to at least three physicians representing the government. Rather than granting Mesmer some land, the government would give him a supplementary ten thousand livres for him to buy or rent the property of his choice. Mesmer rejected this second offer giving two main reasons.

The first was that the agreement was becoming a monetary arrangement which did not reflect the acceptance and recognition of his discovery. The second was also a point of honor: Mesmer could not agree to be judged by people that he would instruct. He wanted commissioners, not students, who would then become judges. To believe that everything could be reduced to a monetary agreement was taken by Mesmer as something akin to an insult. D'Eslon was present also at the meeting and expressed shock at Mesmer's reaction. He professed not to understand why he was rejecting the government's offer, for it was the most substantial one Mesmer had ever received.[10]

This meeting may represent also the first episode of D'Eslon's estrangement from Mesmer. At the end of the meeting, Mesmer returned to his home, and wrote a long letter to the Queen explaining his conduct. In this letter, he reiterated why he could not settle for a mere monetary solution. He told the Queen that he would prolong his stay until September 18, 1781, in order to better care for his patients. This date, however, was symbolic. On the same day a year earlier, D'Eslon had been reprimanded by the Medical Faculty. Mesmer had a flair for the dramatic. This would prove to be the last direct exchange between a government and Mesmer for the next 15 years. Whether or not he subsequently regretted his attitude is not known.

Very soon another conflict, this time with his partner D'Eslon, signaled the beginning of the end of Mesmer's public life. At the end of 1781, following the negotiations with the French government, Mesmer published his second book, *Précis historique des faits relatifs au magnétisme animal jusques en Avril 1781*, in which he described in detail his relationship with the learned societies of both Vienna and France. A few points in this second book deserve attention. The first is of mainly anecdotal interest. As noted earlier, the introduction of the baquet was to become a hallmark of Mesmer's movement. In Paris, it became as fashionable to possess one's own baquet and to invite people to it as it would be much later to possess a hot tub in California. Mesmer protested this popularity. In a footnote to his 1781 book, he wrote that

> People who claim to imitate my methods have furnished their houses with baquets similar to the one I use in my treatment. If this represents their entire knowledge, it is quite limited. One can imagine that if I had adequate installations, I would get rid of the baquets. In general, I only make use of small means if I am obligated to. (cited in Amadou, 1971, p. 202)

This point, however, connected to a much more serious one. Because of the baquet mania, a number of physicians pointed to the possibility of abuses inherent in this new treatment. As mentioned previously, Mesmer himself had been accused of using seductive techniques, and of promoting an indecent form of treatment. Animal magnetism had also been characterized as extremely dangerous for the stability of the nervous system, especially in women. Mesmer attempted to answer some of these criticisms in his book. On the accusation of indecency, Mesmer replied that

> It does not take a lot of common sense to realize that there is no justification in the allegation of indecency surrounding my household. The expressions of pain are not indecent. There is stupidity in supposing that people from all classes, age, and sex, rally everyday at the sign of pain better to offend morality and decorum. (Mesmer, 1781; cited in Amadou, 1971, p. 173)

Mesmer acknowledged, however, that there could be people abusing his system.

> It is possible that among the numerous people who have come to my treatment, some may have had reprehensible behaviors. I do not know them and cannot judge these particular examples. The availability of a medical treatment cannot be conditional upon the life and mores of those who need it. The only thing I ask for is that my house and the people who visit it be respected. (Mesmer, 1781; cited in Amadou, 1971, p. 174)

Mesmer also took the occasion to reassert that these problems could be avoided if his discovery was officially recognized, thus giving him the opportunity to control its dissemination. Once again he attacked what he perceived to be the prejudices of those who deplored the fact that people from all social classes could mingle in his clinic. He noted that real friendship and admiration were more easily found among the modest people than in aristocratic circles. He had a way with words that did not necessarily help him or promote his discovery.

Quarrels with D'Eslon

During the next two years, Mesmer's efforts to institutionalize his discovery were riddled with internal quarrels and discontent. Some of his adepts began emphasizing new political ideas, especially building on his egalitarian principles. Among these disciples, Nicolas Bergasse was the most prominent. In 1781, he published his first satirical pamphlet[11] on the necessity of rejecting animal magnetism for political reasons. His argument showed that the more healthy a population is, the more autonomous and demanding it can be. It then becomes important to control that population through the medical system to ensure that patients are not cured. He argued that any medical system that could and would cure diseases could become a threat to society. Bergasse was equating the role of the legislature with that of the medical establishment. He pointed out that both were devoted to the perpetuation of the power exerted by the ruling class over the general population.

Bergasse developed a love–hate relationship with Mesmer over the years. He acted as his official writer, corrected Mesmer's texts, and taught the elements of animal magnetism. Subsequently, he developed into a powerful political writer, especially in the prerevolutionary years.

Two books written at the end of 1782 illustrate the sentiment of the intelligentsia following Mesmer's conflicts with the Government and the learned societies. The first one, written by a physician, Noël Retz, is a short report on the origins of animal magnetism. According to Retz, Mesmer had plagiarized an author from the fifteenth century, Thomas Fienus (see Chapter 1). For Retz as for Fienus, all of the effects produced by the mesmeric fluid as well as the different cures were only reflections of two human qualities:

imagination and the tendency to imitation. The two main reasons that had been put forth in the previous century to explain the behaviors of the Saint Médard convulsionaries were to surface once again. Although the role played by the imaginative skills of the mesmerized subject had been proposed a number of times since Mesmer's arrival in Paris, it was the first time that both imagination and imitation were proposed to explain away animal magnetism. Indeed, Noël Retz antedated the Royal Commission of Inquiry by two years.

The second book, entitled *Lettre de M. D'Eslon à M. Philips, doyen de la Faculté de médecine de Paris* had, as the title indicates, supposedly been written by Charles D'Eslon after his summons by the Medical Faculty. The book deliberately insulted the members of the Faculty and accused them of charlatanism and overt discrimination. It soon appeared, however, that the book had not been written by D'Eslon but by his adversaries in an attempt to tarnish his reputation. D'Eslon actually asked the police to withdraw the book from the market. It received a great deal of publicity, and the story was reported in many journals of the period (see, for example, in the *Journal de Médecine*, 1782, Vol. 58, p. 188).

Most critics attempted to explain mesmeric phenomena in terms of the disordered imagination of the mesmerized patient. Although both Mesmer and D'Eslon's books attempted to refute this reasoning, it gained prominence in the higher social classes. D'Eslon himself was cited by his opponents as recognizing that mesmerism could be explained partially by the patients' imagination. A passage from his book may have been the most cited in these early years of the history of animal magnetism. It was always cited when one wanted to minimize mesmeric effects. Indeed, these words by D'Eslon were still cited well into the nineteenth century (see, for example, Burdin & Dubois, 1841, whose book represents one of the most acclaimed attempts to demystify the mesmeric movement).

> But even if M. Mesmer had no other secret than being able to use the imagination to favor health, would that not be a marvelous gift? If imaginative medicine is the best medicine, why shouldn't we be doing imaginative medicine?

What is interesting is that not one critic ever cited the next sentence: "In order to settle once and for all these two objections I will describe a fact that will challenge both of them" (D'Eslon, 1780, pp. 46–47).

Four years later, in his reply to the Benjamin Franklin report, D'Eslon could reiterate his position:

> They put words in my mouth when they attribute to me the statement that the imagination played the greatest part in the effects of animal magnetism. Everything they quote from me in this regard is a distortion; they were well aware that this remark was but a momentary conjecture on my part, devoid of serious consideration. (D'Eslon, 1784; reprinted and translated also in Shor & Orne, 1965)

Following his letter to the Queen, Mesmer left Paris for about two weeks. Meanwhile, the faculty had reaffirmed its decision against D'Eslon in a second assembly. If endorsed a third time, he would definitely be dismissed from the faculty. Both Mesmer and D'Eslon continued their magnetic treatment which had become even more popular since their struggles with the scientific community and governmental agencies. Toward the end of July 1782, Mesmer decided to leave for Spa for an extended period. Among the friends that accompanied him were Bergasse, and a banker, Kornmann, whose son had been treated successfully by Mesmer.

During Mesmer's absence, D'Eslon had improved his clinical skills. His clinic had become the center of mesmeric treatment in Paris and was the meeting place of a large number of aristocratic women. Encouraged by his success, he returned to the Faculty to defend his doctrine. This time no mention was made of Mesmer. D'Eslon wished to defend his own ideas, insisting that, though he had been taught by Mesmer, animal magnetism was to be judged through his own practice. As expected, he was dismissed from the Faculty. Quite noteworthy it is, however, that no mention was made of Mesmer. D'Eslon's followers were ecstatic; their leader had seemingly taken over the magnetic movement.

Five weeks passed before Mesmer heard of these events. When he received a package containing D'Eslon's address to the Faculty, he was profoundly distressed. After many conversations and discussions with his friends and followers, he decided to repudiate D'Eslon publicly. To encourage him, Bergasse agreed also to defend Mesmer publicly and to put together a public fund by which Mesmer would be assured of some financial security if he desired to propagate his discovery. On October 4, 1782, Mesmer published a letter that he had sent to Philips, the president of the Medical Faculty, repudiating both D'Eslon's knowledge of animal magnetism as well as his clinical practice. Two weeks later, on October 19, D'Eslon tersely replied to Mesmer's letter. D'Eslon reminded Mesmer that all of his actions had but one purpose: to promulgate Mesmer's discovery. D'Eslon also mentioned the gold snuffbox he had received from Mesmer as a seal of friendship when he first agreed to use Mesmer's discovery. Accompanying the letter was the snuffbox; D'Eslon could not keep it in view of Mesmer's attitudes.

Mesmer's reply was prompt. Two days later he acknowledged D'Eslon's letter and denied that the golden snuffbox had been given as a sign of approval for D'Eslon to use and promote animal magnetism. For those familiar with the history of psychoanalysis, the episode of the snuffbox is reminiscent of Freud's alleged habit of giving a ring to his inner circle of followers, and of taking it back if he believed that they had betrayed his system. History can sometimes repeat itself in interesting ways.

The open conflict with D'Eslon was to prove fatal for Mesmer. Although still supported by a large proportion of the population, Mesmer was losing the support of the higher social classes. D'Eslon was soon to be seen as a more fashionable interlocutor.

Meanwhile, Bergasse with the help of the banker Kornmann had started a public fund to help Mesmer's finances. By the fund's terms, Mesmer would teach his system to the first one hundred subscribers who paid 2,400 francs for their share. It was to be used to publish Mesmer's discovery. The money was deposited with a notary, Margantin, on March 10th, 1783. Bergasse was among the first 20 subscribers along with such prominent figures as the soon to be famous Marquis and Count de Puységur. This group would soon be known as La Société de l'Harmonie Universelle (The Society of Universal Harmony).

During this period, Mesmer began the treatment of a well-known and respected writer, Court de Gébelin. As the treatment progressed and his health returned, Court de Gébelin became an enthusiastic defender of Mesmer's system. He was at times overly enthusiastic. On one occasion, for instance, he called for the extermination of all traditional physicians.

Meanwhile, Mesmer became endowed with supernatural powers in the public mind. An article published in the *Journal de Paris* (1784, Vol. 44) told the following story:

> M. Mesmer walking one day with M. Camp. and D'E. . . along Meudon's pond asked them to go to the opposite side, and to place their walking sticks in the water. Mesmer placed his in the water also. Even with such a distance, M. Camp. suffered an asthma attack while M. E. . reexperienced a pain he used to have on the liver side. Some people were known to be unable to sustain this experience without fainting.
>
> Another day, Mesmer was taking a walk in the woods of a domain past Orléans. Two young women started running playfully after him. He began running also; suddenly he stopped, turned around and pointed his cane in their direction, ordering them to stop running. As soon as he said that, their legs could not support them anymore; they could not walk.
>
> One night Mesmer entered the gardens of Msgr. the Prince of Soubise with six other people. He magnetized a tree and soon afterwards, Mme. the Marquise of . . . and the Mlles de R. . . and L. . . lost consciousness. The Duchess of C. . . was stuck to the tree without being able to move from it. The Count of M. . . had to sit down, his legs unable to support him. I cannot remember what effects M. Aug. . . experienced, but it was terrible. M. Mesmer then called his valet to help remove the bodies. Although used to such a spectacle, he just could not help for reasons that I cannot understand. It took quite a while before each and everyone of them could return to their homes. (see also Thouret, 1784, pp. 65–67)

It is with such a reputation that Mesmer prepared himself to teach his system to the new members of La Société de l'Harmonie Universelle.

The Society of Universal Harmony

The new society founded by Bergasse and Kornmann had two major goals: The first was to ensure that mesmeric doctrine would be taught and disseminated in a controlled fashion. The second was to guarantee that Mesmer would benefit from his discovery, allowing him to be treated according to his aspirations. Like any other mesmeric enterprise, however, it was soon to undergo major turmoil.[12] By the end of 1783, the fund raising was well on its way; more than 48 people had already paid their dues. Among these, 18 members were of very high social status. In addition, there were two Knights of Malta, one lawyer, four physicians, two surgeons, seven or eight bankers or businessmen, two priests, and three monks. All were eager to learn the new doctrine.

Within the next 15 days the fund raising was complete, or nearly so. Ninety-eight members were ready to be taught Mesmer's method. Bergasse was responsible for the magnetic education of the new followers. His eloquence did more to sustain their interest than what he taught. Fortunately, the students gained in practice what their formal education did not provide. Although Mesmer never really taught the subscribers anything, they were free to magnetize under his supervision. By imitating the master, they sometimes elicited surprising effects as the Marquis de Puységur later recognized. Few understood the theory. Fortunately, this did not hinder the successful application of the technique.

The Society of Universal Harmony was organized along the lines of Freemasonry. It was not, however, a Mason enterprise. Although Mesmer had been a Mason since his early days in Vienna, where he and his friend Mozart had become members of the Truth and Union Lodge, he did not affiliate his society with the Paris lodge. At most, he adopted its organizational structure. Bergasse was made responsible for the elaboration of the society's rules and regulations. When Mesmer decided initially to name the society a lodge, he disagreed. He wrote in his *Observations de M. Bergasse sur un écrit du docteur Mesmer* published in London in 1785: "I was asked to provide by-laws for this society, which at first was given, in spite of my wishes, the ridiculous designation of *lodge*" (p. 17, italics in original).

In fact Bergasse's association with the society ended abruptly in 1785 when Mesmer asked him to leave. Following his own political principles, he did not understand why Mesmer did not teach his doctrine once the money had been collected. Even if the rites and rituals of initiation were reminiscent of Freemasonry, the similarities ended there. The initiation was aimed mainly at ensuring that the new disciples would be faithful to Mesmer and his ideas and that they would not teach the new doctrine for their own benefit. It is true, however, that the society had links both with Freemasonry and with the more radical political movements. These appear to have been more accidental than intended. By presenting his doctrine as a new way of life rather than as a mere therapeutic system, Mesmer attracted those contemporaries who thought the moment was right for a change in French society. The sudden urge of the aristocracy to redefine its role as helper of the lower social classes, the political shift to the left exemplified by writers such as Bergasse, as well as the new popularity that scientific discoveries enjoyed were all signs of changing times.

After their initiation, the new disciples established their own magnetic practices. As the motto of the society pointed out, now they had to "Go forth, touch, and cure." As 1784 began, few could foresee that the upcoming year would be crucial for Mesmer and his doctrine. In fact, it was to represent for Mesmer, his final moments of celebrity.

NOTES

1. This letter was written by Heuzer, a Viennese astronomer, to Father Hell. The letter, dated December 21, 1777, basically states Heuzer's opinion of Mesmer's treatment and personality. It stated also that Mlle Paradis had never been more blind and unhealthy than she was at the time of his writing. The letter was quite deprecatory. Mesmer is presented as a charlatan who had been exposed in Vienna:

> He varies his methods of treatment in order to give it more credibility; if helped by chance, or if the patient's imagination endows him, as they did Gassner, with a power that doesn't exist, he [Mesmer] knows how to glorify himself and fill the newspapers, thus acquiring a most undeserved reputation. (cited in Amadou, 1971, p. 197)

2. *Précis historique des faits relatifs au magnétisme animal jusques en Avril 1781* is the most complete document on the early history of animal magnetism. Although written by Mesmer himself, most of the facts are honestly reported (Figuier, 1860; Amadou, 1971). Mesmer contents himself by annotating the facts with some of his own thoughts. It is more than can be said for his adversaries who most of the time manipulated the facts according to their desires. The original text was reprinted in its entirety in Amadou (1971).

3. This was not the last time that a royal court interfered with the medical establishment. Queen Victoria in 1853 upset the British medical world by requesting the use of chloroform for her delivery of Prince Leopold. The Queen was known for her authoritarian although sometimes quite original thinking; in 1857, she chose Ottawa to be the new capital of the colony of Canada!

4. These examples of sensory alterations probably represent the first observations of the ability of some hypnotized subjects to alter profoundly their sensory perception. Most contemporary historical authors report that the Abbé di Faria was the first to demonstrate this ability in mesmerized individuals. The fact that Mesmer knew this certainly points to the experimentation he conducted on his discovery above and beyond its therapeutic value. This point is discussed in greater detail in the subsequent presentation of artificial somnambulism.

5. D'Eslon's book was reprinted *in extenso* within a compendium (the *Recueil général...*) of all the writings on animal magnetism. This collection was put together around 1787. Although it was published in the royal library, the editor is not known. The 14-volume collection is probably the most complete that can be found on the topic (see Amadou, 1971). Apart from reprints of most major books published on animal magnetism, numerous newspaper articles written for and against Mesmerism can be found. The editor annotated the different texts with comments of his own that illustrate his position toward the subject. For example, the following warning can be read at the beginning of Volume One:

> A good example of the foibles of human reasoning will always be extremely useful in preventing such reoccurrence. Where could one find a more striking example than in

most of these collected writings filled with the most ridiculous and absurd ideas that had nonetheless an amazing number of readers?

6. Following this sentence from D'Eslon the editor of the collection (see note 5) wrote in the text's margin: "This way of talking is both modest and well-founded; after having read M. D'Eslon's book, one understands why he could benefit from additional medical knowledge."

7. In the papers of Jean-Pierre Lenoir, Lieutenant General of Police in Paris at the time, can be found the story of the vicar of Sainte Eustache who refused to bury D'Eslon when he died in 1786. Lenoir had to intervene to prevent d'Espréménil from complaining to the government (see Darnton, 1968, p. 87, footnote 3).

8. De Horne's pamphlet was entitled *Réponse d'un médecin de Paris à un médecin de province, sur le prétendu magnétisme animal de M. Mesmer*. In his 1781 book, Mesmer described the pamphlet in the following way: "This opuscule is quite marvelous, in my own opinion, since out of sixteen pages, *in twelve*, there are more absurdities and contradictions than in a full *in-folio* volume" (cited in Amadou, 1971, p. 133, italics in original).

9. It is impossible to convert the livre into modern currencies. To have an idea of its value, Darnton (1984) reported that a skilled artisan made about 500 livres in a year (p. 280). In Chapter 4 of his book, Darnton presents also the general income of different individuals living in Montpellier in 1768. Court presidents received 6,000 livres plus various fees from their offices. Court counsellors received 4,000 livres. University professors earned 1,800 livres whereas the lesser *docteurs-agrégés* obtained only 200 livres. If times have changed, university professors have probably not yet noticed it! Nevertheless, it is evident from these numbers that the government's financial proposals were more than adequate.

10. It should be noted here that however one tries to explain Mesmer's behavior during this period, there is no simple answer. Delusions of grandeur, greediness, paranoia, sense of honor, or humanitarianism might all have been at play in this enigmatic man.

We disagree, however, with authors who have portrayed Mesmer as the epitome of greed. A careful look at Podmore's version of this period of negotiations between Mesmer and the French Government, reveals that some of the facts have been misinterpreted. We will content ourselves to look at Mesmer's letter to the Queen. On page 53 of his book, Podmore (1909/1964) cites 12 lines of Mesmer's three-page letter (see Amadou, 1971, pp. 187-190) leaving the impression that Mesmer was asking for unreasonable amounts of money. The whole letter, however, was written to explain to the Queen that money was not the primary issue that had to be resolved.

Podmore wrote also that Mesmer believed the monetary offer to be "absurdly inadequate" (p. 53) if the King's advisers believed in his discovery. What Mesmer in fact wrote (see Amadou, 1971, p. 183) was: "In contrast, if my discovery was believed in, neither the pride of some delirious scientists, nor the fear of some inevitable expenses should stop the fate of humanity." Mesmer's letter to the Queen is probably the best example of how confused he himself was on his position. That he asked for money is a recognized fact; to limit his intentions to this point, however, is singularly to simplify the complexity of both the situation and the man.

11. *Lettre d'un médecin de la Faculté de Paris, à un médecin du Collège de Londres: Ouvrage dans lequel on prouve contre M. Mesmer que le magnétisme animal n'existe pas*. Published anonymously in 1781 in LaHaye, the book was later attributed to Bergasse (see Barbier, 1822-1827).

12. The history of this society has been reviewed extensively by Darnton (1968). The relationship between the Society and Freemasonry has been investigated and well documented by Amadou (1971). For more details readers are referred to these two books. The orientation of the present chapter differs from the two previously cited books in that we are more concerned with Mesmer's role and fate than the political or spiritualist affiliations of his followers.

4

The Fall of Mesmerism

The year 1784 saw the fall of Mesmerism. In the first half of the year, the movement's momentum was high due to reports of some cures that Mesmer achieved. At the same time, however, there was a renewal of the animosity between the D'Eslonians and the Mesmerists as they became known in the newspapers. These devoted partisans, for the most part women from aristocratic, artistic, and high bourgeoisie circles, took over the written media in order to promote their favorite magnetist. For the first time, the question of morality was raised publicly by both the serious writers and the satirists. The battle between Mesmer and D'Eslon at the end may have represented the struggle of conservatism with liberalism as had been predicted by the more radical mesmeric writers. As the French Revolution drew closer, it soon became evident that by choosing D'Eslon the establishment was acting in accordance with its (far from unconscious) desire to maintain social order.

Some Famous Cases

Among the members of Mesmer's Society of Universal Harmony was the noted chemist, Claude Bertholet who had registered for the courses on animal magnetism. He had retained his right to criticize mesmeric teachings, and within a month, became irritated by the vagueness and unscientific behaviors of his illustrious teachers. When he voiced his discontent, Mesmer accused him of being unfaithful. Bertholet left the clinic, furious. The next day, he publicly denounced the procedures of the meetings. He wrote:

> After having followed more than half of M. Mesmer's classes, since the beginning of April 1784, and after having walked through the treatment and the crisis chambers, I declare that I have not recognized the existence of the

agent that M. Mesmer has called *animal magnetism*. [I declare] that the doctrine that was taught there denies, in my judgment, the best established facts on the world organisation and the animal economy. I did not see anything in the convulsions, spasms, and crises that are thought to be produced by the magnetic processes (when these accidents were real), that cannot be entirely attributed to the imagination, the mechanical effect of massaging highly irritable bodily parts, and this well known law by which an animal will attempt to imitate and reproduce, even involuntarily, the same situation that he sees in another animal. This law is often at play in convulsive diseases. Finally I declare that I consider the doctrine of Animal Magnetism and its practice as totally chimeric, and I agree that, as of today, this declaration be used as anyone will wish to. (cited in Figuier, 1860, Vol. III, pp. 177-178)

Bertholet was anticipating, as had Retz the previous year, the results of the Royal Commission of Inquiry into animal magnetism that were to be published a few months later. It might mean, also, that the members of the Commission, some of whom were Bertholet's friends, may have been influenced by his judgment.

This event was highly publicized by the opponents of the newly formed Society of Universal Harmony. Mesmer, himself, did not consider that the defection of one scientist who had witnessed his practice for less than a month and was a member of the Academy of Sciences was particularly troublesome. His followers, however, thought differently. Bertholet was accused of treason to the written word; allegations of violence soon followed. According to Bertholet himself, some of Mesmer's partisans met him by coincidence a few days following his declaration while he was walking near the Palais Royal. He claimed that they attempted to strangle him. Whether this actually happened is difficult to determine. This incident, however, illustrates the state of rumor, and perhaps of mind, in the year 1784 (see Figuier, 1860, Vol. III, p. 179).

Mesmer on the other hand was doing quite well financially. Paid membership had climbed steadily to 103 persons, and more than 240,000 francs had been deposited in an account bearing his name. He had also just converted a young and energetic priest, Father F. Hervier, to his doctrine. Hervier was so enthusiastic that Mesmer himself had to rectify sometimes what the young priest said about the movement. Before his conversion to animal magnetism, Father Hervier had been known for his demagogic skills. He was invited to preach frequently in many different towns. By preaching about the magnetic movement, he became the first representative of the clergy to take sides, at least officially. With the exception of Father Hell in the early years in Vienna, Father Hervier was the first of a number of Church figures to join the controversy over the mesmeric society.

In the spring of 1784, he was invited to preach at the Saint André Cathedral in the town of Bordeaux. The parishioners were not to forget his preachings for a long time to come. On April 6, Father Hervier was preaching on the consequences of eternal damnation with his habitual eloquence and impetuosity. Throughout his sermon, he stared at the *banc du parlement*, facing his pulpit. On this bench could be found the richest and youngest women of Bordeaux. At the midpoint of his sermon, a young woman developed what appeared to be epileptic convulsions. This event disturbed the sermon, as people watched the convulsing woman anxiously. Father Hervier ceased preaching, descended from the pulpit with great gravity, and approached her. He began magnetizing her with long passes (*longues passes*). In a short time, the convulsions decreased and disappeared. Without losing his calm and dignity, Father Hervier returned to the pulpit and began preaching on the virtue of charity, on miracles of healing brought about simply by Jesus's touch, and ended with a virulent attack on the Bordeaux clergy who had ridiculed him because of his interest in animal magnetism.

Not surprisingly, this magnetic miracle, performed inside a church, created dissension within the clergy. Some considered Hervier to be a saint. Others believed him to be the Devil's advocate. For Hervier himself, the consequences were not positive. When he returned to Paris, he was suspended from preaching. In the same period, five pamphlets were published for and against animal magnetism, directly attacking Father Hervier's recent publication which contained both an account of his own cure as well as a defense of Mesmer's system. The reply was immediate; not only was animal magnetism refuted, but Hervier's honesty was seriously questioned.

These public struggles between Mesmer's sympathizers and his opponents were becoming increasingly frequent. Spectacular incidents were discussed in the newspapers and cafés. For example, on a Sunday, when King Louis XVI was preparing to go to mass, a young man broke into the royal levee, threw himself at the royal feet, and begged "Sire, deliver me from the demon that possesses me! It's that knave Mesmer who has bewitched me" (cited in Figuier, 1860, Vol. III, p. 182). The King turned to his spiritual counselors and stated humorously: "Gentlemen, if it is the Devil, it's a matter that concerns you." According to Figuier, the young man was arrested and sent to the Bastille. In doubtful cases, whether political or religious, this was considered always to be the preferred treatment.

Quite apart from these incidents, a new trend appeared in the pamphlets and books of that year. Having been in a way forced to accept the declarations of many prestigious religious, political, and aristocratic figures who all claimed to have been cured by Mesmer, the medical establishment resorted to doubting either the gravity of the original illnesses cured by magnetism or the validity of such a treatment when a patient suffered a relapse of a disease. A number of publications began questioning the integrity of patients who had described their symptoms. The basic question was to delineate how much suffering and disability were necessary in order to consider someone as a sick person. The second question that followed from the first was to determine the duration of a person's posttreatment in good health in order to validate the cure. It soon became apparent that magnetism could be attacked on both issues with some success. Both Father Hervier and Court de Gébelin had reported highly publicized cures. Both were attacked in a number of pamphlets trying to demonstrate that the patients were not as sick as they had claimed.[1]

When Court de Gébelin quite involuntarily denied these assumptions by dying in Mesmer's house, the lampoonists used his death to symbolize the uselessness of animal magnetism. A number of epigrams announced: "M. Court de Gébelin has just died, cured by Animal Magnetism." Another epigram became popular and was repeated in cafés and theaters: "Here lies the poor Gébelin/ Who knew Greek, Hebrew and Latin/ All should admire his heroism/ He was a martyr of Magnetism" (cited in Figuier, 1860, Vol. III, p. 186).

Although there were many accusations that Mesmer had mistreated the elderly writer, the truth surrounding Gébelin's death was to Mesmer's advantage. Realizing that he was near death, Mesmer lodged him in his house, in a private room. He magnetized Gébelin daily to alleviate his pain. When he died on May 12, 1784, Mesmer decided to conduct an autopsy on his body. The five physicians who witnessed the autopsy corroborated that Court de Gébelin had died from renal failure, a disease unrelated to what he had been treated for by Mesmer[2] (see Grimm, 1830, Vol. 12). It did not prevent, however, the publication of many scurrilous tracts. A number of them sought to document all cases where animal magnetism was thought to have failed. Unfortunately, some of Mesmer's patients had inadvertently contributed to the skeptical attitude by publishing a number of cures that were not well recognized. One of these failures was Mme Poissonnier, the wife of a physician from Paris, who, after having publicized her belief that she had been helped by Mesmer's treatment, died of cancer. Her husband, Dr. Poissonnier, became one of the five members of the Commission named by the Royal Society of Medicine to inquire into animal magnetism a few months later.

The lampoonists were quite active, also, and more to the point, Paulet's book, *L'Anti-magnétisme*, related a number of these cures in a satirical way. The following brief excerpt provides a flavor of what was written at the time:

> Mme the Marquise de la Sourdière, ignoring all of the previous events, implores Mesmer to help her. I can see this poor woman on her knees telling him: "M. Mesmer, you can do miracles. Could you help by giving back a patriot to the state, a good citizen to society, a husband, a father, a friend to his tearful family, and to me an uncle who I cherish deeply. Come, everybody awaits you." He comes, he examines, everyone is breathless; he says: "Your uncle will suffer a terrible agony that will last for three days. Because of his strong constitution, he will go through incredible pain and will only pass away after a long struggle."—"Could you not save him from such suffering," asked Mme de la Sourdière, "and prolong his life even if only for a few days?"— "Yes, Madam, and I will begin now if you retire."—"No, I can't abandon my uncle."—"As you wish, this finger will be more than enough! Up and down, don't you feel anything, sir?" Suddenly a noise comes from the uncle's glottis. "What is it, sir? What have I heard?" says the frightened marquise. "My uncle,

my dear uncle, he does not talk anymore. What! M. Mesmer, would he be. . . ?"—"Madam, I did not fool you; I didn't promise to cure him. Your uncle had to die, and I saved him from all the sufferings of a long agony. You should be happy, he will not suffer further." (Paulet, 1784, pp. 154-155)

Despite adverse media reaction, several more serious books and pamphlets on Mesmer's treatments were published in the first half of 1784. During this year, they numbered more than one hundred books and pamphlets either for or against the theory of animal magnetism. In addition, 1784 saw the first serious published accusations of indecency and immorality; these became the subject of lively discussion.[3]

Although a number of books in favor of animal magnetism were published also (among which was one written by Mesmer [1784a] and edited by Bergasse entitled *Théorie du monde et des êtres organisés*), the majority of the pieces written in defense of the movement were published in newspapers. Here again, however, Mesmer's tendency to reject virtually everything that had not come from himself served to increase the volume of counterattacks from his adversaries.

The most serious attack came with the publication of Thouret's (1784) book, *Recherches et doutes sur le magnétisme animal*, published a few days before the findings of the Royal Commission of Inquiry into Animal Magnetism, presided over by Benjamin Franklin, were released. Thouret's book represents a well-thought-out attempt from the scientific establishment to reject animal magnetism from both a scientific (as was expected from the Commissions of Inquiry) and historical point of view. Thouret had been asked to write the book and publish it before the reports of the Commissions were made public. In this way, it was thought that the population would have an appropriate historical and scientific package by which to judge the uselessness of magnetic doctrines.

Briefly stated, Thouret attempted to demonstrate that most of Mesmer's theory came from traditional magnetic medicine. He sought to demonstrate that Mesmer had plagiarized earlier investigators. In addition, he argued that Mesmer had not even improved upon their theories. Thouret, however, was cautious on the issue of the abuse of the new therapeutic system. He did not emphasize it but contented himself with identifying abuse as a possibility, in much the same manner as Maxwell had previously. He wrote:

> Finally, and this last remark is important, [the old] magnetism could have great influence on the moral. A nearly irresistible impulse formed the basis for the attachment and gratefulness many patients felt for those who had treated them with this new means. Many, and among them Maxwell, even thought that it could be possible under the right circumstances to abuse this means. (p. xxiii)

His most stringent attack was that: "They looked at it [old magnetic medicine] as a powerful means to influence morality. They more specifically thought that it was particularly useful in subjugating the mind or the heart of women" (p. 59).

Thouret ended his book by emphasizing that the main ingredient at play in animal magnetism was the power of the imagination, especially in vaporous patients. It can certainly be hypothesized that Thouret had followed and discussed the topic with some of the Commissioners while writing his book. There is considerable similarity between Thouret's conclusions and those of the official inquiries.

The first of Paulet's two books is similar to that of Thouret. He followed the same general reasoning and arrived at the same conclusion. Paulet, however, was a more satirical writer and preferred a lighter approach to the topic. Indeed, his second book abandoned all vestiges of scientific objectivity at the expense of animal magnetism. This second book, *Mesmer justifié* (1784a), followed those published for and against Hervier and Gébelin. It was the first book to emphasize the role given to women in mesmeric treatment. For example, in describing the different magnetic poles that must be attended to in magnetic medicine, Paulet characterized the breast as one pole having to be manipulated with gentleness and care. He then provided the following anecdote concerning Father Hervier, although he was not specifically mentioned in the excerpt.

> One of Mesmer's main disciples who has propagated his doctrine in Bordeaux seems to be more knowledgeable than anybody else in regard to this pole [the breast pole]; he knows all of its area, its resources and radiations. He was magnetising a young person who he did not believe accustomed to the practices of Animal Magnetism, and asked her in a troubled voice when he was finally at the center of this pole: "Don't you feel anything, Miss?"—To which she replied: "And you, Father?" This answer disconcerted him. (p. 13)

Later in the book, Paulet asserted that the crisis chamber was often the scene of gross indecency: "Maybe out of politeness, or coincidence, or maybe due to the privilege of beauty, nice women are nearly always the first ones to be magnetized, if not the only ones, by the adepts" (p. 20).

Although quite amusing, these reflections gave rise to a number of other publications which were more explicit and far less amusing for the practitioners of the new doctrine. Quite quickly the mesmeric adepts realized that there existed major criticisms that required a response. Surprisingly, Mesmer did not reply to these accusations.

During February 1784, Galart de Montjoie (one of D'Eslon's friends) published four letters in the *Journal de Paris*, attempting to refute the accusations of immorality that had been voiced by a number of writers (cited in *Recueil général*, 1787). Although himself a practitioner of the new therapeutic, he acknowledged that a number of safeguards should be taken by those who practiced or submitted to being magnetized. One of his recommendations was that magnetism should be restricted to the medical profession and preferably performed in group sessions. He also emphasized that patients should be careful in their choice of a magnetist, preferring those who have passed the age of passion(!) which was left unspecified. He concluded his last letter with an exhortation to women:

> To you virtuous women who were so exasperated because I said that Animal Magnetism could create an attachment to the one who magnetizes, be very careful. This attachment is pure; but the impetuosity of your replies could lead one to believe quite the contrary, especially when looking at it from a satirical point of view. You don't need me; but if I pleaded as I did, it is to protect the honor of what is dearest to you. (p. 301)[4]

The letters obviously sought to minimize the impact of the recent attack on the morality of magnetic treatment. Mesmer did not see these attacks in a kindred manner. In two letters written as a reply to Montjoie, he reiterated that his doctrine should be taught to everybody, particularly fathers, mothers, and clergymen who wanted to help humanity. He stressed that animal magnetism was helpful in maintaining morality rather than hindering it. In his second letter, Mesmer emphasized the fact that Montjoie was a close friend of D'Eslon and, as such, was attempting to discredit him. He characterized Montjoie's letters as replete with absurdities and major errors. As discussed earlier, Mesmer defended his honor and his discovery more to his friends than against his adversaries. He did not realize that all of these attacks could be taken seriously; indeed, they were by the authorities. D'Eslon for his part was silent, continuing to magnetize without attracting the attention that was being drawn to Mesmer.

Mesmer was joined by the Baron de Borméo in his refutation of Montjoie. The Baron wrote:

> This danger, the fear of which has been created in the public, is pure fantasy and has been imagined in an attempt to discredit Doctor Mesmer and his disciples as well as his treatment. . . . He [Montjoie] has attempted to raise the public suspicion as to the dangers of Doctor Mesmer's treatment with the weaker sex [*le beau sexe*]. (pp. 36 and 39).[5]

The accusations did not cease, however. They began to circulate in theaters and cafés. Popular songs and doggerel verses began to appear. The following poem was published in Paris in 1784, signed only by the letter D. It was entitled *The Mesmeriad or The Triumph of Animal Magnetism*, and was presented as a "poem in three movements dedicated to the moon." It read as follows:

> Even if the baquet is so widely used,
> It cannot alas, cure a particular discomfort
> That can only be alleviated in a private rendezvous;
> Then magnetism becomes the celebration of love.
>
> And now my hero, charming and magnetizing,
> Behind a locked door will dissipate this burning sensation.
> He knows what to do to make this cruelty vanish
> And never his blessed finger encounters rebellion.

> O sweet ecstasy! O languorous sights!
> The holy baquet of pleasures is the throne.
> Let yourself go, charming things, under the magnetic hand.
>
> Don't listen to all the foolish critics;
> Come, don't be afraid, my hero is discreet;
> He never tells what he does at the baquet.

The last line of the poem carried a footnote that amplified this topic for readers who might not yet have understood fully. It read:

> Of course this will only be known if an unfortunate accident happens; but since these rendezvous have already given birth to some embarrassing imbroglios, mothers and husbands are becoming quite suspicious.

Animal magnetism became the explanation of all emotions. In an anonymous (1784h) book entitled *Le moraliste mesmérien: ou Lettres philosophiques de l'influence du magnétisme*, published in Paris at the Bélin Library, it was stated that the "famous author of the discovery of Animal Magnetism has accomplished for love what Newton did for the world system; his doctrine can explain all of its phenomena" (p. 8). The author acknowledged also the dangers of such a doctrine especially in young and naive women:

> That is why any woman desiring to retain her virtue will avoid the presence of those who desire her, because she knows that by being repeatedly *magnetized*, she could not prevent herself from succumbing to the laws of attraction. You will certainly agree that those who are inexperienced, careless, or so foolhardy as to expose themselves to it, will become its victim. (p. 23)

Charles Devillers (1784) wrote also on the dangers of the magnetic passes, especially when the hand massaged the body: "There are other more active contacts . . . my pen refuses to go into details; all these touchings produce great effects without even depending upon the universal fluid" (p. 7).

The only media missing was the theater. Although slower to jump on the anti-Mesmer bandwagon, the theater was no less vehement than the other arts. Quite a number of plays depicted animal magnetism and the magnetists in a less than reputable light. The first play to attack the subject directly was *Les Docteurs Modernes*. When Duval d'Esprémenil, one of Bergasse's friends as well as a co-founder of the Society of Universal Harmony, heard of the play, he was outraged. D'Esprémenil was known for both his impetuosity and eloquence. Indeed, the former (possibly assisted by the latter) led him to the guillotine ten years later in 1794. Considering that it was an insult for the Government to ridicule Mesmer's discovery, he wrote a long memorandum and delivered it personally to Louis XVI. The King agreed to listen to the manuscript but fell asleep in the middle of its reading. Following his audience with the King, D'Esprémenil returned to Paris and demonstrated in front of the offending theater, distributing copies of the manuscript.

The play did not go well that night. It was interrupted a number of times by booing and shouting people, most of whom were thought to have been either Mesmer's or D'Eslon's disciples. They were so identified partly because one of the demonstrators, perhaps eager to obtain his money, began booing at the end of the play that preceded *Les docteurs modernes*. Arrested, he made a confession to the police. A few days later, the author of the play (Jean-Baptiste Radet) denied in the *Journal de Paris* his participation in what he characterized as a tasteless comedy. He had good reason to do so, being under the protection of the Duchesse de Villeroi, one of Mesmerism's most fervent partisans. A second play, *Le baquet de santé*, was produced also in 1784. Its success, however, did not compare to that of the first play. During the following two years at least two other plays took up the subject of Mesmerism. *La physicienne* and *Le médecin malgré tout le monde* were staged in 1786.

A large number of satirical books were published following the release of the reports of the two Commissions of Inquiries into animal magnetism. One of them should be mentioned here as it was published during the deliberations of the commissions. This book written by a clergyman, the Abbé de Paumerelle (1784), was entitled *La philosophie des vapeurs*. The book presented a satirical version of the history of animal magnetism. Mesmer was depicted as the prince of vapors; the only person capable of curing this intricate disease. The vaporous state was a recognized medical problem encountered particularly in the higher social classes. It was described usually as the onset of migraines, stomach aches, compulsive yawnings, vertigos, palpitations, small convulsions, or losses of consciousness that were not related to any particular physical disability. It was believed also that every aristocratic woman should be knowledgeable in pretending the onset of vapors. Paumerelle took advantage of that situation in his book. He described the vapors in the following way:

> It is well recognized that to be considered an attractive woman, a woman must be continually tossed between this ensemble of feelings, caprices, sudden changes of mood, sulkiness, singularities, grimaces, peculiar habits, and simpering ways. (pp. 5-6)

Mesmer then became the person who could control all of these temperamental displays in women, and for this reason alone, deserved recognition as a great healer. Paumerelle described the episode of Mesmer's decision to leave Paris in 1781 as a great tragedy for both men and women suffering from these torments.

> And women, what will become of women? These delicious convulsionaries, totally submitted to the prestigious enchanter, and who can die and resuscitate with such grace, will you leave them at the mercy of their dark doctors, abandoning them to this sad and mortal boredom from which they will not be able alas to be relieved by any crisis. . . . Ah, mostly ungrateful Mesmer! so you will leave us; and it is in this state that you will leave it to us to console them. (pp. 19-20)

While the many books, pamphlets, and plays focused public attention on Mesmer and his disciples, the major blow to Mesmer's reputation came from an unexpected event. Every year on Good Friday, the Queen attended a spiritual concert given in her honor. On April 16, 1784, the concert took place at the Tuileries. Most of the aristocracy was present at the concert. Mesmer was one of the invited guests. The recital commenced with the music of Rigel and of Gossec. Following Gossec's *Oratorio*, the audience saw a young Austrian pianist accompanied by the Duke de Coigny sit at the harpsichord. Her performance was listened to in silence, which, according to some journalists, was such as to make people forget the preceding offerings. Even Gluck, who was present at the concert, was seen shedding a tear of joy. The audience became ecstatic, however, when it realized at the end of her performance that she was blind. Quite rapidly, it became known that the pianist was Mlle Paradis (see Chapter 1). Mesmer became the center of attention. As one journalist wrote:

> It was obviously the most cruel moment of his life. By coming to Paris the young Viennese pianist was a witness to Mesmer's failure to cure her as well as a reminder of a more than dubious affair he had had. Having to choose between the young pianist and Mesmer, French gallantry did not hesitate. Gibes, pamphlets, even threats were directed against [Mesmer]. D'Eslon was unanimously recognized as the virtuous man *par excellence*. (reported in Figuier, 1860, Vol. III, pp. 193–194)

It is difficult to assess whether Mlle Paradis deserved such an eloquent appraisal. Not all present agreed on her talent. Benjamin Franklin's teenage grandson, Benny, thought that her playing was rather loud and amateurish. Indeed, her popular acclaim may have been more a recognition of her blindness than of anything else. Grimm, nonetheless, in his *Correspondance*, wrote:

> We saw her [Mlle Paradis] three weeks ago at the Spiritual Concert. Her ability on the harpsichord is absolutely astonishing, in spite of her total blindness. One could be led to believe that her appearance in Paris was not a most delightful surprise for Mesmer. (1830, Vol. 12, p. 85, footnote 1)

Subsequently, she returned to Vienna where she taught the piano until her death (see Lopez & Herbert, 1975). The whole scenario was seen by the media as an elaborate construction of the D'Eslonians to discredit Mesmer at a time when the Commissions of Inquiry were beginning their work. Whether true or not, it certainly succeeded in drawing attention to D'Eslon's practice and in endorsing at the same time the Commissioners' decision to examine his practice rather than that of Mesmer. Although the reasons to convene a commission of inquiry were never clearly specified, the atmosphere surrounding the mesmeric movement was certainly disquieting for the government. Apart from the already mentioned political and moral undertones surrounding the mesmeric movement, Grimm (1830, Vol. 12, p. 90) suggested in his *Correspondance* that D'Eslon himself asked for the Royal Commission in an attempt to regain the attention of the public; the latter expected Mesmer to deliver lectures on his discovery since the terms of the fund raising had been respected.

The Commissions of Inquiry

Even though public opinion was polarized on the magnetic movement, the popularity of Mesmer, D'Eslon, and of most magnetists, was increasing among the general public. Paulet reports that more than 8,000 people had already been treated by this new therapeutic approach. On March 12, 1784, the King ordered a Commission of Inquiry into the animal magnetic movement. This Commission would bring together some of the most noted scientists of the time. Nine members were chosen to carry on this royal task. Four were from the Medical Faculty (a surprising decision when one remembers that the King had, a few years earlier, personally rejected this organization in favor of the Royal Society of Medicine). The four chosen physicians were Borie, Sallin, d'Arcet, and Guillotin. Of these, the most remembered is Guillotin, not for his role on the Commission but for his subsequent invention, which became so useful during the Revolution. It may be noted that it was the cause of death for three of the Commissioners, the inventor being one of them. The five remaining members of the Royal Commission were chosen from the Academy of Sciences. They were Bailly, Lavoisier, LeRoy, de Bory, and Franklin.[6] When Borie died soon after the beginning of the Inquiry, he was replaced by Majault.

On April 5, 1784, a second Commission of Inquiry was named, this time chosen from members of the Royal Society of Medicine. All of the documents relating to it were presented as being commissioned by the King to examine specifically the therapeutic value of magnetism. This second Commission consisted of the following five members: Poissonnier, Caille, Mauduyt, Andry, and Laurent de Jussieu. Mesmer had already met both Poissonnier and Mauduyt: His interactions with both had been difficult.

The Benjamin Franklin Commission

The choice of the actual commissioners was difficult to criticize. The President of the Commission, Benjamin Franklin, then the American Ambassador to France, was probably the most well-known scientist of his time. His nomination, however, would prove to be more honorific than practical. He was 78 years old and ill at the time of his nomination. He knew very little of animal magnetism. Although Mesmer had sent him a personal copy of his 1781 book, as well as 12 other copies destined for the American scientific societies, Franklin probably had not read it. In a letter to La Sablière de la Condamine dated March 19, 1784, one week after his nomination to the Commission, he wrote:

> You desire my sentiments concerning the cures performed by Comus and Mesmer. I think that in general, maladies caused by obstructions may be treated by electricity with advantage. As to the Animal Magnetism so much talked of, I am totally unacquainted with it, and must doubt its existence till I can see or feel some effect of it. None of the cures said to be performed by it have fallen under my observation; and there being so many disorders which cure themselves and such a disposition in mankind to deceive themselves and one another on these occasions; and living long having given me frequent opportunities of seeing certain remedies proclaimed as curing everything, and yet soon after totally laid aside as useless, I cannot but fear that the expectation of great advantage from the new method of treating diseases will prove a delusion. That delusion may however in some cases be of use while it lasts. There are in every great rich city a number of persons who are never in health, because they are fond of medicines and always taking them, whereby they derange the natural functions, and hurt their constitutions. If these people can be persuaded to forbear their drugs in expectation of being cured by only the physician's finger or an iron rod pointing at them, they may possibly find good effects though they mistake the cause. (Franklin, 1881, pp. 258–259)[7]

The Mesmerists were not the only group to have attracted the attention of the authorities at the end of the eighteenth century. The water-diviners best represented by Barthélemy Bleton, had been, since the 1780s, subjected to many commissions of inquiry. Their story is quite fascinating, especially in view of the fact that the use of the divining rod began as a means of finding criminals. When Bleton came to Paris, his only pretention was to demonstrate that he could, by his own talent, locate sources of water. He demonstrated his abilities in the presence of Franklin in May 1782. When an official Commission was formed to examine his claims, Poissonnier, D'Arcet, and Guillotin were among its members. Interestingly, even if that Commission demonstrated that Bleton did not have any particular power, the Government still offered him a job in an appropriate ministry based on the fact that he could and had found natural sources of water. Bleton was frequently hired to detect minerals, especially coal mines. Mesmer, by contrast, was not treated as well.

The second movement was led by an enigmatic figure who still fascinates the imagination of many people. His name was Giuseppe Balsamo, alias Cagliostro, who had arrived in France in 1780. Living mainly in Strasbourg, he had built himself a strong reputation as a healer. He described himself as the Grand Priest of Egyptian Freemasonry, initiating people, who had enough money to afford it, into his movement. When he moved to Paris in 1784 he had succeeded in acquiring the protection of the King who had, in a decree, taken him under his personal protection. Supposedly, the King did so to contradict his wife who was allegedly enamored with Mesmer, whom he did not particularly like. Cagliostro never competed with Mesmer, contenting himself with the more esoteric side of healing. He was arrested in Rome in 1791 and condemned to be burned at the stake as a heretic. His sentence was commuted to life in prison, where he is believed to have died in 1793.

Cagliostro was condemned because of his affiliation with Freemasonry which had been rejected by Pope Clément XII on January 14, 1739. The Papal Bull condemned to death, without grace, anyone who identified with the Freemasonry movement or anyone who encouraged affiliation with it. The Bull was later confirmed by Pope Benoît XIV on May 18, 1751. It will be remembered that Mesmer was also a Freemason and that his Society of Universal Harmony was often depicted as a masonic lodge. Some of his problems with the authorities and especially the clergy may have come from this. As will be seen later, when the Church finally took an official position vis-à-vis animal magnetism, it differentiated magnetism from the practice of esoteric sciences. On the other hand, being a member of a masonic lodge could be a wise political move. One has only to remember the problems that Mozart encountered when he ridiculed the rituals of the Freemasons in his opera *The Magic Flute* to realize that many influential political and literary figures were members. In his correspondance, Grimm (1830) noted that the Paris lodge, called the Nine Sisters, gave a commemorative dinner for Voltaire who had become a member in April 1778, a month before his death. Among the invited guests were: Court de Gébelin, the painter Monet, and Benjamin Franklin (see Grimm, 1830, Vol. 10, p. 127, p. 134)!

Finally, Comus, to whom Franklin alluded in his letter, was the pseudonym used by Nicolas-Philippe Le Dru, a peripatetic lecturer on electricity. Le Dru established himself in Paris as an electric healer. It is interesting to note that P. J. C. Mauduyt, one of the Commissioners, had already investigated the benefits of electricity in medicine and was, himself, a partisan of electric therapy (see Sutton, 1981).

Franklin was not the only Commissioner to have some prior contact with the magnetists. In fact, most of them had encountered either Mesmer or D'Eslon. Indeed, Bailly and LeRoy had already acknowledged that the phenomenon was worthy of attention.

When the Royal Commission decided to study the new treatment at D'Eslon's clinic, the Mesmerists expressed outrage. Mesmer wrote a letter to the Commissioners in which he denounced D'Eslon. He accused him of betraying a contract between them by which D'Eslon had promised not to divulge anything he had learned at Mesmer's clinic, and especially, that he should not represent himself as possessing Mesmer's secret. This entente between the two men had been signed and registered more than a year previously. Mesmer pointed out to the Commissioners that by examining D'Eslon's practice, the Commission itself would lower its own honorability. He questioned also the motives of the Commission in rejecting the discoverer of the technique for what he characterized as a questionable student. He had a point. The decision of the Commission was difficult to understand.

In June 1784, Mesmer wrote directly to Franklin. In the letter, he reiterated his earlier demands that the Commission be dismissed. The last paragraph of his letter is worth quoting as it exemplifies what Mesmer thought of himself, his discovery, and his sense of honor.

> I am as you are, Sir, one of those men that one cannot oppress without consequences; [I am of] these men who because they have made great discoveries, can bring disgrace [on their enemies] in a way similar to the authority possessed by powerful men; Whatever will be attempted, I have, as you have, humanity for my judge; and if the good that I have done can be forgotten, and the good that I want to do be stopped, the future will carry on my vengeance. (cited in Amadou, 1971, pp. 241-243)

This is the last letter that Mesmer wrote to the Commissioners before the publication of their reports. He did not receive a reply.

Meanwhile, both Commissions had decided to investigate D'Eslon's practice. The Commissioners began by visiting his clinic daily. They came to it one by one, rather than together, in an attempt to observe independently any potential physical effects of animal magnetism. After having determined that magnetic fluid, in contrast to electricity, could not be measured by any available scientific instrument, they proceeded to observe patients. Some of what they saw intrigued them:

> Nothing is more surprising than to witness the convulsions; if one has not seen it, it is difficult to imagine what it looks like. When one witnesses them, one is surprised by the deep rest in some of the patients, agitation in the others, different accidents that repeat themselves, and the likings that develop. One can see patients looking for each other, running toward each other, smiling and talking affectuously, trying to soften their mutual crises. All are submitted to the magnetist; even when they are apparently asleep, his voice, his gaze, one sign awakens them. We cannot but recognize in the constancy of these effects the great power that seems to agitate and control these patients and of which the magnetist seems to be the possessor. (cited in Figuier, 1860, Vol. III, pp. 204-205)

Surprisingly enough, however, the Commissioners decided to interrupt their observations on the grounds that *"The distinguished patients could not be questioned too closely without risk of annoying them"* (italics added). This was a surprising decision given that this was a Royal Inquiry and that the Commissioners were all recognized as eminent scientists. D'Eslon was infuriated. He wrote in his commentaries on the Commission's report:

> If they had told me before that they would limit themselves in such a way, I would have told them how insufficient a means they were taking; I would have told them that only a small proportion of patients experience instantaneous and noteworthy effects, that a lot of patients are cured without experiencing any effect, and that among those who experience the immediate action of magnetism, its effects vary infinitely. . . . (1784, pp. 6-7)

One of the major criticisms expressed subsequently against the Commission was that it did not investigate both the individual differences in the susceptibility to magnetism and the different manifestations within the same patients. Indeed, half of the Commissioners on both commissions had previously witnessed or heard of many interesting and possibly valid cures. Yet, most of the literature published by the opponents of this new system had emphasized the power of the imagination and the imitative tendencies of human beings. Surprisingly, the Commissioners were inclined to follow this latter approach, looking for examples of imagination and imitation rather than attempting to explain phenomena they did not understand.

Having excused themselves from public scrutiny, the Commissioners decided to experience animal magnetism themselves. They visited D'Eslon's house every other day in order to be magnetized. When they realized that they did not experience any of the traditional effects of animal magnetism, they decided upon a daily group visit for the next seven days. This time, three of the Commissioners experienced some slight symptoms, mainly pain and anxiety. These were dismissed as being caused by the "usual almost ever present variations of one's health status and as such not related to magnetism. . ." (see Figuier, 1860, Vol. III, p. 206). Again, ignoring individual differences, they pointed to the differences between the context in which they were magnetized and that which they had observed previously. Because their own treatment varied so much from the popular one, they concluded that the differences were probably due to the different states of mind of the participants. As a brief example, the Commissioners had decided that they would ignore any sensations that they would experience better to observe objectively the action of the magnetic fluid. In the popular treatment, patients were looking forward to experiencing symptoms. By itself this difference in expectations and attitudes could have been responsible for the differential results obtained. Following these initial observations, the Commissioners decided to experiment with actual patients. Seven people were chosen from the general population and brought to Franklin's home at Passy. Of these seven patients, three experienced some effects, while four reported not experiencing anything.

The Commissioners, however, were not satisfied. They decided to repeat these experiments but this time with individuals chosen from the upper classes: "They selected from the polite world those who could not be suspected of sinister views, and whose understanding made them capable of inquiring into and giving a faithful account of their sensations" (Tinterow, 1970, p. 98).

Four such patients were chosen and brought to the special tub with which the Commissioners were experimenting. Of these four patients, two admitted feeling altered sensations. These were, however, superficial and easily attributed to a form of concentrated attention on the part of the patients. In a third trial, Franklin himself, two of his nieces, and his secretary were magnetized by D'Eslon. Nobody felt anything even though one of Franklin's nieces was in convalescence. These three unsuccessful attempts at magnetizing prompted the Commissioners to alter their strategies.

They began to consider the role of the imagination more systematically and decided to investigate this possibility. To do so they elected to ask Jumelin, a lay magnetist, to submit himself to their experimentation. Although other lines of investigation could have been chosen, the Commissioners limited themselves to the role of the imagination. They were to be severely criticized subsequently both for this choice and for choosing Jumelin who, by his own admission, had not been taught magnetism by either Mesmser or D'Eslon, but had learned it from books. He was a nontraditional magnetist. He ignored the theory of the poles so important in mesmeric practice and had developed his own system of passes. He claimed, however, to be producing as many cures as Mesmer. Based on this, and on the additional claim that Jumelin was also reproducing the same effects as Mesmer and D'Eslon, the Commissioners concluded that Jumelin's practice was identical to the other two. The Commissioners then initiated a series of clever experiments where the blindfolded patients were usually kept unaware of the magnetist's interventions. When this was done, most of the patients magnetized by Jumelin demonstrated effects that did not correspond to what the magnetist was doing. This strategy had already proved successful in the Inquiry conducted on Barthélemy Bleton, the water diviner. When the Commissioners had satisfied themselves that they had demonstrated the same lack of correspondence between the effects elicited and the magnetist's actual behaviors, they concluded that "the imagination is the true cause of the effects attributed to the magnetism" (cited in Tinterow, 1970, p. 114).

In a final attempt to study the more profound effects of magnetism, such as the convulsive crises, they asked D'Eslon to choose one of his most sensitive patients. Accordingly, he brought a 12-year-old boy to Passy who met this criterion. The experiment was simple. One of the garden's trees was magnetized without the boy knowing it. He was then asked to walk through the garden, blindfolded, and to approach four previously determined trees that had not been magnetized. By the time he reached the fourth, he experienced a mild convulsive crisis with loss of consciousness. He was, however, more than 24 feet away from the magnetized tree. Other similar experiments were performed, all pointing to the same conclusion.

All of these experiments led the Commissioners to conclude that imagination, touching, and imitation were the three ingredients of animal magnetism. There was no need to postulate the existence of a magnetic fluid in order to explain the results obtained. Accordingly, their report concluded in the following terms:

> The Commissioners having recognized that the animal magnetic fluid cannot be perceived by the senses; that it did not have any action on themselves, or on the patients who were chosen; being satisfied that the touches and pressures are the cause of changes in the organism that are rarely of a favorable character, and are liable to produce a deplorable effect on the imagination; having definitely shown by conclusive experiments that the imagination without magnetism produces convulsions, and that magnetism without the imagination does not produce anything; they have come to the unanimous decision on the question of the existence and usefulness of magnetism that there is nothing that can prove the existence of the animal magnetic fluid; that this fluid, having no existence, cannot be of any utility; but that the violent effects that are observed in the public treatment are related to the

touchings, to the excited imagination, and to this reflexive imitative tendency that makes us repeat involuntarily what our senses perceived. At the same time they feel compelled to indicate as an important observation that the touchings, the repetitive action on the imagination in order to produce crises can be harmful; that the spectacle of the crisis is also dangerous, because of this imitative tendency which seems to be a law of Nature; and therefore, all public treatment where magnetism is utilized can but only have deplorable effects. (cited in Morand, 1889; a different translation can be found in Tinterow, 1970)

The report was finalized on August 11, 1784. It was adopted officially by the Medical Faculty ten days later. The conclusions of the report were read by Bailly on September 4 at the Academy of Sciences. While more than 80,000 copies of the report were printed and distributed throughout France, the Commissioners prepared a second report that was presented to the King only. This secret report emphasized the moral dangers likely to result from the practice of animal magnetism. Although not published publicly, it was nevertheless available from the Royal Library.[8]

This report represents the first public document denouncing the dangers of animal magnetism. As has been seen already, many authors had already impugned the morality of Mesmer's practice. This was the first time, however, that these moral accusations were in any way substantiated by some form of actual observations. There was, however, little substance to the Commissioners' allegations. Nevertheless, their secret report crystallized the suspiciousness of the scientific intelligentsia of the time, which, in turn, was based on the legacy of the preceding centuries. The accusations are identical; their foundations, however fragile, may indicate that there was some substance to them. The observations on which these allegations were based were not, however, published. By the same token, it is quite possible that some of these alleged dangers may have been "in the eye of the beholder." There is unfortunately no easy proof for such an assertion. In fairness though, D'Eslon agreed that moral danger was possible when he told Lenoir that it was essential that only a physician practice Mesmerism. Self-serving too, perhaps, but still an admission that there might be fire as well as smoke.

This confidential report also provided some insight into the Commissioners' opinion of Mesmer's treatment. The document's major focus is on the moral dangers for women in submitting to animal magnetic treatment. It described women's mental and physical status in a way that would certainly not please the contemporary feminist movement, and it identified women as the prime target of the magnetists. According to the Commissioners, women have a weaker constitution.

> They have a more labile nervous system, their imagination is more vivid and excited. This great nervous mobility although allowing them to have more delicate and exquisite senses, renders them nonetheless more sensitive to sensations of touch. When touched at a specific point of the body, it can be said that they are touched all over.... (cited in Amadou, 1971, p. 279)

This unfortunate state of affairs led them to experience more magnetic crises than their male counterparts. The Commissioners, however, had another idea in mind. Having decided that women were more susceptible to the magnetic crisis, they continued by saying that "some of these crises" (*il en est quelques-unes* . . .) are not caused by the belief in the magnetic fluid, but by the accumulation of the different emotions aroused by the imagination, the touchings, and the imitative reflex. Bluntly stated, the Commissioners believed that some of the crises were actually disguised sexual orgasms:

> Prolonged physical closeness, the essential touchings, the communication of individual warmth, the fusion of the gazes, are Nature's known roads and means to unmistakably communicate sensations and emotions. The man who magnetizes usually places the woman's knees between his, so that the knees and all the inferior part of the body are in contact. The hand is placed on the hypocondriac region, sometimes lower on the ovaries. . . . A woman will lower her head, placing her hands in front of her eyes; her natural modesty is taking over and makes her want to hide. But if the crisis persists, her eyes are troubled: this is an unequivocal sign of the total disorder of the senses. This disorder may not be perceived by her, but has been well identified by the physician's keen sense of observation. As soon as this first sign is present, the eyelids become wet, breathing is shortened, interrupted; the breasts go up and down more rapidly, the convulsions begin along with sudden movements in all parts of the body. In vivid and sensitive women, the last degree, the ending of the sweetest emotion, is often a convulsion. Following this state apathy, enfeeblement, a dullness of the senses takes over. It is the necessary rest after the agitation. (cited in Amadou, 1971, p. 280)

The Commissioners concluded this first part of their report by stating that for weak women, this could signify the loss of their health and of their decency. Although their argument was made very strongly, they did not present any actual cases of such behaviors. Their only argument came from the answers D'Eslon provided to M. Le Noir, a police officer, who was present at one of the meetings. When Le Noir asked D'Eslon "If when a woman is magnetized and in crisis wouldn't it be easy to abuse her?" D'Eslon answered in the affirmative. The reasons for his opinion, however, were not discussed.

The Commissioners then stated that D'Eslon had always insisted on the restriction of magnetic practices to the medical profession; an idea with which Mesmer disagreed. More to the point, they noted that he had never used the crisis chamber in his clinic in order to avoid possible temptation (which obviously Mesmer did not do). Thus, within ten lines or so, Mesmer's morality was twice attacked indirectly. For the Commissioners, this total but sweet disorder of the senses was the only explanation for the manner in which women returned to their allegedly unsuccessful treatment.

Two comments are of importance here. The first regards the continued indirect attack on Mesmer's morality in the last part of the Commissioners' report in the form of equating what they observed in D'Eslon's clinic with what occurred in Mesmer's practice. Even if they did not observe Mesmer's procedures, his and D'Eslon's treatment techniques must have been quite similar, given their earlier close association. Obviously, the Commissioners were judging the whole doctrine and its application without having observed a specific treatment.

The second point will return repeatedly during the following century. In the same way that possessed individuals, or the God-given convulsionaries were unable to control their behaviors, magnetized women were seen as undergoing all of these gentle torments involuntarily and much of the time without knowing what was happening to them. This notion of involuntariness was to become the center of a number of debates on the coercive power of magnetism or hypnotism in the following century.

The confidential report, however, did not play a major public role at the time because of its limited accessibility. It gained prominence, however, subsequently. At this point in time there was not one single case of abuse that had been documented even though one would have thought that Mesmer's opponents would have been delighted to publish such a case. In fact, the first report of an actual attempt at abuse was made two years after the Franklin report by a supporter of animal magnetism in order to demonstrate that it was possible to resist such attempts. Following the secret report, however, there was a major change in the publications of the proponents of the new system. Most if not all of the books published in favor of Mesmerism now devoted at least one section on the possibility of abusing the new therapeutic. They were fast learners.

The Report of the Royal Society of Medicine

The Royal Society of Medicine published its own report five days after the Franklin Commission. Although its conclusions were similar to those of the previous commission, it was not unanimous since Laurent de Jussieu refused to sign the official report and presented his own conclusions, separately. This medical commission had been more preoccupied by the actual therapeutic value of animal magnetism, and de Jussieu could not accept its total rejection. He believed that some of the effects that the Commissioners had witnessed needed explanation. Although he did not accept the theory of animal magnetism, and substituted the term *animal heat* for animal magnetic fluid, he nonetheless believed in the need for further experimentation.

During their investigation, the Commissioners had noticed that depending on the type of disorder treated, the effects of magnetism varied. Three types of diseases were identified: those with severe symptoms and a known cause, those with mild symptoms and no apparent specific cause, and those which might be due to melancholia. The Royal Society of Medicine Commission dismissed the third category in a few words, denying it the status of a real disease. In addition, it reported little to no change in patients suffering from severe diseases. It recognized, however, some benefit stemming from magnetic treatment in people with illnesses of undetermined etiology. These benefits were not attributed to magnetic fluid but to the patients' hopes for a cure, rest and exercise, and, interestingly, their abstinence from medication.

De Jussieu thought that this conclusion did not tell the whole story. He believed that there was a valid phenomenon that merited additional examination and said so. He concluded his own report one month later in the following terms:

> The theory of Animal Magnetism cannot be accepted before it is well developed and solidly proven. The experiments conducted to demonstrate the existence of the magnetic fluid show only that a man can produce some sensitive action upon his fellow man by either rubbing, touching, or even sometimes by just standing nearby a person. This action, believed to be the result of this undemonstrated magnetic fluid, is certainly due to the animal heat existing in each body, that emanates from each body to a certain distance, and can even penetrate other bodies. This animal heat can be developed, increased, or decreased in a body by moral or physical causes. Judging by its effects, it resembles a tonic medication and as such can be either harmful or salutary depending on how much is used and under which circumstances. By using it more, and in a more thoughtful way, it will be possible to know more about its action and its usefulness. Any physician is free to use any means he judges appropriate to cure sickness, but he is under the obligation of publishing these means when they are either new or contrary to the established treatment. Those who have established, propagated or submitted to the magnetic treatment and intend to so continue, are under the obligation of publishing their discoveries and observations. Any such treatment whose procedures are not promptly published must be prohibited [dated September 12, 1784]. (cited in Amadou, 1971, p. 283)

Needless to say, the proponents of animal magnetism viewed the publication of this report with great satisfaction. They endorsed it immediately as supporting the use of animal magnetism and used de Jussieu's name to propagate the doctrine. One reason for doing this can be found in de Jussieu's report. Having recognized that the imagination cannot solely account for the different benefits of the treatment, he proceeded to present his notion of animal heat. He posed the question thus: "Could this heat be the fluid whose existence is so much debated?" For the magnetists, the answer was clear.

De Jussieu published his report, ignoring the protestations of his colleagues who saw this gesture as giving the magnetists undeserved leeway. The Royal Society decided to publish a series of letters it had received from different physicians residing all over France and Europe. They asked Thouret, a prestigious historian, to write the results of this informal inquiry on the benefits of magnetism. His book concluded that, in almost all of France, magnetism was not employed because it was useless and also because of its potential for abuse. He did not, however, substantiate this second claim. As Thouret emphasized, one of the towns where magnetism had not been utilized was Loudun, the site where the famous witchcraft trial of Urbain Grandier (see

Chapter 2) had taken place. "Quite a remarkable fact, that continues to show how previous mistakes are not always useless, the method [animal magnetism] was not accepted; people remembered vividly that during the convulsionaries' processions, similar scenes had happened and ended in tragedy" (Thouret, 1785).

Thouret's book concluded that the only places where magnetism had been accepted were isolated regions of France where the benefits of sound medical advice was not available. This conclusion was greatly overstated.

The Medical Faculty decided also to extend the conclusions of both commissions by making a remarkable decision. It adopted a decree by which all physicians were obliged to sign an official declaration rejecting the practice of animal magnetism. Those who refused to sign were to be expelled from the Faculty. Although most physicians agreed and signed the decree, 30 refused and were expelled. Among the protesters were physicians who had never practiced magnetism and had no intention of doing so, but who felt that the Faculty had no right to limit them in such a way. The formula used by the Faculty stated: "No physician will present himself as a partisan of animal magnetism, either in his writings or in his practice, for fear of expulsion from the list of doctor-regents" (cited in Varnier, 1785). The protesters objected to the language used by the Faculty. In the decree, those practicing animal magnetism were described in scurrilous terms:

> It has been observed that M. D'Eslon and many other doctors from the Faculty, forgetting their oath, and the qualities that make a physician, have chosen to join the ranks of a militia of dangerous and deceitful charlatans who set many pitfalls to the health, morality, and finances of the citizens, by abusing their credulity and promising to give them back their health. (cited in Varnier, 1785, p. 17)

Both Thomas d'Onglée and Varnier, doctor-regents at the Faculty protested publicly; they were ignored.

Reactions to the Commissions' Reports

The reports of both Commissions rapidly became a topic of lively discussion. Apart from the main protagonists, Mesmer and D'Eslon, many people entered the debate. Numerous books, pamphlets, tracts, satires and plays were published at a rapid rate. Letters in the newspapers either attacked or praised Mesmer. The years 1784 to 1785 can probably be seen as the most productive years for the partisans of animal magnetism.

Mesmer, however, did not survive the aftermath of the Commissions, either politically or scientifically. D'Eslon did not survive at all. He died in August 1786, at the age of 55, in intriguing circumstances. While apparently still in good health, he consulted a somnambulist who predicted that he would fall victim to a major illness in the near future. Six weeks later, he suffered a pulmonary congestion, accompanied by a malignant fever and renal colitis. He refused to be treated by the usual medical treatment and died in the hands of four of his student magnetists. His death put an end to the major conflict between the partisans of animal magnetism. Before dying, however, he was able to publish his replies to the reports of the Commissions of Inquiry (see D'Eslon, 1784).

Mesmer's answer to the Commission reports was surprisingly modest. In a first letter, dated August 16, 1784 and addressed to Vicq d'Azyr, he rejected Thouret's contention that he had plagiarized earlier authors, especially Maxwell. It is the first letter in which Mesmer explicitly answered this criticism by stating that he had never read Maxwell. He emphasized also that if Maxwell had elaborated a similar system, it did not alter his own contribution. In a second letter, Mesmer replied yet again to the frequent criticism that he had always rejected the offers of the learned societies to study his system. He reiterated the offer of choosing a number of patients that would be supervised during their treatment. The only reference to the Commission reports in fact was in a postscript where he attacked and rejected the yet unpublished book by D'Eslon. In fact, Mesmer was preparing a major reply. At the end of August, he appealed to the Law Courts directly. Ignoring both the newspapers and the learned societies, he decided to present his protests directly to the legal institutions.

Rather than replying to the reports, however, he once again attacked D'Eslon. As far as Mesmer was concerned, the Commissions were biased from the start. He maintained that they had been influenced by D'Eslon who did not know anything about mesmeric theory, and had been more prone to dismiss new ideas than to attempt to assess them objectively. His entire request to the parliamentary tribunal was concerned with the establishment of a second inquiry along guidelines he proposed. Mesmer did not receive a reply to his proposals. It was the last time that he would address the issues raised by the two Commissions of Inquiry. In the following years, Mesmer attempted to organize better the different chapters of the Society of Universal Harmony; this involved an attempt to resolve a number of internal conflicts.

D'Eslon's reply was better organized. He published a book in which he attempted to demonstrate how the different Commissions had erred. The first criticism was that the Royal Commission had rejected the idea of evaluating the successes and failures of magnetic treatment. He also accused them of being so biased from the very beginning that they knowingly suppressed any information that would indicate a genuine positive effect of the new treatment. For example, they ignored deliberately the fact that one of the Commissioners, M. Caille, had suffered a typical mesmeric crisis during one of his visits to the clinic. This point was made explicit in the report where the Commissioners stated that they would deliberately ignore anything that occurred within themselves. Certainly, this position was peculiarly at odds with people who had agreed to submit themselves to experimentation, in order to evaluate better the effects of the alleged magnetic fluid.

D'Eslon criticized the Commissioners also for social discrimination. He alleged that their overt withdrawal from public treatment, even after they had recognized that many phenomena were occurring during the treatment sessions, was not easily understood. He felt that their rejection of the effects experienced by patients from lower social classes was insulting.

He rejected also the three major conclusions of the Commissions. He accused them of exaggerating their statements. The infamous touchings were, as far as D'Eslon was concerned, always gentle and slight and had nothing to do with long and heavy massage. In addition, individual differences were never studied. This, he believed, would have endangered the imitation hypothesis. The crises, of which the Commissions warned, were occasional occurrences. D'Eslon stated that crises occurred in 6 to 7 of every 50 to 60 patients. In his own three years of practice, involving approximately 500 patients, 20 (4 percent) had actually experienced crisis.

His most vigorous attack was on the issue of imagination. He stated clearly that he had never believed that imagination was the cause of magnetic effects. For him, as pointed out previously, imagination did not play a role in the curative effects of magnetic fluid. Quite to the contrary: *"Is it imagination which eases in a moment the pains of a cruel burn and cures it within a short time?"* (D'Eslon, 1784, p. 24, italics added) It is of interest to note here that even today hypnosis is used in the treatment of burns with some success, although its use is still controversial. D'Eslon concluded his reply by stating that the two Commissions had not succeeded in rejecting animal magnetism. It should be pointed out also that D'Eslon separated himself from Mesmer in his reply. He stated that the Commissions had studied his system rather than Mesmer's and that the conclusions should be confined to him. It was a polite gesture as well as an expression of his belief that Mesmer knew more than he did.

The major replies, however, came from the partisans of both Mesmer and D'Eslon who published a remarkable number of books on the topic; opponents of Mesmerism also published prodigiously. According to Retz, more than 100 books and pamphlets were published in 1784, all purporting to demonstrate the uselessness of animal magnetism. The pro-magnetist books were usually written by patients or members of the different Societies of Universal Harmony. Although most of them constituted a relentless compilation of testimonies of successful cures, some of them were satirical essays attacking the medical establishment, as can be seen by the following title: *Report on the Report of the Commissioners Appointed by the King to Examine the Practice of M. D'Eslon on Animal Magnetism, Written by an Amateur Seeker of the Truth, Excited by the Imagination, the Touching and the Imitation, and Magnetized by Common Sense and Reason* (Anonymous, 1784f). One of these books written by a well-known judicial court member, M. Servan, became quite popular, and for a while it was seen as the answer to Thouret's book. Servan attacked the medical profession directly:

> Physicians have killed me; what I have been left with is not worth looking for a more gentle word. In the last twenty years, I have always been rendered

sicker by the medication I had to take than by my illnesses.... Animal magnetism, if only a chimera, should be tolerated; it would still be useful to my fellow man by preserving many of them from the undeniable dangers of vulgar medicine.... (cited in Figuier, 1860, Vol. III, pp. 220–221)

For the first time, however, authors began publishing statistics on patient successes, the frequency of crisis, as well as detailed information on the treatment used. Servan for example reiterated D'Eslon's claim that only very few magnetized individuals experienced a crisis and that not all of these were of the convulsive type.

In a book compiled by a number of patients, 111 cases were presented. Of these, 6 were completely unsuccessful, 52 had profited from the magnetic treatment but had not been totally cured, and the remaining 53 reported themselves as being completely cured. Among the latter was the case of a 26-month-old child who had been seriously burned on the arm and had been fully cured in nine days. Of the 111 patients, only 12 experienced a crisis, 11 of whom were women. Such statistics can be found in most of the books published following the reports of the Commissions (Anonymous, 1784j).

The public reaction was more directed to the reality of the phenomenon than was the scientific reaction. Most scientists took a middle of the road position asking for a serious study of the question. In fact, many authors recommended that animal magnetism be integrated into the practice of medicine and restricted to the medical profession. Part of the criticism that stemmed from the literate class was an attack on what they saw as an attempt to monopolize the healing arts by the medical establishment. This type of attack was not new. Apart from the previously mentioned conflict between the different factions of the medical and scientific professions, a major area of debate surfaced between physicians and surgeons; the latter were not as yet accepted into the medical field.

The major change in the debate following the reports can be seen in all of the books that were published in favor of animal magnetism. To counteract imputations of immorality and of possible abuse, most writers on animal magnetism incorporated a number of pages, if not a chapter, on the benefits of the new treatment for morality. Not only did they deny the immorality accusation: They adopted an opposite stance, that magnetism was actually good for society. Dating from this period also, most books on the subject incorporated a chapter on the dangers of magnetism. Such a position is readily understood when one looks at the type of accusations that stemmed from opponents of the new theory. In a book entitled *Report on the History of Jugglery in which the Phenomena of Mesmerism Are Demonstrated* (Anonymous, 1784e), there are a number of attacks on Mesmer and his disciples. For example, in discussing Antoine, one of Mesmer's *valets-toucheur* (one who magnetized patients in place of Mesmer), the anonymous author stated: "Mesmer's '*valet-toucheur*' was named Antoine, a most intelligent boy who performed his job, as far as I have heard, in the best of ways, especially with the Ladies" (Anonymous, 1784e, p. 28).

In fact, in his second book, Paulet (1784a) suggested that Mesmer deliberately employed young men with sex appeal to massage the ladies assembled around the magnetic tub. The pro-magnetist books began to take up additional accusations. In his well-written book, Thouret had warned the public that too many magnetizations could shatter the nervous system and lead patients into all types of dementia. The accusations were refuted in a number of reports stemming both from patients and magnetists. This did not prevent the media from publicizing these accusations. A number of epigrams became popular. One of the most popular was:

Le magnétisme est aux abois;
La Faculté, l'Académie
L'ont condamné tout d'une voix,
Et l'ont couvert d'ignominie,

Après ce jugement bien sage et bien légal,
Si quelque esprit original
Persiste encore dans son délire,
Il sera permis de lui dire:

Crois au magnétisme . . . animal!

This epigram became so famous that Bonnefoy reported it in his book, but changed the last sentence to fit the pro-magnetists. The last verse became: "Away from magnetism . . . animal!" By the end of 1785, however, the debate began to recede from the public domain.

This sudden loss of popularity came in part from the infiltration of more radical political ideas into the mesmeric movement stemming from such people as Bergasse, J. P. Brissot, and Jean-Jacques Duval D'Espréménil. This more radical aspect of Mesmerism at the dawn of the French Revolution has been studied by Darnton (1968) in his already cited book. The reader interested in the political aspect of animal magnetism is referred to this source. The politicization of the movement did not, however, have as important an impact on the fate of animal magnetism as did the discovery of artificial somnambulism. On the other hand, this politicization accelerated the decline of Mesmerism, and of Mesmer in particular.

Even though the two reports of the Commissions of Inquiry created a reaction against both animal magnetism and Mesmer, the major blow to both the reports and Mesmer came from one of his most faithful students, the Marquis de Puységur. At the same time that the reports were published, the Marquis published his first observations on a new phenomenon, which he called artificial somnambulism. This new aspect of animal magnetism was to pave the way for the revival of the sensational, of the irrational, and of the unscientific knowledge that had been so painfully dispelled by the previous century of philosophers. Spiritualism was on the upsurge at this time of social turbulence in France.

NOTES

1. The following pamphlets can be found in *Recueil général et complet de tous les écrits publiés pour ou contre le magnétisme animal* listed in the bibliography: Anonymous (1784b), E. F. (1784), F. D. P. (1784), Gébelin (1784), Hervier (1784), M. . . . (1784), M. J. D. F. D. M. (1784). Many of the manuscripts published at that period were either anonymous or signed with pseudonyms or single letters followed by asterisks. As far as possible, we sought to identify these authors more precisely. Unfortunately, in a number of cases, this proved to be unsuccessful. Overall there are 161 entries listed in the *Recueil général*. Most are cited by date and city of publication only. The publisher of most of them is not stated.

2. The 14-page autopsy report can be found in the following manuscript dated May 13, 1784: *Lettre sur la mort de M. Court de Gébelin*. The manuscript is signed by the five physicians who performed the autopsy: Mittié, LaCaze, Cheigneverd, Sué, and LaMotte. They pointed out the possibility that Mesmer's adversaries could profit from Gébelin's death.

3. Many other books had been published in the first half of 1784 for and against animal magnetism. None of these, however, had the impact of two books, Paulet's (1784b) and Thouret's (1784). More striking were the numerous letters published in the newspapers, both scientific and other, on the benefits and dangers of animal magnetism. Although it is quite impossible to give an exact account of all these letters (some of which were more than one hundred pages long), we will try to convey the flavor of the arguments through some examples.

4. The four letters were published on February 13, 14, and 15, and on March 7, 1784. Mesmer's replies were published on February 17 and 18, 1784.

5. These excerpts were taken from the *Lettre de M. L. B. D. B. à M. P. L.-G. H. D. L. B. à Marseille*. Paris: Couturier, 87 pages. The attribution to Borméo was suggested by Barbier.

6. Mesmer had met the famous astronomer Jean-Sylvain Bailly some years earlier and was favorably impressed by him. Among all of the scientists Mesmer had met, Bailly not only showed interest in his theoretical ideas, but even defended Mesmer against some of the people who ridiculed him. Although he had not observed Mesmer's treatment, a lady friend of his had benefited from his intervention. This, according to Bailly, did not prove that animal magnetism was a panacea, but indicated that there existed a phenomenon worthy of investigation.

It is interesting to note in this regard that testimonies emanating from individuals of the higher social classes were usually taken as reflecting some kind of truth. When one reads the first accounts of the numerous magnetic cures, it becomes evident that only the cures of people in the upper social classes were presented in very great detail. This type of behavior irritated Mesmer. In his 1781 book, he wrote:

> In France the cure of a poor individual is easily dismissed; compared to the cure of a marquis or a count, four cures of middle-class people do not count. Cure four marquises, it will perhaps be worth a duke; but cure four dukes, they will be dismissed for the cure

of a prince. This is so different from my own ideas. I believe that I still would merit the attention of people even if I had only cured some dogs. (cited in Amadou, 1971, p. 198)

Although in line with his egalitarian philosophy, this type of comment certainly did nothing to promote the acceptance of animal magnetism by the learned societies. Mesmer, if nothing else, was not known for his diplomatic skills.

7. La Condamine, to whom this letter was addressed, was encountered earlier during the description of the crucifixion of Sister Françoise of the underground Jansenist movement. He was at the time a well-known scientist, as well as a highly regarded government official.

8. The original version of this confidential report can be found in Neufchâteau (1800). The publication year in the original is listed as year VIII using the system adopted following the French Revolution. As far as the authors can ascertain, it should correspond to the years 1799 to 1800 (September 22, 1799 to September 21, 1800).

9. The epigram can be translated as follows: Magnetism is at bay/ The Faculty, the Academy/ Have condemned it unanimously/ Have thrown it in disgrace/ Following this judgment, so wise and so legal/ If some eccentric spirit/ Persists still in his folly/ It will be permissible to say to him:/ Believe in magnetism . . . animal!

It had been popularized at Le Café du Caveau, a café where writers and artists met. The original title was: *Epigramme faite sur le champ, après avoir lu le rapport de MM. les commissaires nommés par le Roi, pour l'examen de cette vieille erreur renouvelée.*

II

From Mesmerism to Hypnosis

5

Artificial Somnambulism

Following the two French Commissions of 1784 a number of developments altered the entire complexion of animal magnetism. The most dramatic change was the serendipitous discovery of artificial somnambulism by the Marquis de Puységur. His observations undercut the negative effects of the Commissions of Inquiry and led Mesmer's system into quite unexpected directions. Because of de Puységur, the conclusions of the reports were challenged by both magnetists and physicians of the early nineteenth century. This, in turn, led to the formation of two new Commissions of Inquiry during its first three decades.

Three additional investigators of some importance also emerged during this period. To begin with, Caullet de Veaumorel, was the first author to abandon the physical basis of the mesmeric system for a psychological one. He emphasized the notion of will in the process of magnetizing, initiating a tradition that is still alive today. It is difficult to evaluate whether it was he or de Puységur who was the first to advocate such a change; all that can be said is that they were contemporaries. The second was a physician, Jacques-Henri-Désiré Pététin, who specialized in the study of hysteria, and made the first observations of the phenomenon known today as *catalepsy*. His most famous contribution, however, was the apparent discovery that in somnambulism there can be a transposition of the senses. This observation endowed artificial somnambulism with a flavor of esoterica and spiritualism that attained its peak in the mid-nineteenth century. The spiritualist development came to be espoused by a third person, the Chevalier de Barbarin, who made the soul the center of his system, and prayer the technique of choice. This spiritualization of the mesmeric system was joined eventually by the American spiritualist movement of the mid-nineteenth century (see Chapter 7). It also awakened the Catholic Church which had been surprisingly quiet since the onset of animal magnetism. This, in turn, led to a classical confrontation with which the witchcraft history has familiarized us. It was not, however, until the 1850s that the Catholic Church would officially state its position on what, by then, was called hypnotism.

Following the Benjamin Franklin report, magnetism enjoyed a brief period of popularity. The onset of the French Revolution as well as the involvement of many Mesmerist leaders in politics relegated the mesmeric debate to the periphery of public interest. It is important to note that the two following years brought about three major trends that have survived until the present: the physical, the psychological, and the spiritualist interpretations of Mesmer's doctrines.

Mesmer's Last Years

For reasons difficult to assess, except that time can be merciless, the years 1784 to 1785 were disastrous for Mesmer. At the time of the publication of the two Commission reports, Prince Henri of Prussia was visiting France. Having heard about animal magnetism, he sought additional information. During a visit to Lyon, he decided to witness a magnetic séance at the local veterinary school. A number of physicians and magistrates were present also at what turned out to be the magnetizing of an old horse. Once magnetized, the horse manifested a severe cough that became worse when passes were made along its throat. The magnetist diagnosed a serious illness, and the horse was immediately sacrificed to the glory of the magnetist who had found what he had so accurately predicted. The Prince, however, was not particularly impressed.

He then visited an army camp directed by the Marquis Tissart du Rouvres, who practiced magnetism with his soldiers as subjects. This experience proved to be more interesting for the Prince. As a last surprise, Mesmer was brought in to magnetize the Prince. Unfortunately, the Prince proved unmagnetizable. Neither Mesmer, nor a tree that he had magnetized for the Prince's benefit, could succeed in altering the subjective experience of the royal subject.

This was a more than humiliating situation for Mesmer. His partisans, however, proposed an explanation for his failure. Recalling Mesmer's aphorisms, they revived the idea that people can demonstrate anti-magnetic qualities. It was thus hypothesized that individuals of royal blood were probably antimagnetic to ensure the security of the State. Although quite a sophisticated explanation, it was soon to play against Mesmer himself.

The Princess of Lamballe, Marie-Antoinette's closest friend, believed that she was of royal blood. To prove it, she decided to undergo all of Mesmer's treatment without experiencing any effect. As she expected, the Princess left the mesmeric clinic triumphantly. Mesmerism was becoming a parlor game of the rich and powerful. Quite discouraged by this time, Mesmer decided to leave France. Before leaving, however, he decided to engage in a final battle with his supporters.

During late 1784 and the beginning of 1785, numerous books were published on Mesmerism. Each author claimed to know of Mesmer's secret and promised to disclose it to the public. The most complete book was written by Caullet de Veaumorel who presented a systematic treatise on Mesmerism. He made, also, the first mention of the power of the human will at play in the magnetizing process. Mesmer replied to Veaumorel in the *Journal de Paris*, denying that the book represented his entire system. He rejected specifically the chapter on magnetizing procedures. Veaumorel replied a few days later that Mesmer's attitude was to be expected since he, Veaumorel, had not paid the dues for instruction in animal magnetism. This was, of course, a blow below the belt.[1]

Veaumorel confronted Mesmer further by maintaining that he had only copied his students' notes and that it was time that Mesmer began recognizing his own supporters. Their epistolary exchange led rapidly to a bitter dispute between the members of the Society of Universal Harmony and their founder. The dispute culminated in the expulsion of a number of the society's leaders, including Nicholas Bergasse. In Bergasse (see Chapter 4) and Kornmann's attempt to establish the Society of Universal Harmony, the contract stated that each new member would not divulge the doctrine, or teach it, before the campaign was fully funded. Mesmer decided that although the money had been raised, and that he had received more than had been promised, he still retained exclusive rights to promulgate his doctrine.

When the Society decided to open the course to the public, without the obligation of having to pay any dues, Mesmer protested. After many unsuccessful negotiations, the Marquis de Puységur suggested that the Society should give to Mesmer the difference between what he had already received and what the French government had promised him in 1781. Everyone agreed, Mesmer included. A few days later, however, Mesmer organized a meeting of the Society without referring to the administrative committee and founded a new organization from which all of his previous supporters were excluded. D'Espréménil who was present at the meeting could not change Mesmer's mind. He then decided to publish a public account of all the money that Mesmer had received from the Society. The letter, dated June 1, 1785, concluded with the following paragraph:

> So 317,040 pounds have already been given to M. Mesmer, plus 26,724 pounds that he certainly cannot have not received, that is a total of 343,764 pounds for a subscription that was only of 240,000 pounds. Is the general public, represented by the Société formed by the subscribers, then at last the owner of the discovery? M. Mesmer contends that it is not.
>
> The author of the *Réflexions préliminaires sur les Docteurs Modernes* has to admit quite naively that he is surprised by such a contention. (cited in Amadou, 1971, p. 264)

Although Mesmer replied to this letter by publishing a small book emphasizing his right to his own discovery, as well as accusing both Bergasse and d'Espréménil of betraying their promises, he was badly damaged in the public eye. Once again, the satirists had a field day. Probably the most serious attack came when a small *montgolfier* (a helium balloon named after its inventors, the Montgolfier brothers), a recent popular scientific discovery, was launched from the Tuileries, with the inscription: "So long magnetic tub, the vintage is done."[2]

Mesmer left Paris for London, where he stayed for a few weeks. He then traveled to Italy and Germany, returning to France for brief periodic visits. When he decided to visit Vienna in 1793 to occupy the house he had inherited after his wife's death, he was evicted. He finally established himself in Switzerland where he completed his final book, published in 1799. We will return later to this book since Mesmer stated his position on artificial somnambulism in this final work. Although many authors have reported that Mesmer was in Paris the day Bailly (the Mayor) was guillotined (see, for example, Figuier, 1860), there is no evidence to substantiate the claim.[3]

In 1802, interestingly enough, Mesmer received a life annuity of 3,000 florins from the French government to compensate for the money he had lost during the Revolution. He did not, however, remain in France. In 1803, he returned to Switzerland. In a letter dated 1809, Mesmer wrote to J. L. Picher-Grandchamp that his life was quiet and happy in Frauenfeld. He subsequently moved to Meersbourg following a prediction of a bohemian who had told him that he would die there in his 81st year. On February 26, 1815, he suffered a relapse from a diseased urinary bladder. He died a week later on March 5 at the predicted age of 81 years old, mostly ignored, if not forgotten.

The Discovery of Artificial Somnambulism

In a satirical comment on the two Commission reports of 1784, an anonymous author had written that "the scholars, by continuously shouting themselves hoarse for or against [animal magnetism], will go husky and will be obliged to shut up. Amen." De Puységur's discovery of artificial somnambulism was to have the same effect on the learned societies. This unusual turn of events at a time when Mesmerism was thought to be done with, disconcerted the medical profession. Magnetic fluid was easily dismissed as an illusion, having no link with physical reality. By contrast, medical practitioners were at a loss when it came to dismissing a psychological phenomenon that closely resembled the miraculous powers of healers of the past. The best they could do was to ignore it, which they proceeded to do.

The Marquis de Puységur was a member of the Society of Universal Harmony; he had followed the teachings of Mesmer and Bergasse, but by his own admission had failed to discover the secret behind the doctrine. Contrary to what the learned societies were publicizing, animal magnetism had become very popular in many regions of France as well as abroad. It had reached America through Lafayette (who was an ardent proponent of the new doctrine), becoming fashionable in many of the colonies of the New World. A German author, Metzger, wrote that "in Dominique, the black slaves show such a passion for the 'bala' [the name given to magnetism], that the authorities were forced to adopt a law to prohibit it" (cited in Figuier, 1860, Vol. III, p. 240).

Another author, in an anonymous French book, wrote: "The Americans whose [physical] system is more sensitive and more irritable than that of the inhabitants of the Old World, are coming from the other pole to praise his [Mesmer's] marvelous art" (Anonymous, 1784i, p. iv).

Perhaps surprisingly, the most ardent advocates of the new doctrine of artificial somnambulism came from the military establishment. The three de Puységur brothers (Maxime, Antoine-Hyacinthe, and Amand-Marie Jacques), as well as Tardy de Montravel, General LaFayette, and Tissart du Rouvres, to name but a few, became central figures in the propagation of the new therapeutic. At this period in time, many military posts had their officer-magnetists. The Marquis Tissart du Rouvres, alluded to earlier, was experimenting on his troops; they are reported to have enjoyed the new treatment. Before elaborating on this phenomenon which soon became a problem for the authorities, we will discuss the initial observations upon which artificial somnambulism were based.

The Marquis de Puységur lived at Buzancy, near Soissons. A gentle man, known for his compassion, he was loved and respected by everyone working or living on his domain. When he began practicing animal magnetism, the population of Soissons was happy to collaborate. He treated the peasants well, and the needy could always find a bowl of soup and some bread at his house.

The Marquis discovered what he called *somnambulistic sleep* quite serendipitously. He had always been intrigued by the fact that in his own practice, he had never elicited the type of convulsive crisis seen in Mesmer's treatment. Quite to the contrary, some of his patients demonstrated what seemed to be a profound and calm sleep. In a short time, de Puységur's reputation brought so many individuals to the domain that he found himself in the impossible situation of magnetizing every one of them. Remembering one of Mesmer's techniques, he magnetized a tree in a public square in the center of the village of Buzancy, and he tied a rope around it to allow more people the benefits of the magnetic fluid. What was surprising, however, was the calmness, the quietness of the crises elicited by the old elm tree. On May 17, 1784, the Marquis made the observation that would revolutionize animal magnetism. He described his discovery in a letter to his brother Chastenet, the youngest of the three brothers, who had followed Mesmer's classes and had also been cured by him of an unspecified illness. He wrote:

> I am still using this marvelous power that I received from M. Mesmer, and I praise him every day because I am quite useful here, bringing out salutary effects on all the sick people of the region. They come in great number around my tree; this morning they were more than one hundred and thirty. It is a

perpetual procession; I spend two hours there every morning; my tree is the best possible tub, all of its leaves communicate health; everyone can feel more or less of its good effects; you will be pleased by such a touching humanitarian picture. I have but one regret, it is that I cannot touch everyone; but my man [Victor], or should I better say, *my intelligence* calms me down. He shows me how I should behave. According to him, it is not necessary that I touch everyone; *a gaze, a gesture, A WILL* is sufficient. And it is the most narrow-minded countryman that teaches me that. When he is in a crisis, I don't know of anyone more deep, more careful, and more *clear-sighted*; there are many others, men and women, who are nearly as efficient, but none can equal him and this saddens me. By next Tuesday, it will be over; this man will not need to be touched any more. No curiosity will lead me to use him and so disregard his health and well-being. If you want to see and hear him, make sure to be here on Sunday at the latest. (de Puységur, 1784-1785, pp. 89-90, italics in original)

This "narrow-minded" peasant was Victor Race, a 23-year-old laborer. For more than four days he had been afflicted by an inflammation of the lungs when, on May 4, 1784, the Marquis visited him at his home. To his surprise, the young man was very rapidly placed into a calm and deep "sleep" without any pain or convulsions. In a letter dated May 8, a full three months before the reports of the Commissions, and even before the Commissions commenced their inquiries, he addressed the Society of Universal Harmony in the following terms:

I pushed the crisis further, but he experienced some vertigos. He talked aloud about his businesses. When I thought that his ideas could affect him negatively, I stopped them and tried to bring up more happy ones. I did not need to expend much effort to do so. I would then see him happy, imagining winning a prize or dancing at a fair, etcetera. *I nourished these ideas in him*, and by doing so made him move on his chair as if he would dance on a tune; what I sang *mentally*, he was repeating in a loud voice. In this way I succeeded in provoking a good sweat on the first day. After one hour of this crisis, *I calmed him*, and left the room. . . . The next day, having forgotten my visit of the previous day, he told me how much better his health was. (cited in Figuier, 1860, Vol. III, pp. 247-248, italics in original)

The basis of what became known as somnambulistic sleep can be found in these two early quotations.[4] The phenomena described in these two excerpts soon became the hallmarks of artificial somnambulism. Thus, a number of observations become pertinent: As far as the magnetized person was concerned, there were no more convulsive crises, but a profound sleep that was followed by amnesia when the subject returned to wakefulness. The magnetized subject appeared to become clairvoyant when in such a sleep which allowed him or her to know how to behave in artificial somnambulism and how to instruct the magnetist. The patient also appeared to become telepathic and seemed to know the unspoken thoughts of his or her magnetist. On the other hand, the magnetist was the depository of the will to magnetize. It was not necessary any more to refer to the fluid. What became important was the will. The strength of the magnetist's thoughts appeared to be translated into the magnetized individual's behaviors. It is the first mention, of what would later be called *le rapport exclusif*, the "exclusive rapport," or the relationship between magnetist and subject. One final comment underscores the fact that already at this early period the idea of suggestion, although not recognized as such, was present. It will be recalled that Mesmer used to suggest olfactory hallucinations to his patients. De Puységur, by contrast, suggested (*Je nourrissais en lui ces idées* [I nourished these ideas in him]) images of events the patient had experienced before. In a sense this technique could be seen as a rudimentary form of age regression to previously known events. At the same time, de Puységur's experiments marked a slow and gradual reversal to some of the attributes that had been seen in earlier years as either the signs of possession or of God-inspired convulsions. These similarities became even more apparent as de Puységur's work progressed.

This idea of rapport took on new dimensions. It acquired a quality of exclusiveness where only the magnetist, having established rapport, could communicate with the patient. Victor, however, could do more than what the Marquis had first thought. Not only did he appear to know what was good for him, but he could identify also illnesses in other people and prescribe the desired treatment. This represented another dramatic change in the system of animal magnetism. Whereas Mesmer avoided, as far as possible, any form of medication, the somnambulists reintroduced its prescription.

The Marquis's description of Victor's behavior while magnetized is of considerable interest. He wrote:

> He is not a stupid peasant anymore, incapable of answering questions by a whole sentence; he is a being that I cannot describe. I do not need to talk to him; I just think, and he understands and answers me. If someone comes to his room, he sees him if *I want him to*, tells him the things that *I want him to say*, although not always as *I have said them*, but rather as the truth is. When he wants to say more than I think would be careful, *I stop his ideas, sentences* in the middle of a word, and *I change his ideas completely*. You will believe it quite impossible that this man should not be particularly grateful for the attention that Mme de P... and myself give him. He never would talk about it in his normal state, but as soon as he is in a magnetic crisis, he opens his heart. He hopes that if it were possible, one could see inside his heart the friendship and the gratitude that he feels. It is difficult not to shed a tear of admiration and sensitivity when one hears so clearly nature's voice. (cited in Figuier, 1860, Vol. III, p. 248, italics in original)

De Puységur was particularly impressed by the difference between the normal state of his clairvoyant somnambulists and their crisis state.

> The line of demarcation is so complete that these two states may almost be described as two different existences. I have noticed that in the magnetic state the patients have a clear recollection of all their doings in the normal state;

but in the normal state they can recall nothing of what has taken place in the magnetic condition. (de Puységur, 1784-1785, p. 103)

De Puységur was quick to publicize his new observations. In 1784, he wrote a book, co-authored with Cloquet, a collector of taxes in Soissons who had spent a month observing the practice of two of the de Puységur brothers. In this, they provided a detailed description of the cures obtained in Buzancy.[5] The book presented 61 cases of which only 8 manifested somnambulistic behavior. It is in this book that, for the first time, somnambulism was mentioned as well as the possibility of patients diagnosing illness and prescribing treatment.

De Puységur's success was repeated rapidly by a number of other people. For one, the Marquis Tissart du Rouvres magnetized a tree in his domain of Beaubourg en Brie, a few kilometers from Paris. He improved on the previous method by providing ropes of different lengths; hanging from the branches of the magnetized tree some of them reached far into the nearby countryside. In this way, sick people did not have to travel a long distance in order to benefit from magnetic treatment. He published a book in June 1784 also describing a series of successful cures.

In the meantime, the Marquis de Puységur had been forced to rejoin his regiment at Strasbourg and thus had to cease treatment at Buzancy. His arrival in Strasbourg, however, was perceived more as the arrival of a new thaumaturgist than as the arrival of a military attaché. He magnetized his soldiers, taught magnetism to many officers, and formed the Society of Universal Harmony of Strasbourg which was to become one of the most active in France. His brother, the count Maxime, was at that time founding the *Société de la Guienne* in Bayonne.

The discovery of somnambulism gave a new impetus to magnetic doctrines, this time with a major difference: Numerous physicians joined the societies. Very rapidly, a number of books were published on the subject. As with the previous books on animal magnetism, these consisted of a listing of all of the different cures obtained by the new treatment. Unlike the previous books, however, they provided an account of the new magnetic state as well as a description of the abilities of somnambulists. Although some of these books were published during the proceedings of the two Commissions of Inquiry of 1784, the Commissioners did not acknowledge them. They were to be criticized for it, especially since they had noticed somnambulistic behavior in D'Eslon's clinic, but had not investigated it.

Furthermore, one of the Commissioners, de Jussieu, in his own report, had actually described one subject in such a crisis. He had, however, drawn "no conclusion from this fact, of which [he] was a witness on several occasions" (de Jussieu, 1784). The new trend was to reject the conclusions of the Commissions on the grounds that they had not studied the most important development of the new doctrine. This rejection was virtually universal. It was best exemplified by the Count Maxime de Puységur's comment in a book published by the *Société de la Guienne* in 1785, where he said: "Of course, if these are the effects of the imagination, the Academy will be compelled to recognize that the imagination is the greatest of all physicians" (de Puységur, 1785, p. 75; cited in the *Recueil général*, Vol. 11, document 132).

This barb was directed at the learned societies; it represented the opinion of the lay public and the literate world of the late 1780s. It is interesting to note that most of the books published between 1785 and 1787 have, as the sole topic, de Puységur's artificial somnambulism. Times had changed.

During this period, de Puységur's youngest brother, Chastenet, was in Brest, continuing his military career. He commanded one of the King's supply ships, the Frédéric-Guillaume. With the help of the officers he had trained in magnetism, the entire ship became a vast magnetic tub. Everything from the ropes to the masts and the sails was magnetized. The entire crew was under the command of magnetism, and the ship's daily journal attests to the numerous cures that were obtained during four months of navigation. Interestingly enough, the observation that the secret of Mesmer resided in the apparent power of the will over the somnambulist, was made not by the Marquis, but by his brother Antoine-Hyacinthe. In his book *Du magnétisme animal* (1807) the Marquis states the following:

> This simple means will always evade the intelligence. There is only one man, as far as I know, who has discovered the mechanism underlying Mesmer's procedures, and this man is my brother, an officer in the navy, known under the name of Chastenet. He discovered in the chaos of the first tubs the *principal cause* of their effects. The next day, he talked about it to Mesmer. The latter, trying to hide his surprise, showed that he was both displeased and worried about the bad consequences that could arise for him and his doctrine from the premature interpretation of this fact. My brother, who approved of the argument, promised to keep secret what he had discovered and seen. (p. 141, italics in original)

This recognition by the Marquis of his brother's role leads one to question whether Mesmer had known about somnambulism before it was first reported by the de Puységur brothers. It is also of interest that according to the Marquis (1807, pp. 29-30), his two brothers began practicing animal magnetism two years before he himself did. Prior to joining the fund raising drive in order to learn Mesmer's techniques and theory, he regarded Mesmer and his own two brothers as charlatans. It is ironic that in most historical accounts of animal magnetism, he came to play such an important role at the expense of his brothers. It must be acknowledged, however, that of the three brothers, the Marquis became the most ardent as well as the most persevering advocate of animal magnetism. As is often the case, it is one thing to observe first, and another to publish first and to thus bear the heat of critical evaluation by peers.

Mesmer and Somnambulism

Only in his 1799 book did Mesmer discuss publicly artificial somnambulism. It is difficult to document whether he encountered phenomena similar to those of artificial somnambulism, and even more difficult to assess their credibility. Nevertheless, there is some circumstantial evidence that he did. Unfortunately, this evidence is found mainly in the writings of some of his supporters, long after somnambulism had been described. There may be some truth in these writings. But regardless of whether Mesmer knew, and perhaps this was his famous secret, he never publicized it. His reaction to Chastenet de Puységur's confrontation over the major role played by the will certainly indicated that Mesmer knew more than what he was willing to divulge publicly. In *L'Hermès*, one of the first journals devoted to animal magnetism and published between 1826 and 1828, Picher-Grandchamp, one of Mesmer's best friends, wrote that he had quite often witnessed cases of somnambulism in the so-called crisis room. Indeed it is quite difficult to believe that he would not have noticed such a phenomenon. Even the Commissioners, and particularly de Jussieu, had observed some somnambulistic behaviors in the treatments they had witnessed. The anonymous author of a small manuscript written and published in 1784 criticized the Commissions' reports on this point in the following way:

> Among the experiments conducted by the commissioners, I wish they would have observed one of those who became somnambules following the magnetic action, and asked him to perform the following experiment. After having blindfolded him as they were doing already, they could have presented him with patients whose illnesses they knew already, and asked him to identify them. If this new type of physician had discovered the illnesses just by mere contact, it would have been difficult to say that the touching produced the sickness, and that imagination and imitation played a role in it. This experiment is a decisive one: *I have seen it done at Mesmer's clinic, and repeated since successfully many times in Lyon.* . . . The difficulty in explaining such phenomena, as well as those seen in cataleptics following magnetism, is probably one of the reasons why the Commissioners did not study them. (Anonymous, 1784g; cited in Figuier, 1860, Vol. III, p. 253, italics in original)

Other indirect evidence that Mesmer knew of somnambulism can be found in Aubin Gauthier's book written in 1842. It is the story of Marguerite, one of the patients who followed Mesmer's treatment. She was usually magnetized by one of Mesmer's collaborators, a Dr. Aubry. In one of her treatment sessions she had been magnetized by another magnetist in the absence of Aubry. At the end of it, nobody could awaken her and Aubry was not available. She suddenly left and walked to the Hôtel Cluny where she entered a room on the second floor. Dr. Aubry was there, quite surprised to see his patient, in crisis with her eyes closed.

"Who told you that I was here?" asked the doctor.
"Nobody," answered Marguerite, "I went to the treatment and you were

not there. Someone magnetized me, but nobody knew how to awake me. I saw that you were here, so I came." (p. 247)

Finally, in December 1784, a report was published in a Swiss journal which described how Mesmer's patients were amnesic following magnetization, but could talk and describe the nature of their illnesses during it (Milt, 1953). Since there is no mention of de Puységur in this report, it could be hypothesized that Mesmer was in fact the discoverer of artificial somnambulism. Bernard Milt (1953) has already proposed this hypothesis, based on the fact that Mesmer had never been particularly keen on sharing his knowledge. In the book *Mesmerismus*, written by Wolfart (1814) and assisted by Mesmer, the author asserted that Mesmer knew about somnambulism, but did not publicize it because of the religious mentality of the time (*Religionsgeist*). If this was the case, Mesmer certainly displayed sound judgment. As will be seen later, the popularity enjoyed by the phenomena elicited in artificial somnambulism set off a conflict between the Church and the magnetists. Whether or not Mesmer knew of the phenomenon of artificial somnambulism will probably never be known. What is important, however, is the perception that he had of this new aspect of his doctrine.

In his 1799 book, Mesmer saw the whole notion of somnambulism (he called it *sommeil critique* [critical sleep]) quite negatively. He warned the reader in his introduction that somnambulism was nothing more than the exaggeration of certain diseases and should not be confounded with animal magnetism. He claimed, also, to have recognized the possibility of clairvoyance, telepathy, and the ability to diagnose one's own illnesses as well as those of other people. He explained it, however, in materialistic terms; man possessed an internal sense that linked him with the universe. It was through the heightening of this sense that the phenomena seen in somnambulism could be elicited. He was also among the first people to point to the similarities between somnambulists and what had been usually described as either demonic possession, divination, or prophecy. He pointed out:

> We still have quite vividly in memory the different persecutions that were carried on by credulous fanatics on people who were unfortunate enough to be the recipients of such wonders or their agents. It is to be feared that even today they could be the victim of some *fanatic disbelief*; they will not be punished as if they were idolatrous or sacrilegious, but they could be seen as impostors or as disruptive of public peace. (cited in Amadou, 1971, p. 308, italics in original)

The remainder of his book was spent attempting to explain all the phenomena of somnambulism according to his own system. He believed that the sole agent responsible for all of the new aspects of magnetism was still the fluid; even in the case of communication of the magnetist's will to the magnetized patient, the active principle was the magnetic fluid. The magnetist used the fluid to extend the influence of his nervous system to that of the other person. This materialistic explanation, however, may have served but one purpose for Mesmer: to avoid a revival of superstitious beliefs that could only be detrimental to the establishment of a scientific system of therapeutics.

Unfortunately for him, his final attempts were not very successful. The sensational aspects of somnambulism were more attractive to the imagination of the magnetists and their clientele than the more rationalistic and materialistic approach that Mesmer was emphasizing. Although animal magnetism was to remain at the core of the somnambulistic movement, the magnetic fluid was not referred to as the sole physical basis of the phenomena anymore. De Puységur's work added to Mesmer's system the notion of the power of the will to influence physical processes. This change marked the first major alteration of this system. It led to a gradual evolution from a materialistic view of the human organism to a psychological and a more spiritualistically inclined description of the human mind.

De Puységur's Conceptions of Somnambulism

If Mesmer's motto had been "Know how to will" (*Sachez vouloir*), in order to be able to be magnetized, de Puységur changed it to "Believe and Will" (*Croyez et Veuillez*). In his 1807 book, de Puységur defined the state of somnambulism in the following terms:

> Any patient, in this state, when correctly directed by an experienced Magnetist, knows not only the cause, the symptoms and the terms of his illnesses, but also can indicate all the means that can help nature in its curative work. . . . First, I would like to talk about the rapport that develops between a Magnetist and the person that he has placed in a complete state of somnambulism. This rapport, as I have said in my first reports, can be compared to the one existing between an iron rod and a magnetic needle placed on its shaft. This rapport is such that the magnetic somnambule will always, with more or less mobility, obey his Magnetist, in the same way that the needle obeys the magnetic rod that makes it move. (pp. 11–12)

Accordingly, not only the individual capable of being placed in a somnambulistic state demonstrated increased sensory and intellectual skills, but he or she was thought, also, to be under the control of the magnetist. Among the different abilities possessed by these new patients, de Puységur listed all of the phenomena usually manifested by electricity and magnetism. In his view, the activation of these phenomena was initiated by an agent that had been identified by Mesmer as the magnetic fluid. De Puységur disagreed with the term, finding it too limited. He preferred to talk in terms of electromagnetic phenomena. He maintained, however, that the agent itself could be activated solely by the human will (*la manivelle de notre volonté*; 1807, p. 14). He added that the magnetist must be able to concentrate his willpower exclusively on the magnetized person. The somnambulist would obey all of the commands of a magnetist who could do this. He wrote:

> I just performed these experiments so that you can see how to do them, how to repeat them by yourselves; one of you who I will place in harmony with this young girl will be able to make her obey, as I did myself, all of the indications of his thoughts. I can only ask for one thing; once you have determined your will, keep it firm, constant, without changing its direction. (1807, p. 19)

It is important to note that the idea of the magnetized person being dominated by the magnetist's will had never been stated so directly. One hundred years later, the famous Nancy school under the direction of Liébeault and Bernheim, re-adopted this position by stating that once hypnotized, a somnambule can be controlled and will respond to suggestions as surely as a rock thrown into water will sink to the bottom. Even the metaphors were the same.

De Puységur also gave public demonstrations of the skills of his somnambulists; as such, he can be seen as the first stage magnetist. He performed in Paris with one of his patients, Magdeleine, in order to better inform the population of the benefits of his discovery. Among the abilities claimed for the somnambulists were that:

1. They could see and hear with their eyes and ears closed.
2. They were controlled by the magnetist's will for everything that is not harmful.
3. They could feel the magnetist's intentions.
4. They could see and describe diseases in themselves and in others.
5. They had a better memory (hypermnesia) during their crises, but were amnesic following them.
6. Their intelligence was increased.
7. They were clairvoyant, although they could often be wrong, and were quite limited.
8. They had to be wisely directed, since they were not particularly humble.

These abilities were certainly reminiscent of the diverse signs that had been described as indicators of demoniacal possession (see Chapter 2).

Among the other changes brought about by de Puységur was the conceptualization of somnambulism as an indicator of diseases. He believed that this notion could be allied with traditional medicine in order to bring about desired cures. Somnambulism, however, was not universal. In all of his books, the proportion of individuals capable of demonstrating some form of somnambulism varied from 10 to 20 percent. If the mesmeric convulsive crisis was seen as a potentially abusive situation, the new development was even more open to criticism. What could be done by a person endowed with such powers over his fellow men (though women would be a more exact term in the present context), became a major point of interest.

The Dangers of Somnambulism

Although less criticized at this point in time than traditional animal magnetism, artificial somnambulism was open to a number of serious criticisms ranging from explicit abuse of the female population to more subtle perversions of morality, such as destroying the religious faith of ordinary people.

It rapidly became evident that the feats of the somnambulists could serve the interests of a dishonest person. Since there was no way of verifying the genuineness of artificial somnambulism, a number of individuals began providing medical advice under its cover. The first example of such behavior came from de Puységur himself, in which he recounted the following anecdote:

> A peasant from Carré d'Etompe, in Burgundy, had experienced a magnetic crisis that had successfully cured a serious illness. When he was in crisis, he had very perceptible sensations, and all of the patients trusted him. He could discover perfectly all of the causes of sickness, as well as prescribe good, sound medicines.
>
> One day, as I passed a nearby cabaret, I inquired why so many people were assembled there. I was told that they were patients coming to consult the "bourguignon."
>
> I imagined then that he was in crisis. I came closer and to my own surprise I saw him with his eyes wide open, touching all these poor people and prescribing all kinds of irrelevant medications. Fortunately, I came around to warn all of these people. I told all of them not to believe anything that had been said in that state; that when not in crisis, he was as ignorant as me or anybody else as to the sources of disease, and I evoked in the cunning peasant an extreme confusion. I reprimanded him fiercely for the deception he was carrying on. He asked for my forgiveness explaining that he had been pestered by a number of people who wanted to know what he was saying during his crises, and that they had offered him money for his consultations. (1784–1785, p. 178)

This first episode of deception was not to be the last one. As will be seen, the medical profession would prosecute somnambulists very early in the nineteenth century for illegally practicing medicine, an offense that professional medical people have always taken very seriously.

As with animal magnetism, artificial somnambulism drew a number of accusations of immorality. The most interesting of these can be found in an anonymous letter to the Soissons's intendant (Anonymous, undated-b).[6] Some excerpts from this letter convey the flavor of the accusations and insinuations voiced against de Puységur. In it, the author described how he and a friend went to Buzancy in order to observe the Marquis's practice. In the following passage, he described how de Puységur magnetized a young woman:

> The M. de P... arrived around eleven o'clock. He entered the circle and touched the daughter of the vinegar maker of Soissons. He placed his hands upon her, on her head, forehead, and neck; he tickled her nostrils; he squeezed

her breast in such a way that the nipples must have felt a slight rubbing; he closed her eyes with his fingers; he moved an iron rod that he had in his hand on her face, directing it from the top of her head to the bottom of her breasts.... (p. 129)

This description was repeated many times in the letter, always emphasizing how the breasts were massaged. He continued:

I had already noticed that Catherine, once touched by M. de P..., experienced some slight convulsions that could be seen by a short but frequent movement in her knees. I was convinced of it when I saw her lack of constraint in the grass. Note that I am talking about a chlorotic [an anemic] ..., that M. de P... is a young man...; you probably know what I mean. [a few lines later] And Catherine lay down on the grass, her eyes red, her complexion inflamed, telling everyone that she had not slept, that she did not know what they were talking about. (p. 132)

The author concluded his letter by asking himself a number of questions on somnambulism and answering them for the reader. His last question concerned the possibility of abusing women in such a state.

Can a young man who takes in his arms a woman with irritable nerves, rubs her vertebrae, her diaphragm, her stomach, her nipples, her navel region, produce a revolution in the subject he is massaging, as the Indians would say? Yes, assuredly; if the imagination is triggered by fear and hope, or by a sensual delirium that cannot be described by any word of our language, the subject will feel a dangerous lack of constraint and the physician will be able, with a guilty boldness ... I have to stop here. (p. 136)

The author left it to the guided imagination of the reader.

As with animal magnetism, a number of books were published alluding to this possibility of abuse in the practice of artificial somnambulism. Contrary to the initial reactions of the proponents of Mesmerism, de Puységur and his followers tackled the problem directly in their writings. Two types of argument were usually advanced against somnambulism. The first one, already mentioned, was the possibility of abusing female patients. The second one was the idea that somnambulism in itself was dangerous for the well-being of patients. De Puységur answered these criticisms with a number of different examples. One of the examples came from a dialogue between Victor, his first true somnambulist, and the Marquis during one of Victor's crises:

P: So I could have you give away all of your possessions and you would not know about it?

V: It would be impossible, sir. Before signing any document, I would know your intentions; and my signature would not be similar to my usual one.

P: But your name alone would be sufficient.

V: If it was sufficient, then you would not even get that. (de Puységur, 1784–1785, pp. 27–29)

It will be remembered that many believed that the somnambulist in crisis could read the magnetist's mind. In this way, he or she could prevent abuse from occurring. A second example comes from an anonymous book, also undated, but probably published around the same period (Anonymous, undated-c). This example represented the first recorded case of intentional abuse of a patient by a magnetist. The case, however, was presented to demonstrate not only the impossibility of such an abuse, but the consequences for the magnetist if he or she made such an attempt. The possibility of abusing the patient was described as a double-edged sword, the consequences of which would be detrimental to the magnetist. The author proposed that if any thought not directed toward the well-being of the patient intruded during the session, it would break down the communication of the fluid. To illustrate his point, he described how a young magnetist had attempted to benefit unduly from the crisis his young fiancée was experiencing: "Immediately, the crisis, even though quite strong, stopped. And from the tender attraction that this young and virtuous person had felt for her Magnetist, developed a feeling of hate so strong and unexpected that she has refused to see him ever again" (p. 47).

This represents the sole report of an attempt of abuse by a magnetist in all of the literature of that period.

When it came to questioning the somnambulists on the possibility of abuse, the Marquis did not hesitate. As the following excerpt illustrates, the questions were direct and to the point:

> One day, I was questioning a woman in a *magnetic state* as to the extent of the power that I could exercise upon her. I had just (without even talking to her) *forced her*, just as a joke, to hit me with a flyswatter that she was holding in her hand. "Well, I said to her, since you seem compelled to hit me, who has done you good, I bet that if I really wanted, I could use you *in any way I want*, for example, ask you to *get undressed*, etcetera...."—"Oh no, Sir," she replied, "it would not be the same thing. What I have just done did not seem to be right; I resisted it for a long time. Since it was a joke, and you looked like you *really wanted me to do it*, I finally yielded to it. But as for your last comment, you will never be able to *force me* to take off all of my clothes. My shoes, my hat, as often as you want; but beyond that, you will get nothing...." (de Puységur, 1807, p. 120, italics in original)

Questioning a second somnambulist, Catherine Montenencourt, the Marquis asked the same questions and received the same answers. But he went further, asking: "Now really, if I absolutely wanted you to get undressed what would happen?"—"I would *wake up*, Sir. It would have the same effects that I suffered when I received this big hit to my side a few days ago. I would *become quite sick*" (1807, p. 120, italics in original).

As de Puységur concluded: "There are limits where the authority ceases, and I could almost affirm that these limits will always be felt instinctively by Magnetists" (1807, p. 121).

As will be seen in forthcoming chapters, the enthusiasm shown by the Marquis in regard to the good instincts of the magnetists was not necessarily to be endorsed by opponents of artificial somnambulism. On the other side of the coin, not all magnetists were to demonstrate such good judgment.

On the question of whether somnambulism was hazardous to patients' health, de Puységur again provided an answer through the voices of two of his most famous somnambulists, Victor and Joly.

The purpose of somnambulism as portrayed by de Puységur was not only to cure disease but also to prevent it. As Mesmer had said previously of animal magnetism in his aphorisms, somnambulism could be seen as an example of preventive medicine. As Joly put it: "Animal Magnetism not only cures the present illness, but it prompts illnesses that are latent, and in this way, acts upon their principle" (cited in de Puységur, 1784-1785, p. 141).

Joly was speaking from extensive experience. According to him, the numerous magnetizations he had undergone had brought upon a state of catalepsy. It did not trouble him, however. When in crisis, he stated that repeated hypnotizations had only triggered an illness that was already latent in him. Without magnetism, it would have come in the following six months, killing him assuredly. Now because of magnetism, he had an opportunity to cure it through his own somnambulistic crisis. He reported that: "It is a great advantage to be able to say: Maybe I will die, rather than I will surely die" (de Puységur, 1784-1785; cited in Morand, 1889, p. 411).

Victor was a little less conciliatory than Joly when his health was in jeopardy. Since the Commissions of Inquiry, a number of authors had pointed to the dangers of magnetism for the nervous system. Some had even asserted that it could lead to death or idiocy. This belief survived into the next century and became on occasion the central point of legal disputes, as will be seen in subsequent chapters.

The incident leading to Victor's contrary judgment concerned de Puységur's desire to convince as many people as possible of the benefits of animal magnetism and somnambulism. He had been asked repeatedly by Mme de Montesson to give a demonstration of somnambulism at her residence. He decided one night to bring Victor to her house and to demonstrate all of the phenomena he had discussed. A number of people were present including Bertholet, who had previously denounced Mesmer as a charlatan in a public letter. The demonstration was far from successful and the Marquis left feeling humiliated. Victor, however, had predicted that his illness would terminate in exactly one week. He predicted that he would bleed from the right nostril after which he would spit out a mixture of blood and water. It was arranged to bring Victor to Mme de Montesson's house on the predicted day.

Victor and de Puységur arrived on the day designated around half past eleven in the morning. The bleeding was expected to take place around midday. Bertholet, who was present, examined Victor's nose. He found some ointment in his nostril as well as a "fatty element." At half past twelve, Victor announced that the bleeding would occur soon. In the following half hour, some blood came through Victor's right nostril, followed, as predicted, by some bloody sputum. The event did not convince anybody, however. The Marquis was embarrassed and as he was leaving, Mme de Montesson informed him that Victor had asked her for a private meeting. The Marquis left leaving Victor still in somnambulism with the other guests.

To the Marquis's own surprise, he did not see Victor for the next two days. On the following Monday morning, the day on which Victor was scheduled to leave his treatment, the Marquis began to show signs of concern. Victor finally arrived late in the afternoon, around four o'clock. He was anxious and depressed; the Marquis was troubled. He magnetized Victor and asked what had happened at Mme de Montesson's residence. Victor's reply saddened the Marquis.

After the Marquis had departed, the guests had accused Victor of lying and faking by having provoked his bleeding deliberately. They had attempted by all possible means to have him open his eyes and had not listened to his protestations. After a long interrogation he was sent back to his home. He was worried and depressed and had experienced a relapse of his former symptoms. He accused the Marquis of having placed him in such a situation without seeing the consequences it would have for him:

> V: What is happening now is pure coincidence. If, as you had asked me, I had left on Monday, my illness would have returned, and I would certainly have died or lost my mind. People would have accused magnetism, where in fact it was your own fault.
> P: It is a good lesson for the future; I will not do public demonstrations anymore.
> V: Without doubt, but it is quite a pity for me to be your experimental subject. (1784–1785, pp. 210–211)

The Marquis de Puységur, however, continued his somnambulistic and magnetic practice. He improved his system and although he always rendered homage to Mesmer as the founder of animal magnetism, he slowly rejected the primary function of the magnetic fluid. For him, *mens agitat molem*, it was thought that moved matter, not magnetic fluid. He slowly identified himself more with the electromagnetic physicians who used a combination of electricity and magnetic passes with their patients, as well as different instruments which included magnets. In 1783, a Commission of Inquiry into the usefulness of magnets had publicly supported their use in traditional medicine. The report (Thouret, 1783) recognized that magnets were useful in a number of diseases and especially with toothaches, nervous diseases of the head and kidneys, in rheumatoid arthritis, in painful afflictions of the face (*tic douloureux*), and generally for all nervous illnesses. Interestingly, the report was not even mentioned in the conclusions of the Commissions of Inquiry on magnetism. It could have provided an excellent argument against the role of magnetic fluid.

One of the well-known "electric physicians," as they were called, J.-H.-D. Pététin, was soon to make a stunning observation that would drive the phenomenon of somnambulism even further from animal magnetism. This "discovery" was to be integrated almost immediately into ongoing thought about the nature of artificial somnambulism and was to render it even more fanciful.

Transposition of the Senses: Pététin's Cataleptic Patients

Pététin was the president of the Medical Society of Lyon. He was not a supporter of animal magnetism although he recognized that the means employed by the Mesmerists were evoking the phenomena of somnambulism, convulsive crisis, and all of the other magnetic effects. In his 1787 book, he presented a number of cases of cataleptic patients. He had always been interested in rare illnesses and catalepsy was one of them. What was more intriguing, however, was some of the symptoms he described and especially what he termed the "transposition of the senses." Although this ability of cataleptic patients was subsequently to be claimed as a phenomenon of artificial somnambulism, it was not, according to Pététin, linked in any way to animal magnetism. For the historian, it is always interesting to see how a trivial incident can acquire wide-spread popularity when it happens to a person who can transform its meaning. It is of value to examine how Pététin discovered this apparently amazing sensory feat in his cataleptic patients.

Pététin published his findings in 1787 in a two-volume work that dealt mainly with the systematization of the different pathognomonic signs of hysteria. He was also typical of those physicians who were called the electric doctors due to their preference for the use of electricity in their therapeutic approach. He was called one day to the bedside of a young woman. He found her totally paralyzed, having also lost the use of her senses. She was thought to be dying, but Pététin knew better. He soon demonstrated that the patient was a typical cataleptic. For more than an hour and a half she hummed a tune and appeared oblivious to her surroundings. She did not hear or feel anything that was happening around her. Suddenly she began to have convulsions, vomiting copious quantities of blood. Following the crisis, she slowly returned to her senses. Pététin ordered an ice-cold bath in which she lay for more than 20 minutes. Upon returning to bed she experienced another convulsive crisis followed by the humming of the same song she had sung previously. In the attempt to stop her singing, he placed the patient in different positions. When he tried to change her position, he fell on the bed. As he was falling, he said:

—It is quite sad that I can't stop this woman from singing.

To which the patient answered to everyone's surprise:

—Eh, doctor, don't get mad, I won't sing anymore.

But in fact she recommenced singing. Pététin gave some thought to what had just happened and decided to repeat the previous fall on the bed. He approached his patient's stomach and said in a loud voice:

—Madam, will you sing forever?
—Ah! You're hurting me. Please talk more softly.

The doctor asked her how she had heard. To which she replied:

—Like everybody else.
—But I am talking to your stomach?
—Is it possible?

She then asked him to talk into her ears, but she did not hear any of the questions. He returned to her stomach and asked her if she had heard any of the questions. Her reply: "No, and I am quite sad."

After a while, however, she stopped answering, and began singing again. Pététin then had the idea of placing one of his fingers on her epigastrium and talking into the fingers of the other hand, as if establishing a communication with her through his fingers. Asked why she sang, she replied:

—I sing to distract myself from a view that frightens me. I can see my insides, the bizarre shapes of the organs surrounded by light. My face must express what I feel, astonishment and fear. Any physician who for fifteen minutes would suffer from my illness, would be happy. Nature would tell him all of her secrets, and if he liked that state, he probably would not, like me, ask for a prompt cure.

The doctor then said:

—Look at your heart.
—There it is. It beats twice and from both sides. When the upper part is constricted, the lower dilates and contracts soon after. The blood is all shiny and goes through two big vessels closed together.

Pététin was impressed. He varied his experiments always keeping contact with her epigastrium. To his own surprise he had to admit that the hearing sense had been transferred to either the fingers or the toes of his patient.

Quite excited, he wanted to know if the effect could be seen in other senses. Having placed some milk-bread (*pain au lait*) into a piece of paper, he deposited it on her stomach. She immediately started chewing and said:

—Oh! This milk-bread is delicious.
—Why are you moving your mouth?
—Because I am eating some milk-bread.
—Where are you tasting it?
—What a question, in the mouth.

Pététin repeated the experiment many times with the same success. It appeared to him that she could hear, smell, taste, and see through her epigastrium. She could hear and see with her fingers. She could even tell which playing cards were placed on her stomach. Any object was quickly and accurately identified. She could also identify objects that were hidden in envelopes, and read sealed letters. As with other somnambulists of this period, she was able to diagnose and prescribe medication (see Figuier, 1860, Vol. III, pp. 272–275).

Pététin continued to explore these phenomena attributing his patients' feats to both their imagination and to the electric fluid. He became quite popular in the following years. The onset of the Revolution, however, would damp down the discussion of the many variations of the Mesmeric system.

A third popular variation of animal magnetism followed a more esoteric development. The Chevalier de Barbarin transformed Mesmer's and de Puységur's systems into a spiritualist one whereby the soul, became the *modus operandi* of the therapeutic intervention. De Barbarin thus was continuing the spiritual movement of Northern Europe, represented mainly by Swedenborg.

A few books were published on these different movements. The most representative is probably the one published by the Ostende Society of Universal Harmony in 1786. The book distinguished between Mesmer, de Puységur, and de Barbarin's followers. This work is interesting because it was one of the first in which proponents of these new systems identified some of the phenomena with what had happened at the Saint Médard Cemetery with the Jansenist convulsionaries:

> We have seen the perfect imitation of what had happened with the convulsionaries of St. Pâris. They were performing on chairs that had been placed to that effect. What was noticeable in women, is the fact that even in their most bizarre contorsions, they were always decent; that showed how modesty overpowers sexuality. (Société de l'Harmonie Universelle d'Ostende, 1786, p. 48)

This type of reasoning became much more frequent in the following years.

The French Revolution and the Restoration Period

The tragic period of the French Revolution saw the disappearance of the magnetic movement. It would reappear in the early nineteenth century with a host of new characters: di Faria, Deleuze, Bertrand, Noizet would become the new apostles of the phenomena elicited in animal magnetism, and of some of its variations. Animal magnetism was, however, still practiced by many physicians and literate people during the Revolution. Deleuze for one began practicing it during its early years. He maintained, however, a discreet silence until the publication of his first book in 1813.

It will be remembered that most of Mesmer's and D'Eslon's followers were from the aristocracy and the upper social classes. These were the people who had to keep a low profile during these years to avoid the guillotine.

Lavoisier and Bailly, then mayor of Paris, as well as Guillotin himself were less fortunate; all of them were executed.

De Puységur, however, continued to magnetize. He had at first espoused the goals of the Revolution. Around 1792, however, he regretted the excesses of the revolutionaries and retired to his estate. Unfortunately for the Marquis, his two brothers had left France. He was soon accused of corresponding with them and thrown into jail, with his wife and children where he stayed for two years. Once liberated, he returned to his house and continued to take care of sick people.

In conclusion, it needs to be realized that if Mesmer popularized animal magnetism, it is the somnambulistic movement that would prevail in the following years. As Mesmer had predicted, in his 1799 book, the popularity of the somnambulistic doctrine provoked hostile reactions from both the religious and scientific communities. For the next 60 years, animal magnetism would linger.

NOTES

1. Mesmer's letter was dated January 4, 1785, and published the 6th. Veaumorel's reply was published also in the *Journal de Paris* and dated January 7. Both letters can be found in Amadou (1971).

2. *Adieu baquet, vendanges sont faites.* The *montgolfier* was named the Harvester (*le Vendangeur*). It also became a popular song.

3. Many authors have described Bailly's execution as one of the worst public scenes of the Revolution. Bailly had been accused of "unfurling the red flag in the Field of Mars, to quell the riot there, on the 17th of July, 1791" (Abbott, 1859, p. 362). Bailly, then mayor of Paris, had sent Lafayette with a detachment of the National Guard, to the scene to disperse the rioters. On the Field of Mars, thousands of people had congregated to support the demands of the Jacobins to depose the King as a perjured traitor.

Confronted by a much larger crowd than anticipated, Lafayette returned to City Hall. As Abbott (1859) described it:

> He soon returned, accompanied by Bailly, the mayor of the city, and all the municipal authorities, and followed by ten thousand of the National Guard. The red flag, which proclaimed that the city was placed under martial law, was now floating from the Hôtel de Ville. . . . M. Bailly, upon horseback, displayed the red flag, in accordance with the Riot Act law, and ordered the mob to disperse. (p. 228)

The confrontation was bloody, and although Bailly's decision was accepted by the National Assembly, he was looked upon as a murderer by the Jacobins. When they came to power, they sent him to the guillotine.

> Bailly was condemned to be executed on the field which was the theater of his alleged crime. Behind the cart which carried him they affixed the flag which he had spread. A crowd followed, heaping upon him the most cruel imprecations. . . . Bareheaded, with his hands bound behind him, and with no other garment than his shirt the sleet glued his hair and froze upon his breast. They pelted him with mud, spat in his face, and whipped him with the flag, which they dipped in the gutters. The old man fell exhausted. They lifted him up again, and goaded him on. . . . Someone cried out, "You

tremble, Bailly." "Yes, my friend, replied the heroic old man," "but it is with cold." After five hours of such a martyrdom, the axe released him from his sufferings. (p. 362)

Even if Abbott has romanticized Bailly's death, it still was an atrocious example of fanaticism. Lamartine, the French writer, described Bailly's death in more poetic terms:

> Few victims ever met with viler executioners; few executioners with so exalted a victim. Shame at the foot of the scaffold, glory above, and pity everywhere. One blushes to be a man in contemplating this people. One glories in this title in comtemplating Bailly. (Lamartine, *Histoire des Girondins*, Vol. 3, p. 282; cited in Abbott, 1859, p. 362)

4. The notion of natural somnambulism was already known at this time although not particularly written about. It had been a subject of discussion in a number of trials in France and England where it had led to a discussion on the moral and legal aspects of criminal responsibility. We will return to these notions in subsequent chapters, especially when we present and discuss the numerous trials where hypnosis was conceptualized as a coercive agent. For the time being, it is sufficient to note that de Puységur identified this new aspect of magnetism in these terms because of its resemblance to natural somnambulism.

5. This book can be found in the bibliography under the Marquis de Puységur's name. If he did not write it entirely by himself, he certainly at least provided most of the details of the different cures. Cloquet, himself, appears to have played a minor role in this undertaking.

6. This letter can be found in the previously mentioned book called *Conservateur* published by François de Neufchâteau. It is listed following the secret report of the Benjamin Franklin Commission. It is unsigned and undated. It seems to have been written, however, soon after the discovery of somnambulism.

6

Between Science and Religion

From the onset of the French Revolution to the second decade of the nineteenth century, very little is known about the fate of animal magnetism and artificial somnambulism. The publication of a number of books in the 1810s suggests, however, that they were still practiced on a relatively large scale. There were, nevertheless, a number of important changes both in the doctrine proposed by the new magnetists and in the attitude of the scientific community.

The first 50 years of the nineteenth century saw the dissemination of magnetic doctrines throughout the world. Not only was animal magnetism practiced and recognized in a number of European countries, but it spread also to the United States. The evolution of the movement, however, was different in these two parts of the world. Whereas the doctrine of animal magnetism struggled in Europe for scientific recognition, most of the disciples of magnetism in the United States tended to spiritualize the movement (Fuller, 1982).[1]

The mesmeric doctrine had already been propagated in the United States long before this second appearance in the nineteenth century. As early as 1784, Lafayette, of revolutionary fame, had written to George Washington to obtain permission to promulgate the new European discovery. Lafayette was opposed by Thomas Jefferson who was appalled by the many irrational beliefs surrounding the mesmeric system. In fact, Jefferson sought to sabotage Lafayette's efforts by distributing copies of the conclusions of the two French Commissions of Inquiry. Lafayette's efforts, however, did not prove fruitless. Although very little is known about the popularity of magnetic doctrines in the United States during the first 30 years of the nineteenth century, the books published at this time bear witness to the fertile ground that Lafayette had cultivated.

The fact that very little is known about the fate of mesmeric ideas between the onset of the French revolution and the restoration of the monarchy is not very surprising. Following the Revolution, France went through the Napoleonic wars for a period that extended until around 1814, at which time

Louis XVIII was finally reinstated to the throne. With the return of the King and the Court, the partisans of Mesmerism reappeared on the public scene. As the newspapers of the period emphasized, the Restoration brought back both the Mesmerists and the Jesuits. This sarcastic comment on the return of at least the remnants of the aristocratic class, proved to be prophetic. The major opposition that the proponents of somnambulism were to confront during the next 20 years or so was the religious establishment.

Of the major representatives of the previous era, the Marquis de Puységur was still prominent. As was seen in the previous chapter, he had been obliged to suffer some inconveniences during the Revolution. When he decided finally to withdraw from politics and return to the care of his peasants, his problems did not end. In 1814, having survived both the "Consulat" and the "Empire,"[2] the Marquis's security was threatened by the invasion of France by the Cossacks. He consulted one of his somnambules, "la Maréchale," who told him that he would be spared any trouble from the invasion, and on this basis he decided to remain at Buzancy. In fact, what saved him from the enemy was his reputation. Although his domain was invaded, the Marquis benefited from the protection of a highly ranked army official, General Czernichef. When the Cossack troops mounted an attack on Paris, the Marquis wrote a letter to the General thanking him for his protection. Unfortunately, the letter was intercepted by the French forces. The Marquis was accused of treason and condemned to be executed by a firing squad. The messenger was captured by the enemy, however, and the orders destroyed (Foissac, 1825). De Puységur continued to magnetize until his death in 1825, publishing in the meantime a number of pamphlets on his successes with animal magnetism.

A word should also be said of Father Hervier (see Chapter 4), the ardent defender of Mesmer's ideas. The priest, after many adventures, was given protection by the Duchess of A., under the condition that he would tend her gardens. He thus spent the remainder of his life magnetizing her trees (Foissac, 1825).

The troubled time that had befallen France relegated the founders of the magnetic movement to a past that did not correspond any more to the liberalism of the new century. The second generation of magnetists were different from their forebears in the manner in which they tackled the incredulity of their opponents. While de Puységur published a few books during these early years of the nineteenth century, mainly documenting instances of therapeutic successes, a number of attacks were launched on his system of ideas. Two major authors concentrated their efforts in an attempt to revive the old conflicts with the magnetists. Fustier (1815), a Catholic priest who wrote under the pseudonym of *Un homme du monde* (a gentleman), illustrated the type of criticisms and accusations that the magnetic movement was obliged to face from some representatives of the Catholic clergy. On the other hand, De Montègre (1812, 1816), a physician, sought to synthesize the new position of the medical community on the question. Rather than trying to denigrate the new therapeutic system, he concentrated on the dangers that magnetism and the treatments proposed by somnambulists were most likely to provoke. This time, however, the magnetists were not as naive as to simply repudiate their adversaries' attacks. They used the systematic attacks of their adversaries as a way of improving upon their theories. As will be seen in this chapter, the magnetists learned to defend themselves faster than their opponents could find new methods to discredit them.

The End of an Era

In 1812, A. J. De Montègre took up the task of reawakening the medical profession to the dangers of animal magnetism. In his first book, he attempted to revive the conclusions of the two Commissions of Inquiry as well as to link, in a more logical manner, the different popular delusions of the previous centuries. His book deliberately attacked de Puységur's morality and seriously questioned the professional ethics of his therapeutic practice. (Mesmer was "passé.") De Montègre objected particularly to the different massages that the Marquis used and strongly criticized his alleged habit of touching women's breasts.

The fact that somnambulists were giving medical consultations as well as prescribing medication outraged physicians. It was to lead the way to legal action against the magnetists and their somnambulists for the illegal practice of medicine. De Montègre pursued his attacks for many years and used the fact that he was editor of the *Gazette de Santé* to make his views known to the general public. In 1816, he published an angry denunciation of the somnambulists and the magnetists who encouraged them to prescribe medication during their consultation. He characterized these practices as "murder attempts" on the part of the culprits, and he asked the authorities to take the necessary steps to prevent such abuses.

Two points are worth mentioning in relation to De Montègre's complaints. The first one, and even some of the more refined magnetists soon agreed with him, was the fact that the medications prescribed by the somnambulists were either what is known today as over-the-counter drugs, or drugs that they knew to be used by physicians for some reason. In fact very often, their prescriptions amounted to nothing more than the applications of leeches, bleedings, or moxas (a tuft of soft, combustible substance to be burned upon the skin). The second point illustrates the changes in perspective since the discovery of artificial somnambulism. Magnetism as such was more or less forgotten. The emphasis now was on this new phenomenon, and as Mesmer had predicted in his 1799 book, it had completely superceded his original theory. The major consequence was to relegate the potential usefulness of magnetism *per se* to the background and to publicize instead the medical "intuition" of the somnambulists. The new doctrine was thus becoming nothing other than medicine practiced by naive people.

Those aspects of magnetism that De Montègre had not attacked, were taken up by Fustier. In a short pamphlet published in 1815, not only was magnetism accused of immorality, but it was also identified as the work of the Devil. Fustier's argument was simple. Since modern science could not explain the various phenomena produced in the somnambulistic trance, they had to be elicited through the Devil's intervention: "I am only saying that this new art ... could be a novel strategy devised by the Devil in an attempt to seduce souls, to increase the number of his believers, and to contradict as far as possible the work of J. C. and his Ministers" (p. 5).

And of course it was the sexual aspects of magnetism that Fustier chose to emphasize:

> A young woman, good magnetic *subject*, consults a well-known adept. Forewarned of what she should be wearing for the success of the operation, she presents herself breast naked down to the waist. ... I will refrain from any comments on these effects that insult morality. ... (p. 26, italics in original)

Fustier's attacks were without basis, and throughout his pamphlet, he was at a loss to provide a single example of these types of immoral abuses. He was not, however, troubled by this minor point. What was important to him was to identify magnetism with Devil worship. His conclusions were clear, strong, and to the point.

> Magnetism has been shown *to be dangerous* for the youth, and for the different sexes and should only be used with great caution. It should only be used from mothers to daughters, fathers to sons, friends to friends, and through the assistance of thoughtful physicians, that is, innocent men that will stand *on principles*; used otherwise it could only lead to dissoluteness. What kind of an art is this where one has to make such careful decisions, be continuously attentive, and watch oneself all the time to avoid transgressing the laws of morality! And one would like us to believe that such discovery came from Heaven, that God favored its establishment, and helped its effects through the use of prayers? (pp. 47–48, italics in original)

In light of the fact that no cases of sexual abuse had been reported at the time, it is interesting to speculate on Fustier's motives. As far as can be ascertained (and this should only be viewed as one possible explanation), Fustier's pamphlet was in reaction to the recent publication of Deleuze's masterful book (1813) on the history of animal magnetism. Deleuze's book was probably the most well-known book of this period and was viewed as such at the time. With the wisdom of hindsight, Deleuze represented the last in the series of traditional magnetists, in the mold of Mesmer and de Puységur.

J. P. F. Deleuze

J. P. F. Deleuze began practicing magnetism in the mid-1780s, at the time of Mesmer's and D'Eslon's fame. As he recounted it, he was at first a skeptic, not taking any of the ongoing controversy seriously. After a brief military career, he dedicated himself to the study of natural sciences. Having heard that one of his friends, M. D. d'Aix, had taken up the practice of magnetism, he visited him and inquired more into this therapeutic system. He began experimenting himself, although his magnetic practice never replaced his first devotion to botany. He never sought public recognition and was content to bypass all of the controversies surrounding the mesmeric system. Only with the publication of his first book, *Critical History of Animal Magnetism* (1813), did he gain belated recognition from the magnetists and from the scientific community.

Deleuze represented, however, a formidable opponent for the medical profession. He was a true scientist, accustomed to the laws of naturalistic observation, and as such could not be dismissed easily. Assistant naturalist at the Garden of Plants, and Secretary of the Annals of the Museum of Natural History, his position on animal magnetism could not be challenged carelessly. When he published his first book in 1813, it signaled, in a way, the beginning of a new era for animal magnetism. Deleuze can be seen today as *the* classical magnetist. He accepted the system as modified by de Puységur totally. He retained, however, his enthusiasm for the classical mesmeric practice of magnetism, over and above his interests in artificial somnambulism.

Deleuze's system can be found in his two books on animal magnetism. His second book in particular, *Practical Instruction in Animal Magnetism* (1825), was written with the clear intention of disseminating magnetic doctrine at a popular level. Written very carefully, and with particular attention to the medical and religious establishments, Deleuze's books were classics in their own time. His care and determination to convince the medical and religious intelligentsia, however, left him with a sour taste. In a small book published posthumously (1834), he wrote:

> When I published the first edition of my *Histoire critique du Magnétisme Animal*, in 1813, I treated with the utmost reserve the delicate and problematic questions. I exposed the facts, so that everyone could verify them, and the principles necessary to use magnetism. I have tried to gain the naturalists' and the physicians' favours by demonstrating the correspondance between the phenomena that I was describing and the laws underlying them and the phenomena and the laws that they already accepted. *This reserve did not serve me well*. Most of those who were well versed in physics and physiology did not pay attention to the proofs that I had put together. *They were as unwilling to examine a particular modification in their accepted view of the world as they would have been to adopt a subversive system, threatening their doctrines.* I will be less shy today. (cited in Figuier, 1860, Vol. III, p. 291, italics in original)

This complaint, however, was not well founded because Deleuze's influence on the scientific and religious communities of his time proved to be enormous. He did not live long enough to reap its benefits. His acute sense of observation can be seen through two different aspects of his work. The first is his description of the different phenomena that are linked to animal magnetism. The second is his careful treatment of the question of morality and spirituality, as seen through the phenomena elicited by animal magnetism.

MAGNETIC PHENOMENA

As we noted earlier, de Puységur was the first investigator to put emphasis on postmagnetic amnesia, though de Jussieu appears to have been the first to document it. In fact, amnesia had to be present in order to conclude that the patient was able to demonstrate somnambulism. Over and above this capacity to forget what had happened during the session, Deleuze was the first to describe a series of phenomena that later became the hallmarks of hypnosis. Two of them should be briefly mentioned as interesting psychological phenomena. The first is the ability to dissociate, although not identified as such by Deleuze. In some of his patients, he had noticed that once in somnambulism, they would talk in the third person as if the somnambulist and the nonmagnetized patient were two different entities. In his 1813 book, he reported this unusual phenomenon in a footnote:

> I must at this point mention a psychological phenomenon that is quite extraordinary. Somnambulists have sometimes been heard talking about themselves as if their individuality in the waking state and in somnambulism represented two different persons. I will give you two examples.
>
> Mlle Adélaïde de F..., who can without having been magnetized, present all the phenomena seen in somnambulism, did not have any idea of her *self* as such. She never acknowledged that Adélaïde was the same as *Petite*, the name that she used and gave herself during her mania.
>
> Here's the second fact: Madam N..., who had a distinguished education, decided, after having lost her fortune in a trial, to become an actress. Her talents brought her success and considerable fees. During these projects she became ill and somnambulist. While she was in somnambulism, she was talking against some decision that she had taken. Her magnetist asked her to explain herself and the answers he obtained were quite unexpected.—Why do you want to become an actress?—It is not me, it is her.—But why don't you stop her?—What do you want me to tell her; she is a crazy woman. (Deleuze, 1813, pp. 177-178, italics in original)

In the following decades such descriptions became the major diagnostic criterion of multiple personality, a concept that appears to have originated from the use of magnetism. Deleuze, however, was quite modest and resisted sensationalizing these phenomena. It is interesting to note that a few years later, these example were resorted to by critics in order to demonstrate that the different personalities in somnambulism were the end result of the Devil's possession.

Another phenomenon, also observed by Deleuze, is still nowadays of particular interest to scientific, clinical, and lay people alike. Deleuze had observed, as had some of his predecessors, that patients in somnambulism displayed an apparently increased memory capacity. Once magnetized and somnambulistic, a patient could seemingly remember much more than in his or her waking state. In some of Deleuze's patients, however, it took a special turn:

> There are somnambulists who retrace with surprizing facility the ideas that they receive in their infancy, and upon whom these ideas exercise more control than those which they have since acquired. A very lucid somnambulist, magnetized by M. de Lausanne, afforded me a remarkable instance of this phenomenon. She was a woman about forty years old. She was born at St-Domingo, from whence she came to France at the age of six or seven years, and she had never afterward been among Creoles. As soon as she was in the somnambulistic state, she absolutely spoke nothing but the peculiar dialect (patois) which she had learned from the negress who had nursed her. In these recollections of infancy, in this return towards the first years of life, we must search for the cause of the opinion of some somnambulists. There are some of them who seem to forget the notion they have acquired by reason and observation, as they regress by degrees towards the period when their minds were but as blank tablets. (Deleuze, 1825, p. 136; p. 96 in Hartshorn's [1843] translation)

This phenomenon, which appeared to occur spontaneously in some highly hypnotized individuals has been called *trance logic* (Orne, 1959) by contemporary researchers of hypnosis. It represents the fact that, in hypnosis, highly hypnotizable individuals have a higher tolerance of ambiguities or incongruities than individuals who are not hypnotized. This capacity to modify reality so as not to be disturbed by incongruous happenings became at the end of the nineteenth century a major point in the demonstration that hypnosis can be used to abuse individuals who submit to it. The phenomenon of age regression, however, did not become popular before the 1880s when psychologists began to pay attention to suggested modifications of personality in hypnosis. It should be added, also that Deleuze, in common with many of his late twentieth-century counterparts, did not attempt to authenticate either her fluency in Creole or the veracity of any of the childhood memories that she reported. At this early stage there was no recognition of the possibility that what is recalled is likely to be an admixture of fantasy and fact.

In the same way, Deleuze documented examples of visual and gustatory hallucinations, postmagnetization suggestions, and the possibility of somnambulists at least being able to self-magnetize. His major emphasis, however, was on the possibility of alleviating pain by magnetism. In fact, Deleuze thought that one of the major effects of magnetism was pain control. Here, it should be emphasized that if Deleuze documented rare somnambulistic phenomena, he was primarily interested in the medical use of magnetism and somnambulism. A major theoretical emphasis that was new was Deleuze's insistence that magnetism did not cure diseases *per se*, but the individuals suffering from them, hinting at individual differences in one's ability to become magnetized. It was thus important to take into account the person's degree of magnetizability, and to adapt treatment accordingly. He did not, however, expand on these individual differences, nor did he analyze the role played by the magnetized individual in eliciting his or her own cure. Some of his advice, however, did not please the medical establishment. For example in the following passage, he stated that

> Many somnambulists are endowed with inconceivable ability and can perform certain operations as well as the best surgeons. I am acquainted with a lady, who, in the state of somnambulism, opened a swelling beneath her breast, and dressed the wound until it was healed. (Deleuze, 1825, p. 124; p. 89 in Hartshorn's [1843] translation)

Not surprisingly, such a statement alarmed physicians and surgeons. Deleuze thought that physicians should be consulted as to the appropriateness of the treatments prescribed by somnambulists. Unfortunately, he wrote also that if the physician was not in accord with the prescriptions of the somnambules, another physician should be sought. This invasion of their field of expertise certainly did not leave physicians indifferent. Like his predecessors, Deleuze believed that magnetism had no effect on healthy people, and that the ability to magnetize or to be magnetized resided within the magnetist. Magnetism was the end result of the magnetist's willpower, his or her strong beliefs in the magnetic system, and above all, the desire to bring well-being. He did not accept, however, the spiritualistic doctrines propounded by some of the practitioners of magnetism; as such his position was seen to be somewhere between Mesmer and the Chevalier de Barbarin who was replacing the fluid by the soul and the passes with prayers. Deleuze maintained that magnetism was, in a sense, a gift from God, and could help human spiritual evolution. He did not believe, on the other hand, that magnetism and somnambulism could by themselves change the basic nature of humanity.

> The discovery of somnambulism having been made, or rather renewed, in our time, without our being prepared for it, and the application which can be made of it demanding a meditative mind, great prudence, severe manners, religious dispositions, gravity of character, positive knowledge, and other qualities which do not accord with the amiable levity and excitable imagination of Frenchmen, it may be doubted whether its sudden propagation has not produced as much evil as good, and whether it would not have been better that this marvellous phenomenon had not been at first observed.... (Deleuze, 1825, pp. 100–101; p. 70 in Hartshorn's [1843] translation)

This jibe at the French spirit may not have been totally unjustified in the light of the conflict that continued between the magnetists, the scientific community, and the clergy. In his two books, Deleuze devoted a substantial chapter to the potential abuse of magnetism, and how it could be avoided.

MORAL AND SPIRITUAL PRINCIPLES

Deleuze was very concerned by all of the unfavorable publicity that animal magnetism had received since its beginnings with Mesmer. Although he did not cite a single documented example of abuse, he nonetheless took special care in elaborating a set of rules and principles that were designed to eliminate the deserved or undeserved bad reputation of the magnetists. Deleuze believed that somnambulism allowed man to unfold his dual nature. He conceptualized it as an external man at play in mundane affairs, and an internal man, a spiritual man who could be reached through magnetism. If Deleuze believed that magnetism and particularly somnambulism could be of some help in demonstrating the presence of man's spiritual nature, he did not spiritualize magnetism. Magnetism, to him, was a medical system, not a spiritual dogma.

Deleuze's concern to establish a sound ethical system can be found in both of his books. The first rule that he laid down was to recognize that only a woman should magnetize another woman. If no female magnetist was available, the father or a relative was permitted to magnetize. He was, however, to follow some safeguards such as sitting by the female patient's side and avoiding eye contact. Four major reasons were presented for his advocacy of such precautions. Since he believed that magnetism created an emotional link between the magnetist and his patient (through the establishment of rapport), safeguards should be instituted so as to prevent confusion in the minds of patients.

From a more pragmatic point of view, he believed that a magnetized woman could feel embarrassed when certain problems arose, and she might hesitate to talk about them to a man. Furthermore, if a crisis was to occur, certain spasms and movements could take place that a man should not witness. Finally, since the magnetic treatment was usually long term, neighbors could see the presence of another man at the household of a woman many times a week as suspicious. The choice of a magnetist was thus a crucial decision. As Deleuze emphasized, these safeguards would not have been necessary if the medical profession had accepted the practice of magnetism. If physicians specialized in magnetism could be found, and treatment was offered under optimal conditions, such precautions became superfluous. Accordingly, the first step toward the elimination of any possible abuse resided in the judicious choice of one's magnetist.

Deleuze was explicit when it came to the possibility of moral abuse. If a man other than a relative magnetized a woman, he should demand the presence of a third party. If, on the other hand, the magnetist attempted an immoral act, the somnambulist would react by experiencing a convulsive crisis. As far as Deleuze was concerned, the somnambulist retained her reason and willpower. At the same time, he was also quite naive in his approach to the problem. To illustrate his reasoning, he provided the following example of a friend of his, M. Passavant:

> Yet suppose the possibility of a lethargic somnambulist and the existence of a being sufficiently depraved to attempt things that would go against decency; it is useless to examine if there would be any danger since we have adopted as a rule without exception that a man who magnetizes a woman must never be alone with her. (Deleuze, 1825, p. 245)

This naivety from such an acute observer is surprising. The English translator appears to have noticed it, since his translation of this passage differs from the original text. In Deleuze's text, it is the responsibility of the magnetist to follow the ground rule. In the English translation, it is the responsibility of the woman to ensure that she is never alone with a male magnetist: "we need not inquire whether any damage might result, if we observe the rule laid down above,—*that a woman, when magnetized, ought always to have a female friend near her*" (Hartshorn's [1843] translation, p. 165, italics added).

Regardless of who was ultimately responsible for the implementation of this ground rule, it did not change the fact that by writing so extensively on the impossibility of abuse, Deleuze provided his opponents fertile grounds for attack and refutation. Many of his detractors suspected that if there was so much smoke, there had to be a fire.

During these first two decades of the nineteenth century, a second person attracted the attention of the public on animal magnetism. If Deleuze represented the typical animal magnetist, the Abbé di Faria was the most controversial figure of the period. Rejected by everyone, scientists and magnetists alike, he came to be seen in future years as the originator of the scientific investigation of hypnosis, and particularly as the founder of the theory of suggestion that the Nancy school championed in the late nineteenth century. Faria was to revise completely the notions surrounding animal magnetism and artificial somnambulism, starting with the names themselves. He came to reject these metaphors as misleading and to describe the phenomena under the new label of *lucid sleep*. This in itself displeased the old guard.

The Abbé di Faria

José Custodio di Faria was born on May 31, 1756, in the village of Candolim in Goa.[3] His parents' marriage ended in a separation when he was seven or eight years old. From that time on, he lived with his father. His father who before his marriage, had received minor orders of the Catholic Church completed his religious studies and became a priest. His mother entered a convent and became a Catholic nun. In 1771, José and his father left India to establish themselves in Lisbon. They stayed for a year in Portugal before moving to Rome where José remained until 1780. Having completed his ecclesiastical studies he was ordained as a Catholic priest and returned to Portugal where he was received at the Royal Court. The story that he was the son of a Catholic priest and a Catholic nun pleased the aristocracy. He remained in Lisbon until the spring of 1788, at which time he decided to leave for Paris. In Paris, his life changed dramatically. Having more or less forgotten his ecclesiastical duties, he became politically involved in the ongoing French Revolution. At the fall of the Convention, on October 5, 1795, Faria became head of a revolutionary group and helped in the establishment of the *Directory*.

Faria's interest in magnetism appears to have begun during this period. In the introduction to his book (1819), he expressed his admiration to the Marquis de Puységur, both for his teaching and his writings. He also expressed the hope that the Marquis would understand their theoretical divergences. A first mention of Faria's work can be found around 1802, in *Les Mémoires d'outre-tombe* of the famous French writer Chateaubriand. In a short passage, Chateaubriand wrote:

> I am not a good subject for Swedenborgism: the Abbé Faria invited for dinner at Madam de Custine bragged that he could kill a canary, using Magnetism: the canary was the strongest, and the abbé, furious, was forced to abandon his attempt to avoid being killed by the canary. . . . (Chateaubriand, 1843, Vol. 2, p. 302; cited in Dalgado, 1906, p. 18)[4]

In 1811, Faria left Paris for Marseilles and Nîmes where he taught philosophy for two years. He returned to Paris in 1813 and proceeded to deliver public lectures on lucid sleep. Having received permission from the police authorities, he began presenting a weekly lecture on Thursdays. Each lecture/demonstration could be attended for the price of five francs.[5] The lecture hall was, nevertheless, usually filled to capacity. On August 11, 1813, Faria presented his first lecture. Each lecture began with a one-hour discourse in which Faria attempted to indicate his disagreements with animal magnetism and artificial somnambulism. A contemporary account, written by General Noizet, who was both a disciple and somnambulist of Faria's, conveys the flavor of these lecture/demonstrations. He wrote:

> The following year, visiting Paris after the military campaign of 1815, I heard that a certain Indian–Portuguese abbé was giving public sessions on Magnetism at his home. I went there and found in his living room a group representing Paris high society. Ladies were outnumbering men to witness this new show, even if one had to endure for more than an hour the reading of an incomprehensible piece of mumbo jumbo (*grimoire*), all poured out in very bad French by a tall old bronzed man with a strange looking face, before the actual quite exciting experiments. (1854, p. i)

His views were so markedly different from the shared beliefs of the time that Faria rapidly became the center of controversy between the scientific, religious, and magnetic communities. Both his popularity and his notoriety increased vastly at the time. Journalists seemed quite happy to ridicule him, and as had happened with Mesmer, he became the subject of a satirical play. In 1813, Mme Victorine Maugirard published a play entitled *La Mesméromanie*, which once again presented animal magnetism in a less than favorable light. Although Faria was not the immediate target of the play, he was nonetheless affected by the bad publicity. Unfortunately, he was also the center of a more important controversy with some members of the clergy. As indicated earlier, some representatives of the Catholic Church were clearly identifying the presence and action of the Devil behind the work of the magnetists.

Ignoring the criticisms, however, Faria continued his Thursday lectures until mid-1816 when a particular event put a finish to his public life. A well-known actor of the time, M. Potier, convinced Faria that he wanted to become his student and adept. During one of the public demonstrations, Potier, who was simulating lucid sleep, opened his eyes and said to Faria: "Well, Mister Abbé, if you magnetize everyone like me, you are not doing anything" (see Dalgado, 1906, p. 33). This story spread through Paris rapidly and Faria was once again seen as an impostor and a quack. But Potier went further. He asked a certain Jules Vernet to write a play, *La Magnétismomanie*, that centered around the character of the Abbé Faria. The play was staged for the first time on September 5, 1816. From this point on, Faria's lectures were a subject of ridicule.

He decided to leave Paris and as Figuier described in his book: "was quite happy to hide his defeat in a boarding school for young women, saying the mass and being their chaplain" (1860, Vol. III, p. 303).

He used this retreat to write his only book, *De la cause du sommeil lucide*, published in 1819. This book was the first of a series of four that Faria intended to write. Unfortunately, on September 20, 1819, he died unexpectedly. He was 63 years old. Although Faria had some followers, he remained an obscure figure in the history of hypnosis. Sixty years after his death, however, his book attracted the attention of the Bernheim's "School" of hypnosis at Nancy. Its members recognized the seeds of their own doctrine in the Abbé's teachings. Faria also survived total neglect when the French writer Alexandre Dumas incorporated the Abbé in his famous novel, *The Count of Monte Cristo*.[6]

FARIA'S VIEWS OF ANIMAL MAGNETISM

One sentence in Faria's book summarizes his position on animal magnetism. He wrote: "One must seek the truth where it is, not where one would like it to be" (1819, p. 322). This he did, even if it was to isolate him from both the believers and nonbelievers in magnetism. His own awareness of these conflicts did not facilitate the clarity of his writing. Nonetheless, hidden in the midst of tortuous philosophical and religious arguments, are the seeds of much of the contemporary thinking about hypnosis. Although his writings reflected the medical knowledge of his time, his explanations of animal magnetism were astonishingly different from those of his contemporaries. It is thus not difficult to understand how his ideas were dismissed during his life, partially revived at the end of the nineteenth century, and are beginning to resurface today.

When Faria wrote his book, he sought to reply both to the criticisms of the clergy on the practice of animal magnetism and to the satirical comments published regularly in the newspapers. He attacked with uncompromising ridicule what he believed to be superstitious behaviors on the part of both magnetists and scientists.

Largely ignored by everyone, he nonetheless influenced some of the newer magnetists, particularly Alexandre Bertrand and François-Joseph Noizet, who proved also to be at the center of the renewed scientific interest that developed during the subsequent two decades (1820–1840).[7]

Faria rejected all of the explanations that had been given up to the time that he, himself, had been a practitioner of animal magnetism. Whether it be the magnetic fluid, the power of the will or the imagination, or the soul, all were dismissed without mercy.

> I cannot conceive how the human race could be so bizarre as to look for the cause of this phenomenon Animal Magnetism in a tub, in a magnetic fluid, in an external will, in animal heat, and in a thousand other extravagances, when this sort of sleep is known to all humans by the dreams, and to all those who rise, walk or talk in their sleep. (1819, p. 33)

His major argument for this rejection was the well-documented observation of individual differences in the ability to be magnetized. As indicated earlier, most magnetists agreed that only a small percentage of their patients could demonstrate such a phenomenon as the somnambulistic crisis. Faria was among the first to explain magnetic phenomena in terms of suggestion and individual abilities. A reading of his book illustrates dramatically how far ahead of his contemporaries he was. It took another 40 years before the notion of suggestion was taken seriously and even more time before scientists began investigating the individual differences underlying the magnetic, or soon to be called, hypnotic response. As acute an observer as he was, Faria was still influenced by the medical, philosophical, and religious beliefs of his period. One must therefore be careful in evaluating his contributions and avoid, as far as possible, reading in more than what was actually written. As will soon be seen, however, what was written was more than sufficient to consider Faria as the founder of the suggestion theory of magnetism.

It should be understood that the concept of suggestion was already present in the early writings of the magnetists. De Puységur, for instance had observed how his commands were obeyed by his patients and his somnambulists. This observation however did not take prominence over the fluidic aspects of the theory. The originality of Faria was to make suggestion and individual abilities the substratum of magnetic behaviors. It is important to understand, however, that Faria did not see these aspects of his theory as two independent variables, but rather as a set of interrelated, interactive aspects of a subject's responses to lucid sleep. In fact he looked at the suggestion process as a trigger mechanism, a necessary but not sufficient condition to produce lucid sleep. Without the necessary individual abilities, suggestion alone was bound to fail in the short term (Faria, 1819, p. 323).

Faria's professional credentials were impressive for the time. He claimed to have attempted lucid sleep in more than five thousand individuals. Of these, he reported that only one in five or six could demonstrate the full range of the then known magnetic phenomena. He created in addition his own vocabulary to describe the phenomenon of animal magnetism. Breaking with the traditional ways of conceptualizing it, he rejected such terms as animal magnetism, magnetist, and magnetized in favor of concentration, concentrationist, and concentrater. The rationale behind his choice of descriptors was to indicate that the subject had an active role to play in the elicitation of the different phenomena. He believed that lucid sleep, as exhibited by the *épopte* (a name used to describe a somnambulist), was elicited by the subject focusing his or her attention on one topic. This was effected by an abstraction of the senses, that is, by relegating both internal and external sensory information to the periphery of attention, and also by relaxation. To the extent that an individual had the ability to do this, he or she would be able to experience what Faria called an ecstatic experience, that is, the state of lucid sleep (p. 12).

In Faria's view, two basic abilities were required from the to-be épopte: psychic impressionability and blood that was thinner than normal.[8] These two abilities coupled with the attentional capacities of the subject made the elicitation of lucid sleep possible. Its actual elicitation, however, depended upon a number of other factors better known today as social psychological variables. This is where suggestion became a necessary ingredient of lucid sleep. Faria saw it as the catalyst that activated the responses elicited by the concentrationist (magnetist). Equally important, however, were the attributions made by the subject. For a suggestion to be effective, the épopte had to falsely attribute to the concentrationist, the power to influence him or herself. The role played by expectations as well as by attributions of the subject were extremely important and Faria emphasized many times in his book that the concentrationist should be aware of them to maximize the responses of his or her subjects and patients.

The notion of nonvolition, that is, the belief that the responses elicited during lucid sleep occurred without the subjects willfully enacting them, was first taken up by Faria. He was in fact fascinated by this aspect of the subjective experience of lucid sleep which he saw as a result of the false attributions of the subjects' own behaviors. He was nonetheless amazed by the manner in which an induced state of mind could produce such subjective experiences: "Is it not paradoxical to say that we influence our own actions, and that we are not aware of our own influence?" (p. 45)

It is interesting to note that Faria thought that most époptes were unaware of their abilities, even though they may have used them in the past. It was this unawareness that led to the involuntariness report. In the clinical context, unawareness could lead to the development of certain illnesses. If the époptes used their abilities (without their knowledge) and were physically affected, Faria called it an *imaginary illness* (*une maladie imaginaire*), whereas, if they were psychologically affected, it was called *chimeras of the imagination* (*chimères de l'imagination*). On other occasions when no physical or psychological problems were activated by these abilities, the unusual experiences reported by the époptes were seen as what he called *premonitions* or *presensations*. Leaving aside, for the present, the issue of what made an individual a good concentrator, it is of interest to examine Faria's thinking about the different phenomena elicited during lucid sleep, and how they could be employed in a clinical context.

EXPERIMENTAL AND CLINICAL USES OF LUCID SLEEP

It may come as a surprise to know that Faria's understanding of animal magnetism was paralleled by an as equally surprising grasp of how it can and should be used. Faria never claimed to be innovative. He firmly believed that the phenomena of lucid sleep had been known and used for centuries. Nevertheless, it is fair to say that he observed and described most of the intricate behaviors and experiences of hypnosis as we know them today.[9] Faria made use of different types of suggestion to demonstrate the abilities underlying the behaviors and experiences of the épopte. He could induce and cancel limb paralyses, suggest visual and auditory hallucinations and illusions, as well as use the state the subject was in to introduce new ideas to memory. One type of suggestion that he particularly enjoyed in a clinical context was to suggest to a patient that a glass of water, for example, drunk during lucid sleep was in fact a specific medicine for an illness. He would then suggest the different effects and side effects to be expected. According to Faria, this clinical use of the lucid sleep state was very efficient with the épopte.

Following Deleuze's examples, Faria also described what is now known as split personality. He went further than Deleuze, however, by proposing that this phenomenon could be manipulated in lucid sleep. He emphasized that amnesia between the two "personalities" was usually present, but could be suggested away. In the same way, he did not believe that the presence of amnesia, at the end of a period of lucid sleep, was a necessary sign of the ability of the épopte to experience this state. Amnesia could be removed by asking the subject to concentrate on particular episodes in the session. In this way, the subject could remember what had happened during his or her "sleep."

An intriguing aspect of Faria's book is his description of induced or suggested analgesia. Although it was known at the time that the magnetized subject could demonstrate analgesia, no major surgeries had been reported. In fact, the first major operation to be reported was the one performed ten years later by Cloquet which is discussed in a subsequent section. Faria's writings however, suggest that major surgeries may have been performed, long before Cloquet. He wrote:

> It can also happen, although quite rarely, that if their distraction is as profound as it can be, rather than experiencing spasms and convulsions when touched unexpectedly, they will not notice even the lightest sensations in serious incisions, wounds, and amputations. These efforts will be seen in all of the époptes if one *paralyses* the limb or part of the body that is to be subjected to a difficult and painful operation. (p. 190, italics in original)

The idea of increasing potential analgesia by paralyzing the target limb first is one of these original ideas that makes Faria such a fascinating author. Finally, Faria was the first to suggest that all of the behaviors and experiences observed in lucid sleep could occur also in the waking state. If the patients' or subjects' expectations were capitalized upon, they had the ability to carry out suggestions in normal awareness. Faria maintained that a good concentrationist was one who could direct épodes to elicit what their abilities allowed them to and who could foresee if the suggestions given would elicit positive, neutral, or negative effects (see his p. 124). The concentrationist's skills were particularly important in the clinical context, where all patients were not necessarily good subjects. Faria believed that everyone could benefit from lucid sleep if the needs of the patients were in harmony with their abilities. By manipulating both the patients' expectations and attitudes, one could bring about desired results. The only difference between an épopte and a less-gifted patient was the time required for healing (pp. 40–41). The non-époptes could experience relaxation and calm during lucid sleep as well as show slow progress in healing (see his pp. 152–160).

In order to profit from lucid sleep, patients had to have an intimate conviction in their abilities to respond to the treatment. Today, we talk about favorable *motives, attitudes*, and *sets* (Barber, 1969). This intimate conviction, however, was differentiated from mere good intentions (*volonté* versus *velléité*). The problem for Faria was that he could find no way of knowing in advance if the subject possessed this intimate conviction. According to him, many of the side effects experienced by subjects and patients (such as palpitations, headaches, anxiety) were the results of conflicts between a negative intimate conviction and a positive attitude to cooperate. This is strangely reminiscent of what would be later called *unconscious conflict*. In fact, Faria went further by suggesting that in épodes lucid sleep brought back to mind spontaneously buried memories, activating the so-called crises of the earlier mesmeric system. Once initiated these cathartic experiences had to occur and be treated appropriately. For Faria, many illnesses were the results of these conflicts between a subject's intimate conviction and the actual state of affairs. The more a subject experienced lucid sleep, however, the more these negative effects decreased.

On the question of free will and the possibility of influencing a person in a state of concentration, Faria was not very clear. On the one hand, he did not believe that the state of lucid sleep could be used to manipulate the épopte. The will of the operator had no direct effect on the subject as the magnetists had believed. He took the example of animal hypnosis that was quite popular at the time (as will be seen later) to demonstrate that it was not the will of the operator that was overpowering the animal, but a state of panic–fear installed in the animal by the situation (Faria must have wished he had known that fact 17 years earlier when he attempted to kill the canary . . .). The manipulation or abuse of an épopte could come about only as a product of persuasion as in any other social situation. On the other hand, he believed also that épodes whose intimate conviction was in conflict with the external situation could be prone to abuse. Once more experienced, however, they regained partially at least their free will: "From that point on, not only do they disobey what is demanded, but they sometimes do the exact contrary to fool the concentrationist" (p. 191).

This brief overview of Faria's theory of lucid sleep certainly indicates how ahead of his time he was. It is not too surprising that his impact on early nineteenth-century ideas was not as dramatic as it should have been. Nevertheless, one should not be fooled. Faria had an impact through some of his followers who subsequently reinstated the study of animal magnetism within medical circles. Starting with the death of Faria, some of his students, especially Noizet and Bertrand, confronted once again the scientific and religious establishments. The events of the following years of conflict certainly illustrated how the intelligentsia of the time were not ready for Faria.

A Resurgence of Sorts

By the end of the second decade of the nineteenth century, animal magnetism had gained acceptance in many European countries. In most of northern Europe, physicians were practicing magnetism. In Russia, the Emperor Alexander formed a Commission of Inquiry in 1815 to examine it. The conclusions of the Commission recommended that the study and practice of magnetism be restricted to the medical profession. The Emperor agreed and published a ukase in line with the conclusions of the Commissioners. Denmark followed in the Russian steps in 1817. In the same year in Sweden, candidates for a degree in medicine were required to write a dissertation on magnetism. In Prussia, also in 1817, the use of magnetism was restricted by law to the medical profession (Figuier, 1860, Vol. III).

Perhaps the most ironic change of attitude toward animal magnetism came from the Berlin Academy of Sciences which, in 1818, proposed a 3,300 franc prize for the best memoire on animal magnetism. In France, the attitude was one of skepticism at best and total rejection at worst. In 1818, in the French Dictionary of Medical Sciences, a lengthy article on magnetism written by Virey showed the negative attitudes of the medical community toward the phenomenon. A number of physicians and magnetists decided to examine animal magnetism more attentively, among them were Alexandre Bertrand, François-Joseph Noizet, both followers of Faria, and J. du Potet, a lay magnetist and one of the most colorful figures of that period. Both Bertrand and Noizet had presented essays on magnetism to the Berlin Academy of Sciences. Their manuscripts were returned for having arrived after the closing date of the contest. Bertrand's manuscript subsequently formed the basis of his first book.

Bertrand was a young physician and an enthusiastic supporter of animal magnetism who was, initially, fully in line with the traditional magnetists. He is an ambiguous figure in the history of hypnosis since in the space of a few years he went from a stance of total support for classical magnetism to one of rejection and dismissal of the traditional doctrine in favor of the theory of imagination. In 1819, however, he was still enthusiastic. During the year he presented a series of lectures at the Hôtel Dieu, one of the most important Parisian hospitals, which proved to be very popular. The following year a number of experiments were conducted at the same hospital under the direction of Husson, then Chief of Staff, on the clinical value of magnetism. For reasons difficult to understand, however, Husson asked du Potet, a lay hypnotist, to conduct these experiments.

Bertrand, who witnessed these experiments, could not but feel wounded for having been overlooked by his own colleagues. During the experiments he took a highly skeptical position. He was not, however, alone. Another physician and long-time opponent of magnetic doctrine, Récamier, was not pleased with the experimentation in the hospital. Having heard that two patients on his ward had demonstrated analgesia during their magnetization, he decided to apply moxas to test their ability to tolerate pain. The first moxa was applied to the upper part of the right thigh of M. Starin and the second one to the pit of the stomach of Lise Leroy. Each moxa, about one inch square, was left on the patient until the skin was totally burnt. The scars produced involved the entire thickness of the skin. Both patients demonstrated no indication of pain. The hypnotist, Robouam, then asked Récamier if the demonstration had convinced him of the usefulness of magnetism. Récamier answered: "No, but my grounds are weakened" (Figuier, 1860, Vol. III, p. 295).

Bertrand continued his investigation of magnetism during the following years and published his second book in 1826. In this, he rejected the doctrine of animal magnetism in favor of a theory of imagination. He proposed that most of the phenomena seen in animal magnetism and somnambulism were the results of an exalted state of mind, what he called a state of ecstasy. It will be recalled that Faria had already described the somnambulistic state as an "ecstatic adventure," a state in which he believed the subject's inner senses were exalted. In fact, most of Bertrand's thinking can be seen as an extreme form of Fariaism, in which the motivating force is the imagination of the subject or patient. He wrote: "As far as somnambulism is concerned, reasonable Magnetists cannot but recognize that *imagination elicits it in most circumstances* and that *in all cases* it at least plays a powerful role in its production" (1826, p. 537, italics in original).

This exalted imagination was responsible for the production of the ecstatic state that Bertrand defined in the following terms:

> A particular state different from awakening, sleep, and illness; a natural state for human beings in the sense that it always appears in certain given circumstances in a similar fashion. For me it is the state that one can see in prophets, in persons miraculously cured, in possessed individuals, convulsionaries, shakers, people in habitual crisis, holy persons that experience ecstasy of all countries and of all times. (1826, p. 3)

It was the first time since the beginnings of the history of animal magnetism that a physician would go to such lengths in identifying and equating most of the mass hysteria phenomena of the previous centuries (some of which were still vividly remembered by the French people) as well as the more individually experienced religious trances as the result of an exalted imagination. If, on the one hand, Bertrand was probably correct in proposing a continuity in the behaviors and experiences of these different phenomena, he, on the other hand, opened a can of worms when he equated holiness and miraculous cure with possessed individuals. The clergy responded with divine anger.

There is another way of looking at Bertrand's contributions that is less flattering for him than has generally been recognized.[10] In a book by Scobardi, published in 1839, previously alluded to, the author explained Bertrand's sudden change of opinion between 1823 and 1826 as due to wounded self-esteem resulting from du Potet being asked to undertake the experimentation at the Hôtel Dieu. As will be recalled, Scobardi seemingly was a member of the sacred congregation of the Index and his book supposedly represented a narrative of the underground attempts by the clergy to banish the animal magnetic movement. He summarized his notes on Bertrand by saying: "This salubrious mood was put to work; *we talked* with Mr. Bertrand in all confidentiality" (p. 53, italics in original). (Bertrand's book was published in 1826.)

In 1825, two major events occurred. The article on magnetism in the medical dictionary was rewritten by a well-known physician, L. L. Rostan, and was seen as supportive of the new therapeutic. At the same time, another physician, P. Foissac, approached the Royal Academy of Medicine in an attempt to reopen the investigation of animal magnetism.

The Medical Dictionary: Rostan's Influence

In the 1818 medical dictionary article, Virey had reported on animal magnetism unfavorably. Rostan's approach to the problem left both proponents and opponents in doubt. For the proponents, it was certainly a victory. Magnetism, in fact classical magnetism based on the power of the magnetist's will, was supported. The major phenomena were presented as real. Rostan particularly emphasized catalepsy (following Pététin), hypermnesia, and amnesia: "The memory of magnetized individuals is certainly what is mostly excited. One can see some who can recite poetry that they have either learned a long time ago, or just read once, with great accuracy and confidence" (1825, p. 18).

At the same time, however, he wrote extensively on the dangers and potential abuses of the magnetic system. Most of his ideas resulted from his assumption that the magnetized individual was exclusively controlled by the magnetist. The magnetized individual was seen entirely as an automaton, a puppet, in the hand of his master. This analogy would plague the image of hypnosis many times in the decades to come.

> The will is nearly absent; it is in such a way under the will of the Magnetist that the individual appears to be his mere instrument; they act through him and [the magnetist] can influence even their desires and their thoughts. They

[magnetized individuals] have such a desire to prove that they can see [clairvoyance] that they will quite often invent fables. (p. 19)

At the same time, however, he wrote that a person could not be magnetized against his or her will. He conceptualized the conditions necessary to successful induction of the magnetic state as a tacit and preliminary agreement between the two parties (see his p. 23). He believed, mistakenly however, that if a person had already been magnetized it became possible to induce this state against his or her will. This yes/no type of answer gave both opponents and proponents of the new system numerous ways of refuting each other. Unfortunately, this notion of the power of the will originated from the magnetists themselves. They were prone to write about their marvelous powers. One of the best examples is provided by a young lay magnetist, Charles Lafontaine, who at the time was demonstrating the powers of magnetism by using it on animals.

It will be recalled that the Abbé di Faria had also, at one point in his early career, attempted to magnetize a canary without apparent success. The traveling magnetist was more successful. In his memoirs, published originally in 1847, Lafontaine (1886) described a number of experiments performed on animals in order to demonstrate how magnetism could be used to kill them. He even maintained that the same results could be obtained on humans. In fact, the misuse of magnetism could produce a number of very serious side effects, including death. These experiments, performed mainly in the following 20 to 30 years, would surface again in the forensic debate of the 1880s.

One example of Lafontaine's work at the end of the 1810s is instructive.

> The first time that I attempted such experiment, it was on a medium-sized frog. I placed it in a glass jar of about fifteen centimeters wide by thirty centimeters high. I looked at it, but at first it moved and jumped a lot. After a few minutes it became quiet and its eyes looked at mine. In a short while, it moved near the wall and back again; its eyes became fixed and looked dilated. I succeeded then at keeping its eyes on mine; it could not look away anymore. I increased my efforts and soon, its mouth opened, its limbs extended and it became rigid. It was dead, but had not exploded like the toad [an earlier experiment performed by a physician friend of Lafontaine]. The experiment lasted thirteen minutes, and I was not in any discomfort. My eyes only were quite tired. (1886, p. 252)

Lafontaine repeated such experiments many times with equal success. He was careful to warn those who wished to replicate these findings, however, not to perform such studies alone. They should always be accompanied by someone. As he put it: "The animal can be stronger than you; it is a duel, and if you fall under its spell, you cannot get out of it by yourself" (1886, p. 252).

To further his point, Lafontaine described how he saved his own son *in extremis* who had fallen under the will of a frog in an attempt to replicate the experiments his father was performing. Such experiments were extremely popular among lay magnetists who offered public séances at the time.

Around the same period, A. Lombard, a well-known magnetist, published a book on the dangers that the magnetists were likely to encounter in their practice. Although most of the book was devoted to means by which the magnetist could avoid being infected by the illnesses of their sick patients, a few pages addressed the issue of abuse. In fact, Lombard reported the first relatively concrete example of an alleged sexual abuse on the part of a magnetist, though, following precedent, in anonymous terms.

> A young and virtuous man, quite profound, had a young female somnambulist. He wanted to experiment on his rational discoveries in order to know if Magnetism could be dangerous. One night *he instructed her.* The young person was quite agitated the next day once she was in somnambulism. One could see on her physiognomy the embarrassment of a vanquished sense of decency. When she was asked how her night had been, she answered in a troubled and painful tone: very bad. Forgetting her natural shyness, she admonished her Magnetist, and implored him not to use his power if he respected her life. I did not allow myself to repeat this experiment. It is sufficient to know that this and many other things are possible. (1819, pp. 101–102, italics added)

Lombard was not content with this apparent example of sexual abuse on the part of the magnetist. He thought in fact that women in general and young women in particular should not be magnetized or if they had to be, they should only be magnetized with extreme prudence. This care was intended to minimize the establishment of an intimate rapport between the magnetists and their patients.

Lombard thought also that women should not magnetize anybody. He believed that their imagination and sensitivity would be counter productive.

> Our love for them [women] should act to prevent their impulsive humanitarian feelings. They have a weaker constitution than men. Magnetism would weaken them even more and soon they could not carry on their sacred duties. Pregnancy and its consequences, breast-feeding, the periodical attacks on their health, the problems they encounter when they stop being fertile, all these require all the strength they can spare. If they were to magnetize in one of these succeeding and encompassing states of their life, they would sometimes be guilty [of transmitting illnesses], and would threaten their own health all the time. . . . (1819, pp. 99–100)

The dangers alluded to by Lombard were taken up by Rostan in his article in the medical dictionary. Rostan was even more specific in his descriptions of the moral and physical dangers that animal magnetism could elicit. Among the physical dangers of magnetic malpractice, Rostan listed the following: headaches, intense pain, weakness, diverse types of neuroses, loss of weight, asphyxia, and many others. He even believed that death could occur by paralyzing the muscles of respiration. Among the psychological side effects, he reported melancholia and mental alienation to be quite frequent. He considered these problems as minimal when one considered the moral dangers. He believed that the possibility of moral abuse stemmed from the complete dependence induced by the magnetic state. Rostan described it as similar to the dependence of a dog on his master. For women, the dangers were obvious to him:

> Which woman, which girl will be assured that she did not suffer any abuse from the part of the magnetist when one knows that she cannot remember anything? (p. 38)
>
> How can one resist repeated touchings, tender gazes, daily contact; it is not possible. Intimacy is established . . . we can predict what will happen. (p. 39)

There was even more than mere sexual abuse. According to Rostan, magnetism could destroy family life and social relationships. It could be used to know the secrets in the lives of people and to elicit confessions. Rostan (1825) is the first author to pinpoint these potential legal problems. Although he did not provide specific examples, he opened up a line of speculation. He concluded his section on the dangers of magnetism by asking the government to restrict severely the practice of magnetism only to those people "who can offer desirable guarantees" (p. 39). He did not, however, specify what these guarantees were.

One might ask why such prominence was given to the potential of sexual abuse of the magnetized person when no documented cases of it had been brought to the attention of the courts. Part of the explanation resides in the medical beliefs of the time. The phenomena of mass hysteria described earlier, the mesmeric crises, and the affectionate relationship between the magnetist and his subjects were all seen as the consequence of a hysterical tendency in the individual who manifested these behaviors. Hysterical symptoms included an exalted sensuality and sexuality. The logical conclusion was to look at the induction of the magnetic state as a method of provoking an enhancement of sexuality. As Figuier wrote when talking about the convulsionaries of the eighteenth century: "Of all the demons that can possess the mind of a girl, the demon of lust is the one most difficult to satisfy" (1860, Vol. I, p. 414).

The Third Commission of Inquiry

The proponents of animal magnetism saw Rostan's article as a victory. P. Foissac, a young physician, who had been practicing magnetism for a few years felt that the time was right to approach the Academy of Medicine once again and request that a new Commission of Inquiry be created.

A Committee was formed to examine his request. On December 13, 1825, Husson, the Secretary of the Committee, presented his conclusions to the Academy. The general conclusion was that the Academy should create a commission to investigate animal magnetism once more. One of several reasons given for this was the fact that the conclusions of the Franklin Commission were already 40 years old and (surprisingly enough) that the experiments performed at the time were doomed to failure due to the negative attitudes of the Commissioners. The Committee also thought that the phenomenon had changed since its early days, especially with the discovery and popularity of artificial somnambulism. The Committee stated also that French medicine should not be considered less advanced than its German counterpart which, a few years earlier, had offered an award for the best memoir on animal magnetism. It was obviously trying to capitalize on French xenophobia. Finally, the Committee reasoned that if magnetism was a useful therapeutic agent, it should be regulated so that charlatans could be stopped from abusing it.

The proposition was debated until the following February 28, at which point it was decided to create a new Commission. The vote, however, reflected the attitude of the academicians: 35 members voted for the Commission and 25 against. The newly formed Commission was not to have an easy life. It took four years to complete its investigation, and its report was not presented to the Academy until one year later. It was read on June 21 and 28, 1831, and provoked heated discussions since its major conclusions were favorable to magnetism. Not too surprisingly, the problems that the Commissioners had encountered during their investigations had been the product of the antagonism of their colleagues. For example, the decision taken by the Council General of Hospitals to forbid magnetic experimentation in the hospitals under its jurisdiction had been a major setback. As a result, the Commission had been obliged to rely upon its own resources. Unfortunately, most, if not all of the Commissioners were not in a position to magnetize patients, thus they were forced to rely on magnetists such as Foissac and du Potet to perform the requisite experiments.

One of the problems created by the use of such people as Foissac and du Potet was the scarcity of patients, on the one hand, and their undue interest in the more spectacular and controversial aspects of mesmerism and somnambulism, on the other. In the five-year period of the Commission's existence, not more than a dozen subjects were observed.

Before reviewing the series of conclusions presented by the Commissioners in 1831, one major fact must be considered since it influenced the manner in which the Commission considered the usefulness of animal magnetism. This major fact was a surgical operation performed by Cloquet in 1829. The operation involved the removal of a cancerous tumor from the breast of an elderly woman, Mme Plantin, using magnetism as the sole anesthetic agent (chemical anesthesia had not yet been discovered, and following Faria, magnetism was thought to produce spontaneous analgesia in some patients). Surgery at the time was a dangerous enterprise.[11] Mme Plantin was a 64-year-old woman who was suffering from an ulcerated cancer of the right breast. She had been magnetized quite often by a magnetist named Chapelain. When Cloquet performed his surgery, the patient did not demonstrate any sign of pain. After the surgery, the woman had no recollection of the procedure and the operation was a success.

The reaction of the medical community was quite violent. Every conceivable argument was presented in an attempt to discredit the case. For Mme Plantin, the debate was superfluous. She died three weeks later, from pleurisy. Her death, however, did not settle the debate surrounding her operation. Having accused her of lying and of simulating analgesia, one British physician suggested that she had probably died of remorse for having deceived the medical profession (Podmore, 1909/1964). This accusation was made eight years after the operation: it is a sure sign that many medical professionals remained very uncomfortable vis-à-vis this unprecedented success. English doctors, as will be seen in the next section, were not particularly enthralled by magnetism. In 1829, following Cloquet's operation, *The Lancet*, one of the two major medical journals of the time, briefly reported the case and concluded in the following terms:

> By far the most interesting of the cases which have yet occurred in the practice of Animal Magnetists, are those in which the patients have been females, and pregnancy one of the results. This curious effect, at one time, made magnetizing a highly popular operation. (p. 384)

Cloquet was not indifferent to these comments and when the British surgeon made his accusations in 1837 (February 4), he wrote a lengthy letter to the *Gazette Médicale de Paris*.

> I would not have talked if my name had not been mentioned; but a fact that I thought forgotten was brought forward. I have the responsibility to answer and reascertain today what I said seven or eight years ago.
>
> When I talked about this quite extraordinary fact, I purposefully avoided any explanation; I was like a mirror, reflecting as accurately as possible the image that was striking me.
>
> The same objections are voiced today as yesterday. People said at the time that I had been fooled, that I was too gullible, that I had misunderstood the power of the will.... But, Gentlemen, I am not as inexperienced in surgery as one would like to believe; I have cut, like many others, thighs and legs; among those I operated upon, I saw some who did not say a word, who did not shout, or complain; but what their mouth did not say, their body movements and gestures did very eloquently.
>
> In no way is this similar to what happened with the woman we are alluding to; her position was quite different. This woman as you know had breast cancer. It was known that she could sleep the magnetic sleep and in an attempt to spare her from the pain of surgery, we thought to profit from this rare ability. I was a total *stranger* to the preliminaries.
>
> I was warned and expressed my doubts. I said that I would perform the surgery as long as the state described was not one of syncope [fainting]. When I met the patient, she was asleep. *I examined her carefully*. Her physiognomy was calm, with no sign of fear or hope; pulsations were calm, regular; her breathing was natural, her eyelids closed.
>
> I began the operation with an incision under the tumor which had not

less than nine to ten inches in length and I *looked at the patient's face*, and could not see any sign of sensation. Her magnetist established rapport between her and me and I asked her if I had caused her a lot of pain. She answered in the negative. I took the scalpel again and made a second incision: *she did not move*. I dissected the ganglia in the pit of her arm and this part of the surgery certainly lasted a full fifteen minutes because I had to spare the axillary artery. Same *impassivity*, same *calm*, same *indifference*. I finally did four or five ligatures and once again the patient did not display any pain, no sensation *as if she was not concerned by what was happening*. Could there be some analogy between the magnetic sleep and catalepsy? One thing is certain; I could understand well the views of the skeptics; if I had not seen it, *I would doubt it myself*.

At the end of the surgery, I plunged a sponge in lukewarm water and washed the bloody parts. It is at this moment only that the first sensations were evident. *The patient started laughing*, and said: "You're tickling me." I finished the dressing and she was brought to her bed.

The wound evolved like all wounds do; until the nineteenth or twentieth day. . . . At that time, it was thought that she could be released from the hospital. Her regular physician agreed and she was feeling well. Three to four days later, new permission to go out. When she came back, she complained that *she had caught a chill*. Rapidly she felt a painful spasm on the operated side; pleurisy; death. That is it, Gentlemen, the fact in all its simplicity. I am telling it because as extraordinary as it may be, *it should be remembered*. I will tell it again today because *I am certain of its accuracy*. (p. 78, italics in original)

The Commissioners were certainly able to profit from this extraordinary demonstration of the anesthetic property of animal magnetism. But rather than emphasize the practicality of the new system, they rapidly became sidetracked by the more sensational claims. When one looks at their conclusions it becomes clear that they were more interested in sensationalism than in a more rigorous investigation of the phenomena elicited in magnetized individuals. This was not because they failed to recognize the importance of the more usual phenomena, but rather because they buried them in a search for the marvelous. Thirty major conclusions were presented. Among the most extravagant claims were the recognition of clairvoyance, the possibility of magnetization using the power of the will, and the diagnosing by somnambulists of their own illnesses and, in some cases, illnesses in other people, and finally the prediction of the ongoing course of their illnesses.

More importantly, however, the Commissioners stressed the importance of being extremely careful in studying these phenomena. They emphasized that they had examined only a few cases and that the investigation of magnetism should be pursued by the medical profession. They recognized individual differences in response to the magnetic process, and described the by now wellknown phenomena of amnesia, analgesia, the various types of hallucination, and the selectivity of the rapport between magnetist and patient. Concerning the clinical usefulness of magnetism, the Commissioners recognized that they had seen such a limited sample of patients that no conclusions could be drawn.

Overall, the report was quite favorable to the magnetic movement. By acknowledging the most curious effects of magnetism, however, the Commissioners were exposing it to new attacks from its detractors. These criticisms were rapidly voiced when the report was presented to the Academy. It was decided after many discussions not to print it, but rather to sign it. In other words, this relatively favorable report was consigned automatically to the already dusty shelves of the Academy of Medicine. One member of the Academy who strongly opposed the publication of the report indicated the main medical concern: He maintained that if the reported facts were true, "they would destroy half of our physiological knowledge" (cited in Figuier, 1860, Vol. III, p. 305). He argued that this could not be permitted. The mere presence of a favorable report, however, was sufficient to create considerable embarrassment among the Academy's more conservative members. A few years later a fourth Commission was formed to definitively resolve the problems created by the magnetists. As will be seen in the following chapter, the French history of magnetism was coming to a temporary halt, just at a time when it began to flourish in other countries such as England and the United States.

NOTES

1. Robert C. Fuller (1982) argues in his recent book that Mesmerism in America was at the forefront of the Second Grand Awakening in the continuous evolution of American spiritualism. His well-documented book is worth reading and offers an interesting interpretation of the influence of the mesmeric movement both on the religious trends in American culture and the development of the most popular beliefs surrounding the beginning of a scientific psychology.

2. The French Revolution has been divided into a number of periods representing the different factions that held political power. The Republic was proclaimed on September 21, 1792, and lasted until 1804 at which time Napoleon established the Empire. The Republic is usually divided into three periods: the Convention, the Directory, and the Consulate. The Empire under the direction of Napoleon ended in 1814 when the Monarchy was restored. Louis XVIII, brother of Louis XVI, was to reign until 1824 (Abbott, 1859).

3. One of the most complete biographies of Faria was published by D. G. Dalgado in 1906. Other biographies are mentioned by Dalgado in his reference section.

4. The book was published in 1843, after the death of the writer. It was published in Paris by Edmond Biré. Although written in a satirical tone, this passage demonstrates that by the beginning of the 1800s, Faria was already known as a magnetist. We will return later to the experiments performed on animals in order to demonstrate the power of magnetism.

5. According to Rudé (personal communication) 5 francs was the equivalent of 100 pennies (*sous*). For 2 pennies, one could buy a loaf of bread. Faria's entry fee was thus the equivalent of buying 50 loaves of bread. It may not have been so modest a price. On the other hand, compared to contemporary fee structures for psychotherapy, 50 loaves

of bread would cost anywhere between 50 and 70 dollars—a more than ordinary price for therapy especially to a capacity audience.

6. Dalgado (1906) provides a complete version and explanation of the presence of Faria in Dumas's novel. Although most probably romanticized, Dalgado's interpretation is most interesting.

7. It is particularly noteworthy that Faria is conspicuously absent from most books on animal magnetism. Not only was he ignored by his contemporaries, but even historians of animal magnetism have constantly ignored his views. It may not be all that surprising when one considers that Faria's views were not in accord with the animal magnetists and the spiritualists. Podmore, for example, mentions Faria's name a few times in his book but attributes most of his thinking to Bertrand. It could of course be due to the fact that Faria rejected the spiritualist movement and its interpretation of artificial somnambulism, whereas Bertrand tended to accept some of the spiritualistic interpretations of magnetism.

8. Faria's physiological knowledge reflected the current medical beliefs of his time. A careful reading of his book, however, reveals that he was in fact talking of the extracellular fluid rather than the actual bloodflow. It was the thinness of the fluid bathing the different organs that was responsible for the intensity with which different suggested behaviors could be experienced. This hypothesis may have come from the observation that in general the épopte was an individual who would sweat profusely. Thinner blood was seen by Faria as the cause of natural somnambulism, a phenomenon akin to lucid sleep. He thought that the two phenomena represented two alternate versions of the same aspect of sleep. As he put it on page 19 of his book: "*Il n'y a d'autre différence entre l'un et l'autre que celle qui existe entre une plante des champs et la même plante soignée dans un jardin*" (There is no other difference between one and the other than the difference between a wild flower and the same flower grown in a garden). Few contemporary writers have evaluated Faria's contributions. For other perspectives, the reader may wish to consult Barrucand (1967) and Perry (1978).

9. It can be quite frustrating to realize that progress in the scientific investigation of hypnosis has been amazingly slow and one can only wonder what such an acute observer as Faria could have done in an appropriate time and place. There are still hypotheses and conclusions drawn by Faria that are waiting to be examined seriously.

10. Most historians have presented Bertrand's work in a favorable light. Podmore (1909/1964), for example, credits Bertrand for the theory of suggestion and rejects Faria by stating in a footnote that although he had talked about suggestion in magnetism, he had no medical training and "had even less influence on educated opinion than Bertrand" (p. 92). What Podmore seems to have ignored is the fact that Bertrand (and perhaps because of his premature death) had no real influence on the intelligentsia of his time. In the report of the third Commission, Bertrand's theory was dismissed in one line. He was rediscovered at the end of the nineteenth century at the same time that Gilles de la Tourette rediscovered the work of Faria.

11. The conditions surrounding the beginnings of surgery were quite difficult. Since it is not the purpose of this book to contemplate the agonies that surgeons and particularly their patients had to face when having to undergo surgery, the reader is referred to Perry and Laurence's (1983) article. This article illustrates the role played by magnetism in alleviating surgical pain.

7

From Europe to America: Times of Change

Contemporary histories of hypnosis usually describe the scientific evolution of animal magnetism as oscillating between moments of uncritical endorsement and epochs of blind rejection. One of the reasons for such descriptions may very well lie in the period about to be described. From the 1830s to the 1860s (give or take a decade according to the country) the scientific establishment may not have been as interested in mesmeric doctrines as it was in the perennial nature of the quarrels surrounding them. Nevertheless, a number of physicians practiced magnetism. The results of their work, however, were not known until the late 1870s, when, as a result of the efforts of such investigators as Charcot and Bernheim, hypnosis regained acceptance in scientific circles.

Up to this point, discussion of the fate of animal magnetism in such countries as England and the United States has been avoided. There are two major reasons for this. First, Mesmerism, or animal magnetism, did not have the same early successes in these countries as it had in France. Nearly 50 years passed before some serious consideration (in the 1830s) was given to the new movement. In both countries, the struggles for acceptance mimicked those seen in France.[1]

What is fascinating about this period is that within a mere 30 years there was a complete transformation of the mesmeric doctrine. In the United States, animal magnetism became intimately linked with the development of spiritualistic movements. In fact, by a curious amalgam of magnetism, spiritism, and social mass movements (such as the Protestant Revival), the original doctrine was lost. In England, the fierce struggle between the proponents of animal magnetism and the scientific community, led to the first scientific investigation of the phenomenon with the work of James Braid. In France, another Commission of Inquiry would reject animal magnetism. In what can be seen as an interesting turn of events, both the French legal courts and the Catholic Church would recognize its therapeutic value.

The Fourth Commission of Inquiry

While the French report of 1831 restored a sense of confidence to the magnetists, it left the scientific community searching for ways to redeem its own reputation. Two years after Husson's report, magnetism was once again brought to the attention of the Academy of Medicine. Two physicians, Georget and Rostan, working at La Salpêtrière Hospital had been conducting experiments on clairvoyance with two of their patients, Pétronille and Braguette. The most unusual experiments were carried out with complete success. What the two physicians did not know, however, was that both women were informed beforehand by the interns of the different experiments. The following year, Pétronille died, but not before having described and acknowledged the different tricks she had used to fool the physicians. The phrase "Beware of the Pétronille" subsequently became a common expression whenever experiments on magnetism were conducted.

This unfortunate event was forgotten temporarily, when in 1836, one member of the Academy reported a case of magnetic analgesia similar to the one presented by Cloquet in 1829. Although the surgery was less serious, it certainly spoke in favor of magnetism. Dr. Oudet had succeeded in extracting a tooth, painlessly, from one of his patients who had been magnetized. The newspapers had publicized the fact, and at a meeting of the Academy on January 24, 1837, Oudet had been severely criticized. He nevertheless presented a report written by the magnetist, M. Hamard, that emphasized not only the absence of pain in a patient who was terrified of dentists, but a complete amnesia for the entire operation. The academicians reacted to this as they had to Cloquet's report. In the heated discussion that followed, one of the academicians proposed that, in order to settle once and for all the question of magnetism, all the members of the Academy should subject themselves to its influence, and "if magnetism produces some effects on only one of them, he would admit it; otherwise he would continue to doubt it" (*Bulletin de l'Académie de Médecine*, January 31, 1837, Vol. I; see also Figuier, 1860, Vol. III, p. 311).

Fortunately, the academicians were spared this challenge. At the following meeting, Berna, a young magnetist, offered to demonstrate the existence, as well as the usefulness, of animal magnetism using his own patients. His proposal was accepted and a special committee was formed to investigate his claims. Ten members of the Academy were to report to their colleagues. Among them were Burdin and Dubois d'Amiens, two of magnetism's most eloquent opponents.

The report was read to the Academy six months later by Dubois. It rejected globally all of the claims that Berna had made. It was extremely negative and Dubois did not lose a single opportunity to denigrate magnetism. From analgesia to clairvoyance, all of the phenomena linked habitually to it were dismissed. Once again, however, the magnetists had shot themselves in the foot. By attempting to demonstrate the more sensational phenomena rather than emphasizing the curative qualities of magnetism, they had opened the door to categorical rejection. The opponents did not permit that door to close again until they had assured themselves that it could never be reopened. Although Husson strongly protested the Commission's conclusions, they were readily accepted by the Academy.

The report was vehemently discussed in the following months. One physician, in an attempt to resolve the debate, offered a prize to the person who could successfully demonstrate the possibility of transposition of the senses, an alleged hallmark of the magnetic trance. This physician, Burdin, was ready to pay 3,000 francs from his pocket to anyone who could perform such a feat. Not surprisingly, there were many claimants, but not one winner. Not only did those who submitted themselves to the test fail to demonstrate this ability: Fraud was discovered in several cases.

Burdin must have known what he was doing, and the magnetists, both lay and professional, showed their inability to understand that "Beware of the Pétronille" was more than just a cynical comment on the part of the opponents of magnetism. Burdin and Dubois published a book in 1841, *Histoire académique du magnétisme animal* that was to become the reference book for those seeking to dismiss the phenomenon. Although attacked vigorously by the supporters of magnetism, the book represented a landmark in its history. Physicians who continued to practice magnetism now knew that discretion was the best politic, as Azam would indicate when he attempted to revive hypnotism in the 1860s.[2,3]

If magnetism was being attacked once again on scientific grounds, it was also encountering problems on the legal front. Although there had been spasmodic controversy surrounding the use of magnetism and somnambulism in the treatment of patients, few had resulted in actual legal battles. This was to change.

Magnetism in French Legal Courts

As indicated earlier, De Montègre had already underlined the dangers associated with somnambulists prescribing medications to the people with whom they consulted. Most European countries had adopted laws restricting the practice of magnetism to the medical community. In France, the battle was fought in the courts of law. Before 1850, most of the trials were won by the magnetists. After 1850, however, the courts usually accepted the views of the professional societies and recognized that magnetists practiced medicine illegally.

Three major topics were discussed by the courts: magnetism as an illegal practice of medicine, magnetism as fraud, and the potential abuse of magnetism to commit criminal acts. The first well-publicized trial was one that involved the famous lay hypnotist du Potet, who for a short time, had practiced in the Paris hospitals. He had been accused of presenting public lectures on magnetism without having been granted the permission by the legal authorities. Although the trial in itself was not very interesting and could be seen as an attempt by the medical profession to maintain its social status vis-à-vis the lay magnetists, the mere fact that it involved du Potet made it colorful. He chose to represent himself at the trial, and his eloquent and often pompous style was given free expression. The following short excerpt conveys his way of discussing the topic:

> Is it a Science or an Art? I am not quite sure myself; the only thing I can say is that I can teach how to induce sleep without *Opium, how to cure fever without Quinquina*; my science forbids drugs, my art ruins apothecaries.... See how we differ from the Scientists: with all their science they can only succeed in shortening life; us, we lengthen it. (cited in Bué, 1906, p. 148, italics in original)

Du Potet was acquitted. His flamboyant style served him well and his reputation gained credibility as a result of the favorable outcome of his trial. In 1840, Aubin Gauthier, one of the most prolific writers of this period, published the first attempt to establish an ethical code for magnetists, outlining a number of potential dangers awaiting the fledgling practitioner. Gauthier was very careful to word his ideas in a manner designed to please both the medical establishment and the magnetists. In 1846, he published a short pamphlet indicating how the magnetists and somnambulists could avoid legal action by the medical associations. Gauthier's work was written following a major trial that had lasted for more than three years (1842 to 1845), involving a lay magnetist, M. Ricard, and his somnambulist, Mlle Virginie Plain. This trial illustrated the more common types of accusations made against the magnetists.

M. Pihoué (the victim) suffered from epileptic fits. Having heard of M. Ricard and his somnambulist, he sent them a tuft of hair to see what type of clairvoyant reading she could perform. The letter he received from Ricard so impressed him that he decided to ask them to visit his town in order to be treated. Ricard and his somnambulist went to Bressuire and commenced the treatment of M. Pihoué. His health improved so dramatically that he decided to continue the treatment in Paris, where M. Ricard lived. At the same time that M. Pihoué was receiving treatment in Paris, the Bressuire public prosecutor became aware of it and decided to lay charges against both the magnetist and his somnambulist. M. Ricard was accused of using fraudulent procedures and deceiving his patients by fostering their belief in an imaginary power, for the purpose of extorting money. Ricard was brought to trial and found guilty. He was given a fine of 50 francs and condemned to 15 days in jail.

What was surprising in this case was the fact that the patient, M. Pihoué, had nothing to do with it. In fact he had expressed outrage since he reported feeling better than he had at any time in his life. M. Ricard decided to appeal, and was once again found guilty. His sentence was extended from 15 days to 6 months in jail. The magnetist took his case to the Court of Cassation (the final Court of Appeal). It decided in favor of the accused and reversed the previous judgments. The Court stated that M. Ricard had not used fraudulent means and, indeed, had been honest about his method of treatment. More surprising was the Court's position on animal magnetism, especially given the conclusions of the most recent Commission of Inquiry. The Court expressed the opinion that magnetism had curative properties and was not merely an imaginary power. Furthermore, it expressed regret that the medical societies had not examined the merits of magnetism more carefully (see *Gazette des Tribunaux*, Saturday, August 19, 1843, pp. 69-70). Needless to say the magnetists celebrated this victory. Whereas the medical establishment had ignored, ridiculed, and condemned magnetism, this court decision afforded them a new official status. As a result of this decision, many trials were abandoned (Charpignon, 1860).

The victory, however, was to be shortlived. On July 9 and 10, 1850, the Paris prosecutor published a public notice stating that somnambulists would be prosecuted for their illegal practice of medicine and for fraud. The notice mentioned also that physicians working with somnambulists would be prosecuted.

At the end of July, M. and Mme Mongruel, magnetist and somnambulist respectively, were arrested and brought before the Court. In addition, Dr. Grabowski, a physician, was accused of signing the prescriptions given by the somnambulist, and M. Sokolowski, a pharmacist, of filling them. The pharmacist was exonerated, but the physician was fined five francs. In contrast, M. and Mme Mongruel, were condemned to 5 days in jail and given a fine of 15 francs. They were found guilty on three counts: the illegal practice of medicine, the use of fraudulent means to extort money, and the interpretation of dreams. This last accusation, as far as the court was concerned, was the equivalent of divination and, as such, a fraud. It is ironic that 50 years later, Freud in his psychoanalytic system made the interpretation of dreams the pivotal point of his new psychotherapy. But these were different times, with different mores!

On appeal, their sentence was extended to 13 months of jail and a fine of 500 francs. When this new judgment reached the Court of Cassation, however, it was modified. The Court rejected the accusation of fraud, but maintained the other two. The sentence was revised and the Mongruels were finally jailed for 5 days on the first count (illegal practice of medicine), and were obliged to pay a fine of 15 francs for divination (interpretation of dreams).

Apart from the recognition that magnetism was part of the medical domain, a reading of the proceedings of the case at the appellate level, reveals an interesting point. The Appeal Court, through the court reporter, M. Thomassy, stated the following:

> An act of will is sometimes sufficient for one man to influence another man. . . . The magnetic sleep is a genuine state that is not simulated and could be amenable to serious inquiries. . . . It is, however, easy to simulate somnambulism; guilty abuses can be performed by magnetism; the magnetized individual can be rendered totally dependent; the will can disappear; the ability to act, even to speak can be annihilated; violence would be easy, seduction even easier; even death can occur (our physicians have said this) by paralysis of the breathing muscles. . . . (cited in Mongruel, 1851, p. 234; see also Charpignon, 1860, pp. 17–18)

These interesting comments were soon echoed in actual cases of abuse. Following this trial, magnetism became regarded as the illegal practice of medicine and subject to the rigor of the law.

The First Cases of Abuse

While magnetism had acquired a less than favorable reputation, it had, nevertheless, attracted a few proponents with medical degrees. The physicians who practiced magnetism published cases claiming that their technique had worked for, rather than against, morality. Charpignon (1841), for example, published an interesting book on the history of animal magnetism linking it to previous phenomena such as exorcism, the shakers of the Cévennes, and the convulsionaries of Saint Médard (see Chapter 2). In his book, he described one case in which magnetism had succeeded in preventing suicide by one of his patients, and another one where magnetism had put an end to the career of a prostitute by modifying her moral standards. As for the potential for sexual abuse, Charpignon was quite conciliatory. He wrote:

> It takes time, a long time before an honest soul be turned away from her obligations; if within a few days the will of an immoral magnetizer succeeds in perverting such instinct, there is no doubt that there already was a strong tendency toward this satisfaction, and that the subject's morality was not very good. (1841, p. 296)

This position, however, was soon to be challenged when the courts had to consider actual allegations of abuse. A number of physicians were already demanding that magnetism be the subject of severe legislation. Robiano (1851), for one, was not lenient with the uses and abuses of magnetism by lay persons. He wrote the following flight of oratory in an attempt to procure the official recognition of animal magnetism:

> Who will contradict me when I say that it is an outrage to see that the first comer, without science, without talent, without aptitude, without morality as without witnesses or sense of responsibility can, no matter how ignorant, brutish, nasty, or corrupt, disorganize constitutions, threaten health, set marriages at odds, disrupt families, poison the credulous people already short of money or mind, propagate impiety, disseminate immorality and the most absurd beliefs under the preposterous excuse that *Magnetism is not recognized as a curative agent by the Faculties*? (Robiano, 1851, p. 184, italics in original)

In order to better understand the conclusions of the first cases alleging abuse, it is important to remember that the only references the experts had in judging the potential dangers of magnetism were either theoretical writings (pro and con) or cases of abuse linked to noctambulism. De Puységur's early observations, for example, seemed to have been forgotten by this time. Forensic medicine was still in its infancy, although some physicians had devoted many years to the topic. In France, names such as Brierre de Boismont and Legrand du Saulle, his student, were respected by all physicians. A number of legal cases involving noctambulism had already reached the French courts and many experts had come to rely on these cases in assessing the dangers of magnetism. In other countries, such as England, sleepwalking had entered the field of law much earlier and already had a set of precedents upon which to draw (Stephen, 1883; Tuke, 1882, 1884).

There was a parallel development in France. Many forensic experts began publishing examples of crimes committed by or against sleepwalkers. Among the most frequently cited cases was one reported by Dyce, and a second one reported by Brierre de Boismont, concerning the case of Dom Duhaguet.

In his classic book, *Hallucinations, or The Rational History of Apparitions, Visions, Dreams, Ecstasy, Magnetism, and Somnambulism* (1845; published in its English version in 1853), Brierre de Boismont devoted a chapter to the hallucinations seen in magnetism and somnambulism. In discussing the value of magnetism, he praised the first Commission of Inquiry for its recognition of the power of imagination: "In recognizing the power of the imagination, we believe that there exist many facts in magnetism and somnambulism from which both psychology and medicine will derive valuable results" (1853, p. 233).

He then proceeded to identify these two states as similar to a state of ecstasy, a nervous condition, where hallucinations were frequent. He believed that in the instance of a patient suffering from these conditions several legal questions could arise. He cited the case reported by Dr. Dyce of Aberdeen of a young woman, Maria C., who was suffering from spontaneous (natural) somnambulism. She was talking in her sleep and answering questions without waking. One of the maids of the house where she lived had noticed that the girl did not remember what had happened during her episodes of somnambulism. One night she introduced a young man she knew into the house. Gilles de la Tourette described what then transpired:

> In this state he had the occasion to treat Maria in the most brutal and perfidious way. These miserable people succeeded in their plan by using the bed sheets as a gag as well as other means to overcome her resistance to their wickedness, even if she was in a state of somnambulism. Upon waking up, she did not remember what she had endured; a few days later, once again in somnambulism, she remembered what had occurred and told her mother all of the odious details. (de la Tourette, 1887, p. 368)

Although nothing is said about whether legal proceedings were instituted, this case was used as the prototypical example of how dangerous somnambulism, natural or artificial, could be. The lack of authentication was not, apparently, seen as a problem. If, in this case, the somnambulist was indeed a victim of her nervous disease, as was alleged, the following case was used to illustrate how the somnambulist could become the perpetrator of a crime. The case was reported also by Brierre de Boismont.

Dom Duhaguet, a prior of a monastery, had a friar under his authority who was known to be a natural somnambulist. One night as Dom Duhaguet was working at his desk, he saw the friar enter his room, in what he perceived as a complete state of somnambulism. He was holding a large knife in his hand.

> He went straight to my bed; appeared to satisfy himself by feeling, that I was really there; after which he struck three heavy blows so powerfully, that the blade, after piercing the clothes, entered deep into the mattress, or rather the mat, which I used instead. He returned as he came, opening and shutting quietly the two doors that led to my cell; and I was soon satisfied that he had gone directly and quietly to his own. . . . The next day I summoned the somnambulist, and quietly asked him of what he had dreamed the preceding night. At this question he was agitated. "Father," he replied, "I had so strange a dream that I do not like to tell you of it; it is perhaps the work of the evil one, and. . . ."—"I command it," replied I, "a dream is always involuntary, and is but an illusion." "Father," said he, "I was hardly asleep before I dreamed that you had killed my mother; that her bleeding ghost appeared and demanded vengeance; at this sight, I was so enraged that I flew like a madman to your apartment and stabbed you. Soon afterwards I awoke, bathed in perspiration. I hated myself for the outrage, and then blessed God that such a crime had not been committed." . . . I then related what had occurred, and showed him the evidence of the blows which he thought were dealt upon me. Upon this, he threw himself at my feet in tears, groaning over the misfortune which had so nearly happened, and imploring such penance as I thought fit to inflict upon him. (Brierre de Boismont, 1853, pp. 247–249)

The prior did not punish the friar, but did make sure that his cell was carefully locked each night. As the author noted following his description of the case, the friar would not have been found guilty if he had actually committed this crime. Due to the alleged somnambulism, the murder would have been considered involuntary. In most European countries, crimes committed during sleep were rarely considered as involving legal responsibility. England, for one, had long recognized the abolition of will during sleepwalking, or any other dream-like state, from which an individual might suffer. The only way to find a person guilty of a criminal act while sleepwalking was to demonstrate that there had been some premeditation about committing this crime. These two possibly apocryphal cases illustrate what the experts had to rely upon when they were asked to investigate allegations of abuse of magnetism and artificial somnambulism. The cases had considerable relevance to what were believed to be similar cases involving animal magnetism.

As indicated earlier, there had been very little evidence to support the dubious reputation animal magnetism had inherited from the very beginning of its mesmeric incarnation. The few cases of abuse that were reported were more anecdotal than legal in nature. Nevertheless, it is very likely that magnetism was used in a number of seduction attempts that went unreported at a legal level. Similarly, numerous accusations of immorality were later made with the discovery of chloroform (a chemical anesthetic). One of the reasons for such accusations (which were as difficult to substantiate as those involving magnetism) was the fact that the early anesthetics (ether, laughing gas, as well as chloroform) were available on the retail market and were often used for entertainment at private soirées. The same may be said for animal magnetism. In fact, in some trials, the judge would ask the medical experts to differentiate between the effects of ingesting an intoxicating substance and receiving a certain quantity of magnetism (Royer-Collard, 1843).

Albert Moll (1889/1982), in his classic book on hypnotism, mentioned only one legal case that occurred in Germany, around 1821. It involved a physician who allegedly sexually assaulted a patient during her magnetic sleep. To avoid the consequences of his act, he offered to procure her an abortion. This offer brought him before a court, but according to Moll, he was finally acquitted. What is intriguing here is the fact that Moll, whose book on hypnosis is certainly one of the best written and well researched of the nineteenth century, could not find more than one reported abuse case in his country. From what is now known, magnetism and hypnosis were, in the first half of the nineteenth century, very popular in Germany. However, they were recognized as curative agents by the German medical societies which had adopted laws governing their utilization.

In France, the story was very different. In 1849, J. Olivier published a treatise on magnetism in which he attempted to minimize the dangers of abuse and maximize the potential benefits of magnetic practices. Together with Charpignon, he reported seeing prostitutes who had suddenly reverted to a moral life, married women who refused to perform their matrimonial obligations to preserve their magnetic fluid, and unfaithful husbands who desired to reform themselves as in the following case:

> One of my somnambulists after having told me spontaneously in one of his sleeps that he had an extramarital affair took a key out of his pocket, gave it to me, and asked me to use magnetism to break this relationship that was both adverse to his obligations and prejudicious to his health. I responded quickly to his demands. The next day as soon as he was under sleep and without me asking he told me the following: "Last night as I was leaving here, I went as usual to the place where we meet; as I arrived, I prepared to place my master key in the doorlock. At the same time, consider my surprise when I felt an iron hand seizing my wrist and turning it away. I resisted but could not succeed in matching the key with the doorlock. I struggled for about ten minutes. Losing patience I turned around and without really knowing where I

was going, I went back running to my home as if some invisible force was pushing me." (Olivier, 1849, pp. 103–104)

Olivier realized that using magnetism could be a profitable way of helping justice. For the first time in the history of the movement, this author proposed that magnetism be used by the justice system to identify those who committed crimes. His enthusiasm, however, was tempered by realism. He wrote: "but as clairvoyant as a somnambulist can be, we should not be satisfied only by his affirmations alone; his mission would be only to provide information that could lead to discovery of a crime and of physical proofs" (pp. 68–69).

This comment by Olivier is as timely now as it was then, and it was to be incorporated into the forensic debate of the late nineteenth century.

Authors like Olivier and Charpignon were a minority. Most of the magnetists were still very much concerned by the potential use of magnetism for immoral purposes. Lafont-Gouzi (1839) warned the public against the predictions of somnambulists by pointing to their innate motivation to please their clients and to promote their alleged abilities: "Their desires to prove that they can see [clairvoyance] is so high that they will often invent fables. One must be on his guard to avoid being deceived" (pp. 6–7).

He indicated that he was appalled by the potential dangers of magnetism. In his opinion, it could be used to kill, mutilate, and even to suggest suicidal ideas in the minds of those who submitted to it (p. 56). Fortunately he represented a minority of extremists who wanted to see magnetism disappear altogether. Other writers like Sabatier-Désarnauds (1838) and Gigot-Suard (1860) were more realistic. Both emphasized the importance of rapport between the magnetized individual and the magnetist in eliciting potential abuses. In common with Deleuze a few years earlier, these authors believed that the basic personality of the subject was not dramatically altered by magnetism. If abuse was to take place, a propitious soil had first to be found.

In the same way that Olivier had pointed to the spontaneous confession of an unfaithful husband, Demarquay and Giraud-Teulon (1860), two physicians practicing magnetism, reported the case of one of their patients who had spontaneously provided details of her life, that could have been deleterious to her, if her audience had not been two honest physicians.

> A woman from the town, while hypnotized and questioned, began replying to our scientific curiosity by revealing secrets that could have satisfied quite a different type of curiosity. The confidences were *so serious, so dangerous for herself*, that we awoke the poor author of those much too free communications, as much because we were afraid for her than we were struck by our responsibility. (p. 33, italics in original)

The two authors obviously had been troubled by the intimate details described by their patient. They concluded that since she had voluntarily revealed details of her life that could have affected her present situation, there were inherent dangers in using magnetism. This report was to be cited repeatedly by the opponents of magnetism and hypnosis during the following years. It was seen also as an example of the truthfulness of revelations provided in hypnosis. The two physicians did not, however, question the motivation underlying the behavior of their patient or check her affirmations, for that matter. Their successors were not to be as naive.

Another case, reported by Royer-Collard (1843) in the *Annales Médico-Psychologiques*, attracted the attention of the public. The editor presented the case with a footnote that was revealing of the attitude of the scientific community toward magnetism. He wrote that by printing the report "we wanted to prove to our readers that we are not afraid to start the discussion on this delicate and quite controversial question of Animal Magnetism" (Royer-Collard, 1843, p. 85).

The case involved a young woman, A., 21 years old, suffering from hysteria with cataleptic tendencies. She was treated by a physician, Dr. M., one of the accused in the case, who had hired her as a servant for his household. During her first days as a servant, she displayed all of the symptoms of natural somnambulism that were followed by a period of illness that persisted many weeks. Soon after her recovery, Dr. M. and M. N., a pharmacist, subjected the young girl to many sessions of magnetic sleep even though, as she later testified, she did not want to be magnetized. The two accused had forced her *manu militari* to undergo their experiments. A few weeks later, as she was walking along a street, she suffered a convulsive crisis. Brought to Dr. C., she revealed what had happened to her. Dr. C. contacted the police and the two magnetists were arrested, and charged with forced magnetization.

The Court decided to consult three medical experts. The question for which it sought an answer was: "Can nervous illnesses found in individuals who have been coerced to submit to a magnetist be similar to illnesses resulting from the administration of harmful substances?" (Royer-Collard, 1843, p. 85).

The question was certainly an interesting one. The experts understood immediately that the Court equated magnetism with the presence of a magnetic fluid and wished to determine the status of this "substance." The answers of the experts were straightforward. As far as magnetism was concerned, they argued that it had not, as yet, been established as a recognized medical technique and as such could not be used to initiate a legal action against a person. The experts were categorical in their characterization of the fluid. They maintained that it did not exist, so it could not possibly have curative value. Accordingly, the case was explained in terms of the young woman's delicate health at the time, as well as by her history of hysteria. The experts could not reject the possibility of simulation and pointed out that many experts had rejected the idea that magnetism could be used in an abusive fashion. The two men were acquitted on the basis that even if magnetism were recognized by science, it was doubtful that it could be used against the will of the patient.

It is interesting to note that after more than 50 years of accusations of abuse and immorality, the first case of alleged abuse to reach the Court was rejected because the experts did not believe in the coercive properties of magnetism. As such, it certainly was a major victory for the magnetists who had struggled to establish the morality of their treatment.

A few years later, A. R. Bellanger (1854) published an account of one patient which was to reopen the whole question of the danger of magnetism. Again the case involved a young woman, Mme B., and a young physician, Dr. X. The events surrounding the case began before the wedding of Mme B. At the time she had developed nervous attacks after having witnessed a display of household violence. Nothing could prevent the onset of these nervous crises. Dr. X. decided to use magnetism in order to alleviate her sufferings. After many months he had finally succeeded in eliminating the crises.

One year later she married M. B., though without great enthusiasm. The crises returned two years later. As the couple was visiting Paris, they met with Dr. X. once again. He attempted to eliminate the crises as he had done before but this time without success. After a few days, however, Mme B. became somnambulistic and revealed her love for her magnetist to his utter surprise.

She was then reported to have begun living a double life, alternating between her usual self and somnambulism up to the day when she found herself pregnant. She could not understand what was happening to her. As far as she knew, she had not had sexual relations with her husband in many months. Her hysterical crises returned with such violence that she had to be institutionalized. Meanwhile, Dr. X. had left the country. Bellanger concluded the presentation of the case by stating: "Mme B. was always innocent; it is the somnambulist in her which was guilty" (p. 287).

This case was particularly interesting since it purported to illustrate how a subject could be totally amnesic to what happened during somnambulism. Bellanger maintained that the woman did not know what she was doing when in her altered state, although once magnetized she became totally aware of her situation and was able to discuss it with her lover. It would have been quite fascinating to see what the experts would have said had the case reached a court of law. It did not, however, and it was not until 1865 that a similar case of abuse would be reported.

Magnetism in England and the United States

As in France, animal magnetism in England and the United States provoked many debates and controversies. For the most part, however, they repeated the French history. This is not very surprising, since the propagators of the doctrine were French immigrants or visitors who had toured these countries, disseminating magnetic doctrines. It is fair to say that it took at least 50 years before Mesmer's teachings provoked heated discussion in these countries, and it was not until the end of the 1820s that Mesmerism began to gain popular support. The nature of the debate took different turns in England as opposed to the United States. In England, the controversy took place primarily within the medical community. Physicians opposed each other and lay magnetists were but spectators. The focus of the debate was upon the notion of quackery rather than on fringe medicine. It rested in the hands of the medical magnetists to demonstrate that the new doctrine carried curative values worthy of interest.

In terms of the forensic history of hypnosis, England has little to offer. One of the major reasons for the sparsity of cases of abuse may reside in the fact that the English legal system equated artificial somnambulism with natural somnambulism. As such, it did not focus much attention on magnetically elicited behaviors. It may also be a reflection of the fact that magnetism from the beginning stayed within the medical community when used therapeutically, or became part of a spiritual movement when it was propagated by lay individuals. A final reason, subtly suggested by Deleuze (1825), was the fact of being British, a factor that was conducive to a proper upbringing, in contrast to the French!

The destiny of animal magnetism was quite similar in the United States. There, as in England, it took approximately 40 to 50 years before mesmeric doctrine found its niche. In contrast to both England and France, Mesmerism in the United States (although used clinically) was assimilated by religious organizations and became part of what contemporary historians have since called the Second Great Awakening in the American Revivalist movement.[4] Nonetheless, magnetism found its way into American medicine more easily than in England and France. This was not surprising as such since, as with so many other scientific developments, Americans have tended to be innovators. It was a time of social excitement, the beginnings of industrialization, and Mesmerism became an ingredient of this social-psychological melting pot.

Animal Magnetism in England

In 1785, a Dr. Bell from France toured many major British cities offering demonstrations of the new art. He was followed in 1788 by de Mainauduc, a pupil of D'Eslon. Although the movement reached the general public, only a minority of physicians actually attempted to use it clinically. Among these, George Winter, a physician attached to The Lyceum Medical Society of London, followed the lectures of de Mainauduc in an attempt to master the principles of Mesmerism. Podmore (1909/1964) based himself on the writings of Winter in order to demonstrate that animal magnetism was being used with success by English physicians. He wrote: "But a physician at Bristol, George Winter, who is our authority for the details given in the preceding paragraph, appears to have used it with success in his private practice for some years, and there were doubtless others" (pp. 123–124).

Fortunately for Podmore, whose proselytizing is sometimes embarrassing, George Winter was dead when this passage was written. In fact, Winter had complained in his short book about how unsuccessful magnetism had been for him, compared to traditional medicine. At the beginning of his book, he wrote:

> The Author's thirst for knowledge being never satiated, he had the curiosity of even learning that science called Animal Magnetism. The cures transcribed into this work are for the purpose of informing the reader that the Author could not cure, *even, one of those patients by Animal Magnetism*, but that such cures were effected by the powers of medicines. (1801, p. 3, italics in original)

And again at the end of his pamphlet:

> These are the principles of Dr. de Mainauduc's lectures; however plausible they may appear, I have not been able to succeed in my expectations. I have kept a register of upwards of one hundred cures, which I could not effect by animal magnetism, but were performed by medicines. (p. 42)

So much for success, although given this remarkable zero rate, it would appear that either Winter was a poor learner, and/or that de Mainauduc was a poor teacher. Perhaps it was an interaction of both.[5]

Winter (1801) indicated that animal magnetism was popular at this time as a source of public entertainment and therapeutic treatment. The year 1790 appears to have marked the height of this initial period of enthusiasm. He reported that at one time a session organized by a certain M. Loutherbourg, at Hammersmith, was attended by three thousand people, and "that some persons sold their tickets for, from one, to three guineas each" (p. 18). (This demonstrates, among other things, that scalpers are not an invention of the postindustrial age!) The interest, however, seems to have faded rapidly. The English had, over the preceding centuries, known many healers. Valentin Greatrakes, a seventeenth-century Irishman (see Chapter 1) remained in popular memory for his healing power through "imposition of the hands." The medical profession greeted Mesmerism with a number of articles describing it as the latest form of spurious healing. It has been seen already how *The Lancet* of 1828–1829 viewed Cloquet's breast surgery with Mme Plantin, seeking to dismiss it with the anomalous moralistic reproach that the side effect of pregnancy in female patients had once made magnetism in France a popular pastime.

The arrival of Mesmerism in England coincided with an offshoot of a fundamentally similar system from the United States. This became know as Perkinism, a variant of the old magnetic medicine. In 1795, Elisha Perkins, president of the Windham County Medical Society in the United States, began writing about his new discovery. Using tractors (small devices fashioned of dissimilar metals, one of a gold, the other of a silver color) he gently stroked the affected parts of the patient's body toward the heart. The stroking seemed to bring relief. The son of the founder of Perkinism, Benjamin D. Perkins visited England to publicize his father's doctrine. He met with surprising success which, in turn, led to the establishment of a Perkinean institute in England. Very rapidly, however, opposition rose and one Dr. John Haygart took it upon himself to demonstrate the fallacies of Perkins's system. Following a logic similar to that exhibited by the members of the Franklin Commission in France, he demonstrated that imagination and suggestion were the two main ingredients of Perkinism as had been found for Mesmerism. He believed, however, that these two phenomena, imagination and suggestion, should be studied in their own right (Haygart, 1800).

Only at the end of the 1820s did magnetism find supporters within the medical community. In 1829, Richard Chenevix who had learned to magnetize with the Abbé di Faria, began to treat young children in Ireland. He then moved from Ireland to London where he continued to treat patients by magnetism in different local hospitals. In 1837, du Potet visited England. He contacted John Elliotson, a British physician and surgeon, who had expressed interest in magnetism, and gained permission to mesmerize patients at University College Hospital. Elliotson was interested in du Potet's work and began to experiment with the new techniques. His experiments on animal magnetism (which he often combined with phrenology) enmeshed him in many sour disputes with his colleagues. In a sense, it destroyed a career which, to this point, had been extremely successful. Part of the problem may have resided in Elliotson's own stubborn character which, in turn, could only be matched by the equal stubbornness of the then editor of *The Lancet*, Thomas Wakley. The dispute over animal magnetism became their personal vendetta. During the 15 years that the conflict lasted, neither of them missed the occasion to attack the other in often quite savage personal terms.

As with the events in France some 70 years earlier, the question of seduction preoccupied the British Victorians. As Wakley described it in *The Lancet*, Mesmerism was regarded as disreputable:

> Mesmerism, according to its advocates, acts most intensily [*sic*] on nervous and impressionable females. What father of a family, then, would admit even the shadow of a mesmeriser within his threshold? Who would expose his wife, or his sister, his daughter, or his orphan ward, to contact of an animal magnetiser? If the *volition* of an ill-intentioned person be sufficient to prostrate his victims at his feet, should we not shun such pretenders more than lepers, or the uncleanest of the unclean? Assuredly the powers claimed by MESMER will eventually prove their own ruin. In endeavouring to raise themselves above ordinary mortals, they lay claims to attributes and powers which must place them, forever, beyond the pale of civilized society. (*The Lancet*, December 15, 1838, p. 450, italics in original; see also Parssinen, 1979)

History was repeating itself.

At the same time that Elliotson struggled for the recognition of animal magnetism, a visit to England by the famous French lay hypnotist Lafontaine, in 1841, generated immense interest within both medical circles and the general public. Among the medically trained people who witnessed Lafontaine's performances was James Braid, a Manchester surgeon, who subsequently began to scientifically investigate animal magnetism. *The Lancet* delighted in attacking Lafontaine's tour of England.

Monsieur Lafontaine, the showman, is in London, for a short time.... It is a reproach to this nation that such persons are capable of practicing their devices amongst us for a single month. When will the age of humbug, credulity, and folly end? The members of the profession in London ought not to meet in consultation any man who still gives an open sanction to the monstrous delusion called "animal magnetism." (*The Lancet*, 1841-1842, p. 216; see also Parssinen, 1979, p. 58)

These attacks did not discourage Braid from studying the phenomenon very carefully or from publishing his results. It was to change the view of animal magnetism for good in the minds of the British medical profession. Braid's careful experimentation led him to conclude that animal magnetism was more of a psychological process than a physical one, although he maintained that it entailed physiological changes. Braid coined the word "hypnotism," a term which was adopted by most medical people interested in the phenomenon.[6]

His work led to the recognition of hypnotism as a genuine psychological process, separated from the claims of the magnetists, and the phreno-magnetists, such as Elliotson, and ironically enough from Braid himself, at the end of his career. His work permitted the separation of the scientific investigation of the phenomenon from its mounting spiritualist association.

In the end, Braid had a major impact in England and the United States, but was merely ignored in France, possibly because some of his views resembled those of Faria. Indeed in the preface of his 1843 book, Braid defended himself against the accusation of plagiarism of certain of Faria's ideas.

A final important contributor to the development of hypnosis in Great Britain was James Esdaile, a surgeon practicing in India, who reported an impressive number of surgical operations performed with magnetism as the sole *anesthetic*. His observations were mitigated, however, by the fact that they coincided with the discovery of chemical anesthesia, so that his remarkable work became lost in the general enthusiasm of this latest discovery. Even less known is the fact that, while in India, Esdaile became involved in an interesting legal case. He reported it in his 1846 book in order to demonstrate that it was possible to literally abduct people by the use of hypnosis.

In this case, an itinerant barber was accused of having stolen a child by using unknown charms. As the child described it, the barber approached him, muttering charms and making passes across his eyes. Following these procedures, the boy felt compelled to follow the barber wherever he went. He had been rescued by a passerby who had noticed the vague expression on his face (described as idiotic).

Esdaile was asked to testify in court on the possibility of being able to carry off a person in the manner described in the evidence. His answer was in the positive. He based himself on an experiment he had performed on a prisoner. He had successfully induced a magnetic state in which the prisoner behaved as an automaton. Upon waking, amnesia was complete for whatever had happened during the magnetic episode. Esdaile demonstrated his technique with two subjects in court. He was so successful that the barber was sentenced to nine years in jail.

The case, however, did not end there. Although the sentence was maintained at the Appelate level, the government decided that Esdaile's demonstrations had unduly influenced the jury, and reversed the verdict. The barber was freed.

Magnetism in the United States

The development of Mesmerism in the United States was uneventful during the first 40 years or so of its introduction into the new country. It will be recalled that Lafayette had attempted to introduce Mesmerism in America in 1784, but had been opposed by Thomas Jefferson who had distributed copies of the Franklin Commission's conclusions. In the 1820s, lectures on Mesmerism were relatively common (Gravitz & Gerton, 1986; Kaplan, 1974). Not until the mid-1830s, however, did animal magnetism find a popular audience. In 1836, Charles Poyen, a French magnetist, toured New England demonstrating the new doctrine. As in England, the United States had seen Perkinism rise at the end of the eighteenth century. Quite rapidly the medical establishment reacted to this "discovery" as it had reacted toward Mesmerism. In 1796, for example, the members present at the Fifth Annual Meeting of the Connecticut Medical Society voted that

> It having been represented to this society, that one of their members, had gleaned up from the miserable remains of Animal Magnetism, a practice, consisting of stroking with pointed metallic instruments, the pained parts of human bodies; giving out, that such strokings will radically cure the most obstinate pain to which our frame is incident . . . causing false reports to be propagated, of the effects of such strokings, especially when they have been performed on some public occasion, and on men of distinction; also, that an excursion has been made abroad, and a patent obtained from under such auspices as membership of this society, and patent above mentioned, the delusion is progressing to the southward, which may occasion disgrace to the society, and mischief abroad; wherefore this society announces to the public, that they consider all such practices as barefaced imposition, disgraceful to the faculty, and delusive to the ignorant. They therefore direct their secretary, to cite any member of this society, practicing as above, before them at their next meeting, to answer for his conduct, and render reasons why he should not be expelled from the society for such disgraceful practices. (cited in Carlson & Simpson, 1970, p. 16)

Just as Haygart had in England, Benjamin Rush (1805) emphasized the importance of the imagination and the will in the production of cures using these new systems. Thus, it took a number of years before the magnetic movement succeeded in gaining a fair number of American adherents. When

Poyen lectured in New England, he met with limited success. He left the United States three years after his arrival to be replaced by Robert Collyer, an English phrenologist, who set out on a lecture tour along the Atlantic coast. Collyer was not a magnetist, but soon realized how closely related the two systems could be.

Although magnetism had met with resistance (see, for example, Charles Durant, 1837), it soon took a new direction. Almost from its beginning, the movement was seen as a way of improving man's spiritual nature and it became incorporated into Protestant revivalism. The *Boston Recorder* in February 1837 printed the following letter:

> George was *converted from materialism to Christianity* by the facts in Animal Magnetism developed under his [Poyen's] practice . . . *it proves the power of mind over matter* . . . informs our faith in the spirituality and immortality of our nature, and encourages us to *renewed efforts* to live up to its transcendent powers. (cited in Fuller, 1982, p. 22, italics in original)

The tendency toward the spiritualization of the magnetic doctrine increased with the years, leading to the foundation of such movements as Christian Science under the direction of Mary Baker Eddy. At the same time, however, many physicians practiced magnetism for its curative values. The translation of Deleuze's book in 1837 by Hartshorn pointed to the perceived importance of the new therapeutic agent. The testimonies of the American public and of the American physicians followed almost word for word those of their European counterparts.

The issue of morality was more rapidly broached in the United States than in England. A number of books and newspaper articles began pointing to the moral dangers associated with this new practice. The criticisms were identical to those that had been raised in France and England. In 1845, an anonymous pamphlet published by a Boston magnetist appeared to confirm public suspicions. In this pamphlet, the author recognized how he had abused his female subjects (see Anonymous, 1845, *Confessions of a Magnetizer, Being an Exposé of Animal Magnetism*; also cited in Fuller, 1982, p. 189).

This image of the powerful magnetist was emphasized also in the literature of the time. When Nathaniel Hawthorne and Edgar Allan Poe decided to incorporate the dark side of magnetism into their stories or novels, the public reacted strongly. One of Poe's short stories, "The Facts in the Case of Mr. Valdemar" (later reprinted in England as "The Last Conversation of a Somnambule," and later still as, "Mesmerism, in Articulo Mortis"), created a major commotion. In this story, Mr. Valdemar requests a friend to magnetize him to avoid dying a death that he knows is impending. Unfortunately, rather than placing him in contact with immortality, Mesmerism traps his soul within his dead body. When a friend finally comes to his aid and demagnetizes him, his body disintegrates instantly. A major controversy arose around this story, and many readers wanted to know if it was wholly fictional. As Fuller

(1982) put it: "Poe wryly refused to comment, but was reported to have enjoyed the furor immensely" (p. 38; see also Chapter 10, this volume).

Such concern, however, was not unique to the public. In 1848, magnetism reached the attention of the American courts. As far as we know, these were the first instances in the United States where magnetism was brought before the legal system. Both cases were reported in the *American Journal of Insanity* of 1848. The first case illustrated how Mesmerism and spirituality were linked together from the beginning of the history of Mesmerism in America. In Cincinnati, Pascal B. Smith was sued by his wife Harriet because he was squandering his property in obedience to certain mesmeric revelations provided by a Mr. James F. Mahan. The revelations were supposedly of divine origin and had been received through mesmeric clairvoyance. The Court found Mr. Smith insane and incapable of managing his affairs.[7]

The second case, *The People v. John Johnson*, was brought to trial in 1846. John Johnson was indicted for the murder of Betsey Bolt, his alleged lover.[8] One of the witnesses, Ann Augusta Burdick, had been kidnapped and nearly killed by Johnson and an accomplice whom she could not identify with certainty. She thought, however, that it might have been her mother. Although the reading of the case is quite confusing at times, it seems that the witness could not recite a consistent story. She was known to suffer from hysterical crises or, as the medical experts put it, she was "subject to hysterics" (p. 344). In an attempt to obtain a uniform story, both the family physician and her husband resorted to Mesmerism.

> I put the questions at Mr. Burdick's request. He and I tried to mesmerize her. He succeeded. I pricked him with a pin and she was startled. She was half an hour in giving the relation. All of it was while she was in the mesmeric state. She was deranged, and talking on every subject, before and after.

Unfortunately her mesmeric version differed from all previous ones. When the experts were called forward to explain this occurrence, they expressed the opinion that she was a hysterical woman. They then confirmed that hysterics tended to fantasize and confabulate, confounding fact and fantasy. John Johnson was acquitted.

The significance of this case is that it is the first known attempt to utilize hypnosis to elicit memories linked to a crime. Although Olivier in France had suggested such a use, it had not been attempted there. One interesting detail of the mesmeric procedure is worth noticing in this case. The physician, in his testimony, indicated that he had determined that the witness was mesmerized by pricking the magnetist, not the magnetized person. This technique underlined the beliefs of the time that a mesmerized individual was in complete rapport with his or her mesmerist. She reported that she felt, through him, that a needle had pricked his skin, as if she had been pricked herself. This type of pseudoscientific test would plague the forensic debates of both the nineteenth and twentieth centuries (see Chapters 10, 11, and 12, this volume).

Thirty years passed before another legal case was reported in a scientific journal. This next case coincided with the renewal of interest in hypnosis in France, and particularly, with the heated debate on the use of hypnosis to abuse patients or subjects and to coerce individuals into the commission of criminal acts. Only toward the end of the nineteenth century did some interest and controversy surrounding the coercive powers of hypnosis emerge in the United States.

Spiritualism, Hypnosis, and the Catholic Church

The expression of an official position by the Catholic Church on hypnosis coincided with the popularity of the spiritualist movements in France, England, and the United States.

A number of events may have led the Church to develop an official position. From the very beginnings in France, Mesmerism had been linked with spiritualism. It occurred under the direction of Chevalier de Barbarin, who had joined forces with the Swedenborgists. Artificial somnambulism had been identified with supernatural powers and many somnambulists had reported seeing and talking with their guardian angels, Jesus Christ, or his mother Mary (see, for example, Ricard, 1836). Many magnetists had written that their somnambulists could see the spirits of the dead, although during the first half of the nineteenth century, the spirits had not yet learned to talk through the somnambulists; at the most, they could produce table-rappings. When, in the second half of the nineteenth century, spiritualism became organized around the Fox sisters in the United States, the movement took on the dimensions of an epidemic in most other countries. The Church's officials were rightfully alarmed.

Whereas many lay magnetists were promulgating spiritual beliefs, the scientific community was attempting to explain away most of the religious epidemics of the previous centuries in terms of hysteria, magnetism, and somnambulism. A scientific consensus evolved that regarded miracles as examples of healing through magnetic-like processes and apparitions as the products of the imagination of naturally gifted somnambulists.

Perceiving itself besieged on both sides, the Roman Catholic clergy was divided on the matter. Accordingly, within Catholic circles, one group believed that magnetism was nothing less than a disguised demonic possession (Frère, 1837; Tissot, 1841). On the other hand, there were members of the clergy who emphatically espoused the magnetic cause, regarding it as a personal gift from God.

In 1840, the Catholic Church published its first official position on magnetism. It recognized that the physical means it employed did not contravene morality and, hence, magnetism was not illicit. However, it maintained that if the answers sought through Mesmerism addressed the supernatural, then it was to be rejected as heretical and illicit. In 1856, however, alarmed by the popularity of spiritualism and the different abuses committed through the utilization of magnetism, the Church published a stronger official stance on mesmerism. In the document submitted to the members of the clergy, the Catholic Church warned against the abuses, either physical or spiritual, that had befallen the magnetic movement. It rejected such use, but did not reject the medical use of it as long as the means employed were consistent with the results sought (see Moreau, 1894).

By the 1860s, very little remained of the original mesmeric system. What may, however, be of interest at this point, is the fact that animal magnetism, and what was to become hypnotism, had been recognized both by the Catholic Church and the legal authorities as a valid therapeutic technique. It is somewhat ironic that it would take approximately 30 more years before the scientific communities at large proceeded to reach the same conclusion.

One final point may be emphasized before the forensic and theoretical debate of the next 20 to 30 years is examined. In the various trials that occurred in three different countries, it is intriguing to note that the use of hypnosis in each of these trials paralleled, in a unique way, the major beliefs held by the respective communities. In the United States, where magnetism was either linked to spiritualism or practiced in a therapeutic context without too much controversy, the first two trials involved either religious delusions or the use of hypnosis to regain a normal memory for traumatic events.

In India, magnetism was regarded as being intertwined with the Hindu tradition of charmers, and as such, translated into the state of fascination used in the kidnapping of a young boy.

In France, where somnambulists had always been seen in terms of their hysterical qualities and were perceived as the victims of their own weakened constitution, the cases reported focused upon the abuses of the hypnotized person by the all powerful hypnotist. It is important to keep these cross-cultural interactions in mind when examining the forensic debate of the late nineteenth century.

NOTES

1. There are already a number of books that have traced the history of animal magnetism and particularly its struggles with the medical establishment, in both England and the United States. A number of scholarly articles have also been published on more specific topics in the history of mesmeric conflict. It must be noted, however, that the history of animal magnetism in the United States is particularly rich and interesting and is the one that has been the least investigated. Although one of the following chapters will cover the psycho-legal history of hypnosis in the United States, there is great need for a careful exploration of the general history of hypnosis in this country.

2. The history surrounding the prize offered by Burdin has been described at length in

Podmore, and need not be repeated here. For those interested in the details of these events, Podmore is a good source of reference. It may be added here that one can find also in Podmore a rejection of Burdin and Dubois's book on the basis of their too obvious antagonism to the doctrine of animal magnetism. Although the book is extremely harsh toward magnetism and magnetists, it is quite accurate historically. Podmore's attempts to denigrate these two authors by emphasizing their intellectual dishonesty may in fact reflect that he, himself, at the time he wrote his book, was an ardent believer in psychic phenomena. Although two wrongs do not make a right, both books are invaluable sources of information and bear testimony to the acrimony of the fights between the proponents and opponents of the magnetic doctrine.

3. In his book, Scobardi (1839) alleged that Dubois had been nominated at the Royal Academy of Medicine provided that he published a book rejecting animal magnetism. As the editor of the book wrote in a footnote:

> Although quite unbelievable, it seems quite certain that the *good fathers* succeeded in their endeavor: M. Dubois (d'Amiens) was nominated to the Royal Academy of Medicine on November 8, 1836, which gave great satisfaction to M. Double, Récamier and *tutti quanti.* (p. 93, italics in original)

Whether true or not, the Commission was formed at the beginning of 1837. Although one may doubt the authenticity and veracity of Scobardi's writings, it is more difficult to doubt the negative attitudes that surrounded the work of this last Commission. As M. Roux, then presiding the Academy, had said at the meeting before the formation of the Commission of Inquiry: "Let us be done with magnetism."

4. Numerous articles and books have been written on the history of animal magnetism in England. We do not feel that it is necessary to repeat here what can easily be found elsewhere. Since the main goal is to follow the legal and moral problems surrounding the use of magnetism, we will satisfy ourselves by referring readers to the following texts: Podmore (1909/1964), Bramwell (1921), Tinterow (1970), Elliotson (1982), Braid (1960), Palfreman (1977), Parssinen (1979), Kaplan (1974), and Sutton (1981). These books and articles convey the flavor of the evolution and struggles of magnetism in England. As far as the history of animal magnetism in the United States is concerned, it is unfortunate that very few books or articles have been written on the topic. Recently, Fuller (1982) published a book entitled *Mesmerism and the American Cure of Souls*. It traces the history of magnetism in its interaction with the spiritualist movements of the nineteenth century. For the historian of hypnosis in America, this first book is a major source.

5. This obvious deviation from the truth is unfortunately not the only one that can be found in Podmore's book. Fuller (1982) has also noted the biases adopted by Podmore in order to secure a positive view of the phenomenon. He wrote:

> I might forewarn the interested reader that Podmore, an active member of the Society for Psychical Research, imposes his own ideological blinders upon the material. Convinced that thought transference is the prime reality behind the occult and supernatural, Podmore does not encourage his readers to take alternative explanations seriously. (p. 186)

This warning notwithstanding, Podmore's account of the beginnings of animal magnetism is informative and entertaining.

6. It should be noted here that already in the early 1820s Hénin de Cuvillers, editor of the *Annales du Magnétisme*, had already listed many derivatives from the Greek word *hypnos*. However, he never used any of them in his writings.

7. The report can be found in the Editorial Correspondence, Letter III, April 19, from the steam boat *Ohio, American Journal of Insanity*, 1848, pp. 83-85.

8. The case can be found in the *American Journal of Insanity*, April 1848, pp. 303-346.

III

The Golden Years of Hypnosis: 1878 to 1905

8

The Entry of Hypnosis into the Judicial System

The trials reported in the last chapter did not capture public attention until the late 1870s. Hypnosis was still controversial at the beginning of the 1860s and few physicians were ready to advocate its use publicly.

During the following 20 years a major change in the conceptualization of hypnosis appeared in France. Divergent theoretical orientations developed from the traditional descriptive approach to the phenomenon. For the first time since the Abbé di Faria, the field of hypnosis began to be incorporated into the mainstream of medicine and psychology. Faria's theoretical views had not been met with acceptance by his peers. Several decades later, the new approaches gave eloquent testimony to his pioneering work.

Few people paid attention to the legal debate that ensued from the various trials involving hysteria and natural somnambulism between 1860 and 1880. This was soon to change dramatically. In the legal battles that took place at the end of the nineteenth century, certain trials attracted popular attention, and the trials that took place during the previous 50 years were examined and re-examined. These trials, which had rarely involved animal magnetism or hypnosis, were to be rethought and explained in terms of the new knowledge. This enthusiastic reconstruction of history proved, however, to be detrimental to the new schools of thought.

Before this fascinating period in the history of hypnosis is reviewed, two facts are worth mentioning. The first is sociocultural. The end of the nineteenth century was extremely important in the development of the sciences as they are currently conceptualized. In the same manner that Mesmer's arrival in Paris coincided with the triumph of the Enlightenment (see Darnton, 1968, 1984), the renewal of interest in hypnosis at the end of the nineteenth century paralleled the development of experimental psychology. The recognition of psychology as a science that could be studied as any other science was a clear break from the traditional philosophical approach to the human mind. Although a vast proportion of the most influential books of the time were more psycho-philosophical than psychological, this new trend continued to flourish. The legal debate furthered the separation of psychology and philosophy by forcing the scientists involved to develop laboratory models that fitted their theoretical arguments. Philosophical speculation was relegated to the back burner.

The second point illustrates the importance of the media's strategic role in modeling the views of lay people on phenomena such as hypnosis. The renewal of interest in the study of hypnosis might not have reached so many and endured for so long without the help of the press. As is the case today, the forensic use of hypnosis produced its fair share of headlines. It is comforting to see that the role played by the media at the time was quite similar to the one it plays today. Above all, it realized, then and now, that hypnosis did not lack entertainment value.

In 1886, 26 years after the publication of his *Histoire du merveilleux dans les temps modernes*, the historian Louis Figuier was still as interested in hypnosis as he had been in animal magnetism, artificial somnambulism, and their related phenomena. In an article published in *L'année scientifique et industrielle*, he wrote:

> M. Charcot never utters the words animal magnetism. . . . Animal magnetism smells of quackery; hypnotism, on the other hand has a scientific resonance; that is why our physicians chastize the former and praise the latter! But for those of us who prefer straight talk, who prefer to name things by their names, and to call a cat a cat, we will say to those trouble-makers of hypnotism that they are only reviving and illustrating those well-known phenomena that had been for, too long a time, negated stubbornly. They are finding finally the place they deserved and were denied by the blind and systematic opposition of physicians and Academies in the first half of this century. As far as we are concerned, animal magnetism and hypnotism are one and the same thing. Consequently, it is our contention that hypnotists, those *legitimate sons of Mesmer* . . . are not smarter than the magnetists, their precursors. As for the alleged miracles by which they hope to dazzle us, they represent a scientific plagiarism disguised under a Greek name. (1886, p. 387, italics in original; cited in Moreau, 1891, pp. 54-55)

Right or wrong, Figuier was reacting to the current scientific debate surrounding hypnosis.

The Beginnings of Judicial Action: 1860 to 1880

At the beginning of the 1860s a number of young physicians were interested in the therapeutic value of hypnosis. Among these, A. A. Liébeault, a country physician, was to become the inspiration of a new generation of researchers and clinicians.[1] From the beginning of his medical career, Liébeault showed an interest in hypnosis. The story is that he usually offered his patients the traditional medical treatment for a fee or a hypnotic treatment without charge. It is said that he soon had a thriving practice from which he derived little income. Indeed, he was regarded by his medical colleagues as a fool twice over: a fool for using hypnosis and also for not charging fees for this service. In 1866, he published his first book, the sum total of his observations and thoughts on the phenomenon of hypnosis.[2]

Liébeault believed that hypnosis, or "artificial sleep" as he often called it, did not differ from normal or natural sleep. He maintained that two basic conditions were necessary to produce artificial sleep in a patient: a conviction that he or she could sleep and a focusing of attention on a single physical stimulus or on a single thought. Suggestion, so as to help the individual focus his or her attention, was the means used by the hypnotist to implement the idea of sleep in a patient. The basic process at play in the eliciting of artificial sleep was the narrowing of the field of attention to such a degree that the hypnotized individual relinquished critical judgment and initiative to the hypnotist. Once hypnosis was initiated and suggestion used, "the sleeper, as immobile as the God 'Terminus,' was transformed into an automaton that one could mold and manipulate at will" (1866, p. 76).

This statement became extremely important in the years to come. It was to dominate the thinking of the Nancy school during the forensic debate. As will be seen in the remainder of this chapter, the notion of the automaton was at the core of many trials involving hypnosis and its alleged coercive power.

At a theoretical level, Liébeault was the first investigator since Faria to identify what are now called cognitive processes underlying the ability to become hypnotized. Many of the phenomena that had been documented in the past were seen as the product of the interaction between specific suggestions and certain abilities of the hypnotized individual. Although Faria had already emphasized the importance of individual differences in hypnotic response, Liébeault extended his ideas by linking certain hypnotic phenomena to specific cognitive abilities. For example, in describing the phenomenon of clairvoyance, a hallmark of the de Puységurian subject, Liébeault recognized that it was related to the hypermnesia that he believed could be produced in hypnosis. He maintained that the subjects who were hypermnesic were also the ones who could easily produce suggested hallucinations. The interaction of these two phenomena had, in the past, been misinterpreted as clairvoyance. In the same way, he observed that vividness of imagery was a sure sign of hypnotizability. The more vivid the suggested images, the more hypnotizable the subject (Liébeault, 1866, pp. 104–105).

Liébeault believed that everyone was hypnotizable to some degree. He wrote in 1866: "I am convinced that with sufficient practice, everyone could sleep at anytime and at will. For most people, however, the sleep produced would most of the time be light" (p. 298).

This is an important point to remember since the Salpêtrière school would seek consistently to distort it by implying that the Nancy school supported the view that everyone could be transformed into an automaton by suggestion.

The most intriguing chapter of Liébeault's (1866) book was one on the interaction of hypnosis and legal medicine. Although Liébeault did not quote a single case of abuse, his chapter on the dangers of hypnosis was the most strongly worded of the whole book. He experimented with antisocial suggestions, but his experiments were naive. He suggested that subjects empty their pockets, untie their shoes, or remove their rings. What appears to have been his most dramatic experiment was his role playing of a priest to elicit confessions from his hypnotized subjects. Even then, the best he could do was to elicit "charming trifles" (p. 524) from one of his female patients. When it came to post-hypnotic suggestion, Liébeault was certain that the "wisest will become immoral, the most innocent will be shameless" (p. 525). He summarized his position thus:

> In the attentional passivity that they experience, they cannot reject the ideas imposed by the beguiler [*l'endormeur*]; they are under his power, they are toys in his hands: illusions, hallucinations, false beliefs, loss of moral values, impossibility of resisting vicious suggestions, carrying on of behaviors harmful to self or others, etc. The beguiler can invoke anything he wishes in the mind of the somnambulists and they will carry it on, not only when they are asleep, but even after they are awakened. (p. 519)

Liébeault's position stemmed from his belief that hypnosis was based on the implantation of a fixed idea in the mind of the subject. By artificially focusing all attentional energies on one specific idea, the subject relinquished his or her freedom of choice and was obliged to carry out any suggestion that had been implanted in his or her mind. Subjects were thus seen as legally and morally irresponsible. The hypnotist, on the other hand, was responsible for whatever the somnambulistic subject did.

It may at first be intriguing that the idea of suggestion became associated with the conceptualization of the hypnotized subject as an automaton (or as Liébeault would later describe it, "as clay in the hands of a potter"). It is less of a surprise when one considers what was believed at the time about altered states of consciousness. Liébeault identified artificial sleep with natural sleep. He saw somnambulism as akin to natural somnambulism, a state described in most legal texts as one in which the sleeper is an automaton (see, for example, Legrand du Saulle, 1863, and Tardieu, 1878). As was seen previously (Chapter 7), numerous crimes were committed by and against natural somnambulists. Liébeault drew his examples from this literature to illustrate the dangers of hypnosis. He made the additional assumption that hypnosis, like natural somnambulism, was a specific physiological state that, once induced, was not under the voluntary control of the subject. The legal cases that arose at about this time were interpreted in the light of the experts' knowledge of natural somnambulism.

While Liébeault was developing his theoretical views of hypnosis based on the notion of suggestion, a second trend of thought from which the Salpêtrière school would ultimately emerge was in the making. Two different groups of physicians sought to link hypnosis to a pathological state akin to hysteria. Lasègue (1865) and Richet (1875) interpreted hypnotic catalepsy and somnambulism as innate hysterical neuroses. They were the first investigators to state that responsivity to hypnosis was a sure sign of hysteria. At the same time, two other physicians, Azam and Broca, began experimenting with hypnosis and especially with hypnotic analgesia.

Azam had become interested in hypnosis while treating a young woman afflicted by numerous hysterical symptoms, notably catalepsy and somnambulism. One of his colleagues, having heard about the symptoms presented by Azam's patient, introduced him to the work of James Braid. Azam experimented for two years with this patient, recruiting the help of a number of his colleagues, among whom was Broca. Broca, more interested in the application of hypnotic analgesia in surgery, performed a series of operations using hypnosis as the sole anesthetic. His work (with another surgeon, Velpeau) led to a first communication at the Académie des Sciences in 1859. Although numerous operations were attempted during these years, hypnosis could not compete with chloroform and this particular use was soon discarded.

Azam's work on the other hand gave impetus to psychological research that in turn, led to the major theories of the 1880s. In 1860, he published a short note on hypnotism in which he described the first case of "double consciousness" in one of his patients, Félida. The interest of this case resides mainly in the fact that Azam followed its progression for more than 35 years. He reported periodically on Félida's progress until well into the 1890s. As has been seen before, other investigators had noticed this unusual condition where consciousness appears to be split into different, even separate, parts. Azam's description of his patient coincided with the discovery that the brain's cerebral hemispheres could function independently. It did not take long before both facts were juxtaposed and the conclusions drawn that hypnosis could tap differential brain processes.

Félida's case is also interesting from a forensic point of view. It appeared to demonstrate that a female patient could have sexual relations while in her "second state" (*condition seconde* as Azam described it), and not be conscious of what had happened to her.

Azam first met Félida in 1858. Among her major symptoms, she suffered from violent headaches and spat blood profusely, although Azam thought that this particular symptom was more psychological than physiological.[3] She worked as a seamstress and had the reputation of being a diligent worker. The first signs of hysteria appeared during her adolescence when she began to suffer a "crisis" every five or six days. By 1858, however, these crises occurred daily. Within a few minutes she would suddenly become more animated, physically stronger, and more verbal. She was more energetic and even "alive to excess" (Binet, 1896, p. 8). Her state of mind when in a crisis contrasted dramatically with her normal state in which she was taciturn, sad, and preoccupied. In her normal state, she had memory lapses that distressed her. In her second state, she was not amnesic. She knew of everything she had done. It was during one of her crises that she had become pregnant. Although many authors have reported that she had been seduced while in her second state, Azam did not describe it as a seduction case. Quite to the contrary, he believed that Félida knew very well what she was doing (at least her secondary personality was aware). The first signs of pregnancy, however, surprised and distressed her. She thought herself sick and it took the indelicacies of a friend who confronted her before she accepted the fact. In her second state, however, Félida welcomed the pregnancy. She loved her fiancé, was happy about what was happening to her, and looked forward to her upcoming wedding.

Félida always described her second state as her normal state. As the years went by, she spent progressively more time in it. She had learned to conceal the switching from one condition to the other so well that only her husband knew of her illness. As she grew older, the second state started resembling the old normal one. The hard life of a mother and a seamstress had taken its toll. It became more and more difficult to differentiate the two conditions. This is as far as Azam reported the case; subsequent developments are not known.

Even if hypnosis was beginning to gain new ground, it was still not accepted by the scientific community. As Richet wrote in 1875: "It takes guts to talk about somnambulism" (p. 348). But the seeds would soon bear fruit. One of the most prestigious figures of medicine in France, J.-M. Charcot, was beginning to investigate hypnosis. Azam's work would soon take on more importance and his patient Félida would not be forgotten.

Before setting the stage for the confrontation between the Nancy and the Salpêtrière schools, a brief exploration of the status of medico-legal expertise at the end of the 1870s is required. This is best effected by looking at some of the actual cases that took place during this period, both in France and in the United States. These cases attracted considerable publicity during the ensuing years and became the focus of the theoretical battle.

Some Legal Cases: Creating Precedents

The cases described in this section all occurred before the theoretical boom of the 1880s. They were thus reported and explained in terms of the knowledge of the period. Hypnosis was seen both as similar to natural somnambulism and as sharing some aspects of the most obvious hysterical symptoms. The similarities between the two somnambulistic states has already been emphasized. What is less known, however, is the fact that two other pathological states had also been written about extensively: catalepsy and lethargy. Both of these states were seen as variants of the hysterical crisis and, as such, had been considered from a medico-legal point of view. A few years later when Charcot conceptualized three "stages" of the hypnotic syndrome (lethargy, catalepsy, and somnambulism), he borrowed these three components from the hysteria literature.

It will be seen how these three hysterical states were used to explain the behaviors and experiences of Joséphine Hughes, a victim of rape and kidnapping in the celebrated Castellan affair.

Apart from the experts' familiarity with hysteria and its diverse manifestations, three other areas of scientific knowledge were to come into play in trials involving hypnosis. Since the discovery of chemical anesthetics, numerous cases of abuse had been reported. Physicians, surgeons, dentists, as well as lay people had appeared in criminal courts for alleged sexual abuse of their chemically anesthetized patients. In the case of lay people, it had mostly to do with the social use of anesthetics. Indeed, ether, chloroform, and the famous "laughing gas" were much enjoyed by the general population, so much so, that most contemporary medico-legal textbooks carried a section on the possibility of sexually abusing an anesthetized individual. Liébeault (1866) cited the case of a dentist who had used chloroform to abuse one of his patients (p. 69).

Experts usually differentiated two types of cases: In the first, a professional profited from the anesthetized state of his patient to abuse her. Here the crime was clear. The patient had voluntarily submitted to the anesthesia for medical reasons and the physician had violated the therapeutic relationship. Most of the reported cases of abuse occurred under such circumstances. In the second type, an anesthetic agent was used by a layman to coerce a woman into having sexual relations. The genuineness of this latter type of abuse was disputed by the scientific experts (see, for example, Taylor, 1881; Thoinot, 1919). All authors, however, agreed that it was possible to rape an anesthetized patient.

They agreed also that anesthesia produced erotic sensations in women; consequently any accusation of abuse had to be weighed carefully against the possibility of confabulation triggered by the normal, pleasurable sensations an anesthetized woman felt at the time of awakening! To quote Thoinot (1919):

> Remember that very often the sleep of anesthesia is accompanied by voluptuous sensations: these sensations may persist on awaking. The woman then believes in good faith that some one has profited by her sleep to perpetrate a criminal act upon her, and she accuses the person who anesthetized her. So you should adopt as an invariable rule in your practice, never to proceed without an assistant or a witness to anesthetize (with chloroform, ether, etc.) a girl or a woman. (p. 94)

The last sentence is certainly reminiscent of what Deleuze (1825) had recommended when a male magnetist magnetized a female patient. As will be seen later, the hysterical patient à la Charcot, suffered also from similar erotic hallucinations. Hysterics were thought to be insatiable liars, who were wanton in the art of false accusation of sexual abuse. Taylor (1881) espoused this position and cited a number of cases both in France and in the United States where the evidence strongly suggested that the victim had either confabulated (that is, fantasized) the allegation or else had lied deliberately.

> There have certainly been many false accusations of rape directed against physicians and dentists who used these vapors [chloroform]. In general listening to the testimony of the victim is sufficient to demonstrate the falsity of her accusation. (p. 199)

Whether one could anesthetize someone against his or her will was more problematic. Although most experts agreed that anesthetics could not be used against the will of a patient, some researchers believed that it could occur occasionally. Dolbeau (1874) in a series of experiments had succeeded in anesthetizing 10 out of 26 human subjects during their natural sleep. He concluded that chloroform could be used against the will of a prospective victim.

Experimenters were less successful when it came to the chloroforming of animals. Fortunately, they could then revert to hypnotizing them so as to demonstrate how hypnosis could be used against the will of an individual. In the past, animals had been prosecuted and magnetized (see Chapter 2). The tradition continued: They were now hypnotized. It was seen earlier how Lafontaine had successfully killed a number of animals using a visual fixation technique. To his credit, however, it must be said that he also tried to prolong the life of animals through magnetism.

> I left them [lizards] by themselves in a jar, without any food. The paper covering the jars was pierced with small holes to provide for an adequate supply of air. All those that I did not magnetize died after nine, eleven, and thirteen days; one lived up to eighteen days.
>
> The two that were magnetized died by *accident*, the first one after forty-two days, the second one after seventy-five days.
>
> For the first one, I had awakened it while I was [standing] at the window; I tilted the jar clumsily and dropped it on the pavement.
>
> As for the other, I had placed the jar on the window, in the sunlight. It was gay and energetic. Unfortunately, I had to leave and I forgot it there. When I came back three hours later I found my poor lizard fried: it had been burnt by the sun. The glass had heated under the sun and because of the small quantity of air available, my poor lizard had fried after seventy-five days of diet and magnetic sleep. (1886, p. 248)[4]

This may be one of the first recorded admissions of an investigator not merely throwing out data, but of cooking it as well. The usual experiments were not as dramatic. Nobody was absolutely certain what hypnosis or magnetism did to animals and this uncertainty was not unreasonable given that animals cannot talk. These experiments originated from the description of a cataleptic state in animals by A. Kircher, a Jesuit priest, in 1643. In a book devoted to the imagination of animals, Kircher described an experiment in which he tied a hen's feet together with a cord and laid the animal on the ground, where, after struggling for a while, it lay perfectly still. Kircher then drew two convergent lines in front of the hen's eyes, and untied the legs. The hen remained motionless, as if not realizing that its movements were no longer restrained. Kircher attributed this amazing result to the hen's innate imagination. As time went by, similar experiments were performed on different animal species. If the hen was quite imaginative, so were crayfish, lobsters, lions, and horses. For some of these animals, however, the method differed. The cataleptic state was obtained either by stroking the animal gently on its abdomen or by visual fixation.

Not until the 1870s was Kircher's theory of the imagination challenged. A number of experimenters replicated these effects with various methodologies (see, for example, Hammond, 1876). They were all successful; all they had in common was the way they captured the animal's attention and focused it on one specific object. It was natural to conclude that this concentration of attention was responsible for the cataleptic state and, as such, similar to what Braid had demonstrated with humans. Only in the 1880s did some experimenters begin showing that the catalepsy resulted more from the induction of a fear response than from hypnosis. The reported experiments were nonetheless impressive. Hammond, for example, reported that

> I have repeatedly performed Czermak's experiments,[5] using young lobsters, frogs, hens, geese, and ducks, with scarcely a failure. Of all animals in my experience, the frog passes into the hypnotic condition most readily. All that is necessary is to hold it firmly for a minute or two by the sides of the body just behind the forelegs, and then gently lay it on its back on a table, board, or palm of the hand. So profound is the hypnotism that a blade of a pair of scissors may be introduced into the lower part of the belly and the animal cut open its whole length, without its moving or apparently experiencing the least sensation. (p. 202)

Moll (1889/1982) reported that in Austria eye fixation and a monotonous verbal repetition could be used to calm aggressive horses. The method was developed by an officer in the Austrian cavalry, Mr. Balassa; it proved to be so effective that the army adopted the procedure under the name of *Balassiren* (see also Lysing, 1892, for a review of hypnosis and animal experimentation). What emerged slowly from animal experimentation, however, was not the fact that they could be hypnotized, although investigators believed this also. The major conclusions were twofold: First, animal hypnosis bore testimony to the physiological basis of the state. Second, repeated hypnotizations led to the deterioration of the nervous system (see Lysing, 1892). This last point was particularly salient in an experiment conducted by Harting and reported by Milne-Edwards to the Paris Academy of Sciences. After having hypnotized repeatedly a number of fowls, most of them developed hemiplegia, and some of them died. It will be seen in the next chapter how this type of knowledge became crucial in the experts' testimony during an American trial, the case of Spurgeon Young.

Natural somnambulism, the use and abuse of anesthetics, and animal hypnosis were thus a part of medico-legal expertise at the end of the 1870s. It extended also to cases of rape and indecent assault. As has been mentioned previously, hysterical and natural somnambulism were not the only states that could lead to potential abuse. Apart from the normal state, hysterical catalepsy and most of all hysterical lethargy were also thought to lead to sexual molestation.

The medico-legal literature of the time strongly suggests that the probability of being sexually abused while suffering an hysterical attack was extremely low when compared to its risk in everyday living. Tardieu (1878, p. 4) reported that more than 3,000 indecent acts were committed every year in France between 1858 and 1869. From 1851 to 1875, 22,017 rapes and indecent assaults were reported to the police (p. 18). Compared to the number of sexual crimes where hypnosis was alleged to have played a role, the disproportion is immense. Still, rape, indecent assault, and hypnosis were certainly a combustible combination when it came to popular and scientific perceptions. Even the use of chloroform or any other anesthetic agent never aroused as many controversies as did hypnosis. Although many authors mentioned numerous reports of sexual abuse with the use of anesthetic agents, none of them went through the pain of documenting actual cases. Why did they do it with such detail when hypnosis was involved? The ultimate threat to the individual's freedom of choice remains the sole obvious answer. Underlying hypnosis, mysterious forces may have been perceived as being at play to deprive of their free will those who submitted to it.

By the end of the 1870s, the etiology of hysteria was believed to be physiological Although the theory identifying the uterus as the diseased organ was no longer fashionable, the relation between the hysterical symptomatology and the malfunctioning of the female sexual organs was still part of the explanation of the syndrome. Psychologically, the hysterical patient was described in the following dismissive terms: "Lies, productions, slanderous simulations, unnecessary robberies, insensitivity, neglect of obligations, of affections, and of the most elementary feelings of dignity and modesty, these are the major hysterical compulsions" (Briand & Chaudé, 1879, p. 141). Legrand du Saulle (1883) corroborated this view by presenting more than 70 legal cases where hysterical patients were found to be lying, simulating, and launching false accusations.

Hysterical patients were not always lying or simulating and some genuine dramatic cases were reported. Despine (1868) commented on a case witnessed by his uncle, a physician living in Aix en Savoie. He had cured a young woman of a hysterical paralysis using magnetism. During treatment, she had demonstrated the ability to experience somnambulism easily. A few years later she developed a spontaneous lethargic state that had all of the appearances of death. Everyone in the village believed her dead, and buried her. When Despine's uncle heard about the case, he suspected foul play and asked permission to perform an autopsy. His conclusions were clear: She had been buried alive (p. 586). In his report of the case, Despine emphasized the relation between somnambulism and lethargy.

All three states, somnambulism, catalepsy, and lethargy, were thought to occur spontaneously in hysterical patients; they were often referred to as *states analogous to hypnosis* (Thoinot, 1919, p. 149). Of these three states, only lethargy was thought to leave its sufferer defenseless. Hysterical somnambulism, because of its delirious qualities, was rarely linked to sexual abuse whereas its hypnotic counterpart, characterized by passive automatism, was frequently implicated with such abuse. Lethargy, on the other hand, happened either by itself or in the context of a typical hysterical crisis. It shared all of the characteristics of an attack of sleep. Thoinot described such an attack:

> The duration of the *attack of sleep* (this expression is synonymous with hysteric lethargy) is very variable; while at times very brief, a half-hour, for example, it may extend over entire days, months, and sometimes, it is said, even years. It is then a case of *apparent death*, and note well that as a matter of fact *all* the celebrated cases of apparent death and marvelous *resurrection* arise from hysteric lethargy.
>
> The symptomatology is, with some very slight variations, that of the sleep of hypnotic lethargy with which we are familiar[6]: movements, excitability, sensations are abolished; if the condition is prolonged it is truly, *to all appearances*, the state of a cadaver. Sometimes the special senses, and hearing in particular, are not extinguished, and the unfortunate lethargic may lie motionless, powerless, and incapable of reacting in the midst of all that is going on about her, and may, in this state, hear the preparations for her funeral if she is too long in waking. . . .
>
> There is no doubt at all that a woman who has fallen into a state of lethargy may be an easy prey for a violator, and, there exist several examples of rape consummated during this state, though they are rare (but the state itself is common). (1919, pp. 150–151, italics in original)

The medico-legal experts were soon called upon to apply this knowledge to a number of criminal cases.

The most celebrated case of the 1860s was certainly the Castellan affair.[7] On March 31, 1865, Thimothée Castellan, approximately 25 years of age, arrived in the little French village of Guiols. Badly dressed, and physically handicapped, he presented himself at the door of an old man named Hughes, and two of his children, a young boy of 15, and a young woman, Joséphine, 26 years old. Castellan claimed that he was deaf and dumb. He was invited to share the family dinner that was already prepared. During the meal, everyone noticed that he had peculiar habits. He would always fill his glass in three attempts, and make several signs of the cross over it before drinking. During the evening, he began explaining (in writing) that he was sent by God, that he was Jesus Christ. He offered to perform a few miracles and to predict the future. Joséphine was especially troubled by his bizarre behavior, so much so that Despine (1868, p. 587) stated that subsequently she went to bed fully dressed, in a state of fear.

Having slept in the barn, Castellan returned the next morning. While Joséphine was cleaning the house, a neighbor who was passing by noticed that the beggar was making strange movements behind her back, and that she appeared quite confused. At lunch time, as they were sitting at the table, Castellan pretended to throw something into Joséphine's bowl. She immediately lost consciousness. Castellan brought her to her room and had sexual relations with her. She later claimed that she was aware of everything that was happening, but could not resist. Even when a relative knocked on her bedroom door, she was unable to call for help.

From that moment on, she was allegedly under the power of Castellan. They left the house together and set out in the direction of another village. They arrived at Collobrières in the evening, and sought hospitality in a farmhouse. They spent two days there, during which Joséphine complained often about her loss of freedom. On the third day, they visited yet another neighboring village where they stopped at the farm of a M. Condroyer. During the day, Joséphine looked disturbed. At times she would praise Castellan, recognizing that he had been sent by God. At other times, she would complain about her powerlessness, pleading for help. The first night she expressed the desire to sleep in a neighboring house. Castellan refused to release her. To overcome her resistance he made passes over her and touched her hips lightly. Joséphine fainted immediately. In that state, however, Castellan made her climb the stairs to the bedroom, counting the steps as she went along. A neighbor who was helping to undress her was struck by the unresponsiveness of the young woman. He tickled the soles of her feet vigorously, but she did not react.

The next two days offered much of the same. Castellan would suggest different behaviors to Joséphine. At times, for instance, she would walk around imitating a dog following such a waking suggestion. At other times, Castellan would suggest pain in different parts of her body.

On the fifth day they left for Capelude. Some distance away they met a couple of hunters who began questioning Castellan. Joséphine profited from this unexpected meeting by escaping, and returned to her home at Guiols.

She was reported to be in a state of intense excitement. To calm her, the family physician prescribed a bleeding, following which, she finally relaxed. A neighbor who was interested in magnetism decided to magnetize her in order to obtain more information about her misadventure. It did not succeed; she did not become magnetized and did not provide any new details of the period of her fugue (if that is what it was) with Castellan. At the trial, the physician described her as a young woman of irreproachable morality, in no way hysterical, and a diligent worker. There was no history of insanity or imbecility in her family.

Castellan was arrested on charges of vagrancy and rape. The judge, however, asked two medico-legal experts, Drs. Camille Auban and Jules Roux, to give their opinion as to the possibility of rape using magnetic maneuvers. The experts had not examined either Castellan or Joséphine. Nonetheless, the vast quantity of material available on the case rendered their task easier. For one,

Castellan himself had acknowledged his use of magnetic passes to take control of his victim. The experts consulted the decision of an earlier case as well as the major books published at the time. Based on this review of the evidence they agreed on the possibility of perverting and even destroying an individual's moral freedom through magnetic maneuvers. They agreed that it was possible to sexually abuse a woman once the magnetic state was induced; they regarded this as a natural consequence of the loss of her free will.

Castellan was judged and found guilty of rape. He was condemned to 12 years of forced labor. Despine described his behavior at the trial:

> During the trial, Castellan displayed extraordinary calmness and effrontery.... He mainly exhibited his magnetic talents. He was bold enough to propose to demonstrate his skills on the President of the Assises. During the closing speech for the prosecution, he did even more: by constantly focusing his gaze on the imperial prosecutor, he threatened to magnetize him. The prosecutor had to force him to lower his eyes. (1868, p. 291)

This decision proved to be extremely important in the years that followed. In reading Thoinot's (1919) report, however, it becomes clear how past events can be reinterpreted if not actually adapted to fit a current fashionable theory. Thoinot was a supporter of Charcot's model, and as such, found that some of the evidence in the Castellan trial did not always follow his master's theory. For example, Joséphine had been described as "in no way hysterical" by her treating physician. This contradicted Charcot's theory based on the analogy between hysteria and hypnosis. Thoinot was not disconcerted by this and presented the item in the following way:

> It is said somewhere in the case that Joséphine Hughes was in no way *hysterical*; we may understand by that merely what is understood in the world at large by that term, that is to say, that she did not appear inclined to the venereal act, and was a girl of good conduct. (p. 126)

Thoinot was saying, in effect, that the physician did not know what he was talking about. As for linking hysteria with being inclined to the "venereal act," Thoinot certainly overstated the lay meaning of the term. In Charcot's theory, there was a direct relation between sexuality and hysteria. As will be seen, Joséphine's descriptions of her ordeal served subsequently as an example of the three basic hypnotic "stages" that Charcot postulated.

The case that the experts had consulted during the Castellan trial had occurred in 1858. As with Castellan, it was a case of alleged rape at the hands of a lay magnetist. Although less sensational, it illustrated another facet of the potential abuse of magnetism or hypnosis.

The case involved Marguerite A., a young girl 18 years old. Feeling ill, she visited the house of C., a magnetic healer, practicing in Marseilles. Starting in November, she attended her treatment daily. At the beginning of April, she noticed that she was pregnant and complained to the authorities.

The police commissioner appointed Coste and Broquier, two medico-legal experts, to determine the origins of the pregnancy and the time from which it dated. They were also to investigate if the young woman could have been deflowered and rendered pregnant against her will, as the result of her being magnetized. The experts were obliged to return to Husson's report of 1831 in order to find an acceptable scientific document on the matter. Based on this document, they concluded that

> if a young girl under the influence of magnetic sleep is insensible to tortures, it seems to us rational to admit that she could experience the act of coitus without her will taking part in it, without her being conscious of it, and that consequently she would not be able to reject by force the act that was consummated on her. (Tardieu, 1878, p. 91; cited also in Thoinot, 1919, p. 117)

They consulted a number of their colleagues, among them Tardieu and Devergie, who agreed with their evaluation. Both of them, however, were of the opinion that in such cases the possibility of both confabulation and simulation was so high that any firm opinion was not possible.

Tardieu (1878) reported a third case in which he was asked to provide an opinion on the possible effects of using electricity, magnetism, or a mixture of the two, to coerce a young woman into the commission of a sexual act. In this particular case, a young woman of 15 years of age, C., had consulted a physician/magnetist, G. The physician had attempted to magnetize her without success. He then decided to administer electric shocks to his patient. She was asked to hold one electrode in her right hand while a second one was positioned on her back. She described the shocks as violent. Following these, she found herself paralyzed, unable to utter a word. It is in this condition that G. was alleged to have abused her. Tardieu rejected the accusation. He did not believe that electricity could cause such paralysis in the way that it had been applied. Magnetism, as C. herself had testified, had not been effective. Hysteria was the most appropriate diagnosis. Tardieu emphasized a careful examination of the patient's state of mind since he believed that it often revealed the hysterical component of her accusations. In yet another case, a young woman of 16 had accused a man who was in the habit of magnetizing her, of having profited from the situation. Tardieu's careful examination of the patient's report had shown that it was almost certainly the result of confabulation (see p. 173).

While cases of abuse were accumulating in Europe, the first American case was being heard in California. In *People v. Royal* (1878), a young woman reported having been sexually abused while magnetized. The accused denied having used magnetism to achieve his goal. The court reached an interesting decision. Based on an earlier ruling, *Commonwealth v. Burke* (1870), the California Court ruled that since force is a necessary element of rape, the use of magnetism could not in itself lead to such abuse.[8] The Court went further: It ruled also that in this case, it was the moral nature of the woman that was so corrupt that she was no longer able to resist her sexual desire. She had been the victim not of rape, but of a shrewd seducer.

One last case merits attention before turning to the beginnings of the theoretical debate between the Nancy and Salpêtrière schools. This case was reported by Paul Brouardel, a forensic consultant and a leader in the field of medico-legal issues. The accounts of the case were published in 1879 at about the same time that the first studies on hysteria and hypnosis at the Salpêtrière were publicized. At the end of April 1879, Mme B., a laundress of Rouen, lodged a complaint against the dentist Lévy, whom she accused of having sexually abused her 20-year-old daughter, Berthe.[9]

Some of the details of the case were particularly difficult to believe. Berthe's mother declared that she had been present at all of her daughter's appointments and had not noticed the dentist abusing her. It was the dentist himself who had recognized what he had done: "Yes; you were pure; you were a virgin. You thought in your simplicity that what I was doing was necessary, and you made no resistance. Save me; save my wife and my children; say that I did not rape you and I will give you everything that I possess" (Brouardel, 1879; cited in Thoinot, 1919, pp. 126–127).

What the Court had to determine was if Berthe had consented to the sexual relations. In the formal complaint, Lévy was described as very handsome and intelligent, whereas the two women were small, ugly, and did not appear very intelligent. They both enjoyed a good reputation. Lévy, however, although married, was known for his indulgence in a life of gross debauchery.

The two women met the dentist at the Hôtel Angleterre. At the first meeting, he asked what appeared to be strange questions. After some inquiry into Berthe's life habits, he told her that it was important to verify if she was still a virgin (for a similar contemporary case see Chapter 11). The treatment depended upon it. After the examination, Lévy informed the two women that Berthe was weak and anemic and would require what he called "a reaction of the blood." According to the mother's testimony, this reaction of the blood had to be performed "from below" (p. 128).

Berthe was asked to sit in the dentist's chair. Lévy then placed the chair in such a way that she was lying in a horizontal position. According to Lévy's instructions, Berthe had to raise her lips and place them against her nostrils and hold them there. After a few minutes, she lost consciousness. The mother, who was sitting at the other end of the room with her back to the dentist and her daughter, reported that she did not notice anything unusual.

The two women returned the next day, and once again the same procedures were followed. On the third day, the mother saw the dentist take a flask from a small table and return to her daughter. She then heard her daughter utter a groan or a cry. Needless to say, she wanted to know what was happening, but the dentist prevented her by pretending that there was nothing unusual in Berthe's behavior. When Berthe awakened, however, she looked "stupefied and a prey to keen pains in her sexual organs" (p. 129).

During the inquiry, Lévy affirmed that Berthe had consented throughout to the sexual relations. Berthe, on the other hand, denied this most vigorously. The question was whether it was possible that Berthe had been deflowered by Lévy without her consent. The experts decided to eliminate the possibility that the dentist had used an anesthetic during the sessions. Nothing in Berthe's account of the incident suggested the use of such an agent. On the other hand, she was four and a half months pregnant, and manifested what was then thought to be demonstrable signs of hysteria. Among these, "the genital organs, the labia majora, could be pierced by needles without the young girl being aware of it" (p. 131). At this point, Brouardel was asked to examine the young woman and to determine the possibility that she may have been the victim of a morbid state resulting from her hysterical symptoms. Brouardel first reported that hysteria by itself could not account for the unconsciousness and insensibility that Berthe had described during the dental sessions. He demonstrated that she was easily hypnotized by compression of her eyeballs. Brouardel concluded that the technique used by Lévy (head back, compressing the nostrils) probably had the effect of inducing a hypnotic state in Berthe.[10] Brouardel believed that she could have been hypnotized by Lévy. She certainly demonstrated all the characteristic symptoms of the hypnotizable patient. He could not, however, answer the question with absolute certainty. He was asked whether Berthe had been hypnotized at the time in Lévy's hotel room. He replied that "This is a question that is impossible to answer" (Brouardel, 1879, p. 56). Nonetheless, Brouardel did present his conclusions to the Court in the following terms: "With reservations on the possibility of simulation, this example is similar to the ones that had prompted them [Devargie and Tardieu] to conclude that a girl can be raped while her will has been annihilated by a nervous or hypnotic sleep" (1879, p. 57).

The jury voted to convict Lévy. He was condemned to ten years of imprisonment.

The Rise of the Salpêtrière and Nancy Schools

As these two schools of thought continued to evolve, the cases reported in the previous section were again brought to the attention of the public. Each school sought to explain them in terms of their theoretical preferences and each met with limited success.

From 1878 to 1884, the Salpêtrière school under the leadership of Charcot put forward its physio-pathological approach to hypnosis and hysteria. It represented the most popular view of the time. The Nancy school officially entered the field in 1884 with the publication of Bernheim's book *De la suggestion dans l'état hypnotique et dans l'état de veille* (Of suggestion in the hypnotic and waking states). He summarized in this first book his ideas on the importance of the suggestive process underlying hypnosis. If Liébeault can be considered to be the founder of the Nancy school, Bernheim was its leader during these difficult years.[11]

Much has been written about Charcot's personality and style. Considered to be one of the most brilliant neurologists of the nineteenth century, he certainly did not need hypnosis to become famous. Most of his biographers have even sought to excuse his incursions into the realm of hypnosis and hysteria, some arguing that everyone is entitled to make errors (see, for example, Guillain, 1955; Ellenberger, 1970). In the forensic debate, however, Charcot and his students did not commit the same mistakes that they had made theoretically. Indeed, their participation in the forensic debate turned out to be a victory, if not theoretically, at least from a practical point of view.

One of the criticisms directed toward Charcot was his stubbornness in giving public lectures, not only to medical students and colleagues, but to anyone who wanted to witness the master in action. The famous lessons had an entertaining quality that was not to please everyone. Delboeuf, for example, visited the Salpêtrière once, only to return home convinced that the phenomena studied by Charcot were so distorted by his approach that it became impossible to discern the essence from the artifact (Delboeuf, 1886a, 1886b, 1889a).

Others were proud to witness such a display of knowledge. Morand (1889) described the atmosphere at Charcot's demonstrations as surprising and exciting:

> The lesson is scheduled for nine-thirty a.m., but the room is already filled by spectators of both sexes. I counted about a dozen women, *students*, I believe, most of whom are ugly, if I dare say. They seem to belong to a third and new species of human beings. This is probably why these strange ladies, most of them foreigners, can listen without batting an eyelid to these lessons where the most realist details and shocking subjects are discussed.
>
> Finally, here comes the professor. He climbs to the podium from the side opposite to the audience. He is accompanied by his guests and assistants. Behind him, a real den of thieves [*Cour des Miracles*]; old women . . . and handicapped patients. . . . Finally, a group of young hysterical women from which the professor will choose the subjects of his live demonstrations. (pp. 104–105, italics in original)

Charcot wanted to do for hypnosis what he had done for neurology. He was not interested in the more sensational claims of the lay hypnotists and magnetists. His goal was to link hypnotic phenomena to identifiable nervous pathways. His approach was patho-physiological. It is only at the end of his life that he came to question his hypnotic theory. But until then, psychological explanations had no place in the description of what, to him, was an obvious neurological syndrome. Hypnosis and hysteria were, for Charcot, intimately related: "In both of them, we can see such similarity in their manifestations that only the etiology can lead to their differentiation: in the latter, spontaneous; in the former, elicited" (Richer, 1885, p. 505).

Paul Richer published his book in 1881 under the supervision of Charcot; this established the entire dogma of the Salpêtrière school. Hypnosis was conceptualized as a hysterical neuropathy, easily diagnosed by the presence of the "major hysterical attack." What Charcot called "the major hysterical attack" was a full blown hysterical crisis that followed a specific and inevitable cycle. Four different periods could be distinguished in a typical crisis: epileptoid, clownish, passionate, and hallucinatory. Each period had its own characteristics; if the physician did not intervene, the onset of the crisis was followed by the four periods, in an inevitable sequence. Although different symptoms alerted the patient to an oncoming crisis, the major one was the *aura hysterica* (reminiscent of the epileptic aura), a characteristic pain in what Charcot called *hysterogenic zones*, usually in the ovarian region.[12] It is difficult not to link Charcot's contentions to Mesmer's own system. There are several striking comparisons between the two men. The mesmeric crisis, although less sophisticated than the Charcotian one, shared many of its characteristics. In common with the mesmerized subject, hystero-epileptic patients could predict the onset and duration of their crises. At a more personal level, both were certainly famous, and recognized for their intransigence; both believed also in a naturalistic, physicalist explanation of the phenomenon he studied.

The major hysteria or *hystero-epilepsy* was characterized by the presence of hysterical stigmata on the patient's body. These stigmata (Charcot's hysterogenic zones) were insensitive areas of the body that were usually randomly distributed, but were quite commonly found around the breasts and ovarian regions as well as on the mucosae (inside the mouth and vagina). These circumscribed regions could be submitted to noxious stimulation without patients being aware of it and were reminiscent of the devil's marks in the old exorcism rituals. One of the interesting characteristics of these zones resided in their ability to induce either a hysterical crisis when the patient reported the onset of the *aura hysterica* or to stop an ongoing one.

The four phases of the hystero-epileptic crisis displayed a number of basic characteristics. In the epileptoid or convulsive phase, a series of convulsions appeared. The patient's body was distorted into an opisthotonic position, where all the muscles of the body were in such a state of contraction that only the back of the head and the bottom of the feet touched the ground. This general convulsion was followed usually by a short period of intermittent, clonic contractions leading to a total relaxation of the body. Sometimes foam could be seen on the patient's mouth.

This first phase was followed immediately by a period of contortions, or *clownism*. In this phase, the patient was once again the victim of a global contraction of the body accompanied by violent and disorganized arm movements as if she was defending herself against an invisible assailant. The third period was more difficult to describe. The passionate phase was characterized by the onset of numerous hallucinations, usually related to a past episode in the patient's life. In some it would be a rape scene that they appeared to relive; in others, a voluptuous and pleasurable sexual event. Morand (1889) reported examples of some of these sexual innuendos professed by hysterical women on Charcot's ward: "One of the patients that we saw at the conferences that I was referring to earlier, said, 'Alfred, come here, let's do it!' and her body movements left no doubt of her intentions" (p. 112).

As Morand specified, eroticism was frequent in hysterical women. In his mind, they even welcomed the erotic sensations they experienced when they had to demonstrate the typical crisis for visitors (p. 112). This period lasted usually from 5 to 15 minutes. It was succeeded by a last phase which was the hallucinatory or delirious one (or as Charcot used to call it, the period of *zoopsia*). This was the shortest in duration, lasting rarely more than a few minutes. At this point, the patient seemed to believe in the reality of the hallucinations she had just experienced. She talked in such a way as to suggest that she was surrounded by all kinds of animals parading in front of her on an imaginary line running from the hyperesthetic ovary to the other one. She would often shout such insults as "Goddamn toads!" or "Dirty rats!" (Morand, p. 114).

Within a few minutes, the patient would awaken and was able to remember what had happened during the crisis, and she could describe the hallucinations that had haunted her. Many variations could take place during the four phases. Although the convulsions were the rule, it was not unusual to see on some occasions the onset of paralysis which could affect the whole body, half of the body, or even a specific limb. It is important to remember here that Charcot was one of the first neurologists to claim that hysteria was not gender-related. Men were susceptible as well as women. The hysterogenic zone *par excellence* in a man would be located in one of the testicles.

The hysterogenic zones had a double function. They could either initiate or block the development of a crisis. Accordingly, the technicians of La Salpêtrière hospital designed an ovarian belt. It was built in such a way as to apply pressure to the side of the ovarian region that had been identified as hysterogenic. In this way, hysterical patients could return to their usual occupations without fear of losing control and convulsing. When a crisis was necessary, as in a demonstration, the belt could easily be removed.

On January 13, 1882, Charcot read his first paper on hypnosis to the Académie des Sciences. He had successfully systematized various hypnotic phenomena into three major classes or stages: catalepsy, lethargy, and somnambulism. These three stages with their inherent characteristics became the hallmark of the Salpêtrière school of thought. They could be observed only in hysterical patients or patients who exhibited latent hysterical symptoms. Pierre Janet was to slightly modify this statement later by describing hysteria as the most, but not the only, fertile ground for the development of hypnotizability (Janet, 1889). As the patient experienced more hypnotizations, the easier it became to hypnotize him or her. As will be seen in the next section, this facility in eliciting hypnotic stages played a pivotal role in many legal trials.

The main characteristic of these three stages was that they resembled strangely their hysterical counterparts, described at the beginning of this section. They showed, however, important differences. Charcot based his observations on his knowledge of the neuromuscular system. Any variation from normality was recorded and investigated in all of its details, usually through hypnosis. The first major observation came from hysterical patients who demonstrated what the physicians of the time called a *contractive diathesis*. As has been seen, muscular contractions played a central role in the hysterical attack. In the cataleptic stage, the patient's limbs might remain in the position they were in at the onset of the stage, or in the position in which they were placed by the experimenter. This happened without any conscious effort from the patient and could last as long as nothing was done to modify the stage. In this stage, the patient could be placed in suspension between two chairs, only head and heels touching them, and remain as rigid as an iron bar. The human plank was often seen as an unmistakable sign of the genuineness of the hypnotic state and as an excellent technique to counteract simulation (Binet & Féré, 1888).

There were also other symptoms peculiar to this stage. Patients occasionally exhibited echolalia and echopraxia, the relentless repetition of either speech or movement. Although the skin was totally insensitive, the visual and auditory senses were usually normal. In this way, the patient was receptive to suggestions. If, for example, the experimenter placed the hands of the subject together, his or her facial expression changed and took on an expression of prayer. If the fists were clenched together, anger could be seen on the patient's face. Finally, the muscles did not hypercontract when they were touched or pinched. Quite to the contrary, muscular stimulation often provoked a general paresis or paralysis in the patient (Richer, 1885). Finally, the cataleptic stage could be induced by visual fixation, by a sudden flash of a bright light, or by a sudden noise; it was canceled easily by puffing air at the patient's eyes. This stage was thought to be dangerous for the patient, and the practitioner was cautioned not to sustain it for too long a time. It was believed that it could bring about a major convulsive crisis that could be deadly to the subject.

The lethargic stage was dramatically different from the cataleptic one. It had all the appearances of profound sleep; the body was totally limp and relaxed. There was no perception of pain. The patient could be hit, pricked, or burned without the slightest reaction. Consciousness disappeared; thoughts and emotions vanished. The cardinal sign of lethargy was a neuromuscular hyperexcitability. A hard pressure on a motor nerve caused a complete contraction of the innervated muscles. A pressure, for example, on the cubital muscle, caused the typical contraction of the fourth and fifth fingers, leaving the first three extended. Pressure on the biceps brought about the arm's flexion. These contractions could be relieved only through the excitation of their antagonist muscles. They resisted any other effort to remove them. Upon waking, however, they disappeared. Lethargy could be induced by closing the eyes of a cataleptic patient. If only one eye was closed, the contralateral side of the body became lethargic while the ipsilateral side remained cataleptic. It could also be induced by compressing the eyeballs or the vertex of the head. It was in this stage that the phenomenon of displacement of the contraction could be most easily observed. A puff of air to the eyes could be used to awaken the subject who would not remember anything related to the lethargic phase.

Finally, and most importantly, the somnambulistic stage could follow either of the two previous ones, or it could be elicited directly by verbal suggestion, eye fixation, passes on the vertex of the head, or a combination of these manipulations. As Morand (1889) illustrated it, the hypnotist might apply some pressure to the patient's vertex while saying: "Sleep, one says at the same time [of the manipulation]; you will sleep, your eyelids are closing, you cannot open them any more; you are sleeping" (p. 142).[13]

Charcot maintained that the somnambulistic patient resembled the lethargic one; completely relaxed, it looked as though he or she were sleeping. There was again a complete absence of pain perception that could be demonstrated in the usual way.

The notion that the hypnotized patient displayed spontaneous anesthesia or at least a spontaneous absence of pain perception came to play a central role in many trials. An illustration of this is a book, *On Obstetrics and Gynaecology*, published by Auvard in 1889, in which a whole chapter was devoted to the use of hypnosis in childbirth. A number of cases were described where it was more or less successful in alleviating the pains of the delivery process. Hypnosis had such limited success overall that the author concluded that its use should be restricted. As part of a global intervention, however, it was seen as very useful. Auvard was a follower of Charcot and was able to demonstrate the presence of the three basic stages in pregnant women. What is of interest is not the use *per se* of hypnosis in obstetrics, it is Auvard's descriptions of his techniques for testing for analgesia in his patients and his medico-legal conclusions on the possible abuses of hypnosis. For Auvard, childbirth represented a unique opportunity to test the degree of pain reduction thought to be brought about by hypnosis. As he wrote in the introduction to his chapter:

> The pains of childbirth are an unmistakable criterion. It seems very difficult to hide such pains, to pretend that one is asleep in so cruel a moment.
>
> This moral guarantee added to the almost pathognomic symptoms of the different hypnotic states increases our confidence in the facts that we have collected recently at La Charité on hypnosis. (p. 247)

These facts may demonstrate how clinicians and experimenters were themselves creating the observations that would lead to their beliefs in the coercive power of hypnosis. The techniques reported by Auvard did not reflect his own idiosyncratic way of practicing obstetrics. The cases reported in his chapter were collected from different clinics and from different countries. The techniques were the same; in many of these observations, the practitioner had been trained at the Salpêtrière: "While practicing the vaginal examination (*le toucher*), Doctor Sergent, who had followed Charcot's lessons for a long time, suggested that this person would be easily hypnotizable" (p. 254).

This report came from Vienna, not Paris. In the same report, Dr. E. Pritzl emphasized that the patient did not resist the vaginal "exploration" (p. 254) at all. These two points, anesthesia of the vaginal mucosa and the nonresistance of the patient to such intimate examination, are at the basis of Auvard's warnings on the potential abuse of hypnosis. Many of the observations reported in his book mention these two facts. The next passage illustrates well the technique employed by the physician. The patient was reluctant to use hypnosis during childbirth. She wanted to have a painful delivery like many women of that period who had been brought up to believe that pain of delivery was a necessary ingredient of childbirth. She was afraid that the absence of pain would affect the baby. The attending physicians succeeded in persuading her that the use of hypnosis would bear no consequences to her child.

> A few minutes later, all resistance had disappeared; she wanted to sleep. The compression of the eyeballs for a period of three minutes brought up a perfect lethargic state during which we were able to perform a complete, extended, and voluntarily slightly brutal examination of the vagina and the hip region. She did not show the slightest suffering. Total insensibility to the injection. The left ovary, quite painful in the waking state, can now be compressed at will. (p. 265)

Not surprisingly, Auvard concluded that there was great potential for abuse of so powerful a state. Unfortunately, he failed to recognize that the tests he performed, though legitimized in an obstetrical context, could scarcely be seen as acceptable beyond this context.

The last section of Auvard's chapter dealt with the medico-legal aspect of hypnosis in obstetrics. Apart from the conclusion that a woman could be abused sexually in hypnosis, he emphasized three major possible consequences. A woman could use self-hypnosis to give birth to an unwanted child and kill it without anyone knowing. Alternatively, in a case of spontaneous lethargy, she could give birth without knowing it and crush her baby under her body weight. The two other consequences were linked to the apparent spontaneous amnesia exhibited by the hypnotized patient. The baby could be stolen or exchanged without the mother ever knowing her own child's fate. Finally, the mother might have no memory of her childbirth and therefore deny that the baby was her own. Because of these problems, he concluded that the physician must ensure that he always had witnesses around him when delivering a child to a hypnotized woman.

A case appearing to illustrate these dangers occurred in Italy in 1883. It was reported by Jules Liégeois (1889a) who found it in an article written by a Dr. Lapponi, entitled: *Di un caso di omicidio in somnambulismo* (On a case of homicide in somnambulism). On June 21, 1881, at about one o'clock in the morning, a young woman, Theresa Dig, age 25, knocked at her parents' door. They lived about one kilometer from her and were surprised to see her at such an hour since she had given birth to a baby girl five weeks earlier. She was dripping wet, explaining that she had just awakened and found herself lying in a nearby pond. She could remember only having fed and put her baby to sleep the night before. Her mother, concerned, ran to the pond, and found that the baby had drowned. Theresa was examined by the court physician and diagnosed as suffering from spontaneous somnambulism and hysteria. She was found not guilty based on the lack of moral responsibility that accompanied her illness.

This illustration from the description of Charcot's main hypnotic stages indicates how experimenters often created their own straw man (or woman) to fit a prevalent theory. In the Theresa Dig case, there was no investigation conducted or evidence presented to rule out other hypotheses, specifically, that she murdered her baby with premeditation.

Charcot believed that in the somnambulistic stage there was neuromuscular hyperexcitability, but this time with a different twist. No heavy pressure, but the slightest touch was sufficient to activate a contraction. The release mechanism was different also. The stimulation of the antagonist muscles did not reduce the contraction. One had to touch the contracted muscles lightly again to see them relax. The senses as well as the strength of the somnambulist were greatly increased. Intelligence was thought to be improved also; this was inferred from the apparent hypermnesia displayed by the subject. In this stage, rapport, or the exclusive relationship between the hypnotized subject and the hypnotist, was the strongest. It was not demanded by the theory that it be exclusive, however. It all depended on which technique was used to elicit somnambulism. If, for example, a finger was used to press on the subject's vertex, exclusive rapport developed. Alternatively, if the hypnotist used an inanimate object, such as a pen or a paper cutter, the somnambulist responded to other people as well as to the hypnotist. This particular stage was labeled indifferent somnambulism; in it, the subject's eyes could either be closed or open. When the eyes were closed, however, the subject became apathetic and could easily revert either to lethargy or catalepsy. Spontaneous amnesia and a heightened suggestibility were also thought to be characteristic of the somnambulistic stage.[14] As the 1880s progressed, the number of alternate stages increased so much that many authors proposed their own classifications. Charcot's three stages were soon considered to be inadequate by most of his own followers.

Not only were new stages described, but new symptoms were found. As early as 1873, Charcot had described the hysterogenic zones. These zones had also been found to be effective in initiating different hypnotic stages in hysterical patients (Pitres & Gaubé, 1885). This new development led medicolegal experts to examine alleged victims of hypnotic crimes for specific areas of the body that could provoke the onset of an hypnotic stage. As Pitres and Gaubé (1885) hypothesized, the presence of these zones, now called *hypnogenic zones*, was probably the underlying cause of a number of sexual assaults for which the victim had no memory. In addition, they considered that these hypothesized new zones explained not only old cases of witchcraft, but also the infamous "deadly assistances" (see Chapter 2). Along the same line of thought, Joséphine's submission to Castellan was reinterpreted as a consequence of pressure applied to her hypnogenic zones. It will be recalled that Castellan had touched Joséphine lightly around the hip region; this movement had led her to lose consciousness.

A second development attracted forensic interest. Chambart (1881b) reported the apparent presence of a third type of zone in the hysterical as well as hypnotic patient. He named these zones *erotogenic*. He believed that they could trigger a sexual experience in a patient. He wrote:

> Certain areas of the patient's body demonstrate a special hyperesthesia, an increase in *psycho-genital* sensitivity. . . . If one touches slightly any area of the body with a fingertip (outside of the erogenous zones) no special reaction will occur. . . . Alternatively, if one touches very lightly for a second, part of the breast, or any other erogenous point, the patient quivers, her face flushes, and quite rapidly, her face, her attitudes, her words, her movements indicate without a doubt the voluptuous sensations that she is experiencing, and over which she has no control. The effects that we just described are even more pronounced *if the patient is hypnotized.* In such a state, it proved sufficient to blow lightly on the palm of our patient to trigger both a sexual orgasm and a complete re-enactment of the coitus. (cited in Ladame, 1887, pp. 333–334, italics in original)

The "discovery" of these zones was soon to become an important aspect of the medico-legal examination. They appeared to offer a possible explanation of why some hypnotized women could not resist an attempted sexual assault. As was seen in *People v. Royal*, the victim, according to the Court's judgment, had been unable to resist her own sexual desires. More importantly, the discovery of such zones in a victim of an alleged sexual abuse could indicate that the woman could experience a sexual orgasm in the absence of any actual rape. This in turn suggested that she may have confabulated the assault in order to explain her sexual reaction. By such means, Chambart (1881b) thought that he might be able to explain all of the cases of false accusations made by hysterical patients against their physicians or caretakers.

Charcot's three stages and their characteristics were rejected by the Nancy school as artifactual of the methods used to produce them. In 1884, Bernheim officially took a position against the Salpêtrière school. In that same year, Liégeois, one of Bernheim's close collaborators, set off the beginning of the forensic debate. The Nancy school of thought was more homogeneous than its counterpart at the Salpêtrière; there were few variations on the central theme. Suggestion was thought to be responsible for the elicitation of the hypnotic condition. Suggestion, or the translation of an idea into an action, became the major concept that Bernheim used to oppose Charcot's conception of hypnosis, though not the only one.

Bernheim recognized that the roots of his theory came from the thinking of Liébeault and Faria. Like many other French experimenters and clinicians, he gave passing reference to Braid's work. He acknowledged that Braid's emphasis on monoideism was correct, but maintained that it was obscured by his sympathy for phreno-magnetism. In fact, Bernheim (1884, p. 40) gave credit to Braid only for his coining of the word hypnotism. His conception of hypnosis differed substantially from that of Charcot. In 1888, he published a small article explaining that there were eight major differences between the two schools. Among these was the recognition that the three basic stages and their accompanying characteristics were the result of suggestion (whether it be direct, indirect, verbal, or nonverbal). Hysteria was not seen as an analogue to hypnosis. Indeed, he believed that hysteria was not a good analogue for studying it. He felt that hysterical patients, because of their own symptomatology (usually resulting from autosuggestion and disordered emotions), changed the phenomena seen in hypnosis in such a way that it became impossible to differentiate what pertained to what.

Bernheim considered hypnosis itself to be a normal physiological state that could be elicited in healthy individuals. It was not a neurosis, nor was it indicative of neurosis. It was, however, subject to individual differences. Not everyone could become a somnambulist; indeed, very few individuals were capable of such profound sleep. Alternatively, very few were resistant to hypnosis. It was a question of degree. Even in the case of a somnambulistic patient, the power of suggestion was not irresistible. As Liébeault had already noted, perhaps one in every six persons, at most, could become what he thought was a pure automaton in the hands of his or her hypnotist. The others were capable of resisting whatever suggestion they chose. This was an important point that the Salpêtrière school would forget often in its debate with the Nancy school. Finally, Bernheim believed that any type of induction was rooted in suggestion and that suggestion was the key to all hypnotic phenomena. He believed, with some justification, that when one knows how to utilize suggestion, a person is able to hypnotize 80 percent of his subjects.

As can be seen from this brief description, the two positions could not but clash with one another. All of the different phenomena that had been studied since the beginnings of animal magnetism were shown by Bernheim to be artifactual of suggestion. Regardless of whether it was Charcot's three stages or more specific motor behaviors, hallucinations, age regressions, personality alterations, or the different forms of post-hypnotic behaviors, Bernheim claimed that all could be elicited through the careful use of suggestive technique. He divided the phenomena exhibited by hypnotized individuals into nine categories. Each category was divided according to the hypnotic item administered to the subject. (This system of classification was a forerunner of contemporary scales of hypnotizability.) Hypnotizability was thus seen as a continuum; the more hypnotizable a person, the more complex or difficult suggestions he or she could experience.[15] Bernheim's classification ignored all of the somatic signs described by Charcot. Indeed, in 1886, he summarized his thoughts on these signs in one brief paragraph:

> Only once have I seen a subject who could demonstrate perfectly the three stages: lethargic, cataleptic, and somnambulistic. It was a young woman who

had spent three years at the Salpêtrière. . . . She was not a naturally hypnotized subject, any more; it was a real suggested hypnotic neurosis. (p. 95)

Neither Charcot, nor his more faithful students (among whom was Gilles de la Tourette who took it upon himself to defend Charcot's position in the forensic debate) appreciated such a barbed dismissal.

Bernheim's experimentation was similar to the type of experimental research that is still conducted today. Although his studies were different methodologically, his observations were nonetheless precise and carefully worded. Indeed, he anticipated many of the modern phenomena of hypnosis, to the extent that current investigators are rediscovering what the Nancy school had described a century ago.[16]

Bernheim's theory evolved over the years to include not only hypnosis, but the domain of waking suggestibility and its application in psychotherapy. He came to place increasingly greater emphasis on the suggestibility of the subject in the waking state, to the extent that he arrived at the position that if hypnosis can increase suggestibility, a subject does not need to be hypnotized in order to respond to suggestion.

The Beginnings of the Forensic Confrontation

From 1884 to 1890, the two schools of thought confronted each other in a number of trials. They attacked each other in numerous articles and books. The most ardent defender of the Nancy school was Jules Liégeois, an administrative lawyer who was fascinated by hypnosis and its potential uses and abuses. At times, he placed Bernheim in embarrassing situations because of his extreme views and intemperate defenses of the Nancy position. On the other side, Gilles de la Tourette, one of Charcot's protégés, defended his master's ideas with violence and arrogance. The public, through the media, witnessed this sometimes less than scientific battle.

In 1884, Liégeois read his first communication on the relations between hypnosis and the civil and criminal codes at the Academy of Moral and Political Sciences. This presentation was to set the tone for the next six years. The main idea that Liégeois sought to demonstrate was the possibility of utilizing hypnosis to coerce individuals into the commission of crimes, or to abuse them psychologically and physically. His fundamental premise was that "any individual placed in a somnambulistic state will become in the hands of the experimenter a complete automaton, both morally and physically" (1884, p. 22).

To support his point, he presented both experimental data and actual cases of abuse, and he drew attention to the consequences of applying the civil and criminal codes to such abuse. On the civil side, he believed that financial extortion and manipulation of the last will and testament of suggestible people were to be feared. On the criminal side, the hypnotized individual could be forced to commit robberies and murders or could be rendered unable to resist sexual assaults. Furthermore, hypnotized individuals could fabricate false testimonies as the result of a prior suggestion that had changed their memories. Bernheim had called these suggestions *retroactive hallucinations*.

Since the Lévy case of 1879, a number of other trials had implicated hypnosis. Liégeois, however, in the examples that he presented to the Academy, reached back to trials predating Lévy. He had discovered a number of trials that he believed could be reinterpreted in terms of Bernheim's theory of suggestion. Not only was hypnosis dangerous; he maintained that suggestion was to be feared as well. He relied in particular on three earlier affairs to substantiate his position. Among these, the La Roncière trial was the most representative of the reconstruction process Liégeois used to convince his listeners. Although hypnosis (or somnambulism) had not been implicated, the victim was alleged by Liégeois to be a hysteric that the Court had failed to recognize. The defense at the time had demonstrated that the victim was a natural somnambulist. It was one of the first attempts to demonstrate that hypnosis and suggestibility could lead to serious miscarriages of justice. To further his point, Liégeois could not resist the temptation of saying that the victim, Mlle Marie de M., had become, in the last years of her life, one of Charcot's most faithful patients.

In 1834, she and her family went to live at Saumur. Soon after her arrival, she began receiving anonymous letters, signed E. de la R. (Emile de la Roncière), a family acquaintance. On September 23, 1834, at two o'clock in the morning, she reported being awakened by the sound of breaking glass. She saw a man enter her bedroom. After closing the door of the room in which her servant slept, he walked toward her bed. Frightened, she tried to hide behind a chair, but to no avail. The man attacked her, tore her clothes off, and tied her up with ropes. He also gagged her to prevent her from screaming. He then proceeded to beat her physically and to stroke her legs with a knife. The servant was awakened by the noises and came to her mistress's rescue. The man escaped before she could enter the room, leaving a letter behind him. Marie described him as normal in height, with a red police cap, and a black scarf covering his face. She thought nonetheless that it was La Roncière. Later on, however, she told her father that she had not recognized her assailant.

What was strange about the case was the fact that nobody else in the house had heard anything. Even Marie, following the harrowing ordeal, resumed sleeping until the morning. At ten o'clock the next day, the servant, Mlle Allen, informed Marie's parents of the night's events, while Marie was looking through the window and reporting that she could see her assailant on the other side of the garden, laughing at her.

For the next two days, nothing was said about the incident. Marie attended a ball; her wounds were not apparent. It was not until three months later that she was examined by a physician who found an almost invisible scar. At this time, however, the anonymous letters resumed. Some were even being deposited in her bedroom. La Roncière was arrested, but letters continued to be delivered.

Although the defense provided evidence to suggest strongly that Marie was suffering from somnambulism, catalepsy, and periods of ecstasy, and that her story was of her own fabrication, the jury was not convinced. It was not convinced either by the judge, who in his instructions had said that he would rather cut his hand off than sign the condemnation of La Roncière. He was found guilty of sexual assault and sentenced to ten years of prison.

For Liégeois, this case illustrated the possibility of a false testimony given in good faith that had been activated by the patient's suggestibility. As was seen in the previous chapter, hysterical patients were often described as suffering from delusions that pushed them to false accusations of rape or sexual assaults. This example, taken from the literature on hysteria, nonetheless supported some of Liégeois's contentions. Fortunately for him, more cogent cases had occurred, and he presented them to buttress his argument. These cases could be divided into two major categories: crimes committed by hypnotized individuals and crimes committed upon hypnotized subjects.

Crimes Committed by Hypnotized Individuals

Very few crimes had been reported before this period which illustrated the alleged power of hypnosis to subjugate the mind and the will of those who submitted to it. Two cases were mentioned by Liégeois: one reported by Dr. Dufay, then working at the Blois jail, and a second one, reported by Dr. Motet. In the first case, Dufay had been surprised to see a young servant he knew incarcerated at the prison. This young woman had been the subject of numerous hypnotizations by one of his colleagues. She told Dufay that her mistress had her arrested because some jewels had disappeared from her house. Dufay hypnotized her and found that the young servant had removed the jewels from one piece of furniture to another, thinking that they would be more secure there. She had done so while in a spontaneous somnambulistic state, and had no memory of her actions. Since her mistress did not know that her servant was a somnambulist, she had pressed charges.

Dufay succeeded in convincing the judge to witness the testimony of the young woman while hypnotized in her cell. The next day, after having heard for himself the hypnotic recall, the judge went to the mistress's house and found the jewels at the exact place the somnambulist had described. She was freed immediately.[17]

The second case, reported by Motet (1881), became a classic in the years to come. It was the first time that hypnosis was performed in court in an attempt to demonstrate the analogy between spontaneous somnambulism and its hypnotic counterpart. It illustrated also the belief current at the time that the somnambulistic individual could not be held responsible for behaviors that bypassed his or her willpower.

On October 18, 1880, around eight-thirty at night, a young man, Emile D., was arrested by two policemen for indecent exposure in a public urinal on Rue Sainte Cécile (Paris). According to the arresting officers, he had spent more than half an hour in the urinal masturbating as well as trying to entice them. Although Emile proclaimed his innocence, he was found guilty and sentenced to three months in prison. While in jail, he became ill and had to be sent to the infirmary. At the infirmary he was extremely confused. He did not remember having been arrested and sent to jail. Fortunately for him, Mesnet, a physician who worked at the jail, remembered having seen him at the St. Antoine Hospital where he had been treated for a serious skin tumor on the chest. While in the hospital, Dr. Motet, his treating physician, had noticed that Emile was a natural somnambulist. Motet had hypnotized him often to demonstrate the various phenomena of hypnosis to interested physicians, including Mesnet.

Emile had a family history of hysteria, having experienced a first crisis in 1877 while in the army. A succession of subsequent crises had brought him to the hospital. The medical investigation concluded that Emile had absolutely no willpower while in crisis. He obeyed any suggestion administered to him and did not remember anything between crises. When Mesnet heard of his arrest, he asked for a medical report, not believing that Emile had committed indecent exposure since his morality had never been questioned during his stay at the hospital. Mesnet believed that his arrest was the end result of a spontaneous crisis. The Court agreed to establish a tribunal to study the case.

Emile was described as "a young man of twenty-eight years with feminine behaviors that could, perhaps, be indicative of homosexuality, although he does not exhibit any sign of this shameful habit" (de la Tourette, 1887, p. 512).

The police officers had testified during the trial that they knew Emile well; that he was often seen at night near the urinal. In his testimony, Mesnet described how Emile suffered from hemoptysis, a condition seen often in hysterical patients. On the day of his arrest, he had experienced several blood losses and had consulted a physician who had prescribed medication. At the end of his workday, he set out to the pharmacy in order to have his prescription filled. On his way, he began once more spitting blood and used two handkerchiefs to absorb it.

Passing by the urinal, he decided to go in to wash them and to clean himself. He began cleaning one handkerchief, but said he could not remember what had happened after that or how long he had remained in the urinal. For Mesnet, it was unthinkable that a man in such a weak condition could commit an indecent exposure. For him, it was even physiologically impossible. He believed that Emile had probably suffered a spontaneous somnambulistic attack; he reasoned that the fact that he had stayed in the urinal for 30 minutes, standing in front of the wall without moving, must have been misinterpreted by the policemen.

Mesnet obtained the Tribunal's permission to demonstrate how easily Emile could pass from his normal state to a state of somnambulism without any memory of the episode. He hypnotized him by eye fixation. While Emile was in this state, Mesnet and the Tribunal's officers retired to another room guarded by two policemen. A few seconds later, Mesnet called Emile in. Emile ran into the room, pushing away the two policemen with surprising strength. In complete rapport with Mesnet, Emile stopped before him, waiting in silence. The judge then decided to test his memory. He asked Mesnet to instruct Emile to unbutton and drop his trousers.

> We tell him: "D..., get undressed."
> He takes off his clothes immediately. Then, on the suggestion of M. le Président, we ask him: "What were you doing in the urinal? Can you remember?" We place him in front of a wall. He takes his handkerchief, gets closer to the wall, and wipes his mouth; he repeats the same movement many times.
> We awaken him by blowing cold air on his eyes, and he looks extremely surprised to find himself where he is. M. le Président approaches him and says:
> "D..., you just got undressed in front of us."
> "I don't think so, sir," Emile replied.
> "All these gentlemen saw you as I did. Look: you are still unbuttoned; your pants are opened."
> "Sir, I don't remember." (pp. 516–517)

Mesnet then demonstrated how Emile was totally analgesic while hypnotized by inserting a large needle through the skin of his neck. Emile was awakened and the trial resumed. The Tribunal decided that Mesnet's demonstration had been more than convincing. Emile was found not guilty and released from jail. He was to pass away two years later.

This case created precedence in the medico-legal history of hypnosis. The expert, Dr. Mesnet, had demonstrated successfully that there was apparently a complete analogy between natural and hypnotic somnambulism; even more important, that the hypnotized individual was more a victim of circumstances than a criminal responsible for his acts. As Liégeois presented it in 1884, the hypnotizable and hypnotized individual could not be held responsible in either a criminal or a civil court.

Crimes Committed upon Hypnotized Individuals

It was generally accepted by the two schools of thought that certain individuals could be abused through the use of hypnosis. They differed, however, on the question of who was susceptible to such abuse. For Liégeois, any individual placed in a somnambulistic state became susceptible to abuse. Relevant to this issue was the fact that during the previous few years two major cases had attracted the attention of the medico-legal experts. The first was the already described Lévy case. The second case (Maria F.) was reported by Dr. L. P. Ladame, of Switzerland. Ladame presented the case as an example of the dramatic consequences that could follow the public demonstrations of hypnosis by stage hypnotists. Thoinot (1919) provided an English summary of this interesting case.

> The German pastor at Chaux-de-Fonds received, in July, a visit from a young girl originally from Zurich, who asked him to write to her parish to obtain authority for her to go to the Maternity Hospital in Bern for her lying-in. This young girl claimed that she had been pregnant since Christmas night. On that night, being alone for a moment with a young man who was accustomed to "magnetize" her, she was raped by him, she said, after he had put her to sleep. The young girl was received at the Maternity and delivered at the end of September. But the letter of the German pastor who asked for her admission into the hospital at Bern fell into the hands of the examining magistrate of Bern, who at once issued a complaint to the magistrate of Chaux-de-Fonds. The latter made an investigation, which he transmitted to the attorney-general of the Republic.
>
> We were then called upon by the attorney general to make a medico-legal report on this case, and to reply in particular to the following points:—
>
> 1. Should the story of Maria F . . . be considered probable in its general statements?
> 2. Could coitus have taken place under the conditions that she described, and without its being possible for her to have been conscious of the acts to which she was subjected?
> 3. Was the will completely paralyzed in this young girl, and was she unable to oppose any resistance [*sic*] to her seducer?
> 4. Is conception possible when a woman is in a state of absolute insensibility? (Ladame, 1882, p. 519; cited in Thoinot, 1919, p. 135)

Ladame consulted the literature (all the cases we have described) and the evidence that had been submitted to the Tribunal. He also consulted with some of his colleagues to better ascertain his knowledge of the hypnotic neurosis. To the first question on the credibility of Maria's statement, he replied in the affirmative. For him, it was clear that Louis V., the accused, was able to "magnetize" (in italics in Ladame's report) the young girl even against her will. The ease with which Maria was hypnotized was one of the consequences of her many earlier hypnotizations. Her declarations stated that she had tried to resist, to shout, but that she was too weak to succeed.

> In this degree of sleep the hypnotized person imagines that he can resist; in reality he does not resist. He consequently has the illusion as to his power of resistance. Consequently, when Maria F. . . affirmed that she wished to repulse her seducer, but that she had no strength; that she wished to cry out, but that she could not, etc., we must admit that she imagined that she could cry out and resist, but that she did not have the will to do so: for it is not strength that is lacking during "magnetic" sleep; it is the will that is paralysed. (Ladame, 1882, p. 526; cited in Thoinot, 1919, p. 136)

Ladame concluded that Maria's story was credible as long as the usual reservations as to the possibility of lying and/or confabulation were also considered.

The second question was more easily answered. Most of the previous literature had maintained that a woman could be raped in hypnosis without any knowledge of what was happening to her. Again, Ladame answered positively, with the usual reservations on the question of simulation. He did, however, make an interesting comment that Thoinot did not care to translate. He alluded to the hysterical patient who had lost all but her genital sensitivity. He maintained that, quite often in such cases, the genital sensitivity was so increased as to cause instances of nymphomania. By contrast, in the hypnotized patient, the genital area usually became analgesic. This comment from Ladame pointed once more to the historical relevance of the decision in *People v. Royal*. It seems evident that there was a general belief in the increased genital sensitivity of the hysterical patient that led to a loss of control over her actions.

Ladame also answered affirmatively to the third question. If Maria had been hypnotized by Louis V., she would have been unable to offer any resistance. Finally, to the question of whether conception was possible in such cases. Ladame answered that conception could occur even if neither the woman nor the man had experienced voluptuous sensations.

Although all of the questions had been answered in the affirmative, the judge still had doubts as to whether Maria's story was genuine. For him, it seemed plausible that she had invented it in order to secure her place at the Maternity Hospital in Bern. To such an objection, Ladame could only answer that it was impossible to determine whether Maria had been hypnotized when Louis V. had allegedly abused her. He suggested that one way to solve this problem was to hypnotize Maria once more and ask her in hypnosis to recall the events of the night in question. Ladame, however, opposed such a use of hypnosis.

> In fact this is a very tricky experiment upon which we do not think it is possible to base an informed judgment. We must remember that the hypnotized individuals have dreams and hallucinations that they confound with reality and describe in the most vivid detail. (Ladame, 1882, p. 531)

Ladame sent his conclusions to the Court. He emphasized the possibility of rape through hypnosis, but could not ascertain if such was the case in Maria's description of events. He warned the Court on the dangers of hypnotizing Maria in order to obtain a complete version of her story. He pointed out, correctly, that such a technique could lead voluntarily or involuntarily to the confabulation of details that would not be verifiable. Taking the medico-legal expertise in conjunction with the other evidence presented in the case, the Court rejected the accusation and exonerated Louis V.

Nevertheless, Liégeois believed that the Court had made an error. Although he considered the case doubtful, it suggested to him that repeated hypnotizations could lead to sexual abuse.

One last case that occurred at the same time merits attention as an illustration of the dangers thought to be related to the presence of the hypnogenic zones in hysterical patients. The case was communicated to de la

Tourette by Pitres in 1883 and is described in both Ladame and Thoinot. It is certainly a doubtful one; nevertheless, it became one of the cases cited as illustrating the coercive aspect of hypnosis. In this case, a young woman was treated for repeated hysterical attacks. She was found to be easily hypnotized. In addition, she was diagnosed as having hypnogenic zones on her extremities (elbows and popliteal spaces), and it was shown that she could easily fall into somnambulism. She was a virgin at the time.

One day, she left the hospital in the company of Theresa, another hysterical patient. They met two men who invited them both to lunch.

> I did not wish to accept; but being urged to do so, I ended by going. We came to a little restaurant outside the village. One of the men wanted to kiss me, and I got very angry; lunch was served without him renewing his attempts. When lunch was over, Theresa left me alone with one of the men. He wanted to kiss me, but I defended myself; I threatened to cry out and I even seized a chair to defend myself. He then rushed upon me and *seized me by the arms.* Then I lost consciousness and I do not know what happened further. When I came to myself again (awakened by Theresa) we were all four in the main room of the restaurant, and it was time to leave. I noticed that I was wet about my private parts, and that I felt a little pain there. I came back to Bordeaux and went home. (Thoinot, 1919, p. 139, italics in original)

Nine months later, she was delivered of a child at full term.

The case was impossible to verify. For Pitres, however, it confirmed his belief in the possibility of forced hypnotization by compression of the hypnogenic zones.

The legal cases were not the only evidence put forward by Liégeois to substantiate his point. A number of experiments had been performed at Nancy to demonstrate the possibility of hypnotic coercion. This signaled the beginning of such experimentation and the next five years would see both schools multiplying their efforts to demonstrate the coercive power of hypnosis. Liébeault's first attempts to coerce his patients into the commission of petty crimes were mentioned earlier. His successors were to become more ingenious and more daring. Many types of experiments were attempted: They involved simulated murders, poisonings, arson, thefts, false bank notes, and many others. Liégeois reported that he had been successful in most of his attempts. In the following experiment, he suggested to one patient that she would poison a man who had just entered the room.

> I dissolve white powder in water, and I say to Mme C. . . (35 years old) that it is arsenic. I tell her: here comes M. D. . . who is thirsty; he will ask for a drink later; you will offer him this drink.—"Yes, sir."—But M. D. . . asks her a question that I had not anticipated. He asks what is in the glass that he is offered. With an innocence that could not be simulated Mme C. . . answers: "It is arsenic!"—I must therefore modify my suggestion. I say: If someone asks you what's in the glass, you will answer that it is water with sugar.
>
> Interrogated by the police chief commissioner, Mme C. . . does not remember anything. She did not see anything, did not do anything, did not give

anything to drink to anyone; she does not understand what people are trying to tell her. (Ladame, 1882, p. 525)

Overall Liégeois's (1884) communication to the Academy of Moral and Political Sciences was not well received. Three major objections were directed against his thesis by M. Franck, Arthur Desjardins, and Paul Janet (Pierre's uncle), all philosophers; they had great difficulty accepting the notion (and alleged power) of suggestion as described by Liégeois. For Franck, it was obvious that the subjects in all of the experiments knew that what they were asked to perform would not bear any consequences. For Desjardins, it was apparent that Liégeois had been duped by his subjects who had simulated everything. He added, for good measure, that even if they had not simulated, existing laws were more than adequate to take care of such undue behaviors. Why should one worry? Finally, Paul Janet regretted the lack of scientific observations in Liégeois's work; here, Janet was pointing to the fact that the speaker was a lawyer, not a physician. He did not, however, reject the results of the experiments *a priori*. He believed instead that much work was still needed.

Whether it had been well received or not, this communication triggered a debate that would extend until the end of the nineteenth century. The Nancy school was proposing a new way of conceptualizing hypnosis. Whether it be experimentally, clinically, or forensically, Charcot's theory was rejected. For the Salpêtrière's followers, it was time to go back to the drawing board.

NOTES

1. A number of books have been devoted to the history of what has been called the "golden years" of hypnosis. We are particularly indebted to Ellenberger (1970), Barrucand (1967), and Sheehan and Perry (1976), all of whom have provided us with the necessary groundwork upon which to build the forensic history of that period. Since most of the academic history of hypnosis is easily accessible, a detailed review of the theoretical struggle of that period will not be presented. It is quite noteworthy, however, that none of these authors have emphasized the importance of the forensic debate in the historical acceptance and/or rejection of hypnosis. It must be said on the other hand that these authors were more interested in the clinical and experimental history of hypnosis. Among the older books that review the forensic debate, the reader is encouraged to consult Moll (1889/1982), and Binet and Féré (1888).

2. Liébeault's book did not sell very well. Depending upon the source referred to, not more than five copies were purchased in the first five years of publication. Although Ellenberger (1970) reported this fact, he also expressed his surprise, since Liébeault was well known in surrounding countries and was probably widely read. It appears that this belief was proposed first by A. W. Van Renterghem in his 1898 book entitled *Liebault [sic] En Zijne School*. Most of Ellenberger's treatment of the Nancy school was taken from this rare book.

3. For additional details of the case, Binet (1896) in his book on *Alterations of Personality* provided an account of Félida's case (see pp. 6–21).

4. These experiments may have been at the origin of Barrucand's hypothesis that the use of magnetism could prolong life. On page 207 of his 1967 book, he listed the age of

death of the major figures in the history of hypnosis, from Mesmer to Janet. The mean age of death was 78 years. This finding prompted Barrucand to write: "Would animal magnetism and hypnotism be elements of longevity?" This question had already been answered in the affirmative by the early magnetists . . . and seemingly demonstrated by Lafontaine's experiments with lizards.

5. Czermak was the first one to explore Kircher's claims systematically. He had a physiological laboratory at the University of Leipzig. For further experiments on animal hypnosis, see Hammond (1876).

6. Thoinot wrote his book in the 1880s after Charcot had published his theory of hypnosis. He was a faithful follower of Charcot's theory and practices. Thoinot's book was translated into English in 1919.

7. The Castellan affair was originally reported in Despine (1868). Thoinot (1919) offers a detailed version in English from which we borrowed the main points of the case. The translation is more than adequate, although the author sometimes overindulges in *post hoc* reasoning. It should be added that what follows constitutes what was written on the case at the time. What might have actually happened is another matter which, by now, may be unknowable.

8. There appear to have been two variations of wording in American rape statutes. On the one hand, there were those which defined rape as obtaining intercourse against a woman's will; on the other hand were those which defined rape as obtaining intercourse without consent. Hypnosis was thus considered under the second definition in the present case (see Solomon, 1952).

9. The Lévy affair has already been presented in an article by Laurence and Perry (1983).

10. The reader is already familiar with Braid's eye fixation technique. Variations of this technique had been shown to elicit a hypnotic state as well. Azam (1860) had reported that there was a relation between the turning upward of the gaze and the ability to be hypnotized. He could not, however, explain it: "I am convinced that there exists between the cerebral phenomena of an epileptic or hysterical attack, and also maybe other purely physiological states, and an upward converging squinting a peculiar relation still unexplained" (1860, p. 19). Compression of the eyeballs was a technique used by the early magnetists. Charcot subsequently retained this method at the Salpêtrière.

11. There was also a third school that evolved in the midst of the controversy between Nancy and the Salpêtrière. It originated from La Pitié Hospital under the leadership of Dumontpallier and two of his students, Magnin and Bérillon. All three became involved in the forensic debate although mainly from a theoretical point of view. Their position was close to the one adopted by Charcot. They introduced, however, the idea of suggestion within a physio-pathological framework. They would almost be forgotten, as Barrucand (1967, p. 157) justly noted, were it not for the fact that Bérillon had been editor of the *Revue de l'Hypnotisme*, an influential scientific journal at the time.

12. It may at first be difficult to follow the ramifications of Charcot's system, since it is not the purpose of this section to discuss his model in detail. We will attempt however to summarize the main points of the theory in a way that will permit the reader to compare it to that of the Nancy model. For the interested reader, Binet and Féré (1888) described the Salpêtrière approach in detail. It is available in an English translation. A brief summary can also be found in Thoinot (1919, pp. 101-110).

13. It is not surprising when one reads such descriptions to see why Bernheim attacked the Salpêtrière's methodology by maintaining that suggestion was the only cause underlying the induction of hypnosis.

14. The three different stages could appear in any order, depending upon the technique used. Although Charcot always maintained the tripartite division of the hypnotic condition, his students and colleagues soon modified his plan. Many intermediate and composite variations of the three basic stages came to be described. The flavor of these variations is conveyed by the following classification: lethargoid state with eyes open or closed, lucid lethargy; cataleptoid state with eyes open or closed, or muscular hyperexcitability; ecstasy, fascination, charm, oneiric, and waking somnambulism (Moreau, 1891). Pierre Janet (1886; cited in Morand, 1889) described nine states, representing different alliances between the three basic ones: catalepsy, lethargic catalepsy, somnambulic catalepsy, cataleptic lethargy, lethargy, somnambulic lethargy, somnambulism, cataleptic somnambulism, and lethargic somnambulism (pp. 157–158).

15. Bernheim's classification can be summarized in the following way: (1) The subject reports that he or she did not sleep, or was only relaxed. Suggestibility, however, is already increased. His or her eyes are opened. (2) Similar to the first degree, except that the eyes are closed. The subject cannot open them. (3) Possibility of a suggestive catalepsy. (4) Possibility of suggestive catalepsy with impossibility to modify the suggested position; automatic rotary movements of the upper limbs. (5) Possibility of suggested contractions. (6) Automatic obedience. In these first six degrees, there is no amnesia upon waking and no possibility of hallucinations. (7) Amnesia upon waking. (8) Amnesia upon waking and hallucinations during sleep. (9) Amnesia upon waking and hypnotic and post-hypnotic hallucinations (for a more detailed description of Bernheim's classification, see Barrucand, 1967, pp. 109–110; Bernheim, 1884, 1886).

16. Particularly interesting is the description in Bernheim's 1884 book of the two different ways high hypnotizable subjects experience age regression. In this quotation, Bernheim had regressed his two subjects to a battle where they had been wounded:

> [The first one] waits for the question of his nonexistent interviewer, and without repeating it, answers. He becomes pale and shakes when he is hurt; he is terrified in front of the police. S. . . , on the contrary, does not become pale when hurt; his heartbeat does not increase; it is another self that he sees and feels in this most curious doubling of his personality of which he has no awareness. He talks to me, answers my questions, knows that he is at the hospital sleeping, and at the same time on the battlefield; he is in no way troubled by this contradiction. (p. 39)

This description of the duality process in age regression is almost identical to descriptions found in Laurence and Perry (1981). It is fascinating to find that in a different century, under different circumstances, hypnotized subjects behaved and experienced suggestions in a similar differential way. In particular, such observations suggest considerable robustness of many hypnotic phenomena and experiences.

17. In this case, nobody mentioned the possibility of simulation.

9

The Public Debate: 1884 to 1890

Liégeois's communication to the Academy set off more than just theoretical interest. For the first time since Benjamin Franklin's Commission of Inquiry, the issue of abuse, whether it be physical, psychological, or moral, was addressed publicly by the scientific community. The general enthusiasm that the questions raised bore testimony to the importance that was given to Liégeois's ideas. Science was ready to tackle a problem that it had avoided carefully for more than a century. In the following six years, books, scientific articles, and newspaper editorials would fuel the debate between the two major schools of thought.

The state of mind in France in the mid-1880s is best illustrated by the words of Anatole France, the famous French writer and poet. On March 21, 1886, he wrote in the newspaper *Le Temps*:

> One fact reassures me; I do not believe that the hypnotists have the power that they believe they have over their subjects. As knowledgeable as they may be, scientists can be fooled. They are error-prone; in fact, they are the only ones who can commit a scientific error. It is an obvious truth that hypnotic experimentation has not up to now been conducted with all the necessary safeguards. I will go farther; we are reliving in 1886 the mesmeric tub and the animal magnetism that captured the enthusiasm of the Parisians in 1778 . . . although hypnotism and suggestion are in better hands than animal magnetism was. But in hypnotic experimentation, it is difficult to avoid deception.
>
> I witnessed the other day a good demonstration of suggestion. The scientist (it was a scientist) who was conducting the phenomena suggested to a young woman that she would feel drunk. He gave her some imaginary wine to drink from an imaginary glass. It should have been sufficient to make the child tipsy. She drank and soon demonstrated all the symptoms of drunken-

> ness. She was too perfectly drunk. I observed her carefully. It was not simply an example of drunkenness; it was its prototype. The young woman played her role as if she were on stage with all the appropriate tricks, with the skills of a talented artist. . . . Everything was perfect. I could not help thinking that this young woman, hypnotized or not, remembered the Montmartre theaters. (cited in Ladame, 1887, p. 294)

Anatole France could not have captured better the core of the debate that occurred at the time. Suddenly it appeared as if Liégeois's communication had unleashed the tongues and writing hands of most practitioners of hypnosis and magnetism. Three major points attracted the attention of these clinical and experimental investigators. Physical and psychological abuses of hypnosis were the major targets of the different expert opinions. To this problem, however, was grafted the issue of moral and legal responsibility. A third area, which had been present since the beginnings of the history of the mesmeric movement but had been ignored for the previous 30 to 40 years, now resurfaced. Stage hypnosis, and more generally lay hypnosis, came to the forefront of the forensic debate. The whole issue of physical and psychological sequelae following the use of hypnosis gave rise to a bitter struggle between some of the most respected clinicians of the period. It culminated in a confrontation between Ladame and Delboeuf at the First International Congress of Hypnosis held in Paris in 1889.

A final, but certainly not minor consequence of Liégeois's communication was the onset of a series of attempts to bring some of the more complex hypnotic phenomena into the confines of the laboratory. Whether human or animal experimentation, the impetus given to research was major.

Lay Hypnosis: The Problems of Sequelae

The idea that hypnosis could lead to some physical and psychological problems was not new at the time. It will be recalled that the secret report signed by Bailly in 1784 emphasized the potential dangers of mesmeric techniques. The Abbé di Faria on the other hand was the first to expand upon the psychological dangers linked to hypnosis, especially in the highly hypnotizable subject (the épopte). As was seen earlier (Chapter 6), the interaction between subjects' expectations and attitudes (conscious or not) and their ability to experience lucid sleep often resulted in the elicitation of cathartic episodes. Legal procedures had already been formulated to prosecute lay hypnotists and their somnambulists following the occurrence of debilitating aftereffects in some of their clients. Charpignon (1860), for example, had reported the case of a lay magnetist who had lost a financial suit after one of his client, a young boy of 13 years, had developed neurotic symptoms. It was not a new story by any means.

In 1880, a major trial involving a well-known lay hypnotist brought back the attention of both the scientific community and the media to this crucial problem. If Lafontaine had obtained recognition in the 1860s and 1870s from the public and the media, two stage hypnotists dominated the scene in the 1880s: Donato and Hansen. Alfred d'Hondt, alias Donato, was a Swiss lay hypnotist who had traveled throughout Europe giving public demonstrations of hypnosis. He had already been held responsible for a series of cases of hysteria that had developed in certain small cities following his itinerant shows.

Hansen was a Danish lay hypnotist who had run into a number of problems on several occasions. Many town councils, including Berlin and Breslaü, had outlawed his demonstrations. In February 1880, while he was performing at the Ring Theater in Vienna, the police were alerted to an allegation that numerous scandalous acts were being suggested on stage. They consulted the Viennese Medical Faculty on the dangers of hypnosis, and a Commission of Inquiry was instituted led by the forensic expert, Hoffman.

At the same time, however, Hansen himself was suing one of his subjects for slander; he had been accused publicly of quackery (and more importantly in front of his Majesty the Archduke Albert who was present at the demonstration on this particular night) by one of the participants. The trial, contemporaneous with the Commission of Inquiry was soon to turn to Hansen's disadvantage.[1]

The facts of the trial were reminiscent of what had happened to Faria. The accused, Henri Fisher, professor in a technical school, wanted to demonstrate that Hansen was fooling the public deliberately by claiming powers he did not have; he had thus decided to denounce Hansen publicly. During the trial, he described Hansen's induction in the following terms:

> Hansen placed his hand on the top of my head, and pressed so hard on the back of my neck that the blood was forced back into my head. It made me feel dizzy. He then placed his fingers on my face, and again pressed them so hard that my mouth was soon filled with saliva as if I had bitten into a sour apple. He continued by moving his fingers in front of my eyes in such a way as to make me squint and tire these muscles. . . . He finally thrusted his thumb into my underarm with a strength only seen in gymnasts, saying "Follow me." I followed him. . . . (cited in Ladame, 1887, pp. 300-301)

When Hansen's turn came to testify, he offered to demonstrate his techniques to the Court. The physicians present at the trial, objected to this exhibition claiming that the technique used by Hansen could be detrimental to the subjects' health. Many of Hansen's subjects testified on the physical problems that his induction procedures had caused them. The experts called upon by the Court were in a delicate situation; none had seen Hansen's demonstrations. In fact, none had ever seen a hypnotized subject!

The human plank phenomenon was at the core of this trial. The Court wanted to know if it was possible to simulate such an amazing feat. All of the physicians thought that it was impossible to endure this procedure without severe consequences. The only one who disagreed with the experts was the accused, Mr. Fisher, who as an ex-gymnast, testified that any good athlete could perform it. He even offered to demonstrate it, but his request was denied by the Court. As the Court pointed out, "the experts think that it is not possible for a man to support such weight when his muscular system is contracted" (Ladame, 1887, p. 302). He was not to be permitted to contradict experts.

Meanwhile, the Commission of Inquiry had been asked to provide answers to similar questions. Of interest to the Court were the expert opinions on Hansen's induction technique, the dangers of the contractions seen in the human plank phenomenon, and the risks inherent in having someone bounce up and down on a contracted individual.

The Commission's opinions in the present case were to assume a particular historical importance. Exactly ten years after Hansen's trial, a young American, Spurgeon Young, died of doubtful causes after having been a subject of many hypnotic sessions, and particularly after having been subjected repeatedly to the human plank feat. As will be seen in the next chapter where the details of this case are examined, the American experts reached similar conclusions.

The Commission of Inquiry concluded that Hansen's induction techniques were particularly hazardous to the health of his subjects and were probably responsible for the many losses of consciousness experienced by those who submitted to it. The human plank phenomenon was seen as deleterious to the human body; it was concluded that the pressure applied to the skeletal system could affect the internal organs. Furthermore, if carried on successfully, it was indicative of the neuropathic tendencies of the hypnotizable subjects. They noted finally that even if a subject appeared normal once dehypnotized, aftereffects could still occur during the following days. In line with Charcot's thinking, the Commissioners concluded that a dormant hysterical tendency could be awakened by a nonprofessional hypnotist. Based upon the Commission's conclusions and the testimonies heard during the trial, the Court decided to ban any further hypnotic demonstration in Vienna. Hansen was not disconcerted. As Ladame (1887) wrote:

> He, Hansen, expressed confidence in the future. He believes that he is the instigator of a new science that will only be recognized by future generations of scientists. He knows very well that he will have battles to fight, but given the importance of the science that he represents, his personal image does not count! (p. 305)

Meanwhile, Donato was touring Switzerland, stirring up many controversies. Newspapers began to relate the negative consequences that had befallen the unsuspecting subjects of his magnetism. Debates arose between different newspapers on the credibility of the alleged negative effects of magnetism and hypnosis. It would, nonetheless, take another six years before public demonstrations of hypnosis were banned in Switzerland. In 1886, the Health Department of Neuchâtel published a report demanding that more stringent legislation be adopted regarding the use of hypnosis. This new direction was based on the reports of many cases of sequelae that had occurred in conjunction with the use of hypnosis by lay individuals. The physical problems were stressed as well as the social impact of the phenomenon.[2]

Ladame had reported two cases of medical complications that had occurred following public demonstrations by a lay hypnotist. In the first one, an 18-year-old woman with no personal or familial history of nervous diseases had participated in two private hypnotic sessions during which she experienced nausea. Eight days later, while at a social gathering, she felt ill and lost consciousness. Following this episode, she had regular hysterical attacks. Never before her encounter with magnetism had she displayed the slightest sign of hysteria (Ladame, 1887).

A more spectacular case was publicized also by the media. In *Le Temps*, June, 1887, one of the editorials was devoted to the dangers of hypnosis. Hughes Le Roux reported the case of an artisan, weak-minded, who had been present at a number of sessions of magnetism. He had been so impressed by what he had seen that he thought himself harrassed by an invisible spirit demanding his death. He became insane subsequently and committed suicide. This fact, which should have found its place in the sensationalistic "yellow" press, was nonetheless reported in one of the most respected newspapers of the time. Magnetism and hypnotism were once again objects of public interest.

The different schools of thought reacted differently to this public attention. Needless to say, they did not agree about the seriousness of the problems elicited by the hypnotization of subjects or patients. Nor were they in agreement on the different problems elicited by the use of hypnosis by lay individuals. Even within each school, opinions differed. In his 1884 communication, Liégeois had emphasized his belief that somnambulists could hallucinate their own death through autosuggestion (p. 43). Other representatives of the Nancy school were less melodramatic. Bernheim differentiated between the problems created by lay hypnotists and the sequelae resulting from either clinical or experimental manipulations. According to him, the use of hypnotic suggestions did not lead to serious problems in healthy subjects. Whatever happened could be corrected by countersuggestion. Ladame (1887) denied also that the suggestive method could be responsible for the onset of hysterical crises; in fact, he recommended the use of hypnosis to calm and control hysteria. The problems publicized were not associated with the use of suggestions, but rather with the use of violent and intimidating induction techniques.

From the Salpêtrière school's point of view, the use of hypnosis by lay individuals and professionals alike could give rise to serious aftereffects. De la Tourette (1887) rejected the concept of hypnotizability in normal individuals. Somnambulism, for instance, was to him either a direct indication of hysteria or the manifestation of a latent neurosis. In his chapter on the use of suggestive medicine, he even proposed that it was better to tolerate a latent neurosis than to risk the establishment of a full-blown hysterical syndrome. Fontan and

Ségard (1887), who followed Charcot partially, reported that the use of hypnosis with healthy subjects could sometimes give rise to headaches, migraines, and nausea. These symptoms could be treated easily by the conscientious practitioner, and were usually of short duration. They were among the first physicians since Faria to report such sequelae. Although the discussion was interminable, with each side refusing to compromise, it was during the 1889 Congress that clinicians banded together in demanding more severe legislation to curtail the use of hypnosis. Their target was naturally lay hypnotists and the dangers of what their mercenary ideas led them to ignore. For instance, in discussing lay hypnotists, Ladame (1889) wrote:

> when he is gone, certainly a lot of talk, but mostly an unnerved population, agitated, suffering from a real psychic epidemic that can only remind us, as it has already been said, of the great mental epidemics of the Middle Ages with their convulsionaries, with their sorcerers, and with their superstitions. (p. 30)

His description of the hypnotized individual was even more dramatic:

> The hypnotized individual, being made a spectacle of himself in front of a crowd devoured by unhealthy emotions, ridiculed publicly, brutally placed in fascination, made to hallucinate deliriously, excited by the grotesque or criminal suggestions imposed by the magnetist, even at the risk of physical or mental harm, the hypnotized individual in public exhibitions is really a victim. (p. 30)

Having summarized a number of cases of negative aftereffects linked to the misuse of hypnosis by lay individuals Ladame asked the Congress to adopt the following three resolutions: (1) that all public demonstrations of hypnosis and magnetism be outlawed; (2) that the curative aspects of hypnosis be integrated into the practice of medicine; and (3) that hypnosis be taught in medical school to ensure that future physicians would be able to practice it safely. The first two resolutions were accepted by the assembly. The third one was modified to read that it would be desirable that the study of hypnotism and its therapeutic applications be introduced into the medical curriculum. It was then adopted by the assembly.

Ladame's request represented more than just a desire of the medical community to halt the potential misuse of hypnosis by lay people. It was also a direct attack on the philosopher Delboeuf who had recently published an article where he opposed violently any legislation of hypnotic practices. He had accused the medical profession of trying to protect its own interest by restricting what was a lucrative practice. Furthermore, he believed that the medical profession as a whole was ignorant in the matter of hypnotism, a subject that it had traditionally relegated to the rank of vulgar trickery. He believed that the criticisms and the warnings proferred by the medical community were nothing other than a reflection of its total incompetence in the matter of hypnotism.

Delboeuf, who was present at the Congress, responded to Ladame's position a few days later. Indeed, it became a personal feud. Each accused the other of falsifying and distorting what the other had said or written. Delboeuf's arguments were simple. A medical degree was in no way an automatic credential of competence in hypnosis. Hypnosis as well as magnetism should become the domain of psychological research. He described himself as a psychologist, and, as such, should be entitled to investigate and use hypnosis as freely as possible. He was not the only one promoting such views; Liébeault had also protested against legislation that would restrict the use of hypnosis to the medical profession.

Nonetheless, there was much documentation showing that lay hypnosis had more than once led to severe aftereffects. Even in its medical use, sequelae had been reported. Often less serious or dramatic, these unwanted and unintended effects of hypnosis activated unwittingly by physicians who had their patients' well-being as their major goal, indicated that the method was not as safe and as secure as everyone wished to believe. Whatever the causes of such consequences, the fact that they had occurred during or after hypnosis was enough to produce a heightened sense of the need for caution among the physicians assembled at the Congress. The topic was to be taken up again at the Second International Congress in 1901 when debating the ethics of hypnotic experimentation.

In general, the power of suggestion to influence the behavior and experiences of patients was taken very seriously. If individuals differed in their explanation of the phenomena of hypnosis, only a few were ready to accept that it could not be harmful. One point that seemed to rally everyone was the importance of canceling whatever suggestion had been given during hypnosis (Bérillon, 1890-1891; Moll, 1889/1982) to avoid unwanted (and sometimes unpredictable) consequences.

> Sexual feeling can also be produced by suggestion. Leopold Casper tells of a case in which Tissié hypnotized a patient, and suggested to him that the right ring finger would indicate sexual desire, and the left, abstinence. When the patient awoke, contact with the right ring finger caused sexual excitement, contact with the left subdued it. Once Tissié forgot to remove the suggestion, and the consequence was that for twenty-four hours the patient was unable to refrain from coitus and masturbation, as well as spontaneous emissions. (Moll, 1889/1982, p. 119)

Even Moll, who did not believe in the dangers of hypnosis, reported nonetheless that nervousness, migraines, and even depression occasionally resulted from the use of hypnosis. He was supported by Bramwell who emphasized the role of expectations and beliefs in the onset of negative experiences during hypnosis (1921).

Most theorists of the period, whether they aligned themselves with Nancy or the Salpêtrière, believed that hypnosis (or suggestion) had a direct physiological effect on the individual who submitted to it. Part of this belief came from experiments using animals as subjects, a number of which were described earlier (see Chapter 8). In 1892 James Lysing published a short review, summarizing the effect of hypnosis on different species: "In animals, hypnotism appears to result from a kind of paralysis of the will. It looks like a capitulation in front of a superior will" (p. 331).

This type of reasoning was not far distant from the one exemplified earlier in the animal trials. It may be noted, however, that in the same article, Lysing reported that some researchers, among them Ernest Hart, explained animal hypnosis in terms of self-hypnosis. The snake did not hypnotize the rabbit; it was the rabbit that hypnotized itself by fixating on the snake. As Lysing put it: "Even at this very early stage, these studies are extremely important; they can produce new data on human hypnology" (p. 335). Meanwhile, it was still customary for articles to appear describing the disastrous effects of hypnosis on the central nervous systems of animals. These experiments were often seen as the best refutation of the suggestion theory of hypnosis proposed by the Nancy school.

> A hypnotized chicken, a lethargic frog lying on its back, a triton that becomes paralyzed when captured roughly experience nervous states analogous to human hypnosis; but did we suggest that they sleep? (Fontan & Ségard, 1887, pp. 20–21)

Sometimes it was the exaggeration of the physicians themselves that reinforced the belief in the dangers of hypnosis. Bramwell (1921) reported a case taken from a certain Dr. X. which illustrated how the so-called dangers inherent in the use of hypnosis could be capitalized upon by ignorant physicians:

> A patient, suffering from torticollis, who had been under my care for a few weeks, shortly afterwards underwent a surgical operation; an important blood vessel was accidentally cut, and about ten days later she died from secondary hemorrhage. I was informed that the surgeon asserted the hemorrhage and death were due to the fact that the patient's constitution had been weakened by hypnotism. If this were true, the relatives felt that they had contributed to the death by permitting the patient to try hypnotic treatment, and I was asked if I could in any way reassure them. This I had little difficulty in doing. I informed them (a) that hypnotism did not weaken the constitution; under its influence Esdaile had reduced the mortality in the removal of the tumors of elephantiasis from 50 to 5 percent, and my own operative cases had all done well. (b) Even granting that hypnotism could weaken the constitution, it was unreasonable to suppose that its influence had spread from the patient to the surgeon, and thereby caused him to accidentally cut a blood vessel. (c) I mentioned the not unimportant fact that I had absolutely failed to hypnotize the patient. (p. 429)

There is a renewed interest nowadays in the problems, both physical and psychological, that can occur when hypnosis is used in the experimental, clinical, and forensic contexts (see Chapter 11 and the Conclusion). A hundred years ago, as today, such problems were seen as more the exception than the rule. But they were present nonetheless, and the practitioner then, as now, had to be aware of the potential for their emergence.

This section would not be complete, however, without mention of the fact that Bernheim, himself, had to submit to a preliminary legal inquiry in 1895, when one of his patients died following hypnosis. The case was reported in the *Revue d'Hypnologie et de Psychothérapie* (1895, Vol. 11, p. 347), the *Revue Médicale de l'Est*, and the *British Medical Journal* (it was also reported later by Bramwell, 1921). The patient, a 37-year-old man, suffered from a phlebitis of the posterior left tibial vein, accompanied by severe pain. To relieve the pain, Bernheim hypnotized him. During the session, the patient experienced periods of respiratory difficulties triggered by anxiety that could only be relieved by removing him from hypnosis. He died two to three hours later, complaining that hypnosis had killed him. The autopsy showed that the patient had suffered an embolism of the pulmonary artery. In the *British Medical Journal*, it was admitted that the case was nothing more than an "unlucky coincidence"; a few lines later, however, the commentator stated that: "It is at least arguable that the psychical excitement induced by the hypnotizing process may have caused a disturbance in the circulatory system, which had a share in bringing about the catastrophe" (cited in Bramwell, 1921, p. 426).

By the end of the nineteenth century, in most European countries, severe legislation had been adopted to restrict the use of hypnosis to the medical profession. In France, hypnosis was only recognized for medical purposes. It was even banned from the Army and the Navy (see Grasset, 1903).

Some Experiments on Coercion

One of the major beneficial consequences of the forensic debate of the nineteenth century was that it stimulated a series of experiments that attempted to investigate the coercive potential of hypnosis. Three aspects of the hypnotic situation were the focus of much attention and criticism. The types of suggestion used to influence the hypnotized individual, the role of rapport or the relationship between hypnotist and hypnotized subject, and the characteristics of the susceptible individual were investigated at both Nancy and the Salpêtrière.

The debate was not cordial, and often exceeded the limits of professionalism. At the 1889 Congress, Liégeois presented a long exposé on the dangers of hypnosis which extended his 1884 communication to the Academy of Moral and Political Sciences. De la Tourette took the floor immediately after Liégeois's intervention and criticized his colleague in severe terms. Delboeuf, who was present at the session, described de la Tourette's comments in the following terms:

> M. Liégeois had just read his superb and courageous report on criminal suggestions. M. de la Tourette stands up and begins to talk in such provocative and denigrating terms of a man of such status and age as M. Liégeois, that my neighbors, foreigners like myself, were flabbergasted.... And I may add that I had never heard someone use sarcasm with such mastery, such volubility, such sureness. (Delboeuf, 1890, p. 31)

Although both schools of thought accepted that it was possible to coerce an individual into the commission of a crime as exemplified by the numerous successes of various contrived demonstrations, they differed in their theoretical explanations for such behaviors. As is still the case (see Chapter 11), the experimental investigation of coercion in the laboratory was extremely difficult to pursue. Critics pointed to the fact that the subjects employed were well aware of the protected milieu in which they were asked to perform. Binet (1900) reported an anecdote about what had happened to Charcot while demonstrating some hypnotic phenomena on his patients. He wrote:

> He [Charcot] wanted one of his patients to write an acknowledgment of a debt for one million [francs]; this incredible amount triggered in the hypnotized patient an invincible resistance, and to finally get her to sign, the debt had to be lowered to one hundred francs. (Binet, 1900, p. 15)

In his laboratory, Liégeois was more successful. Acknowledgments of debts, monetary gifts, falsified documents, and especially falsified wills were easily obtained.

> "I have, as you know, loaned you five hundred francs; you will sign me an IOU that will validate the loan."
> "But, sir, I don't owe you anything; you did not loan me anything."
> "Your memory is not very good, madam; I will tell you exactly how it happened. You asked me for this money, and I agreed to loan it to you. I gave it to you yesterday, here, in pieces of twenty francs."
> Under the influence of my gaze, and confronted by my affirmation spoken with honesty, Madame P ... hesitates; her thinking is disturbed; she searches her memory; finally, listening to my suggestion, she remembers the fact that I had just mentioned; this fact, although imaginary, has become reality for her. Madame P ... is an adult; the IOU for [five hundred francs] ... is written from her hand, as is required by by the article 1326 of the civil Code; the IOU is thus legally valid. If I were to give it to a bailiff, he could request payment. (Liégeois, 1889a, p. 138)

Who was right? Was the IOU legal? How could one interpret Charcot's patient's behavior? For de la Tourette, these crimes would never have happened in real life. As will be seen, however, they were attempted. One aspect of these crimes that Liégeois had ignored was noticed by a number of investigators, among them Ballet (1891), Beaunis (1886), Janet (1919), and Laurent (1891). This aspect was the double-edged effect of a criminal suggestion. Sooner or later, the hypnotized individual would remember the circumstances of the manipulation, and report the trickery to the police. Moreover, Beaunis, who was in agreement with the Nancy school, had noticed that hypnotized subjects could resist an unwanted suggestion in a number of ways. They could refuse to answer, refuse to emerge from hypnosis, or manifest a hysterical crisis. This double-edged effect took on greater importance when the suggestion addressed the issue of crime and sexual abuse. Janet (1894) provided a typical example of this in a report of an alleged sexual abuse on a somnambulist subject. A 17-year-old servant, R., worked for a man who was interested in hypnosis. Her employer attempted on many occasions to use hypnosis to abuse her sexually. He succeeded only in eliciting hysterical convulsions leading eventually to the development of a full-blown neurosis (p. 194).

Here again, an important point should be kept in mind. As was already noticed in the previous chapter, adherents to the Nancy school did not believe that *everyone* could fall victim of a criminal suggestion. They thought that only deeply hypnotizable subjects, the somnambulists, were generally at risk. Although this important theoretical point was continuously downplayed by the opponents of the Nancy school, Bernheim and his colleagues always emphasized it. In fact, following the Eyraud–Bompard trial in 1889, Bernheim himself recognized that hysterical individuals could be even more prone to accept a criminal suggestion than the highly hypnotically responsive person.

Few attempts were made in the laboratory to investigate the possibility of sexual abuse by hypnosis, and quite understandably so. From time to time an investigator would report asking a female subject to remove a skirt, a shirt, or a corset, or to kiss a medical student, but the results were contradictory. Some subjects could prove to be resistant to such demands.

> One day, I told one of our hypnotized female patients that she would upon awakening kiss one of my students, M. X. . . . Once awakened, she approached the student, took his hand, but then, hesitated, looked around, appeared troubled by the attention that was directed at her. She stayed like this for a moment, exhibiting intense anxiety. Questioned closely, she blushed and admitted that she felt like kissing M. X . . . , but that she could never indulge in such unseemly behavior. (Bernheim, cited in Morand, 1889, p. 320)

If a subject complied, however, sequelae were almost certain to develop. More interesting was the possibility of creating a context where sexual abuse could be tested. Bernheim thought that a female subject could be abused if the proper suggestions were used. For example, by suggesting a global negative hallucination where the subject was in a kind of "no man's land" (so to speak), it could be possible to abuse her: "I have seen very austere and prudish ladies who, once placed in such a state [total negative hallucinations], would express neither resistance nor emotion when their dress or shirt was lifted, their leg or thigh pinched . . ." (Bernheim, 1897, p. 44).

The question was whether it could really be so simple a matter. Delboeuf thought not; he rejected the idea that hypnosis could be used to coerce women to participate in unwanted sexual acts. He summarized several unsuccessful attempts to instill in a female subject the delusion that he was in fact her new husband. He suggested to a young girl, for example, that she was in her bedroom, preparing to go to bed. She first looked around as if she did not believe it; she then found something to do like rearranging her bed. After a while, she undid her hair and unfastened her hair clasp. At this point, the hypnotist suggested that he was her husband, and that they had recently married. Each time, the subject rejected the suggestion, and threatened to cry out. Delboeuf was obliged to dehypnotize her to avoid unwanted consequences.

These experiments were of interest not only to the scientific community but also to the general public. This latter type of experiment drew some sarcastic comments from a journalist who had attended one of Delboeuf's conferences. The newspaper *La Meuse* in its May 28, 1888 edition concluded its report by saying: "M. Delboeuf may not have been her idea of the perfect husband."

These comments were paralleled by the bitterness with which the scientists attacked each other. Commenting more than ten years later on this same experiment, and having first expressed sympathy for the death of Mr. Delboeuf, the incisive Liégeois went on:

> Delboeuf, who does not believe in experiments in general, and especially in experiments conducted by others, has from time to time allowed himself to conduct some investigations. From these, he concluded that subjects who received a criminal suggestion are conscious enough either to reject it, or to know that it is not serious, that it will not hurt anyone, that the guns are not loaded, that the knives are made of cardboard, or that it is innocuous to role play, to go along with the experimenters' inoffensive mania. . . .
>
> Well, I have obtained opposite results at Dr. Liébeault's clinic. I used the same suggestion that had failed in Liège with honest young women, and I found, many times, that this idea had been totally accepted upon awakening. One of the young women became so absorbed in her role that she exclaimed once awakened: "I am so happy. I have been wanting to get married for such a long time!" Then, looking at me, she continued: "Tomorrow we *will get up late*, won't we? I love *staying in bed* in the morning." (Liégeois, 1898, p. 236, italics in original)

The belief in the overwhelming power of hypnotic suggestions was reinforced by the results of experiments that attempted to modify normal physiological responses. Many experiments were reported where such phenomena as heartbeat and body temperature change, blister production or elimination, suggested vomiting or micturition, had been successfully suggested. Some investigators had even claimed to have successfully suggested to their male subjects that they were engaging in coitus, and had obtained ejaculations (Ladame, 1887, p. 523). Others had demonstrated that uterine contractions during childbirth could be influenced by suggestions. As Ladame noted, it became easy to conclude that there were potential dangers underlying the misuse of hypnotic suggestions.

These experiments were confounded also by the ability of hypnotized subjects to produce hallucinations or dreams that they later integrated into their memories.

> These dreams are sometimes erotic and women can believe in good faith, especially if they remember the voluptuous sensations that they experienced during their hypnotic sleep, that they have been seduced by their hypnotist, in the same way that medieval witches believed that the Devil possessed them during their demoniacal attacks (incubi and succubi). (Ladame, 1887, p. 333)

This emphasis on subjects' differential abilities and personality characteristics, as well as the different specific phenomena that highly hypnotizable subjects were able to produce, prompted de la Tourette and Brouardel, the two main speakers for the Salpêtrière, to adopt a more middle of the road position:

> The hypnotized subject behaves in line with her personality. She can resist, or she cannot resist. A prude woman will refuse to take off her corset, but a more exhibitionist one will. (de la Tourette, 1887, p. 137)

> If an individual that the somnambulist finds attractive offers a pleasant or neutral suggestion, she will comply; but if these suggestions run counter to her personal values or instincts, she will impose an almost invincible resistance. (M. Brouardel à son cours. *Gazette des Hôpitaux*, November 8, 1887, p. 1125. Also cited in Liégeois, 1889, p. 249)

As will be seen in the next section, this compromise position would lead the courts to look at every instance of alleged abuse on a case by case basis. It would also stimulate the interest of researchers in the investigation of possible interactions between hypnosis, suggestion, and the memory system.

Most investigators, on the other hand, met with success when it came to suggesting criminal behavior to their patients, at least at the level of overt behavior. Poisoning, murder, arson, false testimonies were all carried out successfully in experiments. An example of a suggested murder by poisoning carried out at Liégeois's laboratory (see Chapter 8) has already been presented. Other criminal acts were also suggested: Throwing acid at the face of the experimenter, a less than socially acceptable behavior, was successfully suggested (Liégeois, 1889). The following experiment was carried out at the Salpêtrière by de la Tourette; it involved a suggested murder with a handgun. The patient, H. E., had had some problems with one of the medical interns, Dr. B. Profiting from the natural antipathy between the two of them, de la Tourette hypnotized H. E. and initiated the following dialogue:

> You know M. B.? —Yes, sir. —He is a charming young man? —Oh, no, sir. He does not treat me well. —Really! In this case, we will get rid of him, and another intern will replace him that will treat you in a better way. —I cannot ask for more. —You will take care of this; here is a pistol (we place a ruler in her hand), when you wake up, you will shoot him once; he is supposed to come here, just wait for him.
>
> We blow on H. E.'s eyes, who, once awakened, continues to chat with us while playing with the pistol (or the ruler that she believes is a pistol). As the conversation goes along, she refuses to let go of the pistol. Because the suggestion has still to be carried out, says M. G. F., she will never accept to

give the pistol away. She would rather kill the person who would attempt to take it from her.

At this point, our friend B. comes in; he knows what is going to happen. H. waits until he is near her, and in cold blood, shoots him. B. falls to the floor shouting: "I am dead!" —You have killed M. B. What were the motives that led you to commit such a crime? —M. B. did not treat me well, I had my revenge. —These are not good reasons. —You think so? Oh, well, too bad. Anyway I had a lot of other reasons. In fact he could only be killed by me. (cited in Ladame, 1887 p. 526)

A similar experiment was attempted by Liégeois. In this one, rather than shooting a medical intern, the patient agreed to shoot her mother. Liégeois had taken the precaution of having the patient (Mlle E.) hallucinate the mother as a stranger who had behaved distastefully toward her. As with de la Tourette's experiment, it appeared to be a complete success. This success was potentially tarnished by the fact that following the experiment, the mother accused her daughter of wanting to kill her; the daughter replied: "I did not kill you since you are still talking to me."

These experiments evoked many criticisms, one of which was that the subjects were well aware of the experimental situation, and that they complied with criminal suggestions knowing that nothing would actually happen. Delboeuf (1895) commented on Liégeois's experiment in the following terms:

> M. Liégeois states that Mlle E. ignores that the gun is not loaded. I don't believe it. Why does one assume that a somnambulist is stupid? You, me, everyone understands that M. Liégeois's gun is not loaded. Why would Mlle E. be unable to guess it too? (p. 236)

Other authors criticized all of these experiments, and the following excerpt summarizes well the position taken by many clinicians.

> How can one be so naive as to believe that a subject who has been ordered to commit a crime by scientists, good-mannered experimenters, ignores that he will be stopped in time? Because it is part of his social role as a hypnotic subject to carry on the experiment successfully, and even if needs be to improvise, he will do what his hypnotist is asking for, and sometimes even more. (Foveau de Courmelles, 1890b, p. 208)

The old saying "Beware of the Pétronille" was once again fashionable. This reaction was understandable when one considers that the experiments were usually carried on by suggesting a crime using a hallucinated weapon on a hallucinated victim. Forel, for example, wrote to Liégeois that he had demonstrated the possibility of criminal suggestions in front of the Lawyers' Association of Zurich on March 13, 1888. He had his subject hallucinate that a piece of chalk was in fact a knife, and the room's door the victim. The door had been furiously stabbed! (Liégeois, 1889b, pp. 235–236).

On the other hand, the comment of Liégeois's subject was very ambiguous; it could be interpreted in two different, but plausible ways. For those who did not believe in the coercive power of hypnosis, "I did not kill you since you are still talking to me" meant that the subject was well aware that the pistol was not loaded, that the experiment was a sham. For those, like Liégeois who espoused the opposite position, the subject's spontaneous comment was the perfect illustration that the suggestion to hallucinate a different person had been totally successful. The subject had not shot her mother, but a stranger! As difficult as it was (and still is) to investigate experimentally the coercive power of hypnosis, Binet and Féré (1888) thought that the topic was an important one that should be investigated as thoroughly and carefully as possible: "Experimental suggestions of crime ought not to be lightly made, since we cannot always tell what traces they leave behind them" (p. 200).

The problem of psychological sequelae has already been mentioned in the previous section. One type of sequela that was not mentioned was the possibility that a subject would perpetrate an actual crime as a side effect of his or her participation in these experiments. Not only was it not mentioned, but when it happened at Nancy, it took nine years for it to be reported. The event happened in 1886, three years before the publication of Liégeois's book, but was only reported in 1895 by Liébeault! In October 1886, Liébeault was visited by a certain Dr. X., who expressed the wish to witness an experiment involving a criminal suggestion. Dr. Liébeault decided to use a young patient, N., a good somnambulist, to demonstrate the possibility of suggesting an actual theft. It was suggested to N. that he go the next morning to a friend of Liébeault's house, M. M. F., to steal two small statues that were standing on the chimney ledge. Two days later, he was to bring them back, feeling guilty for his actions. Before N. was dehypnotized, Dr. X. intruded and suggested in an authoritarian voice: "You will steal! Do you hear me? You will steal!"

Two days later, Liébeault's friend, M. F., who was unaware of the suggestions given to N., reported what had happened. The suggestions had been followed completely. Unfortunately, the story did not end there. A little while later, N. was arrested and accused of a series of small thefts, particularly of articles of clothing. The police had no difficulty in obtaining a confession. They found on him also a notebook containing a list of all the articles that he had stolen! Liégeois heard of the arrest of N. through some friends; he went to visit him in jail, and even asked one of his friends to defend him. He, himself, asked for permission to testify on the possible aftereffects of the experiment, but his demand was rejected. N. was condemned to two months in jail. Liébeault, in 1895, commented on the case in the following way:

> For a number of years following his condemnation, I could not stop thinking that the cause lay in the hypnotic suggestions that I and particularly Dr. X. had given. Even now that I know more about the case, I still have the conviction that the general idea of stealing that was suggested by Dr. X. was mostly responsible for the series of crimes that N. committed. (p. 335)

What was this new information that Liébeault referred to? Following this misadventure, Liégeois and Liébeault wanted to rehypnotize N. to ascertain what had happened. Unfortunately, they had to wait for a few years, until N. had attained the age of legal majority; his father had forbidden him any contact with the Nancy clinic (Liégeois, 1898, p. 243). When they finally succeeded in returning him to the clinic, they learned that N. had met again with Dr. X. a few hours later. The doctor had hypnotized him in a café to demonstrate to a few friends the possibility of criminal suggestions. He had suggested to N. that he would steal a number of small objects, specifically, a raincoat that was hanging on the café's wall. N. performed all suggestions readily. Liébeault thus concluded that the interaction between what had happened in the experiment and what had happened in the café had formed in N. a compulsion to steal, particularly, a compulsion to steal articles of clothing. As for Liégeois, he could not refrain from a certain pride in finding a fact that fitted the theory he had been advocating since 1884:

> And now, looking at the moral of this unhappy affair, I will say to my opponents: Is he a real somnambulist or an actor, the one who goes to jail for behaving in this way? You wanted a crime or a real offense! There it is! I have in my hands the proof that you were asking in support of my theory! (1898, p. 243)

One cannot but wonder what Liégeois was thinking. If this was the long awaited proof, one wonders why he and Liébeault waited such a long time before reporting the fact. Guilt, shame, loss of scientific credibility, and lawsuits may all have been contributing factors. It was only in the legal arena that these problems were tackled in a practical way. It is interesting, however, to note that in actual cases, sexual abuse was what was likely to occur and to be believed. By contrast, allegations of criminal suggestions were usually dismissed: the exact opposite of what the experimental work had appeared to show!

There was, however, one area where most experimenters and clinicians agreed. The possibility of using hypnosis to modify or influence testimony in legal proceedings was regarded as one of the most serious threats associated with the use of hypnosis in the legal process.

The Fallibility of Human Memory

If clinicians of the nineteenth century were divided between the two schools of thought at a theoretical level, they were nonetheless consistent in their practice; the interpretation of the results of their experiments varied, but the phenomena elicited by hypnotic suggestion were similar. One area that rallied most of them was the ability to alter the memories of hypnotized subjects. For the Salpêtrière's experts, the problems resided in the fallibility of the memories of the hysterical patient; for the Nancy experts, the memory system of the normal human being was sensitive to suggested (as well as autosuggested) distortions. For both schools of thought, however, the consequences were the same: One should not accept memories elicited in hypnosis without independent corroboration! As Liégeois wrote in his 1889a book on the problems and dangers of hypnotic suggestions: "These facts should force us into a profound and serious reflection on what I will not hesitate to call the terrifying *fallibility of human testimony* (p. vii, italics in original).

If the different experiments were throwing some light on the organization of memory, they were also hinting at the seriousness of using hypnosis as a means of investigating the memories of individuals who were either victims, witnesses, or suspects of criminal behavior. If hypnosis could be instrumental in the creation or alteration of incriminating testimony, just imagine for a moment: "what would be the situation of the individual confronted by such accusations, and who could not for whatever reason be able to produce an alibi? (Liégeois, 1884, p. 57).

This question raised by Liégeois more than one hundred years ago is remarkably contemporary. As will be seen in the following chapters, it activated during the last 20 years of the nineteenth century as much controversy as would be created at the end of the 1960s when once again the use of hypnosis in the legal investigative situation was revived (see Chapter 11).

The expert witnesses were concerned by many aspects of hypnotically elicited testimony. Was the individual simulating hypnosis? Was the subject lying? How reliable was the hypnotic testimony? Could a subject be confabulating or influenced by inappropriate suggestions? Was memory enhanced by hypnosis or hypnotic suggestions?

On all these questions, both schools of thought were in agreement, but for different reasons.

Simulation of Hypnosis

Lying and simulating were considered two separate issues. Whereas simulation automatically raised the issue of deception, lying while hypnotized ran counter to the belief that hypnotized individuals lost control over their behavior. In the past, many authors had espoused the position that hypnotized patients were at risk of divulging information that they wished to remain secret. On the other hand, the linking of hypnotizability to hysteria could not but raise the issue of lying. One of the best documented findings of the time was the propensity for lies and trickery exhibited by hysterical individuals. Most investigators of the 1880s believed that hypnotized individuals could lie. As Moll (1889/1982) stated:

> But all such [hypnotic] statements must be received with caution, for I can safely assert that hypnotic subjects can tell falsehoods as well as if they were awake, and that subtle webs of falsehoods are invented in hypnosis.... In any case, a statement made in hypnosis must be received with caution; it might be an indication, but not a proof. (p. 383)

The issue of simulation was a more intricate one. The problem was of differentiating between a simulating subject and a "genuinely hypnotized" one.

Unfortunately, there was no easy answer. Especially in the forensic field, the issue of simulation was an ever-present one. Most hypnotic phenomena investigated were subjective in nature, and expert witnesses were painfully aware of this apparent shortcoming. As Binet and Féré (1888)[3] wrote:

> We cannot hope to convince judges of the reality of a state in which all the phenomena may be simulated. To accept the fact of hypnotism on the grounds of moral proofs would be to open the door to innumerable abuses of the most serious character. (p. 362)

The answer to such a crucial problem seemed to lie in thoroughly investigating any individual who claimed to have been a victim of hypnosis, or who used hypnosis in an attempt to explain the commission of a crime. In addition, objective signs that corroborated the subjective reports appeared to be required. The Salpêtrière's investigators had already listed a number of physiological characteristics of the hypnotic state (see Chapter 8); unfortunately, Bernheim and his colleagues had demonstrated that most of them were the spurious results of inappropriate suggestions. Most, if not all of Charcot's findings had been shown to be the results of subjects' perception of contextual cues. Even for authors like Binet and Féré whose allegiances were with the great neurologist, it was difficult to ignore the Nancy findings. They then concluded that the classical signs of hypnosis and hysteria were too variable in nature to allow any solid diagnosis of simulation. If physiological signs were dismissed, experts were left with psychological symptoms and their obvious subjective nature. Many authors proposed that simulation could only be detected through careful investigation of the well-recognized phenomena of hypnosis. To them, it became a matter of determining whether the individual was capable of hypnotic analgesia, amnesia, post-hypnotic suggestion, or time distortion. The detection of simulation lay in the experts' ability to unravel it over time; it could never however be ruled out completely (Ladame, 1887, p. 546). As Moll (1889/1982) stated: *"We are never justified in concluding fraud from the absence of any particular symptom"* (p. 305, italics in original).

On the other hand, it was recognized also that simulators had a tendency to exaggerate their hypnotic responses.

> The impostor generally exaggerates, like a person pretending madness. . . .
> The impostor usually accepts all suggestions very quickly, while the experienced experimenter knows that susceptibility to suggestion increases with a certain uniformity. (Moll, 1889/1982, pp. 301-302)

Moll believed that this was especially so with the more difficult suggestions such as analgesia and hallucination. But even the most experienced investigator could be fooled. As will be seen in the final section of this chapter when actual legal cases are presented, the issue of simulation would always be present in the minds of the expert witnesses when they had to express their opinion on the validity of hypnotically elicited testimony.

Conscious simulation was not the only troublesome aspect of hypnotically elicited testimony. Self-deception, or the ability of highly hypnotizable individuals to deceive themselves into believing their own hallucinations or fantasies, was a major concern. The idea of self-deception stemmed from what Richet (1884) had labeled "the imaginary power of resistance" that some subjects reported following their experience of hypnosis. It was a common symptom in hysteria as well. This aspect of the hypnotic experience was most evident in the subjective reports describing responses to challenge items. When it was suggested to subjects that their arm would become stiff and rigid, and that they would not be able to bend it, many reported that they could have resisted the suggestion by bending their arm, but that they did not want to (Moll, 1889/1982, p. 301). The subjective feeling was, however, one of compliance or simulation.

Even in subjects who were determined from the beginning to resist a suggestion, many reported that they would end up by performing it anyway. The question was whether they were compliant or whether they were deceiving themselves. The notion of voluntariness versus involuntariness was (and still is) an extremely slippery one, as exemplified by Bleuler's subjective report of his own hypnotic experience. He had entered the experiment with full intention of being hypnotized, but had attempted to resist the suggestions in order to learn their power:

> My condition was now that of a pleasant and grateful repose; it came over me that I had no need at all to change my position, which under other circumstances would not have been continuously quite comfortable. Mentally I was completely clear, observing myself; my hypnotizer could confirm everything objective that I afterwards told. By the suggestions that followed, the content of my conscious thought was not otherwise more influenced than in waking; nevertheless, they were in great part realized. (Bleuler, 1889)

When given the suggestion that he would not be able to unbend his flexed arm, he felt his biceps tighten, entirely against his will, and counteract the extensors. On other occasions, it rather felt as if he had lost all control over his muscles or that they were paralyzed. This variability in a person's perception of voluntary control over suggested behaviors rendered the whole issue of self-deception even more complicated. As Richet (1884) and Binet and Féré (1888) pointed out, however:

> it matters little that they believe themselves capable of resistance, since as a fact they do not resist. This is what we have to consider, not their illusion as their imaginary power of resistance. (Binet & Féré, 1888, pp. 289-290)

Self-deception could take a more dramatic turn as exemplified by this excerpt taken from Binet and Féré:

> In the first place, the subject may be perfectly honest, and yet the victim of an illusion. When a subject finds on waking that she is suffering from a wound,

or from serious or unpleasant affection, she is apt to look for an explanation for herself. Sometimes, again, she accepts it from a third person, but in all cases she ends by suggesting to herself that she saw things occur as she has explained them; in other words, the explanation has led to a hallucination of memory. Thus a subject who has, during hypnosis, received a blow from a third person, may explain her injury by the supposition that she fell down, and she will maintain the reality of this imaginary fall with the strongest conviction. The medical jurist must be on his guard against the remarks and explanations adopted by the subject to account for the accidents that happened to her, and her assertions should not be accepted without confirmation. (p. 368; for a contemporary illustration of this problem, see Chapter 12, *State v. Mack*)

This raised the question of just how malleable the memories of hypnotized subjects actually were. Many investigations had tried to evaluate the influence of hypnosis and suggestion on the reliability and the veridicality of memories retrieved while patients were hypnotized. The results of these experiments were not to reassure the legal courts.

Hypermnesia and Confabulation: The Issue of False Testimony

No one was surprised that victims, witnesses, and suspects would deliberately lie to gain whatever they sought in a trial. It did not trouble them either. This was a part of the legal process; when caught short, the individual was accused of perjury and punished appropriately. If the rules were changed, however, and the individual lied *in good faith*, without realizing that his or her memories had been tampered with, it was less clear what the courts were expected to do. As increasingly more experts began to realize, this was the major consequence to which the use of hypnosis in the forensic arena could lead.

Once again, the controversy fed on what appeared to be an extravagant statement made by Liégeois. Arguing the possibility of manipulating witnesses, Liégeois stated that he could instill the memory of a specific suspect into the mind of a witness:

> These false testimonies would be even more dangerous, in certain cases, since the sincerity of the false witness would be absolute. (p. 329)

> This criminal will be for them [the witnesses] *the individual that it will please me to designate*. (1889a, p. 334, italics in original)

Could he be correct? As was seen in the previous chapters, it was already well documented that hysterical patients were often the instigators of false accusations. They usually fell victim to their own delusions and hallucinations. The question was whether normal people could also be the victims of memory distortions.

Little experimental work had been conducted on this possibility. The psychological exploration of memory processes was in its infancy, more preoccupied by the rules and regulations of rote recall than by abnormalities of memory. Even Ribot, in his masterful book *The Diseases of Memory* (1882/1977), did not address the issue. As Moll (1889/1982) wrote of the experimental work on memory:

> Suggestion exercises a most active influence. In the first place, hypermnesia can be increased by suggestion; though as far as I know no careful investigations have yet been made on this point. But we possess many accounts of careful investigations into the possibility of inducing errors of memory (paramnesias), or failures of memory (amnesia). . . . (p. 146)

Clinicians, however, had been preoccupied by this problem and had reported many observations of memory distortions. In 1889, W. H. Burnham published a series of articles in the *American Journal of Psychology* reviewing the field of memory. The third part of his review examined the phenomenon of paramnesia or as the author defined it: "I shall use the word paramnesia, suggested by Kraepelin and formed after the analogy of paranoia, paraphasia and the like, as a general term to denote pseudo-reminiscences or illusions and hallucinations of memory" (1889, p. 431, Footnote 1).

Burnham modified Kraepelin's nosology and described three types of paramnesias. In the first type, *simple paramnesia*, the images of the imagination, as they spontaneously arose in consciousness, appeared as memories (p. 434). In normal individuals, a remembered series of events was often completed by imaginary links: "We remember certain points, the imagination fills out the picture" (p. 435).

The second type, *identifying paramnesia*, is better known as the déjà-vu phenomenon, where one has the experience of having been in a seemingly novel situation before. Finally, in the third type, *suggested or associating paramnesia*, an actual impression suggested an illusion or hallucination of memory (p. 449). This third type was also frequent in normal individuals. Memories that are activated in a specific context are automatically influenced by it.

Burnham acknowledged the crucial importance of paramnesias in the medico-legal context. He reported that lawyers usually attempted to influence their witnesses by suggesting repeatedly desired changes in their testimonies over time (p. 460). Burnham's review pointed to the fact that scientists were aware of the fallability of the memory system in normal daily life. What he did not review in detail, however, was the extensive investigation that the Nancy school had conducted on the possibility of manipulating memory by suggestion and hypnosis.

This question evoked more than mere academic interest. It will be remembered that Ladame had reported a case in 1882 (Maria F.) where both simulation and memory alteration could not be ruled out as alternate explanations of her hypnotically elicited recall. Moll (1902/1982) mentioned also a trial before the Aisne Assizes, where an alleged murderer was found innocent in spite of the evidence against him because the judge had ruled that the chief witness might have been the victim of a suggested falsification of memory (p. 381).

The possibility of creating a memory, as well as the tendency of highly hypnotizable individuals to confabulate during hypnosis, was well known to investigators such as Bernheim, Ladame, Forel, and Janet. All had demonstrated the possibility of such memory alterations. Bernheim's term for the phenomenon was "retroactive hallucinations" (1886, p. 164); Forel (1906) called it "suggested falsification of memory" (p. 146); whereas Janet (1889) described the subjects' behavior and experience in terms of "plasticity" (p. 274) and "electivity" (p. 274), alluding both to the malleability of the subjects' behaviors in hypnosis and to the exclusive rapport that developed between hypnotist and subject which, in turn, could lead the hypnotized individual to accept uncritically whatever the experimenter suggested. In Janet's view, however, this did not mean that all subjects would accept and accomplish a criminal suggestion.

Most investigators believed that the memory system was stimulated during somnambulism, and most of them gave remarkable examples of this apparent hypermnesic effect of hypnosis. Binet and Féré (1888), for example, reported that the memory system was more acute during somnambulism than during a wakeful state. They thought that hypnosis increased the power of the retrieval processes accessing memories that one thought forgotten. They did not, however, endorse the position that nothing was ever lost from memory (p. 137). Few authors took the time to check on the accuracy of the retrieved memories. Binet and Féré, for example, asked a subject to remember everything she had eaten during the previous week. Out of hypnosis, she could only remember the previous three to four days. During hypnosis, she could go back as far as seven days (p. 136). Unfortunately, the authors did not indicate if and how they could have verified her statements, apart from asking her if they were correct. Nonetheless, this belief that the memory system of the highly hypnotizable subject was in a state of excitement when hypnotized led to many forms of experimentation; among these were investigations of the possibility of modifying or creating information which would be integrated within the subjects' "true" memories.

The manipulation of memories was tested both in the experimental context (although much more simplistically than in studies performed today) and in the clinical context. In the latter, the modification of memories was demonstrated and reported by Janet in 1886 with one of his patients, Lucie, and particularly in 1889 with another young woman, Marie. This 19-year-old woman was hospitalized because she experienced numerous convulsive crises as well as delirium that could last for a number of days. At the beginning of each menstruation period, she would become very edgy and temperamental. After about 20 hours, she would experience a cold chill, pain in the abdominal and chest areas, and the menstrual cycle would be interrupted. Convulsions were shortly replaced by delirium. After a few days she would return to her usual state, although still suffering from small convulsions, areas of anesthesia, and most importantly from a complete blindness of the left eye. Janet thought of using hypnosis to retrieve apparently forgotten memories of what had happened when Marie had experienced her first menstrual cycle. Once in somnambulism, Marie reported that her first period had happened when she was 13. Feeling ashamed, she had sought to stop it by immersing herself in a cold water bath about 20 hours after the beginning of her bleeding. As a result, she had experienced a cold chill, fever, and delirium for a few days. Her menstrual cycle stopped for about five years. Janet succeeded in removing these symptoms by suggesting to Marie over many sessions that her first cycle had in fact been normal and had only spanned three days. With this new version of the episode accepted, the menstrual cycle returned to normal.

Janet used the same method for all of Marie's symptoms, removing them one by one. When only the hemilateral blindness was left, Janet investigated through age regression Marie's claim that she had been blind since birth. To his surprise, as soon as she reached five years old, she could see perfectly from the left eye. Janet decided to have Marie relive different events of that period (around six years old). He finally found a somewhat seemingly innocuous event that had happened when Marie was forced to share her bed with a child of her age who suffered from impetigo on the left side of his face. Some time later, Marie developed the same symptoms, and lost vision in her left eye. Once again, Janet suggested to Marie that the child was normal and that she could touch him without danger. After two sessions, Marie had regained her normal vision. As far as Janet could ascertain, she never regained any of the symptoms that had been treated in this fashion (pp. 410–413).

Janet's clinical skills at modifying his patients' memories were paralleled by Bernheim's abilities to suggest to his subjects (who were also most of the time his patients) what he had labeled retroactive hallucinations. These sugestions were given to demonstrate how one could create a new memory in the mind of an unsuspecting individual.

> The memory of the scene which was suggested to them in a waking or sleeping state is present in their minds as if it had really happened. I have shown how a false memory can cause false testimony given in good faith, and how examining magistrates can unwittingly cause false testimony by suggestion.
>
> Here is the experiment which you attended yesterday. I found the patient asleep. He is suggestible, afflicted by chronic myelitis, and has often been hypnotized (with hallucinations and amnesia after awakening). While he slept, I said to him, "I know very well why you are sleeping now! You did not sleep last night. Your neighbor in number six did not let you sleep; he coughed, sang, and then opened the window; then he busied himself fixing the fire and made such a racket that every patient was awakened."
>
> Several minutes later, I awakened him. He rubbed his eyes, believed he had awakened spontaneously, and remembered nothing. Then I said to him, "Do you sleep like this everyday?"
>
> "No," he said to me, "but I didn't sleep last night."

"Why?"

"The patient in number six is sick. He choked and complained. I don't know what he did. He also sang as if in a delirium. Then he opened the window and was fixing the fire."

"This is true? You heard him?"

"Of course! Everyone in the room heard him."

Then I made his imagination work on this theme, and I created new memories which were not suggested during his sleep. "And the other patients said nothing? What did the one in number four say?"

"Number four told him to close the window and not to make such a din. Then they exchanged some foul language. Number four got up, went for him, and they fought."

"And a sister was there?"

"The sister could not quiet them down."

"Then the director came? You saw him dressed for the bedroom!"

"He had his bathrobe on and told them he would throw them both out today."

"This is not true, any of it, you dreamed it!"

"I didn't dream it. I was wide awake! All the other patients can tell you about it."

I questioned, in succession, the other patients in the room (all awake). Out of 14, seven had heard and seen it all. They were convinced that it had happened; the scene took place before their eyes. These seven were suggestible subjects who had been hypnotized before.... The patient in number four who was supposed to have caused all this ruckus (and is less suggestible than the others), remembered nothing; the retroactive hallucination was not successful with him....

The experiment is not always successful in the same way. Among subjects questioned as witnesses, some have seen it clearly, whereas others have seen nothing. Others have seen nothing but they have heard their neighbors talk about it, and they recount what they have heard and report their testimony (nonvisual or direct, but auditory and indirect). You see how, with the help of artificial or natural sleep, a false idea, an illusory memory, or a false testimony can slip into the brain. (Bernheim, 1891, pp. 92-94)

Two points are raised by these observations: First, Bernheim chose only individuals who were known to be highly hypnotizable, thus restricting his choice to approximately 10 percent of the population. Second, even with these highly responsive subjects, a fair proportion did not accept the suggested memories. When the expert witnesses confronted each other subsequently during trials, they would often misrepresent this important aspect of the Nancy position. Indeed, de la Tourette himself often accused Bernheim and Liégeois of hypnotizing anything that moved.

A typical example of such accusation happened during the First Congress of Experimental and Therapeutic Hypnosis (1889) held in Paris. Liégeois presented the paper on the dangers of criminal suggestions referred to earlier. Its tone was obviously antagonistic, attacking the position held by de la Tourette and Brouardel who did not believe that the hypnotized individual became a total automaton in the hands of the hypnotist. It generated a heated discussion among the audience. The first to take the floor was de la Tourette. He expressed his disappointment at the superficiality of Liégeois's intervention; he emphasized that he should have expected it since Liégeois, a lawyer, talked about medical questions rather than restricting himself to interpreting the law! He rejected all of the Nancy school's arguments as scientifically untenable; their tendency to hypnotize everyone was more deleterious to the health of the patients and totally unnecessary. He claimed that the Nancy school should restrict itself to hypnotizing only

> diagnosed hysterical patients, for whom there is nothing to lose and everything to be gained. In Nancy, M. Bernheim puts to sleep all the patients under his care; he gloats about his ability to hypnotize nine out of ten tuberculous patients. In this case, if I know what they have to lose, I really cannot see what they would have to gain. (de la Tourette, 1889, p. 268)

Needless to say, Bernheim did not appreciate de la Tourette's remarks. He took the floor a few minutes later in an attempt to correct what de la Tourette had said.

> I never said that I was treating tuberculosis patients exclusively with hypnosis; I put them to sleep when I believe that it will be helpful; I do not stop tuberculosis, but I can get rid of pain sometimes, muscle spasms, increase their appetite, and restore sleep. By doing this I never hurt them, and quite often I help them. (Bernheim, 1889, p. 277)

In his 1891 book, Bernheim discussed the harmless consequences of suggestive psychotherapy. He rejected the possibility of inducing hysteria through hypnosis when it was used by professional people, and attacked people such as de la Tourette, "who cannot free themselves from their *a priori* conceptions" (p. 181) and thus study the subject seriously. Bernheim could not accept the fact that when it came to the manipulation of psychological processes, the medical profession was adamantly hostile toward it. When manipulation was under the pretense of official science, however, anything went, whatever the consequences.

> How strange! I remember that a number of years ago a bloodier practice than hypnotism—the ovariotomy [surgical extraction of the ovaries]—entered medicine. The eminent professors of the Surgical Society said, "This operation again has our full approval." Today, the ovariotomies no longer have any enemies. What am I saying? The ovariotomy is performed upon hysterics under the pretext of curing them. No voice is raised against these practices, while harmless suggestion, which cures hysteria, is anathematized. What a strange twist of the human mind. (p. 180)

When it came time to recognize the possibility of manipulating memories, on the other hand, both schools were in agreement. De la Tourette (1887) expressed doubts about the universality of the role of suggestion in medicolegal cases, but still recognized that it could play a major role when considered in relation to hysteria or other neurotic ailments. Retroactive hallucinations, in particular, were seen as potentially dangerous because the subject believed them to be true (p. 147). In this he was supported by Binet and Féré who also saw the possibility of modifying a person's testimony through indirect (and often unintended) suggestion as a major problem.

> The subject may be mistaken from another cause, the suggestion of the experimenter, who has impressed upon her a recollection which is false. It is impossible for the expert to steer clearly amid all these phenomena, and to make a categorical declaration as to the way the thing occurred. (1888, p. 368)

> ... if the suggestion is clearly defined, the subject's memory will be as intense and as full of details as if the fact had actually occurred. We can see what grave consequences might ensue from these experiments from a medico-legal point of view. (1888, p. 217)

With the publication of de la Tourette's and Liégeois's books, the opposition between the two schools intensified, and it often reached the media for which the possibility of criminal suggestions was a popular topic. It was, however, in the actual trials that this controversy was at its most acrimonious level.[4] When one school was asked to provide the courts with expertise, it would not take long before the other published its own views about the cases in litigation. Contrary to the North American justice system, experts rarely found themselves sitting on the same trial. The Court's judge was the one asking for expertise. If the Nancy school wanted to oppose the Salpêtrière school, for example, its proponents had to publish their views in popular newspapers or in scientific journal.[5,6]

The Legal Battles

At the end of the 1889 Congress, the two schools of thought were as bitterly antagonistic as they had ever been. Numerous trials had taken place during the previous five years, each school interpreting and reinterpreting the outcomes in terms of their own theories. In 1886, one major trial took place that summarized well the opposition between the different experts. At this trial, the Salpêtrière school had been asked to testify; it was represented by Paul Brouardel. In his 1889a book, Liégeois took the opportunity to question the competence of Brouardel's expertise. He summarized it at the end of the forensic session at the International Congress in these terms:

> You will certainly allow me to express my conviction that the doctrines of the Nancy school—which see hypnotism as a physiological rather than a pathological state—are called upon to replace in the near future, nearer than is believed, by M. de la Tourette, the doctrines of La Salpêtrière whose bases are both too fragile and restricted. (Liégeois, 1889b, p. 276)

At the same time that Liégeois was expressing these opinions in 1889, a murder was committed in Paris that was to capture the interest of the population and prove fatal to the Nancy school. For the first time at this trial, both sides were to confront each other in a court of law! A number of other events, however, led up to this major and fatal confrontation.

Criminal Suggestions at Work

By the end of the 1880s, the two schools of thought agreed on one specific point: It was possible to use hypnosis and suggestion to abuse sexually a subject or a patient. Many cases had been documented where the role played by either suggestion or hypnosis in conjunction with some hysterical characteristics of the victim appeared to be central in the commission of a criminal offense. Some of the cases reported bordered on fantasy, and it was very difficult to differentiate what was true from what was imagined. Laurent (1891), a Paris physician, published one of these in a short book on criminal suggestions and attested to its authenticity. The case involved a medical student who had practiced hypnotism. Returning home for the summer holidays, he fell in love with his young cousin. Within a short time, she became pregnant and asked the young man to marry her.

> "Never!" replied her cousin. "I am not a physician yet."—She was already in her second month of pregnancy. At this point, he thought of hypnotism, and talked to her about it; she accepted the idea readily. He put her to sleep and said: "At this specific time on this specific day, you will have great back pains, and your period will begin; with it, what I have unfortunately placed in your belly will go too."—The day before the suggestion was to come to term, four capsules of apiol were administered. At the suggested time, the cousin started her period and lost the potential baby. You will probably say that it is the apiol that provoked the abortion. I don't think so. First of all, apiol is not an abortive agent, and I doubt that it could induce an abortion at a specifically chosen time. (pp. 29-30)

Similar cases had already been mentioned by Auvard (see Chapter 8), and they appeared to be supported by clinical work that had shown the potential influence of hypnosis on the menstrual cycle (Auvard, 1889).

This type of report, however, did not receive as much attention as cases of alleged rape. A case reported by Mabille (1884) did not involve hypnosis *per se*. However, the victim was found to be hysterical, with spontaneous periods of prolonged sleep. For the Salpêtrière school, this was a good example of the possibility of abusing cataleptic or lethargic patients (and by the same token individuals who had been placed in hypnotic catalepsy or lethargy). Part of the experts' report was also instructive in revealing the techniques used at the Salpêtrière to diagnose hysteria and hypnosis.

The case involved four young men who were accused of having raped a 22-year-old woman, Madeleine. Two of the men had met her at a dance and had noticed that she was simpleminded. When she left to return home, they accompanied her against her will. On the road, they held her by the arms, laughing and using coarse language. They were met by two other men, one of whom jumped on the girl and proceeded to rape her. At least one of the other young men followed suit. Subsequent to the rape, they removed her pubic hair and forced her to perform fellatio. The whole episode lasted more than two hours during which Madeleine suffered a cataleptic attack.

When first interrogated, she suffered another attack and slept for more than six hours. The Court ordered a medical expert whose conclusions were categorical. Madeleine was suffering from hysteria and exhibited as a major symptom prolonged periods of nonconvulsive cataleptic sleep for which she had no memory. It was thus obvious to him that she could have been raped without her remembering it. Among other symptoms that she exhibited, one in particular occupied the attention of the experts. Madeleine suffered from variable hemianesthesia, a well-recognized symptom of hysteria.

> By inserting pins or long needles either in the arms, legs, face, or on the chest, one can identify areas of total anesthesia more or less extended surrounded by areas of sensitivity. . . . By inserting the needles more deeply, one can realize that the sensitivity has disappeared not only superficially but also in the underlying deep muscular areas. (p. 87)

Differences in temperature were also found between the sensitive and insensitive areas; when leeches were applied to the anesthetized portions of Madeleine's body (a technique developed by Charcot), it was found difficult to induce bleeding (see Chapter 11 on Bryan's method of ensuring the "truth" of hypnotic recall of a crime defendant; it is a contemporary version of these beliefs and behaviors). Two of the accused were found guilty of rape and sentenced to jail. The youngest two (16 and 17 years old) were exonerated.

The techniques used by the medical experts in this case were reminiscent of those employed to diagnose hypnotizability, mainly insensitivity of the vaginal area, and of the earliest examinations performed in possession cases to identify the so-called Devil's marks (see Chapter 2). Not only did the behaviors perpetuate themselves through time, but so also did the techniques used to discover them! The cases also exemplified what de la Tourette had maintained all along; it was not suggestion that was important in alleged rapes, but the pathological state of the patient (de la Tourette, 1887).

A second case, first reported by de la Tourette in 1887, had been investigated by Brouardel. A man, Alfred T., had been accused of raping Mlle Adèle G. while she was suffering from a hysterical lethargic attack. Adèle testified that Alfred had abused her while she was unconscious. She had only realized it a few months later when she discovered that she was pregnant. Alfred then accepted that he was the father. To complicate matters, however, Adèle protested that she had never had any sexual relationships with anybody. On learning the facts, Adèle's mother accused Alfred of raping her daughter and proceeded to beat him physically. Alfred was arrested and charged with rape.

Brouardel was called upon by the Court to examine both Alfred and Adèle. Alfred was found in good health apart from the remaining souvenirs of the mother's attack. He explained that Adèle had consented to the sexual relations for more than two years. He denied having ever had intercourse while she suffered an attack.

Brouardel's examination of Adèle aimed at answering the question of whether it was possible that she could have been raped without being aware of what was going on. As was to be expected, the physical examination did not reveal anything in particular. Adèle had just recently given birth to a healthy child. She was found to be in good physical health with no familial or hereditary history of nervous diseases. The only point emphasized by Brouardel was her "noticeable obesity" (de la Tourette, 1887, p. 521). Her first loss of consciousness dated from May 1883, following the loss of her father. Since then, she had suffered from periodic attacks (sometimes up to four a month) unrelated to the onset of her period. All of the attacks followed the same scenario: nausea, globus hystericus, loss of consciousness, onset of small convulsions, followed by total body convulsion, hallucinations, and, finally, loss of consciousness (lethargic state) that could last up to six hours. Upon waking, she would invariably suffer from an intense headache and global amnesia. This detailed description of the attacks was provided by her mother. Brouardel expressed the opinion that the description was so complete and in line with Charcot's model of hysteria that it could not really be doubted. He did, however, keep in mind that simulation was always possible in legal cases.

Adèle was sent to Charcot's clinic for further examination. She was found to exhibit some of the typical physiological problems linked to hysteria, particularly a shrinking of the visual field, or tunnel vision in both eyes, most prominently on the right side. She also reported pain upon compression of the right ovarian region.

Brouardel concluded that she was suffering from hysteria and that it was possible that she had been raped in the manner she described. He was very cautious, however, in his conclusion: "We cannot say that the facts happened exactly as Mlle G ... described them; we can, nonetheless, say that it is possible that it happened in such a way" (de la Tourette, 1887, p. 524).

In this particular case, other witnesses had testified that Adèle had had voluntary sexual relationships with Alfred on many previous occasions. The prosecution dropped the case.

Not de la Tourette, however. He used this example as he had in the previous case to buttress the argument that in cases of rape the pathological characteristics of the victims were more important than the use of suggestion. In fact, apart from the Marguerite A. case, the Lévy case, the Maria F. case, and the Castellan case (see Chapter 8), supporters of the Nancy school had very little to offer. However, this did not prevent them from theorizing.

While this trial was underway, another young woman, Annette G., was arrested for having stolen a blanket, convicted, and sent to jail. While in jail, she had to be sent to the infirmary showing signs of both hysteria and morphine withdrawal. Her roommates had noticed that she had been mostly unaware of the events of both her trial and condemnation. Examined by the jail's physician she was found to be hypnotizable, and she responded well to suggestions. When it was suggested to her that she should appeal, she went to the administration offices although it was in the middle of the night. When the lawyer questioned her about the reason for the theft, she answered:

> Mother told me as we were going out that we did not have anything to eat for dinner. We needed three francs. I took the blanket on the bed and went to a pawnshop on Mont-de-Piété where I got three francs; mother had told me so. . . . (see Liégeois, 1889a, Chapter 15, for a complete report on the case)

The lawyer then moved for an appeal: "A. G. is hysterical and hypnotizable; the words of her mother, by the authority that she has over her daughter, had abolished her will, and acted as a suggestion to commit the theft." The Court asked Charcot, Brouardel, and Motet to examine the accused. Following their examination, the experts concluded that hypnosis and suggestion had not played any role in the theft. Charcot attempted to hypnotize Annette, but only succeeded in inducing catalepsy. They concluded, however, that Annette was hysterical, intoxicated, hungry, and miserable; all good reasons to steal a blanket. The withdrawal from morphine in itself was sufficient to explain the amnesic periods. They moved that she be entitled to a defense of diminished responsibility. The Court agreed and she was acquitted.

Liégeois (1889a) did not agree with the conclusions of the experts. He found Charcot's technique deficient and suggested that he should have attempted repeated hypnotizations by different techniques. Annette's testimony was not credible since hypnotized individuals often had the illusion of free will while in hypnosis. He maintained that no physician had corroborated the contention that the suggestion to appeal had been given while in the waking state, hence it should not be accepted readily as established fact that this had been when she had received the suggestion. He added that the amnesic symptom could have been due to the presence of a double consciousness in the same way that Azam's patient, Félida, had exhibited two personalities, one of which was amnesic to the other (see Chapter 8). Finally, he suggested that the experts should have profited from the fact that they had hypnotized her in order to question her about the theft. This latter point, concerning the hypnotic interrogation of suspects, as will be seen in a subsequent section, was not taken lightly and most experts disapproved of it. Needless to say, de la Tourette dismissed Liégeois's comments as unfounded. Annette was a hysteric and a drug addict. Suggestion had nothing to do with the case.

Liégeois's *post hoc* intervention in the case was not surprising. Early in the conflict, Bernheim and he had often attempted to explain major previous trials in terms of their theory.[7] One trial in particular was to illustrate well this tendency of the Nancy proponents to voice their *post hoc* opinions in legal matters. Their methods of explaining most affairs in terms of suggestions or suggestibility was to be detrimental to Nancy when the two schools of thought came to face each other in an actual trial. It would also contribute in an indirect way to the decline of the interest in forensic hypnosis in particular and in hypnosis generally that followed Charcot's death in 1893.

The Chambige Affair

The Chambige case happened in 1888 in Algeria. On January 25, Mme Grille's body was found in a public park, naked, with two bullets in her head. Beside her, still alive but seriously wounded lay Chambige, a 21-year-old man. Chambige was arrested and charged with murder. He explained the situation as a suicide pact between the two individuals; he had failed to kill himself when the time had come.

In order to understand this dramatic story a little better, it is necessary to explore the events that led up to it. Chambige was a law student in Paris. His parents, a well-known family in Constantine (Algeria), were close friends of the Grille family. Chambige had returned to Algeria to visit his mother who was seriously ill. On meeting with Mme Grille, he had developed a violent passion for her, a passion, according to him, to which she finally yielded. Torn between her love for her husband and family and her passion for Chambige, she resolved to give herself to him but only on condition that he kill her subsequently and kill himself at the same time.

Mme Grille, however, enjoyed the best of reputations. She was one of the most attractive women in Algeria, and had the reputation of a faithful wife and a dedicated mother. If she had demonstrated some affection for Chambige, it was thought to be more a sign of pity for the young man whose father had committed suicide, and who was himself obsessed by the idea of suicide. As Bernheim (1891) described him: "Chambige's was, it is true, a perverted imagination belonging to a school of young and decadent psychologists who substitute sensation for sentiment" (p. 114).

Chambige's version was simple; Mme Grille was in love with him, and they had already slept together twice. Because she could not face the situation, they had decided to die together rather than be separated. The prosecution disagreed with Chambige's description of the events. It wanted to demonstrate that he had deceived Mme Grille into following him to the park, where he had raped her before killing her. His own wound was part of a scenario he had contrived in order to escape the murder and rape charges.

The facts did not fit Chambige's story. On the day of the crime, around half past five in the morning, Chambige had accompanied his sister, Mme V., and M. Grille (who had to go to Algiers for business) to the train station. He, himself, was scheduled to return to Paris on this day. He changed his mind at the train station, however, and asked M. Grille permission to visit his wife.

Around eight o'clock, he visited Mme Grille, and left around an hour and a half later. Following Chambige's visit, Mme Grille had breakfast with her two daughters. She then wrote a letter to one of her relatives. The letter was simple, gay, quite different from what one might have expected from a woman about to participate in a suicide pact. She did not complete this letter. In the afternoon, she performed some errands and met with a number of people who all testified at the trial that nothing in the behavior of Mme Grille indicated the tragic events that were to unfold. She even made a rendezvous with a friend of hers for the following Friday. In order to explain Mme Grille's behavior, her husband was asked to testify. The defense lawyer asked him: "The accused says that he had sexual relations with Mme Grille on two occasions."

To which he replied: "If this is true, my wife was either dead or unconscious. Alive, she would have never accepted such dishonor (Lèbre, 1889, p. 28)."

To make his point, the husband related the following facts:

> One day as I was coming back from horseback riding, I found my wife hypnotized in front of a coffee spoon.
>
> I touched her shoulder, but she remained immobile as if in catalepsy. I removed the spoon. She was startled and said: "Oh! I don't know. It seemed like I was completely asleep. Maybe there was a shiny object in front of my eyes? I was like a hen looking at a line." On another occasion, as we were walking under a lamppost, we met three Arabs. She was so frightened that I had to carry her home in my arms. She could not talk, walk, or scream. I had to undress her completely, and she awakened only an hour later. Finally, a similar incident happened as we were looking at a performance of the Assaouas. She was so impressed that she could not tolerate it for more than fifteen minutes. She thought she would start whirling as the jugglers were. (p. 29)

The Lawyer continued his questioning: "Did Mme Grille tell you that she was intimidated by Henri Chambige's gaze?"

M. Grille told him: "Yes, it was a straight gaze, but sparkling and intimidating. We noticed it often, but not malevolently" (p. 29).

This implied that Mme Grille was hypnotizable; given this, she may have made love with Chambige while hypnotized by him. The issue then became one of whether Henri Chambige knew how to induce hypnosis. When his Paris apartment was searched, many copies of the *Revue Philosophique*, which published hypnosis research and clinical work, were found. When questioned about it, the accused denied any knowledge of the subject, claiming it was a mere coincidence.

During the rest of the trial the question of hypnosis was not raised. When the time came to summarize the debate, all three lawyers addressed the question of hypnotism. The prosecution described Chambige's behavior in the following terms:

> What exactly happened, and how did you manage? . . . I do not need to hypothesize the subtle action of a magnetic suggestion; you either found yourself in front of a woman who had lost consciousness, who by herself had fallen into a cataleptic sleep, and you abused her body; or you were more

active, and you prepared the moral and physical destruction of this woman by giving her some poison, or some toxic substance. (Lèbre, 1889, p. 57)

The Attorney General summarized the issue briefly by saying: "We talked both of hypnotic suggestion and of the use of narcotics. Let us put aside these versions which have not been established sufficiently" (p. 70).

The accused's lawyer addressed the issue more emphatically:

> The imagined explanation is bizarre. They tried to establish that Chambige, in this student's environment where he lived, had studied hypnotism, suggestion, and had used it as a threatening weapon to dominate this poor woman. ... The investigation has shown that Chambige has never been interested in hypnotism, that he has never followed the experiments on hypnotism and suggestion. Journals were found at his home that contained articles on the topic, as there are in all journals. They were not even cut out! ... Let us forget hypnotism. Let us guard ourselves against introducing into the conduct of criminal and civil affairs such theories. They could have unwanted consequences and give access to easy justifications. All of the guilty individuals could pretend that they have obeyed an irresistible suggestion, all unfaithful women claim that they were hypnotized. Mme Grille was guided only by the hypnotism of love. (pp. 94-95)

Henri Chambige was found guilty of murder (as part of a suicide pact) and sentenced to seven years of forced labor. The affair was commented upon by many authors. Some, like Tarde (1889) and Lèbre (1889), agreed with the Court's decision. Others, like Liégeois (1894) and Bernheim (1891), disagreed and published their own account of "what probably could have happened" (Liégeois, 1894, p. 238).

This exercise in fantasy (which accepted Chambige's account of the events as truthful) was intended to demonstrate that he had in fact used suggestion either voluntarily, but most probably "unbeknownst to himself"! His passion for this highly hypnotizable woman rendered him blind to the altered state that he was inducing in her. As with Dr. Azam's patient, Félida, Mme Grille was a somnambulist who could experience double consciousness, akin to a double personality. At this crucial moment

> she is not the same person, she has forgotten her husband, children, family, social status, and obligations, etc. All of these have disappeared for her. She sees only Chambige, listens only to his voice, sees through his eyes, thinks through his brain, behaves in line with his impulses. ... He has only one thought; possess this woman for whom he is consumed by love, and because he cannot be happy with her on this earth, bring her with him in death. ... And the drama unfolds more or less as Chambige described it. He possessed her (maybe by saying: "*Your husband, your real husband, it is me!*" and all the insanities that passion can inspire), then killed her, and attempted to kill himself. (Liégeois, 1894, pp. 239-240, italics in original)

The double consciousness experienced by Mme Grille was, according to both Liégeois and Bernheim, the only way to explain her behavior on this tragic day. When Chambige was not present, she would revert to her normal state with no memory for her somnambulistic episodes. As Bernheim concluded:

> Such seems to me to be, clarified by the doctrine of suggestion (as I conceive it) the psychology of this mysterious drama. The honest man who had given her his name knew it well, for he said, "Alive or conscious, she had never been with Chambige." (p. 115)

Such commentaries from the Nancy school's theorists were supported by the media which saw in the debate a fascinating and lucrative subject. This attitude, however, was to prove to be detrimental to Bernheim and his followers more rapidly than they could have anticipated. While the debate was proceeding at the Congress of 1889 on the uses and abuses of hypnosis, a rich bailiff, Gouffé, was found murdered in the vicinity of Lyon. This criminal affair was to captivate Parisians as the drama unfolded. The two schools of thought were finally to meet in the legal arena. Their public was waiting.

The Eyraud-Bompard Trial

The Eyraud-Bompard trial gained notoriety well before it reached the courtroom. The facts in themselves were not remarkable. A rich Parisian bailiff, Gouffé, known for his weakness for streetwalkers, had become the apparent victim of his lubricity. He had a secret rendezvous on the night of July 26, 1889, with a woman, Gabrielle Bompard. His body was found subsequently; he had been robbed, strangled, and hanged.

The murder coincided not only with the First International Congress for Experimental and Clinical Hypnotism but also with the World's Fair of 1889 (where the Eiffel Tower was inaugurated). As was seen earlier, the Nancy school had encountered vigorous opposition at the meeting and perceived the Eyraud-Bompard trial as an opportunity to redress this perceived imbalance.

On July 29, Gouffé was reported as missing for more than 24 hours by his brother-in-law and one of his best friends. Gouffé, who was a widower living with his two daughters, had not returned home on the preceding night. Although he was known for his nights on the town, it surprised the family that he had not first brought home the money he had collected during that day. Both men suspected that something had happened to him. Their fears were well substantiated by a police report stating that on the same evening an intruder had entered Gouffé's office and had fled when surprised by the concierge. Nothing, however, seemed to have been stolen.

For two weeks, the investigation was stalemated. On August 13, the body of a man was found on a hillside near Lyon. It was in an advanced state of putrefaction, such that the brother-in-law was unable to identify the bailiff. Near the body, the investigators recovered a small key. On August 15, the remains of a large trunk were discovered a few kilometers away from the hillside where the bailiff's body had been found. The odors emanating from the trunk, as well as the key that had been found near the body, indicated that the victim had been transported in it. A sticker found on the trunk confirmed that it had been sent from Paris to Lyon on July 27, the day after Gouffé's disappearance. The authorities in Lyon were convinced that the cadaver was the bailiff. The forensic experts subsequently confirmed it (Bérard, 1891).

Dr. A. Lacassagne, a leading forensic physician was able to show convincingly that Gouffé was indeed the victim of this murder. Meanwhile, the investigation had uncovered the relationship between Gouffé and Eyraud, a small-time criminal, who presented himself as a businessman. Eyraud had a mistress, Gabrielle Bompard, in whom Gouffé had a particular interest. The two suspects had disappeared from Paris on the same day that the trunk had been sent to Lyon. A warrant for arrest was issued on November 29, 1889. On December 21, following some brilliant work by the investigative officers, it was found that the trunk had been bought in London, England by Eyraud himself. There were no doubts anymore in the minds of the police; Eyraud and his lover, Gabrielle, were the bailiff's murderers.

From the beginning, the public's curiosity was aroused by the search for the culprits. The press followed the progress of the police investigation and the subsequent manhunt with fervid interest, reflecting the demand of Parisian readers. The investigators traveled to Liverpool, England where they discovered that the suspects had proceeded on to the "New World." They had sailed to Québec and Montréal. From there, they had moved on to Vancouver and Victoria, British Columbia, and then to the United States. They had been seen in San Francisco, Philadelphia, and New York. Then in a dramatic turn, Gabrielle Bompard walked into a police station in Paris with a new lover, Garanger, on January 22, 1890, and confessed to the crime. More precisely, she denounced Eyraud as the murderer and described her role as that of a coerced victim.

Meanwhile Eyraud had fled New York. He evaded capture successfully for more than five months. In June 1890, he was recognized on the streets of Havana, Cuba, and was arrested by the Spanish police. He was deported to France and arrived in Paris on June 30, 1890.

Gabrielle's declarations had been well publicized by the media. While Eyraud was still at large, the Court had ordered three expert witnesses to examine Gabrielle's mental status. The three experts, Brouardel, Motet, and Ballet were from the Salpêtrière. For the next five months, from February to July, these three experts examined Gabrielle. Their final report was dated July 20, 1890 (Lacassagne, 1891).

GABRIELLE'S DECLARATIONS

The experts had been called for by the Court following Gabrielle's intriguing confession in which she presented herself as an observer rather than as a participant. She denied any active participation in the murder and did not seem to understand the gravity of the accusation. She appeared indifferent while narrating the events of the murder, as if she had not realized that a man had been killed. Furthermore, the reasons why she had returned to France and surrendered to the authorities were tantalizing and difficult to explain.

The detailed examination of Gabrielle's life revealed a tumultuous existence. Although a mere 21 years old at the time of her arrest, she had a long history of social maladaptation. There was no familial history of mental diseases or physical illnesses. Her mother had died when she was eight years old, and her father had provided the necessary care for Gabrielle and her brother.

Gabrielle herself had no history of physical or mental disorders. She had experienced her first menstruation at eight years old, and it had been regular since then. Characterwise, however, it was not the same story. As early as eight years old, she was described "as a vicious liar, thinking only of men and fashion" (Brouardel, Motet, & Ballet, 1890, p. 699). At the age of 12, she was sent to a convent in an attempt to instill in her some discipline. After one year, she was sent back home by the nuns because of her unruly conduct and her foul language. She was sent subsequently to several other convents, until at age 18, she returned to her father's home. Everything was harmonious until the day that she discovered that her father was having an affair with his maid. From that point on, Gabrielle's conduct worsened. So much so, that her father asked one of his friends, Dr. Sacreste, if the use of hypnosis could modify his daughter's morality. The physician actually attempted to do this, but to no avail. Though he did not succeed, he nonetheless learned some interesting details. While attempting to remove Gabrielle's promiscuous habits with hypnosis, her lover was using hypnosis to counteract the doctor's influence. Ultimately, the lover was to prove to be the more successful!

Her father described her in terms similar to Dr. Sacreste, but insisted that his daughter was intelligent. As long as it did not involve her passion for men and fashion, she showed good reasoning (p. 701).

Her life in Paris started when her lover decided to leave her. She moved to Paris where she met Eyraud, a 48-year-old man, who introduced her into a world of small-time criminals. About this time, she met another man who hypnotized her virtually every day. She admitted, however, that quite often she simulated being hypnotized (p. 703). She described her relationship with Eyraud as being based on fear. He was in the habit of beating her whenever she contradicted him. In describing the events that led to Gouffé's murder, she said that Eyraud had never mentioned that he intended to kill the bailiff. They were only supposed to obtain money by blackmailing him. When she saw the preparation that Eyraud had undertaken to assure the bailiff's capture she maintained that she did not believe that Eyraud was going to kill his victim. She thought that he was intending merely to scare him. After the murder, however, she spent the entire night alone in her apartment with the dead body at the foot of her bed. She stated that she was too scared to do anything.

She explained her return to Paris by saying that, while fleeing the police, the couple had met a young businessman, Garanger. Eyraud planned to extort some money from him to permit their escape to continue. Gabrielle, however, had other plans. Finding herself in New York with Garanger while Eyraud was in another town, she confessed everything to him. He convinced her to accompany him back to Paris. He also hypnotized her on many occasions, but no details of the goals of this were revealed.

Her physical and mental examination led the medico-legal experts to conclude that Gabrielle had no moral sense; that she was self-centered and ready to do anything to satisfy her wishes. She was diagnosed also as having all of the typical signs of hysteria. These included hyperesthetic areas (increased sensitivity) in such specific locations as under the breasts and in the ovarian region. In addition, her vision was diagnosed as lightly deficient in a typically hysterical way. The experts concluded that she was suffering from mild hysteria. They noticed also the many mentions of the use of hypnosis. They proceeded to hypnotize her, and she turned out to be a good hypnotic subject, at least in their judgment. Immediately upon being hypnotized, she suffered from a mild hysterical convulsive attack accompanied by terrifying visual hallucinations. Once the crisis had passed, she entered into what was described as a deep sleep in which she answered questions automatically. As the experts testified, however: "Needless to say, none of these questions were related to the events under investigation" (p. 708).

She also responded to a number of post-hypnotic suggestions with success. These observations buttressed the experts' diagnosis that she was indeed a neurotic individual. They also took care to note that: "It never occurred to us, and it could not occur to us, that hypnotism and hypnotic suggestion could have had a role in the behaviors that Gabrielle was accused of" (p. 709).

It was not clear at this point, however, if these three experts knew that the physician at the jail, Dr. Voisin, had hypnotized Gabrielle frequently between their visits. Dr. Voisin was also a supporter of the Salpêtrière school. It was thus possible that she could have learned her role through Dr. Voisin's intervention. Unfortunately, as will be seen in the next section, the trial did not illuminate this aspect of the story.

The experts concluded that Gabrielle was responsible for her actions; that she did not suffer from any mental disorder except from an evident lack of moral sense. As they put it, she suffered from

> a break in the development of her moral sense unaccompanied by a similar break in her intellectual development. As profound as her lack of morality is, she has enough of a clear intelligence to know what is right and what is wrong. (p. 710)

Gabrielle was sent to trial.

AT THE TRIAL

The trial had been scheduled initially to begin on November 25, 1890. A number of public events, however, forced the Court to reschedule it for December 15. The first of these events occurred following the jury selection. A newspaper, *Le Matin*, published in its November 13 issue the report of an interview that a journalist had conducted with some of the jurors. According to the article, 21 out of the 36 potential jurors had been interviewed on their prospective role, on their beliefs about hypnosis, and on the outcome of the trial.

> We talked with twenty-one jurors that can be divided into four groups: six agree to the total condemnation of the two accused; two think Eyraud should be sentenced to death, and Gabrielle Bompard sent to forced labor for life; four agree to extenuating circumstances for both; the last nine are implacable for the man, but think the woman is irresponsible, that she should be sent to a health institution until she recovers.
> We have to add here a last detail to be more precise; we have noticed, in at least a few of these lenient jurors, a kind of erethism of the pupil, that reminded us of the one demonstrated by the jurors of the Aeropage who acquitted Phryné. (Bouchardon, 1933, p. 252)[8]

The jurors were dismissed and the journalist sentenced to one month in prison. It turned out, however, that only four jurors had, in fact, been interviewed.

One week later, 19 Parisian newspapers published the results of the medico-legal experts' report. The Court fined all of them, expressing dismay at such a breach of professionalism. Finally, and probably most importantly for present concerns, Bernheim, himself, published in the *Revue d'Hypnotisme* (1889-1890, Vol. 4, p. 226) a short commentary on Gabrielle Bompard. This commentary was published before the medico-legal experts had completed their evaluation and before it was published in the media. In it, Bernheim asserted that Gabrielle had most certainly been a victim of hypnotism and suggestion though he had never examined her! It was this impropriety on Bernheim's part that would lead the court-appointed medical experts to explore the issue of hypnosis.

The trial finally began on December 16, 1890. The public had invaded the courtroom, curious to see the by-now notorious couple. There was such a disorder in the room that the bailiffs could not control the crowd. Judge Robert, who was presiding, became angry and shouted spontaneously: "But there is a bailiff missing here!" (Bouchardon, 1933, p. 265), not realizing that he had just voiced the first memorable sentence of the trial!

The medical experts were not scheduled to appear before the third day of the proceeding. During the first two days, both Eyraud and Bompard testified. The former narrated the events surrounding the murder insisting upon the active role that his lover had played. Gabrielle, on the other hand, denied any active involvement; she was poor, submissive, beaten, and feared for her life. Eyraud had coerced her into prostitution. During her testimony, she displayed the indifference that the medical experts had noticed. At times, it bordered on insolence. When Garanger's turn came to testify, Eyraud asked him how Gabrielle had surrendered to the police. Gabrielle was obviously irritated. She interjected: "How did I surrender to the police? But it is very simple. I took a cab and I went to the police station. That's it" (Bouchardon, 1933, p. 268). Following this sarcastic remark she appeared to enter a hysterical crisis and had to be removed from the courtroom for 15 minutes.

On December 18, the medico-legal experts presented their reports. This was the expected moment of drama. On one side were supporters of the Salpêtrière, on the other were those of Nancy; the atmosphere in the courtroom was tense. The first expert to be called in was Brouardel.

He presented the findings of Gabrielle's examination succinctly. As far as the three experts were concerned, the conclusions were not to be doubted. He testified that Gabrielle was suffering from a mild case of hysteria, but her lack of moral sense was the most important aspect of her personality. He justified the examination of the suspect in terms of her susceptibility to hypnotic suggestions by pointing to the fact that it would have been totally unnecessary had it not been for Bernheim's unwarranted intrusion into the case. In fact, Ballet maintained a few minutes later during his testimony: "It is sufficient to state that we did not see anything in Gabrielle Bompard's case that could be related to hypnotism" (see "Affaire Eyraud-Bompard" in *Gazette des Tribunaux*, p. 1211).

One of the jurors asked Brouardel if it was necessary to place an individual in sleep in order to administer a suggestion for a specific behavior. Brouardel answered by attempting to present both sides' views, albeit slightly tainted:

> We are here in the presence of two doctrines. It can certainly be suggested to a sleeping individual to behave in such and such a way during sleep. We can also, but only with highly hypnotizables, tell them: you will do such and such behavior but only later on; it will always be a simple behavior like kissing a person, hit someone with a dagger made of paper. There seems to be in there a suggestion that could be accomplished once awakened.
>
> The Nancy school goes much further. It teaches that an awakened individual can, controlled by suggestion, enact a behavior, a crime for example, with the same destiny as a falling rock.
>
> I would like to see how it would be possible to recognize deception. ("Affaire Eyraud-Bompard," pp. 1210-1211)

Following the report of the experts, Dr. Sacreste, who had treated Gabrielle so unsuccessfully a few years earlier, testified. He summarized his unsuccessful attempts, but indicated that he had performed a minor but painful surgery on Gabrielle using hypnosis as the sole anesthetic. He concluded that it could be possible that criminal suggestions had been administered to her over time and that they could have been successful.

Sacreste's conclusions were opposed by Brouardel who reminded the jurors that when the physician had attempted to improve Gabrielle's morality over time, he had failed. The conclusion was obvious: "When she had to choose between the doctor and her lover, she went naturally toward the suggestion that she found most pleasant" (p. 1211).

Following the medico-legal report, Gabrielle's lawyer called Dr. Voisin to the witness stand. Many rumors had circulated implying that the physician had hypnotized Gabrielle very often in jail and had succeeded in clarifying many obscure facts of the investigation. When the lawyer asked him to tell the Court what he knew, Voisin answered: "I cannot say anything. I am obliged to respect professional confidentiality, both as a physician, and as a civil servant" (pp. 1210-1211).

This unexpected response from the physician evoked the Court's irritation. The President recognized that he would have to respect the physician's choice, but that he felt obligated to admonish him severely for his intrusion into the due process of the trial. A suspect was not a subject for personal experimentation. This apparently surprising position of Voisin was the element the defense had been waiting for as a prelude to introducing Liégeois, who had been denied permission to examine Gabrielle. On the one hand, Voisin refused to divulge the information that he had, or at least that the Court believed he could have. On the other, the defense's expert had been denied the opportunity of examining its client. What else could the defense do? The Attorney General was not deceived by such an obvious manipulation. He promptly replied:

> I have answered that when three physicians, among which the Dean of the Medical Faculty, have examined day after day for weeks the accused's state, they did not need to be supervised by a professor of law. This is what I have done, this is what I had to do, and I do not think that the Defense should use my denial to further their argument. (p. 1211)

Nonetheless, it was a skillful move; the public began to express its outrage. The Président had to threaten to expel spectators from the proceedings in order to regain control. The defense lawyer called Liégeois to the witness stand to explain the problem and to present his opinions on hypnosis and suggestion. Liégeois was a lawyer, and he decided to remind the court that he knew the intricacies of the legal system. He began his testimony by stating:

> My explanations may be long. I was not allowed to examine Gabrielle Bompard, so I will not be able to restrain my comments to specific points that would concern her. Moreover, I wish specifically not to be interrupted, and I will invoke if need be, article 319.2 of the Criminal Code that specifies that a witness has the prerogative of not being interrupted while he gives his testimony. (p. 1211)

The Président interrupted him: "I do not appreciate your insinuations. You have all the freedom to testify. How long do you think your explanations will take?"

"One hour and a half to two hours," answered Liégeois.

The Court was adjourned until the following morning when Liégeois took the stand immediately. He began by presenting a lengthy account of the history of hypnotism and a detailed explanation of his experiments on criminal suggestion. He then explained by the theory of suggestion many of the cases, if not all of them, that had ever involved hypnosis in the legal process. From the Castellan affair to the La Roncière case, from hypnotism to hysteria, Liégeois did not omit a single case. He had even brought pictures of some new experiments on the formation of blisters by hypnotic suggestion which he maintained were proof of the power of the suggestive technique.

He finally addressed the issue of Gabrielle Bompard:

> What kind of a position do I have? The experts have had three hundred days to examine Gabrielle Bompard; me, not even a minute! I can only base my words on what the newspapers have reported, and on the documents that the Defense gave me. (p. 1213)

By this point, Liégeois had already been speaking for more than two hours and the session was adjourned until the afternoon.

In the afternoon Liégeois attempted to demonstrate how Eyraud could have used suggestion to coerce Gabrielle into the commission of the murder.

> It seems to me that it is possible that Gabrielle was given criminal suggestions, and that she carried them out in a state of double consciousness. She would thus suffer from amnesia which would explain her contradictions and her mistakes. Everyone knows that she is suggestible. It would be sufficient to place her again in this condition to know what happened. Even if she were to lie, one could form an opinion.
>
> She is attached to him like a dog to his master. Can anything explain this? Nothing but suggestion. (p. 1214)

He then blamed the experts who had hypnotized her for their reluctance to question her during hypnosis. As long as she had consented to be hypnotized, it should have been the experts' duty to interrogate her. Liégeois ended his testimony by reminding the jurors that up to 5 percent of the population was highly suggestible and thus not responsible for their behaviors: "I will end here using the word of M. le Président Férey who presided over the La Roncière trial: I would rather have my hand cut off than sign a verdict of culpability against Gabrielle Bompard" (p. 1214). Liégeois's intervention was followed by a rebuttal from Brouardel, Motet, and Ballet. All of them pointed to the fact that Liégeois had presented a number of hypotheses that had no relevance to the case in question. Gabrielle was hysterical, with no moral sense, and, at most, could have been the victim of undue influence. Brouardel rejected most of the legal cases cited by Liégeois. He stated that hysteria was more than sufficient to explain what had occurred in these cases. He opposed also the suggestion to rehypnotize Gabrielle in court, since he maintained that this would impede her free will to such an extent that her testimony would become meaningless. As Ballet concluded:

> We are not talking here of a general theory, but of a specific, precise case. We do not deny the different facts proposed by M. Liégeois in a general sense. We deny, however, that Gabrielle Bompard was hypnotized to accomplish her crime. There are more differences in facts than in doctrines between Nancy

and the Salpêtrière, and still these differences are minimal. There is a greater hurry in Nancy; novelties are accepted more rapidly, with less rigorous control. Even between the supporters of Nancy, there are many divergences. One can not hold against us our own disagreement with the Nancy school. (p. 1215)

The defense motioned for a cross-examination of Gabrielle. This was opposed by the Attorney General and finally rejected by the Président. He ruled that the jury had had the experts' testimonies and had enough information upon which to base its judgment.

THE LAWYERS' CONCLUSIONS

The lawyers presented their final summations on December 19. The Gouffé family lawyer was brief and to the point. He asked for the death sentence for both accused. He barely touched on the issue of hypnosis: In summarizing the events of the night of the murder, he stated:

> It is now six o'clock; they all go to dinner peacefully at a little café in Place de la Madeleine. They are joyous, the waiter notices them; and it is most probably by suggestion and by hypnotism, that Gabrielle was forced to drink half a bottle of champagne . . .
>
> I am very surprised to hear that this girl is irresponsible. I would have much pleasure, and it is quite tempting to discuss the issue of hypnotism, but I think that it is the role of the Attorney General to address it in the name of society. You have been exposed to it by a fanatic of very good faith. If it was to be admitted it would mean the end of all justice. . . . If such doctrines were ever accepted, it would become a first-rate social danger ("Affaire Eyraud-Bompard," p. 1215).

The prosecutor was followed by the Attorney General who addressed the issue of hypnosis at length. He introduced his position by stating: "And then an issue was brought up here that should never have been raised; did she, yes or no, commit this crime while in a state of suggestion" (p. 1217).

The answer provided was long and unfavorable to the Nancy school's position. He presented the work of Charcot in the most eulogistic terms, explaining that post-hypnotic suggestions were successful when simple actions were demanded, but were not possible when the behaviors suggested were both to be complex and to take place over a long period of time. As was the case in the present trial, post-hypnotic suggestions were unsuccessful. He emphasized particularly the lack of legal precedent when it came to evaluating the role of criminal suggestions in contexts outside of the experiment. He flatly rejected the theories of the Nancy school describing them as

> not following the experimental method, but proceeding by argument by authority. . . . *Credo quia absurdum* [I believe to the absurd], it is simpler.
>
> Of course there are no behaviors without an external or an internal cause. Everything on earth is suggestion. Even M. Liégeois, if he allows me to say so,

came to this Court following the suggestion of a young lawyer. Should he then be held irresponsible? (pp. 1217-1219; also cited in Bouchardon, 1933, p. 290)

For the Attorney General, the death sentence was too lenient. The two accused individuals had demonstrated their lack of morality and remorse. They had to be punished accordingly. By contrast, Eyraud's lawyer was surprisingly quiet. He pleaded for extenuating circumstances, invoking the fascination that Gabrielle had held for her lover. Eyraud, this aging man, had fallen prey to the young, beautiful but vicious woman; she had pushed him to murder!

Finally, Gabrielle's lawyer took the floor to defend his client. He must have realized at this point that his position was very difficult. He decided to reverse the argument and to present his client not as the victim of a criminal suggestion, but as a victim of a long life of abuse in which her sensitivity had been made worse. Suggestion had been successfully administered to Gabrielle because she was a sick individual. Once this fact was recognized, it became impossible to punish her; a sick person must be treated, not punished. He barely touched on the question of hypnotism. For him, the mere fact that he had attempted this defense was a proof that science and the law could work hand in hand. Thus, for him, it was important that the issue be raised; it was certainly not to be for the last time.

> As of today, hypnotism has made a triumphant entrance at the Assises. The question is asked. It may not be totally resolved yet, but in the near future, victory will reward long and patient efforts. We should not regret it, gentlemen.
>
> There is no reason to be alarmed. Believe me, M. Attorney General, we are not introducing threatening paradoxes, but soothing truths. We just showed you—as it is taught in Nancy—that, if it is impossible to coerce an individual who knows right from wrong, who has an intact consciousness, into the commission of a hypnotic crime, it is another story when the magnetist has an already well-trained subject like Gabrielle Bompard, *a morally blind person*, who becomes a submissive instrument that will answer to all his desires. In this case, it will always be possible to give and carry out a criminal suggestion. (Bouchardon, 1933, p. 300, italics in original).

The jury retired for its deliberations. It took only two hours to reach a verdict. Both Gabrielle Bompard and Eyraud were found guilty of first degree murder. In Gabrielle's case, however, extenuating circumstances were accepted. Eyraud was sentenced to death. Gabrielle was sentenced to jail and forced labor for 20 years!

THE AFTERMATH OF THE TRIAL

The debate did not end with the termination of the trial. For more than two years, Bernheim, de la Tourette, and many others published articles attempting to justify each school's position at the trial. It left, nonetheless, the impression that the Nancy school had lost a major battle in the ongoing forensic debate. In the words of the Editor of the *Revue de l'Hypnotisme Expérimental et Thérapeutique*:

> The general consensus is that the views of the Nancy school have been defeated in the courtroom. A most regrettable defeat when one realizes that nothing justified the confrontation. They will now have to wait for more favorable circumstances. . . . Until then, Nancy must reflect, complete its studies with new experiments, reaffirm its existence and its strength through solid work that will stand up to criticism. (Bérillon, 1890-1891, p. 407)

On December 23, 1890, three days after the trial, the newspaper *Le Temps* published an interview with Bernheim in which he criticized Liégeois's trial testimony. It transpired from the interview that Bernheim had been consulted by Gabrielle's lawyer; his advice had been that the defence, as far as possible, should avoid the whole issue of hypnosis. He was also the one who should have testified but had to be replaced by Liégeois. According to Bernheim, Gabrielle's lack of moral sense and her extreme suggestibility should have been the central focus of the expert testimony. By broadening the debate to the issue of hypnotism in general, Liégeois had created a polarization of the debate that could only be detrimental to the trial proceedings. For Bernheim, the major issue should have been the question of legal responsibility. He added that he agreed with the medico-legal report, but attacked Brouardel for his unjust accusations against the Nancy school. He maintained that if there was one school that believed in absurd phenomena, it was not Nancy, but the Salpêtrière.

De la Tourette (1891) replied to Bernheim in *La Revue de l'Hypnotisme Expérimental et Thérapeutique*. He also reviewed the debate that had taken place at the trial. He was obviously very happy with the results, and cynical vis-à-vis the proponents of the Nancy school:

> M. Bernheim seems to have denied totally M. Liégeois. He now proposes that in the Gouffé trial the divergent positions of the two schools were not the issue. *This affirmation will come as a surprise for anyone who has followed or read the proceedings*; given more time, we will soon learn that M. Liégeois came to support the report presented by the Paris experts. (p. 247, Footnote 3, italics in original)

Bernheim (1891) replied to de la Tourette in caustic terms. He noted that Liégeois had testified at the trial, not him, and that de la Tourette should not confuse the two. He then launched his attack on the Salpêtrière school:

> I refrain from following M. de la Tourette in his tortuous and humoristic argumentation. What good would it do to rectify wrong assertions, twisted ideas, misquotations? No discussion will settle the argument between us. Humorous jests can please the public; they do not transform errors into truths.

> I affirm, contrary to M. de la Tourette, that hypnotism is not a neurosis, seen only in genuine hysterics; I affirm that it can be obtained, in all of its degrees, in numerous normal subjects that are non-neurotic, as well as in hysterics. I affirm that the conception of hypnosis as presented in the *Dictionnaire Encyclopédique* by our opponent is *totally wrong*, that most experimental facts that he relates are *wrong and filled with mistakes*, that the three phases division of the grand hypnotism, the somatic characteristics, the neuro-muscular hyperexcitability seen in the lethargic phase, the cutaneo-muscular hyperexcitability seen in the somnambulistic phase, the transfer operated by magnets, the localized head pain that follows the transfer, etc., all these phenomena are *genuine artifactual effects of suggestion*; I defy M. de la Tourette to find one hysteric, with no history of hypnotization, who will enact these phenomena *in conditions such that suggestion would not play a role*. (1891, p. 272, italics in original)

If the Nancy school had suffered a defeat in the legal arena, its proponents were not yet ready to hoist a white flag. It is interesting to note, however, that in the following decades, Bernheim as well as Liégeois would be suprisingly reluctant to write about the Eyraud-Bompard trial. In fact, Liégeois never alluded to the trial again.

By exaggerating the role of suggestion, Liégeois had undermined his own credibility. If hypnosis, and particularly suggestion, was present in all everyday behaviors, it became meaningless. Liégeois attempted to ignore the basic facts of the trial, to ignore the pathologies seen in Gabrielle Bompard, and to present on a grandiose scale the dangers linked to suggestion. It was easy to represent him as a "fanatic of very good faith." The Paris experts stayed closely to the facts, presented the psychopathologies, and avoided generalizing the issue. As de la Tourette put it in his article: "Conclusion: twenty years of forced labor from the part of the jury who proved resistant to M. Liégeois's suggestions" (1891, p. 249).

THE ISSUE OF LEGAL RESPONSIBILITY

Among the different issues raised by these different trials, two merit brief discussion. First, if hypnosis could be shown to have played a role in the commission of a crime, there was an issue concerning how the question of responsibility should be evaluated. A second question concerned the role that hypnosis should play in the legal process.

For once, most experts agreed on both answers to these questions. On the issue of responsibility, the victim of suggestion or the hypnotizable hysterical patient did not possess the willpower to resist the suggested ideas. They were neither morally nor legally responsible for their actions. At most, some experts argued that because they had consented to be hypnotized they should at least share a partial responsibility for their actions (Ladame, 1887; Laurent, 1891). In fact, throughout legal history, it had usually been recognized that the victims of suggestions were not responsible for their actions. During the 1890s some

American experts were to oppose this position, claiming full responsibility for those who submitted to hypnosis. The approach was based on the analogy with crimes committed under the influence of drugs. However, this position was not supported by the majority of the interested scientific community.

The issues of whether hypnosis could be used in the legal process and whether a suspect could be hypnotized in order to secure the accurate version of a crime drew a most definitely negative answer from most experts. They maintained that using hypnosis with suspects would be the equivalent of coercing them into confessing their crimes (de la Tourette, 1887; Ladame, 1887; Liégeois, 1889b). They added that the facts revealed by hypnosis would not in any way represent the true state of affairs and that it would be impossible to disentangle fact from fantasy and truth from fiction (Laurent, 1891, p. 54).

Even when hypnosis was used with crime victims, the same problems existed. How did one separate the facts revealed during hypnosis from the fantasies produced during hypnosis? As de la Tourette (1887) recognized: "From a medico-legal point of view, a second hypnotization could be informative, but it could also be biased *a priori*" (p. 152).

He was supported by Liégeois (1889) who recommended that the information revealed during hypnosis should be verified and corroborated independently. He believed that subjects could confuse suggested facts with real ones or be influenced simply by involuntary suggestions.

If hypnosis was to play a role in the legal process, it had to be weighed carefully because of the consequences involved. As Pitres and Gaubé (1886b) concluded: "In summary, in our present state of knowledge, we believe that it would be wise not to consider hypnosis among the practical tools available in medico-legal and investigative work" (p. 348).

Conclusions

By the end of the 1880s, the interest in hypnosis in general, and in its forensic use in particular, began to decline in France. The numerous trials and the relentless quarrels between the two schools had left the scientists, clinicians, and the public disillusioned.

As the interest declined in France, and in Europe in general, it traveled across the Atlantic to the United States. Many American scientists had been present at the International Congress and had become interested in the problems of forensic hypnosis. At the end of the 1880s and throughout the 1890s several trials would involve hypnosis in the United States.

NOTES

1. Hansen's trial is reported in a booklet published in 1880 by Phil. Fr. Walten, entitled: *Der magnetische Schlaf-mit einem anhange: Der process des magnetiseurs*

Hansen in Wien. The trial is also reported in part in Ladame (1887) who has borrowed the facts from Walten.

2. It is around this period that Gustave LeBon (1895) developed his social theory of mass movement, based in part on the idea of mass hypnosis and mass suggestion.

3. The chapter written by Binet and Féré on medico-legal hypnosis is one of the most complete documents of this period. Although both authors were still affiliated with the Salpêtrière, the influence of the Nancy school could already be felt in their writings. Féré had written a book in 1886 entitled *La médecine d'imagination*, whereas Binet was to publish in 1900 a book on the concept of suggestibility. It is interesting to note that in 1888 when they published "Animal Magnetism," at the height of the conflict between the two schools of thought, they pointed to the fact that Féré had been the first author to address the medico-legal issue, and that he had been followed later by Liégeois. In May 1883, Féré had presented a conference at the Société Médico-Psychologique entitled "Les hypnotiques hystériques, considérées comme sujets d'expérience en médecine mentale: Illusions, hallucinations, impulsions irrésistibles provoquées; leur importance au point de vue médico-légal." This was a subtle attempt to indicate that the Salpêtrière had been aware all along of the potential legal problems linked to hypnosis, and that Liégeois had not in any way surprised them. This could certainly be true since Charcot and Paul Brouardel, who was considered one of the leading experts in forensic medicine in Europe, were good friends and worked often together.

A similar attitude can be found in Freud. When Janet published his book in 1889 where he addressed the issue of "fixed ideas" as one of the underlying causes of hysterical symptoms, and how to eliminate them through hypnosis, Freud wrote that Breuer and himself had started using this method before Janet, but had only published their results after Janet's 1889 book. (See Perry & Laurence, 1984, and Prévost, 1973, for a detailed analysis of the Freud–Janet controversy.)

4. During the 1880s and 1890s, hypnosis played a major role in numerous trials. Most of these trials were reported in specialized medico-legal journals or in books written by supporters of both schools of thought. More often than not, the facts presented were minimally explained. It would have been repetitious to survey all of the reported cases, as well as misleading since in a fair proportion of these hypnosis was brought into play as a diagnostic tool for the defense, especially where hysteria was suspected. For the interested readers, a number of books offer a survey of some of these different trials: Bérillon (1892), Bonjean (1890), Delacroix (1887), Garnier (1887), Laurent (1891), Luys (1891a, 1891b). Bernheim (1891) commented also on a number of trials to demonstrate the role that suggestion could have played in the commission of different crimes.

Most of these books covered also trials that involved false accusations made either by hysterical patients against their physicians, or by children. False testimonies made by children were well documented; Bernheim (1891) reported on a trial held in Hungary (the Tisza–Eslar affair) where a judge had used undue influence to coerce a child into accusing and testifying against his father in a murder. False testimonies by children were often seen as similar to the false accusations that hysterical patients were thought to make.

5. The popularity of the experiments on criminal suggestion as well as the media coverage of the different trials revived the clergy's division of opinions on magnetism and hypnotism. Once again, hypnosis was linked to possession and the work of the Devil (see for example, Laënnec, 1888; Moreau, 1891; Régnard, 1887). The population

was certainly interested in the clergy's opinion on hypnosis. A book published in Italian in 1886 by a Jesuit priest, Franco, had reached its third edition by 1888 and had been translated into both French (in 1890) and Spanish. A controversy arose in the *Revue de l'Hypnotisme* at the end of the 1880s when the Archbishop of Madrid published an article in Spain condemning hypnosis. Part of the conflict resided in the tendency of scientists to explain possession cases, miraculous cures, and the subjective experiences of holiness in terms of hypnosis and hysteria in the same way that the discovery of somnambulism at the end of the eighteenth century had touched off the investigation of these same phenomena in tems of animal magnetism and artificial somnambulism (see, for example, Liégeois, 1889). The official position of the Church, however, did not change, and numerous priests protested against the extremist position of their colleagues. The Catholic Church still recognized the usefulness of hypnotic treatment when it was appropriately applied by physicians (see Grasset, 1903).

6. Few lawyers voiced their opinions in the forensic debate. When some did, they were mostly on the Nancy school's side (Bonjean, 1890; Lefort, 1888; Roux-Freissineng, 1887). Others, like Thomas (1885) and Riant (1888), sided with the Salpêtrière in an effort to minimize the effect of some of the Nancy school's extravagant claims.

7. Many of these cases can be found in Bernheim's and in Liégeois's books. While some of them involved hypnosis, most of them did not. These authors drew their conclusions mainly from published accounts of the cases. This most unfortunate attitude drew much criticism from their colleagues. The major one was the fact that suggestion became the universal explanation for all behaviors and, as such, did not explain anything anymore. In the 1890s, Bernheim was to change his strategy and stay more closely to facts. The same could not be said of Liégeois.

8. This last reference to Greek mythology has a flavor of concupiscence. Erethism is defined as "abnormal irritability or responsiveness to stimulation" (*Webster's Ninth New Collegiate Dictionary*, 1985). This state of the jurors' pupils was evoked by the sight of Gabrielle who, like Phryné, was a courtesan. Phryné, who was Praxiteles's (the sculptor) lover, had served as the model for his statue of the goddess Aphrodite. He had created a sensation by presenting the goddess totally nude. The sculpture was described by Clark (1956) as having "a sensual tremor which, for five hundred years, led poets, emperors and boatloads of tourists to linger in the sanctuary of Knidos" (p. 84).

So much so, that a statue of the model, Phryné, was erected in the sacred precincts of Delphi by the grateful community (Clark, 1956, p. 83). Why did the journalist compare Gabrielle to the celebrated courtesan? During her life, Phryné was accused of blasphemy which was at the time a capital charge.

> She was defended by the orator Hyperides. When it seemed as if the verdict would be unfavourable, he tore her dress and displayed her bosom, which so moved the jury that they acquitted her; another version makes Phryné tear her own dress and plead with each individual juror. (Friedrich, 1978, p. 208, citing the *Encyclopaedia Britannica*)

10

Europe Meets America: Hypnosis in the Last Years of the Nineteenth Century

Background

If the 1880s had been a fertile ground for the psycho-legal debate in Europe, the 1890s would see its expansion to North American soil. As was seen before, few cases had yet been reported on the uses and abuses of hypnosis in the American legal literature. By the end of the 1880s, nonetheless, the European forensic debate would finally evoke interest, albeit a limited one, on the part of the American medico-legal experts.

There is a question of why the forensic debate emigrated to America where, at the time, reported cases of misuse were scarce (see Chapters 7 and 8). Two major reasons can by hypothesized. First, improved communications between the Old and the New Worlds allowed many American lawyers and scientists to travel and become exposed to the different issues at stake. Many Americans participated in the numerous International Congresses that took place in Europe in the 1890s. Improved media coverage of major legal issues stimulated the interest of many North American scientists in both hypnosis and psychic phenomena. The Eyraud–Bompard trial, for one, was discussed in the American press, as well as in the scientific journals of the period. Improved communications, however, were not the sole factor responsible for what appeared to be a sudden scientific interest in hypnosis in America.

Experimental research in psychology was developing rapidly in the United States, and a number of laboratories were already exploring the processes of the human mind. On a simplistic level, the positivist tendencies of the more prominent researchers were counterbalanced by the spiritualism of some of their colleagues (see Neal & Clark, 1900). This tendency can be best illustrated by the anecdotal evidence regarding Freud's invitation to Clark University in 1909 to present his recent theories; the organizers decided to invite an experimental psychologist, Titchener, to maintain some balance between the two different views of human nature, as well as to demonstrate that American psychology was interested in other areas of human endeavors: "You might if you like make a sort of justification of pure psychological work as against these other [applied] tendencies which are now certainly very strong" (Titchener, 1880-1927; cited in Evans & Koelsch, 1985, p. 944).

Titchener himself would later write to Meyer that

> I offered to attempt a translation out of this psychology of association into modern psychological terms, and Freud laughed at me, and said that if I came to him for half a year I should see that modern psychology needed to be *revolutionised* in his way. Revolutionised, ye gods! That means, set back just about two human generations. And the man wonders that we do not take his psychologising seriously. (Meyer, 1885-1949; cited in Evans & Koelsch, 1985, p. 945, italics in original)

Whether or not one agrees with Titchener's point of view on dynamic psychology, his evaluation of Freud's contribution to the field of psychotherapy was not exactly prophetic. More to the point, one generation before Freud's introductory lectures to the American public, Janet's conceptualization of subconscious ideas at play in psychopathology was to revolutionize both the scientific and lay concepts of hypnosis.

This new theoretical aspect would be integrated into the debate surrounding the uses and abuses of hypnosis. The "discovery" of the unconscious and the subconscious would give new respectability to the older notion of double consciousness. The work of Janet, Breuer, James, and Freud, to cite but a few, would drastically alter the image of hypnosis, and of the human psyche. James (1936) explained the enthusiasm of his fellow citizens for the more esoteric forms of healing arts by pointing to some basic psychological problems that lay in "their little private convulsive selves" (p. 102). He was probably echoing the French poet Baudelaire who pointed to the existential desperation of human life, toward the end of the nineteenth century in France. In both Europe and America, the end of the nineteenth century evoked the nostalgia for a paradise lost.

The popularity of Janet's subconscious and of Freud's unconscious would modify some of the older beliefs both about hypnosis and the highly hypnotizable individual. These constructs would become very handy when it came time to explain such phenomena as post-hypnotic suggestion, analgesia, amnesia, or hypermnesia. As will be seen in Chapters 11 and 12, it was in the twentieth century that this influence reached its apogee and was translated into theories of the mind that would have caused Titchener to writhe in agony in his grave! (see, for example, Reiser, 1980).

By the end of the 1880s, hypnosis *à la Française* was not popular in the United States. This did not mean that hypnosis was not used; it was just not a popular topic of scientific discussion. As was seen before, Mesmerism and hypnosis had been mostly instrumental in the development of new spiritualistic approaches to the American way of life; it was scarcely a subject of scientific inquiry. In fact, most cases of alleged hypnotic abuse were usually reported in newspapers and few ever reached the courts. When they did, they were most of the time rejected by the authorities.

The topic, however, was a popular one among contemporary writers. It even gave rise to a literary genre of American supernatural fiction that flourished for more than one hundred years (1820-1920; see Kerr, Crowley, & Crow, 1983). Writers such as Washington Irving and Henry James, without forgetting Poe, Hawthorne, and even Mark Twain, expressed to some degree the continuous American schism between faith and doubt, religion and science, transcendentalism and positivism. As was seen earlier (Chapter 7), Mesmerism had been integrated into spiritualist movements in America from its early beginnings. As had happened in France before the Revolution, it had been linked also to all kinds of ideological and political movements.

> Mesmerists and spiritualists often allied themselves with reform and millenarian causes—abolition, communal utopianism, feminism, vegetarianism, and others. . . . Melville debunked the spiritualists' pretensions to social reform by showing their closer affinities with hypocritical, evangelical dogooders. These works showed how easily the supernatural could take on ideological coloring. (Kerr *et al.*, 1983, pp. 4-5)[1]

Many authors attempted to debunk these movements. But for writers in search of the unusual, hypnosis was a gold mine.

> Abhorrent to Hawthorne personally, the "magnetic miracles" of mesmerism nonetheless appealed to him as metaphors for moral and sexual slavery that were especially suitable for romance because they could be ambiguously presented both as occult "necromancies" and as a genuine force that "modern psychology" might yet "reduce . . . within a system." His male mesmerists dominate trance-maidens with the invading power claimed alike by legendary witches ("the evil eye") and nineteenth century followers of Mesmer ("magnetism"). (Kerr *et al.*, 1983, p. 136)

In America, the untamed power of hypnosis was to find more enthusiasm among the general public which enjoyed supernatural tales than in the legal courts which took a decidedly more stern attitude toward the coercive aura surrounding it.

Nonetheless, it is noteworthy that the history of hypnosis in the United States was to become entangled in the struggle between experimental and clinical psychology. From spiritualism to psychic phenomena, both psychology as a science, and supernatural fiction as a literary genre evolved toward dynamic psychology and psychoanalysis. This movement was to be opposed by the rise of materialistic thinking in science that would lead to a stricter behavioristic model of humankind later exemplified in the twentieth century by B. F. Skinner's novel *Walden Two*. The plethora of spiritualistic beliefs, however, was so prominent at the end of the nineteenth century that it finally reached the medico-legal milieu.

One man took it upon himself to sensitize his colleagues to the potential problems linked to the popularity of hypnosis. Clark Bell, a New York lawyer, attempted singlehandedly to awaken in his peers and in scientists in general the enthusiasm that the legal debate had provoked in France. As he wrote, however, in 1889:

> The medical profession in America do not give this subject the attention its importance deserves.
>
> We know of no medical man of prominence in America who has publicly identified himself with the investigation of this science as some of the most eminent men in foreign countries have recently done. . . .
>
> The local press has taken up the discussion in America, which the physicians have neglected. . . . The importance of the subject cannot well be overestimated. Our judicial tribunals are wholly unprepared for the investigation of crimes thus committed. (Bell, 1889, pp. 363-367)

Bell was referring to an editorial published in the *New York Ledger* which emphasized the potential dangers of hypnotic suggestions and the need for legal guidelines. The editorial sought to present both the dangers and the potential therapeutic value of hypnosis. It concluded, however, that the topic had not received as yet the attention necessary to draw appropriate conclusions. In January 1889, the New York Medico-Legal Society formed a committee to investigate the potential uses and abuses of hypnosis.

Bell was a thoughtful man; in order to extend his knowledge of hypnosis, he corresponded, in the following years with the major researchers and clinicians of the time, asking for their opinions of it and related concepts. It was, in a way, a coerced participation. He would then publish their answers in *The Medico-Legal Journal*, since he was in 1889 the President of the New York Medico-Legal Society!

Simultaneous with the publication of the preliminary report of the standing committee on hypnotism, a physician from Providence, Rhode Island, Wm. H. Palmer, published an article on hypnosis in *The Medico-Legal Journal* attempting to summarize the problems raised by its utilization. Palmer's position was one of compromise between the two French schools of thought. He reasoned that if hypnosis was a biological state and its usefulness lay in its potential for revealing the link between the mind and the body, suggestion must be its *modus operandi*. The question of hypnotic crime was emphasized by Palmer as an important but as yet unresolved issue. Deception, simulation, and undue suggestions from the investigator were constant reminders of the elusiveness of the hypnotic condition, especially in the legal context.

The difficulties in the way of obtaining sufficient warrant of sincerity are great, and the medical expert may remember that, as Féré asserts, his duty does not include the finding of victims for the law. He may prove by physical characteristics, that the subject is or is not susceptible to hypnotism, that the phenomena in question may be produced by hypnotic suggestion, but he can do no more than give evidence as to the possibility of such facts. (Palmer, 1890, p. 239)

In the same issue of *The Medico-Legal Journal*, the Standing Committee on Hypnotism published its preliminary report. It recognized hypnosis as a subjective phenomenon that was not necessarily pathological and could on occasions be useful therapeutically. Their last comments concerned its legal aspects and are worth quoting as they would have a major impact on legal thinking at least for the following 15 years:

The illusory impressions created by hypnosis may be made to dominate and tyranize the subsequent actions of the subject. The following legal aspects present themselves:
   1. Has the sensitive sought the operator, or has the operator used undue influence to gain control of him? 2. Are proper witnesses present? 3. Are possible elements of error eliminated, such as self-deception, simulation, and malingering? 4. Is hypnosis a justifiable inquisitorial agent? 5. Do we need a reconstruction of the laws of evidence in view of the perversion—visual and otherwise—created by the trance? 6. Is any revision of the Penal Code desirable in view of these facts? Finally should there be legal surveillance over private experiments or public exhibitions? (*Medico-Legal Journal*, 1890, Vol. 8, p. 264)

Following his customary practice, Bell sent these questions to a number of medical and legal experts asking for their opinions on the different questions raised by the Committee. The answers provided threw some light on the accepted conceptions of hypnosis and hypnotic phenomena. The first to answer these questions was George Trumbull Ladd, then a professor at Yale University:

Science must take full possession of hypnotism, as the essential pre-requisite of any considerable changes in the laws. And in advancing the cause of science over the domain of these phenomena, nerve-physiology and psychology should go hand in hand. I believe that professional psychologists are very eager to learn all they can from physiology on this subject. I wish I could be equally sure that physiologists and physicians were as eager and willing and docile in their attitude toward the science of psychology. . . .
   Of course to determine whether there had been hypnotic control must be a matter of evidence in each case. I do not see then, why we should not have the same necessity for recognizing the value of expert testimony, which arises constantly now in cases of alleged insanity, or "undue influence" of other than hypnotic sort.
   I see no objection to the careful guarded examination of witnesses, or of accused persons, by experts and trustworthy hypnotizers—when sanctioned

by the Court. If my present view of the phenomena is correct, such an examination could rarely or never be very productive of information unless the person under examination consented to be hypnotized. Evidence thus obtained, however, should be used—it seems to me, only as indicating where legally usable and valid evidence might be obtained, and not as itself legally usable and valid. In case of a jury trial, such examination should perhaps be before the judges, but not before the jury. (Bell, 1891, pp. 333-334)

As will be seen in Chapter 12, Ladd's position would find some echo in the forensic debate of the twentieth century. It was paralled by the responses of other experts such as Paul Carus, the editor of the *Monist*:

Hypnosis is a justifiable inquisitorial agent for finding clues, but it has not the slightest value if considered as evidence [in answer to point 4 above] because it is extremely difficult to remove the many sources of error, simulation, and also, perhaps most so, of self-deception. (Bell, 1891, p. 335)

Most experts agreed to the limitations of hypnotic practice to physicians. Not too surprisingly, Bell disagreed with the experts: "As a rule physicians know next to nothing concerning it, especially in New York City. In Chicago it may be different, but here I would not be able to name more than half a dozen who have investigated it" (Bell, 1891, p. 357).

The Medico-Legal Society of Chicago had just proposed to adopt a resolution restricting the use of hypnosis "to properly qualified medical men." Bell's comment was singularly similar to the position Delboeuf had espoused at the First International Congress in Paris (see Chapter 9). Bell, however, could have been correct at the time; few physicians and even fewer investigators were interested in hypnotic phenomena. The answers he received to his enquiries often confirmed his predictions: Most of the experts acknowledged their ignorance on the matter at hand. Bell wanted "students of Science" more than doctors of medicine to become acquainted with hypnosis and its multifaceted aspects.

All experts agreed that public exhibitions of hypnosis should be banned. The reasons given were similar to those given in France. Hypnosis could lead to physical and psychological sequelae in the individuals who submitted to it. In 1891, Cincinnati became the first town to pass an ordinance making it a misdemeanor to give hypnotic exhibitions. In this regard, the Americans were in agreement with the French and the British experts. In Britain, the Psychology Section of the British Medical Association had adopted a similar resolution shortly before (*British Medical Journal*, September 12, 1891) and had appointed a committee on hypnotism at its meeting of 1890. This committee presented its report in 1892. It recognized the genuineness of the hypnotic state, but rejected the theory of animal magnetism. It recognized also its therapeutic properties and its potential for abuse. It expressed the wish that the practice of hypnotism be limited to qualified medical individuals.

If the medico-legal experts as well as physicians in general were not preoccupied by the legal problems surrounding the use of hypnosis, four legal cases would occur in the following years (1890s) that pointed to the necessity of investigating this phenomenon more carefully. These four cases touched upon the three basic facets of potential abuse: physical and psychological sequelae, hypnotic suggestion of murder, and hypnotic testimony.

Hypnosis in the American Courts

Four major cases reached the American courts during the 1890s. Of these, only one, *People v. Ebanks*, was to survive the unawareness of time and be remembered by contemporary writers on forensic hypnosis. Of the other three, only one, the case of Spurgeon Young, actually involved hypnosis. In the other two (*State v. McDonald*, cited in Bell, 1896b, and its follow-up *State v. Gray*, and *People v. Worthington*), hypnosis was brought in by the back door, as a consequence of media fantasies. These four cases, however, would be yoked to similar cases that occurred during the same period in Europe; these had stimulated public interest anew.

The Spurgeon Young Case

In January 1897, Spurgeon Young, a 17-year-old black youth, died of what appeared to be at first glance the consequence of a diabetic coma. The Coroner of Chatauqua County, A. H. Bowen, held an inquest with a jury to determine the actual cause of death. His suspicion had been aroused when he read in the autopsy report that Young had been in the recent past repeatedly hypnotized by lay hypnotists. He called upon Clark Bell to answer a series of questions on hypnosis. Bell, on January 30, received the following letter:

> Dear Sir:—Will you please reply to the following hypothetical question?
> In case of a youth of 17 years of age, of good physical development and medical history, well nourished, weighing about 125 pounds, upon autopsy, with no observable lesion, beyond slight cerebral softening, and trace of kidney deterioration, vital organs normal with cause of disease diagnosed as *diabetes mellitis* [sic]; and it appearing upon conceded evidence that the deceased had for approximately over six months been a chronic "sensitive subject" of extreme susceptibility to hypnotic or "mesmeric influence"; having been protractedly and repeatedly hypnotized many times by amateurs and irresponsible and reckless youthful operators and dabblers in hypnotism; and while under the influence or in a state of statuvolence having been sat or stood on, by men of average or heavy weight, while in a cataleptic state, with head and feet supported, so that he formed a bridge between such supports; and having been thrown into and left in hypnotic or trancoidal states with instructions to emerge therefrom at a given time, and upon emerging apparently from such trancoidal state complaining of nervous chills, physical prostration, and malaise; in your view and opinion, according to the best of your

professional knowledge and belief, according to the best authorities and latest research wherewith you are familiar, in physiology, pathology, and psychology—would physical injury or organic impairment particularly of the renal function, or symptoms of glycosuria, directly or indirectly, follow from the psychic or emotional disturbances or derangement of nerve function, involved in or due to, the morbid innervation incident to such hypnotic practice or experimentation in "mesmerism" or alleged animal magnetism? (Bell, 1896b, p. 530, italics in original)

Despite his addiction to interminably long and tortuous sentences, it is evident that Bowen had taken time to reflect upon his subject of inquiry. Nothing was omitted. The physical, psychological, and emotional side effects of hypnosis and of some hypnotic suggestions were all questioned. And once again, the famous "human plank" phenomenon was at the core of a legal inquiry (see Chapter 9, Hansen's trial).

The physicians who performed the autopsy concluded that hypnosis had caused the diabetes from which Spurgeon died. One of the physicians, on cross-examination, testified that hypnosis could be used to suggest suicide or crime. In his mind, there was no doubt that hypnosis was dangerous both physically and morally.

Clark Bell sent copies of Bowen's request to more that 15 experts in hypnosis and suggestion across America and in Europe. To all of them, he asked for advice on the case. The answers he received were revealing of the state of knowledge at the time. A few excerpts from this privileged correspondence convey the level of sophistication that the American experts could deploy. One of the first to reply was Thomson Jay Hudson, a lawyer in Washington, D.C., author of *The Law of Psychic Phenomena*, and Vice Chairman of the Psychological Section of the Medico-Legal Society. He wrote: "in my opinion, there could be but one inevitable result, namely, a shattered nervous organism, leading eventually, if life is prolonged, to imbecility or insanity" (Bell, 1896b, p. 532).

This extreme opinion was supported, in part, by W. Xavier Sudduth, Professor of Psychology at the University of Minnesota who recognized that the practice of hypnotism by lay individuals was "fraught with grave dangers" (cited in Bell, 1896b, p. 533), and that its practice should be regulated by law. He did not believe that diabetes could be caused by hypnosis. Spurgeon's symptoms, however, could easily have been the results of the suggestions to which he had been submitted. Another expert, Irving C. Rosse, was more colorful in his answer. Having rejected the notion that hypnosis could have had any causative action upon the glycosuria found in Spurgeon's urine, he stated:

> Diabetes of traumatic origin and the association of this disease with nerve changes are familiar pathological facts. The neurosis known as major hypnotism is also a pathological state, since animals become demented after frequent subjection to hypnotic influence, and the best authorities are that vascular changes in the brain with breaking down of nerve tissue associate themselves with hypnotism. . . .

> The injurious tendency of hypnotic practice to exhaust nervous force and weaken the will is spoken of by some authorities as a kind of moral masturbation that should be prohibited or restricted by legal enactment. (cited in Bell, 1896b, p. 534)

Dr. Rosse had probably just read a recent experiment by Gley (1895) published in the *Annales de Psychiatrie et d'Hypnologie* reporting some of the side effects of hypnosis on young frogs. The frogs had been hypnotized and left in this state on the experimental table. Five of the eleven subjects had demonstrated evidence of sequelae: Two had died, two had remained immobile on the table for one hour, and one had finally revived after 20 hours. Gley had concluded that these effects were proof that hypnosis had deleterious effects on the nervous system. In a footnote, he cited a conference by Brémaud in 1884 where the physician had reported an increase in hypnotizability in subjects who were either alcoholic or had indulged in venereal excesses, both conditions known to affect cerebral functioning!

Of all the experts consulted, only four did not see any link between hypnosis, the specific suggestions given, and the onset or aggravation of diabetes. For the others, hypnosis *per se* and particularly repeated hypnotizations coupled with injurious suggestions had to be considered among the factors that had precipitated Young's death. The jury agreed with the experts:

> We find that J. W. Spurgeon Young came to his death at 1033 North Main Street in the city of Jamestown, in said county, on the 24th day of January 1897, from diabetes and nervous exhaustion caused by hypnotic practices; ... that he had also while under such hypnotic influence been carried through the various stages of intoxication and delirium tremens and other hypnotic feats.
>
> We would recommend that the state legislature pass a law prohibiting the practice of hypnotism. (cited in Bell, 1896b, p. 545)

The case was also reported in the *American Law Review* by Joseph Wheless who concluded: "There exists in St. Louis empirics who advertise 'Hypnotism taught in *** lessons'; these constitute a public danger and should be subjected to the police power" (Wheless, 1897, p. 441).

The Spurgeon Young case was paralleled in Europe by a similar case where a somnambulist had died while in a magnetic state. She was performing a psychic reading for a man who was dying at the time of the session. She was so shocked emotionally on discovering his health status that she suffered what appeared to be a heart attack and died (Moll, 1889/1982). Her magnetist, Neukomm, was charged with manslaughter and found guilty (Schrenck-Notzing, 1902). As was mentioned earlier, Bernheim, himself had to undergo a preliminary inquiry when one of his patients died following hypnotic induction (see Chapter 9).

By the end of the nineteenth century, it was thus well recognized that hypnosis could be deleterious to the physical and mental health of those who submitted to it. In 1896, Crocq published the result of a questionnaire study where he had consulted more than 50 European experts (often through their writings) on some basic questions surrounding hypnosis. On the question concerning the dangers of hypnosis, around 70 percent of those responding (35) agreed that hypnosis could be dangerous for the subjects.

Two of the next cases can be summarized briefly. In the yoked cases of *State v. McDonald* and *State v. Gray* (1895), hypnosis played a marginal role in the legal process. As will be seen, however, the case was misquoted so often that it became a common reference in discussions of whether criminal suggestions given in hypnosis could be effective. In this murder case, Thomas McDonald was accused of having shot Thomas Patton on May 5, 1894. McDonald was an employee of Anderson Gray whereas Patton, the victim, was a tenant of Gray, living on a portion of his farm. Both Gray's and McDonald's families lived in the same house. The relationship between the three men was not cordial. Patton had allegedly made vulgar comments about McDonald's wife to Gray. On the morning of the tragedy, McDonald held a discussion with Patton that turned sour. Patton left Gray's house after having hit McDonald and demanded to meet him in the afternoon to settle the dispute.

Gray took the matter into his own hands and apparently convinced McDonald that Patton was a dangerous man who would try to kill him in the afternoon. Gray suggested that McDonald should kill him first; he gave the man a rifle, some cartridges, and took him through target practice. They then went to a grove near Patton's house awaiting his arrival. Gray left him there and returned to his house. When Patton appeared on the road, McDonald shot him. He died a few hours later, accusing Gray of being responsible for his death.

McDonald's trial revolved around the issue of self-defense. The young man had been persuaded by his employer that Patton was dangerous and that his life was in jeopardy. The jury believed McDonald's version of the events and acquitted him. Hypnosis was not mentioned at all during this trial; its use was inferred by journalists who followed it, based on the testimony that Gray had influenced McDonald's actions by his repeated (nonhypnotic) suggestions. Quite soon, headlines announcing that McDonald had been hypnotized by Gray and given suggestions to kill Patton reached the public:

> The only reference to hypnotism in the brief is as follows: "A sensational newspaper reporter startled the world by reporting that in this case Gray had hypnotized McDonald, and that hypnotism was the defense pleaded and allowed and that upon that theory the case tried by court and jury an absolutely false report and purely a product of a most imaginary brain." (Sudduth, 1895, p. 243)

In Gray's trial, the word hypnotism was never mentioned. He was found guilty of being the principal in the murder and accessory both before and after the fact. He was sentenced to death; the sentence was affirmed by the Supreme Court of Kansas.

The case was soon interpreted as an example of the actual culprit being freed while the magnetist or hypnotist was condemned (see Bannister, 1895;

also, an editorial in the *American Lawyer*, 1895, Vol. 3, pp. 5-6). It must be noted, however, that the editor of the *American Lawyer* expressed the wish that Gray's sentence be reversed if it was based on such facts:

> We are ready to admit that the new psychology presents most interesting phenomena, and that in the future, in the hands of science, it will probably show realities that would astound our present comprehension and credulity. But we emphatically assert that in the present stage of its development the power is one upon which courts should refuse to base final judgments. (p. 6)

A similar case had occurred a few years earlier in Europe. The wife of a butcher, Mme. Sauter, had been accused of the attempted murder of her husband and of inciting the murder of nine others. She had fallen prey to a fortune teller who implanted the idea in her mind. Based on the testimony of experts, she was acquitted of both accusations (Schrenck-Notzing, 1903, p. 733), and the fortune teller was found guilty.

In the murder case of *People v. Worthington* (1894), the accused's defense was based on insanity and hypnotism. Hypnotism was rejected by both the lower court and the Supreme Court of California which stated:

> There was no evidence which tended to show that the defendant was subject to the disease, if it be such. Merely showing that she was told to kill the deceased, and that she did it, does not prove hypnotism or at least, does not tend to establish a defense to a charge of murder. (cited in Solomon, 1952, p. 580)

Mrs. Worthington had fatally wounded her lover after her husband had requested she did so to salvage her honor. In a letter addressed to Baddeley, the victim, Mrs. Worthington had written:

> He [her husband] said that he will give me a week's time in which to find you, and, when I do, I must shoot you, or be shot myself. So what I am going to do? I am sure I don't know what to do unless I shoot myself. I think that it is the best thing to do. I would not give you away to save my life. (*People v. Worthington*, p. 690)

When she met her lover again, she shot him four times with a gun her husband had just handed to her! After the shooting, "she seemed not at all excited" (*People v. Worthington*, p. 690). It would have been a perfect case for Liégeois in his defense of hypnotism, or for Brouardel and his colleagues in invoking insanity. In America, however, hypnosis as a defense strategy was not easily accepted! Mrs. Worthington was found guilty and sentenced to 25 years in prison.

As will be seen in the final section of this chapter, other cases in Europe in the last decade of the nineteenth century were to be publicized in America, renewing each time a somewhat lingering interest. The views of the American and the European experts, however, were becoming more and more similar. If the alleged coercive power of hypnosis had played a major role in the reported trials up to this point, confabulation, or what Bernheim had labeled retroactive hallucination, was to become the center of interest of experts on each side of the Atlantic. As Bannister (1895) wrote:

> The greatest danger of the plea of hypnotism in criminal cases, if it is to become a popular or frequent one, is that of false accusation, and the escape of an occasional criminal is an unimportant miscarriage of justice when compared to that of the conviction of an innocent individual.
>
> The value of hypnotism for purposes of obtaining testimony or ascertaining the truth is also very dubious. . . . When an individual is fully in the hypnotic condition he can be made to say anything, and even honest questioning may act as false suggestion. (p. 88)

In this, he agreed with Bell who wrote:

> it would be a very unsafe proposition of law in regard to testimony, to place a witness in a hypnotic trance, and to accept as truth the statements of events that he in that state described as having occurred at a previous time. (1896a, p. 362)

The now famous case of *People v. Ebanks*, heard in the Supreme Court of California on August 23, 1897, was to raise the issue of hypnosis as a guarantee of truthful statements.

Joseph Japhet Ebanks had been charged with the murder of Harriet Stiles and her father, convicted of murder to the first degree, and sentenced to death. He appealed the judgment on 15 different grounds, among which was the fact that the testimony of a hypnotist who had hypnotized him had been excluded by the Court. The Appellate Court supported the motion of the lower court in the following terms:

> Defendant called as a witness one B. A. Stephens, and offered to prove by him that he was an expert hypnotist, that he had hypnotized defendant, and that when hypnotized defendant had made a statement to him in regard to his knowledge of the affair, from which statement witness is ready to testify that the defendant is not guilty, and that the defendant denies his guilt while in that condition. The court sustained an objection to the testimony. The court said: "The law of the United States does not recognize hypnotism. It would be an illegal defense, and I cannot admit it." The court then repeated in substance, what it had said to the jury, and told them to disregard the offer. We shall not stop to argue the point, and only add the court was right. (*People v. Ebanks*, p. 1053)

The Court seemed to follow the position that statements elicited during sleep were not receivable in evidence and that hypnosis was similar to natural sleep.

The position of the Supreme Court was clear. Two facts, nonetheless, are worth mentioning in regard to this case. The first is that three of the five judges added to the decision that this judgment on hypnotism was only valid for the case at hand. Whether or not a crime could be committed while the defendant was hypnotized was not covered by the present judgment. It would have to wait until a specific case reached the Supreme Court. It was also the first time that a Superior Court had ordered the composition of an extensive note on the issue of hypnosis. This note attempted to cover the major areas of hypnotic knowledge "to supply the deficiency of judicial opinion thereon" (p. 269).

The note, written by a certain F. H. B.,[2] covered the field of hypnosis from beginning to end. In it, the author attempted to present contemporary views about its nature and definition, its use as a therapeutic agent, and the issue of criminal suggestions. Based on both the European and American literature, he sought to disentangle the contradicting positions of the scientists on the subject. He did not, however, draw any conclusions; that was for the judges.

The note referred to a number of cases that had been linked to hypnosis in the United States, only to be debunked later. These cases were more a product of media sensationalism than legal proceedings (such as the Hayward-Blitz-Ging affair and the Briggs-Pickens affair[3]). An interesting piece of trivia was mentioned by F. H. B. on a case tried in Tacoma in July 1894, as an illustration of the "power" of hypnosis to influence individuals, even at a distance!

> The plaintiff caused an important witness for the defendant to become confused in manner and in testimony, hesitating and uncertain in statement, by hypnotically making passes with his hands in the direction of the witness, which influence was destroyed by placing a person between the operator and the subject. (F. H. B., 1897, p. 270)

Unfortunately, the note did not mention if anything happened to the person who was required to stand between the two protagonists! This type of report, however, did nothing to explain the factors at play in hypnosis and was reminiscent of the belief in the magnetic fluid. With the wisdom of hindsight, it demonstrates how one's beliefs can influence his or her behavior and experience, a point that will be made more cogently in Chapters 11 and 12. The note made extensive reference to a recent European case, the Czynski affair, which was looked upon as the first instance of criminal suggestions at work over a long period of time. The case was publicized widely on both continents.

The Czynski Affair

The Czynski affair was tried on December 17, 1894 in Munich. The trial lasted for three days, at the end of which Czynski was found guilty and sentenced to three years of jail.

Czynski, a native of Turzenka, Poland was 36 years old at the time of the trial. He lived in the city of Dresden in Saxony, practicing hypnosis and magnetism and giving conferences on occultism. He was married, but had left his wife to live with another woman who had borne his only child. In 1893, he was expelled from Prussia following some misrepresentations. It is in the city of Dresden that he was to meet the Baroness Hedwig von Zedlitz, a member of one of the oldest noble German families (Ellinger, 1896).

Hedwig was 38 years old; she was a "spinster," to use Ellinger's term (p. 152), with an unblemished reputation. She suffered from headaches and stomach pains, and had heard of Czynski's pretensions as a magnetic healer.

In the first months of treatment, Czynski did not succeed in relieving the Baroness of her problems. The medications he had prescribed and the massages he was performing did not alleviate the pain. The relationship between the two, however, grew more intimate with each visit. Nobody knew how intimate until her father and brother received a letter announcing that she had married Czynski secretly in Switzerland. They complained immediately to the police. One week later, Czynski was arrested. He was charged with using hypnosis and suggestion to subdue the Baroness's willpower and to abuse her sexually. He was also charged with fraud: He had arranged to have a false wedding ceremony performed by a friend of his posing as a Protestant minister.

What had happened unraveled gradually as the trial proceeded. Czynski testified that he had never hypnotized Hedwig, and the accusation of sexual abuse was ridiculous. She had consented all along.

> A person as morally pure and as severely religious as the Baroness cannot possibly be deprived of her will power. In order to succeed in such a case the person would have to be subjected to a great many hypnotic operations, and a sickly person is not in a condition to concentrate her thoughts as sharply; this is an impossibility. (Ellinger, 1896, p. 155)

Czynski was not a newcomer to the field of hypnosis and magnetism. He described himself during the trial thus:

> I took a great interest in the subject of hypnotism, studied it thoroughly and wrote several books on it. In 1892, I went to Paris, attended the clinical course at the Charité, and obtained a certificate as a student of medicine. Of course, I am not a graduated physician. On account of my books on hypnotism I received from the Roman Academy the diploma of M. D. *honoris causa*. Before the Medical Society of Constantinople I delivered lectures on hypnotism. I am the author of twenty-two books. (pp. 154–155)

He acknowledged that he had used both massage and metallotherapy in his attempts to cure the Baroness. His sessions were no longer than one minute at a time(!), and he denied that he had ever attempted to suggest undue emotions and behaviors to his patient.

The Baroness's story was different. According to her, he had from the beginning of their relationship harassed her continuously with his passion and his desire to marry her. He had described himself as an unhappy man, a descendant from a noble Lithuanian family. However, political problems did not allow him to maintain the status to which he was entitled. His wife was unfaithful to him, and he wanted to divorce her. Most of these declarations were made to the Baroness while she was in a state of "half-sleep" (p. 158).

During the trial, she described feeling mostly pity for the man rather than love. She had finally yielded to his advances and slept with him. She had then continued to sleep with him.

> His love found, however, no genuine response. But as something sad had occurred I asked myself whether I loved him, and whether I should help him to a better life. Then, I said to myself: Yes, I have surrendered myself to him, and I don't know how that was possible. It was done so suddenly. All of this is so terrible, but I could not help it. Therefore I resolved to marry him, because I felt pity for him.... (Ellinger, 1896, p. 158; also cited in Liégeois, 1898, p. 278)

The Baroness described her reactions as having happened automatically. She was powerless to resist his suggestions, even if she was aware that what she was doing was wrong: "The intimate intercourse with Czynski was not had during a condition of somnolence, only I was influenced to such a degree that I could not resist him. Though I was aware of the wrong I was doing, I was powerless to resist" (Ellinger, 1896, p. 159).

Four expert witnesses were called to testify. Three of the four experts agreed that light hypnosis, on a repeated basis, could have eliminated enough of the Baroness's willpower to prevent her from resisting Czynski's proposals. As Dr. Grashey of Munich testified:

> In a light hypnosis the normal man does not dispose to an equal degree of his accumulation of experiences and of his ability of remonstrating as he does in a condition of full wakefulness. He receives the inspired thoughts more readily, he is more suggestible, he accepts many thoughts which he would have rejected in a wake condition, because he cannot dispose of remonstrative reasoning. I maintain, therefore, that the normal man disposes with less freedom of his will during a condition of light hypnosis. (Ellinger, 1896, p. 161)

Dr. Grashey's testimony was opposed by one of the other experts, Dr. Fuchs of Bonn, who denied that hypnosis had any of the hypothesized coercive power. His opinion was that all the individuals who participated in hypnotic experiments were basically stupid; according to Fuchs, Charcot, for example, could probably not have been hypnotized.[4] He believed that subjects only wanted to be interesting and to please the physicians/experimenters. Such an extreme position would be echoed in America by Dr. Chapin, expert witness on many trials at the time (see F. H. B., 1897, for a sample of Chapin's opinions on hypnosis). Chapin also believed that hypnotized subjects knew that most suggestions were false and that subjects aimed at pleasing the experimenter (F. H. B., 1897, p. 273).

Dr. Fuchs, however, did not convince the jury. Czynski was found guilty of having used hypnosis and suggestion to delude the Baroness. He was sentenced to three years in jail. He was exonerated from the charge of sexual abuse, however, since the Baroness had complied while in her wakeful state.[5]

As Liégeois (1898), Schrenck-Notzing (1903), and Ellinger (1896) recognized, the Czynski trial became the first case where hypnosis and suggestion were recognized by the legal authorities as having played a role in abusing an unsuspecting victim over an extended period of time.

The Last Decade in America

The Czynski case was commented upon extensively in the United States. It became a major source of reference in the report on hypnotism written by F. H. B. in the Ebanks trial. A similar case was to happen a few years later (1905) in Iowa. In *State v. Donovan*, the Supreme Court of Iowa upheld the judgment of the lower court recognizing Mr. Donovan guilty of having used flattery, hypnosis, and lovemaking to sexually seduce his wife's cousin. Donovan had hypnotized the young woman a number of times in the past, especially at family gatherings. With time, he started telling her that he loved her, that his wife made him unhappy, and that he wanted to be with her. He would give her post-hypnotic suggestions to call him at his office. When she called, he would "tell her that she was good-looking, and kiss and caress her, and claimed that he could 'sit down and make a suggestion that she come to his office at a certain time, and she would come.' If she is to be believed, she could not stay away" (*State v. Donovan*, p. 792).

When he found her alone one night at her place, he repeated the story of his love, and made love to her. When testifying, she recognized the fact, but acknowledged that she did not know why she had done so, knowing it was wrong.

On cross-examination, she was asked:

Q: You did not let him have connection with you because he told you he loved you?
A: I suppose it was through his flattery.
Q: What I want to know is which it was done through—hypnotic influence or flattery?
A: I don't know exactly.
Q: Would you have yielded to him if it had not been for the so-called hypnotic influence?
A: I can't say. All I can tell, he had an influence over me in some way— whether through flattery or hypnotism I can't say. I kind of liked him. I don't know if I would have yielded if he hadn't told me that he loved me. I can't tell anything about it. No one knows. I can tell what was done. (p. 792)

Two expert witnesses were called in to give their opinion on hypnosis. Neither of them had any extensive experience with it; in fact, their expertise came from reading a few of the major books on the matter. The Court, nonetheless, received their testimony based on the premise that "Experts, as everyone knows, obtain much of what they know from books, and may express opinions based thereon as well as upon experience" (p. 793).

The victim described how Donovan had used suggestion to control her behavior. To buttress the prosecution's case, other young women were called in to testify that Donovan had also used suggestion to control their behavior. Because the issue of hypnosis was only a matter of evidence, the Supreme Court decided it did not have to rule on the issue. Whether it had been exercised or only pretended, the major issue was that the accused had succeeded in seducing his wife's cousin. The accusation of seduction was thus totally justified. As the honorable Judge concluded: "A careful examination of the record has convinced us of defendant's guilt, and that he richly deserves the sentence imposed" (p. 793).

This case, though almost identical to the Czynski affair, did not, however, benefit from all of the publicity and interest that the latter had received. In the first decade of the twentieth century, enthusiasm was in decline, due mainly to the lack of reported cases that had been substantiated independently.[6]

If the legal note written following the Ebanks case was an indication of the status of hypnosis in America at the turn of the century, especially in regard to its coercive power, it is not surprising to see why the debate did not endure. As was happening in France during the same period, the major problems were associated with its potential effects on memory, not its criminal use. Most American experts agreed that the personality of the subject was a major determinant in the successful realization of criminal suggestions. Even in cases of sexual abuse, the alleged use of hypnosis was not as readily accepted as in Europe. As Sudduth (1895) wrote:

> In other words, hypnosis would be no plea, because a truly virtuous woman would resent the least approach toward familiarity in the hypnotic state, even as she would in the waking condition, and if the immoral suggestions were persisted in they would awaken and woe betide the man who had the temerity to attempt improper advances.
>
> Results, however, depend upon the individual and the conditions under which hypnosis is induced. Perfectly successful cases of surgical operations have been performed upon virtuous women, under hypnosis, that involved exposure of the person, and even operations upon the generative organs themselves. In these cases the operation was for the acknowledged good of the subject and was performed under circumstances calculated to secure her confidence, otherwise it would have been a failure. (p. 254)

Not everyone agreed with such an extreme position. What Sudduth had not counted on were the beliefs and expectations that hypnotized subjects bring to a hypnosis session; some of them can be transformed into self-fulfilling prophecies:

> There are some very susceptible persons who do not know that they can resist the power of the hypnotist. They expect to be influenced, as soon as the effort is made, and yield. All such can resist if they know they can, and will make the proper resisting effort. (Sibley, 1904, p. 499)

Beaudoin (1920) was to reinforce this idea and stress the importance of destroying the superstitions surrounding the use of hypnosis.

This issue raised the problem of assessing moral and legal responsibility in cases where hypnosis was used to suggest a criminal behavior or to sexually seduce a subject. Although American experts were as divided on the issue as were their French counterparts, a majority tended to recognize that at least psychologically and/or morally the hypnotic subject shared partial responsibility. As far as the commission of a crime was concerned, few experts admitted that it could happen to someone who had not already shown criminal tendencies. Gabrielle Bompard's trial was regarded as a legal precedent. But when hypnosis became a seductive technique, the intricacies of the human mind were way beyond the understanding of the experts. As will be seen in the following chapters, contemporary cases of hypnotic seduction still baffle experts. Most of the nineteenth-century investigators accepted the notion of the highly hypnotizable subject as "an automaton." Whether this was caused by the "power" of suggestion or by a side effect of psychopathology (namely hysteria, or as Janet would describe it, as an involuntary shrinking of the field of consciousness), contemporary investigators continue to struggle with the notion of involuntariness in one's own behavior, and with the factors that elicit subjective experiences of loss of control over one's thoughts and actions.

By the beginning of the 1900s, all interest in hypnotism appears to have waned suddenly; very little was written during the next three decades about hypnosis from a scientific and legal approach. Indeed, it took the work of Clark Hull beginning in the 1920s to reinstate a modicum of scientific interest in the topic.

In one of the last articles of this period written on the legal aspects of hypnosis, Ladd (1902) attempted to review and present a general consensus on the problems elicited by the abuse of hypnosis. He recognized that most of these problems represented an extension of the issue of undue influence. He emphasized the notion of "rapport" between the hypnotist and the hypnotized subject, in interaction with the lack of critical thinking on the part of the latter, a point of view similar to what Janet in France had advanced as an explanation of the automaticity seen in both the hypnotized individual and the hysterical patient. Ladd identified sexual abuse and the falsification of memory as the two major areas of potential misuse of hypnosis. In the latter case, he indicated that it could give rise to the "illegal and criminal preparing of witnesses" (p. 179), a point already made by Moll (1889/1982).

Ladd accepted the idea that crimes could be suggested to some individuals and that the law should be aware of this. He did not, however, think that it could be a frequent problem, especially when one considered the scarcity of well substantiated earlier cases. In both areas of danger, he urged the courts to admit and use more frequently the resources of expert witnesses in evaluating the problems at hand. He told the courts also to expect that experts would not all agree on these topics since they still involved many matters of speculation (see also Münsterberg, 1908).

The involvement of the American medico-legal experts in the field of hypnosis lasted approximately 15 years. Although occasional cases were reported during the next six decades (1900-1960), hypnosis was not a central forensic issue in the American legal arena. This was not to last; both lay and professionally trained hypnotists of the 1960s and '70s would do their best to make up for these decades of apathy (see Chapters 11 and 12).

The End of an Era in France

The late nineteenth-century debate in the United States never rivaled the bitterness and antagonism that characterized France in the 1880s and that was still prevalent in the last years of the nineteenth century. As in America, however, the French debate slowly vanished from the public domain in the first decade of the twentieth century. However, in the mid-1890s, it was still raging as is illustrated by an anecdote involving Gilles de la Tourette.

In 1894, de la Tourette was hospitalized, the victim of an assassination attempt by one of his patients. The fact in itself was not surprising; that was one of the occupational hazards of working in an asylum at the time. Many physicians had actually been killed by their patients in the nineteenth century. But on this occasion, as the victim was de la Tourette, the affair was reported in many newspapers. Most of them attempted to explain the reasons for such behavior by his patient. Even the *Journal of Experimental and Therapeutic Hypnosis* added its sarcastic comment:

> The assassination attempt againt M. de la Tourette was commented [upon] in many different ways in the newspapers. It was said that our colleague had fallen victim to "a criminal suggestion" aimed at persuading him of the possibility of their occurrences. In hypothesizing that the author of this assassination attempt did enact a criminal suggestion, it is far from certain that it would have been sufficient to convince M. Gilles de la Tourette. He denies their possibilities with such mastery that we believe that nothing will ever modify his views on this point, not even an experiment of which he would be the victim. (1894, Vol. 7, p. 222)

In reality, de la Tourette had fallen prey to one of his patients' paranoid delusions.

One of the major reasons for the decline of hypnosis in France at the end of the nineteenth century was the disappearance of the two schools of thought that had carried on the interest in hypnosis for approximately 15 years. For the Salpêtrière, Charcot's death in 1893 was the end of an era. Once the famous neurologist was gone, dissensions and discontent took over his ward, and nobody could bring together those who had been under the Master's control. Two of his students would continue to study hypnosis and hysteria: de la Tourette and Babinski. While de la Tourette perpetuated Charcot's thoughts,

Babinski changed gradually, adopting positions quite similar to those of the Nancy school, and of Bernheim in particular. His theorizing however, would not be remembered, partly due to the fact that he denied the role played by emotions in hysterical symptoms; a difficult point to defend against the likes of Bernheim, Freud, and Janet.

Of these, Pierre Janet was to pursue his investigation of hypnosis and psychopathology for his entire life. He did so, however, in Freud's shadow, and despite the opposition of his own colleagues who rendered his life at the Salpêtrière quite difficult. He adopted positions that were similar to Bernheim's in many ways; in fact both Bernheim and Janet can be seen today as the fathers of hypnotic suggestive therapy and psychosomatic treatment.

Ironically, a similar train of events precipitated the fall of the Nancy school. During the 1890s, Bernheim's thought evolved slowly from the notion of hypnotic suggestion to the more global aspect of suggestion and psychotherapy in their interaction with psychopathology. He came to be more interested in the fact that suggestion could be used in the waking state with everyone rather than in hypnosis with a few. He laid down the foundations in France for the proliferation of verbal psychotherapy, in the same way that Freud was slowly building a similar system in Austria. But for proponents of hypnosis, Bernheim was seen as betraying the cause. Particularly on the issue of criminal suggestions, he was to end up promoting a view that partook of both Nancy and the Salpêtrière.

Although it must remain speculation, the decline of interest in the scientific study of hypnosis in France at the turn of the century may have been the result of the extravaganza that the forensic debate had set in motion, in interaction with the fate of the two major schools of thought. The fact that it was contemporaneous with the rise of psychoanalysis and behavioral psychology in both France and the United States added to this complex state of affairs. Forensic hypnosis, however, remained a major topic of gradually diminishing interest during the 1890s and in the first decade of the twentieth century.

The role played by suggestion was to be re-evaluated, and for both Bernheim and Liébeault, the problem of psychopathology became an important factor in the successful completion of criminal suggestions. This position was espoused by many experts at the time. The different legal cases of the previous years had more or less forced its acceptance. It had been recently exemplified in a case in Russia, the Petro-Zavodsk case, where an assistant physician (the equivalent of a male nurse) was found guilty of using hypnosis to seduce a young woman, and then to have her murder her husband. Using a mixture of massage, eye fixation techniques, and magnetic passes, he had succeeded in suggesting the husband's death to the young woman so that she would be the sole inheritor of the family's fortune. Following the husband's disappearance, the correspondence between the two culprits was discovered. They were arrested, tried, and found guilty. On appeal, however, a medical expert demonstrated that the woman had been subjected to criminal suggestions that had been successful because of her neurotic personality. Her sentence was reduced considerably (Akopenko, 1897).

A number of similar cases were publicized during the 1890s. The courts, however, often rejected the defense of somnambulism or hypnotism based on the reports of medical experts who had become more aware of the subtleties inherent in such cases (see, for example, Brouardel, Motet, & Garnier, 1893, on the Valrof case). Crocq (1894, 1896) emphasized the importance of delineating the different factors at play in a criminal trial: what was due to hypnosis, to suggestion, or to hysteria. He maintained that although rare, the successful use of criminal suggestion had been demonstrated a number of times in the past, and should be regarded as possible. He related a case that never reached the legal courts, but was in his view, instructive.

A young physician, Thomas Pitt, was arrested in London and accused of having stolen the jewels of none other than the Baroness de Rothschild. According to Pitt, he had met the Baroness on a train en route to Cologne. They had discussed the fact that he used hypnosis with his patients. Baroness de Rothschild, however, had expressed some doubts about his hypnotic skills; Pitt decided to offer her a lesson. He hypnotized her successfully, and commanded her to give him her jewelry. She obeyed his orders. When he was arrested by the police in London, he explained that he intended to send back the jewels, since he only wanted to teach the Baroness a lesson. Regardless of whether Pitt's stated intentions were true, this case indicated, according to Crocq ((1894, p. 194) that it was possible to use hypnosis for such purposes. What he did not realize, however, was the fact that the physician had been arrested for burglary following the Baroness's recall of the hypnotic procedure he had used with her, exemplifying once more the double-edged effect of using hypnosis in the commission of crimes; this was a fact that he was to acknowledge two years later (1896, p. 285).

In this latter book, Crocq presented the results of a questionnaire assessing the beliefs of the main theorists and practitioners of hypnosis at the end of the nineteenth century. As was mentioned earlier (see Chapter 9), more than 70 percent of those surveyed thought that the use of hypnosis could be dangerous for subjects. Crocq emphasized this finding by citing Azam: "I consider hypnotism to be dangerous for subjects; it exacerbates the nervous system. It is such a profound conviction, that, as a father of two young women, I have never experimented with them" (cited in Crocq, 1896, p. 415).

To the question, "Is rape possible?" 33 out of 34 respondents answered in the affirmative. As far as other crimes were concerned, 24 out of 31 believed that criminal suggestions were possible. On the issue of the alleged automaticity of the hypnotized subject, however, the experts were more divided; twenty-two thought that the hypnotized individuals obeyed their hypnotist blindly, whereas 18 did not think so (see Crocq, 1896, pp. 445–447).[7]

By the end of the nineteenth century, however, few authors continued to espouse either of the two extreme viewpoints. Liégeois and de la Tourette were the only ones who persisted with their original positions. In the books and articles that they published in this last decade of the nineteenth century, each was dismissive of the other, and of everybody else for that matter, who did not agree with them. De la Tourette (1895) was to become more Charcotian than Charcot had ever been, whereas Liégeois (1898) would remain, to the end, his own unique self. But times were changing, and the importance given to criminal suggestions was decreasing. Even Bernheim came to recognize the part played by psychopathology in assessing the responses to a criminal suggestion in a real-life trial. At the 12th International Congress of Medicine, held in Moscow in August 1897, he expressed the opinion that criminal suggestions could be efficient in an extremely small percentage of the population. In most cases that had been reported in the past, Bernheim now rejected the role played by hypnosis and presented them as examples of psychopathology, especially of hypnotic lethargy or as he called it "nervous inertia"! Charcot would have been pleased. What Bernheim was finally acknowledging was the role played by psychopathology in the development of criminal behaviors. He would go so far as to recognize that criminal suggestions would be more efficient with hysterical patients than with hypnotized individuals. This, in fact, appears to have been the position espoused by most investigators by this time.

Five years before, at the Third International Congress of Criminal Anthropology, held in Brussels in August 1892, M. Benedikt had concluded his presentation on criminal suggestion by saying:

> I look at these crimes as the product of an unfortunate scientific fantasy. I do not deny their theoretical possibility, I do not deny that they can be suggested in living-rooms and laboratories, but I deny their practical reality. (cited in Giraud, 1892, p. 353)

In 1898, Benedikt, who was attending the meeting of the Psychology Section of the British Medical Association, commented once again on the earlier theories of the Nancy school, following a presentation by Bramwell who had criticized them:

> Then came the delirious epoch of Nancy, in which no nonsense was too great to be believed. For some time I made no opposition, because paradoxical phenomena must excite paradoxical faith, to enter and to rest definitely in the beliefs of mankind. But this scientific movement was a danger, because it produced a mysticism propagated by novelists and other writers. Then I began to oppose them. Today we can enter quietly into this discussion, and I will state precisely my experience and my conviction. (*Medico-Legal Journal*, 1898, Vol. 16, p. 247)

Unfortunately, Benedikt's convictions were that "there is no place for hypnotic specialists" (p. 248), a more than extreme position. But there may have been wisdom in his words. The "delirious epoch of Nancy" was certainly partly responsible for the fate of hypnosis at the end of the nineteenth century.

But Benedikt pointed also to the influence of popular literature on the behaviors of the general population; a point well-taken if one considers the Svengali of Du Maurier's Trilby, or any other "powerful" mesmerist who inhabited the imagination of many American and European writers (Kihlstrom, 1986). Benedikt was sensitized to this issue; he had to deal on a daily basis with a hundred years of German romanticism at work in the neuroses of his patients (Ellenberger, 1970, 1978).

Toward a Consensual Approach

What seemed to rally most investigators and practitioners of this period were the influences of hypnosis and suggestion on the memory system of the individual. What was already known as the hypnotic subject's potential for confabulation became the central point of concern for the forensic hypnotist. A case in which a patient's alleged past history of sexual abuse became integrated into an ongoing treatment was reported in 1900 by Schrenck-Notzing at the Second International Congress of Experimental and Therapeutic Hypnotism, held in Paris. He, himself, had been called in to explain the facts of the case. An assistant physician, working in Munich, had been accused of having inserted his penis and urinating into the mouth of a 13-year-old girl, Madeleine S. The inquiry had been proceeding for more than three months when Schrenck-Notzing was called into the case. The only testimonies were those of the young girl and of the assistant physician. The version of the facts produced by the man were simple enough. He was hypnotizing Madeleine for therapeutic purposes in her hospital room when he felt a sudden urge to urinate. He left the young patient in the state she was in and urinated in a pot beside the patient's bed. Schrenck-Notzing investigated the young girl carefully, as well as the discussions that she had had with her parents following the event in question. It turned out that Madeleine had incorporated the noises made by the hypnotist into an ongoing hypnotic hallucination and relived a part of the alleged abuse.[8] The discussion with her parents had consolidated the hallucinated memory: "These retroactive pseudo-reminiscences were exaggerated during the waking state by the imagination of the young girl, and her conversations with her parents" (Schrenck-Notzing, 1902, p. 123).

The assistant physician was exonerated. Cases such as this, however, supported the opinion of most investigators that hypnosis had very little to offer in the forensic arena. Even as an investigative technique, too many problems confounded the testimony of the hypnotized subject: confabulation, simulation, lies, self-serving statements were all very difficult to avoid, let along separate from the truth (Baets, 1894). For Bérillon (1896), the problems of suggested false testimonies could affect up to 20 percent of the population. This problem was known also to happen outside of hypnosis; investigators of this period were aware of the natural tendency for the memory system to fill in gaps in the facts to be remembered. This natural tendency (Binet, 1900) seemed nonetheless to increase in hypnosis. As Binet (1900) explained: "These errors have a richness of details seen in true memories. All of our observations demonstrate that a memory can be precise, but totally incorrect" (p. 283).

For Binet, even if part of a memory were true, it did not mean that the entire memory was truthful (p. 286). The problem was compounded by the use of hypnosis, where the pressure to perform increased the suggestibility of the subject. In this particular sense, authors such as Binet (1900) and Wundt (1893), for example, described hypnosis as immoral. Bernheim (1897) specified that imagination, motivation, and the investigative context were all at play in the elaboration of illusory memories. Based on these premises, Bérillon (1896) suggested at the International Congress of Criminal Anthropology that the laws governing the investigation of a criminal case be modified. In France, the details of the investigation were kept secret by the prosecuting party. Bérillon wanted the instruction to be based upon cross-examination. As will be seen in Chapter 12, prosecutorial discretion is still prevalent in such countries as Canada; an unfortunate situation when hypnosis is used indiscriminantly with victims, witnesses, and suspects of crimes.

The use of hypnosis as an inquisitorial agent was thus looked upon very seriously, and with concern. As Philipon (1908) concluded in his doctoral dissertation presented to the Law Faculty of the University of Paris:

> Any confession obtained through the use of hypnosis must be looked at very rationally first, then corroborated, reinforced with more solid proofs. To accuse someone based on such confession would be demonstrating a criminal carelessness. (p. 141)

As far as using hypnosis with victims and witnesses of crime, the experts' opinions were similar to Philipon's position. No one summarized it better than Joire (1900). He maintained that the problem of suggested false testimony given in good faith was even more dramatic since it led involuntarily to miscarriages of justice. Part of the problem resided in the fact that both hypnotist and subject had good intentions.

> Quite to the contrary, it is usually one of those who has the duty and the motivation to help the judicial process in the best way they can that will be the involuntary and unconscious author of a suggestion that can mislead the best directed investigation. (p. 200; see Chapter 12 for contemporary examples of this problem)

This unfortunate suggestion could transform an unsure witness into a confident and very sincere one (p. 200). Even more to the point, whereas other witnesses would hesitate when confronted with the facts of the investigation, hypnotized witnesses would hold their ground steadfastly and to an unshakeable degree. Since some of the details given in hypnosis would be exact, the danger of not questioning the whole content of the testimony was increased.

This regrettable state of affairs was usually viewed as having been brought on by a well-intentioned investigator.

> In the facts under investigation, he sincerely looks for the truth, and it is in the name of this truth that he gives the suggestion that will mislead him. Once the suggestion has been accepted by the subject, the more efforts the investigator will deploy to ascertain the sincerity and veracity of the subject's testimony, the more he will reinforce the suggestion. How could he know that he is giving a suggestion since he is only using the more common investigative techniques, those that everyone uses and that have led to the discovery of the truth in a number of different inquiries. (Joire, 1900, p. 201)

Joire's solution to such delicate problems was to sensitize the legal community to the possibility of confabulation, and to urge the consultation of court-appointed medico-legal experts who could evaluate the questionable testimonies (p. 236).

During the initial decade of the twentieth century, the great forensic debate vanished as suddenly as it had started in 1884 with Liégeois's communication to the Académie des Sciences in Paris. Grasset (1903) was to be one of the last to publish an intensive review of the area in his book *L'hypnotisme et la suggestion*. It was the last upshot of a debate which did not survive its main protagonists. In his review, Grasset presented old facts and old theories. Nothing new was to emerge from the French clinicians on this topic.[9]

Had these troubling questions been answered? In one sense, yes. Practical experience had shown that hypnosis and suggestion did not constitute in themselves a *deus ex machina* that compelled people to behave in ways contrary to their values. The answer did not lie in the surrounding context exclusively, but in the intricacies of the human mind at play in such a context. There were no simple answers to such complex questions. This first entry of hypnosis into the legal arena, however, paved the way for the second that appeared in the United States some 60 years later. The same questions were asked, similar answers given; but in between these two debates, there were six decades of experimental and clinical research that were to take the examination of these issues a few steps closer to an understanding of hypnosis and suggestion.

NOTES

1. The American reader can certainly entertain the thought of comparing Melville's opinion of the spiritualist movement to the contemporary rise of the new "spiritualist" movement in the United States. Then, as now, hypnosis and its legal import were flourishing. Then, as now, a century was coming to an end. Then, as now, scientism prevailed in popular literature. The propagation and simplification of scientific thought through media coverage often led to its degradation and misinterpretation. The beginnings of the age of industrialization were as anxiety provoking as the onset of the nuclear age. Wonder and awe could easily go hand in hand. The idea of freedom of will was an important yet vulnerable construct during this period of dramatic social changes. The same could be said of the contemporary fragile world balance.

2. The individual who wrote the note is identified as F. H. B. It may have been a printing mistake since the Superior Court for the San Diego County appointed shorthand reporter in this case was named *Fred H. Robinson*. Whether or not he is the author of the note, however, must remain a matter of speculation.

3. These two cases will not be discussed since it appears that hypnosis did not play any role in the debate. In the former case, a murder case, Hayward and Blitz were accused of killing Miss Ging. Although Hayward possessed a strong influence on Blitz, he did not ever claim that it was of a hypnotic nature, and the plea was never made by the defense. Hayward had paid Blitz to eliminate Ging and had made him drink to give him the courage [*sic*] to do the job he had been paid for (see F. H. B., 1897). While in jail, a traveling hypnotist was called in to see Blitz, but did not hypnotize him. He only expressed the opinion that he could be hypnotizable. Blitz, himself, denied any hypnotic influence (Sudduth, 1895).

In the latter case, hypnosis was brought up as a *post hoc* excuse for an escapade committed by two young women and a male friend, Pickens. As Sudduth (1895) summarized:

> But when people began to talk about them and shun them the girls found it necessary to hunt up an excuse for their absence from the city and to account for their presence in the place where they were found. The Briggs girl knew something about hypnotism, she is shrewd, sentimental and hysterical. She may even have imagined the commission of a crime during a hysterical moment, or she may have concocted the story to screen her part in the case. There is no evidence of any hypnotic influence in the case, while there are scores of facts pointing to it as a trumped up charge. No one in Eau Clare, who is acquainted with the facts, believes that hypnotism had anything to do with the escapade. (p. 242)

4. Some physicians harbored a less than laudable opinion of the working class. Sudduth, for example, described the subjects in hypnotic experiments:

> The laboratory tests made in this direction in Europe, and on which foreign writers base their beliefs on the possible immoral use to be made of hypnosis, are not to be relied upon, for the reason that they are made upon the peasant class which is notorious for its lack of virtue. (Sudduth, 1895, p. 254)

Liégeois was to support this position a few years later:

> There is no family, rich or poor, wealthy, princely, or even of royal descent that can believe itself out of reach of this danger; nowhere are women, young girls not exposed, and sometimes extensively, to people of a doubtful morality: servants, lackeys, coach-drivers, etc. . . . (1898, p. 274)

So much for the underprivileged classes! If Mesmer had complained one hundred years earlier that curing the lower class had less value than curing the aristocrats as the Benjamin Franklin Commission had emphasized, what would he have thought of these comments?

5. Some authors have reported that Czynski was acquitted by the jury (see Jankau, 1896, for one example). Czynski was acquitted of the charge of having had sexual intercourse with the Baroness while she was in a hypnotic state. He was found guilty on the other counts.

6. Only three other cases are reported in the first decade of the twentieth century. *Austin v. Barker* (1904/1906), a seduction case, will be described briefly in Chapter 12 as it had some influence in the early judicial decisions of contemporary cases. *Parks v.*

State (1902) was the trial of a lay magnetist charged with illegal practice of medicine. This affair was reminiscent of similar ones in Europe throughout the nineteenth century, which were discussed in earlier chapters. Finally, in *State v. Exum* (1905), hypnosis played a peripheral role. In this case, Exum was accused of murdering his wife's son, Guy Walston. During the trial, his wife who had witnessed the murder with two other individuals changed some aspects of her testimony. The modified recall of events could be seen as lending support to the self-defense plea that her husband had entered. When it transpired that she had been hypnotized previously by her husband three times (and although the hypnotic sessions were prior to the murder), she was described as being under the influence of her husband, and her credibility as a witness was questioned. As the court ruled:

> The prisoner testified to the effect that he had hypnotized his wife on three separate occasions, and as explained by him, it tended to show that he had influence over her to a greater extent than usually arise from the relationship between them. If this be correct, the evidence is competent as affecting her credibility, and if not, then we are unable to perceive how the prisoner's case was prejudiced by its admission. (p. 286)

7. Crocq consulted the writings or wrote to 58 hypnosis researchers or practitioners on different topics that had been objects of theoretical dispute in the previous 20 years. Of these, many had either no opinion on a specific question or had never written about it. This explains the different numbers of responses on each question.

8. It must be said, however, that the physician had been suspected, already, of sexual abuse, although he had never been found guilty. Some of the suggestions he employed with Madeleine were sexually ambiguous and may have precipitated this accusation. This case illustrates well the difficulty of disentangling fact from fiction.

9. The legal courts, however, would recognize officially that the practice of hypnosis was part of the medical repertoire on December 29, 1900. This, however, did not stop lay hypnotists from performing their tricks under new denominations. This problem can still be seen today. For example, Reveen, an Austrailian-born hypnotist, is now promoting what he calls a "supra-conscious state" after having been for years a hypnotist and an "impossibilist" [*sic*]. The French experts attempted without success to circumvent such problems by suggesting that both hypnosis and "pseudo-hypnosis" be banned; at the time, the lay hypnotists pretended that their subjects were simulating (Joire, 1902).

IV

The Contemporary Use of Forensic Hypnosis

11

The Twentieth Century: Bust Followed by Boom

In his classic book entitled *Psychological Healing* (1925, originally published in French in 1919), Pierre Janet sought to explain the sudden and abrupt demise of interest in hypnosis that occurred in France during the 1890s. He provided two main reasons for this decline, but was strangely silent when it came to the possible role of the forensic battles even though they clearly played an important role, if not the major role. Enigmatically, he observed that

> The decline of hypnotism has no serious meaning. It has been due to accidental causes, to disillusionment and reaction following upon ill-considered enthusiasm. It is merely a temporary incident in the history of induced somnambulism. (1925, p. 207)

He believed that the struggle between the Salpêtrière and Nancy schools had been "disastrous"; why this was so, he wrote, "will become plain if we consider the actual results of the struggle" (p. 204). Part of the problem, he thought, was Charcot's determination to study hypnosis using the scientific method, which was, unfortunately, the scientific methodology of the field of neurology in which he had been trained. Charcot's interest, however, gave respectability to the field, even among those scientists who saw elements of chicanery and fraudulance as its only distinguishing features.

Janet argued that Charcot's error was to believe that

> hypnotic phenomena were simple physiological happenings akin to those he was used to studying in cases of insular sclerosis or locomotor ataxia, and in believing that an examination of the modifications of the reflexes that occurred in his hypnotized subjects would provide the data on which he could base the definitions and the laws of which he was in search. (p. 204)

In short, Charcot's historically famous error was to adopt the methodology, and the conceptualization, of neurology, rather than of psychology. This was not all together negligent on his part; psychology was still a young field of science. Wilhelm Wundt had opened the first psychological laboratory at Leipzig in 1879, and his experimental work, which was of a ground-breaking nature, had yet to permeate into medicine. Then as now practical applications of scientific data that would help physicians better treat their patients were of paramount concern. Psychology was still in its fledgling years and was not in a position to cater to this demand. Several years earlier, in 1870, Charcot had begun a celebrated study which successfully distinguished between epileptics and hysterical conversion patients whose symptoms closely mimicked epilepsy, utilizing neurological signs. This experience perhaps might have alerted him to the possibility that if a trained observer could not distinguish a hysterical and neurological etiology of epilepsy, the same could be true with other conditions such as hypnosis. Unfortunately, this was not the case.

He realized his error a year before his death in 1893, but by then it was too late. The doctrines of the Salpêtrière, as Janet pointed out, had been clear, simple, and easy to study; now they were overthrown. At the same time, while being instrumental in this act of iconoclasm, the Nancy school, which briefly retained exclusive territorial rights to the field, began to be perceived as having little better to offer—it had only the correct conviction that Charcot had been in error and the doctrine that hypnosis "was a moral state in which suggestibility was enhanced; it was the outcome of suggestion" (Janet, 1925, p. 205). This, according to Janet, appeared to scientists as "superficial, and not really scientific teaching" (p. 205).

The second reason for the demise of hypnosis that Janet proposed centered on more practical matters. Although the Nancy school had compiled accurate norms of hypnotic susceptibility (Bernheim, 1889) which were remarkably similar to what is found in the laboratory today, its proponents espoused the clinical belief that virtually everybody could be hypnotized—at least to a sufficient degree for clinical purposes. Janet reported the figure of 27 persons in 1,000 being unhypnotizable according to the Nancy school; in addition he cited Bernheim as saying that "a doctor who could not hypnotize 95 percent of his patients at the first attempts was a doctor who did not know his business" (p. 206). Janet believed that with scientific data such as these, the proponents of the Nancy school proceeded to hypnotize indiscriminately, and for all types of complaint, although as was seen in Chapter 9, Bernheim objected strongly to these accusations.

Janet's surprising lack of insight into Bernheim's position was a reflection of his years at the Salpêtrière. He never quite abandoned the idea that hypnosis was a pathological state which could only be useful in well-defined psychopathologies. The use of hypnosis as an adjunct to medical treatment, as Bernheim was proposing, did not seem realistic for Janet. It could only lead to patients questioning the adequacy of the treatment that they were receiving. In a very similar way, he would later criticize sharply the extension of his own notion of subconscious into an all-pervasive unconscous à la Freud.

As a reaction to both Charcot's death and Bernheim's modification of the suggestive theory, practitioners started to look for alternative methods of treatment. Janet's own theorizing served as a basis for new hypotheses. His conceptualization of hypnosis as a representation of the automatic tendencies of consciousness led individuals like Babinski and Dubois to propose treatments based on more exalted characteristics such as will and reason. Babinski's "persuasive healing" rejected Charcot's theories as illusory and misleading. He replaced suggestion by an authoritarian structuring of therapy (Babinski, 1911).

The characterization of the hypnotized person as an automaton in the hands of the omniscient hypnotist, which had plagued the field from the days of Mesmer and had been stated most explicitly by Liébeault (Chapter 8) a mere few decades before Janet, once again dominated thinking on the matter. The fatigue, lethargy, and ultimate sense of futility that the forensic debate aroused in practitioners coincided also with the publication of *The Interpretation of Dreams* by Sigmund Freud (1900) who had abandoned an early interest in hypnosis to develop ultimately the new theory of psychoanalysis.

Curiously, however, there is not the slightest inkling in Janet's book that the 1880s and 1890s involved the bitter forensic debates that we described in the two preceding chapters. Indeed, he himself was conspicuously absent from the debate. It was all just a matter of "ill-considered enthusiasm" and while, as has already been seen, this certainly played a role, there was more to it than Janet was prepared to say.

In a sense, Janet was correct when he wrote that the whole episode on criminal suggestions had been vastly exaggerated: "Hypnotism would still be important even if criminal suggestions did not exist; but we should stop bestowing upon it such marvelous powers" (1919/1925, pp. 289-290).

The Nancy school's overstatements had certainly played a role in the decline of hypnosis. He saw it as an unfortunate digression that led his contemporaries to reject the baby with the bath water.

Janet (1911, 1919/1925) recognized the possibility of criminal suggestions. He reported five cases that were for him unobjectionably valid. The problem, however, had been misformulated: "The interesting problem from a medico-legal view is to identify if, in these patients, suggestion was a more efficient and dangerous process than the ones usually used like persuasions and threats" (1919/1925, p. 291).

In Janet's mind, the relationship between the protagonists should have been the main focus of investigation. Quite clearly, he wanted to forget this "ill-considered enthusiasm" and resume the investigation of hypnosis and suggestibility.

One aspect of the forensic debate which placed it almost on the footing of trench warfare deserves particular emphasis. This concerns the very nature of a legal proceeding. It was summed up by Kirby (1984), himself an eminent judge. He wrote:

> In our tradition, the trial process is not simply a search for the truth. Perhaps it should be. But it is not. It is in the nature of a public and ceremonial clash of evidence, conducted in courts for the public resolution of a dispute in society. (p. 153)

As indicated in Chapter 9, with the notable exception of the Eyraud–Bompard trial, this ceremonial clash of evidence occurred rarely in the nineteenth-century French courts. Rather, judges usually called experts from one, but not the other, "school." The advocates of the position not represented in court were usually quick to present their interpretation of a particular case in print, and they did not flinch from the indelicate task of demonstrating that the designated court experts were in gross error. Since these rejoinders were published often in the media, it takes little understanding of human egos to recognize the deep degree of acrimony and bitterness they provoked. Differences of opinion in science can be rancorous at the best of times; making the disputes public augmented the ratio of heat to light by a significant degree. This did not, however, discourage both "schools" from indulging in these public *autos-da-fé*, whenever the opportunity arose. This simple fact appears to constitute the most cogent reason why, as the twentieth century began, hypnosis was in deep decline in France.[1]

The first several decades of the current century were to be dominated by Freud's thinking, and interest in hypnosis became a largely peripheral matter (see Perry & Laurence, 1984, for an account of this period). Janet continued to practice in France until his death in 1946. Other major figures contributed to the understanding of hypnosis: Bramwell, Gurney, and Myers in Britain, Forel and Moll in Germany, and Prince and Sidis in the United States. These, however, despite their important contributions, were but a minority and of little interest to the mainstream of thinking in the health sciences which saw in psychoanalysis the promise that had been thought previously, only a few decades earlier, to be the exclusive property of hypnosis.

Two major developments were ultimately to alter this course of history and restore hypnosis to the high status it enjoys currently. The first of these must have appeared innocuous enough at the time. During the later 1920s, Clark L. Hull established the first experimental hypnosis laboratories at the University of Wisconsin at Madison. This occurred almost a half century after Wundt had formed the Psychology Laboratory at Leipzig. In the Preface to his 1933 book, *Hypnosis and Suggestibility: An Experimental Approach*, Hull presented a brief rationale of this ultimately highly significant historical development. He noted that

> Throughout the history of hypnotism the clinical approach, with its preoccupations with remedial exigencies, has greatly predominated. In contrast to this tendency the approach of the present work is experimental rather than clinical; the persons employed as subjects in the program of research were

normal rather than pathological; the ends sought were principles and relations rather than treatments and cures. This choice was not made through any lack of appreciation of applied science, but rather in the belief that in the long run application itself will be furthered by a proportionate development of pure science. There has accordingly been special emphasis upon the methodology of control experimentation, in which sphere hypnotic investigations of the past have been so largely defective. (p. ix)

Though Hull was subsequently to abandon the study of hypnosis, his legacy was to endure. He was the first to demonstrate that the phenomena were sufficiently robust to survive the transition from the clinic to the laboratory and from the psychiatric patient to the college sophomore. At the time though, this major achievement was not accorded any special significance.

The other major development occurred during the two World Wars. With the exigencies of battle and the need to treat such psychological side effects of warfare as combat fatigue and shell shock quickly and effectively, practitioners of hypnosis rapidly became highly valued by the military. Working under appalling conditions and often faced with shortages of such alternative treatment modalities as sedative drugs and painkillers, these individuals were able, with sufficient frequency, to demonstrate the value of hypnosis as an effective psychological intervention technique.

The subsequent post-World War II development of hypnosis is probably a little too close to be able to chart objectively. It suffices to say that this period has been one of remarkable growth and development at both the clinical and experimental levels.[2] There has not, however, been a pattern of unmitigated tranquility since, beginning in the 1960s and particularly during the past decade, the forensic debate of nineteenth-century France has returned and has become renewed and renourished in North American soil. Perhaps ironic, however, is the fact that many of the participants in the current pleasantries on this matter are blissfully unaware of the large body of documentation of the French debate of a century ago that lies, awaiting fresh inspection, in the Bibliothèque Nationale in Paris.[3]

A Return to the Debate on Coercion

In the Laboratory

Hull's successful demonstration that hypnotic phenomena are robust and can be studied within the benign context of the laboratory was a major turning point in the field's history. Among other things, it held out the tantalizing promise of empirical resolution of the issue of whether a person could be coerced by hypnosis or compelled to act in a manner contrary to his or her moral beliefs. No longer would it be a matter of trusting the word of a magnetized subject, as de Puységur had done (Chapter 5), that he would never be able to induce her to remove her clothes. Now, one could place subjects in controlled situations and see what they would do in response to suggestions that required them to commit acts that were damaging or embarrassing to the self and/or others. It was thought that the experimenter, of course, would be able to contrive the situation in such a manner that no actual harm would occur, while maintaining the fiction that the situation was potentially hazardous. The task appeared to be straightforeward, limited only by the investigator's ingenuity in contriving such situations. Therein lay the rub.

An early attempt to answer this beguilingly simple question owed much, though it was not acknowledged, to the earlier work of French clinicians (see Liégeois, 1889, in Chapter 9). Rowland (1939) conducted a two-part experiment, in the first of which he took four highly hypnotizable subjects, and asked them, while hypnotized, to pick up a large diamondback rattlesnake. The snake had been intalled in its box some three days earlier, and the room had been purposely overheated to ensure that the snake would be "very lively." In addition, holes had been bored in the sides of the box to permit prodding of the snake with a wire.

> The result was a most frightful scene. The snake invariably wound himself into a coil with his head ready to strike, his rattles singing loudly enough that they could be heard within a radius of 100 feet. (Rowland, 1939, p. 115)[4]

Unbeknownst to the subject, however, the seemingly open front of the box was, in fact, covered with glass that was bent in such a manner as to cast no reflection and make it invisible; there was, however, a protective wire screen barrier. Subjects were located 30 feet from the box and two of them were told in hypnosis that "there is a piece of coiled rope in that box. Go up to the box, reach through the screen wire, and pick it up" (p. 115). The other two were told, correctly, that there was a rattlesnake in the box and were similarly ordered to reach inside and pick it up.

The operational test of whether subjects in hypnosis would carry out self-damaging acts was that they put their hand through the wire screen and touch the glass. Three of them did this; one, in fact, began to explore the glass with her hand as if searching for an opening. The fourth subject, upon seeing the snake, came out of hypnosis. Rowland, however, stated that he had been skeptical beforehand of this particular subject's capacity for deep hypnosis, a *post hoc, ergo propter hoc* explanation which was to be invoked on many subsequent occasions when subjects in experiments did not conform to an experimenter's hypothesis.

In the second part of the study, two hypnotized subjects were asked to throw sulfuric acid at the experimenter who, as with the snake, was protected by the nonreflecting glass. To avoid all ambiguity concerning the nature of the task, the potency of the acid was first demonstrated by dipping a strip of zinc into it so that the subjects saw it fume and could have no illusions about the results of their actions. Both subjects threw the acid, one of them with apparent deep disturbance.

As a control, 42 people "of every age and degree of sophistication" (p. 116) were asked to come to the laboratory and pick up the snake. Only one complied, and this (it was discovered when she was subsequently questioned) was because she believed the snake to be artificial. All of the remaining subjects

> were not only badly frightened at the appearance of the snake, but would not come close to the box; only a few were persuaded finally to pick up a yard stick and try to touch the snake. They all seemed bewildered when they touched the glass which they could not see. (pp. 116-117)

Even the one recalcitrant subject became frightened and would not go near the box when, having been assured that the snake was real, she made a closer inspection of it. She knew also that she was protected by the wire screen barrier.

From this, Rowland concluded the "persons in deep hypnosis will allow themselves to be exposed to unreasonably dangerous situations" and "will perform acts unreasonably dangerous to others" (p. 117). As almost an aside, Rowland tempered his conclusion by stating that confidence in the hypnotist might cause subjects to forgo their better judgments and recommended that only professional psychologists and others adequately trained [*sic*] should be permitted to utilize hypnosis.

Despite apparent scientific rigor, it is not at all apparent what really occurred in Rowland's experiment. For instance, it appears that all of the hypnotized subjects had at least some laboratory experience; all were reported as having at least two prior hypnotic sessions. By contrast, it is not clear from Rowland's account how control subjects were recruited and how they were instructed; the implication is that they had no prior experience with laboratory procedures. Perhaps more to the point was the report of the hypnotized subject who made extensive efforts to find an opening in the glass. When questioned a week later, she stated that she did not know why she had exposed herself to such danger, but "she supposed she was confident that the experimenter would not allow her to be harmed" (p. 115). This, indeed, was the unacknowledged problem with the Rowland study, as had been the case in most previous similar experiments in France.

Nevertheless, the finding was replicated by Young (1952) in a study that appears to have been more dangerous for the experimenters than for the subjects. It involved eight highly hypnotizable subjects; they were asked (1) to pick up a water snake (which is not venomous, but resembles the water moccasin, which is), and (2) to throw nitric acid at the exprimenter's assistant. For half of the subjects on each of the two tasks the invisible glass was used. Further, for half of them the task was represented as very dangerous and for the remainder as harmless. The results appeared to be clearcut enough; seven of the eight subjects attempted to handle the snake and to throw the nitric acid. The hazards of this experiment concerned the nitric acid. Having demonstrated its potency by dropping a penny into the dish containing it, the experimenter surreptitiously switched it for a dish of methylene-blue water which was kept foaming by miniscule droplets of barium peroxide. Unfortunately, the experimenter and his assistant could not always distinguish the acid from the water, and a number of burned experimenter hands resulted. In another instance, the switch was not successfully completed and the subject threw actual nitric acid at the experimenter's assistant. It was acknowledged, however, in a footnote that "on account of the promptness of remedial measures, no scars were left on his face; although his heavy uniform (that of an ROTC student) demonstrated in large areas where the acid struck" (p. 405). Clearly, this study took naturalism to a giddy limit, though inadvertantly.

Little, however, can be concluded from Young's study since there does not appear to have been any follow-up questioning of subjects in order to determine their perceptions of how dangerous they actually felt it was. Another experiment from around this period (Lyon, 1954) showed some recognition of the possibility that subjects in experiments will comply with seemingly dangerous requests because they believe correctly that although the task "appears" dangerous, the experimenter has taken steps to protect their well-being. Lyon compared subjects over a number of tasks (such as pouring acid on their hands and tearing up a confidential report) under two different experimental conditions. In the *Command* condition, they were simply ordered to perform the various acts, whereas in the *Justification* one, they were told that although the task might appear dangerous and/or unethical, it in fact was not. Needless to say, there was a much higher incidence of compliance to the experimental requests in the *Justification* condition.

The more important point stemming from this study, however, was that in the *Command* condition a subject who carried out the command did so "because he felt compelled to do so or because he felt the operator wouldn't really let him do anything wrong" (p. 290). In the *Justification* condition, the latter reports were far more common, presumably because of the experimenter's assurances that the task was not dangerous. Lyon's report might suggest two types of response in this contrived situation—that is, some subjects might comply because they correctly recognized that they were in no danger, while others might feel compelled against their will to obey a request that they perceived as dangerous. Historically, as we have seen, the latter alternative has always been the basis of the concern with hypnosis. Clearly, a more incisive experiment was required, and although more than a decade passed before it was attempted, the experiment was a telling one.

Orne and Evans (1965) performed a replication of the essential features of the Rowland–Young procedures and obtained essentially the same results. By the addition of more sophisticated controls, and careful questioning of subjects after the experiment, they were able to evaluate the degree to which both Rowland's and Young's findings were primarily the product of subjects' perceptions of the experiments as "safe." Their theoretical analysis of the issue made explicit what had been largely implicit in the Rowland and Lyon studies. They stated:

> If these actions are to be designated as antisocial or self-destructive it must be shown that they are perceived as such by subjects i.e. truly dangerous or harmful to themselves or others. The implicit cues are of crucial importance. A subject is aware of certain realities imposed by the experimental situation. It is as clear to a subject as it is to any scientist that no reputable investigator can risk injuring a subject during the course of an experiment. A subject knows that an experimenter will outline in advance any possible specific and deliberate danger which could be associated with his actual participation in a study. Consequently, any requested behavior which appears to a subject to be dangerous at face value may be reinterpreted in the context of a laboratory situation. In spite of the apparent objective danger of a task it may nonetheless be perceived to be harmless because the subject realizes that necessary precautions will be taken to avoid possible injury to him.... It is particularly vital in an experiment which depends on a contrived situation to determine what the subject, in different groups, perceives about the experimental situation and what is implicitly communicated to the subject within different groups. (p. 191)

The experiment was performed at the University of Sydney in Australia, so that aspects of the first three tasks may not be familiar to readers in other countries. Subjects were first asked to pick up a thick-tailed gecko (a small harmless lizard), followed by a thin, 14-inch long, green tree snake (which likewise is harmless). Then, invisible glass, similar to that employed by Rowland, was placed noiselessly and without attracting the subject's attention across the opening of the cage and a red-bellied black snake (one of the most venomous snakes of Australia) was placed in the cage. As with Rowland's study, striking the glass firmly with the hand was taken as evidence that the subject intended to pick the snake up.

As in the earlier studies, two other apparently dangerous tasks were set up. In the first, subjects were asked to remove a copper alloy halfpenny from the bottom of a shallow beaker containing fuming concentrated nitric acid. This looks to be a dangerous task, but in fact is not, provided that the experimenter has fast reflexes. No burn will occur if the experimenter can transfer the hand and coin to a basin of soapy lukewarm water within a matter of seconds. Orne was the experimenter in this study and maintained an appropriate reaction time across its duration.

A final task involved telling the subjects that they were very angry at the experimenter's assistant (Evans) for having placed them in the unpleasant situation of the experiment. Indeed, they were told that they were so angry that they had an irresistible urge to throw acid at his face. This part of the experiment was arranged so that a several foot long alleyway box on stilts was placed between the subject and the experimenter's assistant, so that his head and shoulders were visible at the other end of it. The box caught the liquid (since the acid had been switched for a harmless, similarly colored solution) and meant that cleaning up of the experimental room was minimal. Although the instructions implied that only the contents of the beaker should be thrown at the assistant, some subjects took the instruction more literally and threw the beaker as well. Evans, on these occasions, was required to show considerable agility in the art of ducking (which he performed admirably).

There were a number of experimental conditions in this study. Three of them are of primary relevance to the present discussion. Of six subjects who participated in the condition designed to replicate Rowland's and Young's studies, five attempted to pick up the black snake, placed their hands in nitric acid, and threw it at the experimenter's assistant. The sixth subject was so terrified by the gecko that it was not possible to complete the three quasi-dangerous tasks. In the interests of honest reporting, the investigators treated her as a failure on these tasks.

As can be seen, these data replicate the earlier findings of both Rowland and Young. Orne and Evans, however, went several steps further. They included a group of six insusceptible subjects who were asked to simulate hypnosis. The details of this procedure can be found elsewhere (Orne, 1979a; Sheehan & Perry, 1976); it suffices to say here that provided this highly sophisticated quasi-control is properly instituted, it is extremely difficult for even a highly trained and experienced investigator to distinguish nonhypnotized simulation from actual hypnotic behavior. All six of the subjects in this group performed the three seemingly dangerous tasks.

A second "Waking Compliance" control group consisted of six subjects who were not selected for their ability to experience hypnosis. They were simply told that they were being employed as control subjects for an experiment that involved hypnosis. These instructions were minimal, but in every other respect, the subjects were treated identically to subjects in the other groups. Within this group, the performance was only slightly inferior to what had been found in the hypnosis and simulating groups. Five of them performed the two tasks involving the acid, and three of them attempted to pick up the red-bellied black snake.

With these additional controls, the situations presented by Rowland and Young are markedly altered—unhypnotized simulators perform, as a group, slightly better than hypnotized subjects, and Waking Compliance subjects performed slightly worse. Hypnosis now appears to have little, if anything, to do with the carrying out of a seemingly dangerous instruction. The questioning of subjects after the experiment, however, provided data that explained why this was so. Virtually every subject who carried out a requested activity indicated that he or she had felt safe in the experiment. These subjects reported that they had experienced strong emotional reactions of repugnance to the tasks, but that

> they were quite convinced that they would not be harmed *because* the context was an experimental one, presumably being conducted by responsible experimenters. All subjects appeared to assume that some form of safety precautions had been taken during the experiment. (p. 199, italics in original)

They were, of course, completely correct. Interestingly, the same explanations had been offered by Delboeuf and others (see Chapter 9) when they had attempted to explain the Nancy school's experiments.

The range of precautions Orne and Evans's subjects thought had been taken ranged from the practical to the fanciful. Not one of them had anticipated the nonreflecting glass, but many thought that the snake had been defanged or milked of its venom. Some felt that the solution was not really acid, even after they had placed their hands in it. The perception of the acid-throwing task ranged from a belief that the glass screen had been lowered into place to the belief that the assistant was not really there and that what they were seeing was an illusion produced by a complex arrangement of mirrors.

Because of its incisiveness, the Orne and Evans study had a major effect on subsequent experimental attempts to evaluate the coercive power of hypnosis. Investigators quickly recognized the point that because the situation is defined as an experiment, subjects can be confident that adequate safeguards have been taken to protect their well-being, no matter how dangerous the situation "looks." This has not prevented subsequent investigators from devising often ingenious alternative means of testing the coercion hypothesis. While these studies reached similar conclusions to those of Orne and Evans, they deserve brief mention.

Two studies by Coe, Kobayashi, and Howard (1972, 1973) sought to isolate variables that might determine whether or not subjects would carry out an instruction to perform acts contrary to social mores. In the first, the task was to steal a Graduate Comprehensive Examination from the office of the secretary of the department of psychology. All subjects were recruited from approximately the top 20 percent of the hypnotizability continuum, and they were assigned randomly to one of four groups which consisted of various combinations of presence or absence of hypnosis, and presence or absence of a relationship with the experimenter. The variable of subject awareness of participating in an experiment was manipulated also by having half of the subjects instructed in an experimental context and half in a context beyond the experiment. The latter was effected by scheduling subjects for an additional session one week after their first session and then phoning them on the same night, requesting them to meet either the experimenter or an accomplice that they did not know (depending upon whether they had been allocated to a relationship or nonrelationship group) outside of the university library on the following day.

Essentially, the study found that of 30 subjects, 17 of them stole the examination paper. Most of the subjects (71%), however, indicated that they were aware of the fact that the request to steal was a part of an experiment. This awareness was highest in the group which received the request in the context of hypnosis plus a relationship with the experimenter. Of those stealing the examination, 88 percent showed this awareness. Most of the 17 subjects (76%) who stole the examination did so when the context involved hypnosis; nearly all of them, however (85%) showed a clear awareness that the stealing instruction was part of an experiment. By contrast, not one subject who received no hypnosis and was instructed by a confederate (no relationship) stole an examination paper.

The authors candidly acknowledged the potential shortcomings of their study. The most obvious one was that the relationship between subject and experimenter in the "relationship" conditions consisted of two hypnosis sessions; this is clearly less than occurred in virtually all of the nineteenth-century attempts to test the coercive power of hypnosis, where the patient had invariably been hypnotized repeatedly within the context of a therapeutic relationship. Nevertheless, it could be maintained that five subjects (29%) stole the examination while showing that they did not appear to be aware that the request was a part of an experiment. The problem here is two fold: For one thing, not knowing as opposed to saying that one does not know are often very difficult things to separate out in practice. Further, of the five subjects in this category, only two of them received hypnotic instructions to steal.

In the second study (Coe et al., 1973), the same combinations of hypnosis and a relationship with the experimenter were again employed. This time, however, the target behavior involved the selling of heroin. Across the four conditions, nine of the subjects completed the sales transaction (35%), but six of these occurred (67%) in a condition that did not involve hypnosis. As opposed to the previous experiment, selling the heroin was unrelated to whether subjects perceived the request as a part of an experiment. Rather, the variable that appeared to be most related to performing the requested act was the subject's attitudes toward heroin selling; six of the nine subjects who completed the transaction had stated prior to the experiment that it was not contrary to their moral beliefs. As with the earlier study, though, it was difficult to separate out the roles of the individual variables investigated in determining the effect on behavior.

As with Young's (1952) study, the second study by Coe et al. (1973) indicated that experimentation can be potentially harmful to the experimenter. In one case, a confederate was almost physically beaten by two friends of a female subject, and additional complications occurred for the first author since this female subject's father was a professor in another department. He was less than delighted about the task his daughter had been requested to perform as part of a psychology experiment. Another subject indicated that following the heroin transaction, he had intended to attack the same confederate and take the money himself. He had finally decided against this option only because he feared subsequent retaliation. Overall, although the results of these two studies were scarcely decisive, they underscore the difficulty pointed to by Orne and Evans (1965) of performing a clearcut experiment on this topic, while providing some strong hints about what variables are most likely to determine a subject's behavior.

A study by Levitt, Aronoff, Morgan, Overley, and Parrish (1975) tested the interesting idea of attempting to induce hypnotized subjects to perform objectionable, as opposed to dangerous acts. Like Orne and Evans (1965), it employed a quasi-control group of unhypnotizable simulators, but it substituted snakes and nitric acid with the acts of cutting up an American flag and tearing a page from a Bible and burning it. It was found that 93 percent of the hypnotized subjects cut the flag, but so did seven of nine simulators (78%). For mutilating the Bible, five of eight (63%) hypnotized subjects complied with the request, as did four of five simulators (80%). The study was carried out on two different days of testing and the objectionability of the two acts can be seen from the fact that over 40 percent of both hypnotized *and* simulating subjects dropped out of the study at the end of the first session.

As with previous studies, a number of subjects did not see the acts as objectionable because they were requested within the context of an experiment. Two subjects (of seven available for questioning after the experiment) reported what the experimenters perceived as "peculiar reactions" (p. 64). One subject stated that the flag was just a piece of cloth, and he could not think of any reason not to cut it; nevertheless, she was unable to comply with the request. A second subject felt that in cutting the flag, she had been compelled to perform an act that was contrary to her moral beliefs. She stated that she knew that hypnosis could not cause a person to violate personal morality, and the fact that she had complied with the suggestion led her to question her values. Nevertheless, she completed the second session of the study and reported that, although confused as before by the instructions, she refused to deface the Bible and felt better afterward for having done so. It is difficult to determine from these brief reports what may have been happening with these two subjects. These reports plus the high drop-out rate, however, indicate that beneath the surface instructions to perform objectionable acts lead to varying degrees of subjective disturbance—perhaps even in unhypnotized simulating subjects.

A final study (Levitt & Baker, 1983) sought to examine the issue of coercion in terms of what can be characterized as the reverse side of the coin. Here, subjects were offered monetary incentives for resisting each of two hypnotic suggestions that they had previously passed. Of 20 subjects, nine of them resisted both suggestions, six resisted one, and five did not resist either. Whether subjects resisted appeared to depend on the degree to which they perceived the hypnotist as a positive, benevolent person. Indeed, some saw the instructions to resist (which were administered by a person other than the hypnotist) as a request to be disloyal to the hypnotist or even as a betrayal of him.

Taken together, all of these studies suggest that it may simply not be possible to investigate the coercive power of hypnosis in the laboratory directly because no matter how dangerous or repugnant an experimental task may "seem," subjects will always be aware that what they are requested to do is within the context of an experiment. They will tend to assume that where a task "looks" dangerous, the experimenter has taken adequate precautions to protect their well-being.

There may be one alternative way of investigating the coercion hypothesis in the laboratory, although the experimenter contemplating such a study would be well advised (following Levitt *et al.*, 1975, and Levitt & Baker, 1983) to expect a number of subjects to perceive the instructions associated with this procedure as objectionable, even as a violation of the hypnotic relationship. Sutcliffe (1961) reported a study where subjects were given instructions, in various conditions of hypnosis and wakefulness, to act as if they were of the opposite gender. While acting subjects reported some difficulty with this task, they nevertheless complied with the experimenter's request. By contrast, the four highly hypnotizable subjects in hypnosis "resisted the suggestion that they were of the opposite sex and passively but continuously reiterated their true sex" (p. 198).

Given the historical belief in the coercive power of hypnosis, it may well be an astonishing paradox that inducing a change in gender perception is so difficult a task. Conversely, it may be that one's belief in his or her gender identity is basic and all pervasive, and unamenable to alteration by suggestion.

The issue is not unlike a situation that one of the authors encountered some years back with a highly hypnotizable female subject. She had been a subject in several prior sessions and had, until this particular session, passed all hypnotic items presented to her. During this particular session, she had for the first time failed a hypnotic item—this concerned a delusion of a missing number. The item consists of suggesting that subjects visualize a television screen with the digits from 0 to 9 displayed on it. When the subject reports being able to visualize this, it is suggested that the number 5 will fade away and that when it disappears, the subject will no longer be able to say it, think it, or use it: The designated number will be functionally unavailable. The item is tested by having the subject perform a number of arithmetic problems involving the number 5 in the solution, and the subject is said to have passed the item if he or she cannot successfully complete these ordinarily easy arithmetical operations.

This particular subject was able to perform these tasks, and subsequently she was questioned about it. She reported that the number 5 had indeed faded away following which she suddenly thought to herself that the suggestion was foolish, that number abilities are fundamental and cannot be ablated by hypnosis. Accordingly, she had restored the number to consciousness. In many ways, this incident underscores the basic issue implied by the belief in the coercive power of hypnosis. Experimentation does not merely occur in a context of subjects knowing that they are in a protected situation. There is also the consideration that it is not always possible to know what behaviors are truly contrary to a person's most deeply held beliefs. This question becomes quite paramount when one looks at reports of coercion by hypnosis in clinical situations and the apparent domination of the will in field situations such as stage hypnosis. Given that there is a far from perfect correlation between a person's stated moral beliefs and his or her actual behavior, this can become quite a tangled issue. It is rendered even more complex by the possibility that some people may be induced to believe that they can be coerced by hypnosis to behave in a way contrary to their moral beliefs in much the same manner as a self-fulfilling prophecy. What seems to be the major ingredient, however, is the ongoing relationship or rapport between hypnotist and hypnotized individual. This notion of rapport so often mentioned by previous investigators is perhaps best exemplified in the clinical and field situations.

In Clinical and Field Situations

One of the cases most frequently invoked as evidence for the coercive power of hypnosis is described by Reiter (1958). It has shades of Czynski (see Chapter 10) in that there are many elements in the case over and above hypnosis that could have been responsible for the events that transpired. A young man, H., had been imprisoned in Denmark for wartime collaboration with the Germans during their occupation of that country. There he met N., who appeared to be highly knowledgeable about both the occult and hypnosis. They became firm friends, working in the same shop and sharing a cell. They began to experiment with hypnosis and yoga, though they did not ever use these particular terms. N. hypnotized H. and convinced him that salvation could be achieved only by the eschewal of material goods and the adoption of an exclusive preoccupation with the spiritual. N. subsequently permitted H. to hypnotize him. In hypnosis he informed H. that he (H.) was speaking to X., his guardian spirit, through the medium of N. This spirit informed H. that his present life was his final incarnation and that he would be damned eternally if he did not follow his commands uncritically. H. appears to have believed this. Indeed, he came to see N. as a manifestation of X. regardless of whether he was in hypnosis.

H. proceeded to comply with a number of these demands which included becoming a vegetarian (thus doubling N.'s meat allocation) and giving N. his watch. On N.'s demand, he withdrew from all contact with other prisoners. His reward for this, for want of a better term, was to be informed that his mission in life was to unify Scandinavia. N. demanded also that H. fantasize committing criminal acts on the grounds that he was not subject to the dictates of conventional morality and should thus be prepared to commit any act that furthered his mission. This relationship continued after the two men had been released from prison.

Subsequently, N. introduced H. to a woman and demanded that he marry her. Prior to the wedding, N. instructed H. to permit him to have sexual relations with her. When she objected, H. threatened not to go through with the marriage. The threat succeeded, and they were subsequently married. After the marriage, N. continued to make demands on H., such as requiring H. to give him most of his salary. Plans continued apace for the unification of Scandinavia, and N. proposed that the armed holdup of a bank was necessary in order to obtain the money required for this end. H. committed two such holdups, at the second of which he shot and killed two people. He was then arrested by the police.

Reiter's (1958) account of this case placed great store on H.'s account of these events, which was provided in hypnosis. In particular, he relied on the mistaken doctrine that the hypnotized person is unable to lie, and on the slightly more plausible premise that H.'s hypnotically elicited recollections of the events were in substantial agreement with the known facts of the case. Almost exclusively, he focused on the apparent Svengali-like power of an unscrupulous hypnotist at the expense of other ingredients in the situation. For instance, prior to any hypnosis, a strong interpersonal relationship existed between the two men, and H. appears to have accepted, with little resistance, that N. was a medium for the guardian spirit X., that his present incarnation was his last one, and that he had the mission of unifying Scandinavia to perform. In addition, H. does not appear to have resisted any of N.'s demands which graduated from giving him his watch and becoming a vegetarian, to commanding him to marry a woman that N. had chosen, demanding to have sexual relations with her, and the subsequent bank holdups. In short, there appear to be elements in H.'s personality organization and belief systems, which suggest that "behavior such as H.'s could have been performed without the introduction of hypnosis" (Orne, 1960, p. 134).

An earlier study (which predated that of Reiter), was performed by Watkins (1947) in a wartime military setting. It consisted of several naturalistic observations and led Watkins to conclude that an unscrupulous hypnotist could coerce a hypnotized person by utilizing delusory suggestions. For example, in one instance a soldier was induced to attack a commanding officer (a Lieutenant Colonel and head psychiatrist of his division) following the instruction that the officer was, in fact, a "dirty Jap soldier" (p. 257). In another instance, a soldier was hypnotically "coerced" to reveal alleged military intelligence information following the suggestion that the hypnotist was in fact the commanding officer who had given him the information.

In the same study, however, subjects were hypnotically "coerced" to reveal intelligence information following the prehypnotic instruction of "let us pretend I am a German military intelligence officer and you are a prisoner of war" (p. 258). It is very difficult to evaluate what was happening in this field study since the perceptions of the subjects who complied with these and similar requests were not elicited. For instance, it is not possible to determine how an enlisted soldier would interpret a suggestion from one military officer with a degree in psychology to attack another military officer with a degree in psychiatry, and whether it would have made a difference if the officer attacked had been another soldier who had obtained his rank on the field of battle. Again, prehypnotic compliance to instructions of "let's pretend" can scarcely be taken as evidence that an individual has been coerced by hypnosis.

In other cases, both pro and con to the coercion hypothesis, it is likewise not clear what the psychodynamics of the cases reported actually were. Conn (1972) described two cases from his own clinical practice in very brief detail which led him to conclude that hypnosis cannot be used to coerce behavior. In each case, it involved a married woman who said that she loved her husband

and who was seemingly seduced by a hypnotist. In each case, also, the woman stated initially that she was puzzled by her compliance. It is intriguing also that one woman, Mrs. A., took four years to reach the realization that "he (the hypnotist) happened to be the one that came along—any other man would have been the same. He didn't need the hypnosis" (p. 73).

A second woman, Mrs. B., concluded that "I wanted to do the same thing my husband did. Then I couldn't accuse him [of philandering] and I couldn't be hurt" (p. 73). More plausible in this latter case, regardless of whether the insight was accurate, was Conn's observation that despite several attempts, using both clinical and experimental scale criteria, Mrs. B. could be lightly hypnotized at best.

Kline (1972) reported three further cases, two of which are quite favorable to a belief in the potential for coercion by hypnosis. The case reports are of interest (even if one does not accept Kline's interpretation of them) in shedding some light on the psychological make-up of individuals who utilize hypnosis for seductive purposes. All appear to have been highly manipulative individuals who lacked affect in their interpersonal relations, who had no guilt about their activities, and who had only sought professional assistance when it appeared that their activities were about to be unmasked publicly.

The first involved a 56-year-old physician who had been utilizing hypnosis for some years for sexual seduction purposes with a number of female patients. This physician's strategy was to introduce hypnosis into his treatment procedure without there being any real indication of need. He would gradually develop a close, dependent, and initially supportive and reassuring relationship with the patients, following which, with equal care, he would introduce suggestions containing strong erotic content. He would also suggest that the patient have dreams incorporating these feelings. The technique was then to introduce himself into the dreams, following which, if successful, he would seek to instill a strong desire in the patient to act out these impulses in reality. He was not always successful, but his gradualized approach meant that he could beat a superficially honorable retreat at the first signs of resistance.

In one instance, using this approach, he persuaded a 23-year-old woman to take an unpaid position in his office and to have daily intercourse with him. As with many nineteenth-century cases (Chapters 9 and 10) this mode of seduction, however, turned out to be a double-edged sword that was to be his undoing; the woman began having sleep disturbances in which she described while asleep, with a mixture of conflict and pleasure, the details of the day's sexual encounter. Her husband proceeded to tape record these recountings, and it soon became evident what was involved.

A second case involved a 26-year-old homosexual graduate student in psychology who had spent four years in psychoanalysis which had led him to accept his homosexuality. Unbeknownst to his analyst, he had also learned hypnotic induction procedures. As with the first case, he had sought professional help as the result of impending exposure of his activities, which involved inserting advertisements in newspapers indicating his availability as a babysitter. When parents responded to these advertisements, he indicated his availability only when the subject was a boy under the age of ten years. He would then develop a warm relationship with the boy and proceed to involve him in a variety of imaginative activities, at which he was highly adept. At the same time, he sought to impress on the child that he had quasi-magical powers. As with the physician in the previous case, the procedure was graduated, and it was not until he had successfully completed the first steps that he proceeded to introduce hypnosis. Here he would have the boy imagine television programs that he enjoyed, and would seek to have him involved in them; he would use this as a deepening technique.

He would then seek to ascertain if the child was capable of post-hypnotic amnesia. Only when he had established this latter point would he engage the boy in oral copulation and, at times, anal penetration, while utilizing verbal suggestion to disguise the sexual nature of the experience. As with the previous case, he was hoist with his own petard when a child became disturbed and was able to recount most of the sexual details to a psychiatrist.

A third case described by Kline, unlike the previous two, does not appear to be an instance of coercion, but rather one of incompetence in the therapeutic utilization of hypnosis. A 36-year-old gynecologist had incorporated hypnosis into his medical practice and, rather interestingly, had extended it to the treatment of obesity in female patients. A 27-year-old female patient who was highly hypnotizable had been instructed not to eat between meals; she proceeded to ignore the diet he had prescribed and to eat even more. This infuriated him (and presumably this was the underlying psychodynamic reason for her disobedience). Accordingly, and ill advisedly, he suggested in hypnosis that if she continued to eat between meals and to defy his dietary regimen, she would be overwhelmed by a strong impulse to kill her pet poodle, for which she had strong affection.

Following this session, the patient returned home and proceeded to consume a quart of ice cream. She then reported experiencing acute panic, during which she smothered the dog. Upon realizing that it was dead, she drank a bottle of iodine and slashed her wrists. This dismal story of gross incompetence nevertheless had somewhat of a happy ending. Her screaming aroused the neighbors, and police were able to rush her to the hospital; her life was saved by emergency medical procedures.

This case does not appear to be one of coercion, though it may illustrate, as Kline indicates, many of the underlying principles of coercion. Perhaps the main point of the report is that the gynecologist saw the patient in mechanical terms; on the day of the session in which he suggested that she would kill her pet if she disobeyed him, he told her that she had not complied with his instructions and seemed unconcerned about this. He told her that he was displeased and felt that the only way that she could follow his instructions would be if she could experience some anxiety about her noncompliance. He appeared to have no realization of the possibility that patients who merely do not comply, but actually do the opposite to what is suggested, are sending their own imperfectly articulated distress signals.

Kline's first two cases merit one additional comment. They illustrate the difficulties of determining the actual role of hypnosis in the development of a course of events. In the first two cases, Orne (1972) has pointed out that

> we do not know, nor are we given any compelling data to suggest that the distortions of perception and memory brought about by hypnosis, or even the activation of erotic fantasies, significantly facilitated the likelihood of the patient's behavior. In the case of the student reporting the use of hypnosis to seduce children, hypnosis could similarly be thought as yet one additional manipulative tool. One suspects that the student was adept at selecting his youthful partners. (p. 107)

In short, there is a tendency to become trapped in an either/or argument—either hypnosis was instrumental in the cases of abuse reported by Kline, since it was utilized, or it was an adjunctive manipulative technique of minimal significance. Perhaps, though, the main problem with such case reports is that there are some missing data. In each case, the report is based on the account provided by the abusing hypnotist; there is no account of how the abused person perceived what was happening. One can ask, for instance, how an 8-year-old boy can be deluded into believing that oral copulation is really something else. Given the plasticity of human sexuality, one might not always obtain a coherent answer, but by not asking the question at all one is in danger of variously over- or underemphasizing the coercive potential of hypnosis, depending on what side of this great conceptual divide one happens to take a stance.

A more recent case illustrates how it might be possible to understand better the various forces at play in cases involving sexual seduction via hypnosis. The report was based on examination of the court transcript of a legal case (*Regina v. Palmer*, 1976, cited in Perry, 1979) heard before the New South Wales Supreme Court in Sydney, Australia. In this case, a lay hypnotist was found guilty of rape, attempted rape, and indecent assault of two different women.[5] Despite certain limitations imposed by both the nature of court proceedings and the type of questioning that is permitted in this situation, it is one of the few known cases where there is a relatively detailed sequencing of the events surrounding the hypnotic seductions. Although some of the motivational elements remain unclear, due to the adversarial nature of court proceedings (as opposed to clinical interview), the case has some bearing on the traditional issues surrounding hypnotic coercion. Some inferences can be drawn, even if not all are conclusive. The point, however, is that this case has a detailing of the events not only from the point of view of the defendant, but also from the perspective of the female complainants. In addition, the testimony of five expert witnesses (four of whom actually were) was available.

The defendant, Barry Palmer, was born in New Zealand, and at the time of sentencing was 38 years old. His parents died when he was young, and he left school at the age of 15. Subsequently, he completed a course in horticulture, agriculture, dairy farming, and sheep husbandry. In 1960, at the age of 22, he joined a religious organization and soon became one of its officers. He resigned in 1965 shortly after having been convicted of being a "rogue and vagabond" by the Dunedin Magistrate's Court, for having been found in an enclosed yard. This was the first of eight convictions during the next six years for offences which carried such picturesque descriptions as "peep and pry," and which were primarily of a voyeuristic nature. Subsequently, he received a one-year prison sentence in 1974 for making sexual advances toward two different females within an hypnotic context.

During the early 1960s, he learned stage magic and became sufficiently proficient at it to reach the finals of a New Zealand national talent quest. Some years later, he completed a course in hypnosis offered by Dr. Leslie Cunningham in Sydney. He was later to be called as an expert witness for the prosecution at the 1976 trial. It was revealed in court that Dr. Cunningham's doctoral dissertation was entitled "The Use of Hypnosis as a Shortcut to Psychoanalysis" and had been obtained by correspondence from the International Free Protestant Episcopal University in London in 1961. In court, he was able to remember neither the name of his thesis supervisor nor the exact dates when his masters and doctoral degrees had been obtained. When the case was appealed, it transpired that he had been convicted by a Brisbane Magistrate's Court in 1965 for adopting a medical title by inference, and there were two subsequent convictions for similar offences. In 1975, he was convicted of smuggling marijuana into Australia which earned him fines totaling $700 (Australian) and 12 months of hard labor. He served one month of this sentence.

The events leading to Palmer's arrest began on Christmas Day of 1975. Palmer was living at Bondi, a Sydney beach suburb, and was using his apartment, which he shared with another man, to practice as a self-styled "consulting hypnotherapist." One of his neighbors, also New Zealand born, recognized Palmer's accent and invited him to his Christmas Day party. At this party, Palmer performed various stage magic tricks and also demonstrated various hypnotic phenomena. During this demonstration, the host announced that Palmer was available for hypnotic consultation for various nervous tension problems—nailbiting, obesity, and smoking. Three women approached Palmer subsequently and made appointments for the following two days; two were for nailbiting and one for obesity. In the report, they were referred to as Mrs. X., Miss Y., and Miss Z. in order to protect their identities while indicating their marital status.

Mrs. X.'s appointment was for the morning after the party, and her "consultation" was for nailbiting. At the party, she had shown signs of a high degree of hypnotic responsivity; her eyes had closed involuntarily when Palmer suggested it, she was unable to unclasp her hands on a handclasp item, she responded positively to a post-hypnotic suggestion, and also to a suggestion of arm catalepsy. She was not, however, able to sing a song when this was suggested, saying that she did not want to sing in front of an audience. She reported "going all cold." One of the expert witnesses at Palmer's trial was to cite this inability to sing as evidence that Mrs. X. could not be coerced by hypnosis. Subsequent to this failure, Palmer may have wished to demonstrate his omniscience as a hypnotist; he suggested successfully that her hand was stuck to a clothesline, and that each of her legs, in turn, was stuck to the ground. In addition, he successfully had her regress to her first day at school, and she responded also to a suggestion that her head would roll to one side in response to a predesignated cue. It may be quite relevant, also, that Palmer's stage name was Mr. Magic; it implied power over the behavior of others.

Palmer began his nailbiting consultancy by asking her detailed questions about her sexual history, which included both premarital and marital experiences. Of the latter, she stated that "sex was plentiful" (p. 103). Palmer then indicated that he would teach her to have an orgasm with her husband, though it is not clear what led him to make this remark. Hypnosis was then initiated (see Perry, 1979, for a detailed description of the procedure). After some initial hypnotic items, Palmer suggested a heat illusion, the result of which was that she removed all of her clothing. He then suggested that she was on a deserted beach, led her to a bed, and had her lie down. In her court testimony, she reported that it felt like a bed but seemed like a beach.

He then began to fondle her breasts, suggesting that she was "feeling more sexy and just to relax." He inserted his finger into her vagina and was about to replace it with his penis when there was a knock at the door. Mrs. X. stood up, her eyes opened, and she placed her arms over her breasts and asked for a robe. Having dealt with the interruption, Palmer returned her to the bed, told her to relax, and her eyes closed. She then felt a tugging sensation at her pubic area, but it was not until she was washing herself in the late afternoon that she discovered that he had cut off some of her pubic hair.

Palmer then stood her up and attempted to kiss her. For the first time, she resisted. In court she explained: "I pushed him away because he did not have a beard. My husband has a full beard, you see" (p. 194). Palmer immediately began dressing her, while telling her that she no longer would have any worries with her fingernails. He terminated hypnosis, and they discussed his professional fee for these services; she paid him $5, which was one quarter of his customary amount. She then visited a female friend at a nearby apartment, but gave no indication of the events that had just transpired and no indication of subjective distress. Indeed, Palmer arrived there shortly after with a copy of *The Power of Positive Thinking* which he said would give her more self-confidence. He read from it for ten minutes before leaving.

When she arrived home, she found that her husband was still celebrating Christmas (a not uncommon Australian folk custom). She decided not to tell him of what had happened, since she feared that he might assault Palmer. She did not lay charges until two days later and in court admitted that at the time of contacting the police, she knew that another woman had already laid charges against him.

When questioned by both prosecution and defence, she stated that she knew what was happening but that, because she was hypnotized, she felt that she could not do anything to prevent Palmer's sexual overtures, even though they were unwanted. Although Palmer's lack of a beard was given for her only act of resistance, she admitted that throughout the entire proceedings she knew that she was with Palmer. In one answer to the prosecution, she stated that: "I was so relaxed—I did not seem to have any control of my muscles. I knew what he was doing but sort of could not do anything to stop him" (p. 195).

Miss Y. arrived for her hypnotic consultation, which was for weight loss, on the afternoon of the same day. In the prehypnotic interview, little sexual detail was elicited other than that she had not had a boyfriend for two months. In hypnosis, she was asked questions concerning her boyfriend at both ages 18 and 20 and whether she masturbated at these ages. This second client was barely hypnotizable. Nevertheless, Palmer stood her up and embraced her, telling her that she needed a lot of love and understanding. At this point, she reported feeling cold and asked him to terminate hypnosis, which he did, after first suggesting that she would no longer have a craving for sweets or chocolates. As with Mrs. X. they discussed his professional fee, and she gave him a packet of cigars, explaining that it had been given to her at work.

On cross-examination by the defense, she admitted that he had escorted her to her car, with them holding hands. At the car, she invited Palmer to accompany her to a New Year's Eve Party, telling the court she reasoned that "he could show other people his tricks, and maybe there could be some contacts for him in nightclubs because this was what Mr. Palmer wanted" (p. 198).

Miss Y. made no complaint, and her presence in court was at the telephoned request of the police. As with Mrs. X., she admitted under cross-examination that she did not complain to Palmer about his sexual overtures during the post-hypnosis period.

Miss Z., Palmer's third client, arrived on the following morning in the company of her fiancé, a bartender, with whom she was living. She had been upstairs at the time of Palmer's Christmas party demonstration, but had seen her 15-year-old sister manifest body rigidity in response to suggestion. As with Mrs. X., this client's presenting problem was nailbiting. In her court testimony, she stated that the initial conversation was focused generally on nervousness and tension. Her fiancé then left for five minutes to buy cigarettes; during his absence, Palmer asked her whether she and the fiancé were compatible. She replied that they were. Upon his return, the fiancé was asked to leave and to return in an hour. Perhaps because of the self-imposed deadline (which may also have been related to Palmer's clinical insight into the situation) events unfolded quickly. Having induced hypnosis, Palmer asked her if her sex life was happy, to which she answered negatively. Palmer suggested that it was the middle of summer (which it was) and that she was wearing heavy woolen clothing.

He suggested that she remove her clothing and she complied by removing her cotton top and jeans. She said that she was so drowsy and sleepy that she could not stand up to remove her underwear "so Barry Palmer helped me with these" (p. 199). She then reported that he suggested she "would be very sexy— I felt very sexy" (p. 199). He then had intercourse with her. As with Mrs. X., Miss Z. stated that "I felt as if I did not want to do it. I knew what I was doing, but I felt as if there was nothing I could do about it at the time" (p. 199). Her recall of ensuing events was fragmentary; she could not recall dressing and her next memory was of sitting on the bed, fully dressed, talking to Palmer. The fiancé returned to find them sitting in the lounge room discussing nailbiting. He paid Palmer a prearranged professional fee of $5, since Miss Z. was unemployed, following which Palmer prepared lunch for them both. As they left, Palmer inquired about her 15-year-old sister (who had manifested body rigidity at the Christmas party) and requested that Miss Z. "send her over." Once away from the apartment, Miss Z. began to cry, but would not tell her fiancé what was troubling her. They arrived at her father's house where Miss Z., in the words of the fiancé, "went hysterical." She told her father what had happened, and then the fiancé. They proceeded to return to Palmer's apartment to confront him, but second thoughts prevailed, and instead they went to the police station.

There are a number of internal inconsistencies in the accounts that the three witnesses presented in court; these bear repeating if only to communicate the difficulties that are inherent in evaluating the case. Mrs. X. reported that she "was so relaxed—I did not seem to have control of my muscles" (p. 211). Nevertheless she was able to undo her bra strap and stand up voluntarily when the knock on the door occurred. Further, at the Christmas Day party, she was unable to sing when requested to in hypnosis. During hypnosis, she said that her mind was blank to everything but Palmer's voice; nevertheless she was distracted by a knock at the door. Paradoxically, it was Palmer's attempt to kiss her that met resistance; this appears somewhat at odds with her statement that she was aware throughout the experience that she was with Palmer. In addition, she showed no signs of subjective distress following hypnosis.

Miss Y. was obviously not very hypnotizable, but perhaps on account of her beliefs about hypnosis her eyes remained shut when Palmer attempted to kiss her, and she asked to be brought out of hypnosis. She left the apartment holding hands with him, and she invited him to a New Year's Eve party, ostensibly to assist his career, even though she would have been aware, by this stage, of one of its unique aspects.

The behavior of Miss Z. most closely parallels the two cases described by Kline (1972). Hypnotic coercion was successful in the short term in that the hypnotist completed the acts that he had sought to elicit. However, the carrying out of these acts appears to have led to subsequent subjective distress, which in turn led to Palmer's arrest and prosecution. Three differences should be noted, however. First, Palmer was able to achieve in one induction what required a series of repeated inductions in the cases reported by Kline. Second, Palmer made little attempt to alter "the perception of the subject involved so as to shield and protect himself from possible exposure" (p. 89). The suggestion "you are feeling very sexy" is as simple and as direct as it is possible to be. Third, as far as can be ascertained, Palmer did not attempt to induce amnesia.

Miss Z., prehypnosis, said that she and her fiancé were compatible; in hypnosis, however, she indicated that her sexual relations with him were not happy. Like Mrs. X., she was aware of what was happening, but felt that she could not prevent it. She removed her top and jeans herself, but had to be assisted with her undergarments. The most striking inconsistency in her testimony was an admission that she had masturbated Palmer, while being unable to resist what was happening. It is not clear why she volunteered this information which is in some contradiction to her assertion of compliance in the face of overwhelming coercion.

Notwithstanding these anomalies, the case raises the genuine possibility that, at least in the case of Miss Z., her belief of being unable to resist may have created a self-fulfilling prophecy, in much the same manner as that described by Orne (1959). He reported an experiment in which subjects were led to believe that catalepsy of the dominant hand was a defining characteristic of hypnosis. Those who were exposed to this belief manifested this behavior in hypnosis far more frequently than subjects who were not exposed to it. There is still much that is not known about how ideas become translated into actions which are reported as subjectively involuntary, but the possibility that this was the mechanism at work in the Palmer case should not be ignored, especially as at the Christmas Day party he appears to have sought to demonstrate omniscience. Further, his skill at stage magic, coupled with his stage name, may have generated an aura of belief about the irresistibility of his suggestions. One is reminded of the aphorism that some of the people can be deceived some of the time. . . .

Alternatively, it may be, as Orne (1972) has stated, that

> The therapist using hypnosis, like any other therapist, will strive to ally himself with the healthy wishes and aspirations of the patient, but it is of course possible for a disturbed therapist to ally himself with destructive aspects of a patient's personality and facilitate destructive behavior. (pp. 113–114)

This interpretation does not appear to fit the events of the Palmer case. The women showed no apparent signs of psychopathology, of overt disturbance, nor of self-destructive behavior, although there is some evidence that Miss Z. had some interpersonal difficulties the magnitude of which are not possible to assess.

In the end, Palmer was sentenced to 14 years in prison, which can be compared with the usual sentence for rape with physical assault—at that time, approximately 7 years.[6] The judge felt, however, that with his skills at hypnotizing, Palmer did not need to use physical force, which somehow, in his opinion, made his offenses even more serious. This sentence was quashed by the Court of Criminal Appeals because Dr. Cunningham had been permitted to testify for the prosecution, despite credentials of the most dubious kind. The Chief Justice felt also that the delay of two of the women in laying a complaint affected the credibility of the prosecution's case.[7]

One final point concerning the coercive image that hypnosis has for many individuals is their understanding of it through stage hypnosis. On stage, hypnotized individuals are asked to perform a variety of often quite bizarre actions ranging from clucking like a hen (or a turkey) to being Frank Sinatra and singing in his style. To most audiences, the manner in which these inanities occur appears to indicate a preternatural power on the part of the hypnotist, although in fact, subjects for stage hypnosis are recruited from the top 10 to 15 percent of the hypnotic responsiveness continuum, and the skills are really those of the hypnotized person (see the Introduction). Indeed, the skills of the stage hypnotist are confined mainly to those of showmanship. In addition, both authors have encountered not only individuals who enjoy the antics requested of them by a stage hypnotist, but also, highly hypnotizable individuals who categorically refuse to venture onto a stage because they perceive hypnosis in this context as demeaning.

Despite this image of hilarity, usually characterized as being of the "good clean fun" variety, and the apparent display of power over others, the only study that has ever investigated the effects of stage hypnosis presents a somewhat different picture. Echterling and Emmerling (1987) surveyed a group of individuals who had participated on stage at a hypnosis show that was presented at a medium-sized university.

They were able to interview 18 people who had been in hypnosis on stage during the program. Reactions to the experience varied considerably. Seven subjects described it in unequivocally positive terms—their comments characterized it as "fun," "exhilarating," and "fascinating" (p. 151). An additional seven subjects reported the experience as both positive and negative. One subject reported it as "spooky and strange"; another as "generally relaxing, but during one part, when I was seeing the monster, I was tense and scared to death." Another subject reported that "some parts were funny and interesting" but fell off the stage steps when given a sleep command. This awakened her abruptly, and she was subsequently disoriented for a brief period of time (p. 151).

The remaining four subjects characterized the experience as negative. One subject said that "on the stage, I did not want to do what the hypnotist said.... I felt embarrassed and scared" (p. 151).

A second reported that "I knew what I was doing, but I had no control.... It bothered me ... I was scared that I might fall when I was running (p. 151).

A third was frightened throughout that she might be selected to perform a regression to a previous life. A final subject had a serious traumatic reaction. She reported that

I didn't sleep for the next two days. I hibernated and hid from everybody. It has still left me shook up. I'm going to drop out of school. This has messed up everything. I lost control.... This forces me to think about stuff I don't want to. (p. 152)

In short, the demonstration of apparent power over the behavior of others capitalizes primarily on the fact that many volunteers for stage hypnosis are not aware that the feeling of involuntariness they experience is mainly a matter of their hypnotic abilities, rather than domination, even coercion by a hypnotist. This misattribution can lead to negative sequelae; indeed, quite severe ones. They provide, also, some support for the impression that emerges from *Regina v. Palmer* that some individuals may perform acts in hypnosis against their perceived volition, believing that because they are hypnotized, they are unable to resist. The important point to notice however is that when such reports are encountered, they reflect not so much an ability on the part of the hypnotist to somehow distort perceptions and coerce the will, as the subject's *belief* that this indeed can be done and is being done to him or her.

During the long history of hypnosis, however, it has become clear that not all hypnotizable people believe this, as Charcot's students discovered to their own dismay with an hysterical patient. Following a successful demonstration of apparently hypnotically elicited crimes by their master, they had attempted to suggest that the young woman remove her clothes. She flatly rejected the suggestion and subsequently experienced a worsening of her symptoms for several days. There was an attempt to rerun the latter part of this famous incident in hypnotic folklore, described by Hilgard (1971). He wrote:

The late Professor Dorcus, of the University of California at Los Angeles, told me about his confident undertaking to repeat the demonstration, but this young woman subject began unbuttoning so rapidly that he had to call a halt. It turned out that she was accustomed to "stripping in a nightclub," so this was not contradictory evidence after all! It does make the point, however, that something that happens within hypnosis need not happen *because* of hypnosis, and there will always be areas of ambiguity. (p. 576, italics in original)

Indeed, this anecdote may summarize the issue as adequately as it can ever be.

Hypnosis and Memory

In the Laboratory

Most people believe that memory operates like a tape recorder, and as will be seen in the final chapter, this belief took root in many police departments during the 1960s and 1970s and became the justification for an extensive police utilization of hypnosis in the United States. This trend, in turn, was paralleled on a smaller scale in police departments in such countries as Australia, Canada, Great Britain, and Israel. The extent of the belief can be indexed by a survey reported by Loftus and Loftus (1980) who questioned 169 individuals about their beliefs on how human memory works. Of these, 75 individuals had formal graduate training in psychology; the remaining 94 did not. This latter group represented a wide cross-section of the general public. They were lawyers, secretaries, cabdrivers, physicians, philosophers, fire investigators, and so on; in one case, an 11-year-old child was questioned. They were asked to indicate which of the following two statements best reflected their view on how memory worked:

1. Everything we learn is permanently stored in the mind, although sometimes particular details are not accessible. With hypnosis, or other special techniques, these inaccessible details could eventually be recovered.
2. Some details that we learn may be permanently lost from memory. Such details would never be able to be recovered by hypnosis, or any other special technique, because these details are simply no longer there. (p. 410)

It was found that 84 percent of the psychologists agreed that hypnosis was effective for memory enhancement, as opposed to 69 percent of the individuals lacking a graduate psychology training. While this finding may be an embarrassing reflection of the nature of graduate training in psychology, the finding of high rates of belief in the efficacy of hypnosis to enhance memory (overall in this study, it was 76%) has been found by other investigators (see Labelle, Lamarche, & Laurence, 1987; McConkey & Jupp, 1985-1986; Orne, Soskis, Dinges, & Carota Orne, 1984).

The facts, however, are far different. The assumption underlying this belief in hypnotic memory enhancement is that memory is reproductive, that is, that it functions like an accurate recording device. In fact, the scientific evidence is that memory is reconstructive; it is constantly changing in the light of the new perceptual inputs that more or less bombard the sensory systems every moment that a person is awake. Nocturnal dreaming may be another ingredient in this reconstruction process—in some memory systems the effect may be quite marked. But even quite small slippages of memory may be sufficient to reconstruct it to a significant degree.

This reconstructive view of memory was first propounded by the eminent British psychologist, Sir F. C. Bartlett over a half century ago in his classic book entitled *Remembering* (1932). He performed a number of experiments demonstrating that memory is reconstructive in nature. One should keep in mind that these studies involved the normal memory of college students and that none of the studies involved hypnosis.

Even individuals thought to possess an exceptionally good memory demonstrate this reconstructive tendency. A recent case in point concerns the testimony of John Dean, a former aide to former President Nixon at the Watergate hearings. He impressed both questioners and spectators alike with his apparently "photographic memory" for conversations at meetings in the

President's Oval Office over a period of some years. Some media reporters called him the "human tape recorder" though Dean himself disclaimed this highly generous estimate. As it turned out, his disclaimer was not false modesty; Dean had an exceptionally good memory for the general direction of conversations, but when it came to actual details, his memory was as fallible as that of the next person.

As is now well known, Nixon was tape-recording all of his conversations in the Oval Office over a prolonged period, and ultimately a number of the tapes reached the public domain. Thus, it was possible to compare what had been said at these meetings with Dean's recollections. Such an analysis was performed by Ulric Neisser (1984), a noted cognitive psychologist, for two such meetings (September 15, 1972 and March 21, 1973); each was crucial for the Senate Committee's determination of the degree to which Nixon had participated in the Watergate "cover-up."

The September 15 meeting occurred approximately three months after the original break-in at the Democratic National Committee's headquarters, at a time when seven indictments had been handed down by the Federal Grand Jury. Some aspects of Dean's recall of this meeting were totally erroneous. As Neisser put it:

> Comparison [of Dean's recall] with the transcript shows that hardly a word of Dean's account is true. Nixon did not say any of the things attributed to him here: He didn't ask Dean to sit down. He didn't say Haldeman had kept him posted, he didn't say Dean had done a good job (at least not in that part of the conversation), he didn't say anything about Liddy or the indictments. Nor had Dean himself said the things he later describes himself as saying: that he couldn't take credit, that the matter might unravel some day, etc. (Indeed, he said just the opposite later on: "Nothing is going to come crashing down"). His account is plausible, but entirely incorrect. In this early part of the conversation Nixon did not offer him any praise at all unless "You had quite a day, didn't you" was intended as a compliment. (It is hard to tell from a written transcript). (p. 91)

Dean's description of this opening part of the conversation with Nixon implies that the then President had full knowledge (and gave his approval) of the cover-up, whereas a comparison of Dean's recall and the actual transcript of the conversation suggests that his recall may have been a fantasy of how the conversation should have gone. Regarding other aspects of this meeting, Dean mentioned matters that were indeed discussed, but again, the recall was spotty. For instance, he remembered that he left the meeting with the impression that the President was aware of the attempt to keep the White House out of the Watergate scandal, and the transcript of the recording bears him out. He was wrong in his recall of telling Nixon that he was concerned that the cover-up could not be maintained—in fact, he said the exact opposite. Again, as Neisser suggested, he may have wished with the clarity of "20/20 hindsight" that he had warned Nixon on that occasion.

Dean's recall of the March 21 meeting with Nixon was much more accurate, at least for the first hour when he and the President were alone. At this meeting, Dean introduced his memorable metaphor of a cancer growing around the Presidency. Comparison of Dean's remembrances and the tape transcript indicated clear recall of the gist of what was said. There is, however, a reason for this; at this meeting, Dean was presenting a well-prepared report of his perceptions of the current situation. Indeed, he spent 20 minutes describing the events prior to the break-in. Forty minutes were devoted to the cover-up. On this occasion, Dean did most of the talking; Nixon interjected occasionally with remarks, questions, and expletives (deleted). In short, the high level of accurate recall was a function of this meeting having been carefully prepared in advance.

Overall, this analysis demonstrates that much of John Dean's memory was constructed and self-serving, even though much of what was constructed was not entirely wrong. Indeed, Neisser concluded that "there is a sense in which he was altogether right; a level at which he was telling the truth about the Nixon White House" (p. 96). The problem, of course, was to determine what was constructed, what was false, and what was correct. Unfortunately, crimes do not always get taped! When victims or witnesses of crimes remember the gist of the events they went through, it takes careful investigative work to build up a case. Perhaps the greatest value of this report is that it emphasizes the problems inherent in memory of past events. Studies of hypnotically elicited memory in the laboratory reinforce the impressions, obtained both in the nineteenth-century French legal system (Chapters 9 and 10) and in late twentieth-century legal systems (Chapter 12), that the introduction of hypnosis into investigative situations simply compounds the problems of memory.

There are, of course, some differences between investigating memory in the laboratory and seeking to index it in the field, regardless of whether hypnosis is utilized. The great advantage of the laboratory is that the experimenter knows precisely what occurred and what stimuli were presented to subjects. This luxury is often not available to police officers investigating a crime. On the other hand, it may not be possible to duplicate in the laboratory the often intense emotion that may be associated with a crime, such as when a person is being physically assaulted, possibly fearing for his or her life. It is very likely that such emotion may distort memory even more than the benign laboratory context, though it would be very difficult to demonstrate this in practice. The many examples of posttraumatic amnesia, however, are clear indications of the effects of emotions on recall (Mutter, 1979; Raginsky, 1969; Rossi, 1981). When an event has been so traumatic as to be totally eradicated from conscious memory, reconstructing the sequence through hypnosis may become a nearly impossible task. At best, it may offer some investigative leads, but disentangling fact from fiction can sometimes be an extremely arduous task (see Chapter 12 for some contemporary examples). In fact, diagnosing a genuine posttraumatic amnesia as compared to a self-serving simulated one is at best time-consuming and difficult (Shacter, 1986a, 1986b). When these situations arise in the investigative field situation, confabulation and simulation must always be entertained as possibilities as the nineteenth-century investigators had so rightly pointed out (see Orne, Dinges, & Carota Orne, 1984, on the Hillside Strangler case).

A further difference between the laboratory and field situations is that experimental subjects know that they are going to be questioned subsequently about the stimuli to which they are exposed; consequently, subjects are likely to make a special effort to register and retain the stimulus material presented. By contrast, crime victims in particular are likely to be highly inattentive to details that will be of interest to police, especially in situations where they believe correctly or incorrectly, that their lives are in danger.

On the basis of all of these considerations, it is reasonable to think that if there is a hypnotic hypermnesia (memory enhancement) effect, it is best demonstrated in the laboratory since its benign context is the most favorable for documenting it. In addition, given the situation of many actual crimes, there is no guarantee that any hypermnesic effect that can be demonstrated in an experiment will automatically translate to the field. A third quite crucial point is that if it can be shown in the laboratory that there is an increase in error when hypnosis is utilized to enhance recall, this error rate is likely to be magnified in real-life field situations in proportion to the amount of emotion generated. This is particularly so, regardless of whether crime victims are especially eager to assist police in locating the person(s) responsible for a crime against them or are resisting the investigation for fear of retaliation (*Journal de Montréal*, July 27, 1986, p. 8).

An early attempt to investigate the hypermnesia effect was performed by two of Hull's students, Stalnaker and Riddle (1932). They had 12 highly hypnotizable subjects recall poetic and prose pieces (like the preamble to the United States Constitution) that had been learned a year or more before. These experimenters appear to have found an astonishing hypermnesia effect in every one of the 12 subjects; the gains ranged from 18.1 percent to an astonishing 259 percent when hypnotic and waking recall were compared. Over the 12 subjects, the gain was 53.82 percent.

The experimenters, however, made an important error in evaluating the hypermnesia effect—they did not compare what was recalled in hypnosis with the actual written record of the material in question. Indeed, they inadvertantly demonstrated the fallibility of memory in an example they gave of a subject's recall of Longfellow's poem "The Arrow and the Song" which they mistakenly referred to as "The Song and the Arrow." This subject, in the waking state, recalled only: "An arrow and a song went into the sky, I know not why."

In hypnosis, however, the subject appeared to have shown a substantial gain in recall. He wrote:

> I shot an arrow into the air
> It fell to earth I know not where
> And I forgot that this was shot that day
> And picked myself up and went away.

I breathed a song into the air
It fell to ears I knew not where

As I was wandering far and wide
I heard the Song
And as I came to a might oak
I found the arrow still unbroke.

This looks to be a quite spectacular enhancement of memory until one compares it with the original, which is:

I *shot an arrow into the air,*
It fell to earth, I knew not where;
For, so swiftly it flew, the sight
Could not follow it in its flight.

I breathed a song into the air,
It fell to earth, *I knew not where;*
For who has sight so keen and strong,
That it can follow the flight of a song?

Long, long afterward in an *oak*
I found the arrow, still unbroke,
And the song, from beginning to end,
I found again in the heart of a friend.

(We have italicized the exact recalled information.)

It is true that by using Stalnacker and Riddle's scoring method hypnotic recall was superior to waking recall, but this assumes that all other things were equal, and the latter is impossible to either affirm or deny. Of the 12 original lines, only five were correctly remembered in part or in whole. More to the point, of the ten lines "remembered" by this subject, seven were constructed. In an actual field situation, who could say which was which? Subjects were told that the experimental purpose would be defeated if they were to relearn or reread any of the recall material. It is not known if all subjects did this, nor if in the period between the waking and hypnosis recall they made an effort to recall more. Even if they did not, in a way similar to Dean's recall of some of the conversations held at the Oval Office, these subjects had chosen memory targets that had been well learned in the past. By contrast, crime victims and witnesses do not rehearse their traumatic experiences in advance.

For this reason, experimenters since then have preferred to present subjects with material with which they were previously unfamiliar. A large proportion of this research has been carried out in the last several years and represents an attempt by hypnosis researchers to evaluate scientifically the claims made by proponents of a police use of hypnosis (see Chapter 12). As with all research, it is ongoing. Not all of the relevant research questions have yet been addressed appropriately, let alone answered. Nevertheless, there have been a number of consistent findings from studies that have utilized a great variety of stimuli to be recalled which include nonsense syllables,[8] line drawings of familiar objects, slides depicting various stages of a wallet snatching incident in a street, and videotapes of various incidents, such as a bank hold-up or a traffic accident.

One of the most consistent findings is that hypnotized subjects are more prone to be influenced by leading questions. The first study to investigate this was conducted by Putnam (1979). He showed subjects a videotape of an automobile-bicycle accident. Subsequently, half of the subjects were questioned in hypnosis, and half out of hypnosis. The leading questions conveyed misinformation. For instance, subjects were asked such questions as whether they had seen *the* stop sign at *the* intersection, *the* passenger in *the* car, and *the* bent wheel on *the* bike. None of these elements had appeared in the video. There was no difference in recall between hypnotized and unhypnotized subjects when asked nonleading questions. Hypnotized subjects, however, reported significantly more erroneous information on the leading questions. That is, they tended to incorporate into their memories the erroneous material presented in the leading questions and subsequently to report it as "true" memory. A number of other investigators (Zelig & Beidleman, 1981; Sanders & Simmons, 1983) have reported an almost identical finding, though Sheehan and Tilden (1983) were not able to obtain this effect, possibly because of a different experimental procedure.

Some proponents of a police use of hypnosis have criticized these experiments on the grounds that police officers are trained not to ask leading questions. This may be true, but the problem here is that police are not usually present at the scene of a crime at the time it is committed so that often they cannot know what constitutes a leading question. For instance, returning to Putnam's experiment, a police officer who had not visited the site of the traffic accident would not know that there was no traffic sign at the intersection, so that a question about it would appear to be innocent enough, and nonleading.

Hypnosis also increases inaccurate recall. The most striking demonstration of this effect was provided by Dywan and Bowers (1983). Fifty-four subjects of either high or low hypnotic susceptibility were presented with a set of 60 black and white line drawings of common objects. They were then given a response sheet and asked to write down the name of every line drawing that had been shown. They were asked also to indicate which items represented actual rememberances and which were guesses. They were then given take-home response sheets and asked to complete one each day for the following week. At the end of this period, they returned to the laboratory; half of the subjects were asked to recall once more the name of every line drawing that they could remember in hypnosis, and the remaining subjects recalled under a nonhypnotic task motivation condition.

Prior to this final session there was no significant difference between high and low hypnotizables in terms of the number of items recalled correctly at the end of this seven-day period. It was found that subjects in the hypnosis group reported twice as many new items (both correct and incorrect) as "true" memories than did subjects in the task motivation group. In both groups, however, approximately 75 percent of these new "true" memories were, in fact, errors. Nevertheless, one could say that there was a small degree of memory enhancement, but it was at the expense of a large increase in error, emphasizing once again that everything that is recalled in hypnosis needs to be verified independently.

In addition, the effect was most pronounced for the highly hypnotizable subjects in hypnosis; they reported approximately three times the number of new items as "true" memories than did any of the other three groups (that is, low hypnotizables in the hypnosis condition, and high and low hypnotizables in the task motivation condition). Once again, approximately 75 percent of these new "true" memories were, however, incorrect.

This finding of increased error following hypnosis was replicated recently by Button (1986). She used a videotape of an enacted bank hold-up and employed high, medium, and low hypnotizable subjects. Subjects viewed the videotape, which lasted approximately 45 seconds and were asked to recall it a second time. Hypnosis was then induced. Subjects were asked to recall the videotape for a third time. A major difference between this study and that of Dywan and Bowers was that, whereas the recall of line drawings of common objects must by its very nature be either correct or incorrect, recall of a videotape which tells a narrative may be correct, incorrect, or it may be attributional. That is, subjects frequently make statements that cannot be judged as correct or incorrect such as "the man's face was ordinary looking" or "he appeared young for his age."

Button found that regardless of hypnotizability, there was a substantial increase in errors and in attributions, and a modest increase in correct recall when describing the perpetrator of the hold-up. There is the strong implication in these data, as others such as Orne, Soskis, *et al.* (1984) have noted, that subjects increase their productivity without actually increasing their output of correct material substantially. This increase in productivity may be, as in Button's study, mostly in the form of qualitative, attributional material which is neutral with respect to truth or falsity. The consequences of such an increase in attributional material on subjects' confidence in the accuracy of their memories are still to be determined. It may, nonetheless, reinforce the belief of both hypnotist and subject in the "truthfulness" of a hypnotic testimony.

The belief in a hypermnesic effect of hypnosis can have a dramatic influence on a victim's or witness's recall. Whereas in the laboratory, errors of memory can be identified easily, it is much more difficult in a field situation. Two major consequences of this belief have been investigated in recent years, although both had been emphasized already by nineteenth-century practitioners.

The first consequence of a belief in a hypermnesic effect of hypnosis is that it seems to facilitate the creation of false memories that then become incorporated within the individual's memory system. These pseudomemories, or retroactive hallucinations as Bernheim had labeled them (see Chapters 9 and 10), can modify testimony dramatically. This finding has been replicated in a number of laboratories (Laurence & Perry, 1983; Labelle & Perry, 1986; Spanos & McLean, 1985-1986a). For example, Laurence and Perry (1983) demonstrated that a false memory (some loud noises in the middle of the night) could be suggested successfully in about 50 percent of a group of highly hypnotizable individuals. These subjects not only integrated the suggested false information, but were unshakable when confronted with a videotape of their earlier recollection where they had not mentioned any noise during the night to which they were regressed. Even more telling are the results of an experiment constructed in such a way as to allow subjects to deny the reality of a suggested pseudomemory on numerous occasions. Nevertheless, four out of eleven highly hypnotizable subjects still maintained that the pseudomemory was veridical (Spanos & McLean, 1985-1986a). If, as the authors concluded, these subjects finally just "shied away from invalidating their earlier testimony" (p. 158), it could still have appalling repercussions in a legal situation. Whether or not the subjects knew that the suggested memory was false, they chose to maintain their reports; whether they were simulating, giving false testimony in good faith, or falling victim of a memory bias, the legal consequences could be equally dramatic. It remains to be seen which factors facilitate the creation and integration of false memories or of a reporting bias in the subject and whether these could disappear in such a context as a court of law. Researchers have just begun to tackle some of the problems linked to the creation of pseudomemories, and their implications for the psycho-legal use of hypnosis. Many variables—among them cues from the context, and subjects' beliefs, motivation, and skills—need to be investigated to clarify when and how an individual is most vulnerable to memory manipulation, whether it be in or out of the hypnotic context (McCann & Sheehan, 1987a, 1987b; McConkey & Kinoshita, 1985-1986; Schooler, Gerhard, & Loftus, 1986; Spanos & McLean, 1985-1986b). The finding, however, that attributional recall increases during hypnosis may lead to an interesting hypothesis: Remembering unverifiable yet plausible details vividly may increase indirectly the confidence that an individual has about all the other aspects of their memory of an event, including pseudomemories.

This resonance effect could facilitate the integration of a new suggested memory. It is certainly worth noting that in both the Laurence and Perry (1983) and Spanos and McLean (1985-1986a) studies, the pseudomemory was suggested immediately following a detailed hypnotic recall of a previous night that subjects had chosen to remember. In the Laurence and Perry study, the hypnotic recall led to an increase in details that were of a mostly attributional nature. Again, future research will allow investigators to better understand this intriguing aspect of the human memory system.

One fact, however, that is well established, represents the second consequence of using hypnosis to remember past events. It increases confidence in the veracity of both correct *and* incorrect recalled material. This is perhaps the most consistent finding to date; virtually every study that has examined the issue of confidence has found this increase (Laurence, Nadon, Nogrady, & Perry, 1986; Nogrady, McConkey & Perry, 1985; Putnam, 1979; Sheehan & Tilden, 1983; Timm, 1981; Zelig & Beidleman, 1981). Perhaps, more than any other finding in the scientific literature, this is the particular one that indicates the need for exceptional care in the use of hypnosis in the legal investigative situation. It underlines the possibility that with hypnosis an unshakable witness can be created. This, in turn, means that a defendant may lose his or her right to confront an accuser who has become immune to cross-examination (Warner, 1979).

This, however, is not the long and short of the matter. The problem here is not just that hypnotically elicited memory is unreliable, and indeed, less reliable quite often than memory that has not been stimulated by hypnosis. A final set of problems is raised because hypnotic age regression techniques are used typically to aid memory in the legal investigative situation. These procedures themselves pose their own set of problems.

A la Recherche du Temps Perdu

When a person has an incomplete memory of an event of the past, such as a crime in which he or she participated as either victim or witness or even as a self-labeled amnesic suspect, hypnotic age regression techniques are utilized to enhance memory. The person may be taken back to the time segment in which the event occurred and administered the suggestion to relive it. There have been many clinical and experimental demonstrations of this phenomenon throughout the history of hypnosis; because it can be very vivid and compelling, a folklore developed that age regression is "literal." Many people believe that the reports of an age-regressed person constitute truth of a biblical nature. The folklore, which is still quite prevalent, came to be of considerable interest to police during the 1970s when police hypnotechnicians began to proliferate (Chapter 12).

As was seen earlier (Chapter 5), Deleuze (and to some extent de Puységur) may have been the first investigator to stumble upon this phenomenon, but for most of the nineteenth century, it was examined within the context of so-called "personality alterations," where the hypnotized or magnetized person was asked to enact the role of a particular occupational group such as a nun or a soldier. Nineteenth-century investigators such as Janet, Bernheim, Richet, and Binet were conversant with age regression (Chapter 9) both within this personality alteration context and in the manner in which it is currently practiced. It can still be witnessed today in the performances of stage hypnotists who suggest to their volunteers that they are Frank Sinatra or some other such notable person.

The reports of an age-regressed subject are prone to the same forms of contaminant that were seen in the preceding discussion of memory. What is recalled may be fact, it may be confabulated, it may constitute a pseudomemory that has been cued unwittingly by the hypnotist, to mention some of the main possibilities. Since, in regression to childhood in particular, there may be very convincing changes in voice, gesture, and handwriting, an unwary observer may conclude easily and mistakenly that what he or she is witnessing actually occurred and that it constitutes historical truth. This may be even more so when the person relives a painful and traumatic incident in which there are emotional accompaniments such as crying, accelerated breathing, sweating, and nausea (Laurence, Nadon, Bowers, Perry, & Regher, 1985). On one occasion, a subject age-regressed to infancy by Erickson urinated in his trousers when frightened unexpectedly (LeCron, 1965).

One of the more vivid examples that illustrates how age regressed subjects can be cued inadvertantly by the hypnotist was recounted by Orne, Soskis, et al. (1984). It concerned an experiment by True (1949), which was published in the journal *Science*. True reported that 92 percent of subjects, regressed to their tenth birthday, could remember the day of the week on which it fell. In addition, 84 percent correctly identified the day of their seventh birthday, and 62 percent the day of their fourth birthday. This finding could not be replicated by a number of investigators, some of whom sought additional details from True as to how he had performed the experiment. They assumed that he had followed the habitual procedure of administering suggestions to return to the specified ages, and then asked such questions as the subject's age, the date, and the day of the week.

They soon discovered that True had not followed this procedure, but that *Science*, without consulting him, had altered his manuscript in such a manner that it did not reflect his actual procedure. Instead, what True had done was to age-regress the subject, and when he or she reported experiencing the age suggested, he would ask: Is it Monday?, Is it Tuesday?, Is it Wednesday?, and so on until the subject responded by saying "yes." Further, he had a perpetual calendar on his desk and was able to verify instantly the accuracy of the subject's response. This meant also that he was in the position of being able to cue the subject unwittingly via such channels as tone of voice and body language.

Evidence that this is almost certain to have happened was provided by a meticulous study performed by O'Connell, Shor, and Orne (1970). As part of the experiment, they employed a control group of actual four-year-old children and found that not one of them knew the days of the week. Barber (1970) summarized a number of studies that failed to replicate True's finding. He noted a general tendency for hypnotically age-regressed subjects either not to know the day of the week on which a particular birthday had fallen or else to give the wrong answer.

Confabulated recall is best demonstrated by an investigation carried out by Orne (1951). In this classic study, he documented a number of instances of confabulation in the relatively benign context of the laboratory. One subject, regressed to childhood, was able to write the complex sentence, with correct spelling: "I am conducting an experiment that will assess my psychological capacities." This subject was able also to define correctly the word *hypochondriac.* Another subject, when asked the time, looked at a wristwatch "which he surely did not wear at the age of 6" (p. 219). Yet another, regressed to the age of his sixth birthday, reported it as a Saturday; independent evaluation indicated that it had fallen on a Sunday. The memory, however, was partially correct for the subject recalled that he had not been in school. One other subject is of particular interest. He had been born in Germany and did not begin to speak English until his arrival in the United States as a teenager. Regressed to his sixth birthday, he was asked repeatedly in English if he understood English and replied uniformly in German that he did not. Inadvertantly, he demonstrated a clear understanding of a language that he did not speak at the age of six.

Subjects in this study were asked to draw pictures while age-regressed. One subject had pictures that he had drawn at the earlier age. The pictures that he drew in age regression had little more than superficial similarity to what he had drawn as a child, even though it was quite convincingly "childlike." Even when he was shown the pictures he had drawn as a six year old, he still could not reproduce his earlier performance. Karen Machover, the noted child psychologist, was consulted for this study. When shown the drawings that subjects had produced while age-regressed, she characterized them as "sophisticated over-simplifications." This, indeed, may well be the hallmark of hypnotic age regression. Although it is frequently subjectively real for both subject and hypnotist alike, there always remains an adult overlay of learning and cognitions that have been acquired subsequent to the age to which the adult subject is regressed.

Nineteenth-century investigators such as Janet and Bernheim (Chapter 9) were aware that memories could be created in hypnosis. Further, as the previous section indicated, the effect can be reproduced reliably in the laboratory. In all of these clinical and experimental demonstrations, the effect was elicited deliberately; it follows that it can be elicited unintentionally as well. Perhaps as good an illustration as there is of this possibility is provided by the literature on hypnotically induced reincarnation. In comparing the hypnotically elicited reports of previous existences provided by the clients of two British lay hypnotists, Wilson (1982) noted some similarities but one major difference.

He found that, for both of them, the clients remained British in their hypnotically elicited reports of prior lives. Further, not one of them provided a reincarnation report predating the sixteenth century. There was, however, one crucial difference. One of the lay hypnotists elicited fresh reincarnations whose date of birth was nine months to the day of the death of a previous incarnation, suggesting some very human interactions among celestial bodies. By contrast, the clients of the other often took as many as 70 years for a new incarnation to emerge.

The comparison became even more interesting when these British reports were compared with those of three other hypno-reincarnationists (one Welsh and two American). The clients of these individuals tended to report past lives in such exotic places as ancient Egypt and Tibet, but there was a "distinct silence from less fashionable civilizations such as the Hittites, the Assyrians or the Scythians" (Wilson, 1982, p. 90). Taken together, these reports suggest but one explanation; they were pseudomemories that were created by the hypnotist cueing the client unwittingly with his or her beliefs about reincarnation. As will be seen, however, hypnotically elicited reports of reincarnation cannot be understood exclusively in terms of the hypnotist's beliefs about hypnosis and reincarnation, nor the inadvertant communication of them.

An additional ingredient that may contribute to what is provided in a subjective report of age regression is the web of beliefs and needs of the hypnotized subject; these are not always amenable to conscious awareness. A particularly telling example is provided in a case report furnished by Mutter (1979). A woman claimed innocence of being an accomplice to a double homicide. Her male friend was a drug dealer who had swindled his supplier. To avoid retaliation, he visited the supplier's house and shot him to death. He was accompanied by the woman who, subsequent to the shooting, had been sent upstairs to see if there was anyone else in the house. She found a young woman, and despite the defendant's repeated pleas, the dealer shot her also. He then left town. After some reflection, the woman sought immunity from prosecution from the State Attorney's office. The State Attorney said that he would permit this provided she could pass a polygraph test, which she proceeded to fail. She was then referred to Mutter.

He used the ingenious procedure of hypnotically dissociating her left hand and teaching her a reflexive ideomotor response signal with it. She was told during hypnosis that whenever he tapped the dorsum of the left hand, the index finger and thumb would touch each other reflexively. Having established this reflex to his satisfaction, Mutter age-regressed her to the time of the double homicide. He added the suggestion that she would perform the reflex action whenever he tapped her hand and whenever she said anything that was untrue.

She was asked if she had killed the woman. She replied "no." The polygraph indicated deception, but there was no ideomotor response. When asked if she had pulled the trigger of the gun that had killed the woman she again responded in the negative. This time both polygraph and ideomotor indices concurred in supporting her protestations of innocence. Mutter commented:

> The conflicting responses suggested that Kay's unconscious mind believed she killed the girl. Further questioning revealed that Kay felt guilty when she found the female victim and felt directly responsible for her death, even though she pleaded for the victim's life. (p. 48)

One final factor, which has been shown to influence age-regressed reports of reincarnation, and may be at play when an age-regressed technique is utilized to enhance memory, is the phenomenon of source amnesia. First documented experimentally by Evans and Thorn (1966), it involves the tendency of the highly hypnotizable subject to learn esoteric items of general knowledge in hypnosis, following which, they are amnesic to the context (or source) in which the information was learned. For instance, few people know that an amethyst, a blue or purple gemstone, turns yellow when it is heated. Subjects can be informed of this in hypnosis, and when questioned posthypnotically, some will provide the correct answer. When asked how they knew this, some will report that they do not know; others rationalize and reply, for instance, that they have a geologist friend with whom they talked recently. The item is highly difficult and confined to highly hypnotizable individuals; incidences range from 33 to 50 percent within these individuals (Evans, 1979; Laurence *et al.*, 1986).

There are two published reports in which source amnesia was the factor that provided the only plausible explanation of a verbal report of an apparent experience of reincarnation in age regression. Hilgard (1977) reported a case where a college student had been hypnotized at a party and had discovered himself apparently re-experiencing life as it was at the time of Queen Victoria. He was convinced that he was reincarnated and sought Hilgard's assistance in establishing this. Hilgard began with an initial session of nonhypnotic free recall, which, as will be seen in Chapter 12, is mandatory when hypnosis is used in the legal-investigative situation. By taking him through earlier phases of his life, Hilgard established that, years earlier, he had intensively studied the British Royal Family and had forgotten that he had done so. In the meantime, his interests had changed from history to science. The information had resurfaced in hypnosis as a "true" memory, detached completely from the context (or source) in which it had been acquired.

Another case of source amnesia was presented by Lowes Dickinson (1911) to the British Society for Psychical Research. It involved a woman who, when hypnotized by a physician, described in great detail an earlier existence during the reign of King Richard II of England toward the end of the fourteenth century. She showed an almost encyclopedic knowledge about members of the Royal Court and of the customs and costumes of the period. While communicating with this earlier identity, using a planchette (a type of ouija board), in Lowes Dickinson's presence, she inadvertantly revealed the source of this earlier incarnation. It transpired that a book by Emily Holt, entitled *The Countess Maude*, which she had read at the age of 12, contained all of the relevant information. Lowes Dickinson confirmed this in a subsequent hypnotic session, and by reading the book in question.

From the foregoing, it can be seen that what is recalled when a hypnotic age-regression technique is employed should never be taken at face value, even though it is offered in good faith and is accompanied by subjectively convincing behaviors. There simply are too many other factors that may contaminate the report and, at times, render it into blatant misrepresentation of what, in fact, occurred historically. This is crucial in thinking about the police utilization of hypnosis (Chapter 12). Although most researchers and clinicians of hypnosis know that hypnotically regressed reports may be fact or fantasy, there are some who do not. In addition, some of them consult police forces. For instance, a recent police journal carried the remarkable claim by a psychiatrist that "regression has been proved beyond all doubt to be an actual reliving of the experiences, and the subject is remembering things which are beyond recall in the waking state" (Jaffe, 1980, p. 237).

Little wonder, then, that police forces during the 1970s were enticed by the possibility that hypnosis offered a time-saving alternative to the often time-consuming activity that they have been trained to do best. Who could blame them?

While most of this acceptance was in good faith, there are some police officers, as Baker (1986) has amply documented, for whom the means, however illegal, justify the ends. This too, has a long history. As Sir James Fitzjames Stephen (1883) noted during the discussions on the Indian Code of Criminal Procedures in 1872 concerning the uses of techniques that could elicit "involuntary" confessions: "it is far pleasanter to sit comfortably in the shade rubbing red pepper into a poor devil's eyes than to go about in the sun hunting up evidence" (Vol. 1, p. 442).[9]

As will be seen in the following chapter, reports are beginning to surface of police utilizing hypnosis with victims and witnesses, and subsequently not informing the courts of this not insubstantial fact. Given the scientific evidence discussed earlier that hypnosis increases confidence for correct *and* incorrect material, the trend, though currently small, is alarming.

Fin de Siècle

As the end of the twentieth century looms, it is instructive to review the fate of hypnosis. From virtual total decline in France at the beginning of the century, it was rediscovered in the United States, and the fragile seeds of research were planted by Hull. What was lost was the documentation of the bitter legal disputes in France during the 1880s; few people working in hypnosis knew until recently that such a debate had ever occurred. Nor did they know that the leading French investigators of a century ago were highly conversant with phenomena such a confabulation, memory creation, age regression, inadvertent cueing, and source amnesia. Indeed, some investigators of the twentieth century were to reinvent the wheel, as it were, rediscovering phenomena with which nineteenth-century investigators were very familiar.[10]

This necessarily brief and general examination of twentieth-century data on coercion and memory leads to a final set of topics. The following chapter charts the legal history of hypnosis, which occurred mainly in the United States during this century. It examines what courts have had to say about hypnotically elicited recall and the manner in which certain views inherited from the nineteenth century (which saw the hypnotized person as an automaton) were welded with views, derived mainly from psychoanalysis, of unconscious and subconscious mental processes, and of how hypnosis can tap into them. It evaluates, also the dramatic impact of police officers being taught to utilize hypnosis and how this, in turn, led to a major increase in the investigative utilization of hypnosis for a period during the late 1970s and early 1980s. Most of the problems revealed by the nineteenth-century forensic debate and more recently by the laboratory work on hypnosis and memory processes have already found their way into this new development. It is a tangled tale, and it is ongoing. Indeed, the universe may not be unfolding as it should.

NOTES

1. In other countries, notably the U.S.S.R., hypnosis became popular in other areas like obstetrics. Many "hypnotarium" were opened where Russian women could undergo hypnosis as an aid to giving birth (see Chertok, 1957).

2. Following World War II, two national societies (The Society for Clinical and Experimental Hypnosis and the American Society of Clinical Hypnosis) were formed. There was also a regrouping of clinicians and researchers at the international level. Sixty-five years after the Second International Congress of hypnotism held in Paris, the Third International Congress for Hypnosis and Psychosomatic Medicine was held, also in Paris, in 1965. There have been regular triennial meetings of the International Society of Hypnosis that evolved from this Congress ever since. Currently too, there are national societies of hypnosis in Australia, Austria, Brazil, Canada, Finland, Great Britain, India, Ireland, Israel, Italy, The Netherlands, Norway, Scotland, Singapore, South Africa, Sweden, and West Germany. Paralleling these developments within medicine, dentistry, and psychology, there has been a proliferation of lay hypnosis organizations whose members have no higher degrees in one of the health professions; nevertheless, they confer credentials on their members such as Ethical Hypnotist and Professional Hypnotist, and give every indication that they are as clinically qualified as health professionals who utilize hypnosis. Unfortunately, the general public and the media rarely have an inkling that there is a far from subtle difference. Additionally, there has been a spread of hypnosis within Universities, particularly in the United States, and particularly within departments of psychology. This latter development has been of particular importance since it has accelerated the development of the scientific data base which was initiated by Hull (1933).

3. We were surprised to discover recently that there is an entire room of unclassified books and pamphlets, dating back to the time of Mesmer, in the Osler Library of McGill University in Montréal. Other collections of which we are aware are the Albert Moll Collection at Vanderbilt University and the Maurice and Jean H. Tinterow Collection of works on Mesmerism, animal magnetism, and hypnosis at Wichita State University in Kansas. There are bound to be others.

4. Both university research ethics committees and members of animal welfare groups would, correctly, object to such procedures these days, and such treatment of animals would not be permitted.

5. While the charges of "rape," "attempted rape," and "indecent assault" may appear to exaggerate the offences committed by the hypnotist, several observers of the case have suggested that the lack of a Psychological Practice Act in New South Wales meant that under existing laws these were the only charges that could possibly have been laid.

6. This judgment is the complete reverse of that made in *People v. Royal* (1878) where a similar reasoning led to a lighter sentence.

7. In two other more recent cases, in Arizona and Pennsylvania, women were sexually molested in hypnosis by a lay hypnotist. Both cases have similarities to the Palmer case in that there appears to have been a perception by the women involved that they were powerless to resist the sexual suggestions.

8. Studies which have used nonsense syllables as the to-be-remembered items have consistently failed to find a hypermnesic effect when hypnosis was used as a memory enhancement technique (see AMA report, 1985). This can be quite important since hypnosis has been used by police in many cases where finding a license plate number (a stimulus akin to nonsense syllables) of a car used in a crime would have strengthened the case under investigation (see Chapter 12).

9. Sir James was reporting the words of an "experienced civil officer" on the matter.

10. For instance, Perry and Walsh (1978) published a paper documenting for the first time (or so they thought) the phenomenon of duality in age regression. They found that approximately 50 percent of highly hypnotizable subjects report a quasi-literal regression to childhood in which they feel that they are "really" the age suggested and have no sense of their adult identity. The remaining 50 percent report duality; their subjective experience is of feeling both adult and child, either simultaneously or in alternation. Subsequently, Perry was able to ascertain that the highly hypnotizable subjects in the O'Connell et al. (1970) study had been screened for duality; those subjects reporting it in age regression were not included in the main experiment. This makes this study even more monumental given the meticulous screening that was employed to obtain highly hypnotizable subjects. Subsequently, the library research that went into the writing of this book unearthed the fact that duality was well known to the leading nineteenth-century French investigators such as Janet, Binet, and Bernheim. Interestingly, clinicians of hypnosis have recently rediscovered memory creation, also independently. Recent case reports by Baker and Boaz (1983), Domangue (1985), Lamb (1985), and Miller (1986) report successfully using this technique in treating patients—mostly phobics. Only Miller (1986) was aware that Janet had first used memory creation clinically. Most thought that Erickson (1935) had developed the technique. In fact, Erickson appears to have been doing something quite different; he did not seem to be altering the memory, rather, he was altering the affect surrounding a memory (see Perry, Laurence, D'Eon, & Tallant, in press).

A similar wheel was reinvented when Orne demonstrated memory creation on television (Barnes, 1982). Again it was found subsequently that this phenomenon was familiar to Janet and Bernheim. The same can be said also for source amnesia which was known to nineteenth-century investigators.

Although we may appear to be dismissive in using the phrase "reinventing the wheel" to describe how twentieth-century laboratory investigators have independently re-observed phenomena that were investigated by their nineteenth-century counterparts, the real lesson to be learned is that hypnotic phenomena are extremely robust to survive differences of historical occurrence, thought, and culture as well as the transition from the clinic to the laboratory. Motives, attitudes, sets and contextual cues, as some investigators have proposed then and now, are important factors at play in the phenomena observed. They are not, however, the only ones: The time may be ripe to investigate more systematically the characteristics that underlie people's responses in hypnotic contexts.

12

Hypnosis in Criminal Law: History Repeated

Following the Ebanks murder trial (1897) there was a long pause in the utilization of hypnosis as a means of eliciting recollections of the events of a crime.[1] Indeed, it was not until *State v. Pusch* (1950) in the Supreme Court of North Dakota that another unsuccessful attempt to introduce hypnotically elicited testimony was made. As in *Ebanks*, the hypnotic material came from a man accused of first degree murder, and also as in *Ebanks*, the Court refused to admit the testimony. Perhaps ironically, though, the Court, in denying Pusch's appeal showed no awareness of the prior case 53 years earlier. It stated that "no case has been cited by either party relating to the admissibility of the [hypnotic] evidence proferred and no case has been found" (p. 522).

Precedent-Setting Cases

There had been, however, two cases early in the century that were to have substantial bearing on more recent developments of the last two decades. Both of them, at first blush, would appear to be very unlikely candidates for contemporary relevance. *Austin v. Barker* (1904, 1906) in which hypnotically elicited testimony was admitted, was, in its circumstances, almost a rerun of the case of Maria F. reported by Ladame (1882; see Chapter 8), although it was resolved in a vastly different manner. The case was launched by the father of Edith Austin against David Barker. Some years earlier, in August 1901, Edith, much to her surprise, gave birth to a child. Unlike Maria, who was not hypnotized in an effort to learn the origin of her pregnancy, Edith had no idea how the child could have been conceived until she was hypnotized by the attorney representing her father in the case. She then recalled that she had had

335

sexual relations with Barker on a number of occasions during November and December of the preceding year while one of her parents was in the next room. She recalled further that the

> defendant hypnotized her, and so made her unconscious of his unlawful acts with her at the time they were occurring, and that this condition of unconsciousness thereof continued until her father's attorney visited her nearly a year afterwards, and placed her in a hypnotic condition, through and by means of which her consciousness was so restored that it seized hold of events of which she had theretofore been unconscious. (*Austin v. Barker*, 1904, p. 467)

The Court held that this explanation was opposed to ordinary experience and knowledge. It added that if the plaintiff was relying on "some science and theory that was not generally known or understood, it was proper for him to give the jury the light of some competent evidence tending to sustain the probabilities, or at least the possibilities, of what was claimed" (p. 467).

This, the Court pointed out, had not been done in this particular case. The Appellate Court proceeded to reverse the earlier decision in favor of Mr. Austin on the grounds that the lower court had reached a decision that was against the weight of evidence. Many years later, in *Harding v. State* (1968) a Maryland court was to rule that this particular case was the only one relevant to one that it was considering (see next section). Ironically, *Austin v. Barker* (1904) was cited in its decision to accept hypnotically elicited testimony from a crime victim. A double irony was that the *Austin v. Barker* case was retried two years later in 1906. This court also found in favor of the defendant on the grounds that the prosecution case was simply a hearsay account of what Ms. Austin had been told in hypnosis, and it could not be considered as a "true memory."[2] It is perhaps, also of interest that the court was not presented with expert testimony concerning the possibility of confabulation, simulation, and lying, as had occurred slightly more than 20 years earlier in Maria F.'s case in France.

A second major case in the early part of the century which was to have repercussions that are still being felt, was not even connected with hypnosis. This was the famous case of *Frye v. United States* (1923) which concerned the admissibility of evidence derived from what was then picturesquely called "the systolic blood pressure deception test" and is now more inaccurately called "the lie detector." In a historic ruling, the Court ruled that

> while the courts will go a long way in admitting expert testimony deduced from a well-recognized scientific principle or discovery, the thing from which the deduction is made must be sufficiently established to have gained general acceptance in the particular field in which it belongs. (p. 1013)

The Court noted also that the scientific assumption, upon which the polygraph was based, was without foundation. It stated that "the theory seems to be that truth is spontaneous, and comes without conscious effort, while the utterance of a falsehood requires a conscious effort, which is reflected in the blood pressure" (p. 1014).

The Court held that this theory did not have sufficient scientific recognition among psychologists and physiologists as to permit evidence derived from this source to a court of law. This ruling was, subsequently, to be applied to hypnotically elicited recall and used to exclude it from legal hearings.[3]

As an aside, it should be noted that *Frye* has not prevented adoption of the polygraph in quite a gamut of situations, though in general, the evidence elicited from its use has continued to be unacceptable to American courts. An editorial in the *Washington Post* during January 1985 indicates current dimensions of a problem that was recognized over 60 years ago by the *Frye* court. It stated (in part):

> Pentagon officials announce that they have a new machine that will be able to determine the "trustworthiness, patriotism and integrity" of job applicants. It's called a lie detector. You may have thought that a polygraph was just a machine to measure stress—a "fear detector" as one expert called it in testimony before a House Committee. . . . In 1983 the president issued a directive authorizing lie detector tests for 2.5 million civilian and military workers and 1.5 million employees of government contractors with security clearances. After strong congressional opposition was heard, the order was suspended, but a provision in the defense authorization bill allows the Pentagon to conduct a pilot program of 3,500 lie detector tests this year. . . . Even proponents of this scheme will tell you that lie detector tests are accurate only 75 to 90 percent of the time. Others will argue that that estimate is high. Most American courts will not admit lie detector test results in evidence because they are so unreliable. John De Lorean, the recently acquitted auto executive, for example, passed a test administered by his own defense experts and failed one supervised by the FBI. Just as the tests will unfairly deny people jobs and promotion, they will also create . . . a false sense of security if government officials believe they effectively screen out those who shouldn't be hired. . . . (p. 16)

If the history of the polygraph following the *Frye* decision is the appropriate model for what will happen with hypnosis in legal and quasi-legal proceedings, it is likely that issues currently being debated will still be topical during the mid-twenty-first century.

The events of *State v. Pusch* (1950) are of some interest in this regard. August L. Pusch was charged and convicted of murdering his wife, Minnie, by administering strychnine to her. Much of the evidence, which he denied, was provided by his mistress, Lydia Witt, who had borne a child to him. She testified, and it was confirmed by a druggist, that she had bought a quantity of strychnine. She stated that it had been sought on Pusch's behalf. She reported also that Pusch had emptied a number of Vitamin B-complex capsules that had been prescribed to Mrs. Pusch by her physician, and replaced the vitamin material with the poison. Pusch denied this account of what had transpired, but the court found the web of circumstances too compelling and pronounced Pusch guilty. The Appellate Court agreed.

Interestingly, Pusch was subjected both to a polygraphic examination and a hypnotic evaluation. In finding the testimony from these sources inadmissible, the court indicated an unawareness of both *Ebanks* and *Frye*. It knew, however, of cases subsequent to *Frye* that had excluded the polygraph. The polygraphic witness testified that Pusch's record showed "perfectly normal reactions, and that there is nothing about this graph that in any way disclosed any falsification, lying or untruthfulness on the part of the defendant" (p. 520).

The polygraphic witness offered, also, to demonstrate the great scientific recognition of polygraph tests. Despite this, the Supreme Court of North Dakota ruled that the lower court had not erred in excluding the one item of evidence that was potentially favorable to Pusch.

The hypnotic evidence, which was excluded also, is of interest in terms of how an expert witness, possessing a doctorate in psychology from a reputable university, perceived the value of hypnosis in refreshing recollections. According to the Court's summary of the expert's claims about hypnosis:

> he is able to place a person in hypnotic trance, at which time *the person loses all control of the conscious mind and is governed entirely by the subconscious mind*; that when such party is in such an hypnotic trance and is being dealt with in the subconscious mind, the person has *no control over the things being done from the standpoint of the conscious mind and must deal entirely with the subconscious mind.* (p. 521, italics added)

The same expert offered to show that the accused, while under the domination of his subconscious during the hypnotic "state," had been truthful in his answers. This was interesting testimony in that it wedded nineteenth-century views of the hypnotized person being akin to an automaton with beliefs derived from psychoanalysis concerning the operation of an unconscious/subconscious mind. The Court's refusal to admit the testimony can be seen more as a matter of a fortunate blundering than as an incisive understanding of the psychological issues concerned with the nature of mind and of hypnosis.

The Potential for Abuse

Nine years later, in *Cornell v. Superior Court of San Diego* (1959), a court ruled in a more cavalier fashion than in *Pusch*. Harold D. Cornell was an attorney representing Paul Conrey, who had been charged with the first-degree murder of Maria Martin. The facts of the case were straightforward and indicated that Conrey had been implicated in Martin's death; the issue facing the Court was his degree of criminal responsibility. Her body had been found in a ditch on a vacant lot adjacent to a cemetery. Her dress was rolled up to her neck and her panties were found ten feet from her body. She was lying on her face. Large heavy shoes were found on her feet. Tire tracks ran up to and over her body. They then backed away from it and proceeded off the vacant lot. Subsequent police work established that the car was one of five makes manufactured between 1953 and 1954, and that one of the tire marks was of a brand new tire. Thorough and careful police work established that the car belonged to Conrey; this was verified by the finding of a fragment of Mrs. Martin's skull in the framework of the car. Hair matching her hair was found inside the car. Other police evidence indicated that she had been drinking with a man roughly matching Conrey's description at the Quality Bar until at least midnight on the night of her death. There was strong evidence to suggest that Conrey was implicated in Mrs. Martin's death. He maintained, however, that he had been drinking heavily that day and could not recall anything between eleven o'clock that night and the following morning when he awoke in his car, parked the wrong way on a one-way street. This was the period during which the victim had died.

The case was considered at the time to be a landmark decision involving hypnosis. Arons (1967) and Bryan (1962) discussed it extensively in what were to be the first two books written in the United States on the legal, investigative use of hypnosis. Both cited the case with substantial approval. Bryan (1962) went as far as to print the San Diego County Court's decision in full and also a paper by Richard N. Mikesell on the case which had been published in *Hypnosis Quarterly*, a lay journal. Bryan characterized the case as one in which "hypnosis saved a man from the gas chamber." As in *Pusch* nine years earlier, hypnosis was once again characterized as having "truth-telling" properties, although, as will be seen, hypnosis did not establish anything that could be verified by independent means. Nevertheless, the persistence of Cornell, the lawyer, appears to have gained for Conrey a more favorable hearing and a more favorable judgment than he might otherwise have received had hypnosis not been introduced into the case.

The case began when Cornell decided that his client's memory of the events of the night of Mrs. Martin's death might be restored by the utilization of hypnosis. His initial verbal request to the local sheriff was refused. Sensibly, the latter indicated to the attorney that he did not wish to take responsibility for this "unusual" form of questioning. Some legal jockeying then ensued which led ultimately to Cornell requesting and receiving a writ of mandamus from the California Supreme Court in San Diego. The Court, in its ruling, referred to *Ebanks*, two cases involving "truth serum," and four cases involving the polygraph. It found in Cornell's favor, and stated that

> These cases have no application to the problem here presented. They all deal with the admissibility of evidence. Admissibility of any evidence that may be secured during such an examination is not the question here presented. Cornell is now seeking to learn facts that may be of assistance in preparing for the defense of the crime charged. He wants to ascertain, if possible, the accused's whereabouts on the night in question. His hope, of course, is that he may learn of a bona fide alibi. Whether the evidence so secured would or would not be admissible is a false factor. Obviously, it is reasonably possible that evidence so secured, whether or not it is admissible, may put Cornell in possession of facts which, *when followed up*, would result in the discovery

that might constitute a complete defense to the charge. This being so, Cornell, with the consent of his client, is entitled to conduct the proposed examination. (p. 449, italics added)

Mikesell, the lay hypnotist, was now legally permitted to hypnotize Conrey, a task which he approached with some flamboyance. From the lawyer, Cornell, he had learned that Conrey was "honest, sincere and actually innocent," while from the police, the verdict was that he was "cold, hard-headed and calculating" (Bryan, 1962, p. 60). The induction procedure was one designed to convince Conrey that the hypnotist had supernatural powers and centered on the use of a Chevreul Pendulum test in which an object (in this case a moonstone), suspended on a string, is held by the subject. The subject was told that in answer to various questions posed to him, the moonstone would move in a circle when the answer was "no," and in a straight line when the answer was affirmative. The test is one of ideomotor suggestibility and is probably as much as anything a test of the degree to which a subject is cooperating with the hypnotist.

The hypnotist concluded very early that Conrey was resisting this approach. Accordingly, he covered the arm so that the subject could not see his own response. He then resorted to deception; he asked Conrey if he had been with a woman on the night of Mrs. Martin's death. The response from the pendulum was "no," but Mikesell believed that it was deliberately deceptive. He said to Cornell "'It says "yes," doesn't it?'—Cornell agreed. This so threw Conrey that his hand immediately began to shake, sweat started to roll out on his head" (Bryan, 1962, p. 60).

Conrey was asked if he liked the technique and indicated that he did not, since he did not "want his life to depend on a bauble like that" (Bryan, 1962, p. 61). Mikesell indicated to him that this was merely a procedure for beginning the process of hypnosis and that on the next occasion he would utilize an even more effective procedure.

At the next session, Conrey was described as entering deep hypnosis. The only test employed to confirm this came when the hypnotist stuck a pin into his left arm. This, however, is a nonconclusive test and can be simulated, particularly when the reward is the avoidance of a death penalty. We do not mean to say, however, that Conrey was simulating, only that murder suspects have strong motivations to simulate and that no conclusive test appears to have been applied to evaluate this hypothesis in Conrey's case. It should be added that many of the scientific experts in the field of hypnosis have been totally deceived by unhypnotizable simulators when a formal test was applied (see Orne, 1979a), as were their European predecessors.

Nevertheless, this somewhat stagey procedure may have generated an aura of credibility for Conrey's hypnotically elicited narration of the events leading to Maria Martin's death. Originally, Conrey had been charged with rape and first-degree murder. The jury appeared to have been persuaded by his story since it convicted him of second-degree manslaughter (Udolph, 1983).

Remembering that what Conrey recounted during hypnosis could have been fact or fantasy or it may have been simulated, and that there does not appear to have been any attempt to verify any of these hypotheses independently, it is of some relevance to examine his hypnotic recall of the events of Mrs. Martin's death. He stated that he had been drinking with a woman who was divorced from his uncle and had failed to interest her in his sexual overtures. This had begun at four o'clock in the afternoon and took place in a number of bars they visited. Ending at eleven o'clock, the woman left to return home. He proceeded to switch his attention to a waitress with similar negative results. He then remembered a former female friend he had encountered recently. She had given her address as the Star Hotel. He reported that he visited her, opened the wrong door, and had an argument with a man and a woman who occupied the room. Although an attempt was made subsequently to locate these witnesses, they could not be found.

He then went to the Quality Bar where he had what was becoming his habitual bad fortune with one of the female customers. Another female customer, described as having her "hair up in curlers, obviously drunk, big, heavy shoes on her feet, and wearing a white uniform," tried to engage his attention, but he rebuffed her. When he left for his car, she followed him, and although he tried again to rebuff her, she climbed into it. They stopped for hamburgers, and he drove to a vacant lot. He reported that he then passed out. She shook him awake some time later, reviled him in coarse language to which he responded by pushing her aside, demanding to be allowed to sleep, and passed out again. What followed can be only regarded as total conjecture since, of the two parties involved, one died subsequently and the other was reportedly asleep. The woman finished her drink, still swearing, and suddenly (as it was coyly put) "had to answer a call of nature" (Bryan, 1962, p. 63). She shook Conrey to take her home, but he could not be awakened. She stumbled from the car and walked approximately ten feet from it to answer her call. According to Mikesell, this explained why her panties were found off her. To him, it indicated also that rape could not have occurred, since the panties were untorn as he believed would have happened had rape been committed. He reasoned that they would have been torn when being pulled over her heavy shoes. (On the other hand, observant readers of both sexes might want to contemplate whether complete removal of panties over heavy shoes and rolling one's dress up to the neck are plausible actions, even when intoxicated, in response to a call from nature.)

Subsequently, she is conjectured to have tripped and fallen as she returned to the car and cut her chin on the cocktail glass that she was holding. She then attempted to crawl back to the car, but went in the opposite direction. She ended up in the ditch (where her body was found) and immediately passed out. Some time later, Conrey awoke, saw that she was not in the car, and concluded tht she had returned home. He started the car forward. It dropped into the ditch. Realizing that he had gone in the wrong direction, he reversed the car, turned around, and headed for home. He found himself the next morning parked on a one-way street facing the wrong direction.

As indicated, this account of the events surrounding Mrs. Martin's death was believed by the jury, and it may have been what happened. There is, however, no way of knowing, and it may equally have been invented by Conrey while he simulated hypnosis, or it may have been confabulated while he was hypnotized. The alternative hypotheses were never explored. Indeed, there was no indication that any of the principals in the case recognized that there was a need to explore them.

One final aspect of this case deserves comment. In issuing the writ of mandamus which permitted Conrey to be hypnotized, the Court noted that

> The use of hypnotism for the purpose desired is recognized by medical authorities. *Encyclopaedia Britannica*, 1954 Edition, Vol. 12, pp. 22-24. This being so . . . there is no substantial legal difference between the right to use a hypnotist in an attempt to probe into the client's subconscious recollection, and the use of a psychiatrist to determine sanity. (p. 449)

Although the court does not appear to have been aware of it, there had been an important report prepared a year earlier, in 1958, by the Committee on Hypnosis of the Council on Mental Health for the American Medical Association (AMA). Prior to the American report, the British Medical Association had issued a similar favorable report on hypnosis in 1955. During the 1970s, when police officers came to be taught to induce hypnosis via a 32-hour course for the purpose of "refreshing" the memories of victims and witnesses of crime (though not of suspects), this report was cited often as evidence that hypnosis had gained medical acceptability. What is not recognized is that the AMA stipulated severe restrictions both on who should utilize hypnosis and how it should be taught. Its conclusions read in part:

> General practitioners, medical specialists, and dentists might find hypnosis valuable as a therapeutic adjunct within the special field of their professional competence. It should be stressed that all those who use hypnosis need to be aware of the complex nature of the phenomena involved.
>
> Teaching related to hypnosis should be under responsible medical or dental direction, and integrated teaching programs should include not only the techniques of induction but also the indications and limitations for its use within the specific area involved. Instruction limited to induction techniques alone should be discouraged. (p. 187)

In short, it is true that hypnosis received medical recognition in 1958, but the approval was far from being of a profligate and general nature. This fact was to be overlooked often during the ensuing decades.

There were other developments that, at the time, may not have appeared to be amounting to very much but would, likewise, assume importance for the understanding of where things stand currently. In his book of 1967, Harry Arons, a lay hypnotist, described how, in September 1959, he began offering courses on hypnosis to law enforcement officers in New Jersey. In the hope of obtaining official recognition, he offered the course free to designated representatives of police departments; although no police department accepted, 17 detectives paid to take the course. An index of the course's popularity is that in the eight years between first offering the course and writing the book, Arons conducted the course twice a year, and he estimated that 350 individuals associated with law enforcement completed it. They included police chiefs, sheriffs, prosecutors, and detectives affiliated variously with local, state and county agencies. Also attending at various times were investigators from the Internal Revenue Service, employees of insurance companies and private detective agencies, including a number of field polygraphers. In addition to this number, Arons (1967) reported that approximately 75 lawyers and four judges also attended the course. In short, the grass roots of law enforcement in New Jersey and surrounding states were being educated about the views of one individual on the potential of hypnosis within the legal system at an average rate of approximately 50 people per year.

The actual views that Arons promulgated during this period were a curious admixture of astonishing naïveté and acute insight, though it should be said that Arons had his equivalents in the professional hypnosis societies which were beginning to develop at that time. His book demonstrated clearly that he understood that individuals can simulate hypnosis and that they can lie. He also showed some recognition of the fact that individuals can confabulate. In general, he supported the belief in the "truth-telling" properties of hypnosis, as when he stated that "in most cases the fact that hypnosis was used need not be divulged in court at all, as it is not really pertinent to the matter" (p. 27).

In addition, he maintained that the AMA's stipulation concerning restriction of hypnotic techniques to the physician or dentist's area of professional training and competence did not apply to investigative hypnosis. He stated that investigative hypnosis, unlike medical or dental hypnosis, was not concerned with the treatment of human ills; accordingly, he concluded that no restrictions were necessary. Interestingly, this view was soon to obtain endorsement from within police ranks.

In addition, Arons (1967) perpetuated the mistaken belief that memory is reproductive, rather than reconstructive. This view gathered steam during the late 1970s as a result of the teachings of Martin Reiser of the Los Angeles Police Department. Arons wrote, and Reiser must have read: "Scientific research had demonstrated that the mind—or the brain—seems to have the capacity for retaining all impressions that enter it, like a giant tape recorder" (p. 35). He added that "experimentation has shown that almost anything that the mind has ever received can be retrieved under the right conditions" (p. 35).

Without any sense of contradiction, however, Arons proceeded to describe a case in which the giant tape recorder theory of the mind could be seen as somewhat fallible. He described a case in which a witness of a hold-up had provided a license plate number of the getaway car. The number he provided was GNP 554. When this license plate number failed to bear fruit, the witness was hypnotized by Arons and provided the number GMP 545, although subsequently he may have been inadvertently cued to alter the number to GNP 545. A transcript of this part of the session indicates:

> *Operator*: You saw their license plate, didn't you?
> *Subject*: Yes.
> *Operator*: Just call it right out.
> *Subject*: The license plate was GMP 545.
> *Operator*: GMP 545?
> *Subject*: GMP 545.
> *Operator*: Was it N or M?
> *Subject*: Looks like an N.
> *Operator*: N like in Nathan?
> *Subject*: Yes. GNP 545. (p. 45)

Both of Arons's first two questions can be construed as leading questions which communicate to the subject what he is expecting and/or hoping to hear. It transpired subsequently, however, that following arrest of the alleged perpetrators of this hold-up for other crimes, none of the three numbers provided by the eyewitness were correct. Arons maintained that

> the most logical explanation for this apparent failure is that Glassman [the witness] in his anxiety, misread the number to begin with. This points up the need for exhaustive checking out of all information obtained in hypnosis. It cannot be denied that a hypnotic subject, lacking real facts, may hallucinate or contrive or invent information to fit a given situation. (p. 47)

This qualification certainly suggests that a tape recorder theory of memory cannot account fully for all of its phenomena. It underscores also the dangers of not, as Arons recommended, divulging to a court of law that hypnosis has been undertaken with a witness. Often, even without hypnosis, the only testimony against a defendent is the positive identification by a witness, and this can be fallible enough.

Five years prior to the publication of Arons's book, William J. Bryan had published the first American book to be devoted to legal aspects of hypnosis in 1962. Whereas Arons had demonstrated a somewhat contradictory awareness of confabulation, Bryan had no such similar leanings. Like Arons, he saw *Cornell* as a major victory for the forces of enlightenment, and he proceeded to paint the skies in a gaudy hue of false optimism for a brave new world. He wrote of *Cornell*:

> It is significant that the use of hypnotism in this instance was designed to place the defense lawyer in possession of facts which would result in the discovery of admissible evidence. There is only a very short step then from this viewpoint to the admission of testimony under hypnosis as evidence in the courtroom. It is unnecessary (as in the case of the lie detector and truth serum) to even raise the point that testimony under hypnosis is to be considered more truthful than that given in the waking state. Although, of course, this is true nevertheless if this point were not raised, there should be

no difficulty in introducing hypnotic testimony in a courtroom for the benefit of obtaining new facts which could not be obtained in other ways.

It must be remembered that the purpose of the lie detector and truth serum is *only* to produce a truthful response from the subject, but the purpose of hypnotism is not only designed to produce a truthful response, but is designed to uncover certain facts of which the patient himself may be entirely unaware, by examining the patient's subconscious mind. Such an examination is not at all similar to truth serum or lie detector examinations, but, on the contrary, is much more similar to an x-ray examination which attempts to uncover facts regarding the patient's bone structure which cannot be seen with the naked eye. In the same way, hypnotism is used to uncover facts regarding the patient's unconscious mind, which cannot be seen with the patient's conscious mind in the waking state. (pp. 70-71, italics in original)

Elsewhere, in discussing the use of hypnosis in interrogating criminals (p. 244), Bryan (1962) made the extravagantly false claim that "it is extremely difficult for a subject to lie while in a deep hypnotic trance" (p. 245). He believed that, by directing rapid-fire questions to the "subconscious mind," truth is guaranteed automatically, and he described a procedure for effecting this laudable result. It consisted of making the arm analgesic, which to him indicated that the subject must have attained at least "medium trance state." He would then place a number of needles through the arm, with the ideas that if trance lightened, pain would be felt. He believed that "as long as the patient remains in the hypnotic trance he is pain-free as well as subject to truthful answering" (p. 246). He added that the hypnotist can further guarantee truth by removing the needles one by one while asking the various questions, thus indicating that the subject can control bleeding. Again, the assumption was that as long as bleeding was controlled, the interviewee was in a medium-to-deep trance and, hence, in a subconscious state of "truth telling." This technique has unacknowledged affinities with that used by Charcot (see Chapter 9). Overall, Bryan displayed an almost innocent belief that analgesia cannot be simulated, even in conditions where there may be considerable motivation to do so.[4]

A Major Decision in Maryland

Both the Bryan and Arons books centered on the highly problematic use of hypnosis to reinstate the recollections of crime suspects. Both reinforced the notions presented in *Pusch* and *Cornell* that hypnosis represented a royal route to the unconscious which, passively and without struggle, gladly conceded its most lurid and most closely guarded secrets. It was a beguiling but dangerous pseudo-science, though not for crime suspects who could simulate amnesia convincingly; certainly though it was dangerous for defendants who could be convicted solely on the basis of the hypotically elicited recollections of a victim or witness—recollections that might be fact or fantasy and that were likely to contain elements of both. Nevertheless, it is within this context of reemerging false belief that the next major court decision was made. *Harding v. State of Maryland* (1968) was to significantly influence the decisions of courts throughout the United States well into the 1970s, and its effects began to be defused only when a Maryland court (*Collins v. State*) reversed it in 1981. In this more recent case, the court elected to follow a more cautious approach to hypnotically elicited recall. This approach can be traced directly to the *Frye* (1923) ruling on the polygraph.[5]

The *Harding* decision nevertheless merits careful attention because it mirrors recent thinking about the truth-telling properties of hypnosis. It is difficult to determine the details of this case from the Court's judgment; the judge appears to have first outlined the victim's resumé of events, and then added what was subsequently elicited hypnotically. The two accounts leave at least one basic question unanswered.

In September 1966, Harding met the victim, Mrs. Mildred Coley, in a Baltimore bar. They later joined another man and woman and all four of them continued to drink while driving around the city in the man's car. Mrs. Coley was not previously familiar with any of the other three. She sat in the front seat while Harding sat alone in the back seat. At some point, Harding became angry with Mrs. Coley for not sitting in the back seat with him and for refusing his sexual advances. He told her that he had a gun and was going to have sexual relations with her before she left the car. She replied that she would cut him if he even touched her. Subsequently, she opened her purse, and when she turned in his direction he shot her in the chest. Harding then ordered the driver to drive to an isolated backroad, removed Mrs. Coley, who was unconscious and possibly dead, and placed her on the side of the road. She was found by a state trooper early the next morning lying off a road three miles from where Harding had allegedly left her. She was wearing only a black dress, with her underclothes beside her. She was still alive and was rushed to a hospital where emergency surgery was performed on her chest. Further examination revealed semen in her vagina.

When first questioned by police, her story was that she had been abducted at knifepoint in Baltimore by three black males, driven to a nearby county, raped, and stabbed. The police soon learned that she had been shot. The driver of the car was known to police, and she identified him from a photograph. At a third police interview in the hospital, it became clear that she could not recall certain parts of what had happened. She could relate the events up to the time of being shot, and then go on to the point where she had been removed from the car. Beyond that point, she could not recall anything. Approximately a month after the shooting, she was hypnotized by the Chief Clinical Psychologist at a local State hospital.

In the session, she was able to remember lying on the side of the road, and a vehicle, resembling a bread truck or a station wagon, approached. When it stopped, Harding emerged from it, put her in the back and drove off. When they arrived at another location, Harding threw her on the ground and unzipped her dress. She passed out. On regaining consciousness, she found that all of her clothes had been removed except her dress. She realized also, she stated, that she had been sexually assaulted.[6]

The court ruled that "the fact that she had told different stories or had achieved her present knowledge after being hypnotized concerns the question of the weight of the evidence which the trier of facts, in this case the jury, must decide" (p. 306).

The Court noted further that although several American courts had considered the admissibility of hypnotically elicited testimony, only *Austin v. Barker* (1904, 1906) seemed to be "particularly apropos [*sic*] to our question here" (p. 311).[7] The line of thinking appeared to be that in this earlier case, no evidence had been presented in court to document the hypnotic procedures used to restore Ms. Austin's memory; also that two doctors were skeptical of the submission that hypnosis could be used to induce amnesia of her first experiences of intercourse. By contrast, in *Harding*, a professional psychologist had utilized hypnosis with Mrs. Coley and had provided elaborate testimony (that does not appear to have been contested) concerning how hypnosis can facilitate memory for material lodged in the unconscious. In addition, his testimony satisfied the Court that no improper suggestions had been made.

The gist of this expert testimony on the nature of hypnosis was that it involved a focusing of attention away from external, extraneous stimuli, and his views were quoted extensively by the judge. The psychologist testified that

> With the elimination of all this extraneous material you can help the patient to focus their stimulus on occurrences or events that went right through and as a result of reducing the conscious influence which kind of acts as a distraction, this barrier [opens] a little bit, so that now you don't have all this conscious stuff acting as a conscious influence and reinforces the barrier between the conscious and the unconscious. You leave the mind fairly clear to focus on this one subject and as a result quite frequently you can have the subject come back into conscious awareness. (pp. 307-308, syntax as in the original)

With this, and allied statements from the psychologist, the jury was advised that

> The phenomenon commonly known as hypnosis has been explained to you during this trial. I advise you to weigh this testimony carefully. Do not place any greater weight on this portion of Mrs. Coley's testimony than on any other testimony that you have heard during this trial. Remember, you are the judges of the weight and the believability of all of the evidence in this case. (p. 310)

Harding was found guilty, and the decision was to have a major effect on the American legal system for years to come.

The Svengali Squads of the 1970s[8]

Up to this point, hypnosis had been used sparingly in criminal cases. More often than not, its main benefit was perceived as assisting murder suspects to relieve their professed amnesias. The next major development, however, was the wholesale adoption of hypnotic procedures by police departments to assist victims and witnesses in recalling details of a crime. The pioneer of this development was Martin Reiser. This work earned him the American Express/International Association of Chiefs of Police Award for the year's outstanding contribution to the field of international police science and technology in December 1977.

Although Reiser (1980) reports that from 1972 he was receiving occasional requests from LAPD detectives to hypnotize crime victims who they felt should have revealed more information than they had during routine interrogations, it was not until 1975 that his procedures began to be formalized. In June of that year, a one-year pilot project to evaluate the efficacy of hypnosis in police investigations was launched. It was found that

> Of the approximately 70 cases in the data base, at that point, it was estimated that in approximately 77%, information was elicited under hypnosis of importance to the case investigator that was not previously available on routine interview. (p. xv)

These look to be impressive statistics until it is realized that they are "happiness" ratings (to use the parlance of opinion polling). They indicate the extent to which case investigators *believed* they were receiving valuable information, rather than the frequency with which hypnosis was providing additional information that was instrumental in solving a crime. This point, however, did not have any moderating effect on the strong tide of enthusiasm for hypnosis that engulfed many police departments, not merely in the United States, but also in places as remote from the scene as Sydney, Australia.

The upshot was that in 1976, Reiser established a private training institute which he called the Law Enforcement Hypnosis Institute (LEHI) and began training police officers and other individuals in allied professions via a 32-hour course on theory, demonstration, and practice. Figures vary as to how many individuals completed this course over the next several years; estimates vary from 1,000 to 10,000.

Central to the theory underlying this burgeoning practice was the assumption that memory is reproductive, rather than reconstructive. Arons's (1967) metaphor of memory being a giant tape recorder was extended to encompass more recent technology. Reiser wrote:

> Because the perceptual apparatus works in cybernetic fashion, much like a giant computerized videotape recorder, the plethora of information perceived by the sensory system is recorded and stored in the brain at a subconscious level. Much of this data, momentarily nonrelevant, or repressed because of

emotional trauma, is difficult to recall; the problem—one of amnesia. However, hypnosis may provide the key in a significant number of cases by encouraging hypermnesia, relaxing the censorship and permitting suppressed or repressed material to return to conscious awareness. (1976, pp. 39-40)

Other features of Reiser's procedures also created concern about the type of "memory" that was likely to be elicited from hypnotized victims and witnesses. One, in particular, was the utilization of metaphors borrowed from televised sports in which the hypnotized person could be encouraged to "zoom-in" to obtain an "enlargement" of the crime scene, freeze the frame, and reexperience the events of the crime without reexperiencing the affect associated with it. As Reiser (1980) put it:

After an optimal state of hypnosis is achieved, the hypno-investigator indicates that the subject, in imagination, will be watching a special documentary film on television from a safe, secure, and comfortable place. The special documentary can be speeded-up, slowed-down, stopped, reversed, with close-ups possible on any person, object or thing in the film. The sound can be turned-up high so that anything that is said, even a whisper, can be heard very clearly. This will be a documentary film of the incident in question and will depict accurately and vividly everything of significance and importance the subject perceived and experienced in relationship to the crime events. (p. 158)

This use of the zoom-in appears to virtually demand fantasy. If, for instance, a person is asked to zoom-in on an image that, in the original experience, the retina could not resolve, the only source of any additional detail provided by the subject would have to be fantasy. Put in another way, the zoom-in can be, in effect, a potential indirect suggestion to the subject to hallucinate. Indeed, this appears to have been what occurred in *People v. Kempinski* (1980) where a young man was arrested and held in prison for five months while awaiting trial, solely on the basis of a description given by a hypnotized eyewitness. The case was thrown out of court because of testimony that the witness had been 270 feet away from the murder under poor light conditions. An ophthalmologist testified in court that positive identification would not have been possible beyond 25 feet under such lighting conditions.

There are various other criticisms that can, and have been made, of Reiser's procedures (see Orne, Soskis, Dinges, Carota Orne, & Tonry, 1985; Perry & Laurence, 1983).[9] The important point for the present discussion is that Reiser's insistence on police officers, trained by a 32-hour course had a remarkable impact on several justice systems around the world. The hypnotizing of victims and witnesses of crime became a regular and, in some places, a routine police practice. More importantly, because most of the police trained by these procedures did not have a background in experimental psychology and were not aware of research on memory, they tended to accept without question the metaphor of a "giant computerized videotape recorder."

This meant, in turn, that often they took the hypnotically elicited recollections of victims and witnesses at face value and saw no reason (since they had been taught that there was not one) to corroborate independently what the hypnotized person reported. Accordingly, with progressively greater frequency, the practice developed whereby individuals were being prosecuted *solely* on the basis of hypnotic recall. It depended mostly on the level of skepticism within individual police departments whether such prosecutions occurred. Something akin to trial by fantasy emerged in the United States in the late 1970s; it was not long before the courts found themselves faced with some quite extraordinary cases, where the only potential evidence of guilt was of a hypnotic origin. At the same time, though, it should be noted that some professionals trained in medicine, psychiatry, and psychology were not immune to the types of errors made by their briefly trained police counterparts.[10]

Competence to Testify

In 1980, Bernard L. Diamond, a professor both of law and clinical psychiatry, published an important paper in the *California Law Review*. It was to have an important effect on the decisions of a number of legal cases during the 1980s which involved hypnosis as the main, if not the sole, evidence of the accused's presumed legal culpability. Diamond, in concluding that "the only sensible approach is to exclude testimony from previously hypnotized witnesses as a matter of law, on the grounds that the witness has been rendered incompetent to testify" (p. 349), drew heavily on the proceedings of two major, controversial cases of the latter half of the 1970s. These were the combined case of *Emmett v. Ricketts* and *Creamer v. Hopper* in Georgia (1975) and *United States v. Narciso and Perez* in Michigan (1977). Neither involved the utilization of a Reiser-trained police hypnotechnician. They involved a psychologist holding a doctorate degree in education in the former case and a psychiatrist with considerable credentials in clinical hypnosis in the latter.

Emmett v. Ricketts/Creamer v. Hopper (1975) involved writs of habeas corpus brought by two men in prison who had been convicted of murder.[11] Two Georgia pathologists, married to each other, had been murdered in their home in May 1971. There followed a police investigation which the Court was subsequently to describe as inadequate. It stated that

> the many tantalizing clues, the important leads that were never pursued, the controversial prosecutions which resulted, all combined with the sensational nature of the crime to make the case, even to this day, the subject of intense media coverage and general community interest. (pp. 1029-1030)

The investigation floundered for 14 months until the Georgia police assigned to the case received word from the South Carolina police that an informant (Ms. Deborah Kidd) had provided information about the Georgia murders. This information conflicted with known physical evidence and with what she later testified to in court on several major details; nevertheless, two detectives were dispatched from Georgia to interview Ms. Kidd. There is conflicting evidence as to whether this interview was audiotaped; subsequently, one of the detectives testified that Kidd was under the influence of drugs, and gave a rambling and sketchy account of the murders. He added that this account contained some known facts, and "a world of discrepancies" (p. 1034). A month later, in August 1972, Kidd returned to Georgia, where she lived for some weeks at the apartment of one of the detectives with whom she had sexual relations and with whom she claimed to be in love. For at least the following few months, she was supplied with amphetamines by the police.

During this period, she signed a third sworn statement about her recollections of the crime. The Court characterized it, like the two previous ones, as "replete with material discrepancies and allegations that were later dropped from her story" (p. 1035). This statement, again like the two previous ones was presented to the prosecution, but not to the defense. From the very beginning, however, she had told the police who had interviewed her in South Carolina that "she could not remember many details of the crime because she was 'full of pills' during its commission" (p. 1036). This was subsequently to be diagnosed by the police as "partial amnesia." Due to the proliferation of inconsistencies, implausibilities, and gaps in her three recountings of the events of the murder, plus deviations from known facts, this appears to have led to the idea of having her hypnotized. The ostensible reason given for this was to treat her drug dependence. The Court rejected this explanation summarily. It stated categorically that

> it is clear that the dominant, overriding, if not sole motivation therefore was . . . to "further her memory" and to fill in "gaps" in her story. Kidd herself stated . . . that the purpose of these sessions was to have Hall [the hypnotist] place her under hypnosis and by [age regression] help her remember more of the details of the crime which she could not remember because of the time lapse and her use of amphetamine type drugs. (p. 1036)

In addition, the hypnotist, according to Kidd's testimony, instructed her to scan local newspapers and to clip articles referring to the case. He also appears to have attempted to persuade another female, implicated by Kidd, to alter her testimony in return for immunity and release from prison. In its ire, the Court went so far as to accuse the police of providing the hypnotist with their investigation reports, though this allegation was denied by both police and prosecution representatives. It found also that the psychologist's destruction of the audiotapes of the hypnosis sessions with her, which he testified was in the interests of "recycling" them was "incredible." It added that "The Court has further observed his demeanor and considered his responses to questions during his many hours of testimony in this case. The Court does not credit his testimony as to the matters here involved" (p. 1038).

As Diamond (1980) put it,

> The *Emmett* and *Creamer* trials were a veritable nightmare of abuse by police, prosecutors, and a cooperative psychologist-hypnotist. For that reason, the granting of the writs of habeas corpus in those cases does not represent a per se rejection of pretrial hypnosis of witnesses. (p. 325)

This is true; the attempt to suppress Deborah Kidd's testimony resulted, as the Court stated, "in a criminal proceeding that bordered on the Kafkaesque" (p. 1018). It was the main consideration in the Court's permitting habeas corpus for Emmett and Creamer. The only testimony against the two men was provided in hypnosis, by Ms. Kidd. She was described as "a self-admitted former habitual and prolific user of amphetamines, prostitute and shoplifter" (p. 1036). Four separate juries, unaware of a number of discrepancies in the testimony she had presented on these separate occasions, had found her a credible witness. Further, when the defendants attempted to obtain the psychologist's tapes of the hypnosis sessions with Ms. Kidd, an earlier court ruled that they were privileged. In addition, there was not one scrap of physical evidence to link any of the nine accused persons with the murder scene: indeed, Kidd's testimony contradicted much of what the physical evidence at the murder site indicated about the killings. These included numerous fingerprints, none of which matched Kidd, or any of the nine arrestees.

The element that makes the case memorable is the role that hypnosis played in it. What most likely happened, though there is no means of verifying this surmise, is that the police and the professionally trained hynotist they consulted believed firmly in the "truth-telling" properties of hypnosis to the extent of disregarding physical evidence that ran contrary to Ms. Kidd's hypnotically elicited recall. On this view, the belief in hypnosis as a royal road to truth led them, in addition, to disregard inconsistencies in Ms. Kidd's various recalls and also to tamper with evidence that did not agree with what she "recalled." It did not help either that one of the investigating officers established an interpersonal relationship with Ms. Kidd. Such activity is not encouraged in *any* known police training manual.

This case introduced an additional complication; the belief in the authenticity of hypnotically elicited recollections appear to have been a major factor in keeping a number of people in prison for almost two years for a crime in which no physical evidence could be found linking them to it. In a second case reported by Diamond from around this period, hypnosis played a similar role, and illustrates an additional principle. The yoked cases of *United States v. Narciso and Perez* (1977) took place in Michigan. The defendants were two Philippine born female nurses who were working at the Ann Arbor Veterans Administration Hospital durng 1975. For some months previously, there had been a number of incidents where it appeared that some person had been injecting Pavulon (a curare derivative) into the tubing from which patients received medication, leading to a number of suspicious deaths. This had happened to Richard Neely, a patient at the time, who suffered and survived the respiratory arrest that resulted from the curare overdose.

In December of that year, Neely agreed to be hypnotically interviewed by a psychiatrist. At the first session, he vaguely described two individuals who, he believed, were at his bedside on the night of his pulmonary incident, but he made no identification. Later that night, after the hypnosis session, Neely was visited by an FBI agent who encouraged him to recall as much as possible about this earlier night. He received a second hypnosis session. Again, he provided vague descriptions of individuals who had been present that night, but again, he made no positive identification. Subsequently he was shown a line-up of photographs which included one of Ms. Perez; he recognized her as one of his attending nurses, but did not place her by his bedside on the night in question. A little over three weeks later, Neely spontaneously told FBI agents that he knew who had attempted to kill him. When shown the photos he had seen following the second hypnosis session, he immediately, and with great confidence, selected the one of Ms. Perez.

In addition, Neely had conversations with other people which suggested that his memory for the events of the near fatal night was fragmentary. Thus, during one of the hypnosis sessions, he mentioned a Caucasian female nurse and a Mexican male nurse as being in his room immediately prior to his respiratory arrest (p. 278). Following the second session, however, he identified a person who was shown not to have had any connection with the case. He made this identification after being told that this latter person had been born in the Philippines.

Finally, in late 1976, Neely testified under oath that he had known from the very beginning that Perez had been in his room on the specified night and that he had deliberately withheld this information in order to protect her. His story was now complex. He stated that he had deliberately passed over Ms. Perez's photograph three times when first shown the photographs in December 1975. He had changed his mind about the wisdom of this decision following his conversation with the FBI agent approximately three weeks later. He now insisted that he had known this from the beginning and that hypnosis had not in any way altered his memory.

There was, however, one major problem with Neely's memory. A psychiatrist testified at the trial that he had performed an examination and had concluded, on the basis of it, that Neely was a terminally ill patient, who had been an alcoholic for many years; indeed, he had stated that he had drunk between 15 and 25 bottles of beer daily for the previous 25 years. In addition, the psychiatrist diagnosed him as having borderline personality organization. Memory deficits for recently experienced events were indicated. He testified also that Neely was a suggestible individual on the basis of his performance during the hypnotic interviews, which were videotaped. He maintained that Neely idealized the FBI, which he perceived as an embodiment of the Good. Accordingly, during the interviews he had felt severe pressure to please the

FBI agents by helping them with their investigation. This witness concluded that what Neely had reported was not a true memory, but rather an admixture of fact and fantasy that was a direct product of his perceived need to assist the FBI.

The psychiatrist for the prosecution testified, in reviewing segments of the videotape, that Neely was low hypnotizable, possessed an impoverished fantasy life, and tended to use reason and logic in order to reach a conclusion. From this, the expert witness concluded that he was not unduly amenable to suggestion while in hypnosis. The witness expressed, also, great admiration for the skill displayed by the FBI agents in maintaining neutrality during their interviews with the witness. He stated that he believed that there was no more subtle or overt suggestion during these questionings than would occur in a normal social interaction. From this, he concluded that there was no risk that Neely's statements were anything but "true" memories.

The defense psychiatrist thought otherwise. His examination indicated that the FBI may have communicated inadvertent subtle cues which indicated their interest in certain parts of Neely's account of the events of the night in question. He noted that, from the line of questioning, the agents indicated an interest in a woman of Philippine origin and a single hospital room. This, in turn, may have communicated to Neely that they were not interested in a black man and a 20 bed hospital room, for example—both were matters to which Neely had referred spontaneously during hypnosis (p. 280). Further, the FBI agents had posed leading questions on occasions. For instance, instead of asking him "Who do you see?" the agent had asked him "Who could have done this to you?" The essence of this analysis was that

> for individuals, like Mr. Neely, who are subject to light trances, the communicated belief that the hypnotic experience will in fact cause certain results, leads to a strong pressure to provide validation and achieve the experience's objective—in this case a memory. (p. 280)

This may appear to be an esoteric point unless one is familiar with the recently growing scientific literature on eyewitness testimony that has not been aided by hypnosis. For instance, in one study (see Hilgard & Loftus, 1979) subjects saw films of an automobile accident. Subsequently, when questioned about the speed that the cars were traveling, different estimates were obtained depending upon whether the verb used was "hit," "smashed," "collided," "bumped," or "contacted" in the sentence "About how fast were the cars going when they _____ each other?" It should then not be so remarkable that an unhypnotizable person could similarly be led in a hypnotic context.

In its summation, the Court noted that the prosecution had relied upon a highly circumstantial case. Despite calling 89 witnesses, including 17 experts,

> the government submitted no direct proofs of the defendants' guilt on any count. No witness testified that the defendants ever had pavulon in their possession. No witness stated that the defendants ever injected anything into the victims. Nor was there any showing that the defendants were any more

familiar with the drug in question than any of numerous others within the hospital. Instead, the government sought to show through numerous witnesses that certain breathing failures were criminal in nature, that the defendants had the opportunity to commit these crimes, that they were present during the critical time period, during which, according to expert testimony, the drug must have been injected in order to have produced the observed effect and, lastly, that this presence during the critical time period was exclusive. (pp. 306-307)

As in *Emmett* and *Creamer*, there was substantial evidence of prosecutorial misconduct, so much so, that the Court characterized it as "having polluted the waters of justice" (p. 328). It included submission of documents to the defense well beyond the Court stipulated deadline, thus making it difficult to prepare the defense adequately; the deletion of material from documents; and attempts to then conceal that the deletions had been made. As far as the hypnotically elicited testimony was concerned, the Court ruled that it was admissible, on the grounds that it was not, "as a matter of law, the product of unduly suggestive pretrial investigative techniques" (p. 282). It further ruled that it was not sufficiently incredible to warrant it being stricken from the court records. There appears, however, to have been an element of the *Harding* court's thinking in its decision on hypnotic recall. The Michigan Court noted that "courts are always reluctant, except in truly compelling cases, to interfere with the jury's historical role to find the facts and assess credibility" (p. 283).

Further, in ruling that Neely's testimony was not so implausible that it could not be true, the Court added that "this opinion expresses no view as to the credibility or weight that a jury should attach to Mr. Neely's testimony" (p. 284).

In the end, the evidence of prosecutorial wrongdoing led to the two nurses obtaining a new trial, at which it was ruled that the prosecution had failed to prove its case against them.

In addition to citing these two cases, Diamond also cited three additional cases in which he had appeared as an expert witness testifying on the admissibility of witnesses who previously had been hypnotized. One of them (*People v. Diggs*, 1979), illustrates an important point. A woman had been assaulted in the rest room of a bar by a man who had grasped her from behind so that she had not been able to get a good look at him. She knew, however, that he was black, of medium build, and she had seen his eyes briefly. He had run away when she had said that she was pregnant, and that he might kill her baby. Subsequently, she identified a man from both a photo line-up and from a line-up that included the suspect. On both occasions, however, she was not absolutely certain. At trial, she indicated a similar hesitancy; it led to a hung jury and a mistrial was declared.

Following this, she was hypnotized by a psychiatrist, who audiotaped the transactions that occurred. Although the victim had previously stated that she had caught only a glimpse of her assailant, she immediately responded to the hypnotic suggestion that there was a mirror on the rest room wall which enabled her to see her assailant; no mention of this mirror had been made previous to the psychiatrist's suggestion. She now provided more details of the assailant's appearance and clothing as if she were seeing him in a mirror. Toward the end of the session, she was asked if the psychiatrist had suggested anything to her in hypnosis that might have altered her memory, and she replied that he had not. She now became very certain that the defendant was the assailant.

A hearing was held to determine the admissibility of her testimony. The psychiatrist testified that he had not suggested anything to her and that she was in such light hypnosis that he could not have influenced her memory of the assault or of the assailant's description. Diamond brought up the issue of the mirror in his testimony. The Court ruled to admit all testimony that had been given, namely, that of the victim and of the two hypnosis experts. The defendant, however, urged the prosecution and the defense to bargain. In the end, the defendant pleaded guilty to a lesser offense. He still professed his innocence, but believed that another trial might lead to a long prison sentence.

Cases such as these led Diamond to his now famous conclusion of 1980 that witnesses who have been hypnotized should not be permitted to testify in court on the grounds that they are incompetent to testify. This view may ultimately prevail in much the same manner that the use of hypnosis was restricted to physicians in France at the turn of the century. The French have since had no inclination to revive the legal battles involving hypnosis.

Regulation through Guidelines

Two years prior to Diamond's conclusion that hypnotically elicited testimony should be proscribed, an alternative viewpoint was expressed by Orne (1978) in an amicus brief to the United States Supreme Court concerning *Quaglino v. The People of the State of California*. This view argued that if hypnosis were used with a witness prior to trial, the hypnotic interview should follow certain specific guidelines. Orne maintained that

> it must be recognized that the use of hypnosis by either the prosecution or the defence can profoundly affect the individual's subsequent testimony. Since these changes are not reversible, if individuals are to be allowed to testify after having undergone hypnosis to aid their memory, a minimum number of safeguards are absolutely essential. (p. 25)

These guidelines were to undergo a number of revisions during the following years. As originally presented in the *Quaglino* brief, they consisted of approximately four tightly reasoned pages. At that stage, they sought to cover the most typical situation in which hypnosis was likely to be used investigatively. With the experience of less-modal circumstances, they were extended to cover less-typical situations, and in their most recent format (Orne *et al.*, 1985) they are approximately double their original length. In every case where revisions of the guidelines have occurred, the alteration has been in terms of clarifying the appropriate procedures that should be followed when a situation which is an exception to the general norm is encountered.

Thus, for instance, while the *Quaglino* version of the guidelines spoke generally about the court testimony of individuals who had undergone pretrial hypnosis, the most recent version is much more specific. It distinguishes between court jurisdictions that permit hypnotically elicited testimony (where the guidelines make it possible to evaluate the degree of impermissible suggestiveness) as opposed to those that do not (where the guidelines make it possible for the court to determine what matters were *not* reviewed or touched on in hypnosis). In addition, some jurisdictions permit witnesses who have been hypnotized to testify about what they recalled prior to hypnosis, even if some of these events were discussed in hypnosis. Here the guidelines become essential, since most individuals have difficulty in recalling whether the source of a current memory was the prehypnotic or the hypnotic phase of an investigation—especially when court testimony occurs many months, or even some years after a crime took place.

The *Quaglino* guidelines specified, as others had before, that the witness and the hypnotist should be alone in the room in which the hypnotic interview takes place. This has been altered to take cognizance of such situations as when the witness is a frightened child, and it could be appropriate to have a parent present, or when a film technician is needed to operate equipment for videotaping the session. The guidelines also present recommendations for situations where a police artist insists on preparing his composite during a hypnosis session.

Essentially though, the guidelines are designed to permit evaluation of the degree to which hypnotically elicited recollections may be the product, at least in part, of such extraneous factors as inadvertent cueing by the hypnotist or of confabulation. Orne has emphasized consistently that contrary to the belief of many practitioners, the guidelines can never eliminate such factors. All that is ever possible from a stringent utilization of them is an evaluation of the degree to which inadvertent cueing and/or confabulation may have occurred. For instance, if a new and seemingly important detail is first mentioned in hypnosis, despite not having been mentioned in any of the subject's prehypnotic interviews, the videotaped record of the hypnotic interview permits an independent evaluation of whether the hypnotist unintentionally asked a leading question.

The wealth of detail in the guidelines, which is a direct product of the range of actual situations that have been encountered over the last decade, is best communicated by quoting them verbatim in an appendix (see Appendix at the end of this chapter). They represent the most comprehensive attempt to balance the needs of an investigative agency, the rights of a potential defendant, and the psychological welfare of a victim of crime who has become a candidate for pretrial hypnosis.

The Proliferation of Cases Involving Hypnosis

Repercussions of the Harding Judgment

During the 1970s, the American courts were to see hypnosis looming larger in the testimony of witnesses. It was a period in which virtually nothing was heard of the *Frye* and *Cornell* decisions. The latter seems to have disappeared without a trace, despite the enthusiastic affirmations of Bryan (1962) and Arons (1967) of its landmark qualities. It is difficult to know quite why this was so; one possibility is that (as indicated in note 4 of this chapter) it was perceived by the courts as relevant only to the very limited situation of an imprisoned suspect, where the defense attorney should have every opportunity to prepare the defendant's case. Another possibility, not mutually exclusive, was that the courts felt that the *Harding* judgment of permitting jurors to examine the weight of the evidence represented the ultimate in judicial enlightenment. There did not appear to be any great recognition that the *Harding* court was requiring exercises in a highly difficult judgmental art.

Be this as it may, the *Harding* judgment was at the base of a number of cases during the 1970s, with mixed results. Sometimes courts made it the basis of their decision. On other occasions, they rejected it as irrelevant to the determination of a particular case, citing various reasons.

State v. Jorgensen (1971) was one of the first cases to come under the Harding rubric. It involved a double murder 11 years earlier of a young man and woman. The man's body was found the next day in his car; the woman's was found a month later in another location. One of the prosecution witnesses was a woman who had been with the accused and the two deceased for most of the night on which the murders had taken place. They had all met in a restaurant, and she had been instrumental in persuading the two victims to join in a drinking party in the nearby hills. There had been a near collision of the two automobiles involved, followed by a high speed chase of the soon to be murdered young man and woman by the accused. It culminated in a bloody fight at the spot where the man's body had been found.

The witness, however, insisted that she had not seen the actual killing. The state maintained that the witness had suffered a loss of memory as the result of the trauma of the events of that night.[12] She underwent a number of psychiatric interviews, some of which involved hypnosis and sodium amytal. In refusing Jorgensen's appeal, the Court ruled, following *Harding*, that the issues of the case, including hypnosis and sodium amytal, had been fully ventilated in court, and subjected to prolonged and rigorous cross-examination. The Court decided that testimony elicited by both these means was admissible. Further, the Court ruled that

> we do not believe that the fact that they had been subjected to certain psychiatric and medical examinations and procedures prior to testifying,

which were fully exposed in the evidence, would be a basis for disallowing their testimony. (p. 315)

The Court added, as in *Harding*, that the fact that the female witness had furnished different accounts of the events of the night of the murders was not a basis for disallowing her testimony. Finally, it ruled that the defense's objection to the hypnotically elicited testimony, and that derived from "truth serum," went to its weight, rather than to its admissibility. As with an earlier Jesuitical issue concerning the number of angels which could dance on the head of a pin, such intellectual gymnastics became the rule in courts that considered the *Harding* decision as crucial to its deliberations.

Similar thinking dominated *Wyller et al. v. Fairchild Hiller Corporation* (1974), in which the survivors of a helicopter crash sued the helicopter manufacturing company for negligence. One of the plaintiff-appellants, Wyller, had undergone hypnosis for the purpose of improving his limited recall of the events of the crash. Prior to his testifying, Fairchild had moved that he be disqualified on the grounds that the reliability of hypnosis had not been established. A lower court had thought otherwise and had admitted the testimony. The Appelate Court support this decision; it stated that

> we cannot accept Fairchild's argument that Wyller's testimony was rendered inherently untrustworthy by his having undergone hypnosis. Wyller testified from his present recollections, refreshed by the treatments. His credibility and the weight to be given such testimony were for the jury to determine. (p. 607)

An almost identical ruling to *Wyller* was rendered in *Kline v. Ford Motor Co., Inc.* (1975) where the survivor of an automobile accident sued the Ford Motor Company for negligence in the design of a Ford Pinto in which the driver had been killed and she had been a passenger. A lower court had ruled, in Ford's favor, that the survivor was incompetent to testify because she had been hypnotized. The Appeal Court reversed the lower court and, citing *Wyller* almost verbatim, ruled that her hypnotically assisted recall was admissible.

United States v. Adams (1978) represented the first occasion since Jorgensen that the *Harding* doctrine, solidified by *Wyller* and *Kline*, returned to criminal law. Adams was implicated by one of his two accomplices in a murder of a post office employee. The murder had occurred in the course of the robbery of a post office truck which had netted the robbers approximately $3,000 each. An eyewitness to the hold-up, during which Adams was alleged to have shot the truck driver five times, was hypnotized by a lay hypnotist who made no recording (either audio- or videotaped) of the hypnosis session and kept no record of the other persons present.

At the trial, the defense attempted unsuccessfully to have the witness's testimony limited to his prehypnosis statements. It then sought to discredit his testimony by contrasting his pre- and post-hypnosis statements. The defense did not question the contention that the prosecution had laid down an adequate foundation for the acceptance of hypnotically elicited testimony. Rather, it maintained that such testimony should not be admitted on the grounds of its inherent unreliability, and also, that it denied a defendant's right to confront the witness.

Although the Court was not explicit on this point, its decision appeared to refer to the now well-established scientific finding that hypnosis increases confidence for both correct and incorrect information, thereby rendering a hypnotized witness "unshakeable" (Warner, 1979). The Court ruled that, following *Wyller* and *Kline*, testimony based on "memories refreshed under hypnosis" is an issue concerning "credibility but not admissibility" (p. 198). It stated further, that courts considering this problem within the context of criminal proceedings had followed an identical approach, citing *Harding* and *Jorgensen*. It added that reversals of this principle had only occurred when the hypnotic procedures used had not been disclosed to the court; here it cited *Emmett v. Ricketts*. The Court concluded that it believed this to be sound reasoning.

Nevertheless, the Court indicated its concern about how hypnotically elicited testimony was collected, and emphasized the need for great care in obtaining it so as to ensure that what was presented to the Court was "the product of the subject's own recollections, rather than of recall tainted by suggestions received while under hypnosis" (pp. 198-199). As for Adams, the Court noted that he had not objected to the manner in which the foundation for the acceptance of hypnotically elicited testimony had been established, but rather that his attorney had argued that such testimony was inherently unreliable, thus rendering a hypnotized witness legally incompetent to testify. The Court stated that this premise had been rejected in *Kline*; it saw no reason for a different ruling within the context of crime.

One of the more tangled cases involving hypnosis during the 1970s was *State v. McQueen* (1978) in North Carolina. It involved a double homicide of the proprietor and an employee of a brothel in June of 1972. Following the murders, McQueen and another employee traveled widely across the United States before deciding to go their separate ways. McQueen was subsequently arrested in August 1972, in Pennsylvania. He was returned to Missouri to complete a prior prison term and then returned to North Carolina in 1977 to face charges stemming from the brothel slaying.

Meanwhile, shortly after separating from McQueen, his female companion surrendered to the FBI. Hypnosis entered the case as the result of her pleading amnesia for the events of the slayings. She maintained in court that "I knew I saw him kill them and sometimes I really knew I hadn't seen him; I just know, I couldn't remember" (p. 417). In hypnosis, however, she reported being able to regress to the day of the murders and recall that McQueen had shot the women. A remarkable feature of the case was that a tape of the hypnosis session with her was given to the defense attorney a day before she testified. The tape was not offered in evidence and the woman was not cross-examined about her testimony derived from hypnosis. The hypnotist was not asked to testify, although there was nothing to suggest his unavailability. Further, there was no testimony concerning the hypnotic procedure utilized, nor whether anything additional had been elicited in hypnosis.

Nevertheless, the Court ruled that the hypnotically elicited testimony was admissible, and left the jury to determine its credibility. It cited *Kline, Wyller, Jorgensen*, and *Harding* as instrumental in forming its judgment. It likened hypnotic "refreshment" of memory to any other kind of memory improvement procedure such as reading a document, having a conversation with another person, or undergoing a medical or psychiatric treatment. It gave great weight also to evidence indicating that McQueen had possession of weapons and jewelry taken from the murder site and that he had sought to sell the jewelry within hours of the fatalities.

Not all courts, however, of the 1970s followed the *Harding* decision, particularly in cases that involved hypnotizing a defendant. *State v. Pierce* (1974) in South Carolina, was a case in point. Pierce, charged with the murder of a woman, was examined by a lay hypnotist prior to coming to trial. The judge ruled that the hypnotist could testify on anything that assisted a psychiatrist, who was present at the hypnosis session, to determine the defendant's mental status. He ruled further that anything coming from hypnosis concerning Pierce's whereabouts on certain dates or his guilt or innocence, would be excluded. At the Appeals Court, the judge's actions were supported; the Court ruled that hypnotically elicited testimony is not admissible as evidence of the truth of the events of a crime and cited *State v. Pusch* as its legal precent.

By contrast, the Appeals Court in *Greenfield v. Commonwealth* (1974) in the Virginia Supreme Court, actually quoted *Harding* in upholding a lower court's decision to exclude the testimony of a psychiatrist concerning the results of using hypnosis. The Court ruled that in *Harding* the judgment emphasized that the victim's hypnotically elicited statements were substantially corroborated by other evidence. It noted that a number of experts in hypnosis agreed that hypnotically elicited testimony is unreliable, since a hypnotized person can invent or manufacture falsehoods. It lumped hypnosis with statements obtained from sodium amytal, considering that both of them were "unreliable and led to self-serving answers" (p. 421). Finally, the Court stated categorically, without presenting any reasons for its conclusion, that *Harding* rested on entirely different facts compared to *Greenfield*. One can only speculate that what led to this blunt conclusion was the Court's concern over the fact that Greenfield, as a defendant, might be lying. It also may have believed that the hypnotically elicited testimony presented by the witness against Greenfield was corroborated by other evidence. But the Court did not say whether it had considered such possibilities.

Confabulated Memory in Court

State v. Mack (1980), heard before the Minnesota State Supreme Court, was to be a landmark decision. In this case, the Court ruled that if a victim or witness was hypnotized, he or she could not testify in court. It ruled, however, that any additional information elicited in hypnosis could be used by police to construct a case against an ultimate defendant using independent physical evidence. In such a case, of course, as will be seen subsequently in *People v. Woods et al.* (1977), there would be no need for the hypnotized witness to testify, though there would probably be reasons for a hypnotized victim to take the stand. The Minnesota Court was not the first one, however, to take aim at *Harding*; earlier, the Michigan Court of Appeals, in *People v. Hangsleben* (1978), had ruled that the defendant had "failed to establish the reliability of hypnosis as a memory-jogging devise" and that "the only factual foundation offered to the trial court was defendant's assertion that the witness was a qualified psychiatrist" (pp. 544–545). It may not have assisted Hangsleben's case that he had confessed to the murders of two young girls, prior to hypnosis.

State v. Mack (1980) in Minnesota stemmed the tide of *Harding* decisions; it was particularly important, also, in being one of the first clearcut cases involving confabulated memory. Whereas in cases up to this point, it was rarely very clear what was happening (as in nineteenth-century cases such as Lévy and Castellan) there could be no doubt that the witness in *Mack* had confabulated.

The female witness-plaintiff had met Mack at a bar in May 1978, and subsequently he had driven her to a nearby motel where they took a room together on Mack's credit card. They had intercourse, fell asleep, and some time later she awoke to find a pool of blood between her legs. Mack called for an ambulance, and waited until it arrived. The ambulance driver testified in court that the witness appeared "quite drunk"; also that she had told him that it was not Mack's fault. She was taken to a hospital emergency department where she told the attending intern that she had been engaged in "sexual activity with fingers being placed in her vagina" (p. 766). A second intern offered the opinion that the injury could not have been the result of intercourse and also that, because of its length and depth, could not have been caused by a human finger. He said also that this type of injury could be the result of tearing after childbirth. Other parts of the court ruling indicate that at least one intern thought the wound could have been caused by a sharp instrument such as a knife.

Two days later, she phoned the police to report an assault. A police officer interviewed the interns, the defendant, and the defendant's ex-wife. Some six weeks later, he arranged for the woman to be hypnotized by a lay hypnotist. This hypnotist proceeded to suggest that in hypnosis she would remember the events in the motel with Mack as they actually occurred, but as though on a television screen, and without emotion. She now "recalled" that Mack, on entering the motel room had ordered her to get onto the bed and undress. She stated that "He told me to spread my legs . . . he pulled out this switchblade and told me he was going to kill me . . . he kept sticking this knife up me and I remember screaming and screaming" (p. 766).

She was given a suggestion which, if not a post-hypnotic suggestion as the court judgment strongly suggested, was certainly one implying that what she had reported in hypnosis was a "true" memory. She was told that her body and mind had been rejuvenated by hypnosis and that she would now have a very clear memory of the events of the night at the motel. The following day, what she had reported in hypnosis became the basis of a signed statement to the police which led to Mack's arrest some months later, in October 1978.

In finding Mack innocent, the Court emphasized that nothing reported in hypnosis was corroborated independently. In hypnosis, the alleged attack on her consisted of repeated stabbings. Her hospital record, however, indicated a single deep cut inside her vagina, and no damage to the external genitalia. In addition, besides pointing to the major discrepancies between the physical evidence concerning the woman's injury (which was consistent with her gynecological history) and her hypnotically "refreshed" recall of how it had been sustained, the Court noted other minor discrepancies concerning peripheral details. She testified that earlier that day, she had lunched with her father at a restaurant and had eaten a pizza. This particular restaurant did not offer pizza on its menu. She recalled that Mack drove a black Yamaha motorcycle; in fact, Mack owned a maroon Triumph.

In this case, the Minnesota Supreme Court did not merely cite the *Frye* ruling as the standard for considering the introduction of hypnotically elicited testimony; it went beyond *Frye* in ruling that "previously hypnotized witnesses could not testify in criminal proceedings concerning subject matter adduced at pretrial hypnotic interview" (p. 762). The Court stated that

> The crux of the problem is that hypnosis can create a memory of perceptions which neither were nor could have been made, and, therefore, can bring forth a "memory" from someone who cannot establish that she perceived the events she asserts to remember. Neither the person hypnotized nor the expert observer can distinguish between confabulation and accurate recall in any particular instance. After the hypnosis session, the hypnotically retrieved account differs in another way from ordinary human recall. . . . Because the person hypnotized is subjectively convinced of the veracity of the "memory," this recall is not susceptible to attack by cross-examination. (pp. 769-770)

This decision was clearly a major precedent for the issue of the admissibility of hypnotically elicited testimony. It rejected *Harding* on the grounds that this earlier court was mistaken in thinking that the testimony of a hypnotized witness was based on his or her "independent recollection," uninfluenced by suggestions from the hypnotist (overt or covert), and hence was both accurate and reliable. It asserted that, as with the polygraph, so-called "truth serum," and voice prints, the *Frye* ruling prevailed for hypnosis. The Court maintained that the "results of mechanical or scientific testing are not admissible unless the testing has developed or improved to the point where experts in the field widely share the view that the results are scientifically reliable as accurate" (p. 768).

But the Court went one step further than *Frye*. It felt that merely to reassert *Frye* would leave the door open for a case-by-case adjudication of whether hypnotically elicited testimony was admissible in any future case involving a hypnotized witness. Other American states have since done this. For instance, in *State v. Hurd* (1981) the Court ruled that when hypnotized witnessess were to be presented to a court, a pretrial adjudication would be held in which the main factor determining the admissibility of their testimony would be the degree to which the hypnotist had conformed with Orne's guidelines. This, of course raises the spectre of numerous expert witnesses for both prosecution and defense presenting lengthy submissions on whether the witness should or should not be heard. The Minnesota Court recognized this problem in stating that "a case-by-case decision on the admissibility question would be prohibitively expensive, and reveals the difficulty of getting experts qualified to testify about hypnosis as an investigative rather than a therapeutic tool" (p. 766). Clearly, the Court's primary motive was not to save itself time. It was throwing a gauntlet to proponents of an investigative utilization of hypnosis to demonstrate that there could be no danger of trial by fantasy in permitting a hypnotized witness to testify in the absence of corroborating independent evidence. This was to become the prevailing view of the 1980s up to the present time.

Certainly, the *Mack* court had good reason to be concerned about the feasibility of case-by-case adjudications of the admissibility of hypnotic testimony. At the time of the *Mack* decision, there were approximately 500 cases on the books in Minnesota alone awaiting hearing. These were permitted to lapse following the *Mack* decision. The popularity of hypnosis among police forces as a means of obtaining testimony was clearly on the rise during the late 1970s to the extent of reaching epidemic proportions as far as the law courts were concerned.

One final aspect of the *Mack* decision that deserves comment is that it was the first court to specify clearly the role that hypnosis may play in police investigations. The Court stated:

> We do not foreclose, by this opinion, the use of hypnosis as an extremely useful investigative tool when a witness is enabled to remember verifiable factual information which provides new leads to the solution of a crime. A witness under hypnosis may, for instance, bring forth information previously unknown to law enforcement authorities, such as a license plate number, which subsequently aids police in identification of a suspect. Experts see no reasonable objection to the use of hypnosis in this manner, provided the witness is willing, as long as the material remembered during hypnosis is not subsequently used in court as part of an eyewitness' testimony. Even when the use of hypnosis is truly to investigate a crime rather than to create a witness, adequate safeguards should be established to assure the utmost freedom from suggestion upon the hypnotized person's memory recall in the event he or she must later be called to testify to recollections recorded before the hypnotic interview. (p. 771)

Permitting previously hypnotized witnesses to testify about their prehypnotic recall was to raise some further problems, as will be seen in a subsequent section. Nevertheless, the underlying principle for the investigative use of hypnosis was sound. This is well illustrated by a case that had occurred in California a few years earlier.

People v. Woods et al. (1977), which occurred at Chowchilla, California, involved a group of schoolchildren in a school bus who were abducted at gunpoint in July 1976 by three masked men. They were then transferred to several vans, driven to a rock quarry, and sealed inside a rectangular tomb beneath the ground. Subsequently, the driver and two of the older boys were able to dig their way out. In routine police interview, the driver had but fragmentary recall of information of interest to police.

Hypnosis was used because he had made a deliberate attempt to memorize the license plate numbers of two vans but had experienced great fear since he was being watched closely by the abductors. In hypnosis, he suddenly called out two license plate numbers; one was completely wrong, but the other matched the license plate number of one of the vans on six of its seven digits. It should be noted that he had provided three of the correct digits prior to hypnosis. This led to the arrest, conviction and sentencing to life imprisonment of three individuals.

This case is cited often by proponents of police hypnosis who do not see a need for independent corroboration. The point is missed usually, however, that the bus driver did not have to testify in court. There was no need for him to do so. The information he provided in hypnosis was sufficient to permit police to construct an independent case against the defendants which did not rely on the driver's hypnotic recall. Overlooked, on occasions, also, is the fact that one of the licence plate numbers recalled by the driver was erroneous. Overall, the Chowchilla abduction is as good an illustration as any in the literature that what is "recalled" in hypnosis may be fact, may be fantasy, and is likely to be an admixture of both.

Other Major Court Decisions

Since *State v. Mack*, no fewer than 14 other American State Supreme Courts[13] have ruled that if a victim or witness is hypnotized he or she cannot testify in court. Included in the 15 are Maryland and North Carolina which overturned *Harding* and *McQueen*, respectively. Hypnotically elicited testimony has come to be seen as hearsay evidence, and the situation has been likened to other forms of potentially unreliable information that police have at their disposal at the beginning of an investigation. Appearing as an expert witness in the Ontario Supreme Court in *Naeyaert and Elias* (1985), Orne offered this analogy:

> We concluded that hypnosis was useful in investigative context for the simple reason that the police and investigative authorities often have to rely on unreliable sources. In our American idiom I point out that a crime may be committed and a bookey is consulted by the police and he says "well, on the

street they say Lefty did it" now, that sometimes provides a lead and they check up on Lefty and in fact he turns out to be the man that did the crime. That's fine. They then bring that evidence in court and he's tried. They don't bring in the bookey to say. "On the street they say Lefty did it." And so it's fine if you use it in investigation and have totally independent evidence as to the basis for a legal action. But it's likely to lead to a serious miscarriage of justice if you use unreliable bases for testimony. (pp. 26-27, spelling and syntax as in the original)

It is of interest, nevertheless, to describe some of the cases in which the *Mack* ruling was adopted by subsequent State Supreme Courts; some of them clearly involved confabulation of the central facts of a hypnotized witness's testimony. Others illustrate some of the problems that can arise from an investigative use of hypnosis and the manner in which Orne's guidelines can be brought to bear in evaluating them.

In *People v. Kempinski* (1980) (mentioned briefly at an earlier point in this chapter), an eyewitness to murder in Joliet, Illinois had been hypnotized and provided a description that led to Kempinski's arrest and trial, at which he was exonerated. An ophthalmologist testified that at a distance of 270 feet in poor lighting conditions (the actual location of the hypnotized witness relative to the murder) it would not have been possible to make a positive identification. He indicated further that such an identification would only have been possible within a 25-foot radius. Even within this perimeter, as has been noted subsequently, there would still be no guarantee that what the witness recalled in hypnosis was fact as opposed to fantasy (Perry & Laurence, 1983).

The witness's testimony in hypnosis, which was videotaped, showed other discrepancies. At different times during the hypnotic interview which was conducted by a police officer with 32 hours of training, the witness described the person he supposed he had seen variously as "very ugly" and "ordinary looking" and as being "five feet ten" and "six feet one." The witness reported also that he had first met Kempinski when the latter had been a high school senior, and he himself was a sophomore. It was established subsequently, that the accused had not gone further than his second year of high school. Nevertheless, Kempinski stood trial despite these false identifications and because, also, the police in this case did not attempt independent verification of the hypnotic "recall." This, in turn, may reflect additionally the compelling quality of verbal reports elicited in the course of hypnotic age regression (see Chapter 11). Indeed, the eyewitness in this particular case can be seen in the video of his hypnotic session stating, with deep conviction; "I *know* him." Subsequently, in response to a question about the face he was describing, he stated: "I don't forget things like that" (Barnes, 1982).

Kempinski may illustrate one further principle about hypnotically elicited testimony; one that has already been broached in Orne's guidelines. One of them states that the hypnotist should be an impartial expert whose professional status is independent of law enforcement investigators, prosecution and defense. In addition, this person should be minimally informed of the details of the event to be recalled. Kempinski was known to the police through a previous charge against him of entering a house and stealing two firearms. The home belonged to the Joliet Chief of Detectives (where the murder had been committed). He was the head of this particular investigation and was in a position to communicate his suspicions to the police officer who conducted the hypnotic interview. At this stage, it is unlikely that this supposition can ever be confirmed or disconfirmed; the point, however, is that given the circumstances of the case, and the failure of police to notice that the hypnotically elicited testimony provided a weak case against Kempinski, this possibility cannot be overlooked. Perhaps, more to the point, the utilization of guidelines would have made such speculation irrelevant.

People v. Shirley (1982) in California was a case that was somewhat more difficult to pin down in terms of its central details. In its peripheral details, however, there were strong grounds for thinking that hypnosis had produced confabulation. It involved the classic one-on-one situation: The witness accused Shirley, a marine, of having raped her. Shirley, the defendant, maintained that the woman's sexual relations with him were voluntary. Such claims and counter-claims are difficult enough to sort out without hypnosis; the added ingredient of hypnosis often compounds an already confused, and highly charged, situation. This appears to have been the situation in *Shirley*—the Court characterized it as "a classic case of conflicting stories" (p. 1). To add to the dilemmas of *Shirley*, a deputy district attorney hypnotized the victim-plaintiff on the night before she was due to testify in court. Subsequently, she gave self-contradictory testimony which also differed from her testimony at a preliminary hearing.

Some of these discrepancies were noted by the Court. She had been drinking at a bar where she worked and had spoken with Shirley during the evening. All evidence was that she was intoxicated to some degree and was accompanied to her apartment by another marine. She testified that she then passed out fully clothed on the living room couch; and reported in hypnosis that she was awoken sometime later by Shirley standing naked by the coffee table holding a butcher's knife. The Court noted that at different times she described this object as an ice pick and as a screwdriver. At trial, the prosecution did not produce any of these weapons. Shirley is then said to have taken her into the bedroom, ordered her to remove her clothes, and compelled her to orally copulate him for several minutes. Following this, he bound and gagged her with her underclothes, put her head on the bed, and had intercourse with her for approximately one half hour.

Up to this point, she said that the apartment had remained totally dark, and she saw Shirley as a shadow. She testified that he ceased the intercourse abruptly, removed her bonds and gag, and returned her to the living room, where he turned on the light. She claimed that as they entered the living room, Shirley told her that he had intended to take her money, but on seeing a bible on her nightstand next to the bed, had changed his mind. The Court noted that no explanation was given of how he had recognized a bible in the dark. For the next half hour she sat on his lap, both of them naked, on the couch. He then volunteered to bring some beer from his nearby apartment, dressed, returned, undressed, and resumed the conversation in the same position. There is more, but these bare bones of the story convey its gist. It differed in several significant details from her prehypnosis testimony, which was given to the police on the night of these events, and also from her testimony at a preliminary hearing.

Prehypnosis, her account was that she had fallen asleep fully clothed on the living room couch and had awoken in the bedroom naked, bound, and gagged. Also, prior to hypnosis she testified that, while she was bound and gagged, Shirley had intercourse with her both before and after the alleged oral copulation; following hypnosis, she maintained that oral copulation preceded intercourse. There were other discrepancies. Before hypnosis, she stated that her hands were tied during oral copulation; they were no longer so in her hypnotic version of the events. Also, her initial story to the police was that the first time she saw the knife/ice pick/screwdriver was when they returned to the living room following intercourse, while her subsequent story was that she saw it when she awoke on the couch before entering the bedroom.

Seemingly, the question facing the *Shirley* court was which of three accounts were credible—one of her two, or Shirley's. The woman's belief was that her prehypnotic recollections were vague, and it had been for this reason that she had consented to being hypnotized—she believed that hypnosis enabled a person to "remember more than normal" (p. 14). She believed also that hypnosis had filled in a gap in her memory and had helped her to remember that certain events had taken place in a different sequence to what she had recalled originally. The Court thought otherwise.

In a lengthy and erudite decision, the Court traced the history of *Harding* through the 1970s. It noted that courts initially followed *Harding* with little or no analysis of the issue of whether hypnosis does, in fact, "refresh" memory. It was assumed that a witness was testifying from his or her own "true" memory, and that credibility could be tested through cross-examination. Toward the end of the decade, however, courts had become aware of the dangers of using hypnosis for memory enhancement, and had begun to develop legal safeguards for admissibility of hypnotically elicited testimony. This, the *Shirley* court believed, had created an unworkable situation, and it drew on *State v. Hurd* (1981) to make its point. As indicated earlier, the *Hurd* court had ruled for a case-by-case pre-trial adjudication of admissibility of hypnotically elicited testimony. The *Shirley* court considered that this approach

> would provide a fertile new field for litigation. There would first be elaborate demands for discovery, parades of expert witnesses, and special pre-trial hearings, all with concomitant delays and expenses. Among the questions our trial courts would then be expected to answer are scientific issues so subtle as to confound the experts. Their resolution would in turn generate a panoply of new claims that could be raised on appeal, including difficult questions of compliance with the "clear and convincing" standard of proof. And because

the hypnotized subject would frequently be the victim, the eyewitness, or a similar source of testimony against the defendant, any error in ruling on the admissibility of such testimony could easily jeopardize otherwise unimpeachable judgements of conviction. In our opinion, the game is not worth the candle. (p. 31)

Accordingly, this court rejected the notion that is was possible to determine whether either of the plaintiff's accounts of her interaction with Shirley was true, and it recognized, implicity, that both could have been false. It followed the *Mack* court and held "that hypnotically induced testimony is so widely viewed as unreliable that it is inadmissible under the *Frye* test" (p. 32).

A third case illustrated a quite different point. In a grisly rape, torture, and murder of an elderly retired female schoolteacher in Union Mills, North Carolina (Kirby, 1984), four young black men were charged solely on the basis of the hypnotically elicited reminiscences of one of them, Reece Forney; there was no physical evidence linking any of the other three to the murder scene. The "evidence" that the suspects were at the scene concerned the existence of a rake; this particular fact, in accordance with common police practice, was kept confidential on the logic that only the actual killer(s) would know about it. At the trial, much was made of Forney's describing the rake, and it was not until the four men had been found guilty that it became known that Forney's "knowledge" of the rake did not occur until the following interaction in hypnosis:

> *Forney*: (describing walking home after the crime) Seems like I grabbed something and ran back to . . . I walked most of the way because I was so tired.
> *Hypnotist*: (handed a note by the policeman which instructed him to ask about a rake) What did you grab?
> *Forney*: Base of something. Base of something.
> *Hypnotist*: Was it a rake?
> *Forney*: I don't know. It could have been.
> *Hypnotist:* Where did you got the rake from?
> *Forney*: I thing I got it from the yard of a house. I was so mad. . . .
> *Hypnotist*: What are you doing with the rake?
> *Forney*: Running down at them. . . . seems like I was fighting them.
> *Hypnotist*: Did they take the rake from you?
> *Forney*: Yeah.
> *Hypnotist:* And what did they do with it?
> *Forney*: I don't know. (Kirby, 1984, p. 160)

Few cases so well illustrate how, as the result of an inappropriate cue from the hypnotist, a pseudomemory can be created, though the precise mechanism (fantasy or compliance) cannot be reconstructed. Nevertheless, the fact that Forney appeared to know about the rake was sufficient to launch criminal proceedings against him and the three other men.

Not all American courts, however, have followed the *Mack* decision. In Wyoming, for instance (*Chapman v. State*, 1982), the Court ruled that the use of hypnosis does not make a witness incompetent to testify; the credibility of such testimony could, if maintained, be left to the jury to probe and evaluate. It added that the *Hurd* court's strictures for admissibility were likewise unnecessary and maintained that hypnosis was influenced by too many variables to be confined to such a "rigid" procedure. Nevertheless, it felt that compliance with some of these admissibility rules could increase the credibility of such testimony.

A Wisconsin court (*State v. Armstrong*, 1983) ruled that it was legitimate to refresh witness's recollections with hypnosis, provided that it could be demonstrated subsequently that hypnotically affected identification and testimony were not the result of impermissible suggestion, and provided also that the other side was permitted to present expert testimony to the jury concerning the effect of hypnosis on recall. It ruled further, that the *Frye* ruling "applied to the admissibility of 'expert testimony deduced from a well-recognized scientific principle'" (pp. 10-11), whereas, in the case it was adjudicating, it was the post-hypnosis identification of any eyewitness that was in question, not the testimony of an expert.

Despite these variations in Wyoming and Wisconsin, the trend of American State Supreme Courts has been to recognize the severe problems posed by confabulated memory, and to impose *Frye* rulings on hypnotically elicited testimony. They have not been without their critics. Reiser has stated recently that

> It is certainly possible for a witness, hypnotized or not, to lie, confabulate or fantasize *if motivated to do so*. However, my experience over a 12-year period with witnesses or victims who cooperated in an investigative hypnosis interview suggests that *confabulation does not routinely or invariably occur*. The legal-psychological literature on eyewitness problems and the misidentifications of suspects by nonhypnotized witnesses clearly indicate that this is a generic problem involving individual cognitive processes, sensory perceptual mechanisms, apperceptive mass, attitudes, values and belief systems (Buckhout, 1974; Loftus, 1979; Yarmey, 1979). *These human cognitive variables have been labelled incorrectly as a hypnosis problem, leading to confusion, misunderstanding and negative legal consequences* (Diamond, 1980; Orne, 1979). (1985, pp. 515-516, italics added)

It is true that confabulation is not invariable nor routine, but this statement appears to admit that it *can* occur. The question remains one of how it can be detected, and thus far the guidelines proposed by Orne and the *Frye* ruling imposed by 15 American State Supreme Courts provide the only guarantee that an individual will not be tried in court on the basis of another individual's fantasies, which are most likely to be motivated by the desire to please, rather than deceive, police officers. At the same time, however, two recent court decisions by the Pennsylvania State Supreme Court, which adopted a *Frye* ruling in 1981, may upset the delicate balance that has begun to emerge in recent years.

Back to Square One?

In a recent case (*Commonwealth v. Smoyer*, 1984), a man was convicted of aggravated assault, homicide by vehicle, and involuntary manslaughter. The incident occurred as the result of a high-speed car chase in 1977 in which the defendant's automobile allegedly collided with one driven by his wife, which then crashed into a telephone pole. She was killed, but both their son and a male friend of the deceased survived. The latter was hypnotized by a police officer three months after the incident took place.

Prior to hypnosis, he had recalled that Smoyer's car had struck his wife's car on at least two occasions; in addition, he recalled that, on seeing her husband, the wife said: "He's going to kill me." With the introduction of hypnosis, he proceeded to recall that the wife's car had been hit for a third time and that this had caused it to run into the telephone pole. At the original trial, the judge permitted this hypnotically elicited, and damaging, testimony to be admitted, stating that "the use of hypnotism did not render a witness incompetent, but was a factor to be used by the jury in assessing the credibility of the witness" (p. 1306).

On appeal, the Superior Court ruled that the man's prehypnotic testimony was admissible, but that his hypnotically elicited testimony was not. It ruled that the admission of the hypnotically elicited testimony was, if in error, harmless; the defendant appealed this decision to the State Supreme Court. This court ruled that its admission, though in error, had not adversely affected the decision of the lower court. It ruled also that

> Whenever a person previously hypnotized is offered as a witness, offering party must so advise court, and show what testimony to be presented was established and existed previous to any hypnotic process; person conducting hypnotic session must be trained in process and be neutral of any connection with issue or parties; and trial judge shall instruct jury that testimony of witness previously hypnotized should be carefully scrutinized and received with caution. (p. 1305)

More was soon to come. In the following year, the same court made a similar ruling in the case of *Commonwealth v. DiNicola* (1985). The surrounding incident centered on a fire that had broken out in a woman's apartment in a two story building in Erie, Pennsylvania. Her two children and an upstairs neighbor had perished in it. On the night of the fire, which occurred in late August 1979, the defendant, the woman, and her male friend had been drinking beer and smoking marijuana. The latter two had retired to the woman's bedroom to have intercourse, following which they fell asleep. They were awakened by the flames, and all three persons were able to escape.

In her statement to police, a week after the fire, the woman recalled that after putting the children to bed, the three people had continued to smoke marijuana, drink beer, and converse. She had taken a long-distance telephone call, had heard a commotion in the kitchen between the two men, following which she and her male friend had adjourned to the bedroom to have intercourse. DiNicola had used the bathroom to shower, following which she recalled hearing various fumblings around the apartment. She had voiced her concern to her male friend, who said that it was merely DiNicola's intoxication, and was no cause for concern. They began to fall asleep, only to be awakened by the smoke from the fire. It may be of some relevance that she described the marijuana as especially strong, and she believed that it may have been laced with an additive.

Approximately two weeks later she underwent hypnosis, which appears to have been conducted by a lay hypnotist. The session was tape-recorded, but the tape was lost subsequently. All that remained was a portion of a written transcript of the tape. She now recalled that the noises she heard were of DiNicola leaving the apartment, and returning shortly afterward. She recalled also that he had made sexual overtures toward her, which were rejected, and that the children had formed a negative opinion of him. Other details recalled included the substances of both the telephone conversation and the conversation she had with her male friend while DiNicola was showering. At the original trial, neither the fact that she had been hypnotized, nor the testimony's variance from her prehypnotic recollections were revealed to the Court.

The Court ruled in a manner similar to the *Smoyer* court. It held that "Before a hypnotically refreshed witness can testify to his or her prehypnotic recollection, the witness' prehypnotic recollection must be verified by evidence which is clear and convincing" (p. 607).

This may appear to be a cautious and moderate decision, but in fact, it appears to return the debate to the days prior to *State v. Mack* (1980). The very purpose of utilizing hypnosis is to elicit additional information, so as, presumably to build a stronger case. A corollary of this is that normally, but not inevitably, the prosecution believes that it does not have sufficient evidence against a defendant; hence the need for additional, hypnotically elicited detail.[14] When it is realized in addition, that many police officers do not recognize a problem with confabulated recall (see Reiser, 1985), rulings such as this permit prosecutorial fishing expeditions; if sufficient information is not obtained prehypnosis, hypnosis can then be introduced in the full knowledge that if nothing more is obtained, the witness's prehypnotic testimony remains admissible. To compound the matter, this can be done with the most admirable of good intentions that are based on the belief that hypnotically induced confabulations of memory are simply generic to the general problem of eyewitness identification. Finally, this decision raises a particularly complex issue of which more may be heard. The situation could occur where a witness, prior to hypnosis, is not very certain of some detail(s). Given that hypnosis increases certainty, it could happen that this witness would become certain about such a detail(s), even though it may have been erroneous from the very beginning. The legal implications of such a witness testifying about prehypnotic recall in court are mind-boggling.[15]

Investigative Hypnosis Outside the United States

A final interesting point is the consideration of the manner in which other countries have dealt with the introduction of hypnosis into their legal systems. In some of them, there are currently no legal precedents, although there is evidence of considerable activity and utilization of hypnosis.

In Great Britain, hypnosis appears to have been used quite considerably by police, although no court has yet been informed of this fact. Nevertheless, it is known that at least one rape victim in recent years has testified at the Old Bailey, without the Court being made aware that she had been previously hypnotized by a London psychiatrist (Barnes, 1982).

In addition, the procedures utilized by at least one clinical psychologist are of a nature that are at much variance with the American guidelines. Haward (1980) described some of the situations he himself has encountered in his own practice with rape victims. He wrote:

> Hypnotists, especially clinicians, who are used to practicing in the privacy of a therapist-patient relationship and a specially equipped therapy room, may feel overwhelmed when required to carry out a domiciliary assignment in a small bedsitter and in the company of a woman police constable chaperone, the C.I.D. [Criminal Investigations Department] police officer in charge of the investigation, his assistants, as well as the accompanying technicians with recording equipment. Apart from the inhibiting effect such a crowd may have on the hypnotist, they can prove too threatening, frightening or otherwise overpowering to the rape victim to permit her to relax sufficiently for the trance to be induced. Different constabularies tend to work differently, and some are content to leave the hypnotist to undertake the hypnotic session in his own venue and without police officers being present. Others insist on police representatives recording firsthand the statements made by the hypnotized subject. The author has obtained his best results with forensic hypnosis when this has been carried out in his hospital consulting rooms without observers being present, and has been least effective when working in an unsuitable domiciliary environment with numerous police officers in attendance.... One of the advantages of having the senior detective present is that from his overall knowledge of the case he can suggest questions to be put to the witness which arise from the statement being made at the time. When the interrogation is being planned completely in advance and left entirely to the hypnotist, opportunities to explore unexpected but relevant areas of interest may be overlooked. When the hypnotist is asked to carry out the interrogation himself, it is important that he has the fullest possible briefing on the crime, and has access to all the relevant information in the hands of the C.I.D. (p. 11)

Elsewhere, Haward provided information that some British police departments conduct hypnosis interviews in conditions shrouded in the utmost secrecy. He reported:

> British police have been strangely unforthcoming about their use of hypnotists. One constabulary for whom the reviewer had undertaken forensic

hypnosis during the last fifteen years denied all knowledge of it to an investigating journalist. Another constabulary, requesting the reviewer's help in hypnotizing a large batch of witnesses, booked him into a remote hotel under an assumed name in order to conceal his presence as a forensic hypnotist—a situation which led to some embarrassment when on arrival he forgot his nom de hypnose! (1981, p. 26)

Clearly, there is much potential for an inadvertent injustice in Britain in a situation where a clinical psychologist is willing to assist police in situations that he himself considers to be less than optimal, and where strict secrecy is demanded and obtained. In such a situation, a court would probably never know if a witness had been previously hypnotized. In addition, Haward feels it necessary to have full details of a crime. He is seemingly unaware that, as in *United States v. Narciso and Perez* (1977), such full prior knowledge may produce an account of the crime that is more in line with the investigating officer's suspicions than with the witness's actual recollections.

The British Home Office issued a draft set of guidelines for the use of hypnosis by police in the summer of 1984. These guidelines, for the most part, followed those compiled by Orne. They were explicit in stating that hypnosis should only be used in "very serious crime" and as a last resort when all other methods have been tried without success. This specification makes it less likely that the candidate for hypnosis will be cued by the hypnotist concerning the police hypothesis—at least in cases where the police are at a dead end and genuinely have no hypothesis. The Home Office recommended also that where hypnosis had been used, the prosecution and the defense should be informed that some of the evidence has been gained by this means. This suggests that the British Home Office still thought as recently as 1984 that it could be safe to introduce hypnotically elicited testimony in court, despite the recent American legal history of the last quarter century.

A second draft of these guidelines appeared in May 1987. It was still felt by British authorities that there could be situations in which hypnotically elicited testimony might have to be presented in court; in such circumstances "proper corroboration" (p. 7) should exist. The author(s) of the document have felt here that it was best for the legal community to determine what constitutes proper corroboration. This more recent draft reasserted the belief that if hypnosis is used at any stage in the collection of evidence, both prosecution and defense should be informed. It showed, also, an even more acute awareness of the problems that can occur when hypnosis is used in the evidence-collecting process, even when it is done in good faith and following strict procedures. In particular, it emphasized that given the lack of legal precedents on the evidentiary value of hypnotically elicited testimony, and the fallibility of hypnosis as an information-gathering tool, its use should be discouraged, being reserved for very serious crime in situations where the investigating police have no further leads.

In Australia, the police are far more forthcoming about their use of hypnosis, especially to the local media.[16] Since 1980, there have been approximately 20 reports of cases where hypnosis was utilized, almost entirely in Sydney and Melbourne; most of them involved police officers with 32 hours of training. One case, in Melbourne, which occurred in 1966 was still being investigated in 1983. In at least one other (unless it was a journalistic aberration of reporting), confabulation can be suspected strongly. A police officer who utilizes hypnosis presented a lecture on his practice in 1983 at which media representatives were present. At it, he "showed a videotape of a young man who was able to recall accurately the number plate of a car speeding away from him in the dark with its lights out."[17]

The parallels with *People v. Kempinski* (1980) are apparent, though no subsequent prosecution appears to have occurred, and hypnotically elicited testimony has not yet been tested in an Australian court. The videotape of a hypnotic session was shown in a magistrate's court in Sydney in August 1982, and the previously hypnotized female victim was permitted to testify; subsequently, the plaintiff was committed for trial. Again, however, no more has been heard of this 1982 case. It is clear, though, that hypnosis is utilized extensively by the police in Sydney. The police officer who provided the anecdote about the car license plate number reported that in the previous two years he had utilized hypnosis with more than 300 victims or witnesses of crime including rape, hit and run driving, indecent exposure, and murder. While he emphasized that corroborative evidence is essential and that charges are not laid on the basis of hypnotically elicited recall alone, it is possible that, as with Britain, Australian courts may have unknowingly received testimony from witnesses who have been hypnotized.

By contrast to Great Britain and Australia, New Zealand courts have been far more progressive in recognizing the dangers of a previously hypnotized witness testifying in court without the court's knowledge of this fact. One case involved the abduction of a 14-year-old girl who had been held for ransom. She was subsequently located by police and hypnotized in the hope that she would be able to provide added details about the abduction and her abductors. The case reached the New Zealand Court of Appeal, which rendered its judgment in August 1985 on whether her court testimony was admissible, given that she had been hypnotized (*The Queen v. McFelin and McFelin*). The Court ruled that there was sufficient independent evidence to incriminate the McFelins in the abduction, and it refused to overturn their conviction. While recognizing the formidable dangers of utilizing hypnosis investigatively, and noting also that American courts had moved from *Harding* to *Frye* in recent years, the Court left it for the individual trial judge to determine whether it would be safe to admit such testimony in any future circumstances. This could, of course, lead to a New Zealand version of the *Hurd* procedures, and all that this implies at a legal level. On the other hand, the Court ruled that "the fact that the witness was hypnotized should be disclosed to the defense, and all relevant transcripts and information provided on request." The Court added that

> the judge should have regard to whether the hypnotism was carried out by a qualified person independent of the police and the prosecution, and with sufficient safeguards against the influencing of the subject by suggestions or otherwise. (p. 10)

The Court, in short, recognized the problems, even if its solutions may ultimately provide difficulties for a person who is obliged to face charges that are based solely on the hypnotically elicited recall of a victim or witness.

There is less a recognition of these problems in Canada, which, after the United States, has the longest contemporary judicial history involving hypnosis, dating from *Rex v. Booher* (1928) (see Bélanger, Laurence, & Perry, 1984). Canada may have, also, the distinction of the earliest recorded utilization of hypnosis for political investigative purposes. According to Dr. Olivier Robitaille, a Québec physician, animal magnetism was introduced into the province by Edward Gibbon Wakefield, in 1838. Wakefield was one of Lord Durham's associates, and co-author of the famous *Durham Report*. He was a well-known magnetist and used his talents in an original manner. In order to become acquainted with the French-Canadian population, he would visit various families and entertain them on the topic of animal magnetism, following which he would propose magnetizing a few persons. He would then enquire about the political climate and opinions in the country, and report to Lord Durham (Drolet, 1970). It is not possible to calculate the ratio of political fantasy to fact that he obtained by this means.

There has been a small handful of Canadian cases involving hypnosis since *Booher*, but two decisions of the 1980s are perhaps the most relevant to current Canadian law. In *Her Majesty the Queen v. Allan Dale Zubot* (1981), the Court of Queen's Bench of Alberta in the Judicial District of Medicine Hat rendered a *Harding* decision in permitting hypnotically elicited testimony to be presented to the Court, and in instructing the jury that "you are the triers of fact. It is for you to make up your minds what happened" (p. 24). Evidence was presented by the police officer who had hypnotized the sole witness in this case, by Martin Reiser, and by a lay hypnotist for the defense. Zubot was acquitted, but the case had an ironic twist; at a time that the State of Maryland was about to relinquish *Harding* (*Collins v. State*, 1981) and adopt a *Frye* ruling, a Canadian court embraced *Harding*. The case is yet another instance of how, by relying solely on hypnotically elicited recall as evidence of implication in a crime, a legal proceeding can be turned into a trial by fantasy. There was no evidence (other than circumstantial) that Zubot was, as he was charged, an accomplice to murder until a female witness was hypnotized by a police officer. She made a positive identification of Zubot at the murder site on the night that the murder had been committed. She lived nearby and had looked through her bathroom window in conditions of light that may not have permitted positive identification. Further, Zubot had been pointed out to her by police officers as a potential accomplice to the murder. Shortly after this, she was hypnotized.

Following hypnosis, she could now "clearly" see the backyard of the adjoining house where the murder had occurred.

In addition, she had not previously told anyone that she recognized Zubot as being at the murder site until she was hypnotized. Also, when asked why she had been unable to make a prehypnosis identification, she stated that "she was frightened and she didn't want to be involved" (p. 20).

More recently, the same Court of Queen's Bench of Alberta in the Edmonton Judicial District had to decide on the hypnotically elicited recall of a man who had been convicted on two counts of murder, but who pleaded amnesia for the events of the crime. Not until he had been hypnotized did he claim to be able to recall what happened on the night of the shootings; the case was thus one of mental status and degree of criminal responsibility (*Her Majesty the Queen v. Clark*, 1984).

In what can only be described as an unusual role reversal, the expert for the defense was a lay hypnotist who had previously served on the London (England) police force, and now headed a private investigation agency in Edmonton. A Doctor of psychology represented the prosecution. The judge ruled that where the opinions of the two experts conflicted, he accepted the evidence of the psychologist. Indeed, he stated that the lay hypnotist was "not, in my view, an expert in matters pertaining to the human mind and the states of consciousness" (p. 7).

In addressing the issue of the admissibility of hypnotically elicited recall, the judge maintained that, *in principle*, "there would appear to be nothing to distinguish hypnotically-refreshed testimony from testimony refreshed by other means" (p. 9), such as notes written at the time of an event being contested in court. He noted, however, that there were special dangers adhering to hypnosis; in particular, following the prosecution expert, he pointed to an impaired level of critical judgment in hypnosis which could lead to what he called "memory-hardening," and which was left unexplained. Here, he appeared to be pointing to the well-documented finding that hypnosis leads to increased confidence for both correctly and incorrectly recalled information.

In the end, the judge elected for admissibility guidelines modeled on *State v. Hurd* (1980) with a soupçon of *Harding*. He concluded that "the content of the hypnosis session is a proper subject for inquiry at the trial because it bears heavily on the credibility of the witness and the weight to be given his evidence" (p. 12).

Canadian courts have still to battle with the dilemma of hypnotically elicited testimony that is obtained under stringent conditions of adherence to Orne's guidelines, but which contains a high amount of confabulation. The judge's concluding remarks indicated an awareness of this problem, though the solution he offered may be of cold comfort to future jurors who are obliged to implement his recommendations in practice. He closed by saying:

> As the experts often stated in this case, even the most perfectly conducted hypnotic interview does not guarantee that truthful information will be

obtained. A person under hypnosis is capable of lying to the same extent that he would be in his normal state of consciousness. Accordingly, in assessing the credibility of the testimony of the hypnotically-refreshed witness, the trier of fact must consider all those factors ordinarily considered relevant to the credibility of a witness: the demeanor of the witness while testifying, the absence of evidence of previous inconsistent statements and the consistency of the evidence with other proven facts as well as all those other factors usually taken into consideration. (p. 16)

Not all pieces of the Canadian mosaic have been fitted together in precisely this manner. In February 1984, a press conference of La Sûreté du Québec (SQ; one of Canada's provincial police departments) revealed that it employed a psychologist with a Master's degree and two police officers, both with 32 hours of training in hypnosis, to utilize hypnosis on the memories of victims and witnesses of crime.[18] It was reported further that since 1980 they had employed hypnosis on 67 occasions and had solved ten crimes by this means. It was added that the courts of Québec had never been informed of these procedures, since all ten suspects identified by a hypnotic interview, had confessed. Media reports of this press conference did not place any great store on the fact that

> According to the authorities, in every case hypnosis was used because the investigation was faltering, and every other means of investigation had failed to solve the crime. It is surprising that the use of hypnosis not only permitted a breakthrough in the investigation, but also served to obtain a confession! (Bélanger *et al.*, 1984, p. 893)

This issue provided no problem for the police officer who presented the press conference. He explained that

> The delay between the event and the hypnosis session has . . . no importance. According to the "hypno-inquirers" . . . of the SQ, memory records everything, stores information, and compartmentalizes it in drawers. It is sufficient to induce the person to extract the stored information from there. (*LeDevoir*, February 17, 1984)

Without being aware of it, this police officer was in good faith simply reiterating the long-held popular view of the hypnotized person that has been the theme of this book, and the preoccupation of many minds for over two centuries. On this view, the hypnotized person is a passive information storehouse of which "true" memories can be accessed automatically by hypnosis. He appeared to disregard the more telling point that, by his own data, additional information was elicited in 60 to 65 percent of cases, but in only 30 percent could these data be corroborated. There was in this press statement a faith in the belief that, once the information had been corroborated (though the range of corroboration techniques was not touched upon), there was no need to trouble the courts with details of the investigation methodology.

This necessarily cursory summary of the manner in which hypnosis is used investigatively in a number of countries points to one important conclusion. With time, the procedures used in various places will, in most cases, be modified. Some communities will opt for *Frye* rulings that do not permit previously hypnotized witnesses to testify in court; others will exclude hypnosis completely from the judicial system, while still others will adopt various compromise positions that are amalgams of *Frye, Harding,* and *DiNicola.* But whatever position is adopted, one point is essential. It is paramount that laws be enacted that make it mandatory for police departments to inform the courts that hypnosis has been utilized and that it has been performed in strict adherence to Orne's guidelines.

Few have summarized the dilemmas surrounding the investigative use of hypnosis as elegantly as the judge in the *Smoyer* case. It is perhaps fitting that he be given the final word. He stated:

> We have heard, read and studied the experts. We are aware that journeys into the interstices of the mind must be made only by careful and experienced travellers. Happy as we would be to find a final source to confirm memory or retrieve facts, we are yet unconvinced that the senses, under any circumstances, are infallible. (p. 1306)

Appendix

The Guidelines[19]

The present state of scientific knowledge is consistent with court rulings proscribing use of "hypnotically refreshed" eyewitness testimony in criminal trials. It is, therefore, most appropriate to restrict the forensic use of hypnosis to investigative situations where the potential gains are likely to be greater than the risks, provided that suitable guidelines are followed.

As a practical matter, various jurisdictions have taken very different approaches to dealing with the consequences of hypnotically induced recollections. Depending upon the relevant court ruling, different aspects of the guidelines will become essential in resolving the significance that a court would attach to the hypnotic intervention.

First, in those jurisdictions where witnesses are still allowed to testify concerning their "hypnotically refreshed" recollections, the guidelines make it possible to assess the extent of impermissible suggestiveness that may have occurred during the hypnotic session, and the identification of the most serious abuses of hypnosis.

Second, it is generally agreed that hypnosis should not be used simply to fix one particular version of the events in the witness's mind, thereby making him confident that it actually happened that way. However, hypnosis carried out for this precise purpose is often presented later as though it were done with the investigative intent of eliciting new information. The guidelines permit an assessment of what actually occurred and allow inference to be made about the appropriateness of the hypnotic session.

Third, in those jurisdictions where witnesses are not permitted to testify concerning matters about which they have been hypnotized, the guidelines are essential for the authorities to document that certain issues were *not* reviewed or touched upon during hypnosis.

Fourth, some jurisdictions, notably the states of Massachusetts, New York, and Arizona, permit witnesses or victims to testify to events that they recalled *prior to* hypnosis even if the events were discussed in hypnosis; they are not permitted, however, to testify concerning any memories that *changed* subsequent to hypnosis. Since individuals can rarely determine reliably whether a given recollection occurred before or after hypnosis, the procedures outlined in the guidelines are essential to assess what prehypnotic recollections actually were and what effects the hypnotic session is likely to have had.

Regardless of the legal requirements that make it prudent to use the guidelines, it is important to keep in mind that the nature of hypnosis and of its effects on memory leads to the possibility that beliefs of the hypnotist or subject may be transformed into inaccurate memories that the subject reports, believes, and subsequently is willing to testify to under oath. There is currently no available method, including these guidelines, for eliminating this possibility or for recall versus increased distortion that may occur following hypnosis, because ground truth cannot be known with certainty.

Despite these limitations, the use of hypnosis for investigative purposes following the proposed guidelines appears to offer potential benefits—for new leads—that may outweigh the risks of false information or misplaced confidence. This use can be justified, however, only in cases where a suspect has not been identified to the subject, where there has not been widespread publicity involving speculations about the perpetrator, and where law enforcement officials do not have compelling beliefs about what actually transpired. It becomes crucial to follow procedures that provide a detailed record of precisely what has or has not been discussed in the hypnotic interview, and to show that every effort has been made to minimize the potential effect of hypnosis in distorting memory.

To protect the law enforcement agency, the rights of the defendant-to-be, and the health and welfare of the witness or victim to be hypnotized, as well as to allow for the possibility that he can subsequently testify to matters not dealt with in hypnosis, the following guidelines for using hypnosis are proposed. Earlier variants of these guidelines have been adopted by the Federal Bureau of Investigation (Ault, 1979), by the criminal investigative branches of the armed services, and . . . by the New Jersey and Maryland courts.

Qualifications and Knowledge of the Hypnotist

The forensic use of hypnosis should be performed by a psychiatrist, psychologist, or an equivalently qualified mental health professional who has had training both in the clinical use of hypnosis and in its forensic applications. This individual should be an impartial expert whose professional status is independent of the law enforcement investigators, prosecution, and defense (though it is likely that a given expert will have had prior professional contact with these persons).

The expert ideally should know little or nothing about the case. In most situations, however, it is virtually impossible to prevent communications from law enforcement personnel or legal counsel concerning those aspects of the case that they view as important to its disposition. The best solution, accordingly, is to permit no information to be given orally to the hypnotist from individuals involved directly in the case but to require written communications that specify those details that are considered essential for the expert to know in order to carry out the hypnosis interview. This procedure will ensure the possibility of subsequently evaluating the extent of the information available to the hypnotist—information that might be unwittingly communicated to the subject. If the hypnotist has learned about the case from outside sources, such as press accounts, he should record such information in writing prior to the hypnosis session (withdrawing from the case if this prior information is unduly prejudicial).

Complete Videotape Recordings

All contact between the hypnotist and the individual to be hypnotized should be recorded on videotape from the moment they meet until their entire interaction is concluded, including the prehypnosis interview, the hypnosis interview, and the posthypnosis discussion. Casual comments exchanged before or after hypnosis may act as prehypnotic or posthypnotic suggestions and are as important to record as the hypnotic session itself. The camera should be aimed to get *both* the hypnotist and the subject in the picture. A time recording should be incorporated into the record of the session to ensure its continuity. Audio recordings are substantially less useful for the subsequent evaluation of possible biasing, and stenographic transcripts provide no opportunity to record the nonverbal and paraverbal (tone of voice, pauses, etc.) cues by which information and expectations are often communicated to subjects undergoing hypnosis.

Limitations on Those Present during the Interview

Only the hypnotist and subject should be present during any phase of the preinduction, hypnosis, or posthypnosis session. This is important because it is all too easy for observers inadvertently to communicate to the subject what they expect, what they are startled by, or what they are disappointed by (even if the subject's eyes are closed and he has been told to hear only the hypnotist's voice). If investigators or representatives of the prosecution or the defense wish to observe the hypnosis session, they may do so only if they use a one-way screen or a remote television monitor to watch the interview—to prevent jeopardizing the integrity of the session.

Deviations from this guideline must be evaluated carefully. In some situations adequate videotape recording may require the presence of a technician in the room to operate equipment.[20] This individual should not have any prior knowledge of the case and should document this in writing. Other special situations, such as a child who requests or who an involved clinician believes requires the presence of a parent during the session, must be evaluated on a case-by-case basis. The primary consideration here, as in other aspects of conducting the hypnosis session, must be the protection of the witness or victim who has consented to serve as a hypnotic subject.

A more difficult problem arises when no one person possesses all the requisite expertise needed to conduct the hypnosis interview. A psychiatrist or psychologist skilled in clinical uses of hypnosis may lack experience with forensic interviewing techniques. In this situation, a law enforcement professional who is skilled in avoiding leading questions and who has no knowledge of the specific case[21] might conduct the actual interview following hypnotic induction by the clinician and transfer of rapport. The clinician, however, should remain responsible throughout and should terminate hypnosis. A law enforcement professional who participates in the interview should, like the clinician, be given a written summary of the facts he is to know about the case and should submit, in advance of the hypnotic session, a written statement detailing any other prior knowledge that he may have concerning the case.

Prehypnosis Evaluation

At the beginning of the session a psychological evaluation of the subject should be carried out by the mental health professional, and the existence of a full, written, informed consent for the procedure confirmed. *Before* the induction of hypnosis, the mental health professional should elicit from the victim or witness a detailed narrative description of the facts as the subject remembers them, being careful to avoid adding any new elements through direct or indirect suggestions. This preliminary procedure is important because it provides a recorded baseline for evaluating the subject's memories of the incident before anything has been added or changed through hypnosis. Moreover, witnesses are sometimes able to recall more or different memories while talking to a psychologist or psychiatrist than during interrogation by an investigator.

If significant new information emerges during this prehypnosis interview, consideration should be given to stopping the procedure at this point and thus avoiding some of the problems inherent in the use of hypnosis. If the decision is made not to induce hypnosis, the subject should then be interviewed nondirectively as to what he believes happened during this interview, because, having come for the purpose of being hypnotized, the subject may believe that he was hypnotized. In any case, the videotaped record of the entire interaction should be preserved. If the decision is made to proceed with the induction of hypnosis, the subject should be questioned first as to his expectations so that their effect may be evaluated subsequently and any remaining serious misconceptions about hypnosis or its effects may be corrected.

Finally, care must be taken not to suggest explicitly or implicitly before (or during) hypnosis that all memories are accurately recorded in the brain and a particular technique will bring forth these memory traces in their original form. To do so serves as a powerful suggestion that causes most subjects to either "recall" additional less accurate information in hypnosis, or place undue faith in their recollections, or both.

Appropriate Hypnotic Induction and Memory Retrieval Techniques

Hypnosis should be induced by one of the standard methods and incorporate sufficient test suggestions to allow assessment of the subject's hypnotic responsivity. Following the induction of hypnosis, the psychiatrist or psychologist should suggest an appropriate cognitive strategy to aid focusing on the events in question, and first obtain a free narrative report. During this report, the hypnotist should encourage the narrative flow but avoid interrupting, asking questions, or otherwise adding any new elements to the witness's description of his experiences, including those discussed in the preinduction interview, lest the nature of the witness's memories inadvertently be altered or constrained by a reminder of his prior, nonhypnotic memories. Once the subject begins to describe the events in question, minimal verbalization by the hypnotist is desirable. When the subject pauses, comments such as, "Go on," "Continue," "Yes?" "Mm hm?"—indicating the clinician's interest in what the subject says but avoiding communicating concern about specific content—are particularly useful.

If the free narrative fails to elicit needed details, a more directive technique may be employed subsequently, but it should be kept in mind that questioning or otherwise pressuring about specific details will inevitably increase the number of items reported but also increase the probability of inaccurate details being supplied.

In terms of the specific cognitive strategy that the hypnotist uses to focus the subject's attention on the events in question, it is important to note that hypnosis should never be used to encourage a witness to report details when it was physically impossible for such details to have been observed—as when a witness is asked to zoom in on the face of someone who was never viewed except at a distance of 90 yards in semi-darkness or to remove the mask from a perpetrator whom the subject had never seen without a mask! In other words, hypnosis does not retrospectively allow the individual to transcend normal perceptual abilities, and to suggest anything of this kind to the subject, even metaphorically, invites confabulation and increases the likelihood of creating pseudomemories.

Lastly, it should be emphasized that the issues that these guidelines address are not resolved merely because hypnotically induced recollections are brought forth during the *therapeutic* use of hypnosis, such as in the treatment of traumatic neuroses. If such recollections are to form the basis of subsequent testimony, it is essential to follow the guidelines. Some clinicians have argued that the exclusion of testimony following the therapeutic use of hypnosis would deny patients, such as rape victims, the right to their treatment of choice—hypnosis. Hypnosis has not, however, been considered the treatment of choice by any of the leading crisis intervention or rape treatment centers. Without a complete and adequate electronic record of all interactions between a therapist and patient, it would be totally inappropriate to permit an individual to testify on the basis of recollections that occurred during a therapeutic hypnosis session.

Communication with the Hypnotist

There may well be questions that need to be resolved by observers who are not in the room but who are familiar with the case. For this reason, it is desirable for the hypnotist to arrange very brief breaks—leaving the videotape continuously recording the subject—at the end of the prehypnosis interview, and again at the end of the free narrative recall obtained during hypnosis. Observers should put in writing any requests or suggestions for the hypnotist concerning material to be elicited, which can be given to the hypnotist during these breaks. In this fashion a permanent record is obtained concerning when and by whom specific issues are raised during the session; this record should be archived with the videotapes.

Posthypnosis Discussion

During the termination of hypnosis or immediately thereafter while the subject is still in a hypersuggestible state, explicit or implicit posthypnotic suggestions should be avoided concerning the nature, extent, or reliability of the subject's subsequent nonhypnotic memory of the event (e.g., "It will be easy for you to remember things now that you did not remember before"). After hypnosis is terminated, it is important to explore the subject's experiences during hypnosis, which provide needed information about the individual's hypnotic responsivity and whether he felt that hypnosis changed anything concerning his memories. Before ending their contact the hypnotist should invite the subject to reflect on what the subject believes took place during the session, its causes, and implications. Videotape recording of the session should be terminated only after the hypnotist and the subject have parted company and all immediate posthypnotic interviews of the subject by involved personnel have been concluded.

Provision for Clinical Follow-Up

The planning of the hypnosis session should include provisions for making clinical follow-up available to the victim or witness who has served as a subject if it appears to be clinically indicated or if the subject requests it. This follow-up may be provided by the hypnotist, by a clinician who has been working with the subject, or by referral to a suitable clinician in the area where the subject lives. The subject should be informed of these arrangements before leaving the hypnotic session. If repressed traumatic memories have been recalled under hypnosis, these provisions are especially important, and should be an active rather than a passive ("Call if you have any problems") nature.

Technical Considerations

The individual responsible for carrying out the hypnosis should check well in advance the suitability of the setting and whether the videotape recording equipment is working properly. Aside from ensuring that the quality of the picture is adequate and that both hypnotist and subject are going to be clearly displayed in the picture, the hypnotist should ascertain that the audio recording system is carefully tested to ensure that it is capable of picking up very quiet conversation—hypnotized subjects often speak in soft or low voices. As a test of the adequacy of the videotape recording equipment, a brief sample tape should be recorded and evaluated prior to the session. (Obvious errors like placing a microphone on or too near a videotape machine will result in inaudible tapes, thereby completely compromising the intended monitoring of the session.) Finally, provisions should be made to videotape all materials to be shown to the subject.

Cautionary Note on Hypnotizing Suspects

With the increased investigative use of hypnosis, an individual who had been hypnotized as a witness may at some later time become a suspect. In such an event, special procedures must be observed with regard to the subsequent waking interrogation because the memory of the witness/suspect may have been altered by the hypnosis session. During interrogation the authorities may wittingly or unwittingly use the hypnotically induced "information"—especially information that placed the subject at the scene of the crime—in order to elicit a confession.

Because the hypnotically induced "information" may have been confabulated, the witness who has been subjected to hypnosis procedures may be more vulnerable to later interrogation. Therefore, it is essential that the *waking* interrogation of a previously hypnotized witness be recorded—ideally videotaped, but at least audiotaped. The taped record is crucial to determine whether admissions or confessions were elicited voluntarily or whether the interrogator capitalized upon pseudomemories created during hypnosis (e.g., those produced by the "zooming-in" technique) in order to convince a suspect that he must have been at the scene of the crime because he could not otherwise have seen the details reported.

NOTES

1. It is not possible to summarize all of the cases that have involved hypnosis within the confines of a book chapter. Accordingly, we have sought to concentrate on those cases which have been the most instrumental in fashioning American legal thinking during this century, as well as (in some cases) those which best illustrate the hazards of presenting uncorroborated hypnotically elicited testimony in a court of law. For a more comprehensive account of cases that have involved hypnosis, a book by Udolph (1983) is an invaluable source.

2. In the retrial of 1906, the Court seems also to have placed great emphasis on the testimony of two medical doctors who felt that it was implausible that hypnosis could be utilized to disrupt Ms. Austin's recall of her first experiences of intercourse. Overall, the court testimony gives little indication of what actually occurred in this case.

3. The *Frye* ruling of 1923 has been utilized to exclude testimony derived not only from the polygraph, but also from sodium amytal in the days when it was thought to be a "truth serum." In more recent years, it has been the basis for various court decisions to exclude evidence derived from "voiceprints" which have been claimed as valid for identification purposes as fingerprints (for legal discussions of these various techniques, see Burack, 1955; Dession, Freedman, Donnellym, & Redlich, 1953; Imwinkelried, 1983; Patenaude, 1983; Stewart, 1969; Zonana, 1979).

4. Almost 30 percent of Bryan's book is taken up with a chapter entitled "Analysis of a Psycho Killer." This is the case of Mr. H. A. B. who was convicted of first-degree murder, two counts of second-degree murder, and one count of assault with the intent to commit murder. All cases involved older women who were known to Mr. H. A. B. Bryan used hypnosis to examine the defendant and sought to present the results of this examination as indicating that, in his expert opinion, Mr. H. A. B. was insane. The case, *People v. Busch* (1961), was appealed to the California Supreme Court. It ruled that "Dr. Bryan . . . was competent to testify as a medical doctor as to the defendant's mental

condition, but that he was not competent to testify insofar as his opinions were based upon information dependent on the use of hypnosis" (p. 903). Interestingly, while not referring explicitly to *Frye*, it referred to several rulings involving "truth serum" and "lie detectors" which were based on *Frye*. It referred also to *Cornell*, characterizing the case as involving the legal rights of "one confined in a penal institution to consult with his attorney and otherwise prepare his defense" (p. 903).

Bryan's book raises an additional major point, given his belief that the simulation of hypnosis does not present a problem. A recent case, *State v. Bianchi* (1979), illustrates many of the dilemmas surrounding the utilization of hypnosis with accused individuals. Bianchi, suspected of being "the Hillside Strangler," had been charged with the murders of 10 women. The forensic evidence against him was overwhelming. A clinical psychologist (Watkins, 1984) diagnosed him as having a multiple personality disorder as the result of a second persona emerging in hypnosis. It claimed credit for some of the murders, blaming others of them on Angelo Buono, Bianchi's cousin. A psychiatrist (Allison, 1984) also initially diagnosed Bianchi as having a multiple personality disorder; later, he altered his diagnosis to "atypical dissociative disorder" and concluded that Bianchi was not deliberately and consciously faking multiplicity. Subsequently, Orne examined Bianchi and sought to evaluate the possibility of simulation explicitly. In a report of this examination (Orne, Dinges, *et al.*, 1984), the authors pointed out that a diagnosis of multiple personality disorder carried the major secondary gain of avoidance of the death penalty. Since Bianchi had a long history of deception and lying, Orne sought to investigate the truthfulness of his claim of multiple personality in four different ways. In terms of the first criterion—that the structure and content of various personalities should remain stable over time if Bianchi suffered from a multiple personality disorder—it was found that the persona, Steve, who admitted involvement in the crimes, became progressively more hostile and profane over time. Second, Bianchi's manifestations of multiple personality could be influenced by cues; Orne was able to elicit a third personality, Billy, by the simple prehypnosis cue (presented as a casual comment) that Orne believed that Bianchi should have at least three personalities to qualify as a multiple. This occurred shortly after a session with Allison, who had explicitly attempted, without success, to elicit a third personality during hypnosis. In terms of a third criterion, which involved Bianchi's response to a number of hypnotic items—namely, double hallucination, single hallucination, analgesia, and source amnesia—Bianchi's response on most of these items was more like that of a simulator than of a deeply hypnotized subject. For instance, on the double hallucination item, in which he was asked to see both his lawyer, who was present in the room for this part of the session, and a hallucination of him, his response was to assert repeatedly, "How can I see him in two places?" This response appeared designed to assure the hypnotist that his experience was genuine; however, this is something that deeply hypnotized subjects simply do not attempt to do. Finally, nobody in the past had ever seen sudden and inexplicable changes in Bianchi's behavior and identity. All of these data were consistent with the belief that Bianchi had simulated multiple personality in much the same manner as he had been deceitful about many other things in the past. Despite these findings, many experts on multiple personality disorder still insist that Bianchi is a multiple personality. The continuing debate on his mental status suggests that the issue of simulation is far more complex than Bryan represented it. Central to this issue is the question of whether, given the context of murder allegations, Watkins's attempt to treat the suspect by suggesting that during the first hypnosis session there might be another "part" of Bianchi, served to confuse the forensic picture.

5. The *Collins* court ruled that "during the post *Harding* interim to the present, a substantial controversy arose in the scientific community as to the scientific justification for the admissibility of hypnotically induced testimony" (p. 11). Its references to *Frye* were explicit; it referred also to a number of *Frye* inspired rulings on the polygraph and on voiceprints. By the time of Collins, however, a number of U.S. State Supreme Courts, following Minnesota, had adopted a *Frye* ruling regarding hypnotically elicited testimony.

6. The Court, perhaps unwisely, did not go into the issue of whether it was plausible that Harding would have raped Ms. Cooley while she was bleeding from a bullet wound to the chest.

7. In its decision, the *Harding* court chose to ignore the rulings in *Ebanks*, *Pusch*, and *Cornell*, all of which it discussed briefly in a footnote (pp. 310-311).

8. As far as it can be ascertained, the term "Svengali Squad" was coined by *Time* magazine in an article in the September 13, 1976 issue, pages 56-57 (Putnam, 1979).

9. There is, for instance, the procedure of "affectless recall" described by Reiser (1980) in which victims/witnesses are encouraged to recall the events of a crime while distancing themselves from the affect (emotion) which they may have evoked. It is difficult to determine the consequences that this procedure may have for the distortion of memory. For instance, some psychologists consider it important for individuals recalling events to recall associated emotions; they maintain that this procedure leads to better recall. The work of Bower (1981) is cited often on this point; his research tends to show that individuals recall pleasant events best when they are happy and unpleasant events best when they are sad. Affectless recall of the unpleasant events of a crime may thus deprive police investigators of potentially important leads, all other things being equal. Which they may not be.

10. Subsequently, the Society for Clinical and Experimental Hypnosis (SCEH) (October 1978) and the International Society of Hypnosis (ISH) (August 1979) passed identically worded resolutions condemning the utilization of hypnosis by police officers. Both societies

> viewed with alarm the tendency for police officers with minimal training in hypnosis and without a broad professional background in the healing arts employing hypnosis to presumably facilitate recall of witnesses or victims privy to the occurrence of some crime. Because we recognize that hypnotically aided recall may produce either accurate memories or at times may facilitate the creation of pseudo memories or fantasies that are accepted as real by subject and hypnotist alike, we are deeply troubled by the utilization of this technique among the police. It must be emphasized that there is no known way of distinguishing with certainty between actual recall and pseudo memories except by independent verification. (SCEH, p. 452; ISH, p. 453)

These resolutions were, subsequently, characterized by Reiser (1985) in highly negative terms. He wrote:

> A few hypnosis "authorities" with impressive credentials have been on an avowed crusade to "shoot down" the police use of investigative hypnosis. In the process, they have misinformed the courts, colleagues and the public on many key hypnotic and psychological issues. Using assertion and fiat, without the required relevant data, these individuals, claiming to represent the "scientific community" have engaged in scientism in the guise of science and injected proprietary guild interests under the cover of ethical concerns. An underlying territorial motive can be seen in the identical resolution passed

by two separate clinical hypnosis societies declaring it unethical for members to teach, supervise or consult with police who use investigative hypnosis in criminal cases. . . . Attempts are also being made to extend the power play, still in the guise of an ethics problem, to other psychological and hypnosis associations. (p. 513)

The final paragraph of the SCEH and ISH resolutions, however, makes the concerns of these societies explicit. Both stated that they view "it as unethical to train lay individuals in the use of hypnosis, to collaborate with laymen in the use of hypnosis, or to serve as a consultant for laymen who are utilizing hypnosis" (SCEH, p. 452; ISH, p. 453). As can be seen, the two societies were not expressing what Reiser has characterized as an "anti-police bias," but rather their traditional opposition to lay hypnotists. As was noted earlier, this position was expressed also by the American Medical Association in its 1958 report on hypnosis.

Indeed, the AMA was sufficiently concerned that its endorsement of hypnosis in qualified hands as a clinical procedure had been misrepresented to mean that it approved of police hypnotechnicians, that it released a report in 1985 entitled *Scientific Status of Refreshing Recollection by the Use of Hypnosis*. It found no scientific evidence of hypnotic enhancement of memory for meaningless material and for recognition memory for any type of material. It concluded that when hypnosis is used for the recall of past meaningful events, new information is often reported. It stated, however, such new information could be fact, fantasy, or the product of unwitting cueing by the hypnotist, and viewed independent corroboration as mandatory in the legal situation. The AMA reasserted also its belief that "hypnosis should be conducted by a psychiatrist or psychologist, skilled in the clinical and investigative use of hypnosis, who is aware of the legal implications of the use of hypnosis for investigative purposes within the jurisdiction in which he or she practices (p. 1923).

Reiser (1986) responded to this report in the *Newsletter* of Division 30 (Psychological Hypnosis) of the American Psychological Association. He claimed that

> before being unduly influenced by the impressive imprimatur of the AMA on the hypnosis report, Division 30 psychologists also need to take into account the anti-police bias underlying the purportedly "scientific" set of pronouncements. In a prior attempt a short time back, the Orne clique tried to push through Division 30 a resolution making it unethical for members to train or consult with police in the use of investigative hypnosis. (p. 5)

11. *Habeas corpus* is a writ requiring a prison inmate to be brought before a court of law in order to establish whether his or her detention is lawful.

12. As far as can be ascertained, police departments that utilize hypnosis for memory enhancement do not attempt to evaluate whether a crime witness or victim is, in fact, amnesic. Generally, it is assumed that he or she is.

13. The U.S. State Supreme Courts that have adopted a *Frye* ruling on hypnotically elicited recollection are Alaska, Arizona, California, Florida, Indiana, Maryland, Massachusetts, Michigan, Minnesota, Missouri, Nebraska, North Carolina, New York, Pennsylvania, and Washington. In the year since this book was completed, we have heard of two other State Supreme Courts reaching similar conclusions, but we do not have any further details.

14. Karlin (1983) reported two cases in the New Jersey region where there was considerable evidence that what the victim recalled was confabulated. In one case, however, it appeared that the person identified by a hypnotized crime victim actually committed the assault against her. The suspect was an ex-convict who had been

subsequently arrested for a similar crime in a nearby town. Karlin believed that the woman never saw her attacker's face and was either cued to provide a description of his face or else confabulated it. She was later able to identify the aggressor in a photo lineup. Important to the case is that during the week following hypnosis, the victim read a newspaper story about the similar assault in the nearby town. Although no description of the suspect was provided, the store in which he was employed was named. The victim had shopped at this store two months previously, but since it was largely a self-service operation, it is unlikely that she would have picked the suspect out from the 12 employees. Within a few days of reading the newspaper story, she had a dream in which she believed she saw her assailant's face clearly. She reported it during a hypnosis session some days later. Karlin's view was that the description she provided did not resemble the suspect at all; indeed, the description was actually a good description of herself. Since at her previous session, however, it had been suggested to her that she would remember more during the following week, both when awake and in her dreams, she saw this dream as accurate recall. Based on Karlin's testimony about the inaccuracy of hypnotically elicited testimony, the jury did not convict; the suspect received a long prison sentence for the attack in the other town. The utilization of hypnosis in this case may have actually prejudiced an otherwise strong circumstantial case which might better have been dealt with using orthodox police questioning strategies. Unfortunately, however, the photo line-up was not presented to her prior to hypnosis.

15. There are some who would probably wish to argue that we are back to square one on the matter of the admissibility of testimony of previously hypnotized defendants in light of a recent ruling of the United States Supreme Court. A decision in the case *Rock v. Arkansas* was handed down on June 22, 1987, a few weeks before this book was due to go to the typesetter. Ms. Vickie Rock was convicted of the manslaughter of her husband following his attempt to prevent her from leaving their apartment in order to buy a hamburger. She was sentenced to ten years in prison and fined $10,000. Her attorney had her hypnotized by a neuropsychologist; in hypnosis, she recalled that the gun went off accidentally. Arkansas is one of the 15 states that does not admit hypnotically elicited testimony; accordingly, she was not permitted to testify about her recollections in hypnosis to the Arkansas State Supreme Court.

We have not yet seen the U.S. Supreme Court's decision, and have had to rely on a report in *The New York Times* a day after the decision (Tuesday, June 23, 1987, p. B8). By a 5-4 majority, the Court ruled that the Arkansas Court's refusal to admit her hypnotically elicited testimony was an arbitrary restriction on her "constitutional right to testify in her own defense." The majority decision was written by Justice Harry A. Blackmun, who detailed the problems of hypnotically elicited testimony discussed throughout this book; notably, confabulation and increased confidence for both correct and incorrect material. The newspaper report did not state whether the majority considered the issue of simulation and lying—possibilities that must always be considered when the hypnotized witness is accused of a major offense.

Justice Blackmun stated that while the prosecution "may be able to show that testimony in a particular case is so unreliable that exclusion is justified [in the Rock case] it has not shown that hypnotically enhanced testimony is always so untrustworthy and so immune to the traditional means of evaluating credibility that it should disable a defendant from presenting her version of the events for which she is on trial." In reaching this conclusion, he appears to have been upholding the rights of an accused to self-defense in whatever manner he or she deems to be the most effective; indeed, under United States law, one could call a reader of tealeaves, or even a water diviner, to testify if it were thought that such testimony could assist the accused.

Blackmun stated further that the use of Orne's guidelines might reduce, even if not eliminate entirely, the problems of confabulation and augmented confidence, and added that independent experts, with no stake in the outcome, should seek to find other evidence consistent or inconsistent with the hypnotically elicited testimony. In *Rock*, he noted that a defense expert who had examined the gun used in the shooting corroborated Ms. Rock's recollection in hypnosis by indicating that the weapon could be fired without pulling the trigger.

At the same time, the Court stated that "we express no opinion [on] the admissibility of testimony of previously hypnotized witnesses other than criminal defendants." The emphasis on independent corroboration and defendants' rights leaves the strong impression that we will not return to the days before *Mack*, when it was possible to be tried and convicted on the basis of another person's hypnotic fantasies. Notwithstanding, it is clear that some quite crucial cases involving hypnosis can be expected in the coming years, and that exactly 90 years later, the *Ebanks* decision is no more.

16. The following reports were available: *The Sun*, July 10, 1980; *The Sydney Morning Herald (S.M.H.)*, July 10, 1980; *The Sun*, July 15, 1980; *S.M.H.*, August 8, 1980; *The Sun*, August 8, 1980; *S.M.H.*, September 9, 1980; *S.M.H.*, August 21, 1982; *S.M.H.*, August 24, 1982; *The Age*, August 1, 1983; *S.M.H.*, November 18, 1983; *S.M.H.*, January 9, 1984; *S.M.H.*, January 10, 1984; *The Sun*, August 7, 1984; *The Sun*, March 14, 1984; *The Sun*, May 17, 1984; *The Sun*, August 20, 1984; *Daily Mirror*, October 17, 1985; *S.M.H.*, October 18, 1985; *The Sun*, November 28, 1985; *S.M.H.*, January 21, 1986; *The Sun*, January 21, 1986; *The Sun*, January 31, 1986. All but *The Age* (a Melbourne newspaper) are published in Sydney.

17. "Police switch on slow-motion reruns of the mind to catch their crooks." *S.M.H.*, November 11, 1983.

18. There were articles on this press conference in *Le Journal de Montréal*, *La Presse*, *Le Devoir*, and *The Gazette*, all dated February 17, 1984.

19. From Orne *et al.* (1985, pp. 41–49). Reprinted by permission.

20. When police artists are used to help witnesses or victims construct a facsimile of their mental image of the perpetrator, it is most desirable to conduct this outside of hypnosis. The interaction between the police artist and the hypnotized individual is such that the subject's mental image may easily be altered. Nonetheless, some police artists prefer to work with the individual during hypnosis. If this is to be done it becomes absolutely vital to determine any possible preconceptions of the artist concerning the appearance of the perpetrator. Because talented police artists are rare, he may have worked with another witness in constructing a facsimile, making the attempt with the hypnotized subject prone to the effects of his acquired biases. In any case, the careful videotaping of such an interaction in hypnosis would be mandatory (Orne *et al.*, 1985, p. 55).

21. The Federal Bureau of Investigation tries to ensure the interviewer's lack of familiarity with the specific case by using an agent from a different jurisdiction (Orne *et al.*, 1985, p. 56).

Conclusion

> A good historian resembles the ogre of the legend. When he smells human flesh, he knows that there he will find his prey.—Bloch (1974, p. 35; cited in Darnton, 1984, p. 263)

Darnton (1984) emphasized the importance of capturing the mentalities of periods past through the lives of common people, those who did not play a prominent part in traditional "History." He described as closely as possible certain episodes of their lives based on whatever material they had left behind. This approach to history, or "history from below" as it is called, was originally developed by historians like George Rudé (see Hobsbawn, 1985) and is not without its problems; for one, as Darnton himself recognized, how can one be sure that the events investigated were not totally unrepresentative of the period explored? Even more to the point, it is always possible to construct one's own History given sufficient patience and energy.

Post hoc interpretations although in accord with our current ways of thinking may have very little to offer when it comes to understanding what was actually happening in the past. When one looks back at what was, there can be as many answers as one is willing to entertain. Now that we have reached the end of this venture into the grassroots history of hypnosis, we certainly share these doubts. In the often-written and often-interpreted history of animal magnetism, there is not a single, simple explanation that will quench our thirst for understanding. There will always be unresolved questions, and unsatisfactory answers. We may, however, realize the importance of capturing the continuity between phenomena of the past and current concerns. As has been seen throughout the book, the solutions sought by the representatives of the different periods were similar to those that we have to offer today.

Methodologies have changed, approaches have diversified. There is nowadays a consensus between the clinical and experimental views of hypnosis and related phenomena, even though theories abound. It is difficult to ask for any more than this; both experimental and clinical contexts nurture the differences that stem from their specific use of hypnosis, in much the same way that the Nancy and Salpêtrière schools recognized the same phenomena but explained them differently. They must continue, however, to function in parallel, looking at one another for potential sources for advancing understanding.

If many questions remain unanswered, the juxtaposition of the historical and contemporary uses of hypnosis may stimulate new ways of approaching the phenomenon. The addition of the psycho-legal dimension may ultimately broaden the views of both clinicians and researchers, and stimulate the exploration of memory in action. If history can teach a lesson, and if one is willing to consider it, it may be possible to avoid a repetition of what happened in France at the end of the last century.

Individuals who undergo a hypnotic induction are not monolithic sculptures carved by the context. They bring to the situation many idiosyncratic aspects that will interact with the context in eliciting a behavioral response and a subjective experience that may or may not confirm the experimenters' *and* the individuals' perception of the phenomena under study. Beliefs and expectations about both one's self and the situation will mold responses without either hypnotist or subject necessarily being aware of them at the time. In fact, it took 150 years before the importance of demand characteristics (that is, implicit cues in the design and/or procedure of an experiment which communicate the investigator's hypotheses) was emphasized by Orne (1959) in a systematic way. How long it will take before their *modus operandi* is understood is another question!

If experimental contexts are under the control of the experimenter, beliefs about one's self are not. How one expects to react to a given situation is at best conjectural. What shapes one's self-beliefs, and how they influence one's experience of reality are questions that are yet unresolved. Confronted by a new context, there are few other choices than to rely on our past experience and to extrapolate what could be our reactions. Sometimes people are remarkably adept at doing this (Bowers, 1984); at other times they are remarkably inept (Nisbett & Wilson, 1977). Many skills have been hypothesized to underlie the experience of hypnosis: capacity for absorption, imagery, dissociation, some aspects of attention processes. All have been shown to play a role in shaping responses to a hypnotic situation. The intricate structure of an individual belief system can sometimes prove to be quite resilient to change. Even when confronted by reliable evidence, individuals will usually tend to revert in the final instance to their original position (Gray, 1985). When Ellenberger (1970) wrote that one must attempt to cure with means acceptable to the community to avoid ostracism, he was hinting at the difficulty of transcending personal and social beliefs.

A number of issues are worth commenting on at this point. Since the beginnings of animal magnetism, positive and negative side effects of the procedures used have been reported by many authors. Whether they were physical (migraines, dizziness, nausea, etc.) or psychological (anxiety, distress, fright, etc.), the transient experiences that sometimes accompanied the hypnotic experience may be more telling than has been heretofore considered. In investigating more carefully their origins, one may be able to grasp the necessary abilities underlying their production. For example, in many early *and* contemporary reports of hypnotic coercion in the laboratory, subjects who complied to the suggestions often experienced distress following their accomplishment, even though they were aware when interviewed that nothing would be done that could be harmful to themselves or others. As far as can be ascertained through these reports, the more highly hypnotizable individuals were the ones exhibiting such aftereffects, although as some recent data from our laboratory demonstrate, no particular subject is immune to these types of transient experiences (Laurence, Nadon, Bowers, Labelle, Blatt, & Perry, 1987).

What appears to be the case, however, is that the more hypnotizable one is, the more dramatic the effects are, everything else being equal; whether this quality of hypnotizability is high or low, everyone is susceptible to calling up traumatic memories (real or imagined) when such techniques as age regression or hypnotic dreaming are used, and these can have inappropriate repercussions in the forensic setting. In the same way that the early investigators documented that highly hypnotizable individuals could elicit images and emotions that took on reality value upon awakening, one may ask how permanent the images or emotions evoked in hypnosis are and how they become integrated in the subject's memory system (Laurence *et al.*, 1987). Veridical or not, these memories can nonetheless be influential in subjects' perceptions of the recalled events and can interact with the demands placed on them. The subjective reality of suggested experiences may well take precedence over whatever is remembered before hypnosis. The experience of hypnosis in itself could be sufficient to increase one's confidence in the veracity of memories that were only tangential to the hypnotic enquiry; this is what we called in Chapter 11, the resonance effect. The issue of transient experiences, although present for more than two hundred years, has never been the subject of well-structured research and probably should be; subjects' reactions in the Sutcliffe study (1961) utilizing suggestions of gender change are telling.

Probably the most intriguing and elusive issue in the history of hypnosis is the experience of nonvolition. Recognized before the end of the eighteenth century, it has haunted investigators ever since. If the concept of human will has lost its glamour among contemporary researchers (only to be presented under new disguises), it remains a central experience in the reports of highly hypnotizable subjects. Whether the issue is resolved by pointing to the misattributions of which subjects are too often guilty, it still remains to be explained why misattributing could have such repercussions on subjects' behaviors and experiences. One has only to think about the victims' reports of having been sexually abused by an unethical hypnotist to realize how ambiguous such situations are and how unwilling the scientific community can be in acknowledging such possibilities. In the clinical field, however, many pathologies flourish on the inability of both therapist and patient to reinstall the will to change. Obsessions, compulsions, hallucinations, dissociation, to name but a few are all seen by those who suffer from them as being more powerful than their own will to resist or eradicate them, a subjective report that does not cause any problem to most clinicians. The effortlessness with which the pathologies installed themselves is disarming; the great effort deployed to control them is often excruciating. Why then the difference in attitude? Who cannot remember a dream where running was the only escape to a life-threatening situation, but the legs refused to move? No mental effort could change anything in the situation; one had to submit.

If it is recognized today that the hypnotized subject is not an automaton, the issue of effortless enacting and experiencing of suggestions is still present in the subjective reports of those most responsive to hypnosis. What are the underlying abilities? As Faria had pointed out in his 1819 book, except when a subject is aware and convinced of his or her ability to produce some suggested effects, misattributions are crucial in the realization of suggestions. Could this be part of the answer?

In both areas of experimental and field coercion, yesterday as today, the artificiality of the situations has led to much ambiguity. There is still no clear evidence that hypnosis *per se* can be used to coerce people to commit acts contrary to their wills. But the question may be misformulated. Hypnosis, as Bernheim pointed out, does not exist. What does exist, however, is the interaction between a given context and the abilities of the subjects to respond to it. By looking at cases of coercion as self-fulfilling prophecies, the hypnotic context provides an invaluable field of investigation that may lead to the understanding of some intriguing human abilities.

As was pointed to in our final two chapters, popular conceptions of hypnosis and hypnotizability may provide a first answer to the processes underlying self-fulfilling prophecies. Recent research in that area has already demonstrated that common sense knowledge about the influence of hypnosis on one's behaviors and experiences are quite at odds with scientific findings (Labelle, Lamarche, & Laurence, 1987; Loftus & Loftus, 1980; Orne *et al.*, 1985). Especially in the field of memory, these misconceptions can be profitably used in unraveling some of the processes at play in the reconstruction of memories, as well as in the confidence that individuals express on the veracity and reliability of their past experiences. Self-deception (through misattributions) may be what constitutes reality. In the reports of women who have been sexually abused, of subjects who experienced distress following the commission of objectionable suggestions, and of individuals who relived traumatic experiences in contexts that sought to minimize them may lie the substratum that will allow researchers to grasp such an elusive notion as self-deception. In the renewed forensic debate, the same problems can be identified; whether one stresses the dangers of confabulation, of increased but undeserved confidence, or of memory creation (or biases), all of these issues revolve around the notion of self-deception. In the forensic context, it can be even more dramatic since often both the hypnotist and the subject share in the self-deception!

All of these problems have been documented in the last two hundred years, and in the investigators' enthusiasm for unadulterated knowledge, they have been underestimated. The current forensic debate over the uses and abuses of hypnosis has permitted the refocusing of attention on behaviors, thoughts, and emotions in action. It is unlikely, at least in the short term, that the investigative use of hypnosis will be eradicated. In the same way that the polygraph is widely used although not recognized by courts of law, hypnosis will probably still be used by police forces in an attempt to unravel the mysteries of unsolved investigations.

The only trend that can currently be discerned that might alter what seems to be an inevitable course is that some of the individuals who have undergone investigative hypnosis with an operator who did not understand the need for Orne's guidelines, have subsequently been highly dissatisfied by the manner in which they were treated. A small number of police departments and/or city fathers of various municipal governments have been sued. It may take years for these cases to be resolved by the courts, but, whatever they are, the outcomes will have a major effect on where, if at all, hypnosis subsequently finds its niche in the judicial systems of many countries, states, and cities.

Ironically, there always seems to be one more case where the use of hypnosis brought about an unexpected denouement. By the time there is enough information to understand what was the basis of such success, it is often too late to prevent any mishap. If many Supreme Courts in the United States have now espoused a stricter position vis-à-vis the investigative use of hypnosis, the recent decision in *DiNicola* (1985) is a potentially disastrous compromise. The effect of hypnosis on prehypnotic memories could be as dramatic as it is post-hypnosis. This is particularly so in cases where the original prehypnotic memory was erroneous. It is only to be hoped that in cases that follow such decisions, some provision will be made to ensure that the defense and the prosecution are aware that hypnosis was used during the investigation. But by always functioning one step behind the courts, the only part of us that will improve is our wisdom of hindsight. Meanwhile unsubstantiated beliefs will continue to flourish. These may be gloomy conclusions, but we are stuck with them until the courts themselves work hand in hand with hypnosis investigators before permitting hypnosis to be used.

Finally, as the psycho-legal history of hypnosis has shown us, what may be the most remarkable aspect in the continuity of these behaviors and experiences, is their robustness; perhaps history had no other choice in this case but to repeat itself? What remains clear is the necessity of continuing the investigation of these phenomena from whatever perspective possible and, in so doing, of injecting rejuvenated meaning into behaviors and experiences that have always made a point of outlasting their explanations. It may be extremely difficult to transcend our own set of social and personal beliefs, but the discovery of new approaches to some of the complexities of the mind demand that we at least attempt it. Meanwhile the careful laying of the groundwork for investigation of this fascinating aspect of human experience must continue. As Hobsbawm (1985) stated, "There is generally no material until our questions have revealed it" (p. 66).

We may never find an ultimate answer . . . but this is another question!

Bibliography

This bibliography is not intended to be a complete listing of all the publications related to animal magnetism, artificial somnambulism, and hypnosis. It seeks to bring together the most important publications on forensic hypnosis and related issues. The reader is encouraged to consult Barrucand (1968), Darnton (1968), Ellenberger (1970), and Udolf (1983) for references that would not be found in the following list.

Abbott, J. S. C. (1859). *The French Revolution of 1789 as viewed in the light of republican institutions* (2 volumes; reprinted in 1887). New York: Harper & Brothers.

Affaire Eyraud-Bompard. (1890, December). *Gazette des Tribunaux, 1,* 1201-1219.

Akopenko, A. (1897). L'état actuel de la question sur les crimes hypnotiques. *Archives de l'Anthropologie Criminelle, de Criminologie, et de Psychologie Normale et Pathologique, 12,* 705-707.

Allen, G. S. (1934). Hypnotism and its legal import. *Canadian Bar Review, 1,* 14-22; *2,* 80-91.

Allison, R. B. (1984). Difficulties diagnosing the multiple personality syndrome in a death penalty case. *International Journal of Clinical and Experimental Hypnosis, 32,* 102-117.

Amadou, R. (Ed.). (1971). *F. A. Mesmer: Le magnétisme animal.* Paris: Payot. (A nearly complete compendium of Mesmer's writings.)

American Medical Association. (1958). Medical use of hypnosis. *Journal of the American Medical Association, 168,* 186-189.

American Medical Association. (1985). Scientific status of refreshing recollection by the use of hypnosis. *Journal of the American Medical Association, 253,* 1918-1923.

Annales de la Société Harmonique des Amis Réunis de Strasbourg: ou Cures que des membres de cette Société ont opérées par le magnétisme animal. (3 volumes: 1786, 1787, 1789). Strasbourg: Author.

Annales de Psychiatrie et d'Hypnologie. (5 volumes: 1891-1895). J. Luys (Ed.). Paris: Author. (The *Annales* followed the *Revue d'Hypnologie*.)

Annales du Magnétisme Animal. (8 volumes: 1814-1816). Paris: De Lausanne & Dentu. (The *Annales* were followed by the *Bibliothèque du Magnétisme Animal.*)

Anonymous. (1775). *Procès-verbal des opérations merveilleuses qui se sont faites en vertu du sacré nom de Jésus, par le ministère du sieur Gassner, prêtre séculier et conseiller ecclésiastique de S. A. le prince-évêque de Ratisbonne et d'Ellwangen.* Schillingsfurt: Germain-Daniel Lobegots (imprimeur de la cour de S. A. S. Mgr le prince régnant de Hollenlokt et de Waldembourg).

Anonymous. (1782). *Lettre de M. D'Eslon à M. Philips, doyen de la Faculté de Médecine de Paris.* La Haye: n. p.

Anonymous. (1784a). *Histoire du magnétisme en France, de son régime et de son influence pour servir à développer l'idée qu'on doit avoir de la médecine universelle.* (Reprinted in the *Recueil général*)

Anonymous. (1784b). *Mesmer guéri: ou Lettre d'un provincial au R. P. N. en réponse à sa lettre intitulée, Mesmer blessé.* Paris: Marchands de Nouveautés. (Reprinted in the *Recueil général*)

Anonymous. (1784c). *Traces du magnétisme.* LaHaye. (Reprinted in the *Recueil général*)

Anonymous. (1784d). *Eclaircissements sur le magnétisme animal.* Londres. (Reprinted in the *Recueil général*)

Anonymous. (1784e). *Mémoire pour servir à l'histoire de la jonglerie, dans lequel on démontre les phénomènes du mesmérisme.* Paris: Méquignon l'aîné. (Reprinted in the *Recueil général*)

Anonymous. (1784f). *Rapport du rapport de MM. les Commissaires nommés par le Roi pour examiner la pratique de M. D'Eslon sur le magnétisme animal, par un Amateur de la Vérité, excité par l'imagination, l'attouchement et l'imitation, & magnétisé par le bon sens et la raison.* Paris: Couturier. (Reprinted in the *Recueil général*)

Anonymous. (1784g). *Réflexions impartiales sur le magnétisme animal.* Paris: Périsse le Jeune. (Reprinted in the *Recueil général*)

Anonymous. (1784h). *Le moraliste mesmérien: ou Lettres philosophiques de l'influence du magnétisme.* Paris: Bélin. (Attributed to Jean-Baptiste Sulaville.) (Reprinted in the *Recueil général*)

Anonymous. (1784i). *La vision, contenant l'explication de l'écrit intitulé: Traces du magnétisme, et la théorie des vrais sages.* Paris: Couturier. (Reprinted in the *Recueil général*)

Anonymous. (1784j). *Supplément aux deux rapports de MM. les Commissaires de l'Académie et de la Faculté de Médecine et de la Société Royale de Médecine.* Paris: Gueffier. (Reprinted in the *Recueil général*)

Anonymous. (1845). *Confessions of a magnetizer, being an exposé of animal magnetism.* Boston: Gleason Publishing Hall.

Anonymous. (1898). Hypnotism: Report from the Session of Psychology, British Medical Association. *Medico-legal Journal, 16,* 244–250.

Anonymous. (undated-a). *Le magnétisme par un Ami de la Vérité.* (Reprinted in the *Recueil général*)

Anonymous. (undated-b). Lettre à l'intendant de Soissons sur les opérations mesmériennes de M. de Puységur, à Buzanci. In A. F. Montègre (Ed.), *Du magnétisme animal et de ses partisans.* Paris: D. Colas, 1812.

Anonymous. (undated-c). *Nouvelle découverte sur le magnétisme animal: ou Lettre adressée à un ami de province, par un partisan zélé de la vérité.* (Reprinted in the *Recueil général*)

A practical magnetizer. (1841). *Elements of animal magnetism or pneumatology.* New York: Turner & Hughes.

A practical magnetizer. (1843). *The history and philosophy of animal magnetism with practical instructions for the exercise of this power, being a complete compend of all the information now existing upon this important subject.* Boston: No publisher (n.p.) given.

Archives de la Société Magnétique de Caën. (2 volumes: 1845–1846). Caën: n. p.

Archives du Magnétisme Animal. (4 volumes: 1820–1823). E. F. d'Hénin de Cuvillers (Ed.). Paris: n. p.

Archives pour le Magnétisme et le Somnambulisme. (8 issues: 1788–1789). Strasbourg: n. p.

Arnold, G. F. (1913). Psychology applied to legal evidence. In H. J. Wigmore (Ed.), *Principles of judicial proof.* Boston: Little, Brown. (Original work published 1906)

Arons, H. (1967). *Hypnosis in criminal investigation.* Springfield, IL: Charles C. Thomas.

Ås, A. (1962). The recovery of forgotten language knowledge through hypnotic age regression: A case report. *American Journal of Clinical Hypnosis, 5,* 24–29.

Aserinsky, E., & Kleitman, N. (1953). Regularly occurring periods of eye motility, and concomitant phenomena, during sleep. *Science, 118*, 273–274.

Aubin, Nicolas. (1716). *Cruels effets de la vengeance du Cardinal de Richelieu: ou Histoire des Diables de Loudun, de la possession des religieuses ursulines, et de la condamnation et du supplice d'Urbain Grandier, curé de la même ville.* Amsterdam: E. Roger.

Augmentation de 32% des crimes violents aux Etats-Unis depuis 10 ans. (1986). *Le Journal de Montréal*, p. 8.

Ault, R. L., Jr. (1979). The FBI guidelines for the use of hypnosis. *International Journal of Clinical and Experimental Hypnosis, 27*, 449–451.

Austin v. Barker, 90 App. Div. 351, 85 N. Y. S. 465 (4th Dept. 1904).

Austin v. Barker, 110 App. Div. 510, 96 N. Y. S. 814 (N. Y. 1906).

Auvard, A. (1889). *Travaux d'obstétrique*. Paris: Lecrosnier & Babé.

Azam, E. (1860). Note sur le sommeil nerveux ou hypnotisme. *Archives Générales de Médecine, 15*, 5–24.

Azam, E. (1893). *Hypnotisme et double conscience*. Paris: F. Alcan.

Babinski, J. (1906). *Ma conception de l'hystérie et de l'hypnotisme (pithiatisme)*. Conférence faite à la Société de l'internat des Hôpitaux de Paris (séance de 28 Juin 1906). Chartre: Durand.

Babinski, J. (1910). *De l'hypnotisme en thérapeutique et en médecine légale*. Paris: Imprimerie de la Semaine Médicale.

Babinski, J. (1911). Comment concevoir l'hypnotisme: Ses applications thérapeutiques et médico-légales. *Revue Neurologique, 21*, 12–17.

Baets, M. de. (1894). L'hypnotisme en justice. *Le Magasin Littéraire, 1*, 5–28.

Baker, M. (1986). *Cops: Their lives in their own words*. New York: Pocket Books.

Baker, S. R., & Boaz, D. (1983). The partial reformulation of a traumatic memory of a dental phobia during trance: A case study. *International Journal of Clinical and Experimental Hypnosis, 31*, 14–18.

Ballet, G. (1891). La suggestion hypnotique au point de vue médico-légal. *Gazette Hebdomadaire de Médecine, 28*, 522–525, 534–539.

Bannister, H. M. (1895). Hypnotic influences in criminals. *Albany Law Journal, 51*, 87–88.

Barber, T. X. (1969). *Hypnosis: A scientific approach*. New York: Van Nostrand.

Barber, T. X. (1970). *LSD, marihuana, yoga, and hypnosis*. Chicago: Aldine.

Barbier, A. T. (1822–1827). *Dictionnaires des ouvrages anonymes et pseudonymes* (4 volumes). Paris: Barrois l'aîné. (See also Quérard, 1869.)

Barnes, M. (1982). *Hypnosis on trial*. London: British Broadcasting Corporation television program.

Barnes, W. A. (1898). *Psychology, hypnotism, personal magnetism, and clairvoyance*. Boston: Alfred Mudge & Sons.

Barreau, F. (1844). *Le magnétisme humain en Cour de Rome et en Cour de Cassation sous le rapport religieux, moral et scientifique, suivi d'une méthode pratique appuyée sur un grand nombre d'expériences et de faits nouveaux*. Paris: Sagnier et Bray.

Barrucand, D. (1967). *Histoire de l'hypnose en France*. Paris: Presses Universitaires de France.

Bartlett, F. C. (1932). *Remembering*. Cambridge: Cambridge University Press.

Baudoin, C. (1920). *Suggestion and auto-suggestion* (Eden & Cedar Paul, Trans.). London: George Allen & Unwin.

Beaunis, H. E. (1886). *Le somnambulisme provoqué: Études physiologiques et psychologiques*. Paris: J. B. Baillière et Fils.

Beaunis, H. E. (1890). A. Liébeault: Le sommeil provoqué et les états analogues. *Revue Philosophique de la France et de l'Etranger, 29*, 73–80.

Beck, L. F. (1958). Hypnotic identification of an amnesia victim. In L. Huhn & S. Russo (Eds.), *Modern hypnosis*. North Hollywood, CA: Hal Leighton.

Bélanger, J., Laurence, J.-R., & Perry, C. (1984). L'hypnose psycholégale: Une histoire à suivre. *La Revue du Barreau, 44*, 869–899.

Bell, C. (1889). Hypnotism. *Medico-legal Journal, 6,* 363-369.
Bell, C. (1891). Hypnotism and the law. *Medico-legal Journal, 8,* 331-358.
Bell, C. (1896a). Hypnotism in the criminal courts. *Medico-legal Journal, 13,* 351-362.
Bell, C. (1896b). The case of Spurgeon Young. *Medico-legal Journal, 14,* 529-545.
Bell, C. (1896c). Report of the Psychological Section of the Medico-legal Society. *Medico-legal Journal, 14,* 546-561.
Bell, C. (1897). The subconscious mind. Sub-liminal consciousness. *Medico-legal Journal, 15,* 129-144.
Bellanger, A. (1854). *Le magnétisme, vérités et chimères de cette science occulte.* Paris: Guilhermet.
Bérard, A. (1891). L'instruction criminelle à Lyon. *Archives de l'Anthropologie Criminelle et des Sciences Pénales, 6,* 29-37.
Bergasse, N. (1781). *Lettre d'un médecin de la Faculté de Paris, à un médecin du Collège de Londres: Ouvrage dans lequel on prouve contre M. Mesmer que le magnétisme animal n'existe pas.* La Haye: n. p.
Bergasse, N. (1784). *Considérations sur le magnétisme animal: ou Sur la théorie du monde et des êtres organisés d'après les principes de M. Mesmer.* La Haye: n. p.
Bergasse, N. (1785). *Observations de M. Bergasse sur un écrit du Docteur Mesmer.* London: n. p.
Bérillon, E. (Ed.). (1889, Août). *Premier Congrès International de l'Hypnotisme Expérimental et Thérapeutique: Comptes rendus.* Paris: Octave Doin.
Bérillon, E. (1890-1891). Suggestions criminelles et responsabilité pénale. *Revue de l'Hypnotisme Expérimental et Thérapeutique, 6,* 166-170; *7,* 208-214; *9,* 261-266; *11,* 338-342.
Bérillon, E. (1892). Les faux témoignages suggérés chez les enfants. *Revue de l'Hypnotisme Expérimental et Thérapeutique, 7,* 203-212.
Bérillon, E. (1893). Les suggestions criminelles et la responsabilité pénale. *Actes du Congrès International d'Anthropologie Criminelles, 3,* 114-120, 309-332.
Bérillon, E. (1896). Les suggestions criminelles envisagées au point de vue des faux témoignages suggérés. *Revue de l'Hypnotisme Expérimental et Thérapeutique, 3,* 70-76.
Bérillon, E., & Farez, P. (Eds.). (1902, Août). *Deuxième Congrès International de l'Hypnotisme Expérimental et Thérapeutique: Comptes rendus.* Paris: Vigot Frères.
Berna, D.-J. (1835). *Expériences et considérations à l'appui du magnétisme animal.* Paris: n. p.
Bernheim, H. (1884). *De la suggestion dans l'état hypnotique et dans l'état de veille.* Paris: Octave Doin.
Bernheim, H. (1886). *De la suggestion et de ses applications à la thérapeutique.* Paris: Octave Doin.
Bernheim, H. (1889). Le sommeil naturel ou artificiel. In E. Bérillon (Ed.), *Premier Congrès International de l'Hypnotisme Expérimental et Thérapeutique: Comptes rendus.* Paris: Octave Doin.
Bernheim, H. (1890). Du rôle de la suggestion dans les témoignages: A propos de l'affaire Borras, victime d'une erreur judiciaire. *Revue de l'Hypnotisme Expérimental et Thérapeutique, 1,* 8-9.
Bernheim, H. (1891). L'épilogue d'un procès célèbre. *Revue de l'Hypnotisme Expérimental et Thérapeutique, 9,* 270-272.
Bernheim, H. (1897). *L'hypnotisme et la suggestion dans leurs rapports avec la médecine légale.* Nancy: A. Crépin-Leblond.
Bersot, E. (1853). *Mesmer et le magnétisme animal.* Paris: Hachette.
Bertrand, A. J. F. (1823). *Traité du somnambulisme et des différentes modifications qu'il présente.* Paris: J. G. Dentu.
Bertrand, A. J. F. (1826). *Du magnétisme animal en France.* Paris: J. B. Ballière.
Bidon, H. (1894). L'hypnotisme, la défense nationale et la Société civile. *Annales de Psychiatrie et d'Hypnologie, 4,* 94-95.
Binet, A. (1890). Pierre Janet: L'automatisme psychologique. *Revue Philosophique de la France et de l'Etranger, 29,* 186-200.

Binet, A. (1896). *Alterations of personality* (H. G. Baldwin, Trans.). New York: Appleton.
Binet, A. (1900). *La suggestibilité*. Paris: Schleicher Frères.
Binet, A. (1905). *On double consciousness: Experimental psychological studies*. Chicago: Open Court Publishing Co. (Original work published in France, 1889-1890.)
Binet, A., & Féré, C. (1888). *Animal magnetism*. New York: Appleton.
Blanc, E. (Abbé). (1898). *La suggestion hypnotique est-elle licite ou illicite, naturelle ou diabolique?* Paris: Ch. Amat.
Bleuler, E. (1889). Zur Psychologie der Hypnose (Vol. 5). *Münchener Medizinische Wochenschrift*.
Bloch, M. (1974). *Apologie pour l'histoire: ou, Métier d'historien*. Paris: A. Colin.
Boéteau, M. (1892). Automatisme somnambulique avec dédoublement de la personnalité. *Annales Médico-Psychologiques, 1*, 63-79.
Bonjean, A. (1890). *L'hypnotisme, ses rapports avec le droit et la thérapeutique: La suggestion mentale*. Paris: F. Alcan.
Bonnefoy, J. B. (1784). *Analyse raisonnée du rapport des commissaires chargés par le Roi de l'examen du magnétisme animal*. Paris: Prault. (Reprinted in the *Recueil général*)
Borméo, Baron de. (1784). *Lettre de M. L. B. D. B. à M. P. L. G. H. D. L. B. à Marseille*. Paris: Couturier. (Reprinted in the *Recueil général*)
Bottey, F. (1884). *Le Magnétisme animal: Etude critique et expérimentale sur l'hypnotisme ou sommeil nerveux provoqué chez les sujets sains*. Paris: E. Plon, Nourrit et Cie.
Bouchardon, P. (1933). *La malle mystérieuse*. Paris: Albin Michel.
Bourru, H., & Burot, P. (1887). *La suggestion mentale et l'action à distance des substances toxiques et médicamenteuses*. Paris: J. B. Ballière.
Bourru, H., & Burot, P. (1888). *Variations de la personnalité*. Paris: Hachette.
Bower, G. H. (1981). Mood and memory. *American Psychologist, 36*, 129-148.
Bowers, K. S. (1984). On being unconsciously influenced and informed. In K. S. Bowers & D. Meichenbaum (Eds.), *The unconscious reconsidered*. New York: Wiley.
Braid, J. (1843). *Neurypnology: or The rationale of nervous sleep, considered in relation with animal magnetism*. London: John Churchill.
Braid, J. (1960). *Braid on hypnotism: The beginnings of modern hypnosis* (Revised ed. by A. E. Waite). New York: Julian. (This work contains most of Braid's writings.)
Bramwell, J.-M. (1921). *Hypnotism: Its history, practice and theory* (3rd ed.). London: William Rider.
Brémaud, P. (1884). *Des différentes phases de l'hypnotisme et en particulier de la fascination*. Paris: L. Cerf.
Briand, J., & Chaudé, E. (1879). *Manuel complet de médecine légale* (10th ed., 2 volumes). Paris: J. B. Baillière et Fils.
Brièrre de Boismont, A. J. F. (1843). *Médecine légale: Attentats aux moeurs*. Paris: Bourgogne et Martinet.
Brièrre de Boismont, A. J. F. (1845). *Des hallucinations: ou Histoire raisonnée des apparitions, des visions, des songes, de l'extase, du magnétisme et du somnambulisme*. Paris: G. Baillière. (English translation [1853] published in Philadelphia: Lindsay and Blakinston. Reprinted [1976] in *Classics in Psychiatry*. New York: Arno Press.)
Brièrre de Boismont, A. J. F. (1863). *De la responsabilité légale des aliénés*. Paris: J. B. Baillière.
Brouardel, P. (1879). Accusation de viol accompli pendant le sommeil hypnotique. *Annales d'Hygiène Publique et de Médecine Légale, 1*, 39-57.
Brouardel, P., Motet, A., & Garnier, P. (1893). Affaire Valrof. *Annales d'Hygiène Publique et de Médecine Légale, 29*, 497-524.
Browne, J. (1684). *Adenochoiradelogia: or An anatomick-chirurgical treatise of glandules and strumaes, or kings-evil-swellings. Together with the royal gift of healing, or cure thereof by contact on imposition of hands, performed for above 640 years by our Kings of England, continued with their admirable effects, and miraculous events; and concluded with many wonderful examples of cures by their sacred touch* (3 volumes: I. Adenographia, II. Chaeradelogia, III. Charisma Basilicon). London: Theo. Newcomb for Sam. Lowndes.

Bryan, W. J., Jr. (1962). *Legal aspects of hypnosis*. Springfield, IL: Charles C. Thomas.
Bryde, D. (1666). *Wonders no miracle: or Greatrakes healing examined*. London: n.p.
Bucknill, J. C., & Tuke, D.-H. (1858). *A manual of psychological medicine*. London: n.p.
Bué, A. (1906). *Le magnétisme curatif*. Paris: Bibliothèque Chacornac.
Burack, B. (1955). A critical analysis of the theory, method, and limitations of the "lie detector." *Journal of Criminal Law, Criminology and Police Science, 46*, 414-426.
Burdin, C., & Dubois, F. (1841). *Histoire académique du magnétisme animal*. Paris: J. B. Baillière.
Burnham, W. H. (1889). Memory, historically and experimentally considered: III. Paramnesia. *American Journal of Psychology, 2*, 431-464.
Burot, P. (1889). De l'auto-suggestion en médecine légale. In E. Bérillon (Ed.), *Premier Congrès International de l' Hypnotisme Expérimental et Thérapeutique: Comptes rendus*. Paris: Octave Doin.
Bush, G. (1847). *Mesmer and Swedenborg: or The relation of the developments of mesmerism to the doctrines and disclosures of Swedenborg*. New York: John Allen.
Button, J. (1986). The effects of a forensic hypnosis procedure on memory: Does it augment facts or fantasies? Unpublished B. A. Honors Thesis, Concordia University, Montréal, Canada.
Cahagnet, L.-A. (1850). *Sanctuaire du spiritualisme: Etude de l'âme humaine, et de ses rapports avec l'univers d' après le somnambulisme et l'extase*. Paris: n.p.
Campili, G. (1886). *Il grande ipnotismo et la suggestione ipnotica nei rapporti col diritto penale et civile*. Torino: Bocca.
Carlson, E. T., & Simpson, M. M. (1970). Perkinism vs. Mesmerism. *Journal of the History of the Behavioral Sciences, 6*, 16-24.
Carpenter, W. (1877). *Mesmerism and spiritualism: Historically and scientifically considered*. New York: D. Appleton.
Carra, J. L. (1785). *Examen physique du magnétisme animal*. Paris: Eugène Onfroy.
Caullet de Veaumorel, L. (1785). *Aphorismes de Mesmer* (3rd ed.). Paris: Librairie de Bertrand.
Chambart, E. (1881a). *Du somnambulisme en général*. Paris: Octave Doin.
Chambart, E. (1881b). Actions hypnogéniques: Hyperexcitabilité musculaire hypnotique. Hypnose hémicérébrale. *L'Encéphale, 1*, 95-114, 236-250.
Chapman v. State, 638 P. 2d 1280 (Wyoming 1982).
Charcot, J.-M., & Richer, P. (1882). *Contribution de l'hypnotisme chez les hystériques*. In Krauss Reprints, *The origins of psychiatry and psychoanalysis: Pre-Freudian psychology series—France*. (Vol. 28). Nendeln/Liechtenstein: Kraus-Thompson 1978.
Charpignon, L.-J. (1841). *Physiologie, médecine et métaphysique du magnétisme*. Orléans: Pesty.
Charpignon, L.-J. J. (1860). *Rapports du magnétisme avec la jurisprudence et la médecine légale*. Paris: G. Baillière.
Chateaubriand, F. A. R. (1843). *Mémoires d'outre-tombe* (4 volumes). (Re-edited [1949] in Paris: Flammarion.)
Chertok, L. (1957). *Les méthodes psychosomatiques d'accouchement sans douleur*. Paris: Expansion Scientifique Française.
Clark, K. (1956). *The nude: A study in ideal form* (Bollingen Series XXXV.2). New York: Pantheon Books.
Cloquet, J. (1837). Lettre ouverte du 4 février, 1837. *Gazette Médicale de Paris, 5*, 78.
Coe, W. C., Kobayashi, K., & Howard, M. L. (1972). An approach toward isolating factors that influence antisocial conduct in hypnosis. *International Journal of Clinical and Experimental Hypnosis, 20*, 118-131.
Coe, W. C., Kobayashi, K., & Howard, M. L. (1973). Experimental and ethical problems in evaluating the influence of hypnosis in antisocial conduct. *Journal of Abnormal Psychology, 82*, 476-482.
Coe, W. C., & Sarbin, T. R. (1977). Hypnosis from the stand point of a contextualist. *Annals of the New York Academy of Sciences, 296*, 2-13.
Collins v. State, Md. Spec. App. No. 1583, September term, opinion filed 7/13/82 (1981).
Collyer, R. (1838a). *Lights and shadows of American life*. Boston: Brainard & Co.

Collyer, R. (1838b). *The manual of phrenology* Dayton: B. F. Ellis.
Commonwealth v. Burke, 105 Mass. 376 (1870).
Commonwealth v. DiNicola, 502 A.2d 606 (Pa. Super. 1985).
Commonwealth v. Jewelle, 199 Mass. 558, 85 N. E. 858 (1908).
Commonwealth v. Nazarovitch, Pa. - r36 A.2d 170 (1981).
Commonwealth v. Smoyer, 476 A.2d 1304 (Pa. 1984).
Conn, J. H. (1972). Is hypnosis really dangerous? *International Journal of Clinical and Experimental Hypnosis, 20*, 61-79.
Connecticut Medical Society, (1884). *Proceedings (1792-1829)* pp. 39-40, [May 17, 1796]. Hartford: Case, Lockwood & Brainard.
Cornell v. Superior Court of San Diego, 52 Cal. 2d 99, 338 P.2d 447 (1959).
Crampon. (1827). *Magnétisme animal à l'usage des gens du monde, suivi de quelques lettres en opposition à ce mode de guérison.*
Crichton-Browne, Sir J. (1895). *On dreamy mental states* (The Cavendish Lectures). n.p.
Crocq, J. (1893). *Sur quelques phénomènes de l'hypnose.* Paris: Michels et Fils.
Crocq, J. (1894). *L'hypnotisme et le crime.* Bruxelles: H. Lamertin.
Crocq, J. (1896). *L'hypnotisme scientifique.* Paris: Editions Scientifiques.
Cullerre, A. (1886). *Magnétisme et hypnotisme.* Paris: J. B. Baillière et Fils.
Cullerre, A. (1892). L'hypnotisme et le droit. *Annales Médico-Psychologiques, 15*, 256-267.
D . . . (1784). *La Mesmériade: ou Le triomphe du magnétisme animal.* Paris: Couturier. (Reprinted in the *Recueil général*)
Dailey, A. H. (1895). The hypnotic power—What is it? *Medico-legal Journal, 13*, 274-278.
Dalgado, D. G. (1906). *Mémoire sur la vie de l'Abbé de Faria.* Paris: Henri Jouve.
Danjou, F., & Cimber, L. (1834-1841). *Archives curieuses de l'histoire de France depuis Louis XI jusqu'à Louis XVIII* (Ière série 1-15, 2ème série 1-12). Paris: Beauvais.
Darnton, R. (1968). *Mesmerism and the end of the Enlightenment in France.* Cambridge: Harvard University Press.
Darnton, R. (1984). *The great cat massacre and other episodes in French cultural history.* New York: Basic Books.
de Bourzéis, J. A. (1783). *Observations très importantes sur les effets du magnétisme animal.* Paris: Gueffier.
Decroix, M. E. (1895). Tabacomanie, traitement par l'hypnotisme et la suggestion. *Annales de Psychiatrie et d'Hypnologie, 2*, 56-61.
de Jong, A. (1893). L'hypnotisme et la résistance aux suggestions. *Revue de l'Hypnotisme Expérimental et Thérapeutique, 5*, 129-135.
de Jussieu, A. L. (1784). *Rapport de l'un des commissaires chargés par le Roy de l'examen du magnétisme animal.* Paris: Veuve Hérissant.
Delacroix, F. (1887). *Les suggestions hypnotiques: Une lacune dans la loi.* Paris: Chevalier-Maresq.
De Lamenardière, P. (1634). *La démonomanie de Loudun, qui montre la véritable possession des religieuses ursulines, avec la liste des religieuses et séculières possédées* (2nd ed.). La Flèche: G. Griveau.
de la Tourette, G. (1887). *L'hypnotisme et les états analogues au point de vue médico-légal.* Paris: E. Plon, Nourrit et Cie.
de la Tourette, G. (1889). Discussion. In E. Bérillon (Ed.), *Premier Congrès International de l'Hypnotisme Expérimental et Thérapeutique: Comptes rendus.* Paris: Octave Doin.
de la Tourette, G. (1891). L'épilogue d'un procès célèbre. *Revue de l'Hypnotisme Expérimental et Thérapeutique, 8*, 241-249.
de la Tourette, G. (1895). *Traité clinique et thérapeutique de l'hystérie d'après l'enseignement de la Salpêtrière* (3 volumes). Paris: Plon.
Delboeuf, J. (1886a). Une visite à la Salpêtrière. *Revue Belge, 18*, 121-132, 258-275.
Delboeuf, J. (1886b). De l'influence de l'imitation et de l'éducation dans le somnambulisme provoqué. *Revue Philosophique, 22*, 146-171.
Delboeuf, J. (1889a). *Le magnétisme animal: A propos d'une visite à l'école de Nancy.* Paris: n.p.

Delboeuf, J. (1889b). Réponse de M. Delboeuf au rapport de M. Ladame. In E. Bérillon (Ed.), *Premier Congrès International de l'Hypnotisme Expérimental et Thérapeutique: Comptes rendus*. Paris: Octave Doin.

Delboeuf, J. (1890). *Magnétiseurs et médecins*. Paris: F. Alcan.

Delboeuf, J. (1895). L'hypnose et les suggestions criminelles. *Revue de l'Hypnotisme Expérimental et Thérapeutique, 8*, 225-240.

Deleuze, J. P. F. (1813). *Histoire critique du magnétisme animal* (2 volumes). Paris: Mame.

Deleuze, J. P. F. (1825). *Instruction pratique sur le magnétisme animal*. Paris: Germer-Baillière. (Reprinted in 1846)

Deleuze, J. P. F. (1826). *Lettre à Messieurs les membres de l'Académie de Médecine*. Paris: Béchet Jeune.

Deleuze, J. P. F. (1828). Lettre de M. Deleuze à M. M . . . de la Marne. *L'Hermès, 32*.

Demarquay, J. N., & Giraud-Teulon, F. (1860). *Recherche sur l'hypnotisme ou sommeil nerveux*. Paris: J. B. Baillière et Fils.

de Paris, J. (1894). Hypnotisée en omnibus. *Annales de Psychiatrie et d'Hypnologie, 4*, 95-96.

D'Eslon, C. (1780). *Observations sur le magnétisme animal*. Paris: Didot le Jeune.

D'Eslon, C. (1784). *Observations sur les deux rapports de MM. les Commissaires nommés par sa Majesté pour l'examen du magnétisme animal*. Paris: Clousier.

Desnos, A. C. (Comte). (1842). *Les magnétiseurs sont-ils sorciers?* Paris: J. Rouvier.

Despine, P. (1868). *Psychologie Naturelle* (3 volumes). Paris: F. Savy.

Despine, P. (1880). *Etude scientifique sur le somnambulisme*. Paris: F. Savy.

D'Eprémenil, J. J. D.(1784). *Réflexions préliminaires à l'occasion de la pièce intitulée les Docteurs Modernes, jouée sur le théâtre italien, le seize novembre 1784*. Paris: n.p.

D'Eprémenil, J. J. D. (1785). *Sommes versées entre les mains de M. Mesmer, pour acquérir le droit de publier sa découverte*. Paris: n.p.

Dession, G. H., Freedman, L. Z., Donnellym, R. C., & Redlich, F. C. (1953). Drug-induced revelation and criminal investigation. *Yale Law Journal, 62*, 315-347.

Dessoir, M. (1888). *Bibliographie des modernen hypnotismus*. Berlin: C. Duncker.

Devillers, C. (1784). *Le colosse aux pieds d'argile*. Bojolois: n.p.

Diamond, B. (1980). Inherent problems in the use of pretrial hypnosis on a prospective witness. *California Law Review, 68*, 313-349.

Diethelm, O. (1970). The medical teaching of demonology in the 17th and 18th centuries. *Journal of the History of the Behavioral Sciences, 6*, 3-15.

Dods, J. B. (1843). *The philosophy of Mesmerism*. Boston: William Hall.

Dods, J. B. (1850). *The philosophy of electrical psychology*. New York: Fowler and Wells.

Dolbeau, M. (1874). De l'emploi du chloroforme à propos de la perpétration des crimes et des délits. *Annales d'Hygiène Publique et de Médecine Légale, 41*, 168-184.

Domangue, B. (1985). Hypnotic regression and reframing in the treatment of insect phobias. *American Journal of Psychotherapy, 39*, 206-214.

Douliot, H. (1887). L'hypnotisme et la médecine légale. *Revue Internationale, 16*, 411-425.

Dresser, A. (1895). *The philosophy of P. P. Quimby*. Boston: Alfred Budge & Sons.

Dresser, H. (1899). *Methods and problems in spiritual healing*. New York: G. P. Putnam.

Dresser, J. (1887). *The true history of mental science*. Boston: Alfred Budge & Sons.

Drolet, A. (1970). "Le magnétisme animal" chez Lord Durham. In *Les Cahiers d'Histoire: Trois siècles de Médecine Québécoise*. Québec: La Société Historique de Québec, 22, 145-153.

Dubor, G. (de). (1920). *Les mystères de l'hypnose*. Paris: Perrin et Cie.

Dumaniant, A. J. B. (1786). *Le médecin malgré tout le monde*. Paris: Cailleau.

Duncan, M. (1634). *Discours sur la possession des ursulines de Loudun*. Saumur: n.p.

Dupau, J. A. (1826). *Lettres physiologiques et morales sur le magnétisme animal*. Paris: Gabon & Delaunay.

Du Potet, J. (Baron de Sennevoy). (1882). *Traité complet du magnétisme animal* (4th ed.). Paris: Germer-Baillière.

Dupré, E., & Rocher, G. (1901). *L'hypnotisme devant la loi*. Clermont, Oise: Daix Frères.

Durand, J. P. (de Gros). (1855). *Electro-dynamisme vital: ou Les relations physiologiques de l'esprit et de la matière démontrées par des expériences entièrement nouvelles, et par l'histoire raisonnée du système nerveux.* Paris: J. B. Baillière.

Durand, J. P. (de Gros). (1860). *Cours théoriques et pratiques de braidisme ou hypnotisme nerveux.* Paris: J. B. Baillière.

Durand, J. P. (de Gros). (1894). *Le merveilleux scientifique.* Paris: F. Alcan.

Durand, J. P. (de Gros). (1895). Suggestions hypnotiques criminelles: Lettre au Docteur Liébeault. *Revue de l'Hypnotisme Expérimental et Thérapeutique, 1,* 8-23.

Durant, C. (1837). *Exposition: or A new theory of animal magnetism with a key to the mysteries, demonstrated by experiments with the most celebrated somnambulists in America; also, Strictures on "Col. Wm. L. Stone's letter to Doctor A. Brigham."* New York: Wiley & Putnam.

Dureau, A. (1869). *Notes bibliographiques pour servir à l'histoire du magnétisme animal.* Paris: Author.

Dywan, J., & Bowers, K. S. (1983). The use of hypnosis to enhance recall. *Science, 222,* 184-185.

E. F. (1784). *Lettre d'un Bordelais au Père Hervier en réponse à celle que ce savant a écrite aux Bordelais à l'occasion du magnétisme animal.* Amsterdam. (Reprinted in the *Recueil général*)

Echterling, L. G., & Emmerling, D. A. (1987). Impact of stage hypnosis. *American Journal of Clinical Hypnosis, 29,* 149-154.

Eddy, M. B. (1875). *Science and health.* Boston: Christian Science Publishing Co.

Ellenberger, H. F. (1970). *The discovery of the unconscious: The history and evolution of dynamic psychiatry.* New York: Basic Books.

Ellenberger, H. F. (1978). *Les mouvements de libération mythique et autres essais sur l'histoire de la psychiatrie.* Montréal, Canada: Les Editions Quinze.

Elliotson, J. (1982). *John Elliotson on Mesmerism: Collected works* (F. Kaplan, Ed.). New York: Da Capo Press.

Ellinger, M. (1896). The case of Czynski. *Medico-legal Journal, 14,* 150-162.

Emmett v. Ricketts and Creamer v. Hopper. 397 F. Supp. 102 (N.D. Ga. 1975).

Erickson, M. H. (1935). A study of an experimental neurosis hypnotically induced in a case of ejaculatio praecox. *British Journal of Medical Psychology, 15,* 34-50.

Erickson, M. H., & Rossi, E. L. (1980). The February man: Facilitating new identity in hypnosis. In E. L. Rossi (Ed.), *The collected papers of Milton H. Erickson on hypnosis* (Vol. 4). New York: Irvington.

Esdaile, J. (1846). *Mesmerism in India and its practical application in surgery and medicine.* London: Longman, Brown, Green, & Longmans. Reprinted in D. N. Robinson (Ed.), *Significant contributions to the history of psychology, 1750-1920* (Series A, Vol. 10). Washington, DC: University Publications of America, 1977.

Estabrooks, G. H. (1980). *Using hypnotism* (1st ed.). Toronto, Canada: Coles.

Evans, F. J. (1979). Contextual forgetting: Posthypnotic source amnesia. *Journal of Abnormal Psychology, 88,* 556-563.

Evans, F. J., & Thorn, W. A. F. (1966). Two types of posthypnotic amnesia: Recall amnesia and source amnesia. *International Journal of Clinical and Experimental Hypnosis, 14,* 162-179.

Evans, R. B., & Koelsch, W. A. (1985). Psychoanalysis arrives in America: The 1909 psychology conference at Clark University. *American Psychologist, 40,* 942-948.

Evans, W. F. (1873). *Mental medicine: A treatise on medical psychology.* Boston: H. H. Carter.

Evans, W. F. (1876). *Soul and body: The spiritual science of health and disease.* Boston: Colby & Rich.

Evans, W. F. (1881). *The divine law of cure.* Boston: H. H. Carter.

Evans, W. F. (1885). *The primitive mind cure: The nature and power of faith, or elementary lessons in Christian philosophy and transcendental medicine.* Boston: H. H. Carter.

Evans, W. F. (1886a). *Esoteric Christianity and mental therapeutics.* Boston: H. H. Carter.

Evans, W. F. (1886b). *The mental cure: Illustrating the influence of the mind and the body both in health and disease and the psychological method of treatment.* Boston: Colby & Rich.

Extract from "The report of the Commissioners" appointed by the King of France to enquire into

the merits of animal magnetism as a cure for disorders: A new discovery (London: John Nichols). (1784). *The Gentleman's Magazine, 54,* 944-946.
Faria, J. C. (Abbé di). (1819). *De la cause du sommeil lucide: ou Etude de la nature de l'homme.* Paris: Mme Horiac.
F. D. P. (1784). *Lettre d'un médecin de la Faculté de Paris à M. Court de Jébelin* [sic]. Bordeaux: Bergeret. (Reprinted in the *Recueil général*)
Féré, C. (1886). *La médecine d'imagination.* Paris: Delahaye et Lecrosnier.
F. H. B., (1897). *Lawyers Annotated Report, 40,* 269-280.
Fienus, T. (1635). *De viribus imaginationis tractatus.* Lyon: Elsevier.
Figuier, L. (1860). *Histoire du merveilleux dans les temps modernes* (4 volumes: I. Les diables de Loudun; Les convulsionnaires Jansénistes, II. La baguette divinatoire; Les prophètes Protestants, III: Le magnétisme animal, IV: Les tables Tournantes; Les médiums et les esprits). Paris: Hachette.
Flournoy, T. (1900). *Des Indes à la planète Mars.* Genève: C. Eggiman.
Fludd, R. (1638). *Philosophia moysaïca in quâ sapientia et scientia creationis explicatur.* n. p.
Foissac, P. (1825). *Mémoire sur le magnétisme animal, adressé à MM. les membres de l'Académie des Sciences et de l'Académie Royale de Médecine.* Paris: Didot le Jeune.
Fontan, J., & Ségard, C. (1887). *Eléments de médecine suggestive.* Paris: Octave Doin.
Fonvielle, W. (de). (1887). *Les endormeurs: La vérité sur les hypnotisants, les suggestionnistes, les magnétiseurs, les donatistes, les braidistes, etc. . . . .* Paris: Librairie Illustrée.
Forel, A. (1906). *Hypnotism or suggestion and psychotherapy: A study of the psychological, psychophysiological and therapeutic aspects of hypnotism* (H. W. Armit, Trans.). New York: Rebman.
Fournel, J. F. (1785). *Remontrances des malades aux médecins de la Faculté de Paris.* Amsterdam: n. p.
Fournier, M. (1781). *Lettre à Monsieur Mesmer, et autres pièces concernant la maladie de la Dlle Berlancourt de Beauvais.* Beauvais: P. Desjardins.
Foveau de Courmelles, F.-V. (1890a). *Le magnétisme devant la loi.* Paris: G. Carré.
Foveau de Courmelles, F.-V. (1890b). *L'hypnotisme.* Paris: Hachette.
Foveau de Courmelles, F.-V. (1890c). Le magnétisme devant la médecine et devant la loi. In E. Bérillon (Ed.), *Rapport général d'après le compte-rendu des séances du Congrès.* Paris: G. Carré.
Franco, G. G. (1890). *L'hypnotisme revenu à la mode.* St. Amand, Cher: St. Joseph.
Franklin, B. (1881). *The life of Benjamin Franklin, written by himself* (J. Bigelow, Ed.; Vol. III, 2nd ed.). Philadelphia: Lippincott. (Now first edited from original manuscripts and from his printed correspondence and other writings.)
Franklin, B., de Bory, G., Lavoisier, A. L., Bailly, J. S., Majault, Sallin, D'Arcet, J., Guillotin, J. I., & LeRoy, J. B. (1784). *Rapport des Commissaires chargés par le Roy de l'examen du magnétisme animal.* Paris: Bibliothèque Royale. Reprinted *in extenso* in C. Burdin & F. Dubois (Eds.), *Histoire académique du magnétisme animal.* Paris: Baillière, 1841.
Franklin, B., de Bory, G., Lavoisier, A. L., Bailly, J. S., Majault, Sallin, D'Arcet, J., Guillotin, J. I., & LeRoy J. B. (1784). Secret report on Mesmerism, or animal magnetism. In R. E. Shor & M. T. Orne (Eds.), *The nature of hypnosis: Selected basic readings.* New York: Holt, Rinehart & Winston, 1965.
Frère, P.-A. (1837). *Examen du magnétisme animal.* Paris: Gaume.
Freud, S. (1900). The interpretation of dreams. In A. A. Brill (Ed.), *The basic writings of Sigmund Freud.* New York: Random House, 1938.
Friedrich, P. (1978). *The meaning of Aphrodite.* Chicago: University of Chicago Press.
Fromm, E. (1970). Age regression with unexpected reappearance of a repressed childhood language. *International Journal of Clinical and Experimental Hypnosis, 18,* 79-88.
Frye v. United States, 293 F. 1013, 34 A.L R. 145 (D.C. Cir. 1923). (For comments see [1924] *Yale Law Journal, 33,* 771-774.)

Fuller, R. C. (1982). *Mesmerism and the American cure of souls*. Philadelphia: University of Pennsylvania Press.

Fustier (Abbé). (1815). *Le mystère des magnétiseurs et des somnambules dévoilés aux âmes droites et vertueuses par un homme du monde*. Paris: Legrand.

Galart de Montjoye, F. C. L. (dit Ventre de la Touloubre). (1784). Essai sur la découverte du magnétisme animal. *Journal de Paris, 44*, 193; *45*, 195; *46*, 201; *47*, 205-213; *64*, 301.

Garcon, M. (1928). *Le magnétisme devant la loi pénale*. Paris: Henri Durville.

Garnier, P. (1887). L'automatisme somnambulique devant les tribunaux. *Annales d'Hygiène Publique et de Médecine Légale, 17*, 334-354.

Garnier, P. (1896). Vols accomplis en état de somnambulisme spontané; Observations médico-légales. *Revue de Médecine Légale et de Jurisprudence Médicale, 12*, 349-357.

Garnier, S. (1912). *L'affaire F. Ch ...* Lyon: A. Rey. (Excerpt in *Archives d'Anthropologie Criminelle, 27*, 226-227.)

Gaston, Duc d'Orléans. (1635). *Relation de ce qui s'est passé aux exorcismes en présence de Monsieur, frère du Roy*. Paris: Jean Martin.

Gauthier, A. (1840). *Introduction au magnétisme, examen de son existence depuis les Indiens jusqu'à l'époque actuelle, sa théorie, sa pratique, ses avantages, ses dangers, et la nécessité de son concours avec la médecine*. Paris: Dentu.

Gauthier, A. (1842). *Histoire du somnambulisme chez tous les peuples*. Paris: F. Malteste.

Gauthier, A. (1844). *Le magnétisme Catholique: ou Introduction à la vie pratique et réfutation des opinions de la médecine sur le magnétisme, ses principes, ses procédés et ses effets*. Paris: Bureau de la *Revue Magnétique*.

Gauthier, A. (1845). *Traité pratique du magnétisme et du somnambulisme*. Paris: G. Baillière.

Gauthier, A. (1846). *Réforme médicale: Compérage magnétique réprimé, questions et observations d'ordre public sur la pratique du magnétisme, du mesmérisme, et du somnambulisme*. Paris: Dondey-Dupré.

Gébelin, C. de. (1784). *Lettre de l'auteur du monde primitif à Messieurs ses souscripteurs, sur le magnétisme*. Paris: Valleyre l'aîné. (Reprinted in the *Recueil général*)

Gigot-Suard, J. A. L. (1860). *Les mystères du magnétisme animal et de la magie dévoilés*. Paris: Labé.

Gilbert, W. (1600). *De magnete, magneticisque corporibus, et de magno magnete tellure: Physiologia nova, plurimis & argumentis & experimentis demonstrata*. London: Excudebat P. Short.

Gill, M. M., & Brenman, M. (1959). *Hypnosis and related states*. New York: International Universities Press.

Giraud, A. (1892). Chronique: Le 3e Congrès International d'Anthropologie Criminelle à Bruxelles. *Annales Médico-Psychologiques, 3*, 345-362.

Gley, M. E. (1895). De quelques conditions favorisant l'hypnotisme chez les grenouilles. *Annales de Psychiatrie et d'Hypnologie, 9*, 260-262.

Grant, G. (1977). Hypnosis in criminal investigation. *The Australian Journal of Clinical Hypnosis, 5*, 5-72.

Grasset, J. (1881). *Traité pratique des maladies du système nerveux*. Paris: A. Delahaye.

Grasset, J. (1903). *L'hypnotisme et la suggestion*. Paris: Octave Doin.

Gravitz, M. A., & Gerton, M. I. (1986). The Société du Magnétisme de la Nouvelle-Orléans: Its place in the early history of Hypnosis in America. *International Journal of Psychosomatics, 33*, 11-14.

Gray, T. (1985). Changing unsubstantiated belief: Testing the ignorance hypothesis. *Canadian Journal of Behavioural Science, 17*, 263-270.

Greenfield v. Commonwealth, 214 Va. 710, 204 S.E.2d 414 (1974).

Grimes, J. S. (1839). *A new system of phrenology*. Buffalo: O. G. Steele.

Grimm, F. M. (1830). *Correspondance littéraire, philosophique et critique de Grimm et de Diderot depuis 1753 jusqu'en 1790*. Paris: Furne.

Guilhermet, G. (1909). *L'hypnotisme et le droit*. Paris: Encyclopédie Nationale.

Guillain, G. (1955). *J.-M. Charcot, 1825-1893: Sa vie, son oeuvre*. Paris: Masson. English translation [1959] published in New York: Paul B. Hoeber.
Guimbail. (1891). Etude médico-légale sur Gabrielle Bompard. *Annales de Psychiatrie et d'Hypnologie, 1*, 17-23.
Halgan, G. (1901). *L'hypnotisme devant la loi*. Paris: Thèse de Médecine.
Hamard, C. P. G. (1835). *Expériences sur le magnétisme animal*. Paris: n. p.
Hamilton, A. M., & Godkin, L. (1894). *A system of legal medicine* (2 volumes). New York: E. B. Treat.
Hammond, W. A. (1876). *Spiritualism and allied causes and conditions of nervous derangement*. New York: G. P. Putnam's & Sons.
Harding v. State, 5 Md. App 230, 246 A.2d 302 (1968) cert. den. 395 U.S. 949, 89 S.Ct. 2030; 23 L.Ed.2d 468.
Hart, E. (1980). *Hypnotism, Mesmerism, and witchcraft*. Toronto, Canada: Coles. (Original work published 1893; 2nd ed. published in 1896)
Hartshorn, T. C. (Ed. and Trans.). (1843). *Practical instruction in animal magnetism by J. P. F. Deleuze*. Revised edition with an appendix of notes by the translator and letters from eminent physicians and others descriptive of cases in the United States. New York: Appleton & Co.
Haward, L. R. C. (1980). Hypnosis of rape victims. *Bulletin of the British Society of Experimental and Clinical Hypnosis, 3* (April), 11-13.
Haward, L. R. C. (1981). Book review of Martin Reiser's *Handbook of investigative hypnosis*. *Bulletin of the British Society of Experimental and Clinical Hypnosis, 4*, (April), 26-27.
Haygart, J. (1800). *Of the imagination as a cause and as a cure of disorders of the body*. Bath: R. Cruttwell.
Hecquet, P. (1733). *Naturalisme des convulsions, démontré par la physique, par l'histoire naturelle et par les événements de cette oeuvre*. Soleure: Andréas Gymnicus.
Hénin de Cuvillers, E. F. d'. (1820). *Le magnétisme éclairé: ou Introduction aux Archives du Magnétisme Animal*. Paris: n. p.
Hénin de Cuvillers, E. F. d'. (1822). *Exposition critique du système et de la doctrine mystique des magnétistes*. Paris: n.p.
Her Majesty The Queen v. Clark, Court of Queen's Bench of Alberta, No. 8303 2017 C 1 (1984).
Her Majesty The Queen v. Allan Dale Zubot, Court of Queen's Bench of Alberta, Judicial District of Medicine Hat, No. 81-08-0029C (1981).
L'Hermès, Journal du magnétisme animal par une Société de médecins de la Faculté de Paris (4 volumes: 1826-1829). Paris: Lévi.
Herrero, A. S. (1889). L'hypnotisation forcée et contre la volonté arrêtée du sujet. In E. Bérillon (Ed.), *Premier Congrès International de l'Hypnotisme Expérimental et Thérapeutique: Comptes rendus*. Paris: Octave Doin.
Hervier, F. (1784). *Lettre sur la découverte du magnétisme animal à M. Court de Gébelin*. Paris: Couturier. (Reprinted in the *Recueil général*)
Hilgard, E. R. (1965). *Hypnotic susceptibility*. New York: Harcourt, Brace, & World.
Hilgard, E. R. (1971). Hypnotic phenomena: The struggle for scientific acceptance. *American Scientist, 59*, 567-577.
Hilgard, E. R. (1977). *Divided consciousness: Multiple controls in human thought and action*. New York: Wiley.
Hilgard, E. R., & Loftus, E. F. (1979). Effective interrogation of the eyewitness. *International Journal of Clinical and Experimental Hypnosis, 27*, 342-357.
Hilgard, J. R. (1979). *Personality and hypnosis: A study of imaginative involvement* (2nd ed.). Chicago: University of Chicago Press. (Original work published 1970)
Hobsbawm, E. J. (1985). History from below—Some reflections. In F. Krantz (Ed.), *History from below: Studies in popular protest and popular ideology in honor of George Rudé*. Montréal, Canada: Concordia University.
Hoffbaüer, J. C. (1827). *Médecine légale relative aux aliénés et aux sourds-muets*. Paris: J. B. Baillière.

Holden, C. (1980). Forensic use of hypnosis on the increase. *Science, 208,* 1443-1444.
Hull, C. L. (1933). *Hypnosis and suggestibility: An experimental approach.* New York: Appleton-Century-Crofts.
Imwinkelried, E. J. (1983). The standard for admitting scientific evidence: A critique from the perspective of juror psychology. *Villanova Law Review, 28,* 554-571.
Institor (Krämer), H., & Sprenger, J. (1486). *Malleus maleficarum.* (Reprinted in Paris: Plon, 1973)
International Society of Hypnosis. (1979). Resolution (adopted August 1979). *International Journal of Clinical and Experimental Hypnosis, 27,* 453.
Jaffe, J. R. (1980). Hypnosis. *Police Journal, 53,* 233-237.
James, W. (1908). *A pluralistic universe.* New York: E. P. Dutton, 1971.
James, W. (1917). *The energies of men.* New York: Moffat, Yard, & Co.
James, W. (1936). *The varieties of religious experience.* (Reprinted in New York: The Modern Library, 1971)
Janet, P. (1886). Les actes inconscients et le dédoublement de la personnalité pendant le somnambulisme provoqué. *Revue Philosophique de la France et de l'Etranger, 11,* 12.
Janet, P. (1888). Les actes inconscients et la mémoire pendant le somnambulisme. *Revue Philosophique de la France et de l'Etranger, 25,* 238-279.
Janet, P. (1889). *L'automatisme psychologique.* Paris: F. Alcan.
Janet, P. (1894). *Etat mental des hystériques: Les accidents mentaux.* Paris: Rueff & Cie.
Janet, P. (1911). *L'Etat mental des hystériques* (2nd ed.). Paris: Alcan.
Janet, P. (1919). *Les médications psychologiques* (3 volumes). Paris: Alcan. English translation by E. Paul & C. Paul, *Psychological healing: A historical and clinical study* (2 volumes). New York: Macmillan, 1925.
Jankau, L. (1896). L'hypnotisme en médecine légale: Le procès Czynski. *Revue de Médecine Légale et de Jurisprudence Médicale, 12,* 349-357.
Joire, P. (1897). *Etude médico-légale de l'hypnotisme et de la suggestion: Les états médianiques de l'hypnose.* Tournai: n.p.
Joire, P. (1900). Les faux témoignages suggérés. *Revue de l'Hypnotisme Expérimental et Thérapeutique, 7,* 196-202; *8,* 229-236.
Joire, P. (1902). Des rapports de l'hypnotisme et de la suggestion avec la jurisprudence. In E. Bérillon & P. Farez (Eds.), *Deuxième Congrès International de l'Hypnotisme Expérimental et Thérapeutique: Comptes rendus.* Paris: Vigot Frères.
Julliot, C.-L. (1902). L'hypnotisme expérimental devant la loi du 30 novembre 1892. In E. Bérillon & P. Farez (Eds.), *Deuxième Congrès International de l'Hypnotisme Expérimental et Thérapeutique: Comptes rendus.* Paris: Vigot Frères.
Kaplan, F. (1974). The mesmeric mania: The early Victorians and animal magnetism. *Journal of Historical Ideas, 35,* 691-702.
Kaplan, F. (Ed.). (1982). *John Elliotson on Mesmerism.* New York: Da Capo Press.
Karlin, R. (1983). Forensic hypnosis—Two case reports: A brief communication. *International Journal of Clinical and Experimental Hypnosis, 31,* 227-234.
Kerr, H., Crowley, J., & Crow, C. (1983). *The haunted dusk.* Athens, GA: University of Georgia Press.
Kihlstrom, J. F. (1986, September). *The making of the myth: or The two Svengalis.* Paper presented at the 37th Annual Scientific Meeting of the Society for Clinical and Experimental Hypnosis, Chicago.
Kirby, M. D. (1984). Hypnosis and the law. *Criminal Law Journal, 8,* 152-165.
Kircher, A. (1643). *Magnes sive de arte magnetica* (4 volumes). Coloniae Agrippinae: Apud Iodicum Kalcouen.
Kline, M. V. (1972). The production of antisocial behavior through hypnosis: New clinical data. *International Journal of Clinical and Experimental Hypnosis, 20,* 80-94.
Kline, M. V. (1979). Defending the mentally ill: The insanity defense and the role of forensic hypnosis. *International Journal of Clinical and Experimental Hypnosis, 27,* 375-401.
Kline v. Ford Motor Co., Inc., 523 F.2d 1067 (9th Cir. 1975).

Krebs, S. L. (1905). Telepathy and Hypnotism. *Medico-legal Journal, 23*, 30-31.

Kroger, W. S., & Doucé, R. G. (1979). Hypnosis in criminal investigation. *International Journal of Clinical and Experimental Hypnosis, 27*, 358-374.

Labelle, L., Lamarche, M. C., & Laurence, J. R. (1987). Potential jurors' knowledge of the effects of hypnosis on eyewitness identification. Unpublished manuscript, Concordia University, Montréal, Canada.

Labelle, L., & Perry, C. (1986, August). *Pseudo-memory creation in hypnosis.* Paper presented to the 94th Annual Convention of the American Psychological Association, Washington, DC.

Lacassagne, A. (1891). *L'affaire Gouffé.* Lyon: A. Storck.

Lacassagne, A. (1896). *Les médecins-experts et les erreurs judiciaires.* Lyon: A. Storck.

Ladame, P. L. (1882). La névrose hypnotique devant la médecine légale; du viol pendant le sommeil hypnotique; rapport médico-légal. *Annales d'Hygiène Publique et de Médecine Légale, 7*, 518-534.

Ladame, P. L. (1887). L'hypnotisme et la médecine légale. *Archives de l'Anthropologie Criminelle et des Sciences Pénales, 2*, 293-335; 520-559.

Ladame, P. L. (1889). La nécessité d'interdire les séances publiques d'hypnotisme: Intervention des pouvoirs publics dans la réglementation de l'hypnotisme. In E. Bérillon (Ed.), *Premier Congrès International de l'Hypnotisme Expérimental et Thérapeutique: Comptes rendus.* Paris: Octave Doin.

Ladd, G. T. (1902). Legal aspects of hypnotism. *Yale Law Journal, 11*, 173-194.

Laënnec, T. A. (1888). *Rapport médico-légal sur une enquête judiciaire motivée par une fausse accusation de viol porté par une hystéro-épileptique, présentant un curieux dédoublement de la personne.* Paris: Mellinet.

Lafontaine, C. (1866). *Mémoires d'un magnétiseur* (2 volumes). Paris: G. Baillière.

Lafontaine, C. (1886). *L'art de magnétiser* (5th rev. ed.). Paris: F. Alcan. (Original work published 1847)

Lafont-Gouzi, G. G. (1839). *Traité du magnétisme animal considéré sous le rapport de l'hygiène, de la médecine légale et de la thérapeutique.* Toulouse: Sénac.

Lamb, C. S. (1985). Hypnotically-induced deconditioning: Reconstruction of memories in the treatment of phobias. *American Journal of Clinical Hypnosis, 28*, 56-62.

Lancet. (1828-1829). *II*(303), 384.

Lasègue, C. (1865). Des catalepsies partielles et passagères. *Archives Générales de Médecine, 2*, 385-402.

Lasègue, C. (1881). Le Braidisme. *Revue des Deux Mondes, 47*, 914-933.

Laurence, J.-R., Nadon, R., Bowers, K., Labelle, L., Blatt, T., & Perry, C. (1987). Transient experiences in and out of hypnosis. Unpublished manuscript, Concordia University, Montréal, Canada.

Laurence, J.-R., Nadon, R., Bowers, K., Perry, C., & Regher, G. (1985, August). *Clinical encounters in the experimental context.* Paper presented at the 93rd Annual Convention of the American Psychological Association, Los Angeles.

Laurence, J.-R., Nadon, R., Nogrady, H., & Perry, C. (1986). Duality, dissociation, and memory creation in highly hypnotizable subjects. *International Journal of Clinical and Experimental Hypnosis, 34*, 295-210.

Laurence, J.-R., & Perry, C. W. (1983). Forensic hypnosis in the late nineteenth century. *International Journal of Clinical and Experimental Hypnosis, 31*, 266-283.

Laurent, E. (1891). *Les suggestions criminelles.* Lyon: A. Storck.

Le Bon, G. (1895). *La psychologie des foules.* Paris: F. Alcan.

Lèbre, G. (1889). L'Affaire Chambidge. *Revue des Grands Procès Contemporains, 7*, 21-101.

LeCron, L. M. (1965). A study of age regression under hypnosis. In L. M. LeCron (Ed.), *Experimental hypnosis.* New York: The Citadel Press.

Lefort, J. (1888). L'hypnotisme au point de vue juridique. *Annales d'Hygiène Publique et de Médecine Légale, 20*, 152-165.

Legrand du Saulle, H. (1860). *Etude médico-légale sur l'hystérie et sur le degré de responsabilité des hystériques et des aliénés devant la loi.* Paris: V. Masson.

Legrand du Saulle, H. (1863). Le somnambulisme naturel. *Annales Médico-Psychologiques, 1*, 87-99.

Legrand du Saulle, H. (1883). *Les hystériques, état physique et état mental*. Paris: J. B. Baillière et Fils.

Lemesle, H. (1900). Les procès aux animaux. *Revue de l'Hypnotisme Expérimental et Thérapeutique, 12*, 364-367.

Lemesle, H. (1902). L'hypnotisme devant la loi du 30 novembre 1892, sur l'exercice de la médecine. In E. Bérillon & P. Farez (Eds.), *Deuxième Congrès International de l'Hypnotisme Expérimental et Thérapeutique: Comptes rendus*. Paris: Vigot Frères.

Levitt, E. E., & Baker, E. L. (1983). The hypnotic relationship—Another look at coercion, compliance and resistance: A brief communication. *International Journal of Clinical and Experimental Hypnosis, 31*, 125-131.

Levitt, E. E., Aronoff, G., Morgan, C. D., Overley, T. M., & Parrish, M. J. (1975). Testing the coercive power of hypnosis: Committing objectionable acts. *International Journal of Clinical and Experimental Hypnosis, 23*, 59-67.

Liébeault, A. A. (1866). *Du sommeil et des états analogues surtout au point de vue de l'action du moral sur le physique*. Paris: V. Masson et Fils.

Liébeault, A. A. (1889). *Le sommeil provoqué et les états analogues*. Paris: Octave Doin.

Liébeault, A. A. (1895). Suggestions criminelles hypnotiques. *Revue d'Hypnotisme, 10*, 289-299; *11*, 330-336.

Liégeois, J. (1884). *De la suggestion hypnotique dans ses rapports avec le droit civil et le droit criminel*. Paris: Alphonse Picard.

Liégeois, J. (1889a). *De la suggestion et du somnambulisme dans leurs rapports avec la jurisprudence et la médecine légale*. Paris: Octave Doin.

Liégeois, J. (1889b). Rapports de la suggestion et du somnambulisme avec la jurisprudence et la médecine légale: La responsabilité dans les états hypnotiques. In E. Bérillon (Ed.), *Premier Congrès International de l'Hypnotisme Expérimental et Thérapeutique: Comptes rendus*. Paris: Octave Doin.

Liégeois, J. (1890). J. Delboeuf: Le magnétisme animal. *Revue Philosophique de la France et de l'Etranger, 29*, 314-319.

Liégeois, J. (1894). L'affaire Chambige: Etude de psychologie criminelle. *Revue de l'Hypnotisme, 8*, 234-240.

Liégeois, J. (1897). La question des suggestions criminelles: 1. Ses origines, son état actuel. *Revue de l'Hypnotisme, 4*, 97-104.

Liégeois, J. (1898). Les suggestions hypnotiques criminelles: Dangers et remèdes. *Revue de l'Hypnotisme, 7*, 203-211; *8*, 236-243; *9*, 273-279; *10*, 311-318.

Loftus, E. F., & Loftus, G. R. (1980). On the permanence of stored information in the human brain. *American Psychologist, 35*, 409-420.

Lombard, A. (l'aîné). (1819). *Les dangers du magnétisme animal, et l'importance d'en arrêter la propagation vulgaire*. Paris: Dentu.

Lombroso, C. (1910). *Hypnotisme et spiritisme* (C. Rossigneux, Trans.). Paris: Flammarion.

Lopez, C.-A., & Herbert, E. W. (1975). *The private Franklin: The man and his family*. New York: Norton.

Louis, E. (1898). *Les origines de la doctrine du magnétisme animal: Mesmer et la Société de l'Harmonie*. Paris: Société d'Editions Scientifiques.

Lowes Dickinson, G. A. (1911). A case of emergence of a latent memory under hypnosis. *Proceedings of the Society for Psychical Research, 25*, 455-467.

Luys, J. (1891a). Question médico-légale relative à un cas de grossesse inconsciente. *Annales de Psychiatrie et d'Hypnologie, 1*, 84-87.

Luys, J. (1891b). Question médico-légales afférentes à l'hypnotisme. *Annales de Psychiatrie et d'Hypnologie, 1*, 209-217.

Luys, J. (1893). *Enseignement médical libre: Programme du cours d'hypnologie*. Clermont: Oise.

Lyon, W. (1954). Justification and command as techniques for hypnotically-induced antisocial behavior. *Journal of Clinical Psychology, 10*, 288-290.

Lysing, J. (1892). Les phénomènes hypnotiques chez les animaux. *Annales de Psychiatrie et d'Hypnologie, 2*, 330-336.

M . . . (1784). *Mesmer blessé: ou Réponse à la lettre du R.P. Hervier sur le magnétisme animal.* Paris: Couturier. (Reprinted in the *Recueil général*)

Mabille, H. (1884). Rapport médico-légal sur un cas de viol et d'attentat à la pudeur avec violences commis sur une jeune fille atteinte d'hystérie avec crises de sommeil. *Annales Médico-Psychologiques, 1*, 83-98.

Macario, M. M. A. (1857). *Du sommeil, des rêves, et du somnambulisme dans l'état de santé et de maladie.* Lyon: Périsse Frères.

MacNish, R. (1830). *The philosophy of sleep.* Glasgow: W. R. McPhun.

Marc, C.-C. (1840). *De la folie considérée dans ses rapports avec les questions médico-judiciaires* (2 volumes). Paris: n.p.

Mathiot, C. (1891). La législation et la loi devant l'hypnotisme. *Annales de Psychiatrie et d'Hypnologie, 1*, 24-25.

Maugirard, V. (1813). *La Mesméromanie.* Paris: n.p.

Maxwell, J. (1902). *L'amnésie au point de vue de la médecine judiciaire.* Bordeaux: G. Gounouilhou.

Maxwell, J. (1903). *Les phénomènes psychiques: Recherches, observations, méthodes.* Paris: F. Alcan.

Maxwell, W. (1679). *De medicina magnetica.* Frankfurt: J. P Zubrodt.

McCann, T. E., & Sheehan, P. W. (1987a). The breaching of pseudomemory under hypnotic instruction: Implications for original memory retrieval. *British Journal of Experimental and Clinical Hypnosis, 4*, 101-108.

McCann, T. E., & Sheehan, P. W. (1987b). Pseudomemory reports and their variable explanations. *British Journal of Experimental and Clinical Hypnosis, 4*, 112-114.

McConkey, K. M., & Jupp, J. J. (1985-1986). A survey of opinions about hypnosis. *British Journal of Experimental and Clinical Hypnosis, 3*, 87-94.

McConkey, K. M., & Kinoshita, S. (1985-1986). Creating memories and reports: Comment on Spanos and McLean. *British Journal of Experimental and Clinical Hypnosis, 3*, 162-166.

McConkey, K. M., & Perry, C. (1985). Benjamin Franklin and mesmerism. *The International Journal of Clinical and Experimental Hypnosis, 33*, 122-130.

Mead, R. (1746). *De imperio solis ac lunae in corpora humana et morbis in de oriundis* (rev. ed.). London: n.p. (Original work published 1704)

Measuring patriotism. (1985, January 20). *Manchester Guardian Weekly.* (Originally published in the *Washington Post*)

Meige, H. (1894). *Les possédées noires.* Paris: Schiller.

Meissas, A. (Abbé de). (1890). Notice historique sur la découverte du sommeil magnétique. In E. Bérillon (Ed.), *Rapport général d'après le compte-rendu des séances du Congrès.* Paris: G. Carré.

Méric, E. (1891). *Le merveilleux et la science: Etude sur l'hypnotisme.* Paris: Letouzey et Ané.

Mesmer, F. A. (1779). *Mémoire sur la découverte du magnétisme animal.* Paris: Didot le Jeune.

Mesmer, F. A. (1781). *Précis historique des faits relatifs au magnétisme animal jusques en avril 1781.* London: n.p.

Mesmer, F. A. (1784a). *Théorie du monde et des êtres organisés, suivant les principes de M. . . .* Paris: n.p. (Written by N. Bergasse.)

Mesmer, F. A. (1784b). *Lettre de M. Mesmer à M. Vicq-d'Azyr et à Messieurs les auteurs du Journal de Paris.* Bruxelles: n.p.

Mesmer, F. A. (1784c). *Lettres de M. Mesmer à Messieurs les auteurs du Journal de Paris, et à M. Franklin.* Paris: n.p.

Mesmer, F. A. (1784d). *Lettre de M. Mesmer à M. le Comte de C. . . .* Paris: n.p.

Mesmer, F. A. (1785a). Lettre aux auteurs du Journal de Paris. *Journal de Paris, 6*, 22.

Mesmer, F. A. (1785b). *Lettre de l'auteur de la découverte du magnétisme animal à l'auteur des réflexions préliminaires pour servir de réponse à un imprimé ayant pour titre: Sommes* versées entre les mains de M.Mesmer, pour acquérir le droit de publier sa découverte. Paris: n.p.

Mesmer, F. A. (1799). *Mémoire de F.A. Mesmer, docteur en médecine, sur ses découvertes.* Paris: Fuchs.

Mesnet, E. (1874). *De l'automatisme de la mémoire et du souvenir dans le somnambulisme pathologique: Considérations médico-légales.* Paris: F. Malteste.

Mesnet, E. (1894). *Outrages à la pudeur, violences sur les organes sexuels de la femme dans le somnambulisme provoqué et la fascination, étude médico-légale.* Paris: Rueff.

Meyer Papers. (1885-1949). (Available at Welch Medical Library, Johns Hopkins University, Baltimore, MD 21218.)

M. F* * *. (1785). *Essai sur les probabilités du somnambulisme magnétique pour servir à l'histoire du magnétisme animal.* Paris: Marchands de Nouveautés. (Reprinted in the *Recueil général*)

Mialle, S. (1826). *Exposé par ordre alphabétique des cures opérées en France par le magnétisme animal depuis Mesmer jusqu'à nos jours* (2 volumes). Paris: G. Dentu.

Miller, A. (1986). Brief reconstructive hypnotherapy for anxiety reactions: Three case reports. *American Journal of Clinical Hypnosis, 28,* 138-146.

Milt, B. (1953). *Franz Anton Mesmer und seine Beziehungen zur Schweitz, Mitteilungen der Antiquarischen Gesellschaft.* Band 38, Heft 1, Zurich.

Mittié, LaCaze, Cheigneverd, Sué, & LaMotte. (1784). *Lettre sur la mort de M. Court de Gébelin.* Paris: n.p. (Reprinted in the *Recueil général*; first name of authors unavailable.)

M. J. D. F. D. M. (1784). *Remarques sur la conduite du sieur Mesmer, de son commis le P. Hervier, et de ses autres adhérents; où l'on tente de venger la Médecine de leurs outrages.* Paris: n.p. (Reprinted in the *Recueil général*)

Moll, A. (1982). *Hypnotism.* New York: Da Capo Press. (Original work published 1889 under the title: *Der Hypnotismus*)

Mongruel, L. P. (1851). *Le magnétisme militant* Paris: E. Dentu.

Montègre, A. F. (Jenin de). (1812). *Du magnétisme animal et de ses partisans.* Paris: D. Colas.

Montègre, A. F. (Jenin de). (1816). *Note sur le magnétisme animal et sur les dangers que font courir les magnétiseurs à leurs patients.* Paris: Fain.

Moore, R. L. (1977). *In search of white crows, spiritualism, parapsychology, and American culture.* New York: Oxford University Press.

Moran, R. (1981). *Knowing right from wrong: The insanity defense of Daniel McNaughtan.* New York: Free Press.

Morand, J. S. (1889). *Le Magnétisme animal: Etude historique et critique.* Paris: Garnier et Frères.

Moreau, P. (de Tours). (1894). L'hypnotisme en Angleterre. *Annales de Psychiatrie et d'Hypnologie, 4,* 273-274.

Moreau, P. G. (Abbé). (1891). *L'hypnotisme: Etude scientifique et religieuse.* Paris: Ancienne Librairie Religieuse H. Oudin.

Morin, A. S. (1860). *Du magnétisme et des sciences occultes.* Paris: n.p.

Morgan, E., Thwing, E. P., Eskridge, T. P., Funkhouser, R., Kellogg, T. H., Ellinger, M., McDonald, W., & Bell, C. (1890). Preliminary report of the standing committee on hypnotism. *Medico-legal Journal, 8,* 263-264.

Motet, A. (1881). Accès de somnambulisme spontané et provoqué. *Annales d'Hygiène Publique et de Médecine Légale, 5,* 214-225.

Münsterberg, H. (1908). *On the witness stand: Essays on psychology and crime.* New York: Clark Boardman.

Mutter, C. B. (1979). Regressive hypnosis and the polygraph: A case study. *American Journal of Clinical Hypnosis, 22,* 47-50.

Naeyaert and Elias, Supreme Court of Ontario, No. 4062/80 (June 17, 1985).

Neal, E. V., & Clark, C. S. (Eds.). (1900). *Hypnotism and hypnotic suggestion* (4th ed.). New York: New York State Publishing Co.

Neisser, U. (1982). *Memory observed: Remembering in natural contexts.* San Francisco: Freeman.

Neisser, U. (1984). John Dean's memory. *Social Action and the Law, 9,* 87-96.

Neufchâteau, N. F. (de). (1800). *Le Conservateur; ou Recueil de morceaux inédits d'histoire, de politique, de littérature et de philosophie, tirés des portefeuilles de N. Francois (de Neufchâteau) de l'Institut National*. Paris: Crapelet. (The secret report on animal magnetism can be found in Volume 1, pp. 146-158.)

Nisbett, R. E., & Wilson, T. D. (1977). Telling more than we can know: Verbal reports on verbal processes. *Psychological Review, 84*, 231-259.

Nogrady, H., McConkey, K., & Perry, C. (1985). Enhancing visual memory: Trying hypnosis, trying imagination, and trying again. *Journal of Abnormal Psychology, 94*, 195-204.

Noizet, F. J. (1854). *Mémoires sur le somnambulisme et le magnétisme animal addressé en 1820 à l'Académie Royale de Berlin*. Paris: Plon Frères.

Ochorowicz, J. (1887). *De la suggestion mentale*. Paris: Octave Doin.

O'Connell, D. N., Shor, R. E., & Orne, M. T. (1970). Hypnotic age regression: An empirical and methodological analysis [Monograph 3]. *Journal of Abnormal Psychology, 76*, 1-32.

Olivier, J. (1849). *Traité de magnétisme*. Toulouse: L. Jougla.

Olivier, J. (1856). *Magnétisme*. Agen: J. A. Quillot.

Orloff (Professeur-Docteur). (1926). *Une séance de magnétisme: ou Comment devenir sûrement magnétiseur, suivi de la flagellation du curé de Bombon et la vérité sur l'envoûtement*. Paris: Busson.

Orne, M. T. (1951). The mechanisms of hypnotic age regression: An empirical study. *Journal of Abnormal and Social Psychology, 46*, 213-225.

Orne, M. T. (1959). The nature of hypnosis: Artifact and essence. *Journal of Abnormal and Social Psychology, 58*, 277-299.

Orne, M. T. (1960). Book review of P. J. Reiter's *Antisocial or criminal acts and hypnosis*. *International Journal of Clinical and Experimental Hypnosis, 8*, 131-135.

Orne, M. T. (1972). Can a hypnotized subject be compelled to carry out otherwise unacceptable behavior? *International Journal of Clinical and Experimental Hypnosis, 20*, 101-117.

Orne, M. T. (1978). Motion of amicus for leave to file affidavit, and affidavit. *Quaglino v. The People of the State of California*, Supreme Court of the United States, No. 77-1288. October term, 1978.

Orne, M. T. (1979a). On the simulating subject as a quasi-control group in hypnosis research: What, why and how. In E. Fromm & R. E. Shor (Eds.), *Hypnosis: Developments in research and new perspectives* (2nd ed.). New York: Aldine.

Orne, M. T. (1979b). The use and misuse of hypnosis in court. *International Journal of Clinical and Experimental Hypnosis, 27*, 311-341.

Orne, M. T. (1980). On the construct of hypnosis: How its definition affects research and its clinical application. In G. D. Burrows & L. Dennerstein (Eds.), *Handbook of hypnosis and psychosomatic medicine*. Amsterdam: Elsevier/North Holland.

Orne, M. T., Dinges, D. F., & Carota Orne, E. (1984). On the differential diagnosis of multiple personality in the forensic context. *International Journal of Clinical and Experimental Hypnosis, 32*, 118-169.

Orne, M. T., & Evans, F. J. (1965). Social control in the psychological experiment: Antisocial behavior and hypnosis. *Journal of Personality and Social Psychology, 1*, 189-200.

Orne, M. T., & Holland, C. H. (1968). On the ecological validity of laboratory deceptions. *International Journal of Psychiatry, 6*, 282-293.

Orne, M. T., Soskis, D. A., Dinges, D. F., & Carota Orne, E. (1984). Hypnotically induced testimony. In G. L. Wells & E. F. Loftus (Eds.), *Eyewitness testimony: Psychological perspectives*, Cambridge, England: Cambridge University Press.

Orne, M. T., Soskis, D. A., Dinges, D. F., Carota Orne, E., & Tonry, M. H. (1985). Hypnotically refreshed testimony: Enhanced memory or tampering with evidence? In *National Institute of Justice: Issues and Practices in Criminal Justice*. Washington, DC: U. S. Goverment Printing Office.

Palfreman, J. (1977). Mesmerism and the English medical profession: A study of a conflict. *Ethics in Science and Medicine, 4*, 51-66.

Palfreman, J. (1979). Between scepticism and credulity: A study of Victorian scientific attitudes to modern spiritualism. In R. Wallis (Ed.), *On the margins of science: The social construction of rejected knowledge* (Sociological Review Monograph 27). Keele, Staffordshire: University of Keele Press.

Palmer, W. H. (1890). Hypnotism. *Medico-legal Journal, 8,* 233-240.

Parks v. State, 159 Ind. 211, 64 N.E. 862, 59 LRA 190 (1902).

Parssinen, T. M. (1979). Professional deviants and the history of medicine: Medical Mesmerists in Victorian Britain. In R. Wallis (Ed.), *On the margins of science: The social construction of rejected knowledge* (Sociological Review Monograph 27). Keele, Staffordshire: University of Keele Press.

Patenaude, P. (1983). De la recevabilité des preuves fondées sur des techniques non consacrées par la communauté scientifique. *Revue du Barreau, 43,* 51-60.

Patin, G. (1734). Remarques historiques et critiques. In J. A. de Thou (Ed.), *Histoire universelle.* La Haye: M. Rémond de Sainte Albine.

Paulet, J. J. (1784a). *Mesmer justifié.* Paris: Chez les Librairies qui vendent Nouveautés.

Paulet, J. J. (1784b). *L'anti-magnétisme: ou Origine, progrès, décadence, renouvellement et réfutation du magnétisme animal.* Paris: Desennes.

Paumerelle, C.-J. de B. de (Abbé). (1784). *La philosophie des vapeurs: ou Correspondance d'une jolie femme, nouvelle édition augmentée d'un petit traité des crises magnétiques à l'usage des mesmériennes.* Paris: Royez.

Pechlin, J. N. (1691). *Observationum medicarum libri tres.* Hamburg: n. p.

Peebles, J. M. (1905). Spiritism, hypnotism, telepathy. *Medico-legal Journal, 23,* 216-219.

People v. Ebanks, 117 Cal. 652, 40 LRA 269, 49 P. 1049 (1897).

People v. Busch, 56 Cal. 2d 868, 366 P.2d 314, 16 Cal. Rptr. 898 (1961).

People v. Diggs, No. 6490 (Super. Ct. Monterey County, California, April 23, 1979).

People v. Hangsleben, Mich. App. N.W.2d 539 (1978).

People v. John Johnson, *American Journal of Insanity,* April 1848, 303-346.

People v. Kempinski, No. W80CF 352 (Cir. Ct., 12th Dist., Will County, Illinois, October 21: unrep. 1980).

People v. Kenny, 167 Misc. 51, 3 N.Y.S.2d 348 (1938).

People v. Leyra, 98 N.E.2d 553 (1951), 108 N.E. 2d 673 (1952).

People v. Marendi, 213 N.Y. 600, 107 N.E. 1058 (1915).

People v. Royal, No. 1099 (Super. Ct., April 1878). In *California Digest, 53,* 62-64.

People v. Shirley, 31 Cal. 3d 18, 641 P.2d 775, 181 Cal. Rptr. 243 (1982).

People v. Woods et al, No. 63187 ABNC (Alameda County, California, December 15, 1977).

People v. Worthington, 105 Cal. 166, 38 P. 689 (1894).

Perrault, J. (1903). *Essai sur la responsabilité pénale en général et plus particulièrement dans ses rapports avec les passions et l'hypnotisme.* Dijon: Barbier-Marilier.

Perronnet, C. (1886). *Force psychique et suggestion mentale.* Paris: J. Lechevalier.

Perronnet, C. (1888). L'hypnose devant la loi. *Revue du Siècle, 2,* 22-25.

Perry, C. W. (1978). The Abbé Faria: A neglected figure in the history of hypnosis. In F. H. Frankel & H. S. Zamansky (Eds.), *Hypnosis at its bicentennial.* New York: Plenum.

Perry, C. W. (1979). Hypnotic coercion and compliance to it: A review of evidence presented in a legal case. *International Journal of Clinical and Experimental Hypnosis, 27,* 187-218.

Perry, C., & Laurence, J.-R. (1982). Book review of M. Reiser's *Handbook of investigative hypnosis. International Journal of Clinical and Experimental Hypnosis, 30,* 443-450.

Perry, C., & Laurence, J.-R. (1983). The enhancement of memory by hypnosis in the legal investigative situation. *Canadian Psychology/Psychologie canadienne, 24,* 155-167.

Perry, C., & Laurence, J.-R. (1984). Mental processing outside of awareness: The contributions of Freud and Janet. In K. S. Bowers & D. Meichenbaum (Eds.), *The unconscious reconsidered.* New York: Wiley.

Perry, C., Laurence, J.-R., D'Eon, J., & Tallant, B. (in press). Hypnotic age regression technique in the elicitation of memories: Applied uses and abuses. In H. H. Pettinati (Ed.), *Hypnosis and memory.* New York: Guilford.

Perry, C., & Walsh, B. (1978). Inconsistencies and anomalies of response as a defining characteristic of hypnosis. *Journal of Abnormal Psychology, 87,* 574-577.
Peterson, M. J. (1978). *The medical profession in mid-Victorian London.* Berkeley: University of California Press.
Pététin, J. H. D. (1787). *Mémoire sur la découverte des phénomènes que présentent la catalepsie et le somnambulisme.* n.p.
Philipon, E. (1908). *Suggestion hypnotique et responsabilité.* Paris: Bonvalot-Jouve.
Pitres, A. (1885). *Des zones hystérogènes et hypnogènes, des attaques de sommeil.* Bordeaux: G. Gounouilhou.
Pitres, A., & Gaugé, R. (1886a). De l'hypnotisme. *Revue des Sciences Médicales, 27,* 325-348.
Pitres, A., & Gaubé, R. (1886b). De l'hypnotisme (suite). *Revue des Sciences Médicales, 28,* 315-349.
Podmore, F. (1964). *From Mesmer to Christian Science: A short history of mental healing.* New Hyde Park, NY: University Books. (Original work published 1909)
Poyen, C. (1837a). *Progress of animal magnetism in New England.* Boston: Weeks, Jordan, & Co.
Poyen, C. (1837b). *A letter to Col. William Stone.* Boston: Weeks, Jordan, & Co.
Prévost, M. (1973). *Janet, Freud, et la psychologie clinique.* Paris: Petite Bibliothèque Payot.
Prichard, J. C. (1835). *A treatise on insanity and other disorders affecting the mind.* London: n.p.
Prichard, J. C. (1842). *On the different forms of insanity in relation to jurisprudence.* London: n. p.
Prince, M. (1906). *The dissociation of a personality.* London: Longmans, Green & Co.
Putnam, W. H. (1979). Hypnosis and distortions in eyewitness memory. *International Journal of Clinical and Experimental Hypnosis, 27,* 437-448.
Puységur, A. H. A. (Chastenet, Comte de). (1784). *Rapport des cures opérées à Bayonne par le magnétisme animal adressé à M. l'Abbé de Poulizat.* Paris: Prault.
Puységur, A. M. J. (Chastenet, Marquis de). (1784). *Détails des cures opérées à Buzancy, par le magnétisme animal.* Paris: Soissons.
Puységur, A. M. J. (Chastenet, Marquis de). (1784-1785). *Mémoires pour servir à l'établissement du magnétisme animal* (2 volumes). Paris: Cellot.
Puységur, A. M. J. (Chastenet, Marquis de). (1807). *Du magnétisme animal, considéré dans ses rapports avec diverses branches de la physique générale.* Paris: Cellot.
Puységur, A. M. J. (Chastenet, Marquis de). (1812). *Les fous, les insensés, les maniaques et les frénétiques ne seraient-ils que des somnambules désordonnés?* Paris: J. G. Dentu.
Puységur, M. (Chastenet, Comte de) (1785). *Détails de ce qui s'est passé à Bayonne depuis l'époque du 19 août 1784 jusqu'au premier octobre suivant, relatifs au magnétisme animal.* In Société de Guienne (Ed.), *Recueil d'observations et de faits relatifs au magnétisme animal.* Bordeaux: Paul Pallande.
Quérard, J. M. (1869)). *Les supercheries littéraires dévoilées suivie du dictionnaire des ouvrages anonymes par A. A. Barbier* (4 volumes). Paris: Paul Daffis.
Quimby, P. P. (1921). *The Quimby manuscripts* (H. W. Dresser, Ed.). New York: Thomas Crowell.
Radet, J. B. (1784). *Les docteurs modernes, suivi du baquet de santé.* Paris: Brunet.
Raginsky, B. B. (1969). Hypnotic recall of aircrash cause. *International Journal of Clinical and Experimental Hypnosis, 17,* 1-19.
Raymond, F. (1902). Méfaits d'hypnotiseurs amateurs. *Revue de l'Hypnotisme, 12,* 364-366.
Recueil général et complet de tous les écrits publiés pour ou contre le magnétisme animal (14 volumes). Paris: Bibliothèque Royale. (Undated, probably 1787/1788.)
Reese J. J. (1891). Hypnotism and the law. *Medico-legal Journal, 9,* 147-149.
Régnard, P. (1887). *Les maladies épidémiques de l'esprit: Sorcellerie, magnétisme, morphinisme, délire des grandeurs.* Paris: Plon, Nourrit & Cie.
Régnier, L. R., & de Grandchamps. (1890). *Histoire de l'hypnotisme, examen critique de tous les documents qui s'y rapportent et observations personnelles.* Paris: Bureau du *Progrès Médical.*
Reiser, M. (1976). Hypnosis as a tool in criminal investigation. *Police Chief, 46,* 39-40.
Reiser, M. (1980). *Handbook of investigative hypnosis.* Los Angeles: LEHI Publishing Co.

Reiser, M. (1985). Investigative hypnosis: Scientism, memory tricks and power plays. In J. K. Zeig (Ed.), *Ericksonian psychotherapy: I. Structure*. New York: Brunner/Mazel.
Reiser, M. (1986, April). Reader's Forum. *American Psychological Association Division 30: Psychological Hypnosis Newsletter*, pp. 5-6.
Reiter, P. J. (1958). *Antisocial or criminal acts and hypnosis: A case study*. Springfield, IL: Charles C. Thomas.
Retz, N. (1782). *Lettre sur le secret de M. Mesmer*. Paris: Méquignon.
Rex v. Booher, 50 C.C.C. 271 (1928).
Riant, A. (1888). *Les irresponsables devant la justice*. Paris: J. B. Baillière.
Ribot, T. A. (1885). *Les maladies de la personnalité*. Paris: F. Alcan.
Ribot, T. A. (1977). In D. N. Robinson (Ed.), *Significant contributions to the history of psychology, 1750-1720* (Series C, *Medical Psychology*, Vol. 1). Washington, DC: University Publications of America. (Three major books are reprinted in this edition: *The diseases of memory* [English version, 1882]. *The diseases of the will* [English version, 1894]. *The diseases of personality* [English version, 1906].)
Ricard, J. J. A. (1836). *Doctrine du magnétisme humain et du somnambulisme*. Marseille: n.p.
Ricard, J. J. A. (1841). *Traité théorique et pratique du magnétisme animal*. Paris: Baillière.
Ricard, J. J. A. (1843a). *Lettres d'un magnétiseur*. Paris: n. p.
Ricard, J. J. A. (1843b). *Arrêt de la Cour Suprême touchant le magnétisme animal*. Paris: Author.
Richer, P. (1881). *Etude clinique sur l'hystéro-épilepsie, ou grande épilepsie*. Paris: A. Delahaye & E. Lecrosnier.
Richer, P. (1885). *Etudes cliniques sur la grande hystérie, ou hystéro-épilepsie*. (2nd ed.). Paris: A. Delahaye.
Richet, C. (1875). Du somnambulisme provoqué. *Journal d'Anatomie Physiologique, 11*, 348-378.
Richet, C. (1881). The simulation of somnambulism. *The Lancet, 1*, 8-9, 51-52. (New Series)
Richet, C. (1884). *L'homme et l'intelligence*. Paris: F. Alcan.
Robiano, L. M. J. (dit Aloîs de, Comte). (1851). *Charlataneries, abus et dangers des magnétiseurs vulgaires*. Bruxelles: Veuve Wouters. (Excerpts from his book, *Névrurgie*, pp. 177-194.)
Rogers, E. C. (1853). *Philosophy of mysterious agents, human and mundane: or The dynamic laws and relations of man*. Boston: John P. Jewett.
Rossi, D. (1981, October 16). *Guilt as a complication in the investigative use of hypnosis with witnesses*. Paper presented at the Annual Scientific Meeting of the Society for Clinical and Experimental Hypnosis (Symposium entitled: *Issues in Forensic Hypnosis*), Portland, Oregon.
Rostan, L. L. (1825). *Du magnétisme animal*. Paris: Rignoux.
Rous, P. (1887). *Hypnotisme et responsabilité*. Montpellier: Thèse de Médecine.
Roux-Freissineng, A. (1887). *L'hypnotisme dans ses rapports avec le droit*. Marseille: Barlatier-Feissat.
Rowland, L. J. (1939). Will hypnotized persons try to harm themselves or others? *Journal of Abnormal and Social Psychology, 34*, 114-117. Reprinted in L. Kuhn & S. Russo (Eds.), *Modern Hypnosis*, North Hollywood, CA: Hal Leighton, 1958.
Royer, C. (1887). La psychologie physiologique contemporaine. *Revue Internationale, 14*, 5-23.
Royer-Collard, H. (1843). Consultation médico-légale relative au magnétisme animal. *Annales Médico-Psychologiques, 2*, 85-96.
Rush, B. (1805). Observations on the duties of a physician in medical inquiries and observations. In *Collected works* (2nd ed., Vol. 1). Philadelphia: J. Conrad.
Sabatier, J. C. (1835). *Recherches historiques sur la Faculté de Médecine de Paris, depuis ses origines jusqu'à nos jours*. Paris: Deville Cavellin.
Sabatier-Désarnauds, B. (1838). *Du magnétisme animal et du somnambulisme artificiel*. Montpellier: Veuve Ricard.
Salaville, J. B. (1784). *Le moraliste mesmérien: ou Lettres philosophiques de l'influence du magnétisme*. Paris: Bélin. (Published anonymously.)
Sandby, G. (1844). *Mesmerism and its opponents*. London: Longmans, Brown, & Green.

Sanders, G. S., & Simmons, W. L. (1983). Use of hypnosis to enhance eyewitness accuracy: Does it work? *Journal of Applied Psychology, 68,* 70-77.

Sandras, (1859). Sur l'hypnotisme et ses dangers. *Bulletin de l'Académie Royale de Médecine, 25,* 213.

Sarbin, T. R., & Coe, W. C. (1972). *Hypnosis: A social psychological analysis of influence communication.* New York: Holt, Rinehart & Winston.

Schacter, D. L. (1986a). On the relation between genuine and simulated amnesia. *Behavioral Sciences and the Law, 4,* 47-64.

Schacter, D. L. (1986b). Feeling-of-knowing ratings distinguish between genuine and simulated forgetting. *Journal of Experimental Psychology: Learning, Memory and Cognition, 12,* 30-41.

Schooler, J. W., Gerhard, D., & Loftus, E. F. (1986). Qualities of the unreal. *Journal of Experimental Psychology: Learning, Memory, and Cognition, 12,* 171-181.

Schrenck-Notzing, A. (von). (1902). La suggestion et l'hypnotisme dans leurs rapports avec la jurisprudence. *Deuxième Congrès International d'Hypnotisme Clinique et Expérimental, Paris, 1900: Comptes rendus.* Paris: Vigot.

Schrenck-Notzing, A. (von). (1903). De la suggestion en médecine légale. *Archives d'Anthropologie Criminelle, de Criminologie et de Psychologie Normale et Pathologique, 18.* 724-738.

Scobardi (Rev. Père). (1839). *Rapport confidentiel sur le magnétisme animal.* Paris: Dentu.

Servan, J. M.-A. (1784a). *Doutes d'un provincial, proposés à MM. les médecins-commissaires chargés par le Roy de l'examen du magnétisme animal.* Paris: Prault.

Servan, J. M.-A (1784b). *Questions du jeune docteur Rhubarbini de Purgandis adressées à MM. les Docteurs-Régens de toutes les Facultés de Médecine de l'Univers, au sujet de M. Mesmer et du magnétisme animal.* Padoue: Cabinet du Docteur.

Sextus, C. (1893). *Hypnotism: Its facts, theories, and related phenomena with explanatory anecdotes, descriptions, and reminiscences.* Chicago: n.p.

Sheehan, P. W., & McConkey, K. M. (1982). *Hypnosis and experience: The exploration of phenomena and process.* Hillsdale, NJ: Erlbaum.

Sheehan, P. W., & Perry, C. W. (1976). *Methodologies of hypnosis.* New York: Erlbaum.

Sheehan, P. W., & Tilden, J. (1983). Effects of suggestibility and hypnosis on accurate and distorted retrieval from memory. *Journal of Experimental Psychology: Learning, Memory and Cognition, 9,* 283-293.

Shor, R. E., & Orne, M. T. (Eds.). (1965). *The nature of hypnosis: Selected basic readings.* New York: Holt, Rinehart & Winston.

Shortt, S. E. D. (1984). Physicians and psychics: The Anglo-American medical response to spiritualism, 1870-1890. *Journal of the History of Medicine and Allied Sciences, 39,* 339-355.

Sibley, J. T. (1904). The philosphy of hypnotism. *Medico-legal Journal, 22,* 496-504.

Société de l'Harmonie d'Ostende. (1786). *Système raisonné du magnétisme universel d'après les principes de M. Mesmer.* Ostende: Author.

Société Harmonique des Amis Réunis. (1787). *Exposé des différentes cures opérées depuis le 25 d'août 1785, époque de la formation de la Société, fondée à Strasbourg sous la dénomination de Société Harmonique des Amis Réunis, jusqu'au 12 du mois de juin 1786 par différents membres de cette société.* Strasbourg: Librairie Académique.

Society for Clinical and Experimental Hypnosis. (1979). Resolution (adopted October 1978). *International Journal of Clinical and Experimental Hypnosis, 27,* 452.

Solomon, J. (1952). Hypnotism, suggestibility, and the law. *Nebraska Law Review, 31,* 575-596.

Spanos, N. P. (1983). Demonic possession! A social psychological analysis. In M. Rosenbaum (Ed.), *Compliant behavior: Beyond obedience to authority.* New York: Human Sciences Press.

Spanos, N. P. (1985). Witchcraft and social history: An essay review. *Journal of the History of the Behavioral Sciences, 21,* 60-67.

Spanos, N. P., & Barber, T. X. (1974). Toward a convergence in hypnosis research. *American Psychologist, 29,* 500-511.

Spanos, N. P., & McLean, J. (1985-1986a). Hypnotically created pseudo-memories: Memory

distortions or reporting biases? *British Journal of Experimental and Clinical Hypnosis, 3,* 155-159.
Spanos, N. P., & McLean, J. (1985-1986b). Hypnotically created false reports do not demonstrate pseudomemories. *British Journal of Experimental and Clinical Hypnosis, 3,* 167-171.
Stalnaker, J. M., & Riddle, E. E. (1932). The effect of hypnosis on long-delayed memory. *Journal of General Psychology, 6,* 429-440.
State v. Armstrong, Wisc. No. 81-2336-CR (1983).
State v. Bianchi, No. 79-10116 (Wash. Super. Ct. October 19, 1979).
State v. Donovan, 102 N.E. 791 (1905).
State v. Exum, 138 N.C. 599, 50 S.E. 283 (1905).
State v. Gray, 55 Kan. 135, 39 P. 1050 (1895).
State v. Hurd, 173 N.J. Super. 353, 414 A.2d 291 (1980); aff, 86 N.J. 525, 432 A.2d 86 (1981).
State v. Jorgensen, 8 Or. App. 1, 492 P.2d 312 (Ct. App.) (1971).
State v. Lawson, 65 A. 593 (1907).
State v. Mack, Minn. 292 N.W.2d 764 (1980).
State v. McQueen, 244 S.E.2d 414 (1978).
State v. Mena, 128 Ariz. 244, 624 P.2d 1292 *vac. in part,* 128 Ariz. 226, 624 P.2d 1274, (1981).
State v. Morgan, 13 S.E. 385 (no. 14-25) (1891).
State v. Pierce, 263 S.C. 23, 207 S.E.2d 414 (1974).
State v. Pusch, 46 N.W.2d 508 (1950).
Stephen, J. F. (1883). *History of the criminal law of England* (2 volumes). London: Macmillan.
Stewart, W. J. (1969). Hypnosis, truth drugs and the polygraph: An analysis of their use and acceptance by the courts. *University of Florida Law Review, 21,* 541-560.
Sudduth, W. X. (1895). Hypnotism and crime. *Medico-legal Journal, 13,* 239-254.
Surbled, G. (1903). *L'hypnotisme en justice.* Paris: Sueur-Charruey.
Sutcliffe, J. P. (1961). "Credulous" and "skeptical" views of hypnotic phenomena: Experiments on esthesia, hallucination and delusion. *Journal of Abnormal and Social Psychology, 62,* 189-200.
Sutton, G. (1981). Electric medicine and mesmerism. *Isis, 72,* 375-392.
Tarde, G. (1889). L'affaire Chambige. *Archives de L'Anthropologie Criminelle et des Sciences Pénales, 4,* 92-108.
Tardieu, A. (1878). *Etude médico-légale sur les attentats aux moeurs* (7th ed.). Paris: J. B. Baillière.
Tardy de Montravel, A. A. (1785). *Essai sur la théorie du somnambulisme magnétique.* London: n.p. (Originally attributed to "T.D.M.")
Tardy de Montravel, A. A. (1786). *Journal du traitement magnétique de la Demoiselle N. lequel a servi de base à l'essai sur la théorie du somnambulisme magnétique* (2 volumes). London: n.p.
Tardy de Montravel, A. A. (1787a). *Journal du traitement magnétique de Madame B.* . . . Strasbourg: Librairie Académique.
Tardy de Montravel, A. A. (1787b). *Lettres pour servir de suite à l'essai sur la théorie du somnambulisme magnétique.* London.
Taylor, A. S. (1881). *Traité de médecine légale* (H. Coutagne, Trans.). Paris: Germer-Baillière.
Tentzel, A. (1653). *Medicina diastatica, or sympatheticall mummie: containing many mysterious and hidden secrets in phylosophy and physick. By the construction, extraction, transplantation, and application of microcosmical and spiritual mummie. Teaching the magnetical cures of diseases at distance, etc.* Abstracted from the works of Dr. Theophr. Paracelsus: By the labour and industry of Andrea Tentzelius. (Ferdinand Parkhurst, Trans.). London: T. Newcomb for T. Heath.
The Queen v. McFelin and McFelin, Court of Appeal of New Zealand, C. A. 75/84 and C. H. 76/84, August 6, 1985.
Thoinot, L. (1919). *Medicolegal aspects of moral offenses* (A. W. Weysse, Trans.). Philadelphia: F. A. Davis.
Thomas, G. (1885). *Les procès de sorcellerie et la suggestion hypnotique.* Nancy: Imprimeur de la Cour d'Appel.

Thomas d'Onglée, F. L. (1785). *Rapport au public de quelques abus auxquels le magnétisme animal a donné lieu.* Paris: Veuve Hérissant.

Thouret, M. A. (1783). *Rapports sur les aimants présentés par M. l'Abbé LeNoble, ler Avril 1783, à la Société Royale de Médecine par M. Andry Thouret.* Paris: n. p.

Thouret, M. A. (1784). *Recherches et doutes sur le magnétisme animal.* Paris: Prault.

Thouret, M. A. (1785). *Extrait de la correspondance de la Société Royale de Médecine, relativement au magnétisme animal.* Paris: Imprimerie Royale.

Thouvenel, P. (1781). *Mémoire physique et médicinal montrant des rapports évidens entre les phénomènes de la baguette divinatoire, du magnétisme et de l'électricité.* Paris: Didot le Jeune.

Thouvenel, P. (1784). *Second mémoire physique et médicinal montrant des rapports évidens entre les phénomènes de la baguette divinatoire, du magnétisme et de l'électricité.* Paris: Didot le Jeune.

Timm, H. W. (1981). The effects of forensic hypnosis techniques on eyewitness recall and recognition. *Journal of Police Science and Administration, 9*, 188-194.

Tinterow, M. M. (1970). *Foundations of hypnosis: From Mesmer to Freud.* Springfield, IL: Charles C. Thomas.

Tissart de Rouvre, Marquis de. (1784). *Nouvelles cures opérées par le magnétisme animal: Cures opérées à Beaubourg en Brie par le moyen d'un arbre magnétisé, en juin 1784.* Paris: n. p. (The manuscript is followed by a list of seven names attesting the different cures.)

Tissot, J. X. (1841). *L'anti-magnétisme animal.* Bagnols: Alban Broche.

Tissot, J. X. (1856). *Délire des somnambules.* Paris: Meyrueis.

Titchener Papers. (1880-1927). (Available at Cornell University Archives, Cornell University, Ithaca, NY 14850.)

Tonna, C. E. (1847). *Mesmerism: A letter to Miss Martineau.* Philadelphia: William S. Martien.

Touroude, A. (1889). *L'hypnotisme, ses phénomènes, ses dangers.* Paris: Bloud et Barral.

Touroude, A. (1898). *Peut-on hypnotiser quelqu'un sans son consentement?* LaChapelle-Montligeon: Notre-Dame de Montligeon.

Townshend, C. (1844). *Facts in mesmerism with reasons for a dispassionate inquiry into it.* London: Baillière.

Tranquille de Saint-Rémi. (Rev. Père). (1634). *Véritable relation des justes procédures observées au fait de la possession des Ursulines de Loudun et au procès d'Urbain Grandier avec les thèses générales touchant les diables exorcisés.* La Flèche: G. Griveau.

Trevor-Roper, H. R. (1967). *The European witch-craze of the sixteenth and seventeenth centuries.* New York: Penguin Books.

True, R. M. (1949). Experimental control in hypnotic age regression states. *Science, 110*, 583-584.

Tuke, D. H. (1882). *Chapters in the history of the insane in the British Isles.* London: n.p.

Tuke, D.-H. (1884). *Sleepwalking and somnambulism.* London: n.p.

Tuke, D.-H. (1886). *Le corps et l'esprit, action du moral et de l'imagination sur le physique* (V. Parant, Trans.). Paris: J. B. Baillière.

Udolf, R. (1983). *Forensic hypnosis.* Lexington, MA: Lexington Books.

United States v. Adams, 581 F.2d 193 (9th Cir. 1978), cert. denied, 439 U.S. 1006 (1978).

United States v. Narciso and Perez, 446 F. Supp. 252 (E.D. Mich. 1977).

Vacant, A., & Mangenot, E. (1922). *Dictionnaire de théologie Catholique: Hypnotisme.* Paris: Letouzey et Ané.

Valleton, M. de B. (1785). *Lettre de M. Valleton de Boissière, médecin à Bergerac, à M. Thouret, médecin à Paris.* Philadelphia: n.p.

Van Renterghem, A. W. (1898). *Liebault [sic] en Zinjne School.* Amsterdam: Van Rossen.

Van Swinden, J. H. (1785). *Analogie de l'électricité et du magnétisme* (3 volumes). La Haye: n.p.

Varnier, C. L. (1785). *Mémoire pour Me. Charles Louis Varnier, docteur-régent de la Faculté de Médecine de Paris, et membre de la Société Royale de Médecine, appelant d'un décret de la Faculté contre les Doyens et les Docteurs de la dite Faculté, intimés.* Paris: Veuve Hérissant.

Vibert, C. (1881). De l'hypnotisme au point de vue médico-légal. *Annales d'Hygiène Publique et de Médecine Légale, 6*, 399-406.
Virey, J. J. (1818). *Examen impartial de la médecine magnétique*. Paris: Panckoucke.
Voisin, A. (1891). *Un crime d'incendie commis sous l'influence de la suggestion hypnotique*. Paris: Octave Doin.
Voisin, A. (1892). Délit de vol commis sous l'influence de la suggestion hypnotique. *Revue de l'Hypnotisme Expérimental et thérapeutique, 7*, 219-220.
Voisin, A. (1894). Les suggestions criminelles. *Revue de l'Hypnotisme Expérimental et Thérapeutique, 7*, 216-217.
Wadden, T. A., & Anderton, C. H. (1982). The clinical uses of hypnosis. *Psychological Bulletin, 91*, 215-243.
Walmsley, D. M. (1967). *Anton Mesmer*. London: Robert Hale.
Walten, P. H. (1880). *Der magnetische Schlaf-mit einem anhange: Der process des magnetiseurs Hansen in Wien*. Berlin: n.p.
Warner, K. E. (1979). The use of hypnosis in the defense of criminal cases. *International Journal of Clinical and Experimental Hypnosis, 27*, 417-436.
Watkins, J. G. (1947). Antisocial compulsions induced under hypnotic trance. *Journal of Abnormal and Social Psychology, 42*, 256-259.
Watkins, J. G. (1972). Antisocial behavior under hypnosis: Possible or impossible? *International Journal of Clinical and Experimental Hypnosis, 20*, 95-100.
Watkins, J. G. (1984). The Bianchi (L. A. Hillside Strangler) case: Sociopath or multiple personality? *International Journal of Clinical and Experimental Hypnosis, 32*, 67-101.
Wheless, J. (1897). Note: The case of Spurgeon Young. *American Law Review, 31*, 440-441.
Wigmore, H. J. (1913). *Principles of judicial proof*. Boston: Little, Brown.
Wilson, I. (1982). *Reincarnation?* Suffolk, England: Penguin. (Original work published as *Mind out of time?* London: Gollancz, 1981.)
Wilson, S. C., & Barber, T. X. (1982). The fantasy-prone personality: Implications for understanding imagery, hypnosis, and parapsychological phenomena. In A. A. Sheikh (Ed.), *Imagery: Current theory, research, and application*. New York: Wiley.
Winslow, L. F. (1843). *The plea of insanity in criminal cases*. London: n.p.
Winslow, L. F. (1861). The Marvelous [a review of Figuier, 1860]. *American Journal of Insanity, 18*, 14-42.
Winter, G. (1801). *Animal magnetism, history of: Its origin, progress, and present state; Its principles and secrets displayed as delivered by the late Dr. Demainauduc. To which is added, Dissertations on the dropsy; spasms; epiliptic fits; St. Vitus dance; gout; rheumatism; and consumption; with upwards of one hundred cures and cases. Also, advice to those who visit the sick, with recipes to prevent infection. A definition of sympathy, antipathy; the effects of the imagination on pregnant women; nature; history; and on the resurrection of the body*. Bristol: George Routh.
Wolfart, K. C. (1814). *Mesmerismus: Oder system der Wechselwirkkungen, Theorie und Anwerdung des thierischen Magnetismus als die allgemeine Heilkunde zur Erhaltung des Menschen von Dr. Friedrich [sic] Anton Mesmer*. Berlin: Nicholaischen Buchhandlung.
Wundt, W. (1893). *Hypnotisme et suggestion, étude critique* (A. Keller, Trans.). Paris: F. Alcan.
Wyller et al. v. Fairchild Hiller Corporation, 503 F.2d 506 (9th Cir. 1974).
Young, L. E. (1948). *The science of hypnotism*. Baltimore, MD: I. & M. Ottenheimer.
Young, P. C. (1952). Antisocial uses of hypnosis. In L. M. LeCron (Ed.), *Experimental hypnosis*. New York: Macmillan.
Yung, E. J.-J. (1883). *Le sommeil normal et le sommeil pathologique, magnétisme animal, hypnotisme, névrose hystérique*. Paris: Octave Doin.
Zelig, M., & Beidleman, W. B. (1981). The investigative use of hypnosis: A word of caution. *International Journal of Clinical and Experimental Hypnosis, 29*, 401-412.
Zonana, H. V. (1979). Hypnosis, sodium amytal, and confessions. *Bulletin of the American Academy of Psychiatry and the Law, 7*, 18-28.

Index

Académie des Sciences, relations with
  Mesmer, 54-57
Académie des Sciences Morales et Politiques,
  Liégeois's communication (1884), 204,
  215, 219, 223
"Affectless" recall, 387 (*see also* Police)
Age regression
  as literal, 327, 331, 332
  confabulation in, 237, 238 (*see also*
    Confabulation)
  cueing in, 329, 330 (*see also* Demand
    characteristics)
  duality in, 214, 334
  experiments on, 214, 328, 329, 334
  in animal magnetism, 132
  in hypnosis, 214, 393
  in reincarnation claims, 329-332
  physical and psychological aspects, 327,
    328, 330
Altered state of consciousness
  in animal magnetism, 14
  in hypnosis, 182
American Medical Association
  report on hypnosis (1958), 342, 343, 388
  report on hypnosis (1985), 334, 388
American Psychological Association
  Newsletter (Division 30), 388
American Society of Clinical Hypnosis, 333

American supernatural fiction, 170, 171, 265,
  266, 285
Amnesia
  genuine versus simulated, 321, 322
  in animal magnetism, 59, 113, 131, 150,
    159, 164
  in artificial somnambulism, 109, 110, 113,
    115, 131, 170, 171
  in hypnosis, 201, 206, 208, 214, 330
  in Jansenist war, 41, 43
  in Loudun possession, 32, 33
  in lucid sleep, 140
  in medical dictionary, 144
  post-hypnotic, 201
  source, 330-332
  spontaneous, in hypnosis, 201
Analgesia
  in animal magnetism, 143, 148-150, 154,
    168
  in hypnosis, 183, 199
  in Jansenist convulsionaries, 41
  in lucid sleep, 140
Animal magnetism, 3-99
  allegations against Mesmer, 11, 12, 50, 61,
    62, 64-68, 71, 73-83, 89-91, 96-98,
    104-106
  alleged abuse, 77, 78, 80, 116, 117, 128, 129,
    146, 147, 156, 161, 164, 170, 192-194

423

Animal magnetism (*continued*)
  alleged powers of Mesmer, 68
  and Christian Science, 172
  and phrenology, 168, 170, 203
  and Romanticism, 52
  as ecstasy, 143, 159
  as fraud, 156
  as illegal practice of medicine, 128, 156-158
  as investigative technique, 162, 376
  between the Revolution and the Restoration, 126
  criticisms of, 127, 128, 138, 142, 143, 155 (*see also* allegations against Mesmer)
  dissemination internationally in nineteenth century, 126, 142
  explained by animal heat, 92
  female magnetists, 134, 146
  humanitarian aspects, 52, 96
  Mesmer in Paris, 49-68, 104-106
  Mesmer in Switzerland, 106
  Mesmer in Vienna, 3-5, 9-12, 50, 51
  moral and physical dangers, 64, 65, 78, 133-135, 144-147, 158, 162-164, 166
  moral benefits of, 96, 161
  political use of, 376
  rapport, 60, 79, 150
  repeated magnetizations, 187 (*see also* Legal cases in United States [pre-1910], Spurgeon Young)
  safeguards against abuse, 78, 79, 134, 156
  techniques (passes), 60, 75
  used to elicit secrets, 162
Animals
  experimentation on, 136, 145, 186, 187, 213, 222, 271
  trials of, 43-46
Anti-magnetism, and royal blood, 104
Artificial sleep, Liébeault's views, 181-182 (*see also* Hypnosis)
Artificial somnambulism, xix, 106-121, 128, 129 (*see also* Somnambulism)
  as evil force, 129
  as illegal practice of medicine, 116, 128
  confabulation in, 162
  dangers of, 116-121, 128
  de Puységur's views, 114-116
  equated with natural somnambulism in England, 165
  in care and prevention of diseases, 119, 120
  incidence of, 110
  Mesmer's views, 112-114
  rapport exclusif, 109, 114
Assistances, 40-42 (*see also* Jansenism)
Automatism (*see* Involuntariness; Will, loss of)
Automaton (*see* Will, loss of)

B

Baquets, 57, 64
British Medical Association, 342

C

Catalepsy, 184 (*see also* Hysteria; La Salpêtrière school)
  hypnotic, 198
  in the Loudun possession, 32, 33
  of the dominant hand, 316
  transposition of senses, 103, 121-123
Chemical anesthesia
  abuse of, 161, 185, 186, 188
  erotogenous sensations in, 185, 186
Child kidnapping, in hypnosis, 168, 169, 200 (*see also* Obstetrics)
Clairvoyance, 109, 112, 113, 115, 150, 154, 162, 181
Clinical cases
  compilation of success statistics, 96, 98, 99
  finding lost jewelry, 206
  Mlle Paradis and Mesmer, 9-12, 82
  report of zero success with animal magnetism, 165, 166
  successful magnetization of a horse, 104
  successful treatment of adultery claimed, 161, 162
  successful treatment of prostitution claimed, 158, 161
  tooth extraction, 154
Clinical uses of animal magnetism, 91, 92, 161
  in bleeding of patients, 5
  in epileptic convulsions, 75
  in hysterical paralysis, 188

Clinical uses of hypnosis, xx, 297
  during World Wars I and II, 297
  in childbirth, 199, 200
Coercion
  double-edged effect, 118, 224, 283, 309-311, 315
  experimentation on, 182, 211, 212, 215, 216, 223-230, 297-307, 393, 394 (*see also* Suggestion)
  in clinical and field situations, 307-318 (*see also* Suggestion)
  resistance to, 117, 118, 225, 306
  sequelæ to, 225, 229, 305, 306
  sexual abuse, 241, 309-311
Commissions of Inquiry, 83-98
  Benjamin Franklin Commission, 83-91, 126
  fourth Commission (Dubois's report), 154, 155
  reactions to Franklin Commission reports, 93-98, 110
  Royal Society of Medicine, 91-93
  secret report, xvii, 89-91, 98, 126
  social discrimination of, 95, 98
  third Commission (Husson's report), 147-151
Concentration, 139, 141
Confabulation (*see also* Errors of memory; Memory)
  clinical, 210, 236, 237, 285, 286
  confidence and, 286, 287, 326, 327, 360, 377, 394
  experimental, 237, 238, 322, 323
  in low hypnotizables, 354
  in Watergate "cover-up," 319-321
  legal, 145, 162, 192, 202, 209, 210, 227, 233-240, 274, 280, 285, 286, 342-344, 354, 361-368, 370, 375, 377
Control, loss of in hypnosis, 231, 338 (*see also* Will, loss of)
Crisis, convulsive
  explained by imagination and imitation, 42, 88
  hysterical, 184, 196
  in animal magnetism, 6, 30, 37-42, 59, 74, 86, 88, 90, 94, 96, 108, 134
  in assistances (Jansenist), 39-41
  in exorcism, 6, 30, 35
  nervous, 5

D

Demand characteristics (*see also* Social psychological variables)
  in Auvard's obstetrical observations, 199, 200
  in Charcot's theory, 195, 200, 202, 203
  in experimentation, 228, 279, 300, 301, 392
Depersonalization, 9 (*see also* Involuntariness)
Diagnostic tests
  of hypnosis, 345
  of hysteria, 242
Dissociation
  observed by Deleuze, 131
  observed by de Puységur, 109, 110
Double consciousness (*see* Multiple selves)

E

England
  animal magnetism in, 165-169
  Perkinism, 166, 167
Enlightenment, 8, 179, 180
Errors of memory (*see also* Confabulation; Evidence, hypnotic)
  increase in hypnosis, 324, 325
  increased confidence in, 324, 325
  pseudomemories, 325-327, 334
  social psychological factors in, 326
Evidence, hypnotic
  admissibility, 336, 337, 356, 358, 360, 362-364, 367-369, 375-377
  guidelines for, 356-358, 379-385
  mandatory reporting, 375, 376, 379
  pretrial adjudication, 364
  weight of, 346, 347, 358-361, 371, 372
Exorcism, 5-9
  of Emilie, 5-7, 19-22
Expectations, role of (*see also* Demand characteristics; Individual differences; Social psychological variables)
  in hypnosis, 279, 392
  in lucid sleep, 139
Experimentation (*see also* Coercion, experimentation on)
  by the Benjamin Franklin Commission, 87-89
  Hull's laboratory, 296, 297

Experimentation (*continued*)
  memory enhancement, 322-332
  on coercive power of hypnosis (*see*
    Coercion; Suggestions, self-damaging)
Experts, medico-legal
  in Bompard trial, 253-256
  in Castellan affair, 190, 191
  in United States, 278-281, 363, 366, 367, 377, 379, 386, 387
  prior to 1870s, xvi, 159, 184-189, 191, 192

F

Fixed idea, 182
Free recall, 331, 383 (*see also* Memory)
French government, negotiations with Mesmer, 63, 64
French Revolution, xix, 123-125
  Bailly's death, 124, 125
  Restoration, 123, 124

G

Glass harmonica, 15, 23, 51
Guidelines, investigative hypnosis, 356, 357, 374, 379-385, 390, 395
  appropriate induction, 382, 383
  clinical follow-up, 384
  communication with the hypnotist, 383, 384
  hypnosis with suspects, 385
  memory retrieval techniques, 382, 383
  post-hypnotic discussion, 384
  prehypnotic evaluation, 382
  presence of observers, 381, 382
  qualifications of the hypnotist, 366, 367, 380, 381
  technical considerations, 384
  videotape recording, 381

H

Hallucinations
  erotic, 185
  in hystero-epilepsy, 197
  of subject's own death, 219
  of taste, 55, 140
  negative visual, 225
  retroactive, 205, 240 (*see also* Confabulation; Errors of memory)
  visual, 159, 226
Healers, contemporaries of Mesmer, 84, 85
Healing, persuasive, 295
Honor, sense of, Mesmer on, 51, 52, 63, 64, 85, 86
Human plank, 198, 217, 218 (*see also* Legal cases in United States [pre-1910], Spurgeon Young)
Hypermnesia, 115, 131, 132, 144, 159, 162, 181, 190, 201, 206, 234-240, 322-332 (*see also* Confabulation)
Hypnosis (*see also* Simulation of hypnosis)
  alleged powers of, xv, 181, 182, 192, 200, 209, 210, 224-230, 233, 267, 317
  alleged "truth-telling" properties of, 345, 352 (*see also* Lie detector)
  and coercion, xvii, xx, 172, 184, 311-317
  and compliance, 277, 369
  and gender change, 306, 393
  and prolongation of life, 212, 213
  beliefs of subject about, 368
  Bernheim's classification of degrees of, 214
  Charcot's three "stages" of, 184, 185, 188, 189, 197-199, 214
  context of, xv, 232 (*see also* Demand characteristics)
  dangers of, 182, 204, 205, 215, 216, 218, 222, 223, 226, 266, 270-272, 283
  decline in nineteenth century, 282, 293-296
  distortions of cognitive processes, xiv
  electroencephalography (EEG) indices, xiii
  inquisitorial agent, 267, 286
  Liébeault's views, 181, 182
  medical opposition to, xiv
  nature of, xiv, xv (*see also* La Salpêtrière school; Nancy school)
  on stage, 166, 208, 209, 216, 268, 317, 318
  origin of term, xxi, 168, 175, 180
  performed in law court, 206, 208, 255
  physiological signs of, 195, 197-199, 223, 232, 294
  police utilization of, xv
  repeated hypnotizations, 197, 209 (*see also* Legal cases in United States [pre-1910], Spurgeon Young)
  suggestibility, xiv, 201, 296

Hypnotic susceptibility (*see* Individual differences)
Hypnotism (*see* Hypnosis)
Hypnotists
  lay, xx, 148, 156, 220, 221, 333, 334, 340, 342, 362, 377, 388
  police, 342, 349, 350, 376, 378, 387, 388
  professionally trained, xx, 346, 350, 353-356, 366, 367, 373, 374, 377
Hypnotizability (*see also* Individual differences)
  correlates of, xiv-xv, 392 (*see also* Imagery)
  scales measuring, 203
Hypnotized person, seen as automaton (*see* Will, loss of)
Hysteria, 147, 205
  and apparent death, 188, 189
  and confabulation, 171
  and criminal suggestions, 225
  and deliberate lying, 185, 188
  and false accusations, 188, 234
  and hypnosis, 183, 184, 191, 195-199, 203
  and sexual abuse, 188, 189, 241-244
  catalepsy and lethargy in, 188, 189
  differentiated from epilepsy, 294
  in men, 197
  physiological etiology assumed, 188
  simulation of, 242, 243
Hystero-epilepsy, stages, 196, 197 (*see also* Hysteria; La Salpêtrière school)

I

Illegal practice of medicine (*see* Animal magnetism; Artificial somnambulism)
Imagery, vividness of, 181
Imagination
  D'Eslon's view, 66
  in animal magnetism, 5, 55, 66, 74, 78, 87, 88, 95, 143, 159
  in animals, 186, 187
  in artificial somnambulism, 111
  in Jansenism, 42
  in Loudun possession, 32
  in lucid sleep, 139
  in magnetic medicine, 13
  in Perkinism, 167

Imitation
  in animal magnetism, 66, 87, 88
  in Jansenism, 42
  in magnetic medicine, 13
Individual differences
  in animal magnetism, 58, 59, 86, 95, 96, 132, 150
  in artificial somnambulism, 115
  in hypnosis, xiv, 181, 203, 223, 225, 227, 294
  in lucid sleep, 138
Insanity defense, 44, 48, 273
  International Congress of Criminal Anthropology (Brussels, 1982), Benedikt's intervention, 284
International Congress of Experimental and Therapeutic Hypnosis (Paris)
  First (1899), 220, 223, 238
  Second (1901), 221
International Congress of Medicine (Moscow, 1897), Bernheim's intervention, 284
International Society of Hypnosis, 333, 387, 388
Involuntariness (*see also* Will)
  in animal magnetism, 91, 393, 394
  in hypnosis, 233, 234, 239, 280, 283, 295, 318, 332, 393, 394
  in lucid sleep, 139

J

Jansenism (*see also* Amnesia; Analgesia)
  assistances, 40-42
  convulsions, 39
  Jansenist war, 36, 37
  miracles, 38

L

La Pitié school, 213
La Salpêtrière school, 181, 194-199
  Charcot's methodological flaws, 293, 294
  comparison to animal magnetism, 196
  end of, 281, 282
  hypnotic nosology, 214
  patho-physiological approach, 195-204
Law Enforcement Hypnosis Institute (LEHI)
  critiques of courts' decisions, 370, 387
  techniques of hypnotic recall, 349, 350, 387, 388
  views on memory, 348-350

Laws restricting practice of animal
    magnetism and hypnosis, 155, 156,
    218, 219, 223, 289
Lay hypnosis and magnetism, 148, 158, 216–
    220, 289
  alleged sexual abuse, 311–317
  and spiritualism, 172
  Hansen's trial, 217, 218, 260, 261
  in English medical debate about animal
    magnetism, 165
  prosecutions of, 155–158, 216
  Salpêtrière and Nancy views on, 219–221
  societies, 333
Legal cases in Australia and New Zealand,
    374–376
  Regina v. Palmer (Mr. Magic), 311–317
  The Queen v. McFelin and McFelin, 375,
    376
Legal cases in Canada, 376–378
  *Her Majesty the Queen v. Allan Dale
    Zubot*, 376, 377
  Her Majesty the Queen v. Clark, 377
  Naeyaert and Elias, 365, 366
  Rex v. Booher, 376
Legal cases in Europe
  A., 163
  Adèle G., 242–245
  Baroness de Rothschild, 283
  Berthe (Lévy's case), 193, 194
  C., 192
  Castellan, 189–191, 201, 202
  Chambige, 245–248
  Czynski, 275–278, 288
  Du Potet, 156
  Emile D., 207, 208
  Eyraud-Bompard, xx, 248–259
  Félida, 183, 184
  La Roncière, 205, 206
  M. and Mme Mongruel, Grabowski and
    Sokolowski, 157, 158
  Madeleine, 241, 242
  Madeleine S., 285, 286
  Marguerite A., 191, 192
  Maria F., 208–210
  Mme B., 164
  Petro-Zavodsk, 282, 283
  Ricard and Plain, 156, 157
  Theresa Dig, 200, 201
Legal cases in Great Britain, 373, 374

legal guidelines for hypnosis, 374
Legal cases in United States (pre-1910)
  Austin v. Barker, 288, 289, 335, 336, 385
  Parks v. State, 289
  Pascal B. Smith, 171
  People v. Ebanks, 274, 275, 335
  People v. John Johnson, 171, 172
  People v. Royal, 192, 193, 202, 210, 333
  People v. Worthington, 273
  Spurgeon Young, 269–271
  State v. Donovan, 278, 279
  State v. Exum, 289
  State v. Gray, 272, 273
  State v. McDonald, 272, 273
Legal cases in United States (post-1910)
  Chapman v. State, 369, 370
  Collins v. State, 346, 376, 387
  Commonwealth v. DiNicola, 371, 372, 379,
    395
  Commonwealth v. Smoyer, 371, 379
  Cornell v. Superior Court of San Diego,
    338–342, 345
  Creamer v. Hopper (see *Emmett v.
    Ricketts*)
  Emmett v. Ricketts, 350–352
  Frye v. United States, 336, 337, 346, 363,
    364, 370, 375, 376, 379, 385, 388
  Greenfield v. Commonwealth, 361
  Harding v. State of Maryland, 336, 346,
    347, 361, 363, 368, 375–377, 379, 387
  Kline v. Ford Motor Co., Inc., 359, 361
  People v. Busch, 385, 386
  People v. Diggs, 355, 356
  People v. Hangsleben, 362
  People v. Kempinski, 349, 366, 367, 375
  People v. Shirley, 367–369
  People v. Woods et al., 362, 365
  *Quaglino v. The People of the State of
    California*, 356–358
  Reece Forney case, 369
  Rock v. Arkansas, 389, 390
  State v. Armstrong, 370
  State v. Bianchi, 386
  State v. Hurd, 364, 365, 368, 375, 377
  State v. Jorgensen, 358, 359, 361
  State v. Mack, 361–365, 369, 372
  State v. McQueen, 360, 361
  State v. Pierce, 361
  State v. Pusch, 335, 337–339, 345

United States v. Adams, 359, 360
United States v. Narciso and Perez, 350, 352-355, 374
Wyller et al. v. Fairchild Hiller Corporation, 359, 361
Legal trials, adversarial nature of, 295, 296, 311
Lethargy
 hypnotic, 184, 198, 199
 hysterical, 188, 189
Lie detector, 330, 336-338, 363 (*see also* Legal cases in United States [post-1910], *Frye v. United States*)
Lucid sleep, 137-142
 abuse of subject, 141
 clinical applications of, 140, 141
 épopte, 139
 ignored by animal magnetists, 137, 152
 sequelae, 141
 simulation of, 137
Lying, deliberate
 in hypnosis, 209, 231, 308, 345, 361, 370
 in hysteria, 185, 188

M

Magnet, physical, 4
 etymology, 22, 23
 rejection by Mesmer, 5
Magnetic medicine, 4, 12-18
 amulets, magical boxes, 17
 as evil force, 14
 moral dangers, 17
Media
 coverage of hypnosis, 180, 204, 215, 216, 218, 252, 258, 265, 296, 350, 375, 378, 390
 lampoonists, 16, 57, 58, 76, 77, 79-82, 95, 97, 136, 137
 plays, 80-82, 136
Medical establishment, 52, 53
 and lay hypnosis, 156-158
 attacks on Mesmerism, 77, 78
Memory (*see also* Confabulation; Errors of memory; Hypermnesia)
 audio/videotape theory of, 318, 319, 343-345, 348, 378

beliefs about, 319, 378, 394
creation of, 236-238, 325, 326, 329, 330, 334, 369
hypnotic enhancement of, xv, 171, 208, 322-332
in field situations, 321, 322
in the laboratory, 318-332, 334
leading questions, influence on, 324, 344
modification of, by hallucinations or dreams, 226, 227, 389
modification of, Nancy and La Salpêtrière views, 230, 231
"refreshment" by hypnosis, 368-370
reproductive versus reconstructive, 319, 343-345, 348, 378
Mentalities, history of, xxi, 391, 396
Mesmerism (*see* animal magnetism)
Military establishment
 and animal magnetism, 107
 and hypnosis, 223, 297
Mnemonist, John Dean's testimony, 319-321
Multiple selves
 Félida's case, 183, 184
 in animal magnetism, 131
 in artificial somnambulism, 109
 in hypnosis, (*see* Legal cases in United States [post-1910], *State v. Bianchi*)
 in lucid sleep, 140

N

Nancy school
 antisocial suggestions, 182
 Bernheim's veiws, 202-204, 214, 258
 end of, 282, 294
 Liébeault's views, 181, 182
 post hoc opinions of legal cases, 244, 245, 247, 248, 252, 257-259
Natural somnambulism, 30, 184, 205, 207
 cases of abuse, 158-164, 208
 legal responsibility, 160, 182
 linked to hypnotic somnambulism, 208
Neurosis
 hypnotic, 209
 suggested, 203, 204
Noctambulism (*see* Natural somnambulism)

O

Obstetrics, criminal suggestions, 199, 200, 241

P

Pain (see Analgesia; Surgery)
Paramnesias, types of, 235, 236
Paris Medical Faculty, 60-62
  attack on D'Eslon, 61, 62
Perkinism, 166, 167, 169
Poles (see also Zones)
  in animal magnetism, 77-80, 116, 117, 128, 129
  in artificial somnambulism, 116, 117
Police
  artists, 390
  beliefs about hypnosis, 332, 378, 379
  beliefs about memory, 318
  criticisms of research, 324
  "happiness" ratings of success with hypnosis, 348
  malpractice, 351, 352
  slow-motion metaphor, 390
  television technique of induction, 349
  training in hypnotic procedures, xv, 342-345, 349
  "zoom-in" technique, 349
Police utilization of hypnosis, xv, 348-350, 378
  Federal Bureau of Investigation, 380, 390
  in Australia, 374, 375
  in Canada, 376-379
  in New Zealand, 375
  in United Kingdom, 373, 374
  in United States, 335-372
Possession (see also Witchcraft)
  in Loudun's Inquisition trial, 29-35
  signs of, 25-28, 46, 47
  similarities to animal magnetism and hypnosis, xvii-xviii, 24-26, 29, 32, 35, 93, 115, 143, 144, 158, 172, 227, 242
Post-hypnotic suggestion
  antisocial, 182
  cancellation, 221
Pseudoscientific tests
  of animal magnetism, 171
  of hypnosis, 242, 340, 345
Psychoanalysis, 295, 296 (see also Unconscious)
Public conflicts
  between Mesmer and Bertholet, 73, 74
  between Mesmer and D'Eslon, 67
  between Mesmer and Gassner, 8, 9
  between Nancy and La Salpêtrière, 238-240, 244, 253-256, 258-259

Q

Quackery
  accusations of, 217, 218
  in English medical debate about magnetism, 165

R

Rapport, 14, 60, 79, 109, 114, 150, 171, 223, 280
  as cause of abuse, 146, 147, 162, 295, 307
Recueil général . . . , 70, 71, 98
Responsibility, legal, 259, 260, 280
Roman Catholic Church
  and animal magnetism, 22, 24, 25, 103, 104, 127, 128, 144, 153, 172, 173
  conflicts with, 75, 136, 262

S

Scrofula, 17
  royal touch, 45
Sequelae
  hypnotic, 216-223, 225, 227, 229, 309-311, 393
  magnetic and somnambulistic, 88, 89, 117, 118, 120, 141
  stage hypnosis, 317, 318
Sexuality
  abuse of, 225, 241 (see also Coercion; Will, loss of)
  in hypnosis, 192-194, 196, 309, 310

in hysteria, 184, 188, 189, 191, 192, 197
in Jansenism, 42
in witchcraft, 32
Simulation of hypnosis, 192, 231-233, 266, 267, 340
and lying, 231
in experimentation, 302
in lucid sleep, 137
in sexual abuse, 192, 194, 210
Sleep
and electroencephalogram (EEG), xiii
artificial, 181
critical (*see* Artificial somnambulism)
somnambulistic (*see* Artificial somnambulism)
Social psychological variables, 334, 392 (*see also* Demand characteristics)
in animal magnetism, 87
in lucid sleep, 139, 141
in witchcraft, 26
Society for Clinical and Experimental Hypnosis, 333, 387, 388
Society of Universal Harmony, 68-70, 72, 105
and Freemasonry, 69, 72, 85
Sodium amytal ("truth serum"), 358, 359, 361, 363
Somnambulism
alleged abuses in, 146, 161, 162, 209-211
and hysteria, 173
diagnosis of illness and prescription of cures by, 115, 116, 128, 133, 150, 155
hypnotic, 199, 201 (*see also* La Salpêtrière school)
natural, crimes in, 159, 160
spontaneous, 201, 206, 207
Spiritualism, xix, 126, 134, 151, 153, 165
Podmore's bias toward, 152, 165, 166, 173, 174
Subconscious, 264, 295, 332, 338 (*see also* Multiple selves)
Suggestibility
heightened, 201, 204
theory of, 202-204
Suggestion
as self-fulfilling prophecy, 307, 316, 394
as sole cause of hypnosis, 214 (*see also* Nancy school)
beliefs and expectations in coercive, 316

coercive, 223, 276, 277, 295
criminal, 224-230, 261, 262, 279, 280
demand characteristics in coercive, 228, 299, 300, 302
in artificial somnambulism, 108
in lucid sleep, 138, 139
physiological effects of, 226
resistance to, 209, 210, 224-227, 279, 305, 306, 310, 318
uncanceled, effects of, 221
waking, 190, 204
Suggestions, damaging to others
attack on a fellow officer, 308
throwing acid at the experimenter, 227-229, 298-301
Suggestions, self-damaging
betraying the hypnotist, 305
complaints about, 224
H. and N. case, 307, 308
in somnambulists, 225
objectionable behaviors, 300, 303-305
picking up a coin in fuming acid, 301, 302
picking up snakes, 298-301
sequelae to, 225, 229, 230, 268, 305, 306, 313, 314
Surgery
Broca, 183
Cloquet, 148-150
Esdaile, 168
in the nineteenth century before anesthetics, 152
Oudet, 154
Suspects, hypnotized, 337-342, 348, 361, 369, 389
in defense preparation, 274, 275, 338-342, 361, 377, 385, 386, 389, 390
and simulation, 340, 342, 345, 385, 386
Swedenborgism, 136, 172
Sympatheism, 13, 16

T

Testimony, hypnotically elicited
accepted by courts, 350-356, 358-361, 366, 369
as hearsay evidence, 365, 366
as truth, 344, 345

Testimony, hypnotically elicited (*continued*)
  courts notified of, 344
  cued by reading media accounts of crime, 351, 389
  cued inadvertently by questioning procedure, 354, 355, 369
  exclusion recommended by Diamond, 350, 356
  false, given in good faith, 206, 233, 234, 286, 287 (*see also* Confabulation; Errors of memory)
  independent verification of, 268
  instructions to alter, 351
  in the laboratory, 354
  mandatory reporting of, 375, 376, 379
  modified, 230, 240, 274
  rejected by courts, 273, 275, 283, 338, 361-365, 369, 370
  prosecutorial misconduct, 350-355, 372
  uncorroborated by independent physical evidence, 352
Testimony, prehypnotic
  no restriction to, 359, 360
  restriction to, 364, 365, 371, 372
Lancet, The, and animal magnetism, 149, 166-168
Thought transference, 34, 35
Trance logic, 132, 328, 329
Trial, by fantasy, 349, 364
Trees, curative properties of, 15, 58, 107, 108, 110

U

Unconscious, 264, 295, 330, 332, 345-347
Unconscious conflict, in lucid sleep, 141
Unconscious pregnancies, 208-210, 335, 336
United States
  and animal magnetism, 126, 153, 169-172, 174
  and Christian Science, xix, 170
  and hypnosis, 265, 275, 278-281 (*see also* Legal cases in United States)
  and Protestant Revivalist Movement, xix, 153, 170
  and spiritualism, 153, 170, 172, 263-265, 287
  experimental research in Psychology, xiv, 263, 264, 296, 297

V

Vapors, 81
Victims, hypnotized
  alleged posttraumatic amnesia, 346, 347, 355, 356, 365, 388
  confabulation, spontaneous, 367-369
  confabulation, suggested, 355, 356, 361-365
Voice prints, 363

W

Water divining, 84-88
Watergate "cover-up," 319-321 (*see also* Confabulation)
Weapon salve, 14
Will (*see also* Involuntariness)
  and chemical anesthesia, 185, 186
  in somnambulism, 108, 109, 150
  loss of, 144, 145, 181, 182, 188, 189, 191-193, 204, 206, 209, 210, 238, 244, 276, 277, 295, 338, 392, 394
  role of, 103, 114, 115, 138, 141, 145, 169, 295, 318
Witchcraft, 25-35 (*see also* Possession)
  and Montpellier Medical School, 27, 46, 47
  development of, 27, 28
  in the Loudun possession trial, 29-35
  signs of, 25-27
  social aspects, 26, 34
Witness, hypnotized
  competence to testify, 350-356, 359-361, 371, 375
  confabulation, spontaneous, 366, 367
  inadvertent cueing, 351-353, 369, 376, 377
  posttraumatic amnesia, 358, 359, 371
  unshakeable, 327, 360
Writ
  of habeas corpus, 350, 352, 389
  of mandamus, 339

Z

Zones
  erotogenic, 202
  hypnogenic, 201, 202, 210, 211
  hysterogenic, 196, 197, 201
Zoomagnetism, 15 (*see also* Magnetic medicine)
Zoopsia, 197